MANAGING

The Scott, Foresman Series in Management and Organizations
Lyman W. Porter and Joseph W. McGuire, Editors

MANAGING

H. Joseph Reitz
University of Florida

Linda N. Jewell
University of South Florida

Scott, Foresman and Company
Glenview, Illinois
London, England

ACKNOWLEDGMENTS

Acknowledgments for literary selections and illustrations appear at the back of the book on pp. 599–606 which are extensions of the copyright page.

Library of Congress Cataloging in Publication Data
Reitz, H. Joseph.
  Managing.
  (Scott, Foresman series in management and organizations)
  Includes bibliographies and indexes.
    1. Managing.   I. Jewell, Linda N.   II. Title.
III. Series.
HD31.R4425   1985   658   84-14133
ISBN 0–673–15510–2

PREFACE

Why is this book entitled *Managing*, rather than the more traditional *Management*? Because *management* is a concept, while *managing* is an action. Although this book covers the concept and processes of management, it emphasizes what managers *do* to help their organizations, and themselves, succeed.

Our preference for the term managing stems from the fact that, at various times in our careers, we have worked as full-time managers. Not just studied management, but made our living by managing. And our managerial experiences, in industry, small business, and the military have taught us that managers are action-oriented. Surviving, improving, and achieving are the dominant managerial drives. Being a manager is exciting, challenging, varied, and stimulating. Similarly, our teaching experiences have demonstrated that students of management are action-oriented. No great surprise: the principles of self-selection suggest that people who *want to be* managers will be like people who *are* managers in their preferences for doing rather than contemplating.

Out of this background, we have developed a book that differs somewhat from most introductory management texts, although it covers all the topics typically found in such books. Rather than being organized around the traditional management functions, *Managing* is organized around the questions introductory management students most frequently want answered: What's it really like to be a manager? What do managers do? What does it take to be a good manager? What kind of world do managers work in? What opportunities does managing offer? For example, planning and controlling are part of what managers do; behavioral skills and quantitative techniques are needed to be successful; organizational structure and budgets affect the manager's world; entrepreneurial and international careers are some of the opportunities the field offers.

Part 1 responds to the question "Who are managers and what is managing?" It begins with a description of a day in the life of a successful manager, discusses the ways managers typically spend their time, and concludes by showing how contemporary approaches to managing developed.

Part 2 answers the question "What do managers do?" In particular, it explains the functions that managers perform: planning, organizing, directing, and controlling. It shows how these functions affect the decisions that a manager must make on a day-to-day basis.

Part 3 examines what it takes to be a successful manager. Chapters 8 through 13 describe skills necessary to deal with individual and group behavior, communications and decision-making situations, creativity and innovation, and the use of power, influence, and leadership, as well as important tools such as management information systems and quantitative management techniques.

Part 4 describes the world within which managers operate—a world defined by the organization's structure and design, policies, and budgets. We have been careful to describe this world from the perspective of the student and beginning manager, focusing on ways to understand, work with, and use structure, policy, and budgets, rather than how to design organizations and create corporate strategy. This part also discusses the role of staffing and human-resource management in contemporary organizations, and the external forces, including unions, government, and society itself, that all managers face. It concludes with a frank discussion of the problems created by the stress inherent in managing today, as well as the importance of time management.

Part 5 describes in detail two special managerial worlds—those of the entrepreneur and the international manager. Finally it examines management as a career, and the opportunities and challenges it provides.

We use several distinctive features to convey the world of managing and management. Each chapter begins with an original vignette that describes someone in a managerial situation and illustrates a particular managerial activity or principle. Most chapters contain a "Management in Action" that depicts contemporary management problems and experiences. Every chapter ends with "The Bottom Line," which suggests practical applications of the material in that chapter. End-of-chapter cases demonstrate ways to apply the material to managerial problems.

In addition, occasional "Reports from the Field" provide insights into the perspectives of practicing managers who not so long ago were students of management themselves. These reports are drawn from exclusive interviews with successful managers between the ages of 29 and 45. Throughout the book, up-to-date examples from contemporary organizations are used to explain, illustrate, and highlight material. Care has been taken to include examples of managers working in a variety of organizations, from small businesses to multinational corporations, service industries as well as manufacturing, government, education, military, health care, arts, and entertainment.

Our thanks go to all those who reviewed this book in one form or another, especially Joe McGuire and Lyman Porter, who read every word of three drafts, and all those managers and students whose inputs helped shape the content and context of this material.

Diane L. Ferry	*University of Delaware*
Peter J. Frost	*University of British Columbia*
Michael G. Kolchin	*Lehigh University*
John P. Miller	*University of Minnesota*
Stephan J. Motowidlo	*Pennsylvania State University*

H. Joseph Reitz

Linda N. Jewell

MANAGING

CONTENTS

1 / What Is Managing?

Part 1 introduces you to the world of managers and management—the people and their jobs—and to the origins of current approaches to managing.

1 / Who Managers Are and What They Do describes managers as people of action and explains what makes them unique. The manager's environment is shown as both exciting and varied. This chapter discloses some skills and techniques modern managers use to function successfully.

2 / Management Thinking: Its Origins and Development takes us from the beginnings of management thinking through its evolution into current management techniques and approaches. The chapter introduces the managerial concepts of several influential men and women and explains how these principles helped shape current management practices.

1 / Who Managers Are and What They Do

The sky was grey and heavy, with just a few streaks of red, as Pat Fischer pulled into the parking lot. It was just before 7:00 A.M., and it looked like snow, which meant potential problems for the plant's sales and delivery forces making their rounds. Maybe we'll get lucky and get them on the road early today, thought Pat. I'll talk to Chris about keeping the sales staff-meeting brief this morning. Twenty minutes saved might help some people beat the traffic snarls that are sure to come at the evening rush hour.

Pat walked into the office and flipped on the lights. Getting in on Mondays before everyone else was a habit born from experience; everything that could happen usually happened on Mondays. As plant manager Pat had learned that failing to get an early start made it virtually impossible to get through the day's routine without staying late. And tonight there'd be little time to work late—Pat and the company president were taking an important customer to dinner and a basketball game.

Pat sat on the edge of the desk and picked up the "List of Things to do Today" memo pad. There were still three items left from last Friday: Check delivery dates for cartons. Talk to inspector. Pick up tickets. Pat copied these items under

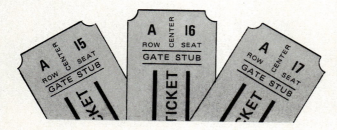

Monday, where "Viking demo" and "See Mel about Ziggy" had already been written. "Viking demo" referred to an in-plant demonstration of an industrial robot by an engineering team from Viking Corporation. Pat had seen a demonstration at a industry convention some weeks earlier and was curious about its potential application in the plant. Having persuaded the company president to attend the demonstration, Pat hoped the Viking people would put on a good show. The reminder to "see Mel about Ziggy" concerned the impending retirement of one of the plant's most skilled workers, Sigmund Wagner, who would have to be replaced.

Before Pat could add to the list, the door opened and Jay, the office manager, came hustling in.

"Morning, Jay. You're in early today," said Pat.

"Hi, Pat. Problem time," replied Jay. "Ann called me at six and said she had the flu and wouldn't be in today. I figured if I got in early I could get to work on her billing, so we can still get invoices out by the afternoon mail."

"OK, Jay, but why don't you call an agency at 8:00 and see if they can't get a temporary replacement over here for the day. We don't want to get too far behind."

"Yeah, OK, Pat," replied Jay, "I'll see what they can do for us."

Pat picked up a clipboard, slipped on a white coat and hard hat, and stepped out into the production area, where work had already begun. "Morning, Doc," Pat said to the government inspector, who was sipping a cup of coffee from the vending machine. "What's up today?"

"Morning, Pat," smiled the inspector. "Everything's humming so far, but I noticed some problems getting steam up again today. It seems like it takes longer each week to get that water up to temperature on the production line. You know, I can't let the line run unless we're getting 150 degrees."

"Yeah, I know, Doc. Thanks for the warning. I meant to talk to you about that last week. We'll be closed down for President's Day. If it'll hold out 'til then, I've got the boiler repair-people coming out to do a full day's maintenance. That should take care of it."

"It should, Pat, but that's two weeks yet. You're taking a chance waiting that long."

"What else can I do, Doc? With one holiday a month as it is, I can't afford to shut down any other time. Keep your fingers crossed!"

Just then Chris, the sales manager, came up, obviously agitated. "Pat, I need to talk to you. I've got Green Mills on the phone. Their regular supplier had a fire over the weekend and they want to give us a big order if we can guarantee delivery today. I've been after that account for over a year. If we can help them out today, we just might get some regular business out of them."

Why is it that chances like this come only when it's toughest to take advantage of them, wondered Pat. The plant was already operating near capacity, and inventories were low because of a big sales drive that had just ended.

"Have you talked to Mel yet?" Pat inquired.

"No," Chris replied, "I couldn't find him, and I didn't want to wait on this. I don't want to lose this sale!"

"OK, Chris, tell them we'll make delivery this afternoon, but make sure you let them know we'll have to extend ourselves to do it."

"Right, Pat, I'll see that they get the message. Thanks!"

"Oh, and Chris," Pat called out as

Chris hurried away, "when you get through guaranteeing delivery, then find Mel and me and let's see if we can figure out how to do it."

"Will do," winked Chris, hustling back to the phone.

Thank God for a production manager like Mel, reflected Pat. Mel generally reacted to special demands and crises with a great deal of bluster but inevitably delivered the goods, and he seemed to enjoy doing the impossible most of the time.

Pat turned and headed for the loading dock to see how the loading of salesmen's trucks had progressed, remembering too late to encourage Chris to cut the sales meeting short. But Chris was already back on the phone to Green Mills, so Pat continued to the dock.

The eleven trucks were all in various stages of being loaded. As drivers and helpers moved about, shouting and laughing, Pat spoke to each in turn, checking their loading sheets and encouraging them to get on the road early. The drivers shared Pat's concern about the weather and paused only briefly to talk. As Pat reached the last truck, the intercom blared out, "Pat Fischer—line 2!" Pat picked up the nearby intercom transmitter.

"This is Pat, Jay. Who wants me?"

"It's Kim Powers at the bank—says it's important."

"Tell Kim I'll return the call in five minutes, as soon as I finish out here," replied Pat.

In reality, Pat didn't return the call for twenty minutes. On the way back to the office Pat met Chris and Mel, and the three plotted a way to fill the Green Mills order without shorting or overly delaying any of the regular customers' orders. Their decisions would move some people from one production line to another and would result in some dangerously low inventory levels, but all agreed the risks were worth the goodwill and potential business that filling the Green Mills order would produce.

When Pat finally called the bank, Kim informed Pat that an $8000 check from one of the plant's customers had been returned for insufficient funds. Pat swore softly and asked Kim to run the check back through in the hope that the customer would have sufficient funds by then. Hanging up the phone, Pat made a note on his clipboard to discuss the problem with Chris and the sales representative who called on that customer.

After a quick phone call to the basketball ticket office, Pat stopped by the sales meeting. Chris kept the meeting to fifteen minutes, and Pat and Chris then discussed the bad-check problem with the sales rep who was to call on that customer late in the day. They decided to use a tactful approach, but the sales rep was to call Chris or Pat before leaving the customer's office to emphasize the seriousness of the problem.

The rest of the morning passed quickly. There were some routine matters: checks to be signed, invoices approved, bills of lading from suppliers to be scrutinized. Pat talked to two important customers who were concerned about deliveries, and made an appointment to see the company's lawyer. A local resident had phoned the company president to complain about excessive plant noise at night. Pat could find no evidence of such noise, but the complainant was threatening a lawsuit and the president had ordered Pat to take care of it.

It was close to 1:00 P.M. before Pat found a chance to go to lunch. Pat and Mel went to a fast-food restaurant a few blocks from the plant, where they developed production plans for the rest of the week. These working lunches for Mel and Pat were routine on Mondays. In fact, the only day Pat didn't have lunch with someone from the plant was Tuesday, when the weekly luncheon meeting of the local association of businessmen and businesswomen took precedence.

After lunch Pat checked the mail and dictated two letters to Ann's temporary replacement. Pat was interrupted by three telephone calls and two plant employees, one of whom was reporting a stockout of a carton used to package products.

By the time Pat had finished dictating, the Viking engineers were ready to demonstrate their new robot system. The demonstration aroused a lot of interest, including that of the union shop steward, who immediately voiced concern over people losing jobs to some "idiot machine." After the president assured the shop steward that such would not be the case in this plant, Pat set up an appointment with the Viking people for the following week.

Following the demonstration Pat made a tour of the plant, stopping to chat with any employee who was so inclined and telling the inventory-control clerk to check on the reported stockout of cartons. As it turned out, the cartons were available but had been moved to avoid getting soaked when a waterpipe valve in the storage area sprung a leak.

The plant engineer had fixed the leak, but the cartons had not been moved back.

After the tour, Pat talked to Mel about the retirement of Sigmund Wagner, to Chris about the sales rep's report on the financially troubled customer, and to the president and the shop steward about robots again. Pat and Chris also spent time overseeing the rearrangements of delivery schedules they had devised to get the Green Mills order out. Pat had Chris call Green Mills when the shipment was on its way, and later to make sure that everything was satisfactory.

About 4:30 the trucks began returning from their routes, some drivers reporting light snow in outlying areas. Pat arranged to meet the customer and the president at the restaurant to allow time to cope with traffic. By the time Pat had gone over the day's production reports, Jay was just finishing up in the office.

"We got all the invoices out in time, but Ann probably won't be back until Wednesday," Jay reported. "Good thing we got the temp in today. We'll need her tomorrow, for sure."

"Good, Jay, that's fine," Pat replied. "I appreciate your getting that stuff out today. You know if we don't bill on time, they don't pay on time."

"No problem, Pat. Well, I'll be in early again tomorrow, until Ann gets back on her feet."

"Don't look for me early," said Pat, "I'm taking a customer to dinner and the basketball game. He's been known to

want to hoist a few afterward, even on a Monday."

"I don't envy you tonight, Pat. Me, I'm gonna take a hot shower, have a nice dinner at home, and put my feet up for the rest of the evening. Goodnight."

But I'm actually looking forward to the rest of the evening, Pat reflected, nosing the car out of the parking lot. Both the customer and the president were congenial people to spend an evening with; the dinner and the game were promising, and there was the challenge of persuading the customer to increase his business. In a way, the evening, like every working day, would provide another set of demands, opportunities, and challenges. One thing for sure, thought Pat with a smile, it was never dull.

Pat Fischer's day provides you with a brief glimpse into the working life of a manager. The day presents a series of challenges, opportunities, demands, and problems that Pat meets with a variety of skills and techniques. For the most part, Pat is successful, although an evening out with a customer remains. Whatever happens that evening, Pat will awaken the next morning to find a fresh set of opportunities and demands.

We provide this vignette because our objective is to do more than define management. We want you to begin to understand what it's really like to be a manager. Ultimately, we want you to learn what it takes to be successful.

If, as is probably the case, you have been employed, understanding what management is all about will be easier. You will have seen your own supervisor meeting challenges, setting goals, handling problems, seeking and giving information, exerting influence, and making decisions.

If you have been a manager, you already know what managing can be like. Yet, because your understanding is limited to personal experience, you must go further.

Whether or not you have worked in an organization, you can reinforce what you learn about management in this course by talking to someone who is a practicing manager. Use that person as a resource to provide insights and examples. For our part, we will share with you the experiences of many other managers. What their experiences and the analyses of their experiences tell us is what this book is all about.

WHO MANAGERS ARE

One way to get some understanding of management is to look at the people who are managers. Exhibit 1.1 includes managers from a variety of fields. What these diverse people have in common is certainly not a set of personal traits. It's what they do, rather than who they are, that makes them managers: each of them accomplishes organizational goals using human, financial, and material resources.

Exhibit 1.1   Managers: A Variety of Opportunities

Frank Borman, former astronaut, now president,
  Eastern Airlines

Marilyn Lewis, entrepreneur, chairman of the board,
  Hamburger Hamlet restaurant chain

Joyce Dannen Miller, national president,
  Coalition of Labor Union Women

Riccardo Muti, music director and permanent conductor
  The Philadelphia Orchestra

Sarah Caldwell, director,
  Boston Opera

Ronald Reagan, President of the United States

Barbara Newell, chancellor of the State University System of Florida

Andrew Young, mayor of Atlanta

Margaret Thatcher, prime minister of Great Britain

Mother Teresa of Calcutta, winner of the 1980 Nobel Prize for Peace,
  founder and head, the Missionaries of Charity

Douglas A. Fraser, president,
  United Auto Workers

Pete Rose, manager,
  Cincinnati Reds professional baseball team

For example, Marilyn Lewis chairs the board of Hamburger Hamlet, a national chain of restaurants. Since she established the first restaurant in California, she has employed people (including her husband, as president), money (from common stock, loans, and retained earnings), information about customer tastes and cuisine, and food and restaurant supplies to accomplish her objectives of controlled growth.

John D. Ong is chief executive officer of B. F. Goodrich. He employs people (particularly production and marketing people), money (an estimated $1.5 billion from retained earnings and sales of assets), and plants, equipment, and machinery. Ong's objective is to switch Goodrich's main focus from tires to chemicals, particularly polyvinyl chloride—a risky venture. His goals are clear: to double sales to $6 billion by 1986 and to raise return on equity from 6.5 percent to 13 percent.

Pete Rose is the field manager of the Cincinnati Reds. By means of people (coaches, trainers, and players), money (provided by the club owners), baseball knowledge, parks, and equipment, he works toward the club's objectives of winning games, increasing attendance, and winning championships.

Most of the managers in Exhibit 1.1 are well known because they manage large organizations. But fame is not a prerequisite for management. Consider the following list of people. Few, if any, are famous, but all are managers:

The manager of the local television station,

The local chief of police,

The coaches of the college athletic teams,

The director of the local theater group,

The instructor of this course,

The chairperson of the United Way campaign,

The managing editor of the local newspaper,

The managers of the restaurants, movie theaters, service stations, and banks you patronize.

Like their more famous counterparts, and, like Pat Fischer, these managers get things done through people.

The chief of police enforces the law and controls crime by means of people (police officers and civilians), money (from the city, state, and federal government), and other resources (the buildings, vehicles, weapons, and equipment under department control). The director of the theater group puts on plays with people (actors, technicians, and community volunteers), money (proceeds from ticket sales, government grants, and donations), and other resources (scripts, the theater building, costumes, props, the news media). The managing editor of the newspaper gets the news printed every day employing people (editors, reporters, printers, and support staff), money (from the publisher's capital, advertising, and sales) and other resources (the building, a wide variety of communications devices, and equipment).

Thus, being a manager does not necessarily depend on who you are or where you work but what you do. A **manager** is *someone who achieves organizational goals through the use of people, money, and other resources.*

WHAT DO MANAGERS DO

From our definition of a manager, then, we can infer that **managing** is *the process of achieving organizational goals through the use of human, financial, and other resources.* But this is a very general definition. To understand what managing really involves, we must take a closer look at that process.

The Managerial Functions

There are certain things every manager does that separate managing from other organizational activities. These **functions of management** are *planning, organizing, directing,* and *controlling the activities of others,* as depicted in Exhibit 1.2.

Planning.   Before a manager can get things done, he or she must decide what things to do, how they are to be done, and when. This is **planning**—*deciding what to do and how to do it.*

Vern O. Curtis, the chief executive of Denny's, Inc., a nationwide chain of restaurants and doughnut shops, inherited a company which had grown too rapidly. Although revenues had increased fifteen percent the previous year, profits had dropped twelve percent. Curtis' new plan was simple— to continue to grow, but to grow in profits as well as revenues. Part of that plan was to open only the 40 potentially most profitable coffee shops of an originally planned 103.[1]

When Lore Harp, president of Vector Graphics, Inc., a microcomputer company got into computers in 1976, she knew little about them and had never held a job. Within five years, the company she helped found had grown to thirty million dollars in sales, with a ten percent after tax profit. Her plan for the company was

Exhibit 1.2   The Managerial Functions

Planning
Setting objectives and deciding how to use resources to achieve them

Organizing
Dividing up and allocating work and resources

Directing
Influencing effort through goals and incentives

Controlling
Maintaining performance standards and progress towards goals

ambitious: a five hundred percent increase in sales. Part of the plan included a public offering of the company stock to help finance this growth.[2]

In both examples, the manager established some objective—a desired state of future affairs for the organization—and decided on ways to achieve that objective.

Organizing.   Having set general objectives, the manager **organizes** by *dividing up the work to be done and allocating it to those who will carry it out.* The manager starts getting things done by deciding which people will carry out which tasks, and establishing the means for coordinating their various activities.

Vern Curtis' organization of Denny's to meet the planned growth in profits included creating levels of management (regional managers, district managers, managers, and assistant managers) to ensure quality and consistency of product. He instituted intensive training and apprenticeship for restaurant managers.

Lore Harp organized Vector Graphics on a functional basis. The friend with whom she first started marketing computers, Carol Ely, became vice-president of marketing. Ely combined advertising, trade shows, packaging, shipping, and service to increase exposure and repeat business. Bob Harp, as technical director and vice-president of engineering, took responsibility for new product development. Dick Tata became vice-president of manufacturing to develop Vector's mass production. Jim Alexander was hired as vice-president of sales.

In these cases the manager divided up the work to be done and allocated it to others. Some managers, like Harp, coordinate these activities themselves; others delegate the task of coordination to a subordinate.

Directing.   Having planned for future events, and organized the work and people to accomplish the plans, the manager then must see to it that efforts are directed toward carrying out these assigned tasks. **Directing** means *insuring that those who are executing the plan know what to do, and that they have some incentives for doing it.*

Vern Curtis has broadened Denny's menu to raise the average amount spent by each customer. He has improved managerial incentives so that the average manager can earn ten percent more than the regular salary in bonuses. He promotes from within.

Lore Harp has sold "solutions to problems" rather than mere hardware. She has emphasized growth through a network of dealers, whom she helped train. She assists dealers with sales aids and started a software library from which dealers can draw. Vector ships on time, provides good manuals, and provides a variety of incentives for dealers to carry and push Vector products. For all of the key people at Vector, there are powerful financial incentives in being part of a fast-growing, well-managed, highly profitable company.

In these examples, the managers made sure that those who were executing the plan understood the plan and exerted their efforts in the appropriate directions.

Controlling.   Despite careful plans, good organization, and accurate direction, performance often deviates from the intended path. Because virtually everything a manager deals with is susceptible to variation, nothing happens exactly as planned.

Variations can be tolerated within limits (temporary delay in shipment; a small unpredicted rise in interest rates; a minor breakdown in communications). Beyond certain limits, however, a manager must get performance back on course. **Controlling** means *seeing to it that performance stays within acceptable limits.*

Control at Denny's has emphasized cost reduction and savings, reflecting Curtis' training as an accountant. The multiple levels of management increase control. Curtis has tightened the criteria used to select sites for new restaurants. He closed 150 units which were not meeting his standards.

Lore Harp's financial control had been tough from the start. She signed all checks, authorized all payments or invoices, and approved customer credit. She signed off on every shipment over $10,000 and personally controlled the 20 most expensive items in inventory, ensuring that none of these items remained in inventory for more than 6 weeks. As a result, Vector's cash flow was excellent.

In both examples, the manager defined acceptable limits and compared actual performance against those standards, taking action when necessary. This is the essence of the control function: seeing to it that performance stays on target, within acceptable limits.

In the introduction to this chapter Pat Fischer carried out each of these functions, planning and organizing the Green Mills order, directing and controlling the treatment of the financially troubled customer. But Pat, like all managers, did more than plan, organize, direct, and control. To get a more complete picture of managing we need to look more closely at what managers actually do.

HOW MANAGERS SPEND THEIR TIME[3]

A police officer's function is to enforce the law, helping society keep the behavior of its citizens within acceptable limits. The officer looks for discrepancies between behavior and standards (violations of the law) and takes corrective action when necessary (warning or arresting offenders).

Yet it would be misleading to describe a police officer's job as one in which the only activities are finding and arresting lawbreakers. Most of the time police work is unexciting. Officers spend many hours filling out reports, talking to or soliciting information from citizens, observing and waiting for something to happen. To be sure, there are exciting moments, but an officer's job is more accurately described as long intervals of routine and boredom, enlivened by occasional moments of action.

In the same way, we can be misled about a manager's job from simply recognizing the manager's functions. To say that a manager plans, organizes, directs, and controls can lead to the conclusion that management is a reflective, sedentary occupation, consisting of decision making and occasional order giving.

Such is *not* the case. Whereas police work is frequently duller than it appears, managing is more active and exciting than its functions suggest. Whatever else managers complain about, few complain that their jobs are boring.

Pat Fischer's day is typical—hectic, not routine. It consists of a variety of activities, most of brief duration, involving a large number of different people. For most

A scheduled meeting can take over an hour of a manager's time.

managers, the job is stimulating, challenging, and unpredictable—long stretches of high activity, relieved by occasional moments of peace and quiet, and even rarer periods of reflective thinking. To be sure, planning, organizing, directing, and controlling do get done, but often in the midst of or in spite of everything else that gets crammed into a manager's day.

Managers' tasks are varied. Most managers regularly carry out five activities: scheduled meetings, unscheduled meetings, phone calls, inspection and observation, and paperwork.

Scheduled meetings can take up the majority of an executive's time. One study found chief executives spending almost sixty percent of their time attending between fifteen and thirty scheduled meetings a week.[4]

What goes on at these meetings? Questions are asked, information given, problems are defined, alternatives compared, and decisions are made—sometimes. At other times, the wrong questions are asked, information is withheld or ignored, problems are glossed over, no alternatives are found, and decisions are postponed. Reports are given; politics are played; status is reaffirmed; compromises are offered; promises and threats are made; coalitions are formed and broken; power is exercised; intelligence, creativity, common sense, stupidity, and lack of imagination are displayed; careers are enhanced or set back. In the course of all this activity, plans are made, resources organized, effort is directed, and control is exercised.

Unscheduled meetings (face-to-face encounters with at least one other person) consume much of the time of middle- and lower-level managers like Pat Fischer. They may take place in the manager's office (a subordinate seeking or giving information, or asking for direction) or outside the office (the manager seeking or giving information or direction to a subordinate at the latter's work station). They may occur in the office of the manager's superior (the manager seeking or giving information or asking for advice) or outside the workplace (talking shop with a colleague at a party).

Inspection and observation, or tours of the work area, are considered important. Managers can see what is going on and can make themselves available to employees and clients. These tours help managers "keep in touch" and demonstrate to employees that the manager is around and interested.

Managers who are successful create a climate for success for themselves and their subordinates. They hire people who have the potential to achieve; they define, encourage, and reward success; they remove obstacles to success; and they set examples for others.

Since personal tours by managers probably have a greater effect on morale than on actual productivity, most managers find time for no more than one such tour a day. An exception is the typical production manager, who might spend a majority of time on the production floor observing, talking, directing, experimenting, and solving the frequent minor crises that occur in a production operation.

Telephone calls are typically to the point. A manager can exchange information briefly without many of the time-consuming social amenities that surround face-to-face meetings. Managers may spend less than ten percent of their time on the telephone but use it to make a large proportion of their contacts easily and quickly. Studies of executives have found that more than one-third of their contacts were made by telephone.[5]

Paperwork is generally disliked by most managers, who read only a fraction of their mail, and reply to or initiate fewer letters than they receive. Nevertheless, reading and answering mail, reading, responding to, and writing reports can take from one-tenth to more than one-third of a manager's time.

Paperwork is usually handled as the opportunity arises. The typical manager has few uninterrupted periods during the work day available for reading and writing. Studies of executives have found that the average length of uninterrupted time is less than fifteen minutes. Only once or twice a week do they have as long as half an hour to themselves![6]

Characteristics of Managerial Activities

Managers do a lot of different things every day. They work *long hours*, and tend to put in more hours as their rank and responsibilities increase. They are *busy*. The number of different activities and interactions is as high as 400–500 per day for first-line supervisors, although the number decreases as rank increases.

Most activities are *brief*, with the exception of scheduled meetings. First-line supervisors spend fewer than two minutes a piece on the majority of contacts. Even chief executives devote fewer than ten minutes per task for half of their activities.

A great deal of their work is *oral*. Upper-level managers may spend as much as ninety percent of their time talking to and listening to others in face-to-face meetings and over the telephone.

Tasks are highly *varied* and *random*. A manager will be confronted with an important problem one minute, and a trivial one the next. Decision making is *fragmented*, as the manager deals with a number of problems simultaneously, often with frequent interruptions.

Differences Among Managerial Levels.   Despite the fact that the workday of all managers tends to be long, busy, varied, and fragmented, with random, mostly brief verbal activities, managers at different levels tend to spend their time differently. (See Exhibit 1.3) At lower levels, managers are most concerned with their specific areas of responsibility. Problems are likely to be short-term. They interact with superiors, subordinates, and peers *within* their departments. Contacts are frequent, brief, and informal.

As managers gain more rank and responsibility, their areas of concern widen. Problems are likely to be longer-term. They interact with more people outside the department and outside the organization. Within the organization, they spend a lot of time with subordinates. Outside the organization, they deal with customers and suppliers, competitors and governmental officials, unions and lawyers. Their contacts are more frequently scheduled, formal, and of longer duration.

Exhibit 1.3   Differences in Frequency and Duration of Activities by Managerial Level

Lower-Level Managers	Upper-Level Managers
More contacts with superiors and peers	More contacts with subordinates
Greater number of contacts	Fewer number of contacts
More time on shop floor	More time in own office
More time in own department	More time outside own department
More time inside organization	More time outside organization
More time in unscheduled meetings	More time in scheduled meetings
Shorter meetings	Longer meetings
Shorter workweek	Longer workweek

Exhibit 1.4   The "Typical" Workweek of Two Honeywell Managers

	Operations Executive	Purchasing Supervisor
Meetings with subordinates (scheduled and unscheduled)	10 hours	16 hours
Contacts with superiors	4 hours	1 hour
Training subordinates	4 hours	4 hours
Receiving training	0 hours	1 hour
Researching feasibility studies	2 hours	1.5 hours
Projects, memos, reports, paperwork	6 hours	3 hours
Telephone calls	10 hours	5 hours
Contacts with vendors or customers	4 hours	10 hours
Thinking about company problems	20 hours	4 hours
	60 hours	45.5 hours

Source: Personal Interviews, Tampa, Florida, June 1980.

Work Away From Work.   Executives report that they spend from sixty to ninety hours a week working. Yet they may spend no more than forty to fifty of those hours "at work." Why the discrepancy?

We know from studies of managerial work that upper-level managers spend a lot of time with contacts outside the organization. We also know they face complex decisions requiring a lot of thinking. They are required to do more long-term planning. Unfortunately, their typical workday leaves little time for extensive outside contacts, reflective thinking, and long-term planning. They are too busy dealing with subordinates, telephones, crises, and meetings.

The answer to this puzzle is simple. As managers move up to higher level positions, they begin to do more of their work away from the office or outside normal working hours. Meetings often take place outside—in the other person's office, at home, at restaurants, or at clubs. Reflective thinking and long-term planning is often done during travel, on weekends, or at home. For many executives, home is the place to think about work.

Exhibit 1.4 summarizes the results of time logs kept by two Honeywell managers during a "typical" week. One is an operations executive responsible for 850 employees; the other supervises a purchasing department of 27 employees. ·

Note that for both managers, paperwork, telephone, and personal contacts take up the "normal" forty-hour week. Reflective planning—thinking about company problems—occurs outside the normal workday.

Contrary to typical differences between upper and lower managers, the supervisor spent less time with superiors than did the executive and as much time with outside contacts. This reflects the nature of their jobs: purchasing departments interact a great deal with suppliers and vendors. Production and operations managers are usually under closer scrutiny of their superiors and typically face crises or changes which require the advice, consent, or at least notification of their superiors.

Managerial Roles

A **role** is a *set of behaviors associated with a particular position in an organization.* One of the behaviors associated with the role of a salesperson is to provide customers with information about products and services; one of the behaviors associated with the role of a noncommissioned officer in the armed forces is to set an example for subordinates to imitate.

Henry Mintzberg, who has devoted much of his career to studying managers, has identified characteristics of managerial roles. He has determined that managers at all levels in a wide variety of organizations have certain roles in common.[7]

Interpersonal Roles. A manager manages people. In an organization, that means the manager has formal authority (the right to give orders and to expect subordinates to obey) and status (one's perceived worth or value relative to others in the organization). As a result of authority and status, a manager performs three functions. As *leader*, the manager influences the group. As *figurehead*, the manager represents the group to outsiders—agencies, clients, suppliers—in ceremonial activities, meetings, lunches, and so forth. As *liaison*, the manager links his or her part of the organization to other social units. For example, the President of the United States entertains visiting heads of state (figurehead), encourages his cabinet members to come up with a plan for reducing inflation (leader), and meets with congressional leaders to discuss the plan (liaison).

Informational Roles. The liaison and leader roles combine to produce three sets of behaviors for managing information. First, the manager *monitors* information, always looking for useful information from all sources. Second, the manager *disseminates* to subordinates information which they need and which might be difficult for them to get. Third, the manager acts as *spokesperson* for his or her group, department, or organization, to provide outsiders with information about his or her area of responsibility. For example, the Commandant of the Marine Corps, attending a meeting of the Joint Chiefs of Staff (monitoring), shares what he has learned about budgets and plans with his staff (disseminating), and returns to the Joint Chiefs to ask for a new weapons system (spokesperson).

Decision-Making Roles. The combination of interpersonal and informational roles leads to a third set of role behaviors: the manager as decision maker. The manager *allocates resources*, deciding who will get what people, money, and equipment. The manager also *handles disturbances*, deciding how to deal with major and minor crises. Third, he or she *negotiates* contracts, treaties, and agreements among parties with conflicting interests. Finally the manager *improves* organizational performance through innovation and entrepreneurial activities. For ex-

A manager needs to understand the behavior of coworkers in order to develop a climate for success.

ample, the manager of a rock group controls the finances and provides the members of the group with spending money when they're on tour (resource allocation). Conflicts within the group, or between the group and the press, police, fans, or technicians must be resolved quickly and smoothly (disturbance handling). The manager works out the details of support services and fees for appearances (negotiating). Finally, the manager looks for new ways to promote the group and its music via talk shows, newspapers, and other media (entrepreneur).

If you reread the manager's day described at the beginning of this chapter, you can identify most of these roles in Pat Fischer's activities. Pat's interpersonal roles included influencing subordinates, representing the company to customers, and providing liaison with government inspectors. Pat spent a great deal of time on informational activities, such as introducing the robotics idea, dealing with the bank, and keeping the president informed. In decision-making roles, Pat reallocated resources to fill the Green Mills order, handled minor crises like the lost cartons and bad check, negotiated with the government inspector and the shop steward, and brought in the robotics demonstration as a possible innovation. Most of Pat's time was spent in interpersonal and informational roles, which is typical for managers at that level.

SKILLS AND TOOLS OF SUCCESSFUL MANAGERS

So far we have described the things that all managers do, the functions they must perform, and the activities in which they typically engage. But not all managers perform their functions well, and not all managers are successful. Those who are successful create a climate for success for themselves and their subordinates. They hire people who have the potential to achieve; they define, encourage, and reward success; they remove obstacles to success; and they set examples for others. In so doing, successful managers use a number of personal skills along with certain managerial tools. Many of these skills and tools are directly related to the manager's most important and variable resource—people.

Understanding Human Behavior

People are a manager's most important resource; they control all the other resources a manager needs: money, energy, supplies, raw materials, land, machinery, and information. People put those resources to work for a manager and consume the product or service the manager creates from these resources.

Exhibit 1.5   Skills and Tools Used by Successful Managers

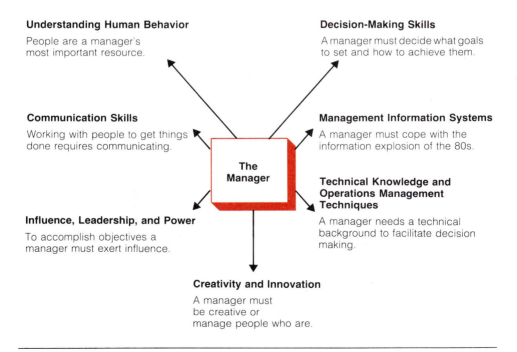

Understanding Human Behavior
People are a manager's most important resource.

Decision-Making Skills
A manager must decide what goals to set and how to achieve them.

Communication Skills
Working with people to get things done requires communicating.

Management Information Systems
A manager must cope with the information explosion of the 80s.

The Manager

Technical Knowledge and Operations Management Techniques
A manager needs a technical background to facilitate decision making.

Influence, Leadership, and Power
To accomplish objectives a manager must exert influence.

Creativity and Innovation
A manager must be creative or manage people who are.

Small wonder, then, that managers who understand human behavior have a significant advantage over managers who don't. Understanding behavior enables the manager both to predict what others will do and to influence them.

Communication Skills

Working with people to get things done requires **communicating**—*using spoken or written words with symbols to convey information.* The manager who doesn't listen to, cannot hear, or fails to comprehend the customers, suppliers, competitors, regulatory agencies, peers, colleagues, superiors, and subordinates is doomed to failure. The manager who cannot efficiently and effectively convey information to these same groups is likewise doomed.

Influence, Leadership, and Power

To accomplish his or her objectives a manager must exert influence. **Influence** is *the process of getting others to behave as one would like them to behave*, while **leadership** is a special type of influence—*the influence of an individual over a group.* **Power** is *the capacity to influence, the traits or conditions which enable one to influence others.*

In the course of a day, a manager influences (and is influenced by) subordinates, coworkers, and superiors. Managers influence suppliers to provide materials, consumers to use products or services, financial institutions to give capital, superiors to give objectives, guidelines, resources, and autonomy, and everyone else to give the information needed to do their jobs.

> *Managing is more active and exciting than its functions suggest. The job is stimulating, challenging, and unpredictable—long stretches of high activity, relieved by occasional moments of peace and quiet. Whatever else managers complain about, few complain that their jobs are boring.*

Decision Making

Management has been described as a decision-making job. It is, of course, much more than that. Managers exert influence, lead, and use power. They collect and disseminate information. They inspect and evaluate. They represent their groups, departments, or organizations.

But much of the managerial function—planning, organizing, directing, and controlling—does involve decision making. A manager decides what goals to set, how to organize to achieve them, how to direct organization effort towards them, and how to control those efforts.

And there is more to decision making than choosing the best alternative. The manager must define problems as well as generate and evaluate alternative solutions. The skill of recognizing problems or anticipating them before they get out of hand is as important as solving them.[8] There are those who contend that *finding* alternative solutions is as important as selecting the best alternative.

Management Information Systems

The increased demand for communications, the great advances in information-processing and communications technology, and the pressures for informed decision making have conspired to give managers another problem: how to deal with all the information so generated.

A leading industrial magazine has warned, "Management's first challenge of the 80s may be to learn to cope with the information explosion which is already inundating executives."[9] Information, and the demands for it, are so great that it can no longer simply be gathered and distributed. Information must be managed, like any other resource, to make sure that accurate, timely information gets to those who need it.

Operations Management Techniques

Technical knowledge means *knowledge about specific products, processes, markets, or services in which an organization deals.* The high demand for MBAs with technical backgrounds provides evidence of the premium many industries place on this knowledge.

Operations management techniques are *special tools developed to help modern managers who are confronted by a wide variety of decisions and surrounded by a world of information.* Many of these techniques can be attributed to the fields of operations research and management science. The use of computers and mathematical models as decision-making aids are central to most of the techniques. Typical matters dealt with by managers who find these analytic techniques useful include planning and forecasting, resource allocation, scheduling, inventory control, demand and supply of services, replacement of plant, machinery, and equipment, information search and retrieval, bargaining, and negotiations.

Creativity and Innovation

This country expects things to improve. Merely staying the same or "holding one's own" isn't good enough. We believe there is always room for improvement, and that those in charge should strive for it.

Improving means changing for the better, finding new and better things to do, and new and better ways of doing them. The demands upon managers to be creative and innovative—or to find and manage others who are creative and innovative—are great.

As the demands for creativity and innovation increase, so do the opportunities for managers who are themselves creative or who know how to find, develop, and manage creativity and innovation. Fortunately, we have learned a lot since World War II about creative people, the creative process, and how managers can create a climate for successful innovation. Given the increasing complexity of problems managers face, and the creative and innovative capacities of competing industrialized nations like Japan and Germany, managers today will have plenty of demand for those skills and talents.

FACTORS THAT DEFINE A MANAGER'S WORLD

Any manager will agree that the job is challenging. For most managers, that challenge comes from trying to achieve organizational objectives in a specific environment, as depicted in Figure 1.6. For example, a new hospital administrator faces the challenge of expanding services in an environment defined by the hospital's organizational policies and structure, the availability of personnel and money, government regulations, unions, ethics, and the pressures of time.

Certain characteristics of the organization itself provide a framework for the decisions and activities of every manager, including chief executive officers. These include the organization's structure and its policies, which are never perfectly suited to any manager and which tend to change slowly and infrequently; finite resources—money, personnel, and time; and the external environment which both guides and constrains a manager's behavior. One influence comes from institutions such as governments and unions. A broader form of influence is social responsibility. Let's examine some of these factors briefly to get an idea of how they define a manager's job.

Exhibit 1.6   Factors that Define the Manager's Environment

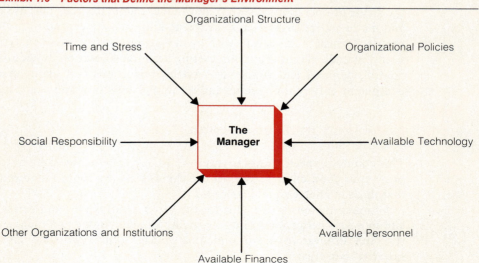

Management in Action
Management Training in the 80s: In School or In House?

Recent changes in the job market for managers are affecting both the content and the methods by which managers are being trained. For twenty years, companies sought out academically trained market researchers, planners, and financial analysts, theoreticians, and "number-crunchers." Today's job market, however, increasingly demands managers who are willing to assume the responsibility of direct supervision, who contribute directly to profits, and who have a broadly applicable set of skills.

Companies are now placing a premium on communication and human relations skills, on the understanding of policy, finance, and international issues. They want managers who can set goals, organize and direct others, take risks, and make decisions on complex problems.

Developing these skills in new managers and retraining veterans will be a demanding task, requiring the efforts of both academic and corporate America. "It's absolutely critical to making this country more competitive, and it is going to take a generation to accomplish," in the view of James P. Baughman the head of management education at General Electric.

One major trend has been a rapid increase in the executive MBA program, in which executives and managers take time away from their jobs to attend courses. Typically, companies pay half the expenses, while the students continue to fulfill all their job responsibilities. In the last ten years there has been a tenfold increase in the number of such programs.

The demand for traditional MBAs has changed as well. Companies are looking for line managers, particularly in sales, manufacturing, and operations. This often means that older students with either industrial or military experience are getting more and better offers than younger, inexperienced peers. It has also meant an increase in summer internships for MBAs to provide them with experience and knowledge in a specific industry.

Many companies are increasing their control over the education of their managerial personnel. Some, like Harris Corporation, have developed programs in cooperation with business schools. Others, like CBS, Bank of America, and Tandem, are starting or expanding their own in-house schools of management. General Electric not only has its own programs, but even sells its managerial education services to other companies. Competition between corporations and business schools to educate and retrain managers for the rest of this century is likely to increase.

Sources: "Who Will Retrain the Obsolete Managers?" *Business Week*, April 25, 1983, pp. 76–80, quotes from pp. 76, 80; "Your Second Chance at an MBA," *Business Week*, March 26, 1984, pp. 138–41; "Job Offers Are Chasing the New MBAs Again," *Business Week*, April 9, 1984, pp. 32–33.

Organizational Structure

The structure and design of organizations to achieve overall objectives is accomplished at the top. Managers must learn to function within the limits that structure creates. For example, consider a company organized by departments. A sales manager who wants to get something done in the shipping department must go through the shipping-department manager. The organization's structure may prevent the sales manager from using the human, financial, or other resources controlled by the shipping department, or at least make it very difficult for the sales manager to use them.

Organizational Policy

A **policy** is *a stated guideline which governs organizational activities.* Policies are set at the highest level of the organizational hierarchy. Even chief executive officers are affected by policies set by the organization's board of directors.

For example, the board of directors of a corporation might establish a policy of "buy American." That is, the organization's managers are restricted from buying products, services, or supplies from foreign vendors when comparable American made products are available. At Vector Graphics, Lore Harp's financial control policy guides her salespeople in extending credit to customers. She alone can approve any order in excess of $10,000.

Personnel

All managers' jobs are affected by the staffing activities of the organization. Coaches and field managers of professional sports teams often have to figure out how to win with mediocre talent provided by the front office. Sometimes owners, in a fit of anger, drive away an outstanding player and expect the manager to make up for the loss by juggling lineups, changing strategy, or performing magic.

Most organizations can find enough warm bodies to fill slots. But having enough really talented people for key positions is a problem that managers must deal with. "If you can't get quality people, nothing else you do really matters," says Marshal Fitzgerald, president of Staford Telecommunications, Inc., a California electronics company.[10]

Finances and Technology

Few managers have enough money and equipment to do everything they want. They have to figure out how to accomplish their objectives with less money than they need. Organizations typically provide managers with a budget—a specific amount of money over a given time period. During his term of office President

Although developing a budget is time-consuming, a manager can use it as a plan for resource allocation and a control mechanism for evaluation of performance.

Reagan made the job of all federal government managers, except Defense, more challenging, in some cases, by cutting their budgets by up to ten percent. Each manager was thus expected to cut back, redesign, or eliminate plans and programs and still accomplish overall department or agency objectives.

Other Organizations and Institutions

Managers in all areas of organizational life deal with unions. Unions influence not only wage rates, but virtually every aspect of personnel management, including hiring, training, discipline, promotion, layoff, transfer, fringe benefits, length of workweek, safety, and working conditions. A big issue in recent airline–labor negotiations has been the size of pilot crews. The airlines wanted a crew of two pilots for the new generation of commercial jets, including the DC–9 Super 80 and the Boeing 757 and 767. The Airline Pilots' Association have argued for three–pilot crews, in the interest of safety (and pilot employment).

Not all organizations are unionized. Every organization, however, is governed by local, state, and federal regulations. At the federal level alone, agencies like the Environmental Protection Agency, the Occupational Safety and Health Administration, the Consumer Product Safety Commission, the Food and Drug Administration, the Energy Department, the Labor Department, the Interior Department, the Justice Department, the Equal Employment Opportunity Commission, and the Securities and Exchange Commission influence managerial activity and cost the company money. In 1981, President Reagan estimated that government regulations "add $100 billion or more to the cost of goods and services we buy."[11]

Social Responsibility

In addition to government and union constraints, every manager deals with and is, to a certain degree, answerable to constituents whose interests conflict. A manager is responsible to his or her subordinates as well as the boss, to consumers and suppliers as well as stockholders, to the community as well as to customers.

More often than not, these interest groups have conflicting demands which the manager must learn to accommodate. Raises to employees are likely to mean higher costs to consumers or lower returns to stockholders. Delaying expansion for fear of environmental damage can cost employees jobs, governments tax revenues, and consumers money and choice.

Managers have values and social concerns like everyone else in society. Translating these values and concerns into action through organizational resources has effects on the interest groups to which managers are, in some way, accountable.

Time and Stress

A manager's typical day is busy, varied, and long, with competing demands for his or her time. Time is the one resource money can't buy; there are but 168 hours per week, some of which must be devoted to concerns other than work.

Successful managers learn to manage their time. They find ways to plan, organize, direct, and control amid all the hustle and bustle of a typical work day, or else they do it outside normal working hours. Time is a relentless enemy.

Stress is a *set of physiological and psychological responses which result from facing an uncertain situation with important outcomes.* "Uncertain situations with important outcomes" is a good way of describing the work environment. Managers face a random array of demands, constraints, and opportunities every day, and these are the stuff that uncertainty is made of.

Some managers can cope with stress; others haven't learned to. For those who haven't learned how much they can tolerate or how to deal with it, stress can be a problem. In mild forms, it can lead to dissatisfaction and occasional inabilities to perform well. In stronger forms, it can lead to forgetfulness, carelessness, hostility, mental or physical illness, and accidents. In some cases, stress results in physical or mental breakdowns. Ultimately, stress can kill.

We know a lot more today than we did ten years ago. We know that different individuals can tolerate different levels of stress. We have learned how to detect and how to cope with it. The manager who learns how to cope will find his or her work easier to deal with. The manager who cannot cope is likely, in one way or another, not to survive.

The Bottom Line

We have given you an initial impression of what it means to be a manager. Those of you who find this image appealing will be curious about what it takes to be a *successful* manager. At the end of each chapter we will provide some guidelines to help you formulate ideas about successful managing.

After studying managers in large, formal organizations for twenty years, John B. Miner has identified six ways in which most of those managers are expected to perform in order to succeed:

1. Be positive toward authority. Managers need the support of their superiors. Alienating your superiors is unlikely to elicit that needed support.
2. Compete and win. The competition for scarce resources is strong, and is not for the fainthearted.
3. Be assertive and active. Managers occupy very active roles which require a great deal of energy.
4. Exercise power. Managers must exert influence over superiors, peers, and outsiders, as well as subordinates, to get things done.
5. Be willing to stand out. Getting ahead requires getting attention for your ideas from subordinates and superiors.
6. Be willing to perform routine aspects of the job. Managers are administrators as well as leaders, and they have a certain amount of routine tasks which must get done.[12]

SUMMARY

Management is the task of accomplishing organizational goals by employing people, information, money, and other material resources. In accomplishing organizational goals, managers plan, organize, direct, and control the efforts of others in the organization.

The job of managing is a busy one. Managers typically work long hours, frequently at a brisk pace, responding to a wide variety of demands and problems. Much of their work is verbal, made up of scheduled and unscheduled meetings and telephone calls.

Most managers spend their time interacting with other people. The manager influences his or her subordinates, represents them to outsiders, and links them to the rest of the organization. The manager monitors information, disseminates it to subordinates, and acts as their spokesperson. As a decision maker, the manager allocates resources, handles disturbances, negotiates, and seeks ways to improve organizational performance.

Managers carry out their functions in the context of an organization. The structure and policies of the organization both guide and constrain their actions. They must achieve objectives with available personnel, finances, technology, and time. Their decisions are influenced by external agents, like governments and unions, and by personal and societal notions of social responsibility.

Because managers spend so much of their time interacting with others, those who understand human behavior, who can exert influence and leadership, and who can communicate effectively are likely to be more successful than those who lack these skills. Other skills and tools particularly relevant to modern management include management information systems, decision-making skills, operations management techniques, and creativity. All of these assets help managers create a climate of success for their organizations.

QUESTIONS FOR REVIEW AND DISCUSSION

1. What are the main activities that occupy a manager's day? How might the proportion of time spent on these activities differ for the president of a bank and the owner-manager of a restaurant?
2. Since executives are interrupted at least every fifteen minutes on the average, it takes them longer to get their work done. Suggest ways to alleviate this problem.
3. What are the three interpersonal role behaviors managers perform? Is any one more important than another? What problems can you see arising if a manager is skilled in one of these role behaviors but lacking in another?
4. Is it more crucial for a manager to be able to disseminate information to subordinates than to act as a spokesman? Why?
5. One benefit of the growth of computer usage has been that the amount of information available to managers has increased greatly. How can this be a problem? How could a manager avoid this problem?
6. In what sorts of organizations or managerial positions would innovative ability be especially important?
7. What does the time constraint imply for people who become or want to become successful managers?

REFERENCES AND NOTES

1. "Denny's: A Brisk Turnaround," *Business Week*, December 15, 1980, pp. 101-5.
2. "Next Stop Wall Street," *Inc.*, Vol. 3, No. 3, March 1981, pp. 36-41.
3. Much of this section is based on research summarized in M. W. McCall, Jr., A. M. Morrison, and R. L. Hannan, *Studies of Managerial Work: Results and Methods* (Greensboro, N. C.: Center for Creative Leadership, 1978) and H. Mintzberg, *The Nature of Managerial Work* (New York: Harper & Row, 1973).

4. H. Mintzberg, "Structured Observations as a Method to Study Managerial Work," *Journal of Management Studies*, 1970, 7, pp. 87-104.
5. *Ibid.*
6. R. Stewart, *Managers and Their Jobs* (London: MacMillan, Ltd., 1967).
7. H. Mintzberg, "The Manager's Job: Folklore and Fact," *Harvard Business Review*, July-August 1975, pp. 49-61.
8. J. Sterling Livingstone, "The Myth of the Well-Educated Manager," *Harvard Business Review*, January-February 1971, pp. 79-89.
9. "Lessons of the 70s for Managing in the 80s," *Industry Week*, January 7, 1980, p. 53.
10. "Money Alone Can't Buy Top Talent," *Inc.*, March 1981, pp. 92-94.
11. "Deregulation," *Business Week*, March 9, 1981, p. 66.
12. J. B. Miner, *The Challenge of Managing* (Phildelphia: W. B. Saunders Co., 1975), pp. 290-307.

SUGGESTED READINGS

M. W. McCall, Jr., A. M. Morrison, and R. C. Hannan, *Studies of Managerial Work: Results and Methods* (Greenshore, N. C.: Center for Creative Leadership, 1978). This analysis provides a summary of the research describing what managers do and how they spend their time.

H. Mintzberg, *The Nature of Managerial Work* (New York: Harper and Row, 1973). The author describes the functions and activities of managers and executives whom he has personally observed.

2/Management Thinking: Its Origins and Development

"Mr. Heard will see you now." The young man thanked the secretary and entered the bank executive's office.

"Well, Brian, how's the restaurant tycoon these days?" asked his host, motioning the young man to a seat.

"Frankly, not too well. We're still not making money, even though business is good. Our gross receipts are up from last quarter, but we still can't seem to show a profit."

"Did you keep a close watch on those cost and inventory figures?" asked the older man, leaning back in his chair.

"Yes, sir, I did, and I asked everyone on the staff to help hold down costs, but the costs are up just the same. No matter how good our business gets, our expenses seem to increase."

"Do you have any ideas, Brian? Right now, my loan committee won't look too favorably on a request for more working capital until you can show a reasonable expectation of profit."

"I just don't know," the young man shook his head. "My father always told me the key to success was to hire good people, pay them well, and keep them happy; they'd take care of the rest. It worked for him, but it doesn't seem to be working for me."

"It's not a bad philosophy," the executive acknowledged, "but what business was your father in?"

"Advertising. He directed the creative department of a big-city advertising firm for twenty years," replied Brian proudly.

"Oh, yes, now I remember." The executive leaned forward and gave Brian a searching look. "Brian, don't you think it's possible that managing your father's advertising department in a big city might be different from running a restaurant in a college town?"

"I don't know; I guess I never really thought of it that way," Brian confessed. "The only business I ever knew much about was my father's, and I know he was very successful."

"I don't doubt that he was," replied Mr. Heard, "but it's likely that what made him a successful advertising executive is different from what might make you a successful restauranteur."

"Well, of course there are differences between the two businesses, but I'm not sure why they would affect the way I manage. What's wrong with hiring good people, paying them well, and keeping them happy?"

"Nothing," replied Mr. Heard, "but I suspect there's more to restaurant management than that. For example, the type of people your father managed in his advertising firm were probably very

different from the people who work in your restaurant.''

"True. With the exception of my chef, they're all college students working their way through school. The people who worked for my father were very creative and were really involved in their projects, as I remember. Advertising was their career.

"So your father's employees were creative, in the midst of their careers, and worked on projects, while your employees are mainly working regular shifts, doing routine work, and using their jobs as a means to an end—to help get them through college. It seems to me those are important differences that might call for different types of management. Not only that, but you're dealing with food and the clientele of a college town, while your father dealt with ideas and probably had national markets to reach.''

"I see what you mean," said Brian. "Let me go home and work on this a while. Maybe I'll call my father and we'll compare notes. Thanks for your help—I'll be back.''

In the vignette above, Brian and Mr. Heard were proposing two different approaches to managing organizations. Brian had tried to use the same techniques that his father had used successfully to manage an advertising firm. Brian was following the *one-best-way* approach to managing, which proposes that certain managerial techniques will be equally successful in all organizations. Mr. Heard, on the other hand, suggested a *contingency* approach, believing that the best way to manage any organization differs from situation to situation, depending on such things as the nature of the organization and the people it employs.

The one-best-way approach that dominated management thinking in the early decades of this century has gradually given way to the contingency approach. By studying the ways in which theories have developed, managers can enhance their understanding of management as it is practiced today and better avoid mistakes of the past.

MANAGEMENT PRACTICE BEFORE MANAGEMENT THEORY

People developed organizations because they learned that groups of people working together can acquire resources and accomplish goals that individuals working alone cannot. The Egyptians created organizations many centuries ago to help build their pyramids, although management, as they practiced it, was little more than supervision: Thousands of laborers worked under the direction and watchful eyes of royal overseers.

How to manage was not a problem then. Social class was the most important determinant of occupation; many workers were actually "owned" by their bosses.

Even those who were not slaves or indentured servants had little choice but to do what they were told, when they were told, and how they were told; the alternative was usually starvation.

Social changes gradually altered these conditions, and technological changes made managing more than a matter of merely supervising. The Industrial Revolution introduced machines into the production process on a large scale. For the first time, the activities of people and machines had to be coordinated, and this coordination fell to managers.

It became obvious that the old ways of running organizations were too crude for a changing and competitive world. Machines increased production and allowed for expansion, but they also required skilled labor, and there was little available. In addition, there were virtually no managers able to successfully handle the expanded duties. Finally, improved communication and transportation methods made competition a reality for more and more firms.

THE SEARCH FOR ORGANIZATIONAL EFFECTIVENESS

With the old ways proving inadequate, the quest for new ways to make organizations more effective began. This search led to formal study of organizations in general, and management in particular.

A group of people become an organization only through management. One or more individuals must set goals, determine tasks, hire workers, determine compensation, acquire raw materials, and perform all the other activities described in Chapter 1. The search for the key to organizational effectiveness started as the search for the single most important of these managerial functions and the best way to perform it. This was called the one-best-way philosophy. In the anecdote that began this chapter, Brian was following a one-best-way philosophy. He expected the management practices that worked for his father to work for him, despite significant differences in their businesses and environments.

The belief that *one aspect of organizational functioning is more important than any other in determining the success or failure of an organization*, and that *there is one best way to carry out this function to achieve the most effective organization* characterizes **one-best-way thinking.** For example, motion picture magnates in the 1940s believed the most important factor in a movie studio's success was its stars, and the best way to ensure having stars was to create them. Thus, studios sought out attractive young hopefuls, such as Lana Turner, Gregory Peck,

Exhibit 2.1   Evolution of Management Philosophies

Classical Management	Transitional Management	Contemporary Management
Scientific Management	The Quantitative Approach	The Open-Systems Model
The Bureaucratic Model	The Human Relations Approach	The Contingency Approach
Administrative Management		

and John Wayne, and put them under long-term contracts while they were carefully prepared for stardom. If the performer caught the public's fancy, he or she went on to become a star. If not, the contract was not renewed when it expired.

It may seem a long way from movies to management, but it really isn't. Concentrating on one part of a complex organization and expecting it to generate success for the whole enterprise is the same kind of thinking whether it is done by Darryl F. Zanuck or the president of a modern multinational corporation. One-best-way dominated management thinking as it emerged from the search for organizational effectiveness in the twentieth century.

THREE STAGES OF MANAGEMENT THINKING

The history of formal management thinking in this century is usually divided into three stages that we will call Classical, Transitional, and Contemporary, as depicted in Exhibit 2.1. However, the times represented by each period overlap, and these three stages should not be thought of as hard and fast divisions.

Classical Management

Those who were searching for the key to organizational effectiveness in what we call the Classical stage examined organizations of 1900–1930. They were the pioneers of the formal study of management.

Scientific Management.   Frederick Taylor, known as "the Father of Scientific Management," was an engineer who used research, experience, and experimentation to improve organizational functioning. The term *scientific management* is derived from his belief that the methods of science could be applied to the study of management.

If the one-best-way framework is applied, the basic premises of scientific management can be described as:

1. The most important aspect of organizational functioning is the actual physical work done in the organization.
2. There is one best way to perform each task, and this way can be determined by scientific analysis.

The implications of these assumptions for the practice of management are clear. To run an effective organization, management should scientifically determine the best way to perform each job, hire employees with the necessary abilities (strength, dexterity, eyesight, and so on) to do the job, train them, and pay them a fair wage.

Taylor's approach to organizational effectiveness was a very specific one. Each organization had to analyze its own particular tasks, but this attention to detail paid off. Scientific-management methods were very successful. The productivity of some of Taylor's clients was reported to have risen as much as 350 percent.

It became fashionable in later years to criticize Taylor's engineering approach to organizational effectiveness as inhumane. To many, scientific management meant "treating people like machines." However, the association of these two ideas is both unfair and inaccurate. Taylor did *not* believe that people were the same as machines. What he did believe was that both workers and management would benefit from the efficient performance of work. Although he saw this benefit in human as well as financial terms, he did emphasize the financial gains.

> *Be it a case of commerce, industry, politics, religion, war, or philanthropy, in every concern there is a management function to be performed, and for its performance there must be principles, that is to say acknowledged truths regarded as proven on which to rely.*
>
> Henri Fayol

Source: *General and Industrial Management,* translated from the French (Durod, 1949) by C. Storrs, London: Pitman Publishing, Ltd., 1971. Quote from pages 41-42.

It is important to remember that Taylor was a product of his times. "A fair day's work for a fair day's pay" was a progressive idea in 1900. Taylor was concerned both that the company receive a fair day's work, and that the worker receive a fair day's pay. In fact, at one time, he was branded a Communist for his outspoken belief in financial incentives for workers.[1]

Viewed from an historical perspective, scientific management was far from an inhumane approach to management. Its methods made work easier and less tiring. For example, Frank and Lillian Gilbreth, two industrial engineers who specialized in time and motion study and job simplification, successfully developed work methods that dramatically increased productivity while reducing worker fatigue. The resulting increases in efficiency provided workers with higher wages, as well as companies with higher profits.

The basic principle of scientific management—using the methods of science to find better ways of managing—flourishes today.

The Bureaucratic Model.   While engineers concentrated on physical work, social scientists thought the key to organizational effectiveness lay elsewhere. Max Weber, a German scholar with wide-ranging social reform ideas, conceived of the organizational form known as bureaucracy. Within the one-best-way framework, Weber's approach can be characterized by the following assumptions:

1. The structure of an organization is the most important determinant of effectiveness.
2. The best way to structure an organization is according to the tenets of his bureaucratic form.

Therefore, to run an effective organization, management should clearly define the divisions of work and the duties and rights of each job position; define the hierarchy of authority and the rules and policies for dealing with work-related matters; and select and promote employees on the basis of ability and job performance.

Weber's bureaucratic model was a broader approach to organizational effectiveness than Taylor's, applying to governmental as well as industrial organizations. The kind of work done in a company was irrelevant to the bureaucratic concept. Almost all modern organizations embody some, if not all, of the characteristics of a bureaucracy: well-defined jobs, hierarchy of authority, rules and policies, and rational selection and promotion criteria.

Although bureaucracy has come to connote an overgrown, inefficient, and rigid organization full of employees who are devoted to rules and forms in triplicate, the blame does not belong to Weber. Like Taylor, Weber was a product of his times. He believed those times created a need for an organizational structure that would be unambiguous, continuous, and allow for quick decisions. He also saw a need for a structure that would counteract the abuses of nepotism and favoritism that were prevalent in the organizations of his time. Weber wanted to create a structure in which "what you know" would be more important than "who you know," so he deliberately built impersonality of work relationships into his structural model. The formation of bureaucracies represented a significant step toward organizational effectiveness.

Administrative Management Theory.   The third direction taken by those who studied organizational effectiveness in the Classical period focused on the performance of management functions. Henri Fayol, a French mining executive, became the most well known of the administrative management scholars.

Fayol recognized that industrial activities included many functions, but he believed that:

1. The management function is the only necessary aspect of organizational functioning.
2. The one best way to perform the job of management is to follow certain universal principles.

One of Fayol's principles of management is the **Unity of Command Principle:** *any employee shall take orders from only one person for any particular work activity.* Fayol believed that this and thirteen other principles were universal truths flexible enough to apply to any situation.[2] Thus, in scope, his theory was on a level with Weber's.

Administrative management theory, of which Fayol's principles are the most characteristic example, has generally escaped the bitter attacks leveled at scientific management and the bureaucratic model.[3] The management functions of planning, organizing, directing, and controlling presented in Chapter 1 can be directly traced to Fayol.

Summary: The Classicists.   The first third of this century was marked by a search for organizational effectiveness that focused on tasks, structure, and administrative policies of an organization. While the writers of this period thought people were important, they assumed that people worked only for pay, and that it was up to the organization to direct and control them to the financial benefit of all.

This assumption was a natural one at the time. Not only were the working classes quite poor, but the study of behavior was still in its infancy and little was known about the more complex aspects of motivation. Ironically, it was a series of experiments in the scientific-management tradition that finally led to a broader view of people in the work environment.

Transitional Management

The second period of management thinking covers roughly the second one-third of this century, 1930–1960. The shift away from the particular interests of the Classical period began inconspicuously enough in Western Electric's Hawthorne production plant in the late 1920s.

Five young women who assembled telephone-relay equipment were selected to work in a carefully controlled environment to see what effects changes in their working conditions would have on their productivity. Initially, when conditions such as lighting, rest periods, and incentives were improved, their productivity increased as well. However, when conditions were then reversed, their productivity continued to climb.

Given these surprising results, the researchers concluded that worker productivity was affected by more than pay and working conditions. Social factors such as the attention and status given the five experimental subjects affected their performances. The Hawthorne studies revealed the influence of social forces at work and produced the principle called the **Hawthorne Effect**—that is, *people are likely to change their behavior when they are aware that it is being monitored.* From these new perspectives emerged human-relations management, one of the pillars of the transitional period in management thinking.

Human-Relations Management. The discovery of the importance of the social environment attracted a diverse group of management scholars, psychologists, and sociologists to the search for organizational effectiveness. They argued for a human-relations approach to management, which proposed that:

1. The most important factor in organizational effectiveness is the way employees are treated;
2. The best way to treat employees is as people first and workers second.

Unfortunately, those who championed this approach could not agree on the meaning of "treating employees as people." Mary Parker Follett, a management consultant and philosopher, argued that management should be aware of the individual psychology of each employee and should stress interpersonal communications, coordination, and cooperation.[4] Douglas McGregor believed it meant changing basic assumptions about the nature of people at work.[5] Chris Argyris insisted that it meant making the workplace conducive to individual growth and development.[6]

In the anecdote that introduced this chapter, Brian adopted a human-relations approach learned from his father: hire good employees, keep them happy, and let them do the rest. That approach had worked for his father, but it wasn't working for Brian. While the human-relations approach produced a big shift in management thinking, it suffered the same flaw that characterized earlier approaches; it held that there was one best way to manage all organizations and employees.

Quantitative Management.   The techniques and theories of quantitative management share a mathematical orientation. They are largely information-processing and mathematical-modeling approaches to the problems of organizations developed in response to the ever-increasing complexities of organizational decisions during the middle years of this century. They were made possible by the technological advances of the time, especially the computer.

As a group, quantitative management practices and theories may be described within our one-best-way framework as sharing beliefs that:

1.   The most important aspect of an organization's functioning is its decision-making capabilities.
2.   The best way to improve decision making in organizations is to improve information access, storage, retrieval, transmittal, and processing.

Quantitative-management approaches offer few clues for the practice of management in the traditional sense. People provide the information and operate the computers, but the heart of the theory is the flow and processing of information. This approach, then, is a natural offshoot of scientific management in its focus on one aspect of the management process and its use of computer and mathematical sciences to find optimal solutions to management problems. Some of its more important aspects will be covered in greater detail in Chapters 11 and 12.

Summary: Transitional Management Thinking.   Most of the proponents of human-relations management were social scientists; most of those involved in quantitative management were mathematicians and computer scientists. These were new perspectives in management as formulated during the Classical period. As a field of study, however, management remained fragmented. The belief that there must be one best way to bring about organizational effectiveness persisted.

Contemporary Management

It took a concept borrowed from an entirely different field of study to push the search for organizational effectiveness beyond the boundaries of a one-best-way approach. That concept led to a new way of thinking about organizations themselves, and thus about managing organizations. It treated organizations like open systems.

The Open-Systems Concept.   A biologist sees living organisms—people, animals, and plants—as systems. An **open system** is a *functioning entity, made up of a number of interdependent parts, that is itself dependent on its environment.* Each part of a system gives something to, and gets something from, the others; that is, the parts work together to make up an organized living being. This being is separated from its environment by a boundary, but it is dependent on that environment for survival. It is this dependency that makes it an *open system.* It must take

Exhibit 2.2   An Open-Systems Model

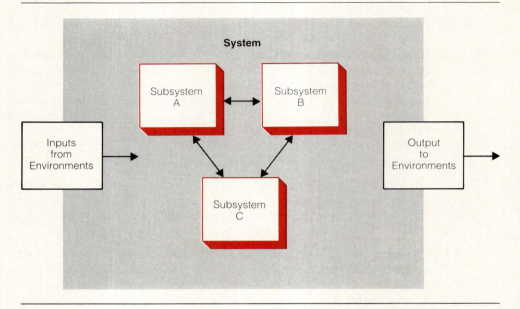

from its environment the raw materials necessary to live and grow, and it must dispose of its waste materials into that environment (see Exhibit 2.2).

You are a very complex open system made up of organs, blood, glands, bones, and other parts. These parts, or *subsystems*, are interdependent. If your liver does not function correctly, you will be very ill, even if your heart and lungs work perfectly. *The reactions of various parts of a system to occurences in other parts* are called **systems effects.**

Like all living open systems, you are dependent on your environment. From it you take air, water, and food; you receive a multitude of stimuli that provide the information you need to get through each day. Into that environment you dispose of unneeded substances, such as carbon dioxide.

General Systems Theory.   In 1951, a biologist, Ludwig von Bertalanffy, proposed that the biological concept of open systems be applied to all levels of science.[7] His **general systems theory** stated that *all functioning entities be viewed as systems composed of subsystems and acting as parts of larger systems.* He believed that this theory held the potential for unifying the sciences at last.

General systems theory was not really new in 1951; it was more an idea whose time had finally come.[8] Others began to elaborate upon von Bertalanffy's basic idea and to demonstrate the practicality of applying a general set of concepts to a variety of areas. One measure of their success is the fact that we meet the term *system* so frequently and in so many contexts today.

Among those who saw the potential usefulness of general systems theory as it was originally put forth were individuals whose particular interests lay in the study

Exhibit 2.3   A Business Organization as a System

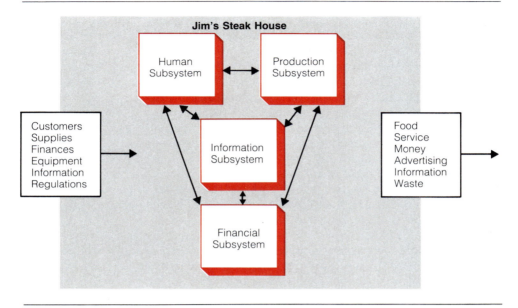

of organizations. By the mid-1960s, the idea that an organization could be likened to a system had gained momentum and began to have a significant impact on thinking about management and organizational effectiveness.[9]

The Impact of a Systems Approach on Management.   To see how the open-systems concept can be applied to a business organization, we will examine a medium-sized restaurant, Jim's Steak House, depicted as a system in Exhibit 2.3.

Jim's Steak House is a system made up of several subsystems. The human subsystem includes cooks, waiters and waitresses, busboys, a manager, two assistant managers, and Jim, the owner. The structure of the organization defines the formal interdependencies, or relationships, among these individual parts of the human subsystem. Other subsystems include the administrative subsystem (rules and policies), the financial subsystem, the production subsystem (preparing and serving food), and the information subsystem.

The primary goal of Jim's Steak House is to make a profit. Jim sees the means to that goal as providing good food at reasonable prices in a nice atmosphere with friendly and prompt service. Therefore, the various employees must perform effectively, since the ineffective performance of any of these functions, from cooking to serving to bookkeeping, can mean failure for the system as a whole. Good food will not make up for consistently poor service, nor will good service make up for consistently being out of several menu items.

The restaurant is obviously dependent upon its environment for customers. It is dependent in other ways as well. The chef may be very good at ordering the right quantities of food and supplies, but this skill is not worth much if the suppliers are not dependable. Likewise, those who maintain the physical appearance of the restaurant may keep it sparkling, but if the garbage pickup is irregular, the smell and unsightly mess outside the building may turn potential customers away.

In addition to being dependent, Jim's Steak House is also *constrained* by its environment. Government regulations and local ordinances dictate many procedures related to the cooking and serving of food. Other regulations control the sale of alcohol, hiring, and firing practices, and set upper limits on the number of customers who can be served on the premises at any one time.

Finally, like all systems, Jim's Steak House experiences systems effects when decisions are made or things happen in any subsystem. A recent decision to expand the menu and add several relatively expensive items (information and production subsystems), met the goal of increasing business. The change also resulted in an increase in the number of job applications from experienced waiters and waitresses (human subsystem). As the number of people seeking jobs at Jim's increased, Jim noticed that his current staff seemed to work harder, perceiving that they could be easily replaced.

The expanded menu included a large number of high quality, perishable items. Jim correctly anticipated the required changes in ordering, delivery, and storage (production subsystem), but not changes in methods of payment. Cash-on-delivery demands from certain new suppliers led to short-term cash flow problems and required changes in bookkeeping procedures. A change in the information and production subsystems affected the financial subsystem.

The foregoing example shows that the idea of describing a business organization in open-systems terms can be useful. Parts of a single subsystem affect each other directly, and changes in one subsystem can produce changes in other subsystems. All subsystems must work together for the larger system to survive and grow, and the larger system must interact effectively with its environment.

> *This statement—the worker is a social animal and should be treated as such—is simple, but the systematic and consistent practice of this point of view is not. If it were systematically practiced, it would revolutionize present-day personnel work. Our technological development in the past hundred years has been tremendous. Our methods of handling people are still archaic.*
>
> F. J. Roethlisberger

Source: *Management and Morale*, Cambridge, Mass.: Harvard University Press, 1941. Quote from page 26, 14th. printing, 1962.

It is necessary to understand the systems approach to understand contemporary management thinking. Systems theory was adopted by those who study organizations. In adopting this model, basic assumptions about organizations as closed, self-determining units had to be changed. In the process, the basic approach to thinking about managing organizations also changed. The major implications of a systems view of organizations are shown in Exhibit 2.4.

As is clear from this exhibit, one of the most important changes brought about by looking at organizations as systems was that it removed the necessity for quarreling over which aspect of organizational functioning was the *most* important to

Exhibit 2.4   Implications of an Open-Systems View of Organizations

System Characteristic	Implications for the Management of Organizations
The system is a whole made up of parts.	The concept of "organization" has meaning only as the sum of *all* its parts—tasks, structure, people, and procedures.
The parts of a system are interdependent.	No *one* aspect of an organization is always the *most* important, because each affects and is affected by the way the others function.
A system is dependent on its environment.	An organization is not a closed entity. External factors affect internal operations.

effectiveness. In a system, *every* part is important; if one fails to function effectively, negative systems-effects occur in others. Every part of an organization—task, structure, policies, people, and information—is an integral subsystem of the larger system, and all must be considered if an organization is to be effective.

Of course, viewing an organization as a system does not mean that everyone interested in organizations in general, or management in particular, must study everything. Most people will be more interested in one aspect than in others. The systems view simply requires that whatever is being emphasized is seen only from the perspective of its role in the overall system.

The second major implication of the systems approach was that it made nonsense out of the search for the one-best-way to structure an organization, design jobs, motivate workers, or make any other organizational decision. From a systems perspective, each organization is somewhat different. Even if the parts appear similar, their interactions are not identical, and neither are their environments.

When organizations are viewed as systems that exist in environments with which they must interact, it makes no more sense to try to treat them all alike than it does to try to treat all people alike.

In short, the acceptance of the open-systems model of organizations requires the adoption of an "it depends" philosophy. In essence, this new way of thinking says that the appropriate action to take with respect to any aspect of organizational functioning depends upon the characteristics of the organization and its current situation. This is the heart of contemporary management. It is called a contingency, or situational, approach.

The Contingency Approach.   Contingency means something that is conditional. Given certain conditions, one thing works best; given other conditions, something else works better. The **contingency approach** means *identifying and employing the most effective managerial action for a particular situation.* It substitutes analysis for predetermined, one-best-way solutions. According to this approach, the more effective organizations are those whose managers and policy-makers recognize the differences between conditions that call for different courses of action.

The basic task in developing contingency theories is to develop guidelines for assessing conditions under which alternative management actions or approaches are appropriate. Contingency theories of leadership, to be studied in Chapter 10, attempt to specify the conditions under which various kinds of leader behavior will be most effective. In contrast, the old one-best-way approach attempted to find the *one* pattern of leader behavior that worked best under all conditions.

The contingency approach does *not* mean that there is not a best way to handle any *particular* situation. Analysis may reveal several suitable alternatives, but one will probably be most effective or efficient. However, this best way is not necessarily best for a different organization, or even for this organization under different conditions.

To illustrate a general contingency approach to management, we will consider two hypothetical department stores, one in Cleveland, Ohio, and one in Dallas, Texas. Even though the department stores in Cleveland and Dallas are both located in cities, are about the same size, and carry merchandise in about the same price range, their external environments are quite different; therefore, there will be different decisions about what is stocked and when it is available.

> *Man can respond to many different kinds of managerial strategies, depending on his own motives and abilities and the nature of the task; in other words, there is no one correct managerial strategy that will work for all men at all times.*
>
> Edgar H. Schein

Source: *Organizational Psychology.* (2nd Ed.). Englewood Cliffs, N. J.: Prentice-Hall, 1970. Quote from page 70.

The environments of the stores are different in other ways as well. Different social traditions in the South and the Midwest mean that differences in clerk training will probably be required. In addition, the accepted pay/benefit program for the Cleveland store will probably be different from that of the Dallas store. Obviously, to attempt to apply the same best-way formula to order stock, train clerks, or reward employees in the two stores may be overlooking differences which will mean failure.

Conditions within organizations are always changing, and today's best way may be tomorrow's disaster. Letting the Dallas clerks decide on their own work schedules, for example, may be to everyone's satisfaction when sales are slow, but may cause havoc during the Christmas rush.

As you can see, the extent to which particular management policies and decisions are appropriate depends to some extent on the organization's external environment and conditions within the organization at any time. Appropriateness also depends to some extent on the kinds of systems effects likely to be created by a particular policy or action. Even if letting the Dallas clerks decide their own work schedules does not interfere with customer service, such a plan will have effects in other parts of the organization. Both personnel and payroll functions will be affected, and if either one cannot adjust as required, the subsequent confusion will likely undo many of the benefits of the original plan.

MANAGEMENT THINKING AND MANAGING

Many people question the practicality of the contingency approach. How, they argue, is it possible for one human being to deal with so many factors and the complex relationships between them?

Application of a pure contingency approach *is* beyond most of us. Even if we had the skills and understanding, we would not have the time to treat each decision as unique. In an effort to combat the enormous appeal of one-best-way solutions to management, theorists may have gone to the opposite extreme.

The more moderate position between the view that each organizational decision is unique (contingency) and the view that all can be treated the same (one best way) is that all organizations have some aspects in common and some that are unique. From this perspective, effective management would consist of being able to determine which aspects of the particular situation were sufficiently standard to allow the application of basic principles and which were different enough to require detailed analysis before action was taken. Management scholar Jay Lorsch states this position quite clearly:

The trend toward more situation theories signifies only a decline in emphasis on universal theories and the techniques they have spawned, not that these theories should or will disappear. Undoubtedly, on a limited number of issues, such generalizations are useful guides to action. The problem for a manager is to identify those issues where a universal theory is helpful, and not confuse them with issues where the solution depends on the situation.[10]

A major purpose of this book is to help you learn what to look for in analyzing the differences between situations. For example, by the time you have completed this course, you should not have to puzzle over whether to accept the general principle that subordinates require feedback on their performances. They do. To that extent, there *is* a best way. But you should also understand that the form and content of useful feedback depends somewhat on the nature of the particular situation. In that respect, the best way is contingent upon the situation.

MANAGING AND MANAGEMENT EDUCATION

In a way, the contingency approach to management is nothing more than a formal statement of what good managers have always known. Studying management through the research, writings, and experience of others can teach us a great deal. We can figure out the questions to ask and some places to look for answers. Successfully applying what we learn, however, is something of an art. Good managers know that theories don't translate directly from the text to the shop floor, and the contingency approach reinforces that knowledge. They are aware that changing one part of the organization will affect other parts as well, and the systems approach makes that explicit.

The future development of management as a formal field of study will depend upon increasing our abilities to translate the art of applying what is known about management into a form that can be passed on to others. Despite current inadequacies in making this transition, formal courses and textbooks in management can clearly help. As one thoughtful student wrote when asked why he was studying management, "I've been hiking and camping all my life, but when I go into new territory, I want a map, even if it is a rough one. I've also been working for quite a while and I've learned that experience isn't everything there either. I expect my degree in management to give me a map of the territory."

This book, then, is an introductory map of the territory of management. Reading it isn't the same as being a manager, any more than looking at a map of Arizona is the same as hiking around in the Grand Canyon. On the other hand, eighty years of collected research and experience ought to provide you with a pretty good start.

The Bottom Line

Those who ignore the past are condemned to repeat it. Those who understand the past can avoid its mistakes. The history of management study suggests:

1. Be wary of those who sell a particular approach or technique as the one best way to manage. Gimmicks or fads appear as often in the world of management as they do in the world of fashion, only at greater cost.
2. Be open to new approaches or techniques that may work in particular situations. At the same time, learn to recognize similarities and differences in those situations where new techniques have worked.
3. Management is not simply dealing with people, handling information, making decisions, acquiring resources, or organizing work. A manager who confines his or her interest to one activity or function is highly vulnerable.
4. A change in one part of the organization will affect other parts. A change in the organization's environment will affect the organization. Anticipating the effect of changes can create opportunities from potential problems.

SUMMARY

Management is relatively new as a formal field of study, dating for practical purposes to the early 1900s. Its development since that time can be roughly divided into three periods. The Classical period, 1900-1930, was characterized by a search for the most effective way to run an organization, concentrating on the physical work to be done, the structure of an organization, and the principles by which its management was to be guided. While the employees of the organization were not considered unimportant, they were basically treated as a constant.

The transitional period of management thinking, 1930-1960, saw quantitative approaches to information processing and management decision-making continue the tradition of emphasizing nonhuman factors in determining organizational effectiveness. At the same time, however, others turned their attention to the importance of employees as individuals whose behavior could not be considered a constant.

Both classical and transitional approaches to management were characterized by one-best-way thinking; there was one aspect of organizational functioning that was the most important, and one best way to perform that function. Not until a new way of conceptualizing organizations themselves was established did this narrow approach begin to change.

The open-systems concept, borrowed from biology, viewed organizations as social systems made up of separate, but highly interdependent, parts. Survival of the system (organizational effectiveness) depended upon all of the parts functioning in successful interaction with one another and with the external environment.

Seeing organizations as open systems removes the necessity for trying to decide which function is the most important. It also makes nonsense out of one-best-way thinking. Since the parts, interactions, and environments of each organization will be a little different, the solution of problems in every case are likely to be a little different.

Current management thinking, called the contingency or situational approach, stresses that the appropriate action to take depends upon the characteristics of the particular situation. Thus, the contingency approach calls for analysis rather than preconceived notions. The systems view of organizations reinforces the importance of including both human and nonhuman factors in that analysis.

QUESTIONS FOR REVIEW AND DISCUSSION

1. Would it be possible to use the ideas of scientific management, the bureaucratic model, and human-relations management simultaneously in an organization? Why or why not?
2. To be sure that you understand the difference between "one best way" and "it depends," consider the problem of excessive absenteeism in one department of a company.
   a. Describe a one-best-way solution to this problem.
   b. Describe some of the factors to be considered if you took a contingency approach to the same problem.
3. Choose an organization with which you are familiar (other than a restaurant) and draw a sketch of it as an open system. Label the major parts, or subsystems, and use arrows to show the most important interdependencies among the parts. You may sketch this college or university, for example.
4. List five factors in the environment of your college or university and describe briefly how each might affect its functioning. Example: Other colleges and universities in the area compete for students and teachers.

5. Your company is considering changing the pay basis for workers in one department from an hourly wage to a piece rate in hopes of increasing production in that department.
   a. Describe one possible *positive* systems effect of the proposed change.
   b. Describe one possible *negative* systems effect of the proposed change.
   Remember: Positive and negative systems effects are *not* the same as reasons why a change will or will not meet the stated goal. (Review the example of Jim's Steak House if necessary.)

REFERENCES AND NOTES

1. A recent review of Taylor's work concludes that most of the more familiar criticisms are unjustified, and that his genius has been generally underrated. *See* E. A. Locke, "The Ideas of Frederick W. Taylor: An Evaluation," *Academy of Management Review*, 1982, 7, 1, pp. 14-24.
2. The fourteen principles are listed and described in an excerpt from Fayol's original work titled "General Principles of Management," in J. N. Shafritz and P. H. Whitbeck, eds., *Classics of Organization Theory*. Oak Park, Ill.: Moore Publishing Co., Inc., 1978, pp. 23-27.
3. The classic criticism of the administrative-management approach was written by H. A. Simon, "The Proverbs of Administration," *Public Administration Review*, 1946, 6, pp. 53-67.
4. M. P. Follett, *Freedom and Coordination*. London: Management Publications Trust, 1949.
5. D. McGregor, *The Human Side of Enterprise*. New York: McGraw-Hill Book Co., 1960.
6. C. Argyris, *Personality and Organization*. New York: Harper & Row, 1957.
7. L. von Bertalanffy, "General Systems Theory: A New Approach to the Unity of Science," *Human Biology*, 1951, 23, pp. 302-36.
8. von Bertalanffy actually introduced general systems theory in the late 1930s, but it was some fourteen years before the idea had impact.
9. One of the earliest publications to make the link between general systems theory and the study of management was probably S. Tilles, "The Manager's Job: A Systems Approach," *Harvard Business Review*, 1963, 41, 1, 73-81.
10. J. W. Lorsch, "Making Behavioral Science More Useful," *Harvard Business Review*, 1979 (March-April), p. 176.

SUGGESTED READINGS

"Hawthorne Revisited: The Legend and the Legacy," *Organizational Dynamics*, 1975 (Winter), 66-80. This interesting perspective comes out of a symposium jointly sponsored by Western Electric and The Harvard Business School on the fiftieth anniversary of the Hawthorne Studies.

Katz, D. and Kahn, R. L. *The Social Psychology of Organizations*, 2nd ed. New York: John Wiley and Sons, Inc., 1978. This is the best and most comprehensive treatment of organizations as open systems.

Lewis, S. "The Cat of the Stars," in M. Schorer, ed. *I'm A Stranger Here Myself and Other Stories by Sinclair Lewis*. New York: Dell Publishing Co., 1962. This story of Adolphus Josephus Mudface the cat, written by Lewis in 1919, is the most delightful illustration we've come across of the meaning of systems effects.

Perrow, C. "The Short and Glorious History of Organizational Theory," *Organizational Dynamics*, 1973 (Summer), 2-15. This highly recommended summary of the clash between the "forces of light" and the "forces of darkness" in the development of management thinking has become a modern classic in the field.

Wren, D. A. *The Evolution of Management Thought*, 2nd ed. New York: John Wiley and Sons, Inc., 1979. Students interested in people as well as ideas, can do no better than Wren's clear, well written account.

2/What Functions Do Managers Perform?

Part 2 defines the basic functions that every manager must carry out to be successful: planning, organizing, directing, and controlling.

3/Planning demonstrates the essential first step of successful management and describes various techniques and methods. Although managers commonly encounter a number of problems in planning, the chapter points out characteristics of plans that can overcome these obstacles.

4/Organizing shows how managers divide up and allocate work among those who will perform it and then coordinate their activities. Methods and problems in defining and allocating work, difficulties managers frequently face in coordinating and mechanisms they use to overcome those difficulties are described.

5/Directing: Goals concentrates on the nature and functions of goals and the relationship between individual and organizational goals. Despite the quality of plans and organization, managers can accomplish little until they successfully direct the efforts of others to achieving organizational goals.

6/Directing: Motivation expands the manager's role in directing the activities of others, as it deals with the intriguing concept of the motivation of work. The chapter offers three different models managers use to understand and influence employee motivation and its effects on work performance. Since all three models emphasize the use of rewards, the chapter describes how managers commonly use and misuse rewards in organizations today.

7/Controlling describes how managers set standards, measure performance, and take corrective action when necessary. Because managers deal with so many variables, they must make sure that the activities they manage are in control—progressing toward objectives and staying within acceptable limits. The chapter concludes with problems and issues of organizational control.

3 / Planning

"John! You got a tie that'll go with this coat?"

John looked up from his book to see his roommate hopping around with one shoe on, sportcoat in hand, a distressed look on his face. "Probably. What's up?"

"I've got a job interview in twenty minutes and I can't find my good tie," Ed replied, grabbing a shirt from the closet.

"What company?" asked John, smiling as he watched Ed buttoning his shirt while retrieving his other shoe from under the bed.

"CSI," replied Ed. "What about that tie?"

John took Ed's sportcoat and searched through his closet for an appropriate tie. "What do they make?" he asked.

"Oh, high-tech stuff—they're in communications and computers."

"Which division is interviewing you?"

"I don't know. What difference does it make?" replied Ed, trying on the tie that John had selected.

John picked up a mimeographed sheet marked CSI-Position Description. "What's a radiation-tolerant flash A / D converter?"

"Who cares? Where's my belt?" snapped Ed.

"CSI cares, I bet. It's a new development they expect to be their number one profit-maker next year. One of the positions they're looking to fill is administrative assistant to the director of that project."

"No kidding? Think they might ask me about it? How should I know what it is? I'm no physicist."

"You're also no electrical engineer, Ed. The division that's interviewing is their semiconductor division. That's mainly electrical engineering."

"No kidding? Well, I'm in management, not engineering. They can't expect me to know that technical stuff."

"Maybe not, but I bet some of the people they're interviewing will. This is a very high-technology outfit. Why are you

interviewing them anyway?"

"Well, it was a company I've heard of, and they're offering a good starting salary. Why?"

John walked over to Ed and put a hand on his shoulder. "I think maybe this job interviewing is more competitive and serious than you think. You're graduating this spring and need a job. I suggest that for your next interview, my man, you're gonna need a plan."

"A plan? For a job interview? Get serious. All I need to do is be my usual charming self and the job's mine."

"I am serious, and so are the interviewers," replied John. "I'm sure they see plenty of charming candidates every day. They're probably looking for some evidence of maturity and management potential."

"Which means what?" asked Ed, as he started for the door.

"It probably means being well-prepared for the interview—having specific objectives, knowing something about the company and industry, and knowing your own strengths and weaknesses relative to the job you're interviewing for. In other words, having a plan."

"That takes too much time," said Ed, glancing at his watch. "I haven't got time to plan."

"Au contraire, mon frere," John rejoined, as his roommate dashed down the stairs, "you haven't got time because you don't plan."

A manager's creed says, "Give me the resources and I'll accomplish the objective." The resources which a manager uses are both human and nonhuman: people, money, materials, and technology. The objective may be as broad as increasing profits or surviving a recession, or it may be more specific, such as marketing a new perfume or winning an election.

Planning involves both setting objectives and determining how resources will be used to accomplish them. The planning John suggested to Ed would involve setting an objective for his next job interview (to be invited for a plant visit), and determining how to achieve that objective (to dress and perform appropriately during the interview).

Planning is largely a conceptual function; it requires thinking about the future. It requires a manager to:

1. Set an objective—a future state toward which effort will be directed. For example, a law enforcement agency sets an objective of reducing the number of crimes by five percent over the next six months.
2. Assess the organization's resources—what the organization is going to have to work with. In the case of law enforcement, the department head would evaluate the number of officers and their skills, the agency's budget, the status of its equipment, and its standing in the community.
3. Assess the current and future environment with which the organization must contend to achieve its goal. The agency would consider the current and projected rates of violent crimes; patterns in types, times, and areas of crime; and forecasts of other environmental factors, such as economic conditions and weather, which might affect crime rates.
4. Determine how and when to allocate resources to accomplish the objective. This step, of course, is based on the information generated in steps 2 and 3—

the current and future state of the organizational resources and its environment. In our example, the agency might conclude that its current personnel and equipment are sufficient to cope with violent crime, if concentrated efforts are made in certain high-crime areas. Then the agency would evolve a plan for a temporary reorganization, in which more officers were assigned to the target areas.

From the activities described we can generate a formal definition. **Planning** is *selecting objectives and determining a course of action, including allocating resources, in order to achieve those objectives in a specific time period.* Simply put, a plan states *what* is to be accomplished, *when* it is to be accomplished, and *how* it is to be accomplished. Exhibit 3.1 outlines a hardware store owner's plan to conduct an annual inventory.

This simple plan has all the ingredients—an objective, an assessment of organizational resources and the environment to be dealt with, allocation of resources, and a time frame. While it need not be slavishly followed in order to achieve the objective, the plan has uncovered the essential elements—assistance to finish the inventory before reopening, and seven or eight hours and $35 to accomplish the objective. Uncovering essentials is only one of the things good planning can do for an organization.

THE PURPOSE OF PLANNING

In the anecdote that introduced this chapter, John advised Ed to prepare for his next job interview with a plan. In fact, we are all frequently advised to "plan ahead." But this takes effort, resources, and time. Is planning worth all this? What can it accomplish? Since managers are doers rather than thinkers, they sometimes see planning as interfering with doing. They often need strong incentives to plan.

In fact, planning improves doing. In Ed's case, a plan could have given him a goal to help coordinate his efforts, identify opportunities, and avoid problems. In theory, anyone who has immediate access to unlimited resources can probably get by; but because most resources are limited, and it takes time and effort to acquire and prepare them for use, setting up guidelines is essential to effectiveness.

Acquiring and Preparing Resources

Planning ahead enables a manager to be ready to act, to have the resources necessary to do the job when it needs to be done. A manufacturer expanding operations to meet increased demand will need capital, trained workers, machinery, equipment, materials, operating and warehousing facilities, and sales personnel. Planning enables the firm to acquire the facilities, hire and train the personnel, locate and purchase the raw materials, and have all of them ready to go. Without a plan, workers may be hired with no place to work, material may be ordered without capital to finance it, production may be delayed for lack of trained workers or appropriate equipment, goods may be produced with no place to be warehoused.

Exhibit 3.1   Planning for an Annual Inventory

Objective: To obtain an accurate physical count of all stock.

Resources Available: Inventory forms; hand calculator; two assistants, one being the owner's daughter, the other living an hour's drive from work.

Environment: 3,000 square feet of floor space containing an estimated $80,000 in stock ranging from nails and screws to power tools.

Resource Allocation: Since at this time of year, the store has customers from opening at 8 A.M. to closing at 6:30 P.M., inventory will be done Friday after closing by owner and daughter. Set aside $10 for meals and snacks, and $25 in overtime pay for daughter.

Plan: Notify local police patrol that staff will be working in store past midnight on Friday night.

Give daughter Friday off. Have her come in to work at 6 P.M.

At 6:30 P.M., Friday, close store; send other assistant home; owner and daughter conduct inventory.

Have son-in-law bring in hot meal around 10 P.M.

Finish inventory around 1–2 A.M. Drive daughter home.

Have assistant open store Saturday morning and staff it alone until 10 A.M.

Controlling Costs

Planning makes doing easier and cheaper. Acquiring resources under crisis conditions is expensive—you have to take what is available and pay whatever price is demanded. Predetermined acquisition makes it easier to buy a commodity, often at more favorable prices. For example, travellers who buy airline tickets at the last minute pay full fare if they are lucky enough to get the flight they want. Those who plan ahead have less trouble getting the desired flight and can sometimes save through special discounts for early ticket reservation and purchase.

Companies in the food industry, who face seasonal price variations, can save by planning for early purchases. A meat-packing company can take advantage of high demand for ham at Easter if it has cured hams ready to sell at that time. The firm can wait until the last minute and buy fresh ham for immediate processing at 60 cents per pound or $18,000 per carload lot. Planning ahead for such purchases enables the firm to buy the same product in January for 40 cents per pound or $12,000 per carload lot.

Directing and Coordinating Efforts

When the work of more than one individual or unit is involved, planning provides direction and makes it possible to coordinate effort. For example, the objective of every major transcontinental air carrier is the safe, timely, comfortable transportation of satisfied passengers from one city to another. The flight plan for the late-afternoon Philadelphia to Los Angeles run calls for the pilot to provide sufficient time in the air to allow the attendants to serve beverages and dinner and show a movie. The time schedule also coordinates the activities of the ground personnel—baggage handlers, gate agents, aircraft maintenance, and food service—with the ground time of the aircraft. Without adherence to a plan, such a complex operation could become chaotic.

Management in Action
Planning in Family-Owned Firms

Richard Beckhard, a management consultant for thirty-five years, has worked extensively with family-owned firms. His research and experience in this area have uncovered a particular weakness of such companies—the failure to plan for the company's survival after the founder's retirement or death.

Only about three out of every ten family-owned firms survive the founder. According to Beckhard, "The thing that has kept the family firm from surviving is inadequate planning for continuity." Because surveys show that nearly half of all business failures result from the appointment of an incompetent chief executive, it is essential that family firms plan for the successor to the founder, whether the successor is to be a family member, a nonfamily member of the firm, or a complete outsider.

Without such planning, Beckhard predicts, "The firm will rapidly fall apart, key employees will leave after the founder goes, and the family will disintegrate as they squabble over the allocation of power and assets."

One of the keys to Beckhard's success in family businesses is in recognizing the importance of integrating the family into the planning process, usually by bringing the family and the top management team together. Sometimes, however, it is difficult, if not impossible, to carry out such a joint effort, either because family members are scat-

tered around the country or because they are unwilling to face the inevitability of the founder's absence. Founders themselves are often unwilling to get involved in planning for their succession, because it seems like planning for their own funerals. As one founder put it, "It is really digging your own grave in a way . . . a kind of *seppuku*—the hara-kiri that Japanese commit . . . you're ripping yourself apart . . . I've found to work through that is terrible." Sometimes, therefore, the founders and their families remove themselves from the planning process entirely, and leave the process up to the board of directors. Whoever is involved in planning for the succession, nothing will happen until the founder initiates the process.

Among the unique and most difficult issues that planning for the founder's successor raises are those of the selection criteria used to evaluate family and nonfamily members, provisions for the continuation of employment for family members, and the consideration of inlaws.

Sometimes the family personalities and conflicts prolong the succession question past the founder's death or retirement. One contingency plan that can be used to avoid the problems created by such a delay is to arrange for an interim president to take over until these problems have been resolved and a permanent successor has been chosen.

Sources: "Conversation with Richard Beckhard," *Organizational Dynamics*, Summer 1983, pp. 29–38. Quotes from p. 30. "Challenges and Issues in Managing Family Firms," *Sloan*, Winter 1983, pp. 12–15. Founder's quote from p. 15.

Avoiding Problems

Red tape refers to *bureaucratic procedures and requirements which often frustrate managerial action.* There are times when regulations can bring operations to a halt, and ignorance of such regulations is no comfort to a manager facing a shutdown. In one memorable instance, a federal inspector closed down a coal mine because of inadequate toilet facilities. That was bad enough. The mine owners alleged, however, that shutting down the mine prevented routine maintenance. Subsequently, a part of the mine collapsed. A federal court ruled that the miners were not entitled to sue the inspector for the collapse of the mine. This situation might have been averted if management had discovered the rules and regulations beforehand and had dealt with them either by compliance, legal action, or alternatives.

Early identification of potential problems makes it possible to lessen or eliminate their impacts on performance. For example, Bear Archery, Inc. decided to move its operations from Michigan to Florida. During the planning process, Bear discovered a lack of skilled labor in the area. Negotiations with the Chamber of Commerce at the plant site in Florida led to the development of a course in bowmaking at the community college. By the time the company had built its plant, a pool of trained bowmakers was ready to be hired. Without planning, the plant would have stood idle until skilled personnel had been recruited or trained.

Identifying Opportunities

In assessing the environment and evaluating available resources, planning can identify previously unexploited opportunities. An individual preparing for retirement may discover tax-exempt investments that not only provide growth and safety for the future but reduce current income taxes as well. Companies planning to meet long-term goals may run across opportunities which are profitable in the short run as well.

Delta Air Lines is a case in point.[1] After the airline deregulation in 1979, Delta began working on a five-year plan. The new Atlanta airport, the world's largest, was to open in late 1980. Delta had already contracted for a large number of gates in the new facility, doubling the number of passengers it could serve. In assessing unknown air routes for possible future expansion, Delta discovered a number of routes, abandoned by other carriers after deregulation, which could be served using Atlanta as a hub. Delta capitalized on this discovery by adding nonstop service between Atlanta and Salt Lake City, Seattle, and Portland. Long-term planning had uncovered short-term opportunities.

Does planning pay? One way to answer this question is to compare the performances of firms emphasizing planning with those of firms not emphasizing planning. One study compared the sales and profit performances of ten selected firms. Five of the firms (3 from the drug industry and 2 from the chemical industry) actively and formally planned at least three years in advance. The other five firms (3 similar drug and 2 similar chemical companies) did not carry out formal long-range planning.

Exhibit 3.2   Increases in Profits for Formal vs. Informal Planners

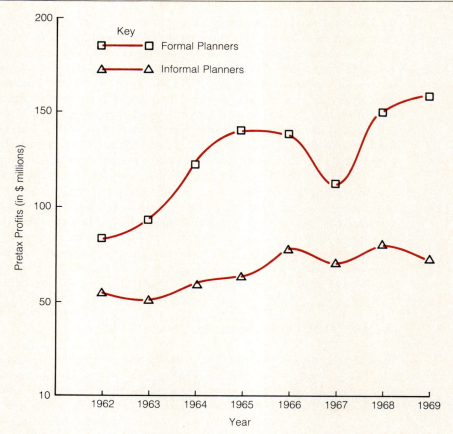

Source: Herold, D. M., House, R. J., and Thune, S. S., ''Long-Range Planning and Organizational Performance: A Cross-Validation Study,'' *Academy of Management Journal* (March 1972).

Over the seven years of the study, the five firms which actively and formally planned for the long term consistently outperformed the informal planners. The profits of the five formal planners increased by 139 percent, while profits of the informal planners increased by only 59 percent. The yearly profit figures for the formal and the informal planners are given in Exhibit 3.2.

Planning is just as crucial for small companies as it is for large corporations. In Florida, which led the nation in 1982 in small-business growth, only sixteen percent of small businesses survive as long as five years. Failure to plan their financial futures is a major reason for their financial failures. According to the state's Small-Business Development Center in Tampa, ''For small businesses, good management is more important than money.''

THE PLANNING PROCESS

In the anecdote that introduced this chapter, John advised Ed to prepare a plan for future job interviews. The process Ed eventually used for his interview contained these elements:

An objective: to be invited for a plant visit

Resources: personal appearance, dress, education, previous work and interview experience

Forecast: appearance and behavior expected by interviewer questions likely to be asked

Plan: select and prepare clothes for interview

gather information from company reports, other business literature

attend placement-center program in interviewing techniques

prepare questions to ask interviewer

rehearse answers to likely questions

A plan requires managers to carry out four different kinds of activities: setting objectives, evaluating resources, forecasting, and deciding how to reach the objectives. The essence of a plan is the last activity, deciding what is to be done, but its utility and value are based on the first three activities—setting objectives, evaluating resources, and forecasting. Telling a company exactly how to develop a new product is of little value if the company can not get the necessary resources, or if there is no demand for the product. A good plan tells us more than simply *how* to do something: it tells us *why* we should do it and *if* we can do it.

Setting Goals

A **goal** is simply *a desired future state: the way we would like things to be sometime from now.* Goals serve to provide direction and coordination to efforts and activities. Most goals describe specific states toward which an organization strives. For example:

- The Republican Party wants to control the House of Representatives.

- Nissan Motor Company hopes to produce 120,000 Datsun mini-pickup trucks in the United States annually.

- American Leisure Corp. plans to operate a luxury 1000-room hotel/casino in Atlantic City.

Each of these goals provides direction for future activities. The Republican Party must get 59 more Republican congressmen elected to gain control of the House. Nissan Company must build and staff a new $300 million automobile plant in the United States.[2] American Leisure must build and staff a new hotel/casino in Atlantic City.[3] Each of these objectives can trigger thousands of different activities by thousands of people and result in the expenditure of hundreds of millions of dollars.

Some goals are better than others for direction and coordination. "Good" goals are consistent with overall objectives, clear and unambiguous, measurable and attainable, and objectively operational.[4] The first three characteristics are easily understood. The fourth, "objectively operational," simply means that subordinates can understand how they can contribute toward that goal. Goals which are clearly defined and measurable lend themselves to being understood by subordinates.

A good test for a goal is the following question: Will we, at some time in the future, be able to tell whether we have achieved the goal? If you can answer "yes," the goal most likely meets criteria 2, 3, and 4.

Evaluating Resources

In light of predetermined objectives, an organization will find it has certain strengths and weaknesses. For example, manufacturers considering international expansion often have the technological and financial resources needed to build and operate overseas plants, but they lack the managerial expertise required in the international arena. A manufacturer expanding overseas must decide whether to develop its own managers, hire different ones away from competitors, or use managers who are native to the new countries.

The Japanese, whose foreign investments are growing at a phenomenal rate, use a mixed strategy. For example, initially Hitachi, the electronics pioneer, sends its own managers from Japan to run its plants in Michigan, California, Britain, and Singapore.[5] These managers identify promising local people who are sent to Japan to learn about Hitachi, then returned to their native countries to take over the plants. Hitachi's assessment is that it has the expertise, but not enough Japanese managers, so it plans accordingly.

Forecasting

Forecasting is *attempting to predict environments that might affect organizational objectives.* We are all familiar with weather forecasts used in planning picnics and trips to the beach. (Weather forecasting is, in fact, an important part of the planning process for many organizations, including shipping companies, resort hotels, agricultural concerns, and military operations.)

Almost all managers make short-term forecasts of their personnel, equipment, and financial requirements, trying to anticipate changes in the use and availability of these resources to avoid being caught short-handed. These kinds of forecasts are well within the capabilities of most organizations with experienced managers. Other kinds of forecasts are so complicated that companies have to rely on outside experts.

Exhibit 3.3   Projected Additions in Bank Personnel Required Annually, 1980–1985

Year	Total Personnel Requirements	Personnel Loss* (Mortality)	Additional Personnel Required
1980	57,574	1085	4430
1981	61,145	1151	4722
1982	64,976	1223	5054
1983	69,099	1300	5423
1984	73,540	1382	5823
1985	78,328	1471	6258

* Based on actuarial estimates of a death rate of 2 percent annually for bankers as a group. This figure does not, of course, include attrition by discharge or withdrawal.

Source: W. Andrew McCullough and Jerome L. Duncan, *Florida Banking: A Personnel Forecast Through 1985*, (Gainesville, FL: University of Florida College of Business Administration, 1977).

In the volatile financial environment of the 1980s, accurate forecasting has been literally worth its weight in gold to managers planning a company's next financial moves. Few forecasters anticipated the abrupt rise and fall of interest rates in 1980-82. As a result, financial managers became reluctant to make long-term commitments. Whereas bond issues of 25- to 30-year maturities were common before the 1980s, shorter-term bonds became the rule as interest rates became harder to forecast.

On the other hand, specialists forecasting the future value of the world's major currencies were highly accurate. Financial managers following their advice were making as much as 33 percent annual return in currency trading.[6] Large companies like Gulf Oil, which trades $3 billion annually, often subscribe to these forecasts at $15,000-$25,000 per year to verify their own in-house forecasting.

Forecasting ranges from judgmental to data-based. In professional football, judgmental forecasting (the coach's hunch about an opponent's next offensive or defensive ploy) has gradually given way to data-based, computer-generated forecasts of opponents' tendencies in given situations.

Labor-intensive industries such as banking must be aware of future personnel needs in order to plan for orderly growth. The forecast in Exhibit 3.3 was prepared for the Florida banking industry, which has one of the fastest growth rates in the nation.[7] The forecast is both judgmental and data-based, reflecting past growth trends in commercial bank deposits, personal income, and bank personnel as a function of deposits and incomes. Changes in past trends were built into the model to adjust for the addition of limited branch-banking and automatic tellers.

The forecast indicates that Florida bankers will have to fund, recruit, and hire 27,281 additional personnel between 1980 and 1985, almost 50 percent of the total number of people employed by Florida banks in 1980. Further details reveal that the state's banks will need an additional 7000 middle-managers, and that their needs for computer specialists and technicians will increase by 150 percent, from 4400 to 11,200 between 1980 and 1985! These forecasts make personnel planning a critical item for Florida bankers.

Exhibit 3.4 Basic Forecasting Techniques

	A. Qualitative Methods		B. Trend Projection	C. Causal Methods (Quantitative)	
	1. Delphi Method	2. Market Research	1. Trend Projections	1. Regression Model	2. Econometric Model
Description	A panel of experts is interrogated by a sequence of questionnaires in which the responses to one questionnaire are used to produce the next questionnaire. Any set of information available to some experts and not others is thus passed on to the others, enabling all the experts to have access to all the information for forecasting. This technique eliminates the bandwagon effect of majority opinion.	The systematic, formal, and conscious procedure for evolving and testing hypotheses about real markets.	This technique fits a trend line to a mathematical equation and then projects it into the future by means of this equation. There are several variations: the slope-characteristic method, polynomials, logarithms, and so on.	This functionally relates sales to other economic, competitive, or internal variables and estimates an equation using the least-squares technique. Relationships are primarily analyzed statistically, although any relationship should be selected for testing on a rational ground.	An econometric model is a system of interdependent regression equations that describes some sector of economic sales or profit activity. The parameters of the regression equations are usually estimated simultaneously. As a rule, these models are relatively expensive to develop and can easily cost between $5,000 and $10,000, depending on detail. However, due to the system of equations inherent in such models, they will better express the causalities involved than an ordinary regression equation and hence will predict turning points more accurately.
Accuracy Short term 0–3 months	Fair to very good	Excellent	Very good	Good to very good	Good to very good
Medium term 3 months–2 years	Fair to very good	Good	Good	Good to very good	Very good to excellent
Long term 2 years and up	Fair to very good	Fair to good	Good	Poor	Good
Turning point identification	Fair to good	Fair to very good	Poor	Very good	Excellent
Applications	Forecasts of long-range and new-product sales, forecasts of margins.	Forecasts of long-range and new-product sales, forecasts of margins.	New-product forecasts (particularly intermediate-and long-term).	Forecasts of sales by product classes, forecasts of margins.	Forecasts of sales by product classes, forecasts of margins.
Data required	A coordinator issues the sequence of questionnaires, editing and consolidating the responses.	As a minimum, two sets of reports over time. One needs a considerable collection of market data from questionnaires, surveys, and time series analyses of market variables.	Varies with the technique used. However, a good rule of thumb is t use a minimum of five years' annual data to start. Thereafter, the complete history.	Several years' quarterly history to obtain good, meaningful relationships. Mathematically necessary to have two more observations than independent variables.	The same as for regression.
Cost	$2,000 +	$5,000 +	Varies with application	$100	$5,000 +
Computer calculation required?	No	No	No	No	No
Time required to develop forecast	2 months +	3 months +	1 day—	Depends on ability to identify relationships.	2 months +

Exhibit 3.4 describes several of the more common forecasting techniques used in organizational planning today. *Market research* and *trend projections* are used by virtually all companies that sell products, although levels of sophistication vary greatly from company to company. *Regression* and *econometric models* are taught by most business schools and used by many firms needing economic forecasts. The *Delphi method*, developed by Rand Corporation, can be used in all kinds of forecasting, from air-passenger traffic to zoology.

A particular advantage of these models is the ability to predict the effects of different plans, which is of obvious help in choosing among several alternative plans. The pharmaceutical manufacturer, American Hoechst, uses a computer mapping-system to project revenue increases. By simply touching a computerized map with a light pen, an executive can forecast changes in sales revenues resulting from different sales alignments.[8]

The federal government uses econometric models to assist in planning tax increases or decreases, regulating the money supply, and so forth. Unfortunately, the accuracy of this method leaves a lot to be desired. One major model forecast that an immediate tax decrease was essential, while another forecast that such a tax cut would be a disaster.[9] The chances are that neither forecast was correct.

Formulating a Plan

Putting together the objectives, Evaluating organizational resources, and forecasting the environment leads to the actual formulation of a plan stating what should be done, by whom, when, and with what resources.

Because most forecasts are somewhat uncertain, a plan may contain some **contingency**—*an alternative course of action to follow if a given change in the environment occurs.** For example, a short-term financial plan might include borrowing from banks when long-term interest rates are high. Realizing that long-term interest rates might decline during the life of the plan, the financial manager might build in a contingency: If long-term interest rates drop below ten percent (and bond prices rise accordingly), then the corporation can issue bonds and use the proceeds to pay off the high-cost, short-term borrowing.

Plans often involve several steps and can easily become complicated, particularly in the case of a long-term plan involving several projects. Two techniques developed to aid such planning are known as PERT (Program Evaluation and Review Techniques) and CPM (Critical Path Method). PERT was designed by the United States Navy to aid in the management of its Polaris Missile program. CPM was initially developed to aid in the management of large construction projects. Both techniques have been applied in numerous other areas, and are regularly included in the computer software for managerial analysis offered by almost every software company.[10]

---

* (Contingency planning is part of the contingency approach to management described in Chapter 2. It recognizes that there may not be one perfect plan, but that the relative effectiveness of different plans depends upon changes in the environment.)

Both techniques list all the activities required to complete a project or program and arrange them visually in the sequence in which they must occur. For example, in building a new plant, a company must first acquire the land on which to build. Before it can acquire the land, it must locate the site. Before it locates the site, it must decide what characteristics a new site must have. These activities must occur in sequence—the company cannot build before acquiring land, and it cannot acquire land before locating it.

A PERT representation of these activities would look like this:

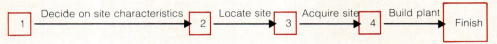

By estimating how long each activity will take, the company can decide when each step should begin, given a desired date for the project's completion. Let us suppose the time estimates are nine months for plant construction, three months for site acquisition, two months to locate the site, and one month to decide on site characteristics. If we want the plant built by June 30, 1986, then construction must start no later than October 1, 1985. We must start looking for a site by August 1, 1985, and start deciding on site characteristics by July 1, 1985.

To see how PERT would apply to a more complicated project, consider the production of a major motion picture. It is not uncommon for producers to spend $10 million on a film. At current interest rates, long production schedules are extremely costly. Tight schedules result in lower costs, early release dates, and quicker return on investment. Such scheduling, however, requires an efficient plan for the sequence of events required in film production.

There are five major activities involved in producing a film. Assuming the producer has the necessary financing, the steps are 1) acquiring a script, 2) writing the screenplay, 3) hiring director, cast, and crew, 4) shooting the film, and 5) releasing the film. Some of these activities cannot occur before others have been

Exhibit 3.5   A Preliminary PERT Network

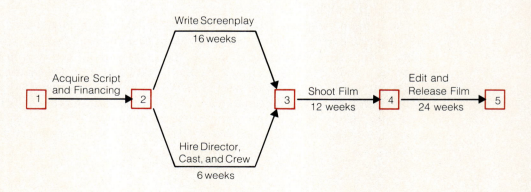

completed—the film cannot be released (5) before steps 1–4 are completed; the film cannot be shot without a script (1), cast and crew (3), and *some* screenplay (2), although screenplays are seldom complete before shooting begins. Step 1 must occur before steps 2 and 3, but cast, crew, and director can be signed without a screenplay. So a basic PERT network might look like Exhibit 3.5.

Financially, the crucial time is between steps 2 and 5—the time that the investors' money has been committed before it starts showing any return. Let us suppose that the targeted release date is mid-December, in time for the big holiday movie crowds. Given the estimated times in the figure, the network suggests that the latest to begin writing the screenplay and hiring for the movie would be 24 + 12 + 6 weeks = 42 weeks before mid-December, or about mid-February. This assumes that the crew would start shooting after only 6 weeks' work on the screenplay, and that most of the screenplay would be finished while the movie was being shot. If the director wanted to wait until the screenplay was complete before shooting, writing would have to start 24 + 12 + 16 weeks prior to mid-December or by mid-December of the previous year.

Of course, other things have to take place prior to shooting and releasing a film. The director must find a location and acquire a set and props. The film must be edited and publicized. Editing the film is perhaps the most time-consuming of all the steps and can make the difference between a good film and an outstanding one. Editing sometimes involves months of 10-15 hour days. A final PERT network might look like Exhibit 3.6.

Note that the PERT network in Exhibit 3.6 calls for several activities to be carried out at the same time. This is an essential feature of PERT: identifying activities which can be performed concurrently. Carrying out several activities at the same time, rather than in sequence, shortens the overall time for the project.

Exhibit 3.6   A Final PERT Network

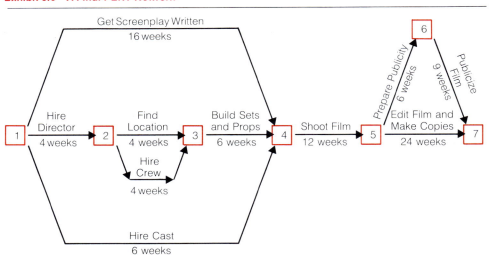

By identifying critical activities, PERT permits a manager to shift resources (including his or her attention) from noncritical activities. This increases the chance of completing critical activities on time, and helps avoid big delays in the project.

The critical-path method of planning attempts to find the path through the network of activities which takes the longest time. In Figure 3.2 the critical path is through points 1–4–5–7: 16 weeks + 12 weeks + 24 weeks = 52 weeks. The path through 1–2–3–4–5–6–7 is only 41 weeks, and through 1–2–3–4–5–7 is 50 weeks. The total time required to produce the film is represented by this "critical path" 1–4–5–7. Any delays in one of those activities will delay the entire project. Delays in activities *not* on the critical path, such as hiring the cast, may not necessarily delay the total project, if they can be carried out simultaneously with events on the critical path.

TYPES OF PLANS

Having discussed the benefits of planning and described the process itself, we now examine the different types of plans that managers commonly use. Plans are usually categorized along two dimensions—scope and time. In scope, organizational plans range from the strategic level down to budgets and schedules. In time horizons, plans range from short-term to several years.

Strategic Plans

Strategy is really a military term, from the Greek word meaning "generalship." It means the deployment of forces to meet the enemy under advantageous conditions. Just as strategy is developed at the highest military and political levels, strategic planning is a top management function. A **strategy** *evaluates and develops the organization's purpose, mission, and overall objectives and policies to place the organization in an advantageous position in its operating environment.* For example, Kodak developed a strategy around its traditional strengths in optics and chemistry, maintaining its dominance in photographic fields, while moving into ultrasophisticated electronics technologies. To implement that strategy, Kodak spends upwards of $1 billion in research and development, and increased the number of electrical engineers it hired by 900 percent over a three-year period.[11]

Tactical Plans

Tactical planning is carried out by managers at all levels. It involves *directing the organization's activities to achieve overall strategic objectives, consistent with the organization's mission and policies.* Tactical plans include policies, programs, projects, budgets, procedures, and rules. The two major types of tactical plans are standing plans and single-use plans.[12]

The sharing of information between managers and their subordinates is important in recognizing and working out problems.

Standing plans are *plans developed for repetitive activities:* problems or processes which the organization will deal with more than once. They include policies, standard operating procedures, and rules, so that personnel can accomplish recurrent activities in a consistent and efficient manner. The concern over efficiency is obvious: having discovered through research or experience a feasible and efficient way to handle a situation, the organization uses a standing plan to influence its members to follow that procedure, rather than spend time evolving their own, possibly less efficient, procedure.

The concern over consistency is apparent upon reflection: Consistency throughout the organization makes cooperation and control easier. For example, if branch plants follow a standard operating procedure (SOP) of reordering supplies two weeks in advance of an anticipated stock-out, the central warehouse can maintain efficient inventory and delivery systems and keep branch stock to a minimum.

Single-use plans are *plans developed for unique situations or problems.* A budget is a single-use plan. It considers objectives, current resources, and the future environment and allocates resources accordingly. It is unique because it covers a specific, never-to-be-encountered-again time period—for example, fiscal year 1986.

A **program** is a *large-scale, complex plan designed to achieve a specific objective.* Programs are typically broken down into **projects**—*short-term plans designed to achieve objectives within programs.* In 1979, TWA's annual fuel cost increased 55 percent, far more than most of its competitors, mainly because of the inefficient nature of the airline's fleet of aircraft.[13] TWA then began a program designed to increase the fuel efficiency of its fleet. Part of that program involved several projects acquiring and phasing into operation ten Boeing 727-200 aircraft, four 747s, and two L-1011s. Another more distant project was to acquire ten new Boeing 767s by 1983 to carry more passengers while using 21 percent less fuel than the present aircraft.

Short-Range vs. Long-Range Plans

Plans can cover time horizons varying from a few hours to several years. Their classification as short-range, medium-range, or long-range is arbitrary. What most people mean by short range is one year, and by long range more than three years. Strategic plans tend to have longer time horizons than tactical ones, and higher levels of management are more involved in long-range planning than are lower levels. Long-range plans tend to be less detailed, less formal, and less certain than short-range plans, to allow greater flexibility for the increased uncertainty that goes along with longer-range forecasts.

WHO PLANS WHAT

Although top executives do more strategic and long-term planning, all managers plan to some extent. The amount of time spent in planning, and the type of planning carried out, varies with managerial level and with the type of organization.

Planning and Managerial Level

Strategic planning remains the province of top management, although other people will provide information useful for the planning process. In 1980, General Electric established a strategic objective of increasing productivity by a six percent annual rate. Based on forecasts from labor, and research and development specialists, the plan was simple but revolutionary: install robots into GE production wherever possible over the next five years.[14]

Managers at lower levels of the organization's hierarchy will spend more of their planning time on intermediate or short-term plans. First- or second-line managers will be most closely involved in procedures, schedules, and budgets. Exhibit 3.7 gives a rough idea of how planning functions might be distributed over several levels of managers in a "typical" company.

Planning and Organizational Characteristics

The differences between the planning of a "typical" company and that of an "atypical" company generally occur in the areas of strategic and long-term determinations. Very large companies may spend a great deal more time in long-range planning for two reasons. First, it takes longer to coordinate changes for a large

Exhibit 3.7 "Ideal" Allocations of Time for Planning in the "Average" Company

	Today	1 Week Ahead	1 Month Ahead	3 to 6 Mos. Ahead	1 Year Ahead	2 Years Ahead	3 to 4 Yrs. Ahead	5 to 10 Yrs. Ahead
President	1%	2%	5%	10%	15%	27%	30%	10%
Executive Vice-President	2%	4%	10%	29%	20%	18%	13%	4%
Vice-President of Functional Area	4%	8%	15%	35%	20%	10%	5%	3%
General Manager of a Major Division	2%	5%	15%	30%	20%	12%	12%	4%
Department Manager	10%	10%	24%	30%	10%	5%	1%	1%
Section Supervisor	15%	20%	25%	39%	3%			
Group Supervisor	38%	40%	15%	5%	2%			

Source: George A. Steiner, *Top Management Planning* (New York: Macmillan, 1969), p. 26.

company. The company's size may reduce its short-term adaptability, making accurate long-range planning more crucial. Second, a large company is more likely to have the managerial and financial resources necessary for long-range planning.

Size, however, is not the only factor affecting planning modes. Organizations involved in heavy expenditures for advanced technology need more long-term planning because of the lead time involved in acquiring and using the technology and because of the long payback periods such investments usually require.

A good example is the multibillion-dollar watch industry, where the struggle for market share has revolved around traditional mechanical watches versus digital watches based on electronic technology. Timex, which once produced half of all watches sold in the United States, dismissed digitals as a fad. Watchmakers in Hong Kong invested so heavily in electronic digitals, which became popular, that by 1980 they and Texas Instruments had captured an increasingly large share of the world's watch business. Although Timex realized by 1976 that digitals were not a passing fad, and began heavy investment, by 1980 their market share had dropped to one-third of the American market. Development and marketing of a successful line of digital watches is a long-term project, even for the largest producer.[15]

> *Planning is just as crucial for small companies as it is for large corporations. According to Florida's Small-Business Development Center in Tampa, ''For small businesses, good management is more important than money.''*

On the other hand, organizations less dependent on heavy capital investment or advanced technology do not need to put so much effort into long-term planning. While long-range planning is an important managerial task at corporate headquarters of fast-food franchises like Burger King, McDonald's, or Wendy's, management planning at the individual restaurant level seldom exceeds one year. The demands for long-term planning for service organizations like high schools, police departments, and symphony orchestras are considerably less than those in the airline or automobile industries. The steel industry has been involved in long-term planning for decades, while the banking industry is a relatively new user of this type of formal planning.

Formal Planning

Over the past twenty-five years, formal planning has proliferated. In the 1950s, only one of every twelve major American corporations had a full-time long-range planner. By the late 1960s, ten out of twelve used long-range planning. Today virtually all American corporations with sales over one hundred million dollars prepare long-range plans.[16]

A number of organizations have formalized planning to such an extent that they have developed special departments. Such organization permits the development and use of a group of specialists with the forecasting and decision-making skills that planning requires.

Organizations which use these departments are typically large, centralized, high-technology, complex organizations. They have a recognized need for continual intermediate- and long-range planning *and* they have the financial and managerial resources to operate a full-time planning department. Smaller companies usually do not have sufficient resources, and organizations which are less centralized and integrated, with simpler technology, do not have as great a need for specialized planning departments. Exhibit 3.8 lists the internal and external forces that influence organizations to adopt formal or informal planning.

WHY MANAGERS DON'T PLAN

Despite the increased need for greater knowledge of the process, there are still organizations that do little or no planning. Some managers believe the costs of planning are too great for the potential benefits. Organizations with few managerial resources or little financial slack are going to devote their resources to immediate problems. Their goal is survival in the short run, and they will worry about the future when it comes.

Organizations which operate under very simple structural arrangements have less need for formal planning than complex organizations operating in competitive, changing environments.[17] For example, the citrus fruit industry is made up of organizations with relatively simple technology and structures that spend most of their efforts in day-to-day operations and little on planning.

"Resistance to change" is another reason often cited for managers' reluctance to plan. This resistance is based on certain facts:

1. Many managers are too busy to plan. As pointed out in Chapter 1, managers have plenty to do, and planning is only one of those activities.
2. Managers usually prefer to work on immediate problems. The rewards for solving current problems and the punishments for ignoring them are immediate. The rewards and punishments associated with planning are long-term. Behavior which is rewarded or punished immediately takes precedence over that which has only long-term payoffs.

Exhibit 3.8   How Internal and External Factors Influence Planning Characteristics

Factor	Planning tends to be more formal and detailed	Planning tends to be less formal and detailed
Type of Organization	Large companies	Small one-plant companies
Top Management Style	Policy maker Authoritarian Inexperienced planner	Intuitive or day-to-day thinker Democratic/Permissive Experienced planner
Organization's Environment	Stable Little competition Many markets and customers	Turbulent Severe competition Single market and customer
Production Process	Long lead times Capital intensive Integrated manufacturing process High technology Market reaction time for new product is long	Short lead times Labor intensive Single manufacturing process Low technology Market reaction time for new product is short
Problems Organization Faces	New, complex, long-range problems	Short-range problems
Purpose of Planning System	Coordinate activities	Train managers

Source: Adapted from George A. Steiner, *Strategic Planning* (New York: Free Press, 1979), p. 54.

3. Good planning is hard work. It requires the generating, processing, and verifying of a lot of information. It requires checking assumptions, assessing forecasts for errors, building in contingencies, and obtaining the cooperation of others.
4. Planning can reveal a manager's poor performance. Planning starts with setting objectives, and managerial performance can be evaluated against these objectives. Some managers are reluctant to specify objectives for fear of failure.
5. Managers prefer to be doers, not thinkers. However , planning involves thinking, paperwork, and time alone. For many managers, time alone is available only away from the office—at the expense of leisure activities.[18] Chapter 1 suggests that most managers are so busy that they must either do their planning away from work or they must exert a great deal of effort just to find time to plan. The fact that most managers, nevertheless, do find time for planning is strong evidence of the importance they place on this function.

WHEN PLANNING DOESN'T WORK

Even when managers find time to plan, they have no guarantee of success. Poor planning may be worse than none at all. A manager can spend long hours trying to develop a plan so that individual, departmental, and organizational objectives are met, but without the support of employees who must implement the plan, reliable information and forecasting, and a stable organization, even the best of plans will not work. Reorganizing and replanning will occur on a regular basis, and maintaining employee motivation will be almost impossible.

It is important for a manager to know what *can* go wrong so that he or she can develop plans to overcome each eventuality. Instead of accepting the future, a manager can try to change it by developing a strategy to resolve the dilemmas brought about by poor implementation, poor plans, and instability and change in the organization.

Poor Implementation

The reason cited most often for the failure of planning is not a poor plan, but lack of support from those who are crucial to its success. A survey of over three hundred American and European firms concluded that planning does not work if it is not accepted by all levels of management.[19]

One problem with formal planning departments is that they can become so specialized as to become totally separated from other areas.[20] Remember that managers spend most of their time dealing with present crises, face-to-face interaction, phone calls, and meetings. A group spending all its time in the future can become very different from one rooted by environment and preference in the present. If

```
                          New Product Analysis

Command ===>                                                    Define Mode

------------------------------------------------------------------------------

                                  YEAR_1      YEAR_2      YEAR_3      YEAR_4

TAXRATE   Tax Rate              22          22          22          22
INFLATE   Inflation Rate         0           7           8           6
D_UNITS   Delta Units            0
D_PRICE   Delta Price            0


              -------------------------------------------------------------

UNITSOLD  Units Sold             50,000      57,500      66,125      76,044
PRICE     Selling Price           8.50        9.00        9.50       10.00

REVENUE   Revenue               425,000     517,500     628,187     760,437


RAW_MAT   Raw Material          150,000     184,575     229,242     279,446
DIR_LAB   Direct Labor          100,000     123,050     152,828     186,297
PACKAGE   Packaging              25,000      30,762      38,207      46,574
DISTRIB   Distribution           37,500      46,144      57,311      69,862

GROSS_P   Gross Profit          112,500     132,969     150,600     178,258
FIXED_C   Fixed Costs            40,000      40,000      40,000      40,000


NET_BTAX  Net Before Taxes       72,500      92,969     110,600     138,258
TAXES     Taxes Payable          15,950      20,453      24,332      30,417



NET_INC   Net Income             56,550      72,516      86,268     107,841
```

Forecasts are simply predictions of the future and should be used only as indicators of what might happen.

the rest of the management team views planning and planners as out-of-touch with the real world, they will withhold support. Planning departments which do not communicate regularly and frequently with those for whom they are working are doomed to frustration and isolation. They will work on irrelevant problems, lack the cooperation needed to get necessary information, and see their plans largely ignored.

To compound the problem, if specialists are doing the planning, other managers may view this function as outside their responsibilities, and fail to do any planning of their own. Given an excuse to pass the responsibility onto other shoulders, many managers will do so. "Planning? I leave that up to the bright boys and their computer games. Me? I've got enough to do dealing with the real world today." Boasts like that in an organization indicate that planning is not integrated into the management system. Unless things are changed, the usefulness of planning will be wasted.

Poor Plans

Poor plans result from poor information, poor forecasting, and poor decision-making. Planners must rely on information they collect from others, and information is a valuable commodity in organizations. It requires effort and resources to get it and check its accuracy. Planners without resources, without the cooperation of other managers who put little effort into acquiring information and checking its validity will generate poor plans.

Forecasts can be wrong if, among other reasons, they are based on false assumptions. The plan to rescue the American hostages from Iran in 1980 failed partly because of poor forecasting. A minimum of six helicopters were required for the rescue; if the team started the mission with eight helicopters, then at least six would be available for the rescue effort. Two false assumptions were made: (1) that the helicopters were in perfect condition and (2) that no extraordinary events would occur. Unfortunately, at zero hour, only five helicopters were serviceable, and the mission was aborted. The planners were too optimistic. They disregarded one of the most important laws of planning—if something can go wrong, it will.

Forecasts are *not* plans, only parts of plans. Despite the sophistication of today's forecasting techniques, forecasts are simply *predictions* about the future. A plan must be flexible enough to deal with environments that turn out to be different from those that were forecast. The plan to rescue the hostages was locked into the forecast. No one had a contingency plan available to carry out the mission with fewer than six helicopters. When the forecast failed, the plan failed.

The topic of decision making will be thoroughly discussed in Part 3. However, one particular cause of poor decision making in the planning process is that the wrong people are making the decisions.[21] Even if planning is specialized, those who must carry out the plans can and should be involved in making the decisions. Had the military personnel executing the rescue mission in Iran had their way, the decision would have been to start with more than eight helicopters.

Instability and Change

Good plans specify alternatives to changes in the organization or its environment. However, sometimes the organization or the environment is so unstable that formal plans are useless—conditions alter more rapidly than plans can be executed.

High turnover, changing markets, uncertain financing, and rapid technological change all create problems for plans and those who must execute them. Periods of instability and variation seem to produce different reactions to planning. Some organizations sit back and wait for uncertainty to subside before resuming plans. A few increase planning efforts in an attempt to take advantage of others' hesitation. Some argue that while instability makes detailed plans impossible, strategy is more important than ever as a tool for coordinating activities during periods of uncertainty. For example, the unstable economy and increasing competition caused RCA to suffer an 83-percent profit decrease in 1981. The new chairman has

A successful manager finds the time to plan.

emphasized getting RCA "back to what it was" as a rallying point for the corporation's management. "What it was" means industry leadership in entertainment and electronics. That means getting out of fields into which it has diversified, such as real estate, rental cars, frozen foods, and carpets.[22]

The Bottom Line

Planning is the logical first function of management—setting objectives and deciding how they will be achieved. Good planning is not a substitute for doing, but makes it easier. A good plan helps a manager acquire necessary resources, reduce costs, direct and coordinate effort, and identify opportunities. What we know about managers and planning today suggests that:

1. If you're too busy to plan, you're too busy. Lack of planning may be one reason for being too busy. If you can't find time to plan, make time.
2. A plan is no better than the information it is based on. Check out assumptions and verify information. Be wary of relying on information that comes from a single source.
3. A forecast is only a statement about what is *likely* to happen. Build contingencies into the plan to allow for errors in forecasting.
4. A good plan is worthless if it is not carried out. Many a plan fails because the planner fails to check it out with colleagues, subordinates, or superiors whose cooperation is required. Unless there are strong reasons for not doing so (such as security), those who will be involved in carrying out the plan ought to be involved or represented in the planning process.

SUMMARY

The process of planning includes four sets of activities: setting goals, evaluating the organization's resources, forecasting the environment, and formulating the plan. Sophisticated management information systems have improved forecasting and scheduling activities, and are of particular use in complex, integrated planning.

All managers plan, but strategic planning remains essentially a top-management activity. As one descends the managerial hierarchy, planning becomes tactical rather than strategic, and involves shorter time horizons.

Because of their increased need and greater resources, large, complex, high-technology organizations do more formal planning than smaller, simpler organizations. In some of these larger organizations, planning is carried out on a full-time basis by a formal planning department.

Despite the benefits of planning, many managers avoid it. Planning requires thinking time, and managers often find little time to do much more than react. Planning can be expensive, and the payoffs are not usually immediate. Finally, managers are often held accountable for the success or failure of their plans.

Poor planning usually results from poor forecasting, inadequate information, faulty assumptions, or failure to involve the right people. But even a good plan is worthless if it is not implemented. Failure to integrate planning into the other managerial functions is the biggest drawback to its success.

QUESTIONS FOR REVIEW AND DISCUSSION

1. What are the characteristics of goals that provide the most direction and coordination?
2. How do strategic and tactical plans differ in organizational objectives and time horizon?
3. What are standing policies? What are their objectives and why? How do they differ from single-use plans?
4. What is a program? How is it organized?
5. How might large and small firms differ in their strategic and long-range planning? Why?
6. How do expenditures for high technology and capital investment influence planning?
7. What types of organizations use formal planning? How and why do they integrate it into the organization? How has the use of formal planning changed over time? What are some of the problems that may arise?
8. How are forecasts related to plans?
9. Why is the manager-employee relationship so crucial to planning?
10. Why do many plans never get implemented? How can this problem be corrected?

SUGGESTED READINGS

W. H. Brickner and D. M. Cope, *The Planning Process* (Cambridge, Mass: Winthrop Publishers, 1977). The authors are careful to identify key factors which contribute most to the successful use of planning in organizations.

G. A. Steiner, *Strategic Planning* (New York: Free Press, 1979). This book provides a clear understanding of strategic planning and its implementation.

P. Lorange, *Corporate Planning: An Executive Viewpoint* (Englewood Cliffs, N. J.: 1980). This book describes corporate planning, based on Lorange's own model.

REFERENCES AND NOTES

1. *Business Week*, May 19, 1980, pp. 124-5.
2. *Business Week*, June 16, 1980, p. 161; p. 93.
3. American Leisure Corporation. Ross Stebbins Inc., June 1980.
4. H. J. Reitz. *Behavior in Organizations* (Homewood, Ill.: R. D. Irwin, Inc., 1980).
5. *Business Week*, June 16, 1980, p. 95.
6. *Business Week*, June 2, 1980, pp. 79-80.
7. W. A. McCullough and J. L. Duncan, "Florida Banking: A Personnel Forecast through 1985" (Gainesville, Fl.: University of Florida, College of Business Administration, 1976).
8. *Business Week*, June 16, 1980, p. 106.
9. ABC Nightly News, June 15, 1980.
10. A. V. Cabot and D. L. Harnett, *An Introduction to Management Science* (Reading, Mass.: Addison-Wesley, 1977), p. 100.
11. "Kodak's Bright Picture," *Barron's*, Dec. 27, 1982, pp. 12-13.
12. J.A.F. Stoner, *Management* (Englewood Cliffs, N.J.: Prentice-Hall, 1978), pp. 99-101.
13. *Business Week*, May 19, 1980, pp. 106-7.
14. *Business Week*, June 9, 1980, p. 64.
15. *Business Week*, May 5, 1980, pp. 92-100.
16. W. H. Brickner and D. M. Cope, *The Planning Process* (Cambridge, Mass.: Winthrop Publishers, 1977), p. 11.
17. R. S. Webber, *Management: Basic Elements of Managing Organizations*, rev. ed. (Homewood, Ill.: R.D. Irwin, Inc., 1979), pp. 291-92.
18. W. F. Glueck, *Management* (Hinsdale, Ill.: Dryden Press, 1980) 2nd ed., pp. 204-5.
19. K. A. Ringbakk, "Why Planning Fails," *European Business*, Spring 1971, pp. 15-27.
20. P. S. Stonich, "Formal Planning Pitfalls and How to Avoid Them," *Management Review*, June 1975, pp. 1-11.
21. Webber, *Management*, op. cit., p. 288.
22. L. Laudro, "RCA Tries to Combat Its Growing Problems by Returning to Its Roots," *Wall Street Journal*, March 4, 1982, pp. 1 and 22.

Case Belmont-White Company

Two months ago, at an operating committee meeting, the president of the Belmont-White Company asked Thornton Peet, the general sales manager, and Paul Robb, manager of the organization planning and procedures department, to get together and determine if better forecasts of sales and of inventory requirements could be made available in order to improve factory schedules, financial planning, and so on.* Bert Kent and Charles Stevens, both of whom worked for Robb, and Robert Henry, Edwin Merrill, and David Spitz of the sales department, were assigned by Robb and Peet, respectively, to work on the problem. Stevens and Henry, being older and more experienced, and being regarded as rather senior men, immediately became the informal leaders of the work group. The five men worked out the technical problems to the satisfaction of both Stevens and Henry. The group attempted to consult with its immediate superiors as the work progressed.

After the study had been under way for some time, Henry told Stevens that he, Merrill, and Spitz seemed to be blocked by the opposition of the product division managers. Henry also told Stevens that he felt "he could not go over the division managers' heads" to Peet; and he asked Stevens to have his boss, Robb, inquire of the sales manager whether a conference might not be held to appraise the progress of the work. Stevens told Robb of Henry's request and the reason for it. Accordingly, Robb talked to Peet about the matter. Peet acquiesced, as he believed the problem ought to be solved as rapidly as possible.

Peet invited the four product division managers, Robb, and the five-man working group to the conference and set the time for it. Peet told Henry to go ahead with Stevens and set up the presentation to be made at the conference.

As Henry and Stevens planned the conference, they decided that the group from the sales department—Henry, Merrill, and Spitz—were really on the spot. The three men all agreed that in order not to embarrass themselves or their bosses, the presentation of the joint conclusions of the working group ought to be made by Stevens.

At the meeting, Peet, the four product division managers, and the three men from sales who worked on the study were present, as were Robb of the organization planning and procedures department and his two assistants, Stevens and Kent. When Peet asked who was going to report progress, Henry suggested that Stevens was the best man to present their findings. Peet asked Robb if that was O.K. When the latter agreed, Stevens used half an hour to outline the concept of their work; he stated that both groups had agreed upon details and believed their recommendations would work; they were prepared to take personal responsibility for them. Both Merrill and Spitz asked Henry to amplify certain points during the presentation. It seemed to Robb that they had in mind clarifying matters for their own bosses who might be opposed or might not understand.

Following Stevens' statement, the sales manager called upon his product division managers to give their reactions

Exhibit 1

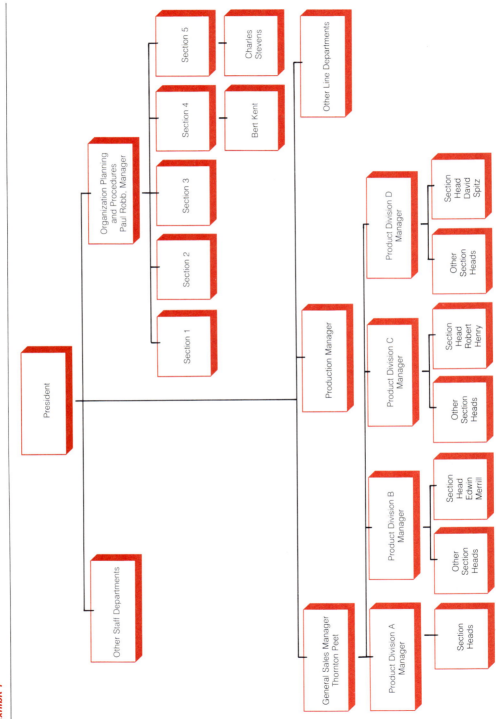

to the proposals. One of them gave the plan lukewarm support; the three others said it could not be accomplished. There was much discussion among the three who were opposed. Occasionally, Henry, Merrill, and Spitz tried to "get a word in edgewise," without much success. Once, Kent asked the Division B manager a question; the effect seemed to be mild anger at being interrupted.

Robb watched the whole proceeding with interest. He recalled that it had seemed to him that for the past two years, this same group of four product managers had opposed every step involving changes in methods or procedures. In his opinion, their "delaying tactics" had been costly to the company. Robb knew that the president

expected him to break some of these bottlenecks. Robb was only a staff adviser, but he knew he "had the president's ear" whenever he needed it. He considered the sales manager to be progressive and thought Peet could not tolerate these conditions much longer. It seemed to Robb that Peet had line responsibility to get something done in this area. Robb liked these "old-line" product managers and did not want to hurt them if he could avoid it.

While Robb was in the midst of these musings, and after two hours of apparently fruitless discussion, Peet turned to him and said: "Robb, you have heard this whole discussion; what do you think we ought to do next?"

CASE QUESTIONS

1. What kinds of plans are the team of Kent, Stevens, Henry, Merrill, and Spitz concerned with?
2. Why are the product managers resisting the plan to improve planning?
3. What kinds of problems does the planning department face in working with line departments?
4. Why didn't the plan for the meeting work?
5. If you were Robb, how would you answer Peet's question?

Report from the Field *Coordinating Activities*

Charlotte Sharp is shift coordinator at Shands Hospital, a large, privately owned medical facility in the Southeast. As shift coordinator, she is the top management person in the hospital for the 3 P.M. to 11 P.M. shift. Her job is to coordinate the needs and activities of the twenty-eight medical units in the hospital, particularly the staffing needs of the nursing units on her shift.

"My day starts by coordinating with the previous shift. First I listen to medical-report tapes on the patients. They tell me the number of patients in each unit, their conditions, and any problems that I might have to deal with. Once I've been updated I get together with the staff-supplement staffing coordinator to discuss staffing needs and changes for the evening. If any nurses scheduled for my shift have called in sick, we decide whether we have to call in more nurses or whether staffing is adequate.

"Once we've made this decision, I start my rounds of the units, checking for problems, like a shortage of beds or staff. I make two rounds, one at the beginning of the shift and one at the end. They're time-consuming and hard on the feet, but they're the only way to really get the information and make the decisions needed to coordinate all the units. Making rounds and writing reports are the only real 'routine' tasks in this position.

"On a typical evening I may deal with problems ranging from finding extra beds for a crowded unit to coordinating a full-scale emergency. For example, the other evening my first call was from a nurse who had a patient scheduled for surgery the next morning. The patient wanted to sign a statement prior to surgery that she should not be kept alive by life-support systems if she was brain dead after surgery. I coordinated her request with the hospital's attorney, who advised me to have her make a written request to pass on to her family. They would ultimately be responsible for those kinds of decisions.

"During my first rounds that evening few problems arose. I usually vary the order in which I visit units, but I always start with the Recovery Room. I've learned that if things are crazy there it will affect staffing everywhere.

"We had only one crisis that night, a STAT code from the Pediatric Intensive Care Unit, where a young girl had gone into cardiac arrest. I respond immediately to the scene of all such crises. In this case, by the time I arrived, we had six people at the patient's bedside reviving her. Things went very smoothly. It always pleases and amazes me how efficiently and well people work together in instances like this. One of the real satisfactions of the job comes from seeing a life saved through the coordinated efforts of competent people.

"The STAT situation with the young girl required my presence for a hour and a half, so my second rounds were pretty quick. I finished the evening by picking up the nightly report on positive hepatitis tests. I am responsible for notifying the appropriate charge nurse that the patient must be isolated. My last task was to discuss staffing needs and changes with the staff-supplement staffing coordinator and to tape my own medical reports for the next shift coordinator."

Source: Personal Interview, October 1983.

4/ORGANIZING

"Come on in, Walt, and shut the door." The young man closed the door and dropped into the last empty chair.

"Well," began Diane, restraining her excitement, "we got it—twenty minutes before the executive committee to make our pitch for the new oxygen mask! I asked for half an hour, but would have settled for fifteen minutes. It'll be tight, but we can do it."

"You bet we can," agreed Walt, who headed up the team that had designed the new self-contained oxygen mask for fire fighters. "When they see the test data and the market potential for this thing, they'll give us everything we want."

"I hope so," said Diane, "but let's leave nothing to chance. I want a really professional presentation for this one— no holes, no loose ends. I've broken the content down into six parts: introduction, product, market potential, finance, legal, and closing. I'm giving each of you the task of providing the necessary data and materials for one part. Walt, you obviously get the product; and I want

three working models for the presentation. Elizabeth, you do the workup on the financial end, including capital costs and per-unit costs."

"I'd like to tackle the legal end," offered Don. "I've had enough business law to know how to talk to the legal staff."

"OK, Don," Diane replied. "Carol, you take the marketing section. I'll give you a hand, because I know what the committee looks for."

"I want all your materials to me in ten days. I want them marked in order of their importance, because we have only twenty minutes. There'll be a lot of editing to do. Jim will do the initial write-up of the presentation. He's had plenty of experience. Once he's got that done, we'll have another meeting and go over it together. That will give us about a week for revision and rehearsal. Right now, I think Walt and I will make the actual presentation, but I'll want you all there, if possible."

"Diane, do you want Carol and me to coordinate our data? There might be some overlap between marketing and finance."

"Good idea, Elizabeth. That should make it a lot easier to coordinate the marketing and finance sections. It makes a good impression with the board when figures from different areas complement each other, rather than look like they've got nothing to do with each other.

"As a matter of fact," Diane continued, "I'd like all of you to check your figures with Elizabeth before you give them to me. That'll save me the trouble of doing it myself and give me more time to work on coordinating the overall presentation."

"What about art work?" asked Carol. "Do we want to use slides, overhead transparencies, or charts?"

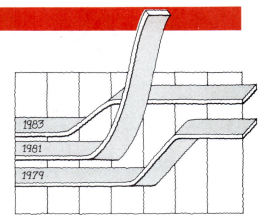

"Let's go with charts," Diane replied. *"We can get better use of color and larger figures that way. I want everyone to have at least two charts sketched out for me when you give me the rest of your material. I'll have one artist do all of them. They'll look better that way.*

"Any other questions? OK let's do it. Let me know how you're coming from time to time. I want to keep right on top of this one."

The meeting between Diane and her group provides an example of organizing in action. Diane has set objectives and has determined a course of action to achieve those objectives. She then has broken up that course of action into manageable pieces and has coordinated them for efficiency and effectiveness.

Organizing means *deciding what tasks must be accomplished, dividing up and allocating those tasks to individuals or groups, and coordinating their activities.* Diane plans to get the executive committee to back her group's new product by making an effective presentation. She organized the presentation itself by dividing up the work, allocating it among her group, and coordinating their efforts.

Diane broke the task into several parts: preparing the data and materials, writing up the presentation, and making the presentation to the committee. She gave the write-up task to Jim, and reserved the presentation for Walt and herself. She further divided the preparation task into four parts: product, marketing, finance, and legal, and assigned those tasks to Walt, Carol, Elizabeth, and Don, based on their individual expertise and experience. Dividing up the work allows each individual the time to apply expertise by working on only one part of the presentation.

The disadvantage of dividing up the work among several individuals is that the work must be coordinated. If the individual reports are inconsistent, repetitive, or fail to cover important areas when taken together, the presentation will be a failure. Diane coordinated the efforts in three ways: First, she directed each individual to check data and materials with Elizabeth, the financial expert. Second, Jim was given the job of writing the first draft of the presentation, putting together all the materials supplied by the individual members. Finally, Diane and the group will meet to rehearse their parts.

It may appear that the manager is putting a lot of effort into coordinating the group's activities. In fact, she is doing no more than is necessary. Diane could reduce her job by allocating the tasks to fewer people or by doing it herself; but if she did everything herself she'd be wasting the expertise of her group, while leaving herself with less time to do other things. The function of organizing can be seen as balancing the advantages of specialization and division of labor against the cost of coordination. A successful manager like Diane learns how to balance those advantages and costs.

THE PURPOSE OF ORGANIZING

Organizing allows managers to accomplish more objectives in a better way by using the coordinated effort of many people. They can take advantage of individual differences in skills and abilities to develop those skills to a high degree, and use them in conjunction with technology and other resources to produce goods and services far beyond the capacity of any individual. Thousands of scientists, working alone, could not put a human on the moon, but the coordinated efforts of thousands of specialists did just that in 1969. No writer, no matter how brilliant, can inform or entertain a nation by working alone. But organized effort, providing that writer with hundreds of thousands of copies of his or her work and with nationwide advertising and marketing programs, can reach a national audience.

Organizing involves dividing a task into several parts and then rebuilding it through coordination. We organize work at several levels: the work of an individual, the work of several individuals into groups or teams or departments, and the work of an entire organization.

DIVISION OF LABOR AND SPECIALIZATION

In 1832 Charles Babbage, an Englishman, who designed the first mechanical calculating machine, proposed four advantages of dividing up work to permit workers to specialize:

Simplification of Training.   It is quicker and cheaper to train a worker to perform one operation in a manufacturing process than to train the worker to perform all the operations.

Elimination of Changeover Time.   A worker performing several operations will be required to change activities and tools. Time is lost as the worker readjusts himself or herself and his or her tools to the new process. An individual performing the same task all the time with the same tools loses no time to changeover.

Enhancement of Skill Development.   The repeated performance of the same operation will enable the worker to develop his or her skill to the highest degree.

Improvement of Technological Development.   An individual concentrating on a single operation will devise an easier and better way to perform the operation, which may lead to the development of improved machines or tools. (The carpenter's plane was devised by a worker who mounted a chisel in a frame to keep from cutting the wood too deeply.)

Babbage saw the benefits of division of labor coming from **specialization—** *doing a small number of operations expertly rather than a great number of operations unskillfully.*

Babbage applied the principles of division of labor and specialization of function to, among other things, the manufacture of pins. He observed that there were seven operations involved in pin-making: drawing the wire, straightening the wire, pointing, twisting and cutting heads, putting a head on the pin, applying a coat of tin, and affixing the finished pins to paper. Division of labor and specialization allowed skilled workers to concentrate on highly skilled tasks, while the bulk of the work could be performed by workers of less skill. Babbage observed that the efficiencies thus gained enabled ten specialized workers to convert raw material into a pound of pins for only 28 percent of the cost of one individual performing all the operations.[1]

The Development of Specialization

Although Babbage may be credited with the first well-planned applications of the principles of specialization in industry, he was by no means the first to realize the advantages of specialization and organization. The history of warfare reveals that these principles have been understood and applied for thousands of years. Well before the time of Christ, the Egyptians divided the art of warfare into three operations and trained each soldier as a specialist in one of the operations—as a charioteer, infantryman, or archer.

By 331 B.C., the principles of specialization and organization spread to other parts of the world, where they were best understood and applied by Alexander the Great of Macedon. He not only divided his army into infantry and cavalry, but further subdivided their tasks. Alexander's army consisted of light infantry, heavy infantry, bowmen, and men specializing in the use of slings and pikes. He had engineers, artillerymen with a battering ram, and medical personnel. Finally, he used cavalry to finish off and pursue enemy infantry fatigued at the end of a long battle. This specialization, and the organization of these masses into a coordinated phalanx of over 16,000 men, enabled Alexander to conquer Egypt and the rest of the known world by the time he was twenty-five years old. Unfortunately, two thousand years passed before these principles were applied in industry.

> *Specialization has enormous advantages in the use of human skills and technology. However, there appears to be too much specialization. In recent years, job rotation, job enlargement, and job enrichment have been used to increase both employee efficiency and satisfaction.*

Frederick Taylor, whom we briefly described in Chapter 2, is credited with founding the scientific management movement which focused on improving productivity through careful attention to job design.[2]

Taylor believed that management needed to take a more active role in developing specialization by studying work to determine the one best (most efficient) way of performing each operation. Workers would be trained to do each task ef-

Exhibit 4.1   Taylor's Functional Foremanship

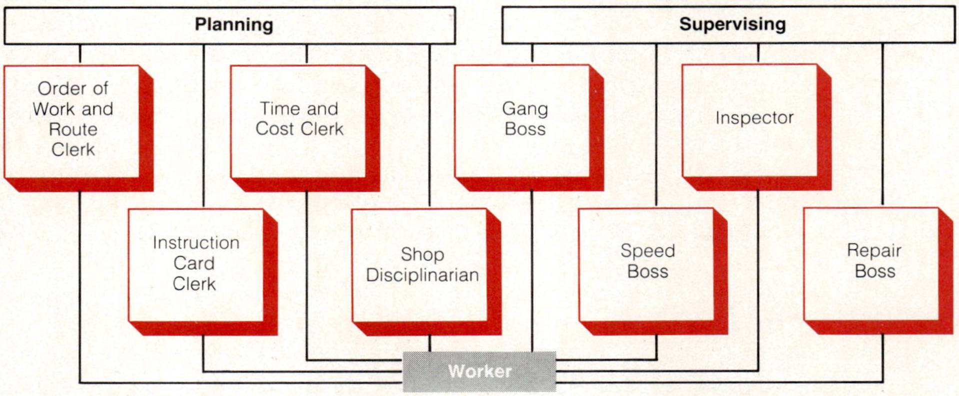

ficiently and would be provided with an incentive to do so by being paid on a piece-rate rather than by a daily wage.

According to Taylor's associate, Frank Gilbreth, such simplification and standardization benefited all. He used the example of a worker who, on his own, could produce ten units a day for $4.00:

> *. . . by analyzing the methods of working, down to the minutest motion, and by discovering a new method that took less time with less effort and was subject to less delay, the worker was able to put out 25 pieces for which he received 25 cents apiece. The man's pay here is raised more than 56 percent, and the production costs have been lowered 37 percent.*[3]

Taylor realized that a foreman's job could be broken down into several operations as well, each of which required different skills. The job, as he proposed it, required a set of skills, the sum of which were beyond the capabilities of most foremen of that time; but individuals could perform a particular function on the basis of individual skills, then be trained to carry out that function in an efficient manner. Taylor's concept of "functional foremanship"[4] broke the foreman's job into two broad categories: planning and supervising. Each of these two categories was further divided into four subfunctions, as depicted in Exhibit 4.1. A foreman was trained in one of these eight areas so that in the planning department, one determined the most efficient way of ordering and routing work, another prepared written instructions for each job, a third computed time and costs for each operation, and a fourth devised the means for keeping workers operating more efficiently. On the shop floor, one foreman coordinated individual work, another paid attention to the workers' speed, a third controlled quality, and a fourth supervised machine maintenance and repair.

Exhibit 4.2   A Typical Manufacturing Organization Incorporating Functional Foremanship on a Departmental Basis

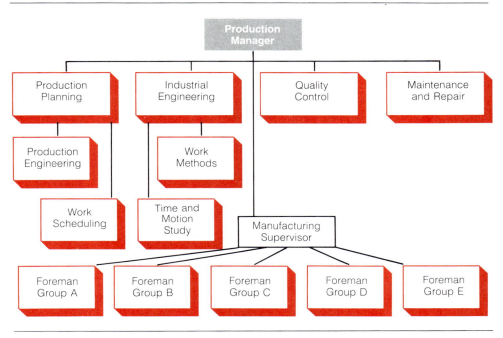

Functional foremanship as proposed by Taylor was awkward, because each worker was subject to the orders of eight bosses; yet the functional process survived. Today, many of the activities are carried out by entire departments of specialists rather than by a single individual, as shown in Exhibit 4.2. The job of the order-of-work and route clerk is now carried out by the work scheduling department. The instruction card clerk has been replaced by work methods. Time and cost functions are performed by industrial engineers in time and motion studies. Inspection has become Quality Control, while Repair is now Machine and Shop Maintenance. The functions of disciplinarian, gang boss, and speed boss have generally been absorbed by the direct supervisor or foreman. The day-to-day supervision is carried out by the foreman under guidelines established by production planning, quality control, and maintenance.

The Design of Work Today

The manager's role is not much different today from Taylor's time: to organize work to take advantage of specialization and then to coordinate the efforts. However, we have learned a good deal about both defining and coordinating work since Taylor's time.

Management in Action
Leaner Organizations

From the 1950s through the early 1980s, organization at the corporate level meant bigger and bigger staffs of middle managers to deal with increasing growth, complexity, and diversity of large businesses. The purpose of such staffs was to gather and analyze information on markets, financial affairs, and products to assist executives in their decision making. But executives quickly lost control of these staffs, which often continued to grow even when they had outlived their usefulness. The end results, in many cases, were excessive managerial costs and an increasing bureaucracy that reduced the ability to adapt and change.

The recession of the early 1980s, coupled with stiff competition from Japanese corporations unburdened by large layers of middle management, has reversed the trend toward centralized decision making. Corporate staffs have been reduced or eliminated, and operating executives have reclaimed their power. At Xerox Corporation, general managers are now making decisions on new products that corporate staff once made; Brunswick Corporation reduced its headquarters staff by forty percent. Crown Zellerbach has eliminated three layers of management by increasing the power of its plant managers. Each of these managers now controls credit, marketing, labor, and sales decisions formerly made at corporate staff level.

Some analysts see this trend toward leaner organizations as only an intermediate step in an evolution toward much less structured and more flexible, decentralized organizations. The organizations of the future are envisioned as being based not on a formal hierarchy of authority as in the past, but on the expertise of individuals and groups who organize themselves to meet different situations. The emphasis will be on special task forces created to solve problems, meet challenges, and exploit opportunities as the occasion arises. According to these experts, the bureaucratic, highly structured, multilayered organization in which most people work today is on its way out, doomed by its own inefficiencies and lack of flexibility.

International Business Machines is the primary example of the large organization that has moved away from a traditional structure to a more flexible, decentralized approach. General Electric, Rank Xerox Ltd., and Connecticut Mutual Life Insurance Company are other large firms that have turned to trimming corporate staffs and creating smaller, decentralized groups. While some analysts believe that this organizational trend will persist, others believe that it is just another trend. Because managers are always looking for new ways to organize and coordinate work, corporate staffs will be "rediscovered."

Sources: Personal interviews and "Special Report: The Shrinking of Middle Management," *Business Week*, April 25, 1983, pp. 54–60.

Exhibit 4.3   The Process of Job Design

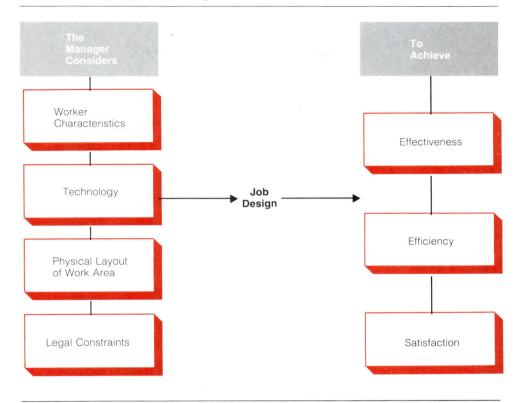

Job design is a *process which specifies the content of a job, the tools and techniques to be used, the work environment, and how the job is related to other jobs.* A manager's objectives in designing a job are effectiveness (accomplishment of task), efficiency (minimization of resource waste), and satisfaction (maintenance of individual and group employee morale).

However, the design of work is not an exact science. Determining what, how, and where a job will be done requires a manager to consider the following factors, summarized in Exhibit 4.3:

1. Worker characteristics: How much will a typical worker be able to do?
2. Technology: What tools and equipment are available?
3. Layout of the work area: What facilities are available?
4. Legal constraints: What union agreements or governmental regulations apply?

Consider the organization of work in a fast-food restaurant. Because the restaurant pays minimum wages, the typical employee is young, inexperienced, untrained, and will quit after fifteen months. The available technology includes high-speed grills, large freezers, timing devices, electronic cash registers, and pre-packaged and premixed products. The building is large enough to permit six people to serve four lines of customers, leaving room for fifty diners. The legal constraints include safety requirements, hour limits on young workers, sanitary regulations on cooking and storing foods, and work break and overtime payment requirements. Evaluation of these factors causes the manager to divide the work into two parts: food preparation and counter work (taking and serving orders and operating the cash register). Simplification, specialization, and standardization are the manager's guidelines to simplify training and take advantage of technology.

Defining Job Content

The first step in job design is to specify what the job entails. Content (what is to be done) is one of the major determinants of method (how it will be done). If you're going to tune up your car, you need to know the content of the job (changing the spark plugs, points, gas filter, and adjusting the timing) before you can decide what methods to use.

Content also aids the job holder in learning the necessary methods instead of wasting time learning unnecessary methods. Unfortunately, this simple principle is violated in many training programs. For example, there has been a strong tendency to prepare business-school students for managerial careers by teaching them a multitude of techniques without regard to job content. Students may spend a great deal of time learning mathematical and statistical techniques and little, if any time, developing creative and verbal skills. The most common complaints voiced by business leaders about business-school graduates are that these graduates rely too heavily on quantitative methods, display too little creativity, and lack basic communication skills.[5]

Task Attributes

Classifying the tasks to be done according to certain attributes or characteristics may enable a manager to make better decisions about the job in light of the three criteria of effectiveness, efficiency, and satisfaction.

Research conducted at Harvard on industrial jobs determined a method of classifying work according to six important job characteristics, called *Requisite Task Attributes* (Exhibit 4.4).[6] Behavior of the worker in a particular job is divided into three elements: the different physical *activities* performed in the job; verbal *interactions* with other people, particularly face-to-face communications; and the *individual characteristics* associated with the job. The task itself is analyzed in two ways—elements which are *required* by the job, and those which are *optional* or available, but not required.

For example, the requisite task attributes of a ticket seller in a theater box-office would be the following: required activities such as dispensing tickets, receiving cash, and making change; required interactions such as asking customers about the number of tickets desired and answering inquiries about schedules; required knowledge and skills such as the ability to add, subtract, multiply, and make change, and the ability to deal with customers pleasantly.

Despite the freedom from direct supervision there are very rigid job rules— little autonomy. Optional interaction with customers on the job occurs infrequently. While responsibility for handling large amounts of money is required, a ticket seller may also take responsibility for recognizing potential problems such as fake passes, counterfeit money, and limited available seating.

Job Analysis

Job analysis is *the gathering of information about a job to establish wage rates, to define jobs for employees, and to aid in the redesign of work.* (We will discuss the use of job analysis for setting wage rates in the chapter on staffing). Conducting job analysis is of great benefit in staffing positions. It points out the skills required, those skills not absolutely required but of benefit, and special limitations which might affect employee satisfaction (for example, limited opportunity for optional interaction). The analysis can also suggest ways to organize the job to improve employee satisfaction or performance. The manager of the theater can increase the ticket-sellers' skills by providing them with a chart showing the amount for various numbers and combinations of tickets (two adult and three children = $13.50). This simple tool might reduce errors and time per transaction.

Exhibit 4.4   Requisite Task Attributes: A Scheme for Analyzing Work

Elements of Behavior

		Physical Activities	Verbal Interactions	Individual Characteristics
Elements of Task	Required	Variety in Objects Dealt with and in Physical Activities	Required Interaction	Knowledge and Skill
	Optional	Autonomy	Optional Interaction (on or off the job)	Optional Responsibility

Adapted with permission from Arthur N. Turner and Paul R. Lawrence, *Industrial Jobs and the Worker: An Investigation of Response to Task Attributes.* Boston: Division of Research, Harvard Business School, 1965, Exhibit 1.4, p. 27.

Too often, managers, harassed for time, assume employees can learn a new job on their own, only to be disappointed later to find that the expectations about job performance differ sharply. In a typical case, a machine operator described his introduction to his new job.

The clicking machine assigned to me was situated at one end of the row. Here the superintendent and one of the operators gave a few brief demonstrations, accompanied by bits of advice which included a warning to keep hands clear of the descending hammer. After a short practice period . . . I was left to develop my learning curve with no other supervision than that afforded by members of the work group.[7]

This worker's response to such vague job definition was to guess at the minimum amount of work output and quality required to stay on the job. He spent a good deal of time participating in games and rituals that his fellow workers had devised to pass the time of day.

Ambiguously defined or undefined jobs can result in employee performance which differs from managerial expectations. Ambiguity can also take its toll in employee stress, absenteeism and turnover, and dissatisfaction at work.

Job definition allows a manager to communicate the content and standards of jobs to employees. It provides information about content and required worker characteristics, which not only aids in employee selection but helps determine whether a job can be designed to improve effectiveness, efficiency, and satisfaction.

The design or redesign of work presumes knowledge of the tasks to be performed. Job analysis describes what is done in a particular job, how it is done, and why.

There are a number of job analysis methods currently in use. No one method is clearly superior to the others: one may be better for performance appraisal, another for job selection, and a third for setting wage scales.

A complete job analysis provides for:

1. Task activities—what is done and how it is done.
2. Human behaviors—physical activities, communications, special demands.
3. Machinery and equipment used.
4. Materials used, products made, services rendered.
5. Standards for output or performance.
6. Physical environment of the job, work schedule, pay, and other incentives.
7. Skills, knowledge, education, and experience required.

This information is provided in several different ways, any or all of which may be used in analyzing a particular job:

1. Observing the job being performed.
2. Interviewing those who perform the job and others who deal with them.
3. Questionnaires filled out by workers and/or their supervisors.

4. Requiring the worker to keep a diary or log.
5. Filming or recording the work being done.
6. Analyzing similar jobs or job descriptions, machinery used, and job location and layout.

Environmental Factors Affecting Job Design

Specifying the content of a job is often influenced by both the physical and the social environments in which work takes place (See Exhibit 4.5). The *physical environment* includes the product, production processes and quotas, the available machinery and the way it is laid out. Realistically, one cannot redesign a welder's job to completely disrupt a $20 million assembly line.

The *social environment* includes union agreements, governmental restrictions, worker preferences and satisfaction. For example, both union and government may require that potentially hazardous work, such as sewer inspection or high tension wire installation and repair, be done by pairs of workers rather than alone. And industrial history is replete with examples of technologically sound job designs that failed because they violated strong worker norms or preferences.

Exhibit 4.5   Environmental Factors Affecting Job Design

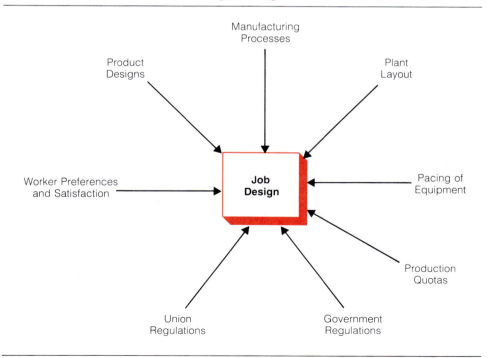

DETERMINING JOB METHODS

Once content (what is to be done) has been defined, the next step in job organization is to determine the method (how it will be done). In addition to content, the designer of work methods considers the psychological and physiological capabilities of the work force, principles governing the flow of work, and factors such as fatigue and work schedules.[8] In industrial jobs, work methods are usually designed by industrial engineers and individual psychologists. In nonindustrial jobs, work methods are left up to the foreman, supervisor, manager, administrator, and the job holders themselves.

Factors to be Considered

Industrial engineers consider three factors when establishing job methods. One factor, of course, is the nature of the work to be done, or *job content*. The second factor is the *environmental factor:* namely, what technology is available, the scheduling and flow of related jobs, and government and union restrictions. Finally, there is the *human factor*, which includes the physiological capabilities of the workers, their psychological characteristics, and limits for fatigue and stress.

Among the human factors important in job methods are manual dexterity, strengths and forces of body movements, and speed and accuracy of responses, as well as perceptual capabilities such as workers' abilities to see and hear information from dials, displays, and other signalling devices. For example, the shape and design of information displays can dramatically affect the percentage of mistakes that an average worker will make in reading them.

Industrial engineers and psychologists also know something about the effects of job design on worker fatigue and stress, but unfortunately knowledge in this area is not as precise as that dealing with other physiological factors. We know that light and noise affect performance, output, and quality, but stress tolerance is a highly individualized characteristic that makes measuring stressors and establishing guidelines for the work design very difficult. However, stress at work is important enough that we devote an entire chapter to the topic in Part 4.

Human-Machine Systems

It is no secret that advances in technology are largely responsible for the fantastic productivity of modern workers compared to their counterparts of a hundred years ago. In deciding whether and how to use improved technology in job design, the manager must consider the relative capabilities of people and machines.

We can divide human functions in job performance into three categories:

1. Receiving information (hearing, seeing, touching)
2. Making decisions based on the information received plus information stored (memory)

3. Acting (reflexive or repetitive, well-learned responses or actions based on reasoning and complex information processing.)[9]

In which of these functions can machines provide the greatest assistance? Although machines are very specialized, within their limits of specialization they can exceed most human physiological capacities (for example, strength, speed, endurance). Given proper maintenance, machines are also more reliable. Human beings, on the other hand, enjoy greater flexibility, can perform a much greater variety of functions, and can maintain themselves. A famous scholar of man-machine systems makes the following comparisions.[10]

Humans can outperform existing machines in:

1. Detecting small amounts of light and sound.
2. Recognizing and organizing patterns of light and sound (seeing and hearing).
3. Improvising and using flexible procedures.
4. Storing large amounts of information for long periods.
5. Recalling relevant facts at the appropriate time.
6. Reasoning inductively (drawing a general conclusion from evidence).
7. Exercising judgment.
8. Developing concepts and creating methods.

Existing machines, on the other hand, can outperform humans in:

1. Responding quickly to control signals.
2. Applying great force smoothly and precisely.
3. Performing repetitive and routine tasks.
4. Storing information briefly and then erasing it completely.
5. Performing rapid computations.
6. Performing many different functions at the same time.

Organizing involves dividing a task into several parts and then rebuilding it through coordination.

The preceding general principles serve as guidelines for designing human-machine systems to perform work. Consider the job content of a travel agent - making airline reservations and writing tickets. For certain activities, the human is superior—recalling information about a client's particular preferences or travel circumstances, improvising when flights are cancelled or overbooked, and exercising judgment and reasoning.

Machines, on the other hand, are superior in quick response (automatic phone answering devices), performing routine and repetitive tasks (automatic dialing of frequently used numbers), storing information briefly and then erasing it completely (computer-assisted storage, updating, and retrieval of schedules and

These robots in GM's Lordstown, Ohio plant can check with absolute accuracy 12 points on each side of a car's body and can detect a problem before it occurs.

fares), and performing rapid computations (calculating charges and comparing costs of alternative travel plans). Thus, modern travel agencies, hard pressed to keep up with increasing business and vacation travel by Americans, have redesigned travel-agents' jobs by supplying them with computers, calculators, and communications technology.

In many organizations we still find people doing jobs for which machines are clearly superior. In some cases this inefficiency is due to the lack of information about available technology or the lack of imagination in putting technology to work. In most cases, however, it is a matter of economics: new technology costs too much, or manual labor is cheap enough to warrant inefficiencies. Nevertheless, in industrialized countries like the United States and West Germany, and even in countries where human labor is traditionally inexpensive like Japan and Taiwan, increases in labor costs are making the incorporation of technology more feasible.

In recent years, technological breakthroughs in computer-assisted technology have led to the development of industrial robots which may revolutionize the field of job design. Robots are machines with some of the capabilities which until now only humans enjoyed, including the capacity to recognize and interpret patterns of light, sound, and substance (to "see, hear, and feel"), the capacity to make decisions by combining information so received with stored information, and an increased flexibility.

A major advantage of robots is their ability to take over dirty, dangerous, strenuous, or stressful jobs—for example, spot welding, spray painting, and drilling in a noisy, high-speed assembly process. At General Electric, robots are used to remove white-hot metal for turbine engine blades from forging furnaces. Before the robots were installed, workers removed the metal using only tongs, requiring them to stay within feet of a furnace heated to 1700 degrees Fahrenheit.[11]

ALTERNATIVES TO JOB SPECIALIZATION

How far is the division of labor to be carried? Early proponents of specialization saw no limits other than economic. Jobs would be broken down into the smallest components allowed by the economies of specialization. More recently, however, some job analysts claim that too much specialization leads to worker boredom and alienation, and deprives work of its meaning.

Other means of increasing the content of individual jobs have been proposed to increase worker satisfaction and the meaningfulness of work. Four basic approaches to defining job content have evolved: *job specialization*, which has already been discussed, *job enlargement*, *job enrichment*, and *job rotation*.

Job Enlargement

Job enlargement is an *attempt to reduce boredom and increase the meaning of work by increasing the number of operations in a process performed by a single worker*. It is a move away from specialization. In terms of Exhibit 4.4, showing Requisite Task Attributes, job enlargement increases both the variety of required activities and the required knowledge and skill of the worker.

Ideally, a job is enlarged until one person is able to complete an entire subprocess or subunit. For example, in a very specialized clerical department of an insurance company, the operations of opening and sorting client mail, locating files, evaluating claims, requesting payments, corresponding with clients, and updating files and reports could each be handled by a different individual or section. One could enlarge any of these jobs by combining operations. For example, one individual could open and sort client mail and locate the appropriate files. The individual could also forward any inquiries, together with the files, to another clerk whose job has been enlarged to include claims evaluation, payment requisition, and correspondence.

The theory behind job enlargement is that combining tasks reduces boredom, increasing task variety and strengthening the worker's identification with his or her job. Job enlargement is expected to produce increases in both worker satisfaction and productivity. In one company, the task of assembling centrifugal water pumps had been specialized. Initially, each of six assemblers performed one operation. The average time required to assemble a pump this way was about 130 seconds. Then the jobs were enlarged so that each worker assembled an entire pump and checked its quality. The average time required to assemble a pump dropped to about 90 seconds, and production costs dropped by 10 percent.[12]

The overall success of this strategy has been mixed. Not all jobs can be easily redesigned. Enlarged jobs sometimes exceed individual worker capability or outstrip the capability of highly efficient specialized machinery. Further, not all employees want their jobs to be enlarged. They prefer specialization to task variety, and resist attempts to increase job content.

Job Enrichment

The goals of job enrichment are similar to those of job enlargement: to reduce boredom and to increase worker satisfaction and the meaning of work. However, the means are somewhat different. **Job enrichment** is an *attempt to give workers more control over their tasks and more responsibility for design, execution, and output.* The worker assumes some of the functions previously carried out by his or her immediate supervisor or by other staff. In some job enrichment programs, the worker may plan and schedule the work, carry it out through several stages, and be responsible for quality control.

Thus, job enrichment, like job enlargement, increases variety, knowledge, and skill requirements. In addition, job enrichment increases the autonomy in a job, as well as the responsibility assumed by the employee. In a simple case, maintenance jobs are enriched by allowing the crews to decide when and how equipment should be maintained. Air Canada allows aircraft maintenance personnel to decide when aircraft windows should be replaced.[13]

In a more complete enrichment program, General Foods used a team approach for production employees at a new plant. The teams not only produced the products, but helped evaluate their own performances, decided on their pay schedules, and corrected customer complaints.[14]

Once the content of work has been defined, job methods can be determined. Deciding how a job is best accomplished is an inexact science. Factors which influence the choice of work methods are worker characteristics including psychological as well as physiological capabilities, environmental factors including technology, plant layout, and government and union restrictions, as well as job content.

In the world of sports management, job enrichment has enjoyed recent notoriety. At the college level, some football coaches have also become athletic directors, directly controlling athletic department budgets and establishing policies as well as spending money and executing policies as coaches. At the professional level, several organizations have combined the jobs of field manager and general manager, again giving the person responsible for day-to-day managing more control and discretion in hiring, firing, and paying coaches and players.

By rotating employees among different jobs, management hopes to minimize boredom and routineness. Employees are also given the opportunity to develop other skills and have a perspective of the total production process.

The overall success of job enrichment, like job enlargement, is mixed. Obviously, whether such a strategy works depends upon the nature of the work and the available labor force. Some jobs resist enrichment; some workers do likewise. Management sees it as giving workers too much discretion at the expense of management. Unions feel it blurs the distinctions between management and labor, and requires labor to take on management functions without adequate additional compensation.

Job Rotation

Job rotation is perhaps the simplest answer to job specialization. The objectives again are reduced monotony and fatigue and increased satisfaction through greater task variety. **Job rotation** is a *practice whereby each employee learns several operations in a manufacturing process and rotates through each in a set period.*

In job rotation a fast-food employee might operate the grill one week, work the counter the next week, the drive-in window the third week, and then return to the grill. An obvious benefit of job rotation is a more broadly skilled work force. This makes it easier to fill in for absent or tardy workers or to respond to unusual situations, such as a busload of customers ordering 125 Big Macs.

The Sociotechnical Systems Approach

In some industries there have been experimental attempts to formally involve workers in job design. With this **sociotechnical systems approach,** *groups of workers share responsibility for some set of tasks forming a meaningful part of a production process.* For example, a group might have the responsibility of converting corrugated paper into shipping boxes and containers. Given the raw materials and the available technology, the group determines individual job content, work methods, work flow, and production schedules.

In some ways the sociotechnical approach is like job enrichment, except that it is extended to the group, rather than the individual. In many instances group members share pay, as well as responsibility, for job design and production. Large organizations currently using a sociotechnical approach to some degree are Proctor & Gamble and Mead Containers. They report that it results in lower production costs, greater productivity, and higher employee satisfaction.

Worker characteristics, the nature of the jobs, technology, and the physical and social environments of work will determine the success of a given approach to job design in any organization.[15] The point is that the manager has several approaches to choose from. The way work is designed will affect organizational effectiveness, job performance, and employee satisfaction.

Exhibit 4.6   The Balance Between the Advantages of Division of Labor and the Costs of Coordination

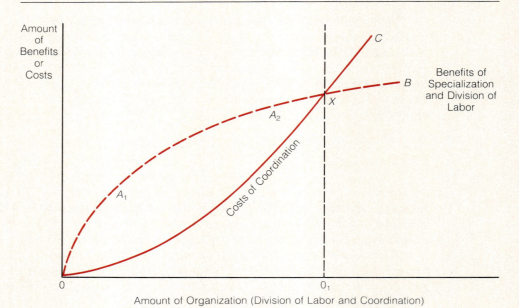

COORDINATING WORK

We have said that organizing consists of defining work, dividing it into jobs which can be handled by one person or one group, and then coordinating those jobs to achieve organizational objectives effectively, efficiently, with satisfied workers. We have described job definition, job specialization, and the principles of dividing up work. We must now consider the problem of coordinating all the activities which comprise the work to be done.

Coordination is *the process of integrating activities and getting individuals or groups to work together to achieve objectives.* The manager's task in organizing work can be viewed as one of balancing the benefits of division of labor and specialization against the costs of coordinating the diverse activities created by division of labor and specialization. This task is depicted in Exhibit 4.6, in which the curve *OB* represents the benefits of increasing division of labor and specialization and *OC* the costs of coordination.

Curve *OB* indicates that dividing up work tends to benefit the organization, but at some point (A_1) the additional net benefits from further specialization begin to decline; the costs begin to grow faster than the benefits. As specialization continues to increase, the net benefits eventually level off (A_2). That is, further specialization provides at best only minimal increases in net benefits.

Why does the *OB* curve level off? As specialization increases, so do its costs. These costs include the costs of machinery and other technology, and the costs of hiring and training personnel to perform these more specialized jobs. Further, there is evidence that, at some point, work that becomes too specialized loses meaning and interest for workers, increasing the cost of job dissatisfaction.

As division of labor and specialization increase, the demands for coordination also increase, and so do its costs, as depicted by the *OC* curve. At point *X*, where the two curves *OB* and *OC* intersect, the net additional benefits from further specialization are exceeded by the additional costs of coordination. Economics dictate that the prudent manager would divide up work no further. Until some breakthrough such as a new technological advance raises the *OB* curve or lowers the *OC* curve, further specialization is too costly.

The Need for Coordination

Interdependence—people working together to achieve common goals—requires coordination of effort. Specialization increases interdependence; specialists are dependent upon the activities of others to perform their specialities well.

Examples of interdependence in organizations are everywhere: An accountant depends on other departments to report figures for computation; a spot welder on an assembly line depends on others to provide the frame and chassis for welding; a recording star requires backup musicians, audio technicians, and mixers to produce a record; an actor depends on scriptwriters, make-up artists, costumers, scenery designers, camera operators, and other actors to film a scene. In each of these examples, poor coordination can make it impossible for specialization to succeed. If the backup musicians can't fathom the tune or beat or if the studio isn't wired correctly, the recording star's session is doomed to failure.

The need for, difficulty in, and costs of coordination increase as specialization increases because of four differences that develop between specialized units in an organization:

1. *Differences in goals.* On a newspaper, for example, the goal of the reporting staff may be up-to-the-minute reports, calling for late copy deadlines. The printers' goal, however, is a clean, smooth running production process, calling for early copy deadlines.
2. *Differences in time orientation.* Long-range planners are oriented toward the future, five or more years hence. Those who must provide them with information to develop the plans and who must ultimately implement those plans are likely to be preoccupied with immediate problems and relatively unconcerned about the more distant future.
3. *Differences in interpersonal orientation.* Time pressures in production-oriented specialties may result in quick decisions with tense businesslike communications. Other specialties like planning, research, and development may have a more participative, relaxed style of communicating.
4. *Differences in formal structure.* Accounting and production departments are likely to be more centralized and more formally structured than sales and public relations departments.

Coordinating Mechanisms

The differences described above make coordination both necessary and difficult. In most organizations, the ways in which the work is to be done are generally dictated by the nature of the work and existing technology. But coordination must come from **coordinating mechanisms**—*deliberate managerial activities that integrate the efforts of work units.*[16]

Direct Supervision and the Managerial Hierarchy.   The supervisor is responsible for coordinating the activities of his or her subordinates by planning, issuing instructions, and monitoring performance. The city editor on a newspaper assigns reporters or approves their requests to cover stories, insuring that major news is covered and that several reporters aren't working on the same story. In turn, the work of the various reporting departments—local, state, national, international, sports, and financial—is coordinated by the managerial hierarchy by the managing editor.

The **managerial hierarchy** is *a system by which an organization coordinates the efforts and activities of its supervisors.* In a managerial hierarchy, every member of an organization is responsible to a supervisor who coordinates the efforts of first-line workers. Each supervisor, in turn, reports to a manager, who is re-

Exhibit 4.7 A Managerial Hierarchy

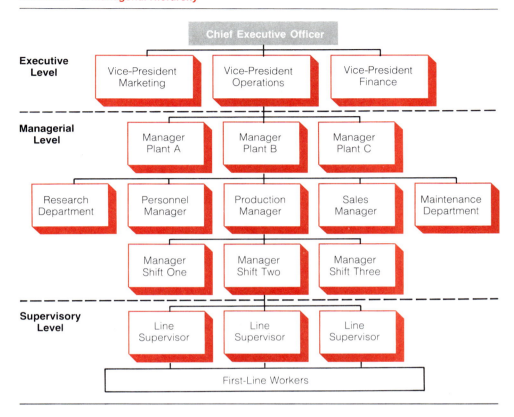

sponsible for coordinating the efforts of two or more supervisors. Each manager is responsible to another higher-level manager. The hierarchy continues to the top of the organization, as shown in Exhibit 4.7.

The hierarchy is intended to help the managers at all levels coordinate the efforts of large numbers of work units by giving them authority over their subordinates. At the top of the organization the chief executive officer (CEO) coordinates the efforts of his or her staff and others at the executive level. The term *executive* usually denotes someone who has been promoted through the managerial ranks to a position in the head office or headquarters of a large organization. An executive usually has a staff and reports directly to the chief executive officer. Those at the executive level coordinate their own staffs and the activities of the managers who report to them. This process continues down through the managerial hierarchy to the level of supervisor. A supervisor is one who directs the activities of first-line workers; a manager is one who directs the activities of supervisors.

A most common method of organizing work in business and industrial organizations is **departmentalization**—*grouping together under a single manager or* supervisor *a number of people who perform the same, similar, or related tasks.* In Exhibit 4.7, at the Managerial Level, we find plants A, B, and C organized by departments. Each plant has a research department, a personnel department, a production department, a sales department, and a maintenance department. Departmentalization permits a manager to specialize—to coordinate the efforts of people doing similar or related tasks. Departmentalization and organization structures different from that shown in Exhibit 4.7 will be discussed in Chapter 14.

Mutual Adjustment.   Supervision and the managerial hierarchy alone cannot coordinate the work in today's complex organizations. Sometimes informal communications are sufficient coordinating mechanisms, such as two secretaries adjusting their lunch hours so that the office will be covered at all times. Sometimes more formal communications procedures must be developed by management, including systems of signs, signals, or other special languages which permit the rapid and clear transmission of plans, changes in plans, or activities. In baseball, infielders signal who will cover a certain base if a bunt or steal is attempted. In police work, officers in the field communicate with each other using codes to allow other officers to pursue a fleeing suspect or to back up officers needing assistance.

> *Organizing allows managers to accomplish more objectives in a better way by using the coordinated effort of many people. They can take advantage of individual differences in skills and abilities to develop those skills to a high degree, and use them in conjunction with technology and other resources.*

Sometimes more formal coordinating devices, such as *committees* or *liaison personnel*, must be developed to make decisions affecting several different specialties, to provide a means for regular communication of information among specialties, or both. The medical board of a hospital is a good example of such a committee, composed of representatives of each of the medical specialties using the hospital's facilities. A liaison person is sometimes designated to pass information back and forth between the departments or groups who have problems (distance, language, time) in communicating with each other frequently or accurately.

Standardization.   A final way of achieving coordination is to establish regular ways of doing things so that units required to cooperate can know what to expect from each other. The term **standard operating procedure** (SOP) means that *one way of performing some task has been defined and understood by all who might participate in or be affected by it.* If it is SOP for a company's truck drivers to schedule preventive maintenance for their vehicles every 5000 miles, the maintenance department can plan its activities by keeping track of each vehicle's mileage. If it is SOP for every individual aboard ship to report to a preassigned station as soon as a fire or an imminent collision is reported, coordination of these diverse specialties is infinitely easier and faster.

Using SOP is an example of standardizing *work processes.* Coordination can also be facilitated by standardizing *work output* and *worker skills.*

Standardization of work outputs is important when one department or specialty must work with the output of other departments or specialties. A waiter who knows the ingredients of dishes and sizes of portions prepared by the cook can answer customers' questions and recommend changes to suit particular customer desires. An assembler of furniture will not have to search for pieces that fit together if all components are manufactured within certain tolerance levels.

Standardization of worker skills is achieved through employee selection and training. A surgeon depends on those assisting an operation to have particular skills and knowledge of SOP. If there is great variation in worker skills, other personnel usually have difficulty coordinating their activities. A faculty member teaching a class in which students range from barely literate to graduate status experiences great difficulty in finding an appropriate level at which to pitch the course. One who teaches a class of seniors, all of whom have the necessary prerequisite courses, experiences no such difficulty.

These coordinating mechanisms (summarized in Exhibit 4.8)—direct supervision and the managerial hierarchy, internal communications, and standardization—are part of the design and structure of an organization. Organizational structure and design will be described and discussed in Chapter 14.

Exhibit 4.8   Mechanisms for Coordinating Work

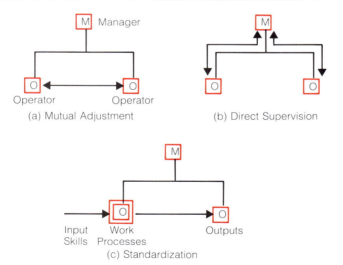

Source: Henry Mintzberg, *The Structuring of Organizations* (Englewood Cliffs, NJ: Prentice-Hall, 1979), p. 4.

From *The Structuring of Organizations: A Synthesis of the Research* by Henry Mintzberg, p. 4. Copyright © by Prentice-Hall, Inc. Reprinted by permission of Prentice-Hall, Inc., Englewood Cliffs, N.J.

The Bottom Line

In organizing work, the successful manager will consider the following:

1. The objectives of organization are increased efficiency, effectiveness, and satisfaction, *not* the convenience of the manager. A job definition or coordinating activity that makes the manager's job easier at the expense of the effectiveness or satisfaction of the manager's department is not destined for success.
2. A job should be defined before determining job methods. That is, decide what is to be done before deciding how it should be done. Developing or hiring employees skilled in performing useless tasks is not an efficient use of human resources.
3. Specialization is attractive, particularly as it permits the use of advanced technology. However, specialization has its costs, both economic and human. There are alternatives to specialization which increase the scope of employee performance.
4. Direct supervision is only *one* form of coordination. A manager who relys solely on direct supervision condemns him or herself to spending too little time planning. Standardization takes planning, but can relieve some need for direct supervision. The efficient manager encourages employees to coordinate their own activities through mutual adjustment processes, freeing up time for other managerial activities.
5. Because specialization requires coordination, a manager who becomes overly specialized is more likely to become *coordinated* than to become a *coordinator*. A manager who becomes increasingly specialized may enjoy the fruits of that expertise for a while. However, knowing more and more about less and less carries the danger of eventually knowing everything about nothing.

SUMMARY

Organizing is the process of defining work, dividing it up in ways to take advantage of division of labor and specialization, and then coordinating the activities of those performing it. It begins with defining job content—what work is to be done.

Specialization has enormous advantages in the use of human skills and technology. However, there appears to be too much specialization. In recent years, job rotation, job enlargement, and job enrichment have been used to increase both employee efficiency and satisfaction.

Once the content of work has been defined, job methods can be determined. Deciding how a job is best accomplished is an inexact science. Factors which influence the choice of work methods are worker characteristics including psychological as well as physiological capabilities, environmental factors including technology, plant layout, and government and union restrictions, as well as job content. In recent years, greater awareness of the relative advantages of humans and machines respectively has led to increasingly sophisticated human-machine systems in all types of organizations. The use of robots appears to be a particularly promising means for relieving humans of dangerous, unpleasant, or stressful work.

The division of work requires coordination—integrating individuals and activities to achieve objectives. Because specialization produces certain differences among specialized units in organizations, such as differences in goals and time orientation, coordination is both necessary and difficult. The primary mechanisms by which diverse efforts are coordinated in organizations include direct supervision and the managerial hierarchy, internal communications, and standardization of processes, outputs, and worker skills.

QUESTIONS FOR REVIEW AND DISCUSSION

1. What are the objectives of job design and the organization of work? How are these objectives sometimes in conflict?
2. If it is so clear that specifying job content is imperative before determining work methods, why do you think many training programs and schools don't do this?
3. Use the six requisite task attributes to analyze the following jobs: a) counter attendant at McDonald's, b) college professor, c) newspaper reporter, d) long-distance truck driver.
4. What are the advantages of division of labor? How can it ba harmful to an organization?
5. How has technology helped workers? What negative consequences can it have for workers? How is the organization affected by these consequences, and how can it avoid or correct them?
6. What are the objectives of job enlargement? What constraints affect it?
7. How does job enrichment differ from job enlargement? Why is it sometimes opposed?
8. What is the sociotechnical systems approach to job content determination? How successful has it been in practice? Why might first-line supervisors oppose it?
9. How have technology and economics influenced the development of human-machine systems? What are some likely effects of increased use of industrial robots on the function of organizing?
10. What methods of job analysis are best for performance appraisal, job selection, and wage setting? (The use of a method for one does not preclude its use for another.) What problems could arise from using one method of analysis for both performance appraisal and wage setting?

REFERENCES AND NOTES

1. C. Babbage. *On the Economy of Machinery and Manufactures*, 4th ed. (London: Charles Knight, 1835), pp. 169–86.

2. F. W. Taylor, *Principles of Scientific Management* (New York: Harpar & Bros. 1911).
3. *Ibid.*
4. *Ibid*, pp. 36–37.
5. "What are They Teaching in the B-Schools?" *Business Week*, November 10, 1980, pp. 61–69.
6. A. N. Turner and P. R. Lawrence, *Industrial Jobs and the Worker: An Investigation of Responses to Task Attributes* (Cambridge, Mass.: Harvard University Press, 1965).
7. D. F. Roy, "Banana Time," *Human Organization*, Winter 1959–60, Vol. 18, pp. 158–68.
8. E. S. Buffa, *Modern Production Management*, 4th ed. (New York: John Wiley & Sons, 1973), p. 368.
9. Buffa, *op. cit*, p. 370.
10. E. J. McCormick, *Human Factors Engineering*, 3rd ed. McGraw-Hill, 1970.
11. "Robot as the Magic Word of the Future, or so G.E. Hopes." *Gainesville Sun*, March 19, 1982, p. 1c.
12. M. D. Kilbridge, "Reduced Costs Through Job Enrichment: A Case" *The Journal of Business*, 1960, 33, pp. 357–62.
13. Cited in W. F. Glueck, *Management*, 2nd ed. (Hinsdale, Ill.: Dryden Press, 1980), p. 345.
14. R. E. Walton, "The Diffusion of New Work Structures: Explaining Why Success Didn't Take." *Organizational Dynamics*, Winter 1975, 3, pp. 3–22.
15. J. R. Hackman and J. L. Suttle, *Improving Life at Work* (Santa Monica, Calif.: Goodyear Publishing Co., 1977).
16. H. Mintzberg, *The Structure of Organizations* (Englewood Cliffs, N.J.: Prentice-Hall, 1979).

SUGGESTED READINGS

J. Galbraith, *Organization Design* (Addison-Wesley, 1977). Galbraith tackles the problem of organization by integrating what we know about human behavior in organizations with what we know about organizing. He provides a useful framework for recognizing the ways in which organizations can be designed.

H. Mintzberg, *The Structure of Organizations* (Englewood Cliffs, N. J.: Prentice Hall, 1979). Based on a synthesis of the empirical literature in the field, the author introduces five basic configurations of organizational structure—the Simple Structure, the Machine Bureaucracy, the Professional Bureaucracy, the Divisionalized Form, and the Adhocracy.

J. Woodward, ed. *Industrial Organization: Theory and Practice* (Oxford: Oxford University Press, 1965). This is a classic book that explains the importance of technology for organizational design. Woodward's analysis of industrial organization shows how different technologies require different forms of coordination and control.

Case Hovey and Beard Company

Part 1

The Hovey and Beard Company manufactured wooden toys of various kinds: wooden animals, pull toys, and the like. One part of the manufacturing process involved spraying paint on the partially assembled toys. The operation was staffed entirely by women.

The toys were cut, sanded, and partially assembled in the wood room. Then they were dipped into shellac, following which they were painted. The toys were predominantly two-colored; a few were made in more than two colors. Each color required an additional trip through the paint room.

For a number of years, production of these toys had been entirely handwork. However, to meet tremendously increased demand, the painting operation had recently been re-engineered so that the eight women who did the painting sat in a line by an endless chain of hooks. These hooks were in continuous motion, past the line of women and into a long horizontal oven. Each woman sat at her own painting booth, so designed as to carry away fumes and to backstop excess paint. The woman would take a toy from the tray beside her, position it in a jig inside the painting cubicle, spray on the color according to a pattern, then release the toy and hang it on the hook passing by. The rate at which the hooks moved had been calculated by the engineers so that each woman, when fully trained, would be able to hang a painted toy on each hook before it passed beyond her reach.

The women working in the paint room were on a group bonus plan. Since the operation was new to them, they were receiving a learning bonus which decreased by regular amounts each month. The learning bonus was scheduled to vanish in six months, by which time it was expected that they would be on their own—that is, able to meet the standard and to earn a group bonus when they exceeded it.

Part 2

By the second month of the training period, trouble had developed. The women learned more slowly than had been anticipated, and it began to look as though their production would stabilize far below what was planned for. Many of the hooks were going by empty. The women complained that they were going by too fast, and that the time-study man had set the rates wrong. A few women quit and had to be replaced with new women, which further aggravated the learning problem. The team spirit that the management had expected to develop automatically through the group bonus was not in evidence except as an expression of what the engineers called "resistance." One woman whom the group regarded as its leader (and the management regarded as the ringleader) was outspoken in making the various complaints of the group to the foreman: The job was a messy one, the hooks moved too fast, the incentive pay was not being correctly calculated, and it was too hot working so close to the drying oven.

Abridged and adapted from "Group Dynamics and Intergroup Relations" by George Strauss and Alex Bavelas in *Money and Motivation* by William Foote Whyte. Copyright © 1955 by Harper & Row, Publishers, Inc. By permission of the publishers. Note: This is a segmented case. Your instructor may wish to have you discuss Part 1 of the case before reading subsequent parts.

Part 3

A consultant who was brought into this picture worked entirely with and through the foreman. After many conversations with him, the foreman felt that the first step should be to get the women together for a general discussion of the working conditions. He took this step with some hesitation, but he took it on his own volition.

The first meeting, held immediately after the shift was over at 4:00 in the afternoon, was attended by all eight women. They voiced the same complaints again: The hooks went by too fast, the job was too dirty, the room was hot and poorly ventilated. For some reason, it was this last item that they complained of most. The foreman promised to discuss the problem of ventilation and temperature with the engineers, and he scheduled a second meeting to report back to the women. In the next few days the foreman had several talks with the engineers. They and the superintendent felt that this was really a trumped-up complaint, and that the expense of any effective corrective measure would be prohibitively high.

The foreman came to the second meeting with some apprehension. The women, however, did not seem to be much put out, perhaps because they had a proposal of their own to make. They felt that if several large fans were set up to circulate the air around their feet, they would be much more comfortable. After some discussion, the foreman agreed that the idea might be tried out. The foreman and the consultant discussed the question of the fans with the superintendent, and three large propeller-type fans were purchased.

Part 4

The fans were brought in. The women were jubilant. For several days the fans were moved about in various positions until they were placed to the satisfaction of the group. The women seemed completely satisfied with the results, and relations between them and the foreman improved visibly.

The foreman, after this encouraging episode, decided that further meetings might also be profitable. He asked the women if they would like to meet and discuss other aspects of the work situation. The women were eager to do this. The meeting was held, and the discussion quickly centered on the speed of the hooks. The women maintained that the time-study man had set them at an unreasonably fast speed and that they would never be able to reach the goal of filling enough of them to make a bonus.

The turning point of the discussion came when the group's leader frankly explained that the point wasn't that they couldn't work fast enough to keep up with the hooks, but that they couldn't work at that pace all day long. The foreman explored the point. The women were unanimous in their opinion that they could keep up with the belt for short periods if they wanted to. But they didn't want to because if they showed they could do this for short periods, they would be expected to do it all day long. The meeting ended with an unprecedented request: "Let us adjust the speed of the belt faster or slower, depending on how we feel." The foreman agreed to discuss this with the superintendent and the engineers.

The reaction of the engineers to the suggestion was negative. However, after several meetings, it was granted that there was some latitude within which variations in the speed of the hooks would not affect the finished product. After considerable argument with the engineers, it was agreed to try out the women's idea.

With misgivings, the foreman had a control with a dial marked "low, medium, fast" installed at the booth of the group leader; she could now adjust the speed of the belt anywhere between the lower and upper limits that the engineers had set.

Part 5

The women were delighted, and spent many lunch hours deciding how the speed of the belt should be varied from hour to hour throughout the day. Within a week the pattern had settled down to one in which the first half hour of the shift was run on what the women called medium speed (a dial setting slightly above the point marked "medium"). The next two and one-half hours were run at high speed; the half hour before lunch and the half hour after lunch were run at low speed. The rest of the afternoon was run at high speed with the exception of the last 45 minutes of the shift, which was run at medium.

CASE QUESTIONS

1. Define the job content of the women in the painting operation.
2. What factors were taken into consideration in the original job redesign effort? What factors were not taken into consideration?
3. Is the change in job methods implemented in Part 5 an example of job enlargement or job enrichment? Why?
4. Identify the various coordinating mechanisms used for the work in the painting operation.

5 / Directing: Goals

Alex McCall sipped his coffee and reflected with pleasure on the dinner. Surprisingly good for a college town, he mused, and the service was decent, too. Eating well was the one indulgence he granted himself when on recruiting trips.

"Now to the task at hand," he said to himself. McCall followed the same routine whenever he was on a college recruiting trip. After the last interview of the day, he would return to his hotel room and select the top two or three candidates. He would then reward himself with a nap, shower, and good dinner before choosing the most promising applicant. This ranking was important, he knew, because the top-ranked applicant almost certainly would be invited for a plant visit.

Today's interviewing had made the initial decision relatively easy. Two young candidates, both graduating in May, were clearly superior to the others in the four categories McCall looked at—academic performance, work experience, personal appearance, and interview performance. Now he had to choose either Cathy, a 22-year old finance major, or Sharon, who had a double major in management and marketing. McCall opened their folders and reviewed their data as he finished his coffee.

Their majors, he knew, were not a factor. Both had solid business educations, perfectly suitable for an entry-level managerial slot. Both had been on the Dean's List several times, had worked to help finance their educations, and had found time to be campus leaders in extra-curricular activities. Both had earned highest marks for their personal appearances and conduct during the interview. The decision wasn't going to be easy!

His eye stopped near the end of the interview form he used, where he jotted down responses to certain questions. The questions which drew his attention concerned the applicants' goals.

The first asked, "What are your personal goals in seeking this job?" Sharon, he recalled, had been slightly taken aback, but then had responded confidently, "Like everyone else's, I guess. I want to use the skills I've developed in college, to get ahead, and to make a good salary." Cathy, on the other hand, had been equally confident but more precise. "My goal is to be a division head in five years. After that, I'll set a new goal."

The second question was tougher. "What will be your managerial goal if you get the job? That is, what will you try to accomplish for us?" Both young women had taken time to gather their thoughts before replying.

"I'd like to make enough of a contribution to earn the respect of both my immediate superior and my subordinates," Sharon had said, "and to be given more responsibility and challenge."

Cathy, on the other hand, had specified two goals. "First, to get half of my subordinates promotions or better-than-average raises every year. Second, to find a way every year to save the company an amount of money equal to at least double my salary."

McCall asked for the check and closed up the two file folders. "Goals," he thought, "it often comes down to goals. Everybody talks about them, but few interviewees really understand what goals mean. At least, today, one of them does." His decision made, McCall returned to his room to write his recommendation.

The two previous chapters described the managerial functions of planning—deciding what will be done—and organizing—deciding who will do what to get it done. Once a manager plans and organizes the work, it is up to others to carry it out. Now, the manager's function is to get people to do the work in the way it has been organized in order to carry out the plan. This function is the essence of management: getting things done through people.

You may have noticed that, for each of these first managerial functions, goals have played an important part. Planning starts with a goal, a desired state of future affairs, which begins the process of evaluating the requirements and availability of resources and leads to deciding what must be done with those resources. Organizing is also goal-directed, as the manager divides up, allocates, and coordinates tasks to achieve goals of effectiveness, efficiency, and satisfaction.

Now we look at directing, which is comprised of two major elements, goals and effort. **Directing** can be defined as *inducing others to exert their efforts toward the accomplishment of organizational goals*. Because goals are such an important part of directing, in particular, and of managing, in general, this entire chapter will focus on them. Chapter 6 will move to the more general element of directing the motivation behind human effort.

The first part of this chapter examines the nature and functions of goals. The second part discusses the relationship between individuals' goals and the goals of the organizations they work for. The third part describes the relationship between goals and effort.

THE NATURE OF GOALS IN ORGANIZATIONS

A **goal** is *an end toward which people direct effort*. For example, the reasons for your academic efforts may include becoming highly educated, receiving a college degree, acquiring a good job, getting high grades, earning self-respect. These or similar goals help direct your efforts into academic activities and away from activities that might interfere with these goals, such as playing video games or sleeping all day. In the story that introduced this chapter, Cathy's goal of becoming a division head in five years directed her efforts toward those activities which would lead to that goal, such as learning the skills that a division head needed, and away from the activities that might interfere with that goal, such as alienating those who might help her.

Goals or organizations exist not just for individual members, but for collections of individuals—groups, departments, divisions, and even for the organization itself. Collective goals serve to direct human effort; they differ from individual goals only in scope.

A **collective goal** is *any particular combination of individual interests that becomes an agreed-upon objective for all parties.* These agreed-upon objectives serve a variety of purposes for those who aspire to them. They serve a *coordinating function* by providing guidelines for decision making, and an *evaluative function* by providing standards against which to weigh the results of decisions. They also perform an *image function;* statements of goals are the primary way that organizations describe themselves to outsiders such as possible investors, prospective employees, and potential customers. Finally, collective goals can serve an *incentive function* by influencing an individual to join the group or organization and work hard.

In the last chapter we discussed the importance of coordination in organizing work. Goals increase the effectiveness of both direct supervision and mutual adjustment as coordinating mechanisms. In Chapter 3 we discussed the importance of evaluating plans. Goals allow a manager to evaluate the effectiveness of a plan so that it can be changed before it's too late. That goals have meanings beyond the mere fact of reaching them is summed up in the description of a goal as "an image of a future state."[1] Daydreaming about what it will be like to be a college graduate or a division head is part of maintaining interest and effort in many activities. Finally, goals provide incentives for individuals or groups to choose how they will direct their efforts and how much of those efforts they will apply to a given activity.

Formal Organizational Goals

When most people think of organizational goals, they think of formal goals. A **formal organization goal** is *a statement of the organization's reason for existence* (See Exhibit 5.1). Formal organizational goals define the end toward which effort is directed. Such goals typically appear in a formal statement similar to that of St. Jude Children's Research Hospital:

"St. Jude Hospital . . . (is) dedicated solely to the conquest of the catastrophic illnesses that destroy the lives of little ones."[2] Shortened forms of such statements often become slogans with which organizations are identified. For example, ITT's formal research goals are summarized in the slogan, "The best ideas are the ideas that help people."[2]

Slogans and formal statements such as these may serve image and incentive functions quite well. However, you will notice that both examples are vague. They say nothing about how one organization will conquer childhood illnesses or where the other will look for ideas that help people. As guidelines for coordinating and evaluating decisions about what people in the organization will do, formal goals aren't very helpful. These purposes are served by another type of organizational goal.

Exhibit 5.1   The Image Function of Organizational Goals

Southwest Forest Industries.
A Fortune 500 company committed to growth in the Southeast.

We're Southwest Forest Industries. We are a major Fortune 500 company, employing over 7,000 people across the country. And our recent acquisition of over 400,000 acres of timberland in Alabama, Florida and Georgia, a pulp and paper mill in Panama City, Florida and the Atlanta & St. Andrews Bay Railway Company, means we are making a commitment. A commitment to the continued growth of our company. And the economy of the Southeast.

We're headquartered in Phoenix, Arizona with plants and facilities in over 100 locations in 32 states. We convert trees into paper, packaging and building materials. And in 1979 we had sales of $778 million and $30.3 million in net income, our third consecutive record year.

If you would like to know more about us and our plans in the Southeast, send for our annual report.

Simply write to: W. A. Franke, President, Southwest Forest Industries, Post Office Box 2560, Panama City, Florida 32401.

Southwest Forest Industries Ⓢ

Courtesy Southwest Forest Industries.

Operative Organizational Goals

Operative goals guide the activities of those in an organization. Formal goals provide the "what," operative goals the "how."[3] Thus, an **operative goal** is a *goal that specifies the means by which a formal goal is to be pursued.*

The formal goal of eliminating childhood diseases, for example, can be pursued in a variety of ways. St. Jude Hospital goes about it by providing a treatment center for young patients which serves as a living laboratory for research into causes and cures of their illnesses. Its major operative goals, then, might be described as research and treatment.

Operative goals coordinate organizational decision making by providing guidelines for organizational policy. A hospital that emphasizes research, for example, will allocate resources differently, have different kinds of jobs, and expect different kinds of behaviors from one that emphasizes the treatment of crisis victims. In business organizations, differences in operative goals may be seen in different policies as to the relative priorities of quality, quantity, long-term profit, short-term profit, diversification, employee morale, and customer satisfaction.

Because they guide policy, operative goals provide a baseline for individual managers, who translate these goals into plans for their own parts of the organization. Managers may do this on their own or together with superiors.

Exhibit 5.2   Organizational Goals of a Restaurant from Top to Bottom

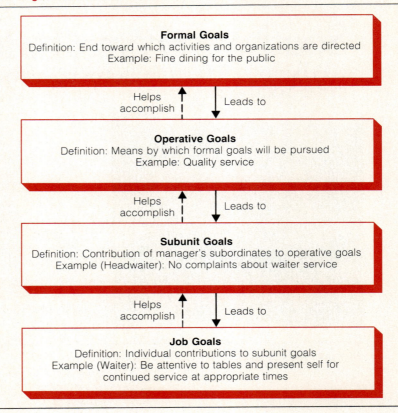

However they are set, the purpose of goals at a manager's level is to define the contribution of his or her subordinates to broader organizational goals. As we saw in Chapter 3, goals serve this purpose best if they are expressed in specific, measurable terms such as how many items must be produced in what time period to what quality standards. *Goals at the manager's level* are called **subunit goals.**[4] They specify the collective performance for which the manager is responsible. Once these goals have been set, a manager can go on to set individual **job goals**—that is, *goals that specify the contribution of each subordinate to collective performance.* The spreading of organizational goals throughout the organization is illustrated in Exhibit 5.2.

HOW GOALS ARE SET IN ORGANIZATIONS

Most goals, from organizational to job goals, evolve through a series of interactions among several individuals or groups. Both internal and external processes determine an organization's goals.

Internal Processes

Most formal, broad operative goals in organizations are established by means of an ongoing bargaining process between key individuals, such as owners, executives, boards of directors, and upper-level managers. Each individual brings to this process his or her own interests and perceptions of what the organization can and should do.

The "particular combination of individual interests" that becomes an organizational goal depends largely upon the balance of power among the key individuals involved. In some cases, the situation becomes a power struggle for the leadership of an organization. The various news media frequently carry stories of executives who leave their positions when their ideas about company goals are rejected.

> *June and July were the worst months in (the London) zoo history, an appalling start to the summer made worse by an ill-tempered spat between Lord Zuckerman, the 76-year-old President of the Zoological Society, and his one-time protege, Michael Hanson, who quit his job as the zoo's administrative director after submitting a report suggesting various ways in which the zoo might be made more profitable and, incidentally, more fun. On the face of it . . . it's the traditional clash between old guard and new; science versus showbiz.*

Although the ideas and preferences of those at higher organizational levels usually have the greatest impact on the nature of organizational goals, these key individuals do not have free rein. To meet any goal, an organization must be able to attract and keep employees. Thus, goals must be consistent with the values of most employees. Some large chemical companies had trouble getting and keeping certain employees in the 1960s. They manufactured substances used in the unpopular Vietnam conflict, and the goal of making a profit through the sale of these substances was inconsistent with the values of many young job seekers and employees.

The expectations and values of the employees cannot be ignored in setting organizational goals, especially operative goals, since these are the goals that most nearly affect what employees do. However, the employer's range of decision-making freedom still tends to be wide since employees are always free to work elsewhere. External expectations and constraints tend to be more confining.

External Factors

No matter how powerful it may be, no organization has complete goal-setting freedom. People and other organizations with which it interacts have expectations about what it should do and place constraints on what it can do. These people and other groups make up an organization's environment, and the organization's dependence on that environment means that these cannot be ignored. It is from its

Exhibit 5.3   A University's Goals as Proposed by its Environment

Thus the clangor of the anvil chorus, singing in many voices, and in many keys, these discordant themes:

Yes, provide a broad, liberal-arts, humanistic education.

No, teach people practical things, so as to guarantee them jobs.

Yes, focus on research and education for the elite.

No, train dental technicians, hotel managers, accountants, and also provide professional education for lawyers, doctors, and engineers.

Yes, stop lowering academic standards, but be sure to enroll more poor persons and members of minority groups as a way of creating a more egalitarian society.

And also, while you're at it, provide compensatory education for those victimized educationally by inadequate public schools, provide opportunities for part-time students, especially for women caught in the homemaker's trap, provide continuing education for job enrichment for workers as well as executives, and, by the way, become the vehicle through which income redistribution can be achieved.

Source: W. Bennis, "Managing the Unmanageable," *The Chronicle of Higher Education*, 1975, p. 20.

environment that an organization gets its inputs, distributes its outputs, and, indeed, draws its very survival, as we described in Chapter 2.

Outside opinions of what an organization may and should do can be both extensive and conflicting. Warren Bennis, a former president of the University of Cincinnati writes vividly of what can happen when these demands clash head on, with the organization in the middle. An excerpt from that article is reproduced in Exhibit 5.3.

An organization's environment can affect goals in other ways. It is a source of information about the probability of attaining certain goals. For example, a significant drop in contributions decreases the likelihood that a charitable organization can reach its goals. It also provides signals, such as increased competition, that goals may need revision. For example, the auto industry was badly crippled by OPEC's price increases in the 1970s. Therefore, the goal of making a profit by providing the American public with large, fancy "gas guzzlers" had to be changed.

Goal Displacement

Obviously, setting broad organizational goals is a complex, ongoing process. There are many people and forces to be accommodated. In addition, goals are not made to last forever. If conditions change, goals may change. Some goals also get lost along the way.

In 1968 the Boy Scouts of America announced a *formal* goal of making scouting more relevant to the American society. One of its *operative* goals, or means by which this formal goal was to be pursued, was to bring one third of all eligible boys (those between the ages of eight and twenty) into the program by 1976. This goal was translated into specific enrollment quotas at the Boy Scout district (*subunit*) level.

Management in Action
Alcan Wants to be Number One

Until 1928 Canada's Alcan Aluminum was a subsidiary of Aluminum Company of America (Alcoa), the world's largest producer of that valuable and much-demanded metal. Even after Alcan spun off from Alcoa in 1928, its headquarters remained in the United States until the 1960s, when it moved north of the border. For decades the chief executive officer of Alcan was an American, and the company set conservative goals, concentrating on markets outside the United States, trying to upset neither American nor Canadian interests. Then, in 1979, David M. Culver became the first Canadian president of Alcan, and many things changed. The extent of the changes is reflected in Alcan's new goal: to become the largest aluminum company in the world. "There is a strong desire for us to be a recognized No. 1," according to Alcan vice-president Ihor Suchoversky. Alcan's rivals are quick to agree.

Historically Alcoa has dominated the world aluminum industry in revenues, net return on sales, and return on common equity. But Alcan has been catching up in revenues, exploiting its traditional strong presence in foreign markets.

First of all, Alcan is trying to acquire Atlantic Richfield Company's (Arco) aluminum operations. Achieving this objective would increase Alcan's sales by ten percent to 5.5 billion and double its American assets, opening up the profitable U. S. market and creating an instant rivalry with Alcoa. Part of the Arco deal would include a $450 million rolling mill in Kentucky that would double Alcan's market share for beverage-can aluminum sheet, a $3.4 billion market in its own right. Should Alcan fail to achieve this objective because of antitrust objections of the U. S. Justice Department, it will continue to seek other acquisitions around the world. Further, according to Culver, Alcan will expand in the United States one way or another: if it can't buy assets, it will simply build its own plant.

Alcan has established objectives of improved profitability to help make up the $100 million lead in profits currently enjoyed by Alcoa. A key to improved profitability is a $3 billion efficiency drive at its smelters in Quebec, which currently comprise fifty percent of its aluminum smelting capacity. Alcan already claims to be the lowest cost producer in the industry, primarily because of its electricity costs. Fifty years ago the company had the foresight to acquire ownership of the hydroelectric plants that supplied its power. Electricity costs Alcan roughly one-sixth what its competitors pay.

Culver concedes that Alcoa has always had a technological advantage, spending over $80 million on research and development in 1983. To meet that goal Alcan plans to increase R & D funding some 10 to 15 percent a year.

Source: "Alcan Goes Toe to Toe with Alcoa for the No. 1 Spot in Aluminum," Business Week, *August 27, 1984*, pp. 95–96.

In 1974 the *Chicago Tribune* described widespread cheating among Boy Scout professional staff trying to achieve membership enrollment goals.[5] One Detroit supervisor allegedly instructed his staff to meet its quota even if it had to use names from local cemeteries to do so (*job* goals). Clearly, fictitious Boy Scouts are not going to help achieve the goal of "making scouting more relevant." What we call "goal displacement" had occurred.

Goal displacement is the *process by which efforts to accomplish a goal set up new goals that are pursued instead of the original one.* In other words, the original goal loses its "place" as a guide for decisions about the activities of organizational members. Thus, not only do hard-won organizational goals shift in focus as they are disseminated throughout the organization, they may become unrecognizable in the process.

Job specialization and division of labor can easily contribute to goal displacement. In many businesses production and marketing are specialized activities carried out by different departments. If the overall goal of a business is stated as maximizing profit, operative goals may be established to minimize production costs and maximize sales revenues, given that profits equal revenues minus costs.

> *Formal organizational goals define the end toward which effort is directed. ITT's formal research goals are summarized in the slogan, "The best ideas are the ideas that help people."*

While these basic goals may work for a while, when increased competition begins to threaten the company's market share, the marketing department may respond by drastic price reductions. Marketing meets its goal of high sales revenues, but at prices so low that profits vanish. (Examples of profitability being sacrificed for market share abounded in the American automobile and airline industries of the 1970s and 1980s.)

The danger of goal displacement is another strong argument for the effective coordinating mechanisms described in Chapter 4. Someone needs to ensure that the pursuit of operative goals does not cause the organization to lose sight of its formal goals, and that different operative goals are consistent with each other. Before George Ball assumed command at Prudential-Bache Securities, for example, it was not uncommon to find three sales campaigns with conflicting goals operating at the same time.[6]

ORGANIZATIONAL AND PERSONAL GOALS

Directing has been defined as channeling the efforts of others toward defined organizational goals. As we have noted, organizational goals can serve an incentive function; a person who finds an organization's goals attractive may be more likely to exert effort on the job. The belief that this incentive function was the *key* to motivation was popular for some time. It seemed that the way to get employees to

The relationship between personal goals and organizational goals is very important. When there is goal congruence, the result is usually a satisfactory level of effort.

exert sufficient effort to accomplish organizational goals was to get them to accept these goals as their own.[7] As in so many of these one-best-way prescriptions, there was some truth in this one. As we shall see, however, things weren't quite that simple.

Goal Congruence

Since goals define a desired state of affairs toward which effort is directed, there can be no doubt that personal goals affect individual behavior. The extent to which such goals affect behavior at work obviously depends upon how closely related they are to work. The goal of ''being a division head in five years'' is obviously more relevant to work behavior than is the goal of ''being able to run five miles a day.''

Fortunately for managers, most people have certain personal goals that are related to work—high status, financial security, professional challenge, social interaction, and contributions to society. Organizational goals serve as incentives to achieve such personal goals. We call this happy circumstance goal congruence. **Goal congruence** is a *situation in which the same behaviors help to accomplish both individual and organizational goals.*

In the narrative that introduced this chapter, Alex McCall had no trouble finding congruence between Cathy's goals and those of the organization. Her short-term goals were to get promotions or raises for her subordinates and to save the company twice as much money as it paid her. Cathy correctly perceived that those goals (developing talent and saving money) would be consistent with any company's profit goals. She also saw them as a means to her five-year objective of becoming a division head.

For a manager, achieving goal congruence does not necessarily mean that employees must take on organizational goals. All that is required is the recognition that making a contribution to these goals is a way of achieving their own goals.

Goal Congruence and Work Behavior

As long as the job allows the worker or manager to do things that help accomplish both organizational and personal goals, that individual is likely to do well and to get ahead. A manager with imagination, interpersonal skills, good judgment, and lots of energy will probably move swiftly up the hierarchy of a company that demands and rewards such traits. As the manager moves up, congruence between personal and organizational goals tends to get stronger. Creating and meeting challenging organizational goals may, in fact, become a personal goal.

Those at the top of an organization are generally perceived as being highly committed to organizational goals. Individual and organizational success are mutually dependent. That is why people at the top tend to work longer and harder than anyone else. If the organization meets its goals (increases profits, defeats the enemy, reduces unemployment, wins the Super Bowl), so does the person at the top (gets a bonus, receives a hero's welcome, is reelected, signs a new long-term contract). If the organization consistently fails to meet its goals, the person at the top is most likely to be retired, shamed, defeated, or fired.

Despite the tendency for personal and organizational goals to become more congruent at upper levels of an organization, the link can be broken at any point up to and including the top. The Coca-Cola Company's popular president, J. Lucien Smith, resigned five years before his scheduled retirement because the job "just wasn't fun anymore."[8] When the behaviors required to meet Coca-Cola's goal of remaining the world's largest soft drink manufacturer no longer allowed him to achieve his personal goal of enjoying his work, Smith chose to leave.

Goal Congruence and the Manager

There are two ways managers can try to bring about congruence between their subordinates' personal and organizational goals. As we shall see in the next chapter, managers can select employees whose expressed goals agree with the organization's. They can also show subordinates ways in which helping to meet organizational goals will help to meet their personal goals as well.

The second approach forms the basis for the path-goal theory of leadership, to be discussed in Chapter 10. The **path-goal theory** proposes that *effective leaders clarify and clear paths that lead to subordinates' goals.* For example, if Cathy gets the job for which she interviewed, she can clarify the path to a subordinate's goal by telling him or her what skills and experience are needed for promotion. She could help clear the path to that goal by giving assignments in which the subordinate can develop the skills and acquire the experience that promotion requires.

A manager can not only point out the way to achieve job goals to meet personal goals, but can also support this congruence by giving careful attention to the way job goals are set. Research on job goals and job performance consistently indicates that:

1. Goals affect employees' performance by mobilizing their efforts, directing their attention, increasing their persistence, and inducing them to develop strategies for achievement. Goals help to control performance by keeping individuals aware of what they need to produce and by channeling their efforts in those directions. Goals influence people to work, rather than slack off, and to use imagination and ingenuity.
2. Specific, challenging goals lead to higher performance than easy goals, goals that simply state "do your best," or no goals at all. Some ninety percent of the research surveyed indicates that specific, challenging goals lead to superior performance.[9]

The research suggests that a manager who is not clear about the behaviors expected of a subordinate, or who sets goals that are too easy or too hard, can "waste" subordinate goal congruence. For example, your goals of acquiring knowledge and getting an A in this course may be congruent with the instructor's goal of having you learn the information. However, if the instructor does not clarify what you have to do to get an A, you may become discouraged and decrease your effort. You may also exert too little effort if what you have to do is clear, but too difficult. If getting an A is too easy, you may still exert less effort than the instructor believes is necessary to learn something, even if you work hard enough to get an A.

PARTICIPATIVE GOAL SETTING AND EMPLOYEE EFFORT

One way suggested for bridging the gap between personal goals and organizational goals is to involve employees in the setting of goals at the job-goal level. This has led to various participative goal-setting techniques, including management by results; working, planning, and review; and management by objectives.

How Participative Goal Setting Works

Participative goal setting is *the process by which supervisors and subordinates jointly determine subordinate goals for some period of time.* At least four conditions are necessary for this process to be effective:

1. Goal setting should be preceded by a diagnosis of the subordinate's job and the place of that job in the organizational system.

The job goal-setting process is a possible way to elicit the subordinate effort required to accomplish organizational goals. Participative goal setting does this directly.

2. Supervisor and subordinate should be committed to the process and willing to participate.
3. The goals that are set should benefit the subordinate as well as the organization; they must be attainable.
4. The goal-setting interview should be followed by periodic feedback and counseling.

Note that Condition 3 specifically recognizes the importance of goal congruence. A complete model of the actual participative goal-setting process used by one large organization is shown in Exhibit 5.4. The four requirements listed above for a successful program appear in this model as follows:

1. Diagnosis for goal-setting readiness
2. Preparation for goal setting
3. Goal setting and anticipated goal-setting results
4. Intermediate review, final review, and feedback cycle.

If Cathy's new boss were to use a formal process of participative goal-setting with her, they might proceed as follows: Cathy and her boss would discuss several goals, including the boss' goals for Cathy and her department and her own goals for her department and herself. Among goals they would agree on would be to get half her subordinates good raises or promotions each year. Then Cathy would sit down with her subordinates and discuss their own goals and her goals for them. She and several of her subordinates would set individual objectives that will help subordinates receive promotions or raises.

Exhibit 5.4   A Model of the Participative Goal-Setting Process

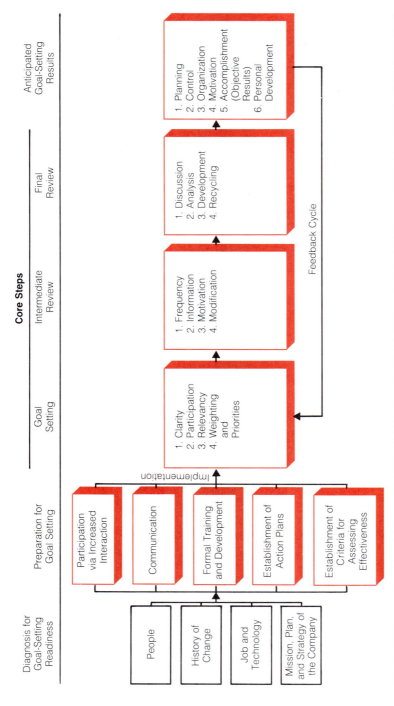

*After the preparation phase is completed it is necessary to develop a systematic plan implementation.
From J.M. Ivancevich, J.T. McMahon, J.W. Stredl, & A.D. Szilagyi: "Goal Setting: The Tenneco Approach to Personal Development and Management Effectiveness."
Organizational Dynamics, Winter, 1978, pp. 58-50.

Exhibit 5.5   Do's and Don'ts of the Participative Goal-Setting Interview

Do	Don't
Do ask, "How are *we* going to do this? What can I contribute to this effort? How will *we* use this result?" thus implying your joint stake in the work and results.	Don't imply that it is the employees' total responsibility, that they hang alone if they fail. Individual failure means *organization* failure.
Do use an interested, exploring manner, asking questions designed to bring out factual information.	Don't play the part of an interrogator, firing questions as rapidly as they can be answered and usually requiring only a "yes" or "no" reply.
Do keep the analysis and evaluation as much in the employees' hands as possible by asking for their best judgments on various issues.	Don't listen to what they present and then sum up your reaction on an emotional basis.
Do present facts about organization needs, commitments, strategy, and so on, which permit them to improve and interest them in improving what they propose to do.	Don't demand a change or improvement in a peremptory tone of voice or on what appears to be an arbitrary basis.
	Don't take their planning papers and cross out, change dates, or mark "no good" next to certain activities.
Do ask them to investigate or analyze further if you feel that they have overlooked some points or overemphasized others and to return with their plans after factoring these items in.	Don't redo their plans for them unless their repeated efforts show no improvement.

Source: From Putting Management Theories to Work by Marion S. Kellogg, revised by Irving Burstiner, Ph.D. Copyright © 1979 by Prentice-Hall, Inc. Reprinted by permission of Prentice-Hall, Inc., Englewood Cliffs, NJ 07632.

The most widely known formal participative goal-setting procedure is **Management by Objectives (MBO)**, *a formal process for setting employee job goals and for evaluating employee performance.*[10] As with all such procedures, there is a strong emphasis on building a partnership between the participants. The importance of this idea is illustrated by the Do's and Don't's in Exhibit 5.5.

Is Participative Goal Setting Effective?

Like many management tools, MBO and related procedures were greeted by noncritical enthusiasm, followed by a period of intensive research into their effectiveness. The results support the contingency approach to management: the effectiveness of MBO depends on certain conditions.

The usual criteria for judging the effectiveness of formal participative goal-setting techniques are improved performance and reported employee satisfaction. Taken as a whole, the participative goal-setting research tells us that sometimes the process is associated with improved performance and sometimes it is not, and some people report satisfaction with the process and some people hate it.

Research makes clear that such techniques are not the one best way to raise employee effort. The success of MBO and related methods depends upon the nature of the job, the extent to which the goals set are measurable and attainable, the degree of support the program receives from top management, the extent to which a job is independent of other jobs, and a great variety of individual traits, including the ability of managers and subordinates to understand what the process requires.

Whether the criterion for evaluating the effectiveness of formal goal-setting procedures is performance or satisfaction, one result will be clear, measurable, and attainable goals and improved performance, if the process is carried out as it is designed. In addition, since such goals are more likely to be attained, we would expect them to be associated with greater employee satisfaction than vague or impossible goals. A major factor in the successes of formal goal-setting techniques, then, may be that the process requires the participants to focus closely and specifically on job goals.[11]

A full-scale participative goal-setting program is extremely time-consuming and, therefore, expensive. There is no hard evidence that its benefits could not be achieved at less expense. However, the principles of techniques such as MBO—diagnosis, goal definition, feedback, and counseling—are sound. If having a formal framework within which to use them is the only way that they will become part of ongoing management activities, then the expense of formal participative goal-setting programs may indeed be worth the benefits.

Organizational goals, their clarity, their difficulty, and their perceived relevance to personal goals do play an important role in determining what people do and don't do in organizations. So do a great many other factors, as we will see in the next chapter which turns to the sticky business of getting people to accomplish organizational goals.

◢◢◢ The Bottom Line ◣◣◣

Managers can and do use goals as an important tool in carrying out their directing functions. Goals can do a number of things: help coordinate efforts, evaluate performance, provide incentives, and enhance the organization's image. In their use of goals in organizations, managers find that:

1. No single goal can do everything. When setting a goal, it is best to decide on the goal's purpose—to present an image, provide an incentive, coordinate effort, or evaluate performance. Does this mean that managers need goals for their goals? Yes.
2. Ultimately, organizational goals are accomplished through the efforts of individuals and groups that comprise the organization. People are more likely to exert efforts to achieve organizational goals when those efforts also help them achieve their personal goals.
3. Various participative goal-setting techniques can help create greater congruence between personal and organizational goals. They are not, however, always the best way to direct employee effort. And, if they are used merely to make employees believe that what's best for the organization is best for them when it really isn't, then they will only succeed in alienating employees from organizational goals.
4. A "good" goal is one that is clear, objective, specific, feasible, challenging—and consistent. By consistent, we mean that it fits in with the goals of those it is designed to influence and with other organizational goals. An employee in an organization who sets goals needs to understand other organizational goals. That, in turn suggests that:
5. There are no good secret goals.

SUMMARY

The directing function of management is channeling the efforts of others toward defined organizational goals. These organizational goals are established through an ongoing bargaining process involving key individuals and groups. This process is not totally free since no organization has complete goal-setting discretion. Goals must satisfy certain internal and external expectations and constraints.

Two major categories of organizational goals help direct individual and group effort. Formal goals describe the desired end and are usually general formulations of the organization's reason for being. Operative goals guide day-to-day operating procedures. They guide the formation of subunit goals, which define the contribution of the various parts of the organization to organizational goals. Individual job goals define the contribution of the individual to subunit goals.

Various participative goal-setting techniques have been developed in an attempt to create greater goal congruence between personal and organizational goals. MBO and related techniques have had both successes and failures in application. The large number of factors upon which the success of such programs depends has made it clear that they cannot be considered one-best-way techniques for bringing about sufficient employee effort to meet organizational goals.

QUESTIONS FOR REVIEW AND DISCUSSION

1. State the differences among organizational, operative, subunit, and job goals.
2. Put yourself in the place of a professor of introductory management and
    a. Write a *formal* goal statement to be used in official notices about the course.
    b. Set two or more *operative* goals for accomplishing this formal goal.
3. In Question 2, there is only one "key individual" and so no bargaining is necessary to set goals. However, there are still internal (class) and external (environment outside classroom) influences on the goals. List as many of these influences on the goals as you can.
4. Make a list of the personal goals that are most important to you right now.
    a. Identify those that are related to your academic work.
    b. Of those identified in (a), further identify those that are *congruent* with the formal and operative goals for this course that you listed in Question 2.
5. What functions can goals serve? Why would it be difficult for one goal to serve all functions?
6. What is the difference between goal congruence and goal displacement? How could lack of goal congruence lead to goal displacement?
7. Would you expect the subunit goals of the managers of each of the following groups to be similar or dissimilar? Briefly explain your answers.
    a. Telephone operators and telephone repairpersons
    b. Regular floor nurses and emergency room nurses
    c. Bank tellers and grocery checkers
    d. Car salespersons and real-estate salespersons
8. Give an example of goal displacement from any organization. State the original goal as specifically as you can, as well as the goal that displaced it.

REFERENCES AND NOTES

1. A. Etzioni, *A Comparative Analysis of Complex Organizations.* New York: The Free Press, 1975 p. 103.
2. *1979 Annual Report of ALSAC*, St. Judes Children's Research Hospital, p. 2.
3. A complete discussion of the distinction between formal and operative goals can be found in C. Perrow, "The Analysis of Goals in Complex Organizations." *American Sociological Review*, 1961, 26, pp. 854–66.
4. These goals are more commonly called *operational goals.* We have avoided that term because its similiarity to *operative goal* creates confusion.
5. *Chicago Tribune*, June 10, 1974.
6. "Special Report: The Shrinking of Middle Management," *Business Week*, April 25, 1983, p. 55.
7. E. A. Locke, "Toward a Theory of Task Motivation." *Organizational Behavior and Human Performance*, 1968, 3, pp. 157–89.
8. *Time*, August 18, 1980.
9. E. A. Locke, K. N. Shaw, L. M. Saari, G. P. Latham, *Goal Setting and Task Performance: 1960-1980.* Office of Naval Research: Technical Report GS 1, 1980.
10. A complete presentation of the philosophy and the principles of implementation of MBO may be found in K. Albrecht, *Successful Management by Objectives.* Englewood Cliffs, N.J.: Prentice-Hall, Inc., 1978.
11. See P. D. Tolchinsky and D. C. King, "Do Goals Mediate the Effects of Incentives on Performance?" *Academy of Management Review*, 1980, 5, 3, pp. 455–67, for a summary of the research on this topic.

SUGGESTED READINGS

Etzioni, A. "Two Approaches to Organizational Analysis: A Critique and a Suggestion." *Administrative Science Quarterly*, 1960, 5, 2, 257–78. The earliest systems model of organizational effectiveness is proposed as an alternative to the standard "does it meet its goals?" model. Etzioni is particularly strong in the use of images and examples.

Kast, F. E. "Organizational and Individual Objectives." In J. W. McGuire, ed. *Contemporary Management: Issues and Viewpoints.* Englewood Cliffs, N.J.: Prentice-Hall, Inc., 1974, 150–80. This reading covers briefly most of the material in this chapter plus discussion on the means by which organizations adapt to multiple and conflicting goals.

Simon, H. A., "On the Concept of Organizational Goal." *Administrative Science Quarterly*, 1964, 9, 1–22. A short discussion by one of management's leading theorists on the difficulty of defining organizational goals, and the role of organizational goals in organizational decision making, and the differences between "goals" and "motivation." Do not be alarmed by the mathematical terminology. You can skip it, if necessary, and still get a lot from this reading.

Vandivier, K., "Why Should My Conscience Bother Me?" In J. B. Ritchie and P. Thompson (eds.), *Organization and People*, 2nd ed. St. Paul, Minn.: West Publishing Co., 1980, 204–17. The story of a data analyst and technical writer who resigned from a major corporation because of what was perceived to be direct pressure to falsify reports. His belief that the goal of a particular project was to make the product look good, no matter how, is a first-rate illustration of the concept of goal displacement.

Case *Management By Objectives (or) The $500,000 Misunderstanding*

"The thing to remember," Ted Shelby intoned, "is that, no matter how high up in The Company we are, we are all subordinates to somebody.... From this perspective," he went on, "it becomes crystal clear that superiors and subordinates up and down the line must have a clearly spelled out understanding of what is expected of each. I might add that this comes out loud and clear in our interviews with top management subordinates. Briefly stated, the objective of Management by Objectives is to totally eliminate all possibilities of misunderstandings between superiors and subordinates, and to assure that each ... has a crisp and hard-hitting set of objectives to measure ... against."

"Now, I want each of you to have the opportunity to talk to a plant manager in person. I want each of you to get a hands-on feeling of how this program works ...."

One of the new women management trainees, Nella Allen, was assigned to interview Ben Franklyn, the plant manager at the old plant in Providence. Several days later she drove up there and was ushered into Ben Franklyn's office. "So, you're the gal that Shelby sent to get some 'hands-on' experience with management by objectives?" Ben pronounced the words with exaggerated clarity, as he invariably did with words he found distasteful ... "You would probably like to see my objectives as plant manager at Providence. I hope you've got a little time today, because they need some explanation.

"You know, the guys who write these things up, why I don't believe they've ever been in a plant in their lives, except when Mr. Marsh makes one of his speeches here. These things are clear and—what's that word they use—'objective' (distaste again) to them only because they haven't got the first god-damned idea of what goes on in a manufacturing plant." ...

Nella pulls her chair over to Ben's big desk, and Ben opens up a file and spreads some papers and graphs out. "Now," says Ben, pulling out a sheet titled "Production Objectives," these are more or less okay, even though I don't have any real control over them. Let's take this one: 'Scrap as percent of finished product.' Know how I handle it? Well, now I inspect all the raw material coming in twice as carefully as I used to. That's because it isn't only what my boys do; a lot depends on the job they do in the foundry at Fayetteville. It used to be that I could play ball with those guys; if the stuff they sent wasn't completely lousy, I'd give it a try. But not now. Now I send it back unless it's top grade. What else can I do? It's a waste of time and money, but I make my objective."

"Here's another one: 'Production man-hours as a percent of standard time.' Now, that one's easy enough to meet. Maybe you don't always get your production up, but you can look okay if you...." Ben went on to describe his procedures for claiming downtime on machines and a lot of other things that Nella didn't understand, except that they didn't sound very productive. Next, Ben pulled out a set of objectives labeled "Behavioral."

"I know you're going to find these perfectly clear, just like me—har." Ben started off. "Here, look at these...."

Source: R. R. Ritti and G. R. Funkhouser, *The Ropes To Skip and The Ropes To Know.* Columbus, Ohio: GRID, Inc., 1977, 161–63.

There followed major headings such as "Morale," "Subordinate Readiness," "Interpersonal Sensitivity," and the like. Ben took a sarcastic tone: "... shall act to improve man-manager relationships at all levels of plant management." ...

"But here, look at this. This is what I really wanted to show you. What's today, December 20, right? Okay, now here's my expenses as percent of budget—108 percent. That's fine, they give us a leeway of 10 percent over. And take it from me, I busted my tail to hold it there. So, yesterday, what comes down to me from New York? This!"

Ben is holding a sheet with a lot of figures on it but Nella was never much at accounting, and looks mystified. "Let me tell you about this," says Ben. "If you read between the figures, what it says is, "Mr. Franklyn, you now have $500,000 of additional expense as of December 19. We regret that this may cause you to miss your expense objective." ...

"But what could happen from that?" says Nella. "Surely, anybody can see that your missing the objective is simply a misunderstanding."

"Anybody that wants to see it that way will," said Ben. "And if anybody finds that it's convenient to forget it, they'll do that too. And sooner or later, nobody will remember how it happened. All that's in the books is that I missed the objective."

CASE QUESTIONS

1. Find an example of goal displacement in the case.
2. Evaluate the goal "shall act to improve employee-manager relationships at all levels of plant management" in terms of the two goal characteristics known to help produce improved performance.
3. Give an example of one or more plausible negative systems-effects likely to be created by Ben Franklyn's actions on behalf of meeting his 'Scrap as a percentage of finished product' goal.
4. What would you expect the effect of the New York office's action on Ben Franklyn's future performance to be? Explain your answer in terms of what you learned in this chapter.
5. The Company, in this case, called what it was doing with respect to goal setting, management by objectives. Review the case in light of this chapter's discussion of participative goal-setting techniques and decide whether you think this label is justified. Give evidence from the case for your conclusion.

6/Directing: Motivation

"When you signed up, you in effect declared, I want to do this job and I'll give it my heart and soul. By signing up for the project you agreed to do whatever was necessary for success."[1]

So Tracy Kidder explained the commitment of company engineers to the monumental effort required to build a new computer. Kidder's Pulitzer prize-winning book The Soul of a New Machine recounts the true story behind Data General's Eagle project. In it he analyzes the motivation behind the effort of the key individuals.

DATA GENERAL OFFERS 'SUPER' MINICOMPUTER

For Tom West, who conceived and shepherded the project, it was the challenge of managing a unique project under severe time pressure, with limited resources and many inexperienced young engineers. The chances for failure were enormous. If they succeeded, because the company needed the product desperately, West and his project team would be heroes.

Carl Alsing, West's righthand man, signed on because he admired and was fascinated by West. He felt that West was brilliant, unpredictable, successful, and driven when enthusiastic about something that was his own, like Eagle. West made Eagle seem like an adventure.

Steve Wallach, the architect for the new computer, at first turned down West's offer. He felt the constraints were too great, since his previous design work had been on canceled projects. But West

eventually won Wallach over. First, he convinced Wallach that Eagle was the only project that would allow Wallach to use his talents as a computer architect. Second, he allowed Wallach to take his fears about another cancellation to Data General's president. Convinced by the president that a successful project would, in fact, lead to a commercially marketed product, Wallach signed up.

Chuck Holland headed up the group who wrote the software for the computer—the Microkids, newly graduated microcode specialists. Holland felt he had been overlooked so far. Eagle gave him an opportunity to do something dramatic, and to choose and organize the team with which to do it.

Ed Rasala, exhausted from a previous project, at first declined to join. Finally, convinced by West that he was desperately needed, he agreed to head the Hardy Boys—the team that built the computer's hardware. They had to bring Wallach's design to life, to put together the machine that would do what Wallach said it would do, using Holland's software. Their success required great

effort—and lots of "debugging," or correcting technical problems. Rasala saw himself as "not the smartest designer in the world . . . but I'm dumb enough to stick with it to the end." To Rasala, Eagle was his highest challenge, a test of strength.

Every worker in the project enlisted for a different reason. Bob Beauchamp, while working on a low-priority, low-pressure project, was attracted to Eagle by the intensity and fervor of the team. When offered the chance for some grueling work, "I jumped on it," he said. Dave Peck and Neal Firth designed simulators for the project, driven by a spirit of competition to see who was the better programmer. Rosemarie Seale couldn't quit, even though she sometimes hated the job and the pressure. "It's like one of those terrible movies," she explained. "I just have to see how it comes out."

Most practicing managers agree that setting goals is easier than getting people to work effectively and diligently for their accomplishment. For Tom West, the ultimate managerial challenge was to get this group of brilliant, hardworking people to commit to the creation of a new computer, and have it ready for production within a year. They had to give maximum effort until the goal was accomplished. He knew that each of his recruits was capable of such effort. But what would it take to get each one to undertake the work? And once committed, what would induce them to continue directing their efforts toward his goal?

What Tom was concerned about was **motivation**—*the reasons for which people exert effort.* He had to find ways to induce different kinds of people to exert full effort toward his goal for a year or more. Tom was facing one of the greatest challenges for contemporary managers, because the people he was concerned about had great freedom. They were free to refuse, free to leave the company for other good jobs, free to give minimum effort, free to do things other than work for his goal.

MOTIVATION: MYTH VS. REALITY

To sort out myth from reality, let's go back to what motivation is. Motivation identifies the causes of human choice and effort. It is the answer to the question "why?" as in, "Why did Steve agree to work on the project?" or "Why are the Hardy Boys working eighty hours a week?" Steve became a part of the team because the project afforded him his only opportunity to design a computer. The Hardy Boys worked eighty hours a week because they faced a series of intellectual challenges that fascinated and compelled them.

Myths and misunderstandings have emerged largely because the "why" of doing things is not readily apparent. Take the term *highly motivated.* When you hear of someone, a young executive, for example, described as highly motivated, what do you think of? A person who comes to work early, stays late, asks questions, seeks challenges, takes on responsibility, sets goals. While this description is not wrong, it is a list of *behaviors,* not motivations. What we see in observing others are the products of motivation: effort, behavior, and performance. We are often left to guess at the motivation, the "why."

One myth is that motivation is a "mysterious inner spark" that some have and others don't. The reality is that sleeping and apathy are motivated, just as achieving and curiosity are motivated. The reasons for sleeping differ from those for achieving, but both behaviors have reasons behind them.

A second myth is that motivation is a "switch" that others turn on and off. The excuse often given for low effort is that "my boss (or my instructor) doesn't motivate me." That excuse ignores the fact that a boss (or instructor) is only one source of motivation. Each individual is capable of providing reasons for his or her own effort, or self-motivation.

A third myth is that motivation and job satisfaction are the same thing, or job satisfaction is the primary cause of motivation. This one is usually expressed as, "A happy worker is a good worker." However, forty years of research have failed to produce any evidence to support this statement.[2] Satisfied workers are not necessarily good workers, nor even highly motivated workers. The engineers on Data General's Eagle project were often dissatisfied—with pay, working conditions, top management, their own immediate superiors, and with the success of their project. They worked hard, month in and month out, and their effort was not the same as nor the result of job satisfaction.

MOTIVATION AND PERFORMANCE

Managers are by no means solely responsible for the motivation of their subordinates. The reasons people choose to pursue goals are as many and varied as the individuals themselves; but managers control or influence many parts of the work environment. Managers, therefore, can influence the effort that others expend. To do this successfully, they must understand the role of motivation in the performance and effort of subordinates.

The balance of this chapter will be directed toward achieving that understanding. In Chapter 8 we will discuss the factors that influence human behavior.

Factors that Determine Performance

Ability and motivation (individual characteristics) and work environment, including other people (environmental characteristics) combine in the **Performance Equation** (See Exhibit 6.1). *Performance is a function of the interaction between ability and motivation, and the environment in which the performance takes place, or* $P = f[(A \times M) \times E]$.

Abilities are the basic physical and mental equipment, such as eyesight, strength, intelligence, adaptability, dexterity, and specific skills an individual brings to a job. Motivation puts abilities to work. The environment can help or hinder.

Ed Rasala was identified by Tom West as a key individual for the Eagle project. Ed had the unique ability to be able to manage the computer's "debugging" process, to correct all the thousands of problems and mistakes which might keep

Exhibit 6.1   Factors that Determine Performance

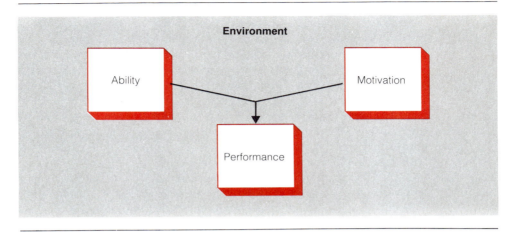

Eagle from being a useful, marketable product. Ed was the person who could take a new computer and "get it out the door." But that ability would not have affected Eagle if Ed had not chosen to sign up and put forth the months of grueling effort required. It took motivation—"opportunity, responsibility, visibility," in his words—to provide the effort that translated that ability into performance.

However, it is ability, not motivation, that sets the upper limit on performance. We cannot do what we lack the basic equipment to do, no matter how much we want to. The point is well illustrated by a guitarist who was once asked why he played back-up for recording stars rather than becoming a solo artist. His reply was brief and to the point, "Stubby fingers!"

Even when ability is adequate, motivation does not lead to much except frustration and disappointment if the environment contains major obstacles to performance. Faulty parts, lack of diagnostic computers, or top management interference all could have doomed Ed Rasala's efforts to debug the Eagle.

Which factor is the most important? In some situations, the required abilities may be so standard that motivation is the more crucial factor. In others, the requirements may be so high that virtually no amount of effort can compensate for ability limitations; however, a manager is not likely to meet this situation often. On a day-to-day basis, the amount of effort expended by subordinates will make a substantial difference in their performances. The Eagle project, despite the team's superior abilities, would have failed without their unflagging efforts.

The Basic Motivation Principle

The definition of motivation reminds us that we are studying effort. However, it says nothing at all about why this effort does or does not come about. To be successful in influencing the effort of others, we must know something about why they expend effort as they do. The answer, which we call the **Basic Motivation Principle,** simply states: *People expend effort on activities that reward them.* The rewards involved may be *extrinsic* (given by others), such as praise, or they may be *intrinsic,* (not dependent on others), such as feelings of accomplishment. These rewards may come immediately (a clean car after you have washed it) or be far in the future (graduation after four years of effort). They may be big (an Olympic medal) or small (a "thank you"). They may be easily understood as rewards by others (a promotion) or seem strange to most (risking death or defeat).

Rewards are also relative. Certain behaviors are rewarding, but other behaviors may be *more* rewarding. For example, an executive may find going to a football game more rewarding than clearing up the paperwork brought home in Friday's briefcase. Bob Beauchamp, on the other hand, found working on the Eagle project more rewarding than most off-the-job activities. We will discuss rewards and their effective uses in a later section of this chapter. For now, let's look at what motivation theories have to say about the Basic Motivation Principle.

THEORIES OF MOTIVATION

There are three leading approaches to motivation, in general, and the motivation of workers, in particular—need theories, expectancy theories, and the reinforcement model. Although these three approaches are often presented as conflicting alternatives, they really address elements of the Basic Motivation Principle, as summarized in Exhibit 6.2. Need theories consider *what is rewarding;* expectancy theory primarily addresses *what factors influence the belief that a behavior will be rewarded;* the reinforcement model consists of principles about the *outcomes of behavior,* especially those which lead to reward. We will consider each approach briefly before turning to their implications for the practice of management.

Need Theories

A **need** is *a physiological or psychological requirement.* According to one general theory of motivation, needs drive us to behave in ways that will satisfy needs. Hunger is a physiological need. When we are hungry, we do things to obtain food. We may go to the refrigerator for a snack or to a restaurant for a meal. The need can be satisfied in a variety of ways.

Need theories of work motivation are based on this principle. **Need theories** are *theories stating that people exert effort at work to meet needs that are unsatisfied.* This idea gets common-sense support from the fact that a major reason for working has always been to earn money for food, shelter, and clothing.

Three Need Theories of Motivation.   By far the best-known theory of work motivation is a five-category list of needs hypothesized as common to all people.[3] These needs are arranged in order from basic (lower-order) *physiological* and *safety* needs, up through less basic (higher-order) *social* and *esteem* needs, to the need for *self-actualization,* or self-fulfillment.

According to this *stepwise theory*, developed by A. H. Maslow, lower-order needs must be met before behavior is directed toward satisfying higher-order needs. Only when the first four needs have been met will the need for self-actualization determine behavior.

What this theory of needs implies for managers is that motivating workers is a matter of arranging for their needs to be met (at whatever levels they are operating) on the job. A second such theory, offered by Frederick Herzberg, goes even further to argue that only the two highest levels of needs motivate performance on the job. Lower-order needs are relevant only to job satisfaction. Therefore, managers who provide for employees' lower-order needs (such as working conditions, job security, fringe benefits, and pay) but ignore higher order needs (such as advancement, achievement, and recognition) can expect, at best, satisfied but unmotivated workers.

A third well-known need theory is considerably narrower in scope than the two already discussed. Harvard psychologist David McClelland focuses on two needs, the needs for achievement and power. One basic premise is that some people are challenged by the opportunity to achieve something (have a high need for achievement) and others are not (have a low need for achievement). Other things being equal, McClelland asserts, those with a high need for achievement will exert more effort at work than others. A second premise is that successful managers generally have a high need for power, which they use to achieve organizational, rather than simply personal, goals. A unique feature of McClelland's theory is the assumption that these needs are *learned*. Thus, his theory does not assume that all people have the same needs.

We can use these three theories to explain the efforts and choices made by the engineers on the Eagle project. Tom West's motivation lay in the project's ultimate managerial challenge—self-actualization (Maslow). The Hardy Boys worked long hours, despite poor working conditions, because the endless series of challenges helped them satisfy their esteem needs, giving them opportunities for recognition and achievement (Herzberg). The entire team gave their all because they were high achievers (McClelland).

Exhibit 6.2   Three Theories of Motivation

	Need Theories	Expectancy Theory	Reinforcement Model
What the Theory Says	People make choices and exert effort in order to satisfy needs important to them.	People make choices and exert effort consistent with their expectations about the outcomes of that effort and the value they place on those outcomes.	People make choices and exert effort because of the outcomes of their behavior.
What the Theory Emphasizes	The identification of the need(s) most important to a person at a given time and how to satisfy the need(s).	The individual perception of the links between effort, performance, and outcomes and how those outcomes are valued.	The outcomes of a person's behavior and their effects on it: reinforcement, punishment, or extinction.

Need Theories and Research.   Management scholars have carried out a great deal of research on need theories over the years. In general, these theories have not fared well. Research has failed to demonstrate that most people have similar sets of needs arranged in a fixed pattern[6] or that only higher-level needs affect effort on the job.[7] Research on the need for achievement has fared better; successful individuals in the business world are usually found to have higher needs for achievement and power than others.[8]

As these theories were put into practice in organizations, attempts to increase worker motivation have usually focused on job design, as described in Chapter 4. Most of these practical applications have been one-best-way efforts based on the assumption that people are very similar in their responses to work situations. Research into the effectiveness of these applications has found the usual mixture of successes and failures.

More recent work in the area has attempted to improve the success rate by giving greater attention to the role of individual differences in responses to work.[9] Practical applications of the need-for-achievement theory have generally focused on individuals as well. Since it is a learned need, achievement-oriented training can raise the level of this need, and so raise the level of effort.[10]

Need Theories and the Basic Motivation Principle.   Despite the weak premises on which general need theories are based, they reveal that people will exert effort to acquire what they feel is necessary. A manager who knows how a person evaluates his or her *own* needs has an idea about what will be *rewarding* to that individual and how to direct effort. Need for achievement theory reveals that even people who do not generally put much effort into work behavior can learn that their efforts have rewards.

Expectancy Theories

The role of choice in determining where effort will be made is emphasized by a group of theories of motivation called expectancy theories. An **expectancy** is *a belief about the probability that something will happen.* According to a basic expectancy theory of motivation, there are two such beliefs that influence effort.[11]

The Effort-Performance Expectancy is *a belief that effort will lead to the successful performance of some task.* In other words, "If I try hard enough, can I do it?" This belief depends upon a number of factors, the most important of which is the individual's assessment of his or her own skills and knowledge relevant to the difficulty of the task being performed. It also depends upon other beliefs, such as whether the right tools and equipment (if needed) are available and whether there are major obstacles to performance in the environment.

The Performance-Reward Expectancy is *the belief that a reward may follow performance.* "If I do it, will I be rewarded?" This belief depends upon what has happened when the performance has occurred in the past, what the individual has been told will occur if the performance is accomplished, and/or what he or she sees happening to others who perform successfully.

The general expectancy model of motivation also includes the concept of values. A **value** is *the worth an individual places on a reward.* It is personal and not necessarily predictable by others. An individual may place a high value on family life, and little or no value on getting ahead in the organization. Such a person is unlikely to work hard for a promotion to a job that will require extensive travel. Not only does the promotion have a low value, but it would take time from the highly valued family interaction.

According to a basic expectancy theory of motivation, values, the Effort-Performance Expectancy, and the Performance-Reward Expectancy combine to determine how much effort will be expended; that is the level of motivation. The greatest motivation occurs when both expectancies are high and the expected reward is strongly valued. If either expectancy is zero, no effort will be expended.

What we see in observing others are the products of motivation: effort, behavior, and performance. We are often left to guess at the motivation, the "why."

We can use this concept to explain the effort and choices made by Steve Wallach from the Eagle team. He didn't sign up at first because he believed that the project was likely to be canceled (performance-reward expectancy was low). When that belief was changed, he agreed because he saw the project as the only way he would get to design a computer—a highly valued outcome.

Research on Expectancy Theories.   The general expectancy theory of motivation gets very complicated. In full form, the general expectancy theory of motivation presents measurement difficulties and implies a complex "mental arithmetic" that makes it impossible to test in its entirety. However, hypotheses drawn from various elements of the model have been supported.[12]

Expectancy Theories and the Basic Motivation Principle.   Despite the measurement difficulties, the expectancy theory of motivation adds to our understanding of the basic motivation principle.

First, it emphasizes the role that expectations for success (the Effort-Performance Expectancy) play in motivation. Most people (like Steve Wallach, at first) who figure they can't possibly accomplish something are unlikely to choose to expend effort in that direction regardless of the incentives. As we shall see, this apparently small point has substantial implications for influencing employee effort.

Second, expectancy theory makes clear that incentives and motivation are not necessarily the same thing. The concept of *value* in expectancy theory demonstrates that an incentive may or may not be seen as a reward. In any case, it will be only one of the relevant determinants of effort.

Finally, expectancy theory adds the concept of *value* to our understanding of what is rewarding to people. As with what people say they need, what they say they value offers some clues to the ways in which they will expend effort.

The Reinforcement Model

The last major approach to understanding work motivation is a set of laws derived from systematic observation and data collection. The usual process of theorizing and then making observations to see if they fit the theory is reversed. The reinforcement model is a picture of reality based on observation that emphasizes the effect of the environment on behavior.

Outcomes of Behavior.   The reinforcement model directs attention to what happens *after* behavior occurs. So far we have discussed only rewards. There are two other possibilities. The behavior may be punished; or nothing relevant may happen at all. The reinforcement model tells us what is likely to happen to behavior as a result of its outcome.

Rewards increase the likelihood that the behavior they follow will occur again. If the reward means receiving something attractive, such as an "A," a bonus, or praise, we say the behavior has received *positive reinforcement.* If the reward stops or reduces something unpleasant or painful, we say the behavior has received *negative reinforcement.* In either case, the behavior is likely to occur again under similar conditions.

Some salespeople make deliberate use of the principle of negative reinforcement. They come back again and again until eventually a customer buys just so they will go away. When this happens, a salesperson has been *positively reinforced* for being persistent; the customer has been *negatively reinforced.* Both "being persistent" and "purchasing from a pest" will occur again in similar circumstances.

Punishment reduces the likelihood that the behavior it follows will occur again. Punishment may be administered by the physical environment (going into the woods to get wildflowers and coming out with poison ivy), or it may be applied deliberately by someone else as a means of changing behavior.

Punishment is a very common approach to behavior change in our society, but it is not very well understood. It is only a means of eliminating, or temporarily suppressing, *undesired* behavior. It has no effect at all on the *desired* behavior because there are always any number of alternative behaviors from which to choose. For example, a worker who is punished for exerting little effort may quit, pretend he's working hard, or seek revenge instead of exerting more effort.

There are times when punishment is appropriate, especially if the behavior is dangerous or harmful to others. The important thing is to stop the undesired behavior. If the situation is an emergency, what the person does *instead* is of little interest. From a *motivation* standpoint, however, punishment puts the emphasis in the wrong place—on the undesired behavior instead of the desired behavior.

If the outcome of behavior is neither rewarding nor punishing to the individual concerned, the behavior will eventually stop. In other words, if there is no relevant outcome, behavior is *extinguished.* Extinction works more slowly than punishment in *suppressing* behavior, but it is the most certain way to *eliminate* behavior.

Consider the manager who has an "open-door policy." Employees are told they may come in at any time to talk over problems, make suggestions, or ask questions.

Management in Action
Will Merit Pay Improve Teaching?

Large school systems in this country have been paying teachers on the basis of seniority. Raises have typically been a function of the teacher's previous salary, number of years in the school system, and level of education. The past few years, however, have witnessed an increasing concern with the state of education in this country, as functional-illiteracy rates continue to be appallingly high, and foreign competition in industrial technology has made increasing inroads into U.S. shares of markets.

In 1984 Florida became the first state to adopt a statewide merit-pay program for its public school teachers. The program initially allows each school district to designate up to one third of its teachers as Associate Master Teachers. The criteria for this designation are a master's degree, ten years' experience, a superior score on a standardized test for teachers, and a superior evaluation of classroom performance by a three-person evaluation team. Teachers who meet these criteria will be awarded a $3000 bonus.

Shortly thereafter Tennessee enacted an even more comprehensive merit-pay bill calling for incentive bonuses ranging from $2000 to $7000, with the higher bonuses available to more experienced teachers who teach year-round.

In both states the strongest opponents of merit pay for teachers were the teachers themselves, as represented by their unions. Their major objections were that merit pay would introduce competition, as teachers vied with one another for bonuses, and that such bonuses would reduce the amount of money available for the rest of the state's educational budget, including regular salary increases for teachers. Another major objection to merit-pay programs is the difficulty of accurately evaluating teacher performance. Teachers' unions have also argued that administrators would use bonuses to reward favorite, rather than better, teachers, and that the programs would threaten the job security of teachers who failed to meet standards.

The arguments in favor of merit pay were that the programs would attract more bright young people into the teaching profession, and that these programs would encourage high levels of effort and performance in teaching. Lamar Alexander, the governor of Tennessee, has been one of the outspoken advocates of merit pay for teachers. In explaining his position, Alexander indicated that his state could not afford to give all teachers high raises, so that the money should be used to encourage and keep the best ones. The old system, he said, featured "low wages, lifetime contracts, little real evaluation—and not one penny of extra pay for outstanding performance." As a consequence, he said, the system rewarded mediocrity. "The longer we reward mediocrity, the longer we'll get mediocrity."

Sources: "Tennessee Governor Signs Merit-Pay Bill," Associated Press, March 7, 1984. Quotes from "Merit Pay for Good Teachers?" *U.S. News & World Report,* July 14, 1983, pp. 61–62.

Exhibit 6.3   The Effects of Outcomes of Behavior on Future Behavior

Outcome	Effect on Future Behavior
Positive or Negative Reinforcement	Increased likelihood of same behavior in similar situation.
Irrelevant Outcome (Neither reward nor punishment)	Eventual extinction
Punishment	Decreased likelihood of same behavior in presence of punishing agent.

Behaviors

Suppose, however, that when employees attempt to take advantage of this policy, the manager's office is empty. If this happens *every time*, they will eventually stop going. The only thing they will be getting out of going to the manager's office is the exercise, an outcome that is irrelevant.

Remember that rewards positively or negatively *reinforce* (strengthen) the behavior they follow; punishment *weakens* the behavior it follows; and no relevant outcome leads to *extinction*. These conclusions are summarized in Exhibit 6.3.

Performance is a function of the interaction between ability and motivation, and the environment in which the performance takes place.

The Eagle team came to work every day because working on the project gave them the opportunity to solve challenging technical problems and earn the respect of their colleagues (reinforcement). They persisted in trying to solve difficult problems because experience had taught them that persistence is eventually rewarded (reinforcement). They avoided using techniques that had not been successful in the past (extinction). They stopped seeking advice from a senior member who berated them all the time (punishment).

Research into whether the laws of reinforcement hold up in the work situation has generally been favorable.[13] Rewarding desired behaviors appears to be a very effective way of influencing employee effort in many, although not all, situations.

The Reinforcement Model and the Basic Motivation Principle.   The most important contribution of the reinforcement model to the basic motivation principle is that it clarifies the roles of other outcomes of behavior. The basic motivation principle tells us that people devote effort to activities that are rewarded. The reinforcement model tells us that they stop doing things that are not rewarded. Both pieces of information are necessary to understand the motivation behind choice and effort in the work place.

IMPLICATIONS OF MOTIVATION THEORIES FOR INFLUENCING EMPLOYEE EFFORT

Our discussion of the practical implications of what we know about motivation will focus on selection, placement, and promotion; training; performance appraisal; and job design and physical working conditions. Keep in mind that an organization is a system; the motivation of its work force is affected by *all* of its personnel practices. The individual manager is important, but he or she is not solely responsible for employee effort.

The Significance in Selection, Placement, and Promotion

Need and expectancy theories strongly suggest the importance of achieving a match between employee characteristics and the job into which he or she is placed or promoted. At the selection level, this agreement may also be useful as a predictor of whether the individual will fit into the organization at all.

Need theory suggests that early sharing of information about the needs of the employee and the rewards that the organization in general (or a specific job in particular) can offer will benefit all concerned. A job applicant who feels the need for social interaction at work is not likely to find working alone rewarding.

Expectancy theory tells us that matching individual values, as well as individual needs, to job characteristics may also have positive motivational effects. We remind you, however, that in both cases, we are speaking of *information* (from the person being selected or promoted) about needs and values, not *assumptions* about universal needs and values.

Expectancy theory also emphasizes the importance of matching employee abilities, skills, and knowledge to the requirements of the job. Hiring, placing, or promoting people to jobs for which they lack the required abilities can lower the effort-performance expectancy, and so lower motivation (effort). A particularly dramatic example of this was provided when a maintenance worker was observed half-heartedly cleaning a mirror that soared from the level of her waist to some four feet over her head. In response to a remark that she needed to be a little taller for the job, the woman replied, "I need to be a *lot* taller. There's no use in even trying. All I do is make a worse mess. They won't give me a ladder either; it isn't in the specifications."

The worker lacked the height to do the job as it was defined. What observers may have chalked up to a sloppy job performance, resulting from laziness or poor attitude was, in fact, lack of a very basic ability. The worker wasn't exerting much effort (wasn't very motivated) because she believed (accurately, in this case) that it wouldn't do any good. In expectancy theory terms, her effort-performance expectancy was very low.

We can hope that this kind of gross mismatch between physical attributes and job requirements occurs infrequently. Mismatches between job requirements and other abilities and skills occur frequently however. They may even exist through promotion, since the ability to do one job does not guarantee the ability to do another one higher on the ladder. However they occur, such mismatches are an unfortunate and unnecessary source of reduced employee motivation.

Implications for Training

Obviously, one way to avoid mismatches between what employees can do and what they are required to do is to supply training. There are probably no jobs for which some form of training would not increase new workers' confidence that they would be able to perform satisfactorily; that is, in general expectancy theory terms, increase the effort-performance expectancy. The assumption that a job is too easy to require training overlooks this confidence factor and probably costs more than it saves in the long run.

Motivation and Performance Appraisal

On the whole, there tends to be considerably more discussion than understanding of the motivational qualities of performance appraisals. A student once remarked, for example, that his poor test score wasn't very motivating. He was saying that bad news was not going to inspire him to do better. The fairly common assumption that it would do so is probably valid for a limited number of people. Feedback is *important* to improved performance, but it doesn't *guarantee* it. Expectancy theory suggests three functions of performance appraisals that are related to motivation.

1. Whether the results of an evaluation are good, bad, or average, they provide information about the relationship between effort and performance. Therefore, they influence the belief that effort may or may not lead to success (the effort–performance expectancy). An employee who exerts a great deal of effort on the job, but consistently gets average evaluations, is getting a message that effort is not achieving the desired performance.
2. For many workers, good performance evaluations are necessary if they are to get valued rewards such as raises, promotions, educational opportunities, and the good opinion of others. In this sense, a good evaluation is an *incentive* for performance so long as there is faith in the validity of the appraisal methods.
3. The perception employees have of the methods by which performance appraisal is accomplished leads to the third connection between performance appraisal and motivation. Because performance appraisal results are often the

means to valued organizational rewards, their relevance, accuracy, and general fairness are of great concern to those evaluated. Performance appraisal methods perceived to be unfair, inaccurate, or irrelevant may be expected to lower the performance-reward expectancy and so motivation.

Implications for Job Design

Much has been made of the implications of need theories of motivation for job design. One argument for job enlargement and enrichment programs described in Chapter 4 is that they allow employees to satisfy higher-level needs. This strategy is based on the assumption that most employees have satisfied lower-level needs and will exert more effort only if it helps meet higher-level needs.

Research has not generally supported one-best-way solutions to motivating employees through job design, but that does not mean the idea has no merit. If it is possible to redesign an existing job, and if the job holders express a desire that it be done, enlarging or enriching jobs can increase the rewards of performing well. In that case, effort, or motivation, should be increased according to the Basic Motivation Principle.

Notice the "ifs." They are big ones. Job redesign requires adjustments in the overall system, and usually some employee retraining, so it is not a matter to be lightly undertaken. Original job design oriented toward making work more interesting requires less investment, but remember the remarks on selection, placement, and promotion. The contingency approach applies here: interesting, meaningful work is best done by people who want interesting, meaningful work. The Eagle project team was made up of such people. The comment of a Ford employee after four weeks at the Saab plant in Sweden indicates that meaningful work is not a universal reward. "If I've got to bust my ass to be meaningful, forget it. I'd rather be monotonous."[14]

Motivation and Working Conditions

For a variety of reasons, management writers, in recent years, have devalued the influence of the physical work environment on motivation. It just didn't seem that there could be a connection between something so complex as motivation and something so mundane as working conditions. In addition, many seemed to believe that giving attention to general working conditions, tools, and equipment smacked of so-called mechanistic scientific management. Fortunately, that seems to be changing. The authors of a recent article about working conditions note, "In many work situations, persons who are both willing and able to successfully accomplish a task may be either inhibited or prevented from doing so due to situational characteristics beyond their control."[15] These authors identified eight groups of situational characteristics. General expectancy theory tells us that trying to per-

Exhibit 6.4   Situational Resource Variables Relevant to Performance

1. **Job-Related Information.**   The information (from supervisors, peers, subordinates, customers, company rules, policies, and procedures, etc.) needed to do the job assigned.

2. **Tools and Equipment.**   The specific tools, equipment, and machinery needed to do the job assigned.

3. **Materials and Supplies.**   The materials and supplies needed to do the job assigned.

4. **Budgetary Support.**   The financial resources and budgetary support needed to do the job assigned—the monetary resources needed to accomplish aspects of the job, including such things as long distance calls, travel, job-related entertainment, hiring new and maintaining/retaining existing personnel, hiring emergency help, etc. This category does not refer to an incumbent's own salary, but rather to the monetary support necessary to accomplish tasks that are a part of the job.

5. **Required Services and Help from Others.**   The services and help from others needed to do the job assigned.

6. **Task Preparation.**   The personal preparation, through previous education, formal company training, and relevant job experience, needed to do the job assigned.

7. **Time Availability.**   The availability of the time needed to do the job assigned, taking into consideration both the time limits imposed and the interruptions, unnecessary meetings, non-job-related distractions, etc.

8. **Work Environment.**   The physical aspects of the immediate work environment needed to do the job assigned—characteristics that facilitate rather than interfere with doing the job assigned. A helpful work environment is one that is not too noisy, too cold, or too hot; that provides an appropriate work area; that is well-lighted; that is safe; and so forth.

Source: Lawrence H. Peters and Edward J. O'Connor, "Situational Constraints and Work Outcomes: The Influences of a Frequently Overlooked Construct." *Academy of Management Review*, 1980, 5, 3, 391–397, page 396.

form as required when there are serious deficiencies in any of these areas (described in Exhibit 6.4) can reduce the effort-performance expectancy, and so, motivation.

Job-related information, tools and equipment, materials and supplies, time availability, and environment are working conditions that can directly enhance or hinder effort and performance. Among the many threats to the success of the Eagle project, at least two fit this category. One occurred when a breakdown of the cooling system made working conditions in the windowless computer lab impossible. A second was when lack of a source for new computer chips called PALs almost terminated the project.

Implications for the Organization's Reward System

By the *reward system*, we mean all those incentives formally offered by an organization for service and performance. Examples include salary, raises, promotions, vacation time, bonuses, private offices, or the traditional key to the executive washroom; that is, any reward that depends on meeting certain standards.

Since what is rewarding depends on the individual who receives the reward, there is no guarantee that incentives will be perceived as rewards. Assuming they are, however, the performance-reward expectancy makes clear that it is important that employees believe they will be rewarded if they meet performance standards.

Exhibit 6.5   Equity of Rewards

Roll call of American Incomes (Median 1981)	
Retail clerk	$ 10,000
Typical hourly worker	$ 13,000
Blue collar factory worker	$ 16,500
Typical supervisor	$ 28,000
Plant manager	$ 36,000
Typical major-league player	$ 162,000
Top corporate executive	$ 450,000
Top 10 baseball players	$1,100,000 (each)
Top 10 corporate executives	$3,000,000 (each)

Source: R. Poe, ''Moneyball.'' *Across the Board*, September, 1981, 12–21, page 17.

There are any number of circumstances that result in rewards not following the accomplishment of specified work performance as expected. Standards may be changed or raised, performance appraisal may be poor or occur too infrequently, or promised rewards may not be available (the company didn't make enough money to pay a bonus, for example). However it occurs, if rewards are not forthcoming as the result of meeting standards, both general expectancy theory and the reinforcement model predict that effort will be reduced. Other guidelines for the use of rewards are presented in the next section.

REWARDS IN ORGANIZATIONS

The effective use of rewards is subject to the contingency approach. When, how, and in what form a manager should reward depends on a variety of individual and organizational factors. There are guidelines that are applicable to any situation.

Guidelines for the Use of Rewards

The following guidelines have to do with formal rewards; that is, with those extrinsic rewards, whatever they may be, deliberately given to an individual or group for meeting or exceeding certain performance standards.

1. Rewards that are perceived as fair relative to the skills required, the effort exerted, the time invested in training, and what other people receive, are more effective than those not so perceived. A recent survey of salaries in certain occupations is reproduced in Exhibit 6.5. You can test your own perceptions of fairness by comparing the position of these occupations with your own ranking.
2. The behavior (or performance level) that will lead to the reward must be clear and understood. Remember the relatively greater effectiveness of measurable goals over ''do your best'' instructions, discussed in the last chapter.
3. In general, the more closely the reward follows the behavior that earned it, the more effective it will be. Rewards based on once-a-year performance appraisals,

for example, have very weak connections with performance. They will be most effective in influencing effort as appraisal time draws near.

4. System rewards, such as group insurance, across-the-board raises, recreational facilities, legal and medical care, and other fringe benefits that come from being members of the organizational system have little effect on effort.[16] They are primarily effective in keeping employees in the organization.

5. The reward should fit the accomplishment. One author illustrated the point as follows: Lavish praise for something which the individual views as routine . . . may backfire. The feeling that relatively minor or marginal work receives as much recognition as the successful completion of a complex task brings with it the feeling that neither is understood or appreciated.[17]

It is interesting to note that many companies are redesigning their management compensation systems so that pay is more closely tied to performance rather than position, tenure, or inflation. In the past, it was common for every manager to receive a raise, regardless of performance. Now, however, many companies are making increases in salary and benefits explicitly dependent upon performance evaluation. At Beneficial Corporation, these new performance-based incentives extend from the top of the company down to assistant vice-presidents. GE changed the stock-option plan for its six hundred top executives so that the best performers will get more options while poor performers will get none. For the five thousand GE managers making over fifty thousand dollars a year, bonuses are contingent upon meeting short-term financial goals, as well as longer-term objectives.[18]

Common Mistakes in the Use of Rewards

The previous guidelines are directed primarily toward those rewards that we have called formal. However, rewarding and punishing go on all the time in organizations, quite independently of formal intentions to reward or punish. There is an informal reward system as well as a formal one.

The informal reward system consists of the day-to-day outcomes of behaviors that result from organizational policies and the reactions of managers and coworkers. It generally receives little attention, despite the fact that it is always operating. The rewards of working with brilliant, dedicated engineers kept the Eagle project team going without formal rewards. The admiration of colleagues was positively reinforcing. Because it is informal and spontaneous, the informal reward system is particularly susceptible to errors. These errors are often unintentional, but that does not alter the damaging effect on employee motivation. The Basic Motivation Principle clearly implies: reward the behaviors you want. The reinforcement model tells us that there are predictable consequences if you do something else.

One common mistake managers make is to *ignore* desired behavior, usually behavior managers take for granted, because they believe it should be automatic. Examples are attendance, punctuality, following standard procedures, and being pleasant to others. All three approaches to motivation that we have studied make it clear that "management by shoulds" is impossible. People don't do what we think they should—they do what they are rewarded for doing.

Strange as it seems, managers often *punish* desired behavior. Suppose, for example, that your boss asked you to fill in and write the monthly report while the employee whose regular task this is, is in the hospital. "Sure," you say, "glad to help out." A week later your boss comes to see you all smiles. "You did a dynamite job on that report! In fact, we liked it so well that we are going to let you do it every month from now on."

The example above illustrates the sad fact that too often the "reward" for doing a good job is getting to do more of it with no extra pay and no reduction of old duties.

On still other occasions, undesired behavior is rewarded. Often these rewards come, however unintentionally, from managers or from organizational policy. The individual who comes late for a meeting, for example, quite often finds that the meeting has been held up until he or she arrives. One way to look at this situation is that it saves the time of repeating what the latecomer misses. Another way to look at it is that the undesired behavior (being late) has been rewarded. The tardy employee is able to finish his or her work without missing any of the·meeting.

Sometimes coworkers provide rewards for behavior that interferes with organizational goals. An employee who is engaging in horseplay instead of working, for example, is usually receiving rewards in the form of attention and appreciation from his or her peers. A manager may be able to suppress the undesired behavior by punishment, but chances are good it will continue in some form when the manager is no longer there to punish.

There are usually conflicting rewards in any situation. By conflicting, we mean that there are rewards from different sources for alternative behaviors, such as working versus horseplay. Social rewards that come from coworkers are likely to conflict with organizational or manager-controlled rewards, and they can be very powerful. Except for such extreme measures as breaking up work groups or transferring individuals, there is little a manager can do to control such rewards.

Sources of rewards beyond managers' control will occasionally maintain undesired behavior. All they can do is try to watch over the outcomes that they *can* control. One part of being successful in the job of managing is knowing the difference between the two.

The Bottom Line

We have come to the end of a two-chapter discussion of the management function of directing. Taken together, the material in these chapters allows us to draw certain conclusions for a practical approach to this important activity:

Chances of increasing employee effort and directing it successfully toward activities that help to accomplish organizational goals are greater when managers (or others in the organization):

1. Set clear goals, the accomplishment of which is possible and can be measured in some way.
    a. Where possible, set goals by means of a joint process involving both the employee and manager.
    b. Make the *behaviors* that will help accomplish the goals (the operative goals), as well as the goals themselves (the formal goals) as clear as possible.

2.   Arrange the environment in ways that will help the performance of the behaviors that meet organizational goals. The details of this arranging depend upon the situation, but the general approach includes the following:
     a.   Select, place, and promote employees with the greatest possible match between individual abilities and job requirements.
     b.   Provide some form of training for every job.
     c.   Give employees the tools and other resources needed to perform the job.
     d.   Remove or reduce as many environmental obstacles (such as noise, confusion, overcrowding) to performance as possible.
     e.   Spend the time, effort, and money required to develop a workable performance appraisal system that seems fair and makes sense to the majority of those evaluated.
3.   Reward the desired performance or other behavior.
     a.   Select, place, and promote employees with an eye toward matching, if possible, the expressed needs and values of employees with the rewards that the job can offer.
     b.   Deliver promised formal rewards when behavior meets standards.
     c.   Informally reward, from time to time, those behaviors that are consistent with goals, even if employees are believed to have an obligation to perform them.
     d.   Avoid, to the extent possible, the punishment of desired behavior.
     e.   Avoid, to the extent possible, the rewarding of undesired behaviors.

SUMMARY

Motivation is a word used to explain observed differences in the choices people make and the amount of effort they exert in various activities, such as work. All behavior is motivated, but it is easier to see effort and performance, rather than the motivation behind them.

The quantity and quality of work performance is determined by a number of factors in the environment as well as by the ability and motivation of the individual. Ability sets the upper limit, motivation puts the abilities to work, and the environment can help or hinder the performance.

The Basic Motivation Principle holds that people expend effort on activities that are rewarding. The three leading approaches to work motivation address different aspects of this principle. Need theories are concerned with what is rewarding. Expectancy theory examines the factors that affect the expectation of a reward, and the reinforcement model focuses on what actually happens as an outcome of behavior.

QUESTIONS FOR REVIEW AND DISCUSSION

1.   What role does motivation play in performance? What is the manager's role in employee motivation?
2.   What are the basic components in expectancy theory? How do they differ from those in the reinforcement model?

3. To understand the difference between factors determining effort that others do and don't have influence over, make two lists, one of factors affecting your effort in this class that the professor has some influence on, the second of factors influencing your effort that are strictly personal.

4. Why do you think need theories of motivation are so popular, despite the lack of evidence for their basic principles? Why is the reinforcement model relatively *unpopular*, despite the considerable evidence that it works?

5. Distinguish negative reinforcement from punishment and from positive reinforcement.

6. A basic message of this chapter is that the level of employee effort in an organization is influenced by the full range of staffing policies and practices. If you view the organization as a system, what is the implication of this message for the individual manager who is attempting to influence employee effort?

7. What are the probable effects on:
    a. a desired behavior that is ignored by the person or organization that desires it?
    b. a desired behavior that is punished by the person or organization that desires it?
    c. an undesired behavior that is rewarded by the person or organization that does not desire it?

8. How might a manager go about influencing a chronic absentee's effort to come to work regularly, using positive reinforcement or punishment? Why is ignoring the behavior probably not going to bring about its extinction?

REFERENCES AND NOTES

1. T. Kidder, *The Soul of a New Machine*. New York: Avon Books, 1981, p. 63.
2. A recent review of this issue is C. D. Fisher's, "On the Dubious Wisdom of Expecting Job Satisfaction to Correlate with Performance." *Academy of Management Review*, 1980, 5, 4, 607–12.
3. A. H. Maslow, "A Theory of Human Motivation." *Psychological Review*, 1943, 50, 370–96.
4. See F. Herzberg, B. Mausner, and B. Snyderman, *The Motivation to Work*. New York: Wiley, 1959.
5. D. C. McClelland, "That Urge to Achieve." *Think*, 1966, 82–89.
6. Maslow's theory was first published about 40 years ago and subsequently excited considerable research interest. This interest has largely died out because of consistent findings that there is little or no support for the foundations of the theory. A good review of both the research and the problems of that research is M. A. Whaba and L. G. Bridwell, "Maslow Reconsidered: A Review of Research on the Need Hierarchy Theory." In R. M. Steers and L. W. Porter, eds., *Motivation and Work Behavior*, 2nd ed. New York: McGraw-Hill, 1979.
7. A representative review of research relative to the two-factor theory may be found in R. J. House and L. A. Widgor, "Herzberg's Dual-Factor Theory of Job

Satisfaction and Motivation: A Review of the Evidence and the Criticism." *Personnel Psychology*, 1967, 20, 4, 369–89.

8. See McClelland, pp. 82–89.
9. A review of this research may be found in E. J. O'Connor, C. J. Rudolf, and L. H. Peters, "Individual Differences and Job Design Reconsidered: Where Do We Go From Here?" *Academy of Management Review*, 1980, 5, 2, 249–54.
10. D. C. McClelland, "Achievement Motivation Can Be Developed." *Harvard Business Review*, 1965, 43, 4, 6–24.
11. The discussion in this section is after the model presented by L. W. Porter and E. E. Lawler, III in *Managerial Attitudes and Performance*. Homewood, Ill.: Irwin, 1968.
12. See J. P. Campbell and R. D. Pritchard, "Research Evidence Pertaining to Expectancy-Instrumentality-Valence Theory." In M. D. Dunnette, ed., *Handbook of Industrial and Organizational Psychology*. Chicago: Rand-McNally, 1976, 84–95.
13. See W. C. Hamner and E. P. Hamner, "Behavior Modification and the Bottom Line." *Organizational Dynamics*, 1976, 4, 4, 3–21.
14. Saab is noted for its experiments in designing "intrinsically meaningful work." The Ford employee is quoted in R. Schrank's *American Workers Abroad*. Boston: MIT Press, 1980.
15. L. H. Peters and E. J. O'Connor, "Situational Constraints and Work Outcomes: The Influences of a Frequently Overlooked Construct." *Academy of Management Review*, 1980, 5, 3, 391–97; quote from 391–92.
16. A full discussion of system versus individual rewards may be found in D. Katz and R. L. Kahn, *The Social Psychology of Organizations*, 2nd ed. New York: Wiley, 1978, 409–17.
17. M. S. Kellogg (revised by I. Burstiner), *Putting Management Theories to Work*. Englewood Cliffs, N.J.: Prentice-Hall, Inc., 1979, p. 10.
18. "The Shrinking of Middle Management," *Business Week*, April 25, 1983, p. 5.

SUGGESTED READINGS

Hamner, W. C. "Reinforcement Theory and Contingency Management in Organizational Settings." In H. L. Tosi and W. C. Hamner, eds., *Organizational Behavior and Management: A Contingency Approach*. Chicago: St. Clair Press, 1974, 86–112. This is an easy-to-read summary for the beginner of the reinforcement approach to influencing employee effort.

Nadler, D. A. and E. E. Lawler, III. "Motivation: A Diagnostic Approach." In J. R. Hackman, E. E. Lawler, III, and L. W. Porter, *Perspectives on Behavior in Organizations*. New York: McGraw-Hill, 1977, 26–36. The article gives a short overview of the expectancy approach to motivation.

Salancik, G. R. and J. Pfeffer. "An Examination of Need-Satisfaction Models of Job Attitudes." *Administrative Science Quarterly*, 1977, 22, 427–56. Alderfer, C. P. "A Critique of Salancik and Pfeffer's Examination of Need-Satisfaction Theories." *Administrative Science Quarterly*, 1977, 22, 658–669. Together, this pair of articles summarizes the pro and con positions about a need theory approach to motivation.

Skinner, B. F. *About Behaviorism*. New York: Vintage Books, 1976. Its leading spokesman talks about the reinforcement model. J. B. Rule of *Newsday* says, "*About Behaviorism* is an opportunity to match wits with one of the great men of psychology and to participate in some of its great debates." We agree.

Case *Sunrise Service*

It was a trying time for everybody, the year The Company built its new extruded expandrium plant in Pocatello. Finally, the business office, the planning office, the architects, and Top Management got everything ready, and construction was begun. Ben Franklyn was to be plant construction superintendent, and Ted Shelby and Stanley were his staff. Their task was to coordinate the efforts of the contractors, the mechanical engineers, the electrical engineers, and the operations people.

Soon they found that this was not easy, and about a month after the ground was broken, Ben found it necessary to call a staff meeting. "I don't like the way this project is going," he told Ted and Stanley.

"Yes, in fact, I analyzed the situation yesterday myself," said Ted. "As I see it, there's a problem in getting everybody together on what's to be done."

"Listen," said Stanley, "I can tell you exactly *what's going on*. One of the electrical engineers comes and says that his group needs another generator installed. So you go to the mechanical engineers to see about the structure to house it, and they're busy working on the ventilating system, and anyhow they can't do a thing about the generator structure until the contractor hires some ironworkers. So you go to the contractor, and he's busy on the main building, and anyhow, he can't submit any plans until the operations people okay the specifications for the generator installation. So you go to the operations people, and they're busy making modifications in the materials flow charts, and anyhow they can't pass on the specifications until the electrical engineers explain to them why they want the extra generator in the first place. All those guys have their own priorities and their own schedules, and none of them worries very much about the others."

"That's right," said Ben, "but what can we do about it? I've tried talking to them about it, but you know how it goes. Everybody gives you smiles and promises, but they just won't get together."

"How about a meeting?" Ted suggested. Ted likes to have meetings.

"Meetings!" says Ben, "We've wasted enough goddamned time already!" Ben doesn't like to have meetings. But then he thinks for a moment and says, ". . . but you know, maybe that's the answer. We'll get those guys together and figure out what everybody is going to do . . . each morning before work."

"But work starts at 7:30," says Stanley.

"Well, an hour should be enough time," says Ben. "We'll meet every morning at 6:30 to coordinate the day's activities."

"Wait a minute," says Ted, who doesn't like meetings that *much*, "if we can't get those guys together now, we certainly can't get them together when we're all half asleep."

"Never you mind," says Ben. "I know what I am doing."

Ben schedules a series of meetings every morning at 6:30 A.M. for the foremen and engineers from his various groups, and he notifies them all that they are expected to be there. For two straight weeks they are there, and though not happy about it, they do manage to solve some of the problems.

The first meeting of the third week, Ben begins by saying, "I can't say how pleased I am about the progress we're making in getting this project straightened out. In fact, if things go well today, I don't know that there is any reason to have a meeting tomorrow morning."

Things go beautifully that day, and Ben skips a day on the meeting. The next meeting ends with Ben saying, "I don't see why

Source: C. Ritti and G. R. Funkhouser, *The Ropes to Skip and the Ropes to Know: Studies in Organizational Behavior.* Columbus, Ohio: GRID, Inc., 1977.

we can't just coast until next week, the way things are going. You guys are really hitting it off now, and as long as you've got the project under control like you do, we don't really need to meet in the mornings. Let's see how things go, and maybe we'll have a meeting next Monday morning."

As it turned out, everything got going so smoothly, and kept going so smoothly, that next Monday's meeting was the last "sunrise service" that anybody had to attend for the duration of the project.

CASE QUESTIONS

1. What was the basic problem facing Ben Franklyn with respect to the management function of directing? Based on what you have learned from this chapter, why do you think "talking to them about" the problem had not worked?
2. Ben was obviously not enthusiastic about the idea of trying to solve his problem with meetings, yet he set them up anyway. What was his purpose? What principle from the chapter does this illustrate? Be specific.
3. Suggest an alternative strategy Ben Franklyn might have used to accomplish his desired goal based on what you have learned in this chapter. Be specific.

Report from the Field *Developing Employee Motivation*

To Roger Boeger, general agent for Connecticut Mutual Life Insurance in Kansas City, the agent in the field is the key to the agency's success. "We try to find the very best individuals and recruit them for our company. Then we do everything we can to develop them, to help them educate themselves in this extremely complex, competitive, and changing business. At the same time we give them challenging goals and personal incentives to develop and produce, surround them with role models—super agents—and create an atmosphere that makes them want to succeed and stay with us.

"Most agents choose a career in insurance for three reasons: they want freedom of action; they want to make money; they want personal satisfaction from their work. So I try to gear their training and supervise along lines that will enable them to do those three things. As general agent, I can provide them with a number of things:

1. broad and specialized services;
2. pride in being with a winning team;
3. opportunities to share ideas with super agents;
4. senior/junior agent relationships;
5. attitudes that are more expansive about our business;
6. tremendous motivation to succeed; and
7. leverage with the home office in solving problems.

"But I don't think that's enough. In talking to ten heads of what I'd call super agencies, I found that we all agreed that a crucial factor was if the general agent found time to give of himself for the agents' benefit. First, that means knowing each agent well enough to be able to give him or her the means for success. That means not treating each agent the same, because they each need some different things. I provide them with an example, in my sincere belief in what we are doing, in my constant enthusiasm, in displaying good work habits and time management, in keeping my financial house in order, in self-discipline, in learning something new and useful every day, in continually looking for and passing on new opportunities, in helping them believe that life insurance can be sold anytime, in setting goals and planning.

"Joint activities, encouragement, incentives, and personal example all contribute to an atmosphere of success. Does it work? I have an agent who led our entire company in disability income premiums in only his sixth full year in the business. One day he told me, 'There is such a success atmosphere in this agency that it would be impossible for anyone to fail.' Obviously that is not totally accurate, but over the past ten years we have retained fifty-one percent of our agents. I am proud of that. In 1980, nineteen of my agents exceeded my income, and for that I am proud, not jealous. After fourteen years in the role of a general agent, I have learned not to compete with an agent for ego superiority, but rather to share the success as an extension of my personal success."

Source: Personal Inverview, December 1983.

7/Controlling

"Dessert? How about Bananas Foster, Chris? They do it well here."

"Fine with me, Cathy. No sense counting calories now, after a meal like that. But level with me," Chris went on, as the waiter left to prepare their dessert, "what's on your mind? You've been biting your tongue all evening."

"Okay," Cathy sighed, "you asked for it. I've been offered a chance to finish my management training early and do a special project for the personnel director."

"Sounds like a pat on the back to me. They don't often give management trainees a chance like that. What's the project?"

"The director wants me to set up a system for 'evaluating and monitoring the engineer/management program' as he put it," replied Cathy.

"Engineer/management? Is that the one where they select bright young engineers from the different company divisions and put them through three months of intensive coursework?" asked Chris.

"That's the one," confirmed Cathy. "Each of the twenty division-heads sends one or two people to each program. They get the equivalent of five semester-long MBA courses in accounting, finance, marketing, economics, and human-resource management in twelve weeks."

"Sounds pretty intense," remarked Chris, "and expensive as well. You figure the salary for thirty or so engineers for three months, plus transportation and living expenses, plus the cost of the instruction—you're talking about half a million dollars for each program. How many do they do?"

"They do three a year; about 150 engineers have gone through the training so far."

After the waiter had served their Bananas Foster and coffee, Chris observed, "The director wants a system for evaluation and monitoring—sounds to me like someone thinks the program needs more control."

"Me too," agreed Cathy. "I've done some checking around. The objective of this program is simply to provide the company with a supply of technical people who can move into management positions when the need arises. It's consistent with the president's idea that managers in this company need to be good technicians first.

"But there's been some grumbling, beginning with the program's cost. Also, some division heads are increasingly reluctant to lose key people for three months. And some engineers are less than eager to be away from their work too long. So somebody, probably the president, decided to find out if the program was measuring up."

"Measuring up," echoed Chris. "That's it in a nutshell. Sounds like you're going to have to specify the program's objectives, get people to agree on some standards, and then see how the program measures up."

"Not only that, but I've got to figure out what to measure and how to measure it before I begin doing the evaluation."

"To say nothing about suggesting ways to determine when corrective action should be taken," added Chris. "I assume this is all being done with the idea of improving the program?"

"I would hope so," replied Cathy. "I imagine the corrective action will be taken care of by the director and the president. Knowing that they'll be using my system—well, it's a great chance to be a hero or a bum."

"I think you ought to take it. The visibility will be great for you. And you'll do a good job."

"All I can do is try," Cathy said, finishing her dessert and calling for the check. "And after this meal, I'm going to have to get my eating back under control. Fortunately, my standards are objective, and measurement is simple—my scales do not lie. Unfortunately, the only corrective action is to diet."

As Chris and Cathy's conversation suggests, control is an essential part of everyday life, both on and off the job. The president of Cathy's company wants to control the expensive engineer-management program. Cathy wants to control her weight. Whether the target is something as simple as weight control or as complex as program control, the basic principles are the same. **Control** is *the process of keeping something within acceptable limits.* Cathy has been asked to design a system to control a training program—to keep it within acceptable limits of success (management-trained engineers) and costs (money, time, and inconvenience).

In management, the control function is a realistic response to the significant difference between a plan and its execution. Exhibit 7.1 summarizes the four managerial functions and describes the role of control in the management process.

Corrective action is necessary either when the plan is not being followed or when it is not working. For example, suppose Cathy discovers that some division heads are not sending their best people, or are actively discouraging their engineers from attending the program. Corrective action would be necessary because they were not carrying out the plan. On the other hand, suppose many of the engineers who completed the program left the company for other jobs. Corrective action would be necessary because the plan was not working.

Management can take corrective action only when it is aware that a plan isn't being followed or isn't working. This awareness is essential to any control process.

Exhibit 7.1   The Role of Control in the Management Process

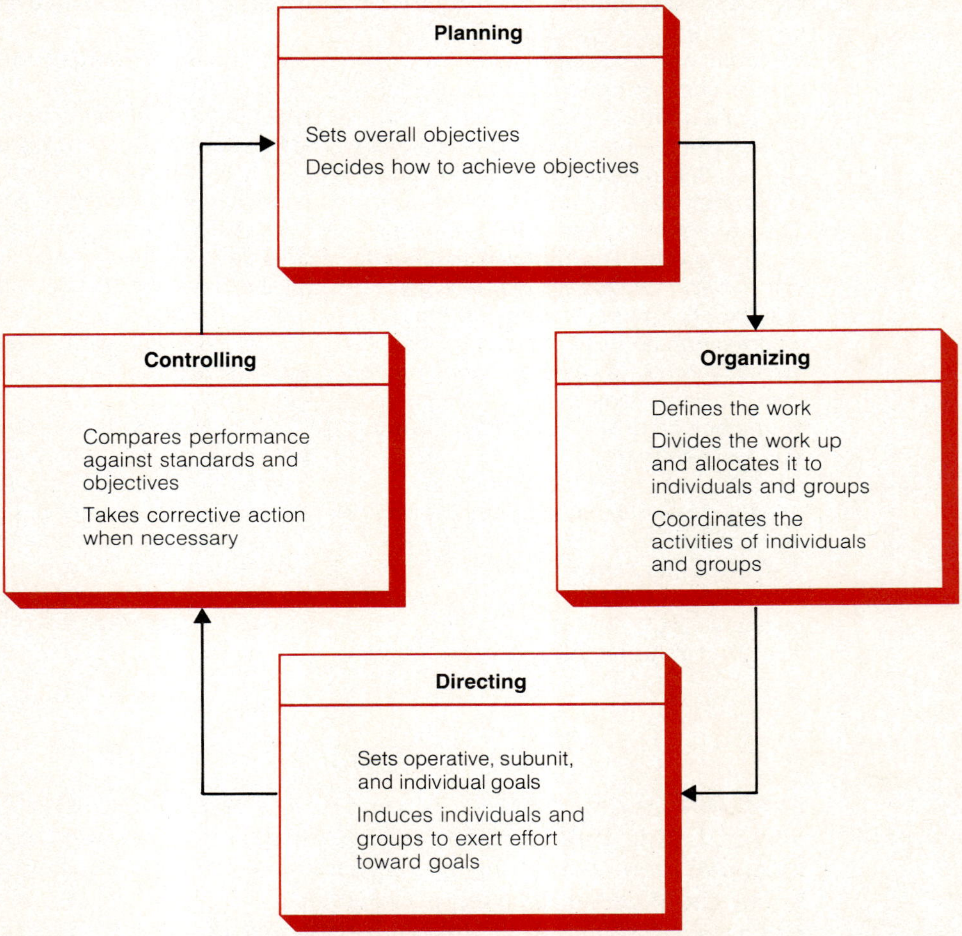

Planning

Sets overall objectives

Decides how to achieve objectives

Controlling

Compares performance against standards and objectives

Takes corrective action when necessary

Organizing

Defines the work

Divides the work up and allocates it to individuals and groups

Coordinates the activities of individuals and groups

Directing

Sets operative, subunit, and individual goals

Induces individuals and groups to exert effort toward goals

THE CONTROL PROCESS

The control process depicted in Exhibit 7.2 is simple. It consists of four steps: (1) setting standards, (2) measuring performance, (3) comparing performance against some standard, and (4) taking corrective action when Step 3 shows that it is necessary.

For example, a baseball manager sets standards for evaluating the performance of a starting pitcher (Step 1). The manager has a coach chart the number of pitches thrown and the number of hits given up by the pitcher (Step 2). Inning by inning, the manager compares this figure against the pitcher's normal standards (Step 3).

By the fifth inning, the pitcher has thrown ninety pitches and given up nine hits; he normally uses only seventy pitches and allows five hits. Based on this informa-

Exhibit 7.2 A Simple Control Process

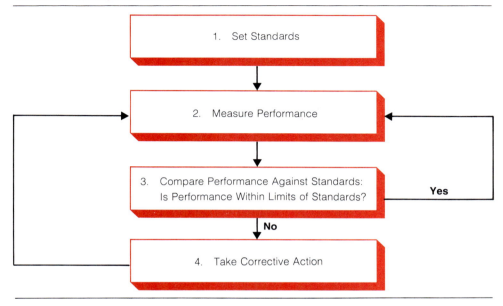

tion, the manager decides that the pitcher is "out of control" and takes corrective action. The manager replaces the starting pitcher with a relief pitcher (Step 4).

In attempting to control more complex systems, the control process itself becomes more complex. A government, in attempting to achieve certain economic goals by controlling inflation, must measure the inflation rate, no mean feat given the countless goods and services consumed by the public every day. The standards, which must be agreed upon, may be influenced by economic and political forces in the country and the world. Finally, the corrective action that will be taken if inflation is "out of control" will be more complex than replacing an individual.

Establishing Methods and Setting Standards

Before performance can be measured or compared against standards, two preliminary steps are required. First, the organization must establish methods for measuring performance, and then it must set standards and control limits for that performance, but these preliminary steps (discussed later in the chapter), will not be effective if performance is poorly measured or standards are carelessly established.

One example of particularly inaccurate measurement in a control process is provided by the management of great cattle ranches in the Old West.[1] Absentee owners relied on local cattlemen to manage their investments. The control system included an annual audit of the herd to compare against expected growth. Discrepancies between the audit figure and expected size indicated problems needing corrective action, such as mismanagement, dishonesty, rustling, or all three.

Unfortunately for the owners, the method for measuring performance was not a physical count of the animals, which might include 50,000 head spread over 5 million acres of unfenced land. Instead, the managers estimated how many cattle there ought to be based on estimated cows, estimated calves, and estimated purchases. These estimates were inevitably overly optimistic, with the result that the discrepancy grew larger each year. In one notable case, a company which showed 39,000 cattle on its books could find only 9000 when it came time to liquidate the herd.

Carelessly set standards can result either in standards which are too restrictive, resulting in overcorrection, or in standards which are too loose, and which do not indicate a need for corrective action until it is too late. The fire at the MGM Hotel in Las Vegas in November of 1980 was a tragic example of loose standards. An inspection of the hotel prior to the fire revealed that the hotel's fire prevention devices conformed to the city's standards for hotels built before 1970. Unfortunately, those standards did not require safety doors in stairwells, smoke alarms, or sprinklers on all floors. Thus no corrective action was taken, and eighty-three people died in the fire.

Types of Control Systems

Managers have borrowed a number of engineering techniques from other professions to enhance their exercise of control. All of these are consistent with the control loop depicted in Exhibit 7.2—standards are set, performance measured, comparisons made, and corrective action taken as necessary. The loop is closed by the line from corrective action back to performance measurement.

Feedback Systems.   A *feedback system provides information about past performance to permit corrective action.* A grade on an exam is feedback for the student about the effects of his effort and intelligence upon his grasp of certain course material. Changes in monthly sales receipts provide to retail stores feedback on the effectiveness of advertising and promotional techniques. The important thing to remember about feedback is that it looks backward—it provides information about how things went, usually in the very recent past—to correct action in the future.

Feedforward Systems.   A *feedforward system attempts to provide information about the future, to avoid errors before they occur.* These systems make some kind of forecast about what will happen if things continue as they are. They enable corrections to be made to keep performance "on course." Feedforward systems are often referred to as *steering controls.*

Updating of plans is a feedforward control when organizational activities are altered to meet forecast changes in the environment. For example, the number of college-age (18–22 year old) Americans has peaked and will continue to decline for the next twenty years or so. Colleges can act now to maintain enrollment in the future by increasing their efforts to serve older Americans, who will constitute a larger potential market.

Go-No-Go Systems. One special kind of control device, a **go-no-go system,** simply *segregates targets into acceptable or nonacceptable categories.* These systems, often called *screening systems,* are particularly useful when safety and speed are objectives.

Airport screening of passengers is a good example. The goal is to allow no one to board an airliner with a lethal or potentially lethal weapon. Screening devices scan passengers and their carry-on baggage for suspicious objects. If nothing is detected, the passenger is allowed to board with his or her baggage. If anything suspicious is detected, the passenger and baggage are detained for closer scrutiny. These systems have been very effective in controlling airline hijacking in the United States.

Management Information Systems. Any control process requires a flow of information concerning standards, actual performance, action taken, and effects of that action. **Management information systems** are *communication systems designed to provide management with accurate and timely information needed for decision making.* As organizations become more complex, the need for efficient and effective management information syspems grows.

One of the steps Cathy could take in her new assignment would be to set up a management information system to monitor the costs and effects of the program. Management information systems will be discussed fully in Chapter 11.

TARGETS OF CONTROL

One way of classifying control systems is by their targets—what kinds of things are being controlled. In organizations we can identify three types of targets—inputs, processes, and outputs, consistent with the systems view of organizations depicted in Exhibit 2.3.

Controlling Inputs

Ultimately, organizations are concerned with output—the number, quality, and costs of goods and services they produce. But, as one of the oldest economic sayings goes, "You can't make a silk purse out of a sow's ear." In other words, it's very difficult, if not impossible, to convert low-quality inputs into high-quality outputs. Computer users echo this by stating, "Garbage In, Garbage Out." You can't get high-quality information output if the data input is sloppy, inaccurate, or irrelevant.

Organizations seek to control both human (personnel) and nonhuman (materials) inputs. The quality and quantity of personnel are controlled through recruitment, selection, and training. Typically, recruitment and selection employ a go-no-go method, in which employees must meet a minimum set of standards to be selected. Sometimes quantity is controlled to meet fluctuations in supply and demand for labor by raising or lowering entrance standards. In this case, a combination of feedforward control, based on forecasts of labor needs and supply, and

Management in Action
Controlling Computer Usage

In recent years the dramatic increase in data tampering and the illegal use of computers for embezzlement and industrial espionage has highlighted the need for better control over the use of computers. The problem is greater than a few spectacular crimes, such as the embezzlem nt of $21.3 million from Wells Fargo in 1981. The growing number of personal computers and clerical terminals makes theft and accidental or planned damage to information possible from every side and at every level of the organization. A computer consultant for Security Pacific Bank used its electronic funds transfer code to send over $10 million to his Swiss bank accounts. Two employees of a Virginia bank procured a computer printout of its securities' customers and took it to a rival bank. A technician at a major corporation got access to the firm's most sensitive files through its computer.

As a consequence, computer manufacturers, users, and cons ltants are developing and experimenting with a variety of control systems to combat this growing and expensive problem. Most of the current systems employ a form of input or process control.

The two major types of input/output controls urrently in use include access control and system integrity. Access controls are physical barriers such as locks on doors, storage devices, terminals, consoles and other input/output devices. System barriers require proper authorization, such as passwords, before permitting access to information. System integrity prevents a user from gaining access to unauthorized parts of the system. A system has integrity when no other paths or processes are available to a user except those for which he or she is explicitly authorized. A particularly perplexing problem for designers of these controls systems stems from the fact that computer experts who want to beat a system can use their computer to generate and test huge numbers of attempts to defeat the controls. Another problem is figuring out how to prevent computer theft by employees who have authorized access to systems.

Firms that use process controls employ both auditing and encryption devices. Auditing is a managerial control tool for verifying that a system is running as it should. Auditors make scheduled and unscheduled checks of users and procedures to look for variations which might suggest actual or potential information leaks. The recent U.S. Foreign Practices Act legislates the use of systems controls, making auditing a necessity, not an option, for many companies. Encryption means coding, storing, and transmitting information in a form that renders it useless to those who do not have access to the code. Although all codes can be broken, the objective of encryption is to make the cost of breaking the code exceed the value of the information encoded. One computer security expert says, "Encryption is the control of the future."

Sources: "How to Achieve Computer Security," *Business Week*, April 20, 1981, pp. 88–92; "Crackdown on Computer Capers," *Time*, February 8, 1982, pp. 60–61; quote from p. 61.

screening control, by adjusting minimum standards, could be used. The topics of recruitment, selection, and training will be discussed at length in Chapter 17.

Controlling the quality and quantity of materials is generally the function of the purchasing and receiving departments. In controlling quantity, purchasing develops inventory-control procedures based on historical data (feedback). These procedures are designed to signal when and how much of a particular material or good should be ordered. The objectives are to meet the economic criteria of minimizing total costs which include costs of the goods, maintaining them in inventory, and running out of the goods (stockout costs). Inventory-control models require accurate feedback on inventory levels as well as on lead times required for delivery of goods purchased.

To control quality, purchasing departments rely on a feedback system while receiving departments use a screening system. The feedback used by purchasing deals with the quality of goods and materials received from particular suppliers. Feedback that a supplier's quality is slipping will usually initiate corrective action in the form of complaints to the supplier, requests for price adjustments, or demands for replacement of low-quality goods (See Figure 7.3). Longer-term corrective action may consist of replacing a poor supplier with a better one.

Exhibit 7.3   An Input Control Process: Controlling Quality of Incoming Parts and Materials

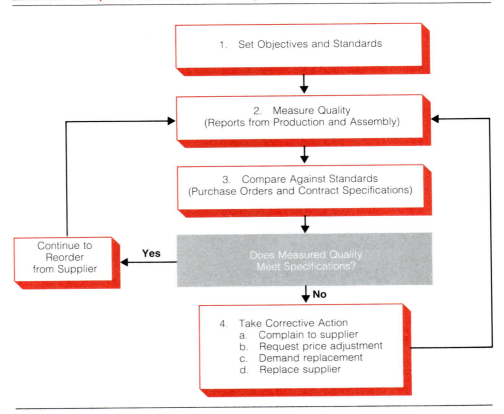

Receiving departments screen incoming shipments to see that they conform to quantities and characteristics indicated on purchase orders. When shipments do not conform (feedback), the discrepancy is usually turned over to purchasing for corrective action, although sometimes receiving may have the authority to refuse a shipment which significantly differs from that which was ordered (go-no-go).

Controlling Processes

By process control the organization seeks to insure that inputs are being transformed into outputs in prescribed ways: that policies, procedures, and plans are being followed. Like input control, process control is used with both human and nonhuman inputs. For example, a hospital must control the transformation of human inputs (sick people) into outputs (healthy people). To this end, hospitals establish process control systems for monitoring admittance and diagnostic procedures, treatment and surgical procedures, dietary, recovery, and discharge procedures.

In many cases, process controls evaluate behavior rather than objects, to see if what is being done conforms to standard rules and procedures. Sampling is used to observe behaviors for a short period of time and compare them with standards. The boss's daily tour of the plant is a form of process control. The measurement is his or her personal observation, the standard is his or her personal standard, and corrective action is an immediate, personal, directive rebuke or reward: control leads to direction.

Management can take corrective action only when it is aware that a plan isn't being followed or isn't working. This awareness is essential to any control process.

A more subtle form of process control is the undercover inspection, in which behavior is observed by an inspector posing as a client or customer. Many bars use undercover inspectors to insure that bartenders are mixing drinks in the prescribed fashion, not overpouring or underpouring, and not pocketing receipts. The FBI conducts undercover operations to discover if public officials are using their offices for financial gain.

Process controls are typically of the go-no-go variety: either the procedure is being followed or it isn't. If it isn't, corrective action is taken.

Obviously, process controls are not confined to observing human behavior. Observing machine operations, reading pressure gauges and thermometers, listening to the sounds of engines are also examples of process control.

Not all process control is formally designed by the organization. Employees and members exercise informal control over each other's behaviors through interpersonal systems involving group norms and sanctions. For example, workers encourage each other to maintain certain standards of efficiency. These important informal control systems are discussed more fully in Chapters 8 and 9.

Mary Ann Sanford makes over 20 critical checks on seat belt systems in GM cars.

She is only one of over 1,800 GM people who make more than 6,000 safety inspections on GM cars built in America.

Checks are made on many things from seat belt retractors to anchor bolts. Latch buckles. Warning lights and buzzers. Every seat belt in every car gets checked. We do this because it's all part of building safer cars. That's important to you. And to us.

We believe in taking the extra time, giving the extra effort and paying attention to every detail. That's what it takes to provide the quality that leads more people to buy GM cars and trucks than any other kind. And why GM owners are the most loyal on the road.

That's the GM commitment to excellence.

Chevrolet • Pontiac • Oldsmobile • Buick • Cadillac • GMC Truck

Safety is a full-time job.

Let's get it together. Buckle up.

Nobody sweats the details like GM.

General Motors publicizes the quality controls made on their seat belt systems.

Controlling Outputs

For some organizations, output controls dominate the control process. This is particularly true when the outputs are tangible material goods. Automobile producers and television manufacturers publicize the extent and tightness of their output controls. Ford advertises that 29 different inspections are performed on its automobiles. Zenith contends that "the quality goes in before the name goes on." BMW emphasizes process *and* output controls, describing them as both "exhaustive" and "traumatic."

Output controls may include feedforward, screening, and feedback systems. Screening is used to limit the number of subquality products that are actually sent out of the organization. Test-driving a car is a form of screening: if it doesn't meet the inspector's standards, the car is reworked until it can pass. Customer and dealer complaints are a form of feedback control. A significant number of complaints indicates that corrections to inputs or processes need to be made, or that screening of outputs needs to be tightened. Feedforward control of outputs might consist of changes in option packages or colors to meet changes or unexpected trends in consumer tastes. If market research indicates a stronger preference for red and white cars, more cars can be produced in those colors to meet the anticipated demand. Of these three systems, screening and feedback are used most often in output controls.

Output controls of less tangible outputs are more difficult to devise. If we consider college graduates as outputs of universities, it is difficult to measure their outgoing quality. Grades, for example, are notoriously unreliable predictors of postgraduate success. Universities tend to alter inputs (through admittance policies) and processes such as programs or courses when the environment seems to call for changes in their outputs, but little effort is made to measure the characteristics of these outputs directly. Feedback from employers is usually erratic and hard to evaluate, and colleges have backed away from comprehensive program examinations as methods of controlling final outputs.

EVALUATING A CONTROL SYSTEM

Before we describe specific organizational control methods, we need to establish some criteria for evaluating their worth.[2] Keeping these criteria in mind will help you judge the extent to which different control methods will work. Characteristics of good control systems are listed in Exhibit 7.4 and discussed below, using Cathy's control system for the engineer/management program as an example.

A Description of a Good Control System

Accurate.   An accurate system is a reliable measure or comparison of performance against standards. An inaccurate system (1) fails to detect problems or (2) signals a problem where none exists. Suppose Cathy relies solely on comments from graduated engineers to assess the program's effectiveness. Having invested three months in the program, they are unlikely to offer evidence of its failure (Type 1 error). Suppose she relies solely on comments from division heads. Those who oppose the program are likely to overstate failures and downplay successes (Type 2 error).

Timely.   The sooner a control system detects and signals the need for corrective action, the more easily can corrections be made. If Cathy's system detects errors at the input stage (i.e., the wrong people are being sent to the program), corrections are easy (replace them with the right people). For every week the system delays in detecting or reporting wrong inputs, considerable time and money are wasted.

Exhibit 7.4   Characteristics of Good Managerial Control Systems

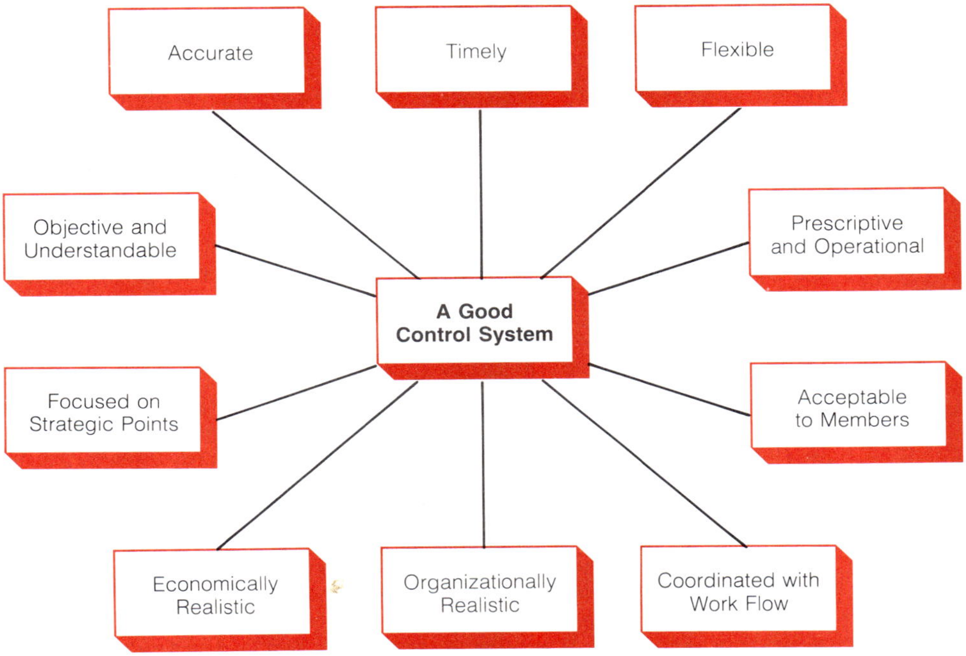

Objective and Understandable.   A good system can be understood and used reliably. A report that "fifty percent of the graduates have moved into management positions, thirty percent remain in technical positions, and twenty percent have left the company" is objective and understandable. A report that "many graduates feel the program has helped them but many others don't" is subject to bias and misinterpretation.

Focused on Strategic Points.   Control systems cost money and effort. Using them efficiently means ensuring that good controls are at work where they really count, points at which detecting problems can really save money, time, and effort; those at which failure to correct problems can be disastrous; or those at which the number of errors or problems is likely to be greatest. Strategic points for Cathy's system to monitor include those points where uncertainty, confusion, or stress are most likely—at the beginning of a program, when participants have no experience in it, and near the end, when they're most anxious about returning to their old jobs and applying their new knowledge. New programs are usually subjected to heaviest scrutiny early in their lives.

Economically Realistic.   The economic realities of control systems indicate that cost/benefit analyses be applied before and during system operation. Systems costing more to run than the savings they generate are economically unrealistic.

Sampling is a method of making control economically realistic. A relatively small percentage of objects is randomly selected from the population to be controlled. (Statistical methods allow controllers to make inferences about the quality of inputs, processes, or outputs involved without inspecting every item in the population.) Instead of investigating the careers of all 150 graduates of the program, Cathy could analyze in some depth the careers of twenty or thirty graduates selected by careful sampling techniques.

Organizationally Realistic.   A control system is organizationally realistic when it is consistent with the organization's status and authority systems. The program Cathy is evaluating was designed by people two and three levels above the engineers in the managerial hierarchy. The engineers in the program may be reluctant to criticize those of considerably higher status. Additionally, those with the power to take corrective action might be reluctant to rely heavily on evaluations of people untrained in measurement and observation of training programs. Therefore, one alternative to relying solely on the feedback of the engineers would be to bring in outside consultants.

> *While policies serve as general guidelines, procedures control specific actions to be taken in certain circumstances. Procedures often, though not always, specify the means by which policy will be implemented in certain regularly occurring conditions.*

Coordinated With the Work Flow.   Control systems that disrupt the normal flow of work may cause more problems than they solve. Cathy should avoid measurement methods that might interrupt classes during the training program or take people's time away from their work. Unobtrusive measures such as looking at job and project assignments and performance evaluations will help Cathy collect information with little disruption.

Flexible.   A flexible control can be adapted to meet unusual circumstances while still meeting standards of objectivity and consistency. Special requirements of handicapped engineers attending the program could be included in the costs of the engineer/management program without disrupting standards.

Prescriptive and Operational.   Prescriptive and operational systems indicate the action to be taken to maintain control and ensure that corrective action is both feasible and flexible. Cathy's system might include formal recognition of achievement in the program and counseling for participants experiencing academic, personal, or family problems during or after the program.

Acceptable to Members.   Problems can arise if controls are not acceptable to those who must implement them. Cathy's system should consider not only the people running the program, but the participants, their superiors, and those who will be designated to take corrective action. For example, attempting to control learning by stating that any participant receiving a C will be terminated is likely to be unacceptable. Faculty will be unwilling to give Cs, and likely candidates will be unwilling to enter the program.

An Example of a Good Control System

A good control system with which many people are familiar is the subway fare-collection system used in many major cities. Its purpose is to control access to the subway trains so that only those who have paid the proper fare can ride. All passengers enter the system through turnstiles. These turnstiles rotate far enough to admit one passenger only when the proper token has been inserted.

The token is the measure. It is compared against standards using a go-no-go method (the token or coin either passes through a template or doesn't), and action is taken. If the token passes through the template, the turnstile is released for one rotation. If the token does not pass, the turnstile remains locked.

The system is accurate. Only a prescribed token will operate it, and each token may be purchased only for the correct fare. It is timely. It screens the passengers before they gain access to the trains, rather than during or after their rides. It is objective and comprehensible. Posted signs clearly indicate the cost of tokens and their use, and the turnstile admits each passenger who presents the proper token.

Focusing the turnstiles at strategic points—between the street and the boarding platform—makes observation and detection of attempted cheaters easier. The system is both economically and organizationally realistic. A machine will collect several times its cost in fares every day. It is simple to operate and easily repaired.

The overall system is flexible and coordinated with work flow by locating outlets which sell tokens between sets of turnstiles. People without tokens can purchase them easily, out of the way of people with tokens, thus interrupting the flow of passengers as little as possible. Agents selling tokens provide the flexibility. They can automatically open a special gate for emergency use, admitting passengers with monthly passes, or repair or maintenance personnel.

Finally, the system is prescriptive, operational, and acceptable to both the riding public and the personnel. Everyone knows what to do or can learn. The system works, and people pay their fares. Personnel guard the system, and make every effort to insure that no one beats it. Like every system, this one is beaten occasionally, but the risks involved make wholesale cheating too expensive.

METHODS OF CONTROL

Now that we have a set of criteria for evaluating control systems, we can discuss several techniques managers use to control organizational activities. The most common techniques can be categorized according to their primary control targets—inputs, processes, or outputs (Exhibit 7.5).

Exhibit 7.5   Organizational Control Targets and Methods

Target	Inputs	Processes	Output
Examples	Personnel Equipment Supplies Money Information	Routine Activities Methods Projects Emergencies	Goods Services Information
Methods	Standards Training Budgets MIS	Policies Audits Standard Operating Procedures Performance Appraisal Project Control	Goals MBO Quality Control Public Relations

Methods for Input Control

The inputs organizations need in order to function are people, equipment and supplies, money, and information. Information as both an input and a process is controlled by the management information system, discussed in detail in Chapter 11. People, equipment, and supplies as inputs are controlled primarily through the use of standards, while money is controlled through the use of budgets.

Standards.   In Chapter 4 we discussed the role of standardization in organizing work. Tasks are divided up to permit specialization, and standardization is used as one means of helping to coordinate specialized work. By using standards to screen incoming personnel, equipment, and supplies, management makes it easier to integrate these inputs into the organization's activities and processes.

If all management recruits meet certain standards of education, intelligence, and aptitude, they can all be sent through a management training program designed for people meeting these standards. *Training* is a way of further controlling human inputs. It insures that employees have sufficient skills and knowledge of company procedures and policies to function effectively in their work.

The use of standards in purchasing and receiving goods and machinery was discussed earlier in this chapter. Organizations also purchase services, which are, likewise, inputs to which standards can be applied. The kinds of services purchased range from janitorial and secretarial help to market research, product research, bookkeeping, and executive recruiting. Companies buy transportation, waste and disposal, and catering services.

Service inputs are usually controlled by performance standards written into service contracts. These standards indicate both the quality and quantity or frequency of the services to be rendered. Such contracts usually include statements about corrective action to be taken if standards are not met.

Budgets.   Budgets, the subject of Chapter 16, are used to control the amount of money (financial inputs) an organization has to work with over a given time period. Budgets may also control how financial inputs are used. For example, a college athletic department may have a budget of $2.4 million for 1986, of which $400,000 is budgeted for administration, $500,000 for scholarships, $100,000 for maintaining facilities, and the remaining $1.4 million for operating the various sports offered by the athletic department.

The extent to which internal budgets (the way a department spends the money it is allocated) are controlled may vary. Typically, the overall budget is rigid: the athletic director will get no more and no less than $2.4 million in 1986. However, the director may spend a little more on operations than the budgeted $1.4 million, making up the difference by saving on maintenance expenses. Internal budgets are usually established or approved by the athletic board, whose approval may be required before any major reallocation can be made.

Methods for Process Control

Controlling the everyday processes of an organization, as well as emergencies and special projects, requires a number of methods. The most common methods used include audits, policies, standard operating procedures, performance appraisals, and project control methods.

Audits. An audit attempts to provide an accurate picture of an organization at a particular time, to see if its processes are functioning as they should. Like a medical checkup, the ideal audit is a critical appraisal by an objective expert who looks for problems and determines whether policies and procedures are being followed.

There are three types of financial audits—external, internal, and management. People tend to be more familiar with *external audits*, which are conducted by chartered or certified public accountants. Their purpose is to prove that the company has adhered to generally accepted accounting principles in conducting its financial affairs. External audits typically use sampling procedures to insure that the company's reported figures are accurate. These inspections are a major way of controlling fraud and embezzlement.

Internal audits are designed to go beyond verifying the accuracy of financial reporting. They attempt to assess the efficiency and effectiveness of control systems, and whether or not these systems are being followed. For example, the sales control system may require that each sales invoice be checked for accuracy of quantities billed, prices used, calculations, and credit terms, as depicted in Exhibit 7.6. This procedure makes it possible to pinpoint responsibility should discrepancies arise. An internal audit can determine if these checks are being performed, and if the control is sufficient.

Personal observation can be thought of as a type of internal audit. It is unsystematic and generally haphazard, yet most managers find some time every day to conduct "a tour of the plant." The direct effectiveness of personal observation as a control device is limited. Employees are likely to modify their behavior when the boss is coming, so the chances of observing deviations from SOPs are small. How-

Exhibit 7.6   Internal Control Questionnaire for a Sales Audit

Client _Kingston Company_ Audit Date _December 31, 1984_
Names and Positions of Client Personnel Interviewed: _Mr. Samuel Corboy (Controller)_
Mr. Julian Grace (Chief Accountant)
Auditor _Harold Groody (Senior Account)_ Date Completed _September 17, 1984_
Reviewed by _Titus Balstrade (Manager)_ Date Reviewed _September 20, 1984_

Question	NA	Yes	No	Remarks
SALES				
1. Briefly describe method of recording sales.				Billing clerk matches invoice with sales order, enters prices, extends and foots. Sends daily batches to keypunch for EDP preparation.
2. Are customers' orders subjected to review and approval before invoice is prepared:				
a. By sales or order department?		✓		
b. By credit department?		✓		
3. Are blank invoices prenumbered?		✓		
4. Are blank invoices available only to authorized personnel?		✓		
5. Are sales and order department personnel denied custodial access to assets?		✓		
6. Are bill of lading forms prenumbered?			✓	Potential loss of data control.
7. Are back orders or pending files reviewed periodically? How often?		✓		Weekly
8. Are invoices checked for accuracy of:				
a. Quantities billed?		✓		
b. Prices used?		✓		
c. Mathematical calculations?		✓		
d. Credit terms?		✓		
9. Are completed invoices compared with customer orders?		✓		By billing clerk.
10. Are returned items cleared through the receiving department?		✓		
11. Does the system provide control over:				
a. Sales to officers and employees?		✓		
b. Sales to subsidiaries and affiliates?		✓		
c. Scrap and waste sales?		✓		
d. Sales of equipment?		✓		
e. C.O.D. sales?	✓			
f. Cash sales?		✓		
12. Are there accuracy checks on date prepared for EDP departmnts:		✓		Control totals are prepared but not used for control.
a. Control totals?				
b. Key verification?		✓		
13. List and describe programmed EDP controls. _Self-checking customer code_ _Limit check on sales account_				Unique code for each customer for sales over $5,000.

Source: J.C. Robertson, *Auditing* (rev. ed.). Dallas: Business Publications, 1979, p. 202.

ever, plant tours may be indirectly effective. They reinforce employee perceptions of authority, demonstrate that there is interest in what they are doing, and sometimes provide an opportunity for upward communication about work problems.

Management audits are conducted by outside agencies employed to evaluate several aspects of management and company performance. Areas include such diverse targets as health of earnings (certain financial ratios compared to industry norms), research and development, corporate structure, sales effort, and executive ability and integrity.

Outside experts are usually retained to ensure objectivity. Metropolitan police departments have come to rely on civilian review boards to evaluate police policies and procedures. These review boards evolved out of the public's mistrust of internal police review procedures.

The problem of subjectivity in internally performed management audits is common. Archie McCardell, the chief executive officer and chairman of International Harvester, was lured to IH from Xerox in 1977.[3] Inducements included a $1.8 million loan. The conditions of the loan were tied into Mr. McCardell's performance. If he succeeded in raising Harvester's profits to the average rate of six competitors within seven years, the loan would be forgiven. However, one additional contract clause permitted even earlier forgiveness of the loan for "spectacular performance." Spectacular performance was not specified in the contract, but its definition and measurement were left up to the board of directors.

Harvester enjoyed one good year under McCardell. But a strike in 1980 lead to a $400 million loss. In May of 1982, McCardell resigned as chairman, having presided over losses so great that Harvester was threatened with bankruptcy.[4] Nevertheless, the board was generous in its evaluation. In 1980 it applied the "spectacular performance" clause, and forgave his $1.8 million loan in a unanimous decision, thus demonstrating the difficulty of maintaining objectivity during an internal evaluation.

Policies.   A policy, as first discussed in the chapter on planning, is a governing principle, a guideline for action. It can be thought of as a written standard which helps control decision making. Policies are types of feedforward control—they serve to steer or guide future organizational activity.

Policies typically evolve from an organization's past experiences. Informal procedures that work well and help achieve organizational goals often become written policies. These serve as reminders of actions that have worked to the company's benefit, in hopes that, if decisions continue to be made in that way, the organization will continue to benefit.

Policies also evolve from past mistakes. For example, one metropolitan police department recently adopted a stringent policy for the use of firearms by its officers.[5] Officers may not fire their weapons as warnings, to apprehend, arrest, or stop fleeing felons, but only to prevent someone from being killed. The chief instituted the policy in response to a number of incidents. In two cases, teenagers were paralyzed after being shot by police; in another case, an officer killed a fellow officer whom he had mistaken for a suspect.

Most small businesses start with very few policies, but develop them from their experiences. Owners eventually learn to create rather rigid policies controlling the handling of cash, inventory, and access to computers and long-distance telephones. Failure to institute such controls has bankrupted many naive small businesspeople.

It has become increasingly common for organizations to enact policies in direct response to outside agencies or pressures. Many companies have adopted affirmative-action policies in response to social and legal pressures to hire more women and minorities. These policies serve as guidelines for managers by directing them to actively recruit female and/or minority employees and by providing them with incentives and resources to do so.

Occasionally the control processes of certain governmental agencies are themselves subjected to review and corrective action. In 1983 an Eastern Airlines jumbo jet lost power in all three engines and nearly ditched in the Atlantic, because its mechanics had failed to install oil seals. Monitoring aircraft maintenance procedures is the airline's responsibility, but the Federal Aviation Administration is responsible for overseeing the airline's procedures. In its review, the National Transportation Safety Board concluded that the incident reflected serious control problems at both Eastern and the FAA. The Board discovered that a dozen incidents of faulty maintenance had occurred before the near-tragedy, but neither Eastern management nor FAA inspectors recognized them as signals of serious problems and did nothing to change maintenance procedures. NTSB chairman Jim Burnett, in discussing the Board's corrective action, said, "It is not simply enough to punish the mechanics involved when we had management people that were not developing a system that would be foolproof."[6]

Procedures.   While policies serve as general guidelines, procedures control specific actions to be taken in certain circumstances. Procedures often, though not always, specify the means by which policy will be implemented in certain regularly occurring conditions. For example, most department stores have procedures for employees to follow in dealing with customer refunds, returns, or exchanges of merchandise. A typical policy is to permit no refunds thirty days after purchase. A typical procedure to implement that policy is to require a customer to prove the date-of-purchase with a sales slip before approving a refund, return, or exchange.

Project Control Methods.   In Chapter 3, we described the role of projects in planning. A project plan is a single-use plan designed to cover a set of activities leading to a specific goal.[7] There are a number of methods that seek to coordinate the various activities in order to complete the project on schedule.

The simplest project control method is the *Gantt chart*. It is used to help control unrelated projects by providing a visual display of actual progress compared to targeted progress. When kept up to date, it shows the manager whether each task is ahead of, behind, or on schedule. When tasks are behind schedule, it is up to the manager to take corrective action. In Exhibit 7.7, which shows the status of five projects as of November 22, projects one and two were started and completed on time, project three started a week late, four is on schedule, and the last is scheduled to get under way shortly.

PERT and CPM are two methods for controlling related projects. We have already described these methods in Chapter 3. They serve the same function as a Gantt chart: keeping the manager aware of actual progress versus scheduled progress. In addition they indicate interrelationships on projects: what activities must be accomplished before other activities or projects can be started.

One of the advantages of PERT and CPM in project control is that they identify the most critical activities having the greatest potential for delaying a project. We stated earlier that good control systems concentrated on strategic points. Using PERT or CPM to identify critical activities enables a manager to concentrate efforts and resources on those activities which are crucial for successful completion—a strategic use of control.

Performance Appraisal. The performance appraisal, introduced in Chapter 6, is a systematic evaluation of an individual's or group's job-related behavior. It measures the efficiency with which the organization is using its human resources, and helps maintain organizational control.[8]

As a control device, performance appraisal measures job performance and evaluates that performance against some standards. Information from that evaluation is used to control current job performance and also provide feedback for the staffing system—if performance is deficient, perhaps hiring or promotion criteria need to be changed: Current methods might be putting the wrong people in certain jobs.

The measurement of job performance is a difficult task for a manager. First of all, most jobs involve a lot of different activities requiring many different skills. Second, a manager usually has more than a few people to evaluate, some of whom

Exhibit 7.7   A Gantt Chart Showing the Status of Projects

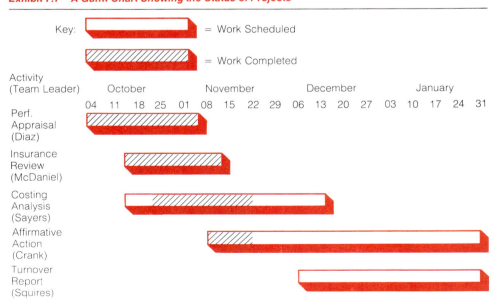

may work in different areas. Thus, a great deal of effort has been expended to find ways for managers to evaluate their employees. Some methods include personal observation, self-assessment by the employee, ratings by the employee's peers, and evaluation by client or customer. Others include the use by managers of questionnaires, checklists, and videotapes. Finally, objective measures are used such as units produced, units sold, net profits, or material wasted.

Evaluating the performance once it is measured is usually done in one of two ways. The first is *evaluation by comparison:* how well did the individual perform compared to his or her peers? Academy awards, selection of allstar teams, and grading on a curve are all examples of evaluation by comparison. The second is *evaluation against predetermined standards:* how well did the person perform compared to some impersonal criterion? When we say that a person should sell $150 per day minimum, or that 80 units is a standard day's production, or that a student needs to answer 90 percent of the test questions correctly for an A, we are evaluating against predetermined standards.

Performance appraisal as a control device is somewhat unique in that the target is part of the control process. Any performance appraisal eventually provides feedback to the employee. This feedback may come directly in the form of a review between the employee and his or her boss, or indirectly in the form of promotions, raises, or other outcomes, and thus may affect motivation and effort. Employees can use this feedback for self-control. If their appraisals are satisfactory, they can continue doing what they've been doing. If their appraisals are not satisfactory, they may take corrective action and change their job behaviors.

Methods for Output Control

Ultimately, organizations are evaluated by their outputs. Most of what occurs in selecting, receiving, and processing inputs goes on internally, away from public scrutiny. The quality, number, and cost of goods and services produced are the things for which organizations are known and upon which their eventual success or failure depends. Thus, most organizations pay a great deal of attention to controlling their outputs. Three kinds of output control will be discussed here—goals, management by objectives, and quality control.

Goals. Goals (introduced in Chapter 5) measure not only outputs which the organization provides for its customers and clients, but also outputs which departments, groups, or individuals within the organization provide for each other. For example, an army recruiter may have a goal of enlisting thirty recruits per month. These recruits and others go through training, where the commanding officer has a goal of providing 1500 skilled recruits every six weeks. These graduates join others and are assigned to various army units throughout the world, each of which has specific manpower and training goals.

The use of goals as control devices has several advantages. First, as we discussed in Chapter 5, goals are effective devices for channeling and directing human effort. They serve as steering or feedforward control devices. Second, goals provide some room for flexibility and ingenuity on the part of the individual or group being managed. This alleviates the need for the manager to stress input and process controls; the individual or group can assume some of that responsibility. Finally, goals concentrate attention where it matters most.[9] Any organization is complex enough to lose sight of the important objectives. A manager who spends all his or her time worrying about subunit inputs and processes may neglect the bottom line—productivity and output.

Management by Objectives.   Management by objectives (MBO), as described in Chapter 5, is basically a joint goal-setting process. In simple form, managers and their subordinates each set individual goals for themselves and for their areas of responsibility. They then meet to negotiate differences and reach joint agreement on their goals. Finally, they meet periodically to review goal progress and to take corrective action if necessary.[10]

Management by Objectives

1.   *Set goals individually.*
2.   *Meet to negotiate and jointly agree on goals.*
3.   *Periodically review progress and take action.*

If we look at MBO in terms of our basic control model in Exhibit 7.1, we can see its major advantages. First, MBO facilitates the evaluation process. When managers and subordinates sit down to discuss and negotiate goals, they are communicating about each others' standards. If this negotiation process leads to jointly agreed-upon goals, then the standards by which performance is to be evaluated should be clear to all concerned.

Second, MBO facilitates the corrective action phase of control. Periodic reviews of progress are designed to find out whether sufficient progress is being made, whether performance is under control. If performance is not under control, decisions about corrective action can be made or initiated during the meeting.

An especially good feature of the MBO review process is that if a problem exists which is beyond the subordinate's control, the manager's help can be immediately enlisted. For example, slow progress may be the result of manpower shortages, a problem which must be corrected by the manager.

MBO does not, however, provide much help in the measurement phase. It does tell us what things should be measured, but leaves the problem of how to actually measure performance up to the individuals concerned.

Quality Control.   Controlling the quality of outputs is a two-phase process. First, of course, quality must be built into the product. Seeing that quality goes into the product is really a form of process control, making sure that procedures are followed correctly.

Production control systems can be very elaborate, such as this one in a large bakery. The system can evaluate a batch of products in an attempt to ensure the quality. Then a decision to accept or reject an entire batch can be made based on the sample.

One of the most publicized quality-control programs is **zero defects**—*a quality control program with a stated objective of attaining error-free performance.* "Do it right the first time" is a common slogan in a zero-defects program.

The zero-defects concept was begun at the Martin Company in Orlando, Florida, in 1962 and gained wide acceptance among military and defense contractors. A typical program includes frequent in-process inspections and special bonuses or other incentives for error-free performance.

The problem with zero-defects is in economic reality, one of the criteria we discussed earlier for evaluating control systems. For most goods and services, the additional cost incurred as a process moves from high quality (a few defects) to perfect quality (zero defects) is going to exceed the additional savings or revenues obtained from that higher quality. If it cost $100,000 more to increase quality from one-percent defectiveness to zero-percent defectiveness, while additional sales increase only $80,000, the move to zero defects is economically unrealistic.

The second method of controlling quality is through inspection, to reduce the number of defective goods and services which actually reach the consumer. An inspected product either meets or exceeds some minimum quality standards and is okayed for shipment, or it fails to meet the standards and is scrapped or sent back for rework.

Acceptance sampling is an inspection process designed to control output quality by insuring that no more than some specified percentage of outputs fail to meet minimum standards. In acceptance sampling, inspectors analyze a random sample of outputs. (Inspecting *every* item of output is used only where the costs of a single defect are very high). Based on the characteristics of the sample, the inspectors then decide whether to accept or reject the batch of outputs from which the sample was drawn. For example, suppose inspectors analyzed a sample of fifty toys from a run of a thousand and found three defective ones. If the company had decided to keep defective products to three percent or less, the run would be rejected because the probability that the run was more than three percent defective would be very high.

Acceptance sampling is preferred to 100-percent inspection when:

1. The costs of letting defects go are not high.
2. The costs of inspection are high.
3. Mental or physical fatigue would reduce inspector performance.
4. Inspection would destroy or flaw the product.

Whatever the inspection procedure, remember that inspection is only a *part* of the control process. Inspection must be linked to corrective action to achieve control.

PROBLEMS AND ISSUES IN CONTROL

The control process raises a number of issues for managers. One is that of *cost*. Controls cost time, effort, and money. Setting standards which are stricter than necessary or using corrective action which is more drastic than needed are costly misuses of control systems. Other issues arise in the areas of measurement, standards, and corrective action.

Problems in Measurement

Measurement Error. The accuracy with which a control target is measured is a problem when objective measures are not available . When control relies on human perceptions, all sorts of error can take place.

In one study, 245 experienced inspectors were tested on their ability to use the precision micrometers they normally used in inspection.[11] The results found that a large majority of the inspectors failed to use the instruments to the standard levels of precision. In fact, 91 percent of the inspectors failed the tests for two of these instruments. Training and periodic updates of training are clearly needed in any control system which relies heavily on human judgment.

Right to Privacy.   In systems requiring information about people for control purposes, the right to privacy is at issue. The control of selection processes for hiring is an area where this issue has become noteworthy. May prospective employers require applicants to take lie detection tests, to divulge information about their military records, police records, marital status, and plans for parenthood? In recent years, courts have protected the rights of applicants, ruling, for example, that employers do not have the right to an applicant's arrest record or parenthood plans.

In attempts to control the quality of public officials, laws have been passed requiring political candidates to divulge everything from information about possible conflicts of interest to complete financial records. These requirements have led many prospective candidates to withdraw. Some candidates felt the office wasn't worth the loss of privacy, particularly in cases when the information requested was irrelevant to the job. The Public Information Act may be a control system which costs more than it is worth, since it may result in the loss of some highly qualified candidates.

Problems in Evaluation

Contradictory Evaluations.   A control system can be stymied when there is disagreement about whether the object meets or falls short of the standards. Refer back to Exhibit 7.1. That figure indicates clear responses to unambiguous evaluations. When standards are met, the response is simply to continue monitoring. When standards are not met, the response is corrective action. But when it is not clear whether or not standards are met, the response is not clear.

Control systems designed to monitor human behavior may have a built-in response for contradictory evaluation—an appeals process. When a defense lawyer evaluates the defendant's behavior differently from the way it was evaluated by the judge or jury, the evaluation can be appealed to a higher court. When an employee disagrees with a superior's evaluation of the employee's performance, appeals are sometimes possible. But in most situations and most organizations, contradictory evaluations lead to internal conflict which can bring the entire control process to a grinding halt. To a certain extent contradictory evaluation problems can be alleviated by clear, agreed-upon standards and well-trained evaluators.

Obsolete Standards.   Sometimes standards remain fixed while times or situations change. The system continues to control performance in ways that no longer make sense. Using only the husband's salary to control credit extended to a husband and wife is obsolete in an era when it is common for both spouses to be equally employed or for the wife to be the better paid or more stable wage earner of the two. Limiting the interest paid by banks and savings and loans to five and one-half percent in a year when the rate of interest charged by banks exceeds twenty percent is an obsolete standard. Control systems to monitor control systems and take corrective action when necessary may not be popular. However, they may become so as instances of obsolete standards become more frequent.

Determining Who Sets Standards. Determining who should set performance standards has generally been settled on the basis of power rather than of effectiveness. That is, setting standards is an act of power, and those with power and authority in organizations have been the ones to set standards.

In some instances, society wrests some power from organizations by imposing standards on them. Auto-emission and gasoline-mileage standards have been imposed on the automobile industry, medical-care and physical-plant standards have been imposed on the nursing-home industry, and return-on-investment standards have been imposed on certain segments of the utility industry. Organizational effectiveness and efficiency were not the issues in these cases; power was. Controls were imposed to rectify an imbalance of power which these industries were perceived to have over the consuming public.

Fear of externally imposed standards has led many professions to attempt self-regulation. Accountants, lawyers, and doctors have established standards in the hope that setting and enforcing their own standards will prevent the public from imposing outside control.

There has been a recent trend toward allowing members at lower levels of an organization to have some say in the standards by which they are governed. There is as yet little evidence that such participation in standard-setting improves its efficiency or effectiveness.[12]

Problems in Corrective Action

Reject vs. Rework. When a product fails to meet standards, a major issue is whether that product can be salvaged: Will it be cheaper to scrap the item or to correct the defects? The same issue arises when an individual fails to meet standards. Should rejected applicants be given remedial training and another chance? How many opportunities should an employee be given to meet promotion standards before being terminated? How often should a student be allowed to try to pass a required course before being dropped from the program?

Organizations tend to give individuals who fail more chances than they give products. Nevertheless, costs of additional training or opportunities can become excessive, particularly when there are other people whose opportunities to succeed or fail are being blocked.

Determining Who Gets the Feedback. Performance feedback is more likely to go to those who set and enforce standards than to those who must try to meet them. This again reflects the fact that those in power set standards and control feedback.

From an effectiveness standpoint, however, those whose performance is being motivated should be included in the feedback process. Performance improves with feedback and deteriorates without it. Preventing individuals from getting accurate performance feedback is a very expensive means of demonstrating power. From the standpoint of organizational effectiveness, accurate feedback is an important asset.

╱▟ ▟ **The Bottom Line** ▰▰▰▰▰▰

Most managers would like to have more control. If they were satisfied that inputs, processes, and outputs were "under control," they could spend more time planning, organizing, and directing effort toward greater opportunities, efficiency, and effectiveness. In striving to increase control, successful managers should take into account the following:

1. Control is a tool to help achieve goals; it is not an end in itself. Good control systems do not dominate an organization, but are coordinated with work flows.
2. Controls which are misunderstood or not accepted by those who must use them will not work. Few managers have sufficient power to coerce their subordinates into using or being controlled by systems they reject. Most people, however, are capable of exerting at least some self-control when the mechanisms and objectives of control are clear and reasonable. Involving those who must use control systems in their designs is a way of increasing the likelihood that the systems will work, while at the same time lightening the manager's workload.
3. Corrective action does not necessarily mean punishment. Activities and processes can be kept in control through the use of direction, feedback, and incentives. Remember that punitive control is much more complex than positive control and creates incentives to avoid punishment by escaping detection.
4. Managers have a variety of methods to use to help control inputs, processes, and outputs. The contingency approach is applicable in control: the best control method depends upon the target and the situation.
5. Economic realities of organizational life mean there will be no perfect control systems—the costs are too great. Therefore, managers should focus their controls on strategic points at which the costs of control will reap the greatest benefits.
6. Control systems, in themselves, can have systemic effects throughout the organization. Managers aware of this will avoid designing control systems that create larger problems than they solve.

SUMMARY

The purpose of control is to keep the organization, its activities, plans, and personnel moving toward their objectives. Control is needed because there are always differences between a plan and its execution. Managers can control these differences by measuring performance or objects, comparing them against predetermined standards, and taking corrective action when necessary.

Organizational control systems depend on the accurate and timely flow of information. In feedback systems, information about what has happened is used to determine the need for and kind of corrective action to be taken. In feedforward systems, information about what is going to happen determines corrective actions. In screening systems, individuals or objects are compared to minimum criteria and either pass or fail.

Managers control inputs and processes as well as outputs. Input control systems typically rely on screening techniques, while process control emphasizes both feedback and feedforward control. Input controls usually combine screening with feedback systems.

Standards and budgets are the most common forms of input control. Processes are controlled by audits, policies, procedures, project control methods, and performance-appraisal techniques. Output controls include goals, management by objectives, and quality control methods.

In addition to being accurate and timely, good control systems are objective, understandable, and concentrate on strategic points. Good control systems do not dominate an organization, but are coordinated with work flows and are economically and organizationally realistic. Finally, they are understood and accepted by those in the organization who must operate them.

QUESTIONS FOR REVIEW AND DISCUSSION

1. What are the characteristics of good control systems? Can not having control systems sometimes be better than having them? Give an example.
2. What are the characteristics of good standards in control systems? How can communication affect their effectiveness?
3. Are measurement systems always important? How do they differ between production output and services output?
4. How are feedback and feedforward systems different? How are they related?
5. What are the advantages of go-no-go systems of control? In what sort of situations are they effective and inappropriate? What sort of measurement systems should they use?
6. How do prescriptive and operational control systems differ? How do they enhance each other?
7. Evaluate the following: "Control systems should be flexible enough to be acceptable to all members who are affected by them."
8. How do input control methods for acquiring personnel differ from those control methods used for acquiring material inputs? Which is harder to control and why?
9. What are the problems associated with measuring the performance of employees? What characteristics must performance appraisal have to overcome these?
10. What role do budgets play in control?
11. How do internal and external audits differ in methods and objectives? What purpose do management audits serve, and what problems arise with these?
12. What agencies does the federal government use to control its own operations? Name three and the operations they oversee.

REFERENCES AND NOTES

1. J. A. Michener, *Centennial* (New York: Random House, 1974).
2. J. A. F. Stoner, *Management* (Englewood Cliffs, N.J.: Prentice-Hall, 1978), pp. 586–89.
3. "Archie McCardell's Absolution," *Fortune*, December 15, 1980, pp. 89–98.
4. "Harvester Reaps Corporate Changes," *Associated Press*, May 4, 1982.
5. *Gainesville Sun*, "Warren Restricts Use of Firearms," December 16, 1980, p. 5A.
6. "Safety Board Blasts Eastern, FAA for Maintenance Lapses," *Associated Press*, January 25, 1984.
7. P. Lorange, *Corporate Planning: An Executive Viewpoint* (Englewood Cliffs, N.J.: Prentice-Hall, 1980), pp. 165–68.
8. L. L. Cummings and D. P. Schwab, *Performance in Organizations: Determinants and Appraisal* (Glenview, Ill: Scott, Foresman and Company, 1973), Chapter 5.
9. E. A. Locke, K. N. Shaw, L. M. Saari, and G. P. Latham, "Goal Setting and Task Performance: 1969–1980," *Office of Naval Research Technical Report GS-1*, June 1980.
10. S. J. Carroll, Jr. and H. L. Tosi, *Management by Objectives: Application and Research* (New York: MacMillian Co., 1973).
11. E. S. Buffa, *Basic Production Management*, 2d. ed. (New York: John Wiley and Sons, 1975), p. 648.
12. E. Locke, et al. *op. cit.*

SUGGESTED READINGS

R. D. Harris and R. F. Gonzalez, *The Operations Manager: Role, Problems, Techniques* (St. Paul: West Publishing Co., 1981). Section V, Control, describes basic control processes in the management of production activities in industry, including quality control and cost control. These descriptions provide ideas for control of nonproduction processes as well.

R. Henderson, *Performance Appraisal: Theory to Practice* (Reston, Va.: Reston Publishing Co., 1980). An exhaustive and detailed description of performance appraisal techniques and processes, this book clearly explains the role of appraisal in organizational control.

J. Pfeffer and G. R. Salancik, *The External Control of Organizations* (New York: Harper & Row, 1978). The authors offer a different perspective on control by describing how organizations themselves are controlled by the environments in which they operate.

Case Rockwood National Bank

In an effort to control costs of servicing customer accounts, the vice-president of Rockwood National Bank charged Ray Shingle, manager of systems, to make a study and subsequent recommendations to reduce the operating expense of the department.

Thirty days later, Mr. Shingle's recommendations were put into operation. Six months later, costs of operating the department were reviewed against costs for the preceding six month period. It was found that costs had decreased by $6715. This decrease was due primarily to savings in salaries charged against the customer-service department. During the preceding six month period, 9037 customers had been provided service. Under the new system, 4812 customers had been provided service.

When the vice-president of the Rockwood National Bank reported the savings in the customer-service department to the president of the bank, the president expressed surprise that the vice-president thought a savings had taken place. "In the first place," the president said, "you moved the customer-service department from the main floor to the sixth floor so that fewer customers would take the trouble to check their balances and review their statements; furthermore, you require customers to show positive identification before they can obtain any information about their accounts; on top of this, you have instructed the personnel in the customer-service department absolutely to refuse to give out any banking information to anyone requesting it over the telephone. It's my opinion," continued the president, "that you should revert to the old system and give our customers the kind of service they deserve."

CASE QUESTIONS

1. What was the intended target of Mr. Shingle's control system?
2. What were the characteristics of Mr. Shingle's control system?
3. Suggest other methods that could be used to control the cost of servicing customer accounts.

3/What Skills and Tools Do Managers Need?

Part 3 describes the skills and tools managers need to plan, organize, direct, and control work today. The development and use of these capabilities are major determinants of managerial success.

8/Understanding Individual Behavior *discusses how an individual's personal characteristics combine with physical and social environments to shape behavior. Because managers get things done through people, successful managers must understand human behavior.*

9/Understanding Group Behavior *describes the behavior of people in groups and the strong forces groups exert on members' behavior in organizations.*

10/Power, Influence, and Leadership *delves into the power, influence, and leadership skills needed by managers to achieve their goals. It describes different kinds of power and influence and when each is most appropriate. Leadership is treated as a special form of influence—that of an individual over a group.*

11/Communication Skills and Management Information Systems *covers oral, nonverbal, and written communication and offers suggestions for improving skills both as a communicator and as a listener. It concludes with a discussion of management information systems and their roles as major tools in modern organizational communications.*

12/Decision-Making Skills and Operations Management Techniques *concentrates on decision making—individual and group decision processes and factors that influence quality. It describes several quantitative techniques used in making decisions today.*

13/Creativity and Innovation *argues that these qualities are essential for survival in today's competitive environment. It describes creative processes for individuals and organizations, and ways that managers can manage more creatively and more effectively.*

8 / Understanding Individual Behavior

Ellen James was angry. She strode to the door of her office and snapped at her secretary, "Karen, get Art on the phone—now!" Karen, who had been in the process of cleaning up her desk to go home, did as she was told.

"Art? Ellen. Where are the cost figures? I told you I wanted them by five o'clock, and it's five after five now."

"I was just getting ready to call you. I'm still working on them, but I'll have them to you within the hour," explained Art.

"Art, you don't seem to understand. I said five o'clock, and I meant it. I'm leaving this office in ten minutes. I've got to catch a plane at seven-thirty and I'd like to pack and see my kids before I go. Besides," she added, "I thought you delegated that job to Sandra. Why are you working on them?"

"One of her kids got sick, and she had to go home to take care of him. So we're a little behind, but I'll finish them up and get them to your house by six-fifteen."

"You let her go home? Wonderful. You'd better listen to me, Art," she said. "Get your act together. While Sandra's home with some flimsy excuse again, you're holding the bag. I'm not paying you to do her work. You're supposed to be a manager, not a cost accountant. She's using you, and you're too weak to make her knuckle down. Those people who work for you have your number, Art. You buy any story and then do the work for them. That's not good enough for me and you know it."

"But what am I supposed to do?" asked Art. "Her kid got sick. I can't expect her to ignore him."

"Her kids are her problem, not yours," Ellen replied. "You're on some Mr. Nice-Guy trip, always getting involved in your employees' personal problems.

"You know what? I think you really enjoy playing father-confessor to all your female employees. Well I'll tell you this—you're doing them no favor. You're holding them back in this company. If they want to get ahead here, they've got to learn to keep home and work separate. Until they can demonstrate that, they're not going anywhere. And neither," she added, "are you.

"Art, did you ever stop to think that you're not the solution to their problems—you're just another problem? I'll see you and those cost figures at six-fifteen at my house!"

Art stared at the telephone and shook his head. What made Ellen so

184

wasn't as ambitious as she was, and that to some people, home was more important than work.

"You're just another problem," she had said. He liked that. She was the problem—he had to protect his people from tyrants like her who only cared about power and success. She'd chew up some of his people if he let her, and he knew they appreciated his protection.

Art flicked on the intercom and told his secretary to get his wife on the phone. "I'm sorry, Mr. Conway, but I was just leaving to. . . . "

"Mary, I told you to check with me before you left. Get my wife on the phone—now!" As Art picked up the phone, a chilling thought struck him, "Suppose I am the problem?"

tough, he wondered. Had she always been that way, or had climbing up the corporate ladder made her that way? Maybe she didn't realize that everyone

Managers are people who get things done through other people—subordinates, peers, coworkers, and superiors, as well as customers, suppliers, government officials, and others outside the organization. It should come as no surprise, then, that the first chapter in this section on managerial skills and tools is about understanding human behavior.

In the story that introduced this chapter two managers were having problems with this very concept. Art saw Ellen, his immediate supervisor, as a woman driven by success, insensitive to others' problems. If Art's diagnosis of Ellen is correct, then Ellen's drive for success is likely to be frustrated.

Because managers depend so heavily on other people, insensitivity, which usually stems from ignorance about, or indifference to, human behavior, can be a fatal flaw. A study which emphasized this liability compared twenty chief executive officers with twenty-one otherwise successful executives who failed to reach the top.[1] Why did the twenty-one fail? The study cited insensitivity to others more than any other reason.

But perhaps Ellen isn't insensitive, only realistic. Suppose Art is the problem, being too protective of his subordinates, and doing too much of their work. The same study that cited executives' insensitivity also found two other flaws which derailed executives on their way to the top—inability to delegate (overmanaging) and inability to adapt to a boss with a different style of managing. Perhaps it is Art, not Ellen, who needs to develop skills in understanding human behavior.

Most likely, both Art and Ellen could improve their skills, given the problems they seem to have with each other. Each seems to have miscalculated his or her impact on the other, a problem that can be very damaging to a superior-subordinate relationship. As you read this chapter, keep in mind that managers who are skilled at understanding human behavior understand how they interact with other people, as well as understanding the behavior of others.

LEARNING TO UNDERSTAND BEHAVIOR

Learning to understand human behavior is like learning any other skill—it takes time, patience, and effort. It requires discipline to avoid jumping to conclusions about people. It involves analyzing both the personal and environmental factors that influence the behavior of a particular person at a particular time.

Astute managers take into account both personal and environmental factors in trying to understand others' (or their own) behavior, because they recognize that behavior seldom has a single cause. Ellen assumed Art let Sandra go home because he was weak. Art assumed Ellen was driven by success. Neither really tried to analyze the others' behavior. For a manager's purposes, analyzing human behavior does not have to be formal or complex, but it does require going beyond simplistic assumptions.

Attribution

Attribution is *the process of making assumptions about the causes of behavior.* Attribution has two important identifying characteristics: it assumes a single cause of behavior, and it is usually based on something other than firsthand knowledge of the person and situation involved. For example, one common basis for attribution is a single obvious or well known piece of information about the person involved. Ellen James attributed Art's letting Sandra go home to a single cause. To Ellen, Art was "too weak to make her knuckle down." Ellen's attribution focuses on one aspect of Art's personality. It ignores Art's other personal characteristics and the role of his environment (Sandra, her coworkers, Ellen herself) in explaining his behavior. The chances are slim that Ellen's simplistic diagnosis is accurate. Behavior is determined neither solely by personal characteristics, nor by the environment, but by a more complex interaction of the two.

In general, attribution takes the form of statements such as: "He/she did that because *(a single reason).* We all make such statements. There is a general tendency for people to attribute their successes to personal characteristics and their failures to environmental characteristics, such as bad luck. Those who study attribution have identified a number of common bases such as the four shown in Exhibit 8.1.

In themselves, the kinds of attribution statements shown in Exhibit 8.1 are neither good nor bad. What they are is oversimplified. Whether or not this creates a problem depends upon the situation. If Ellen decides to fire Art because he is "weak," it's a problem. If Art decides Ellen's toughness is the sole source of his problems with subordinates, it's a problem.

Managers like Art and Ellen have to make, or provide information for, important decisions about the retention, promotion, or firing of subordinates. While it may be sufficient for a worker's friend to attribute his or her behavior to "weakness" or "toughness," that worker's manager has a responsibility to look a little deeper. Attribution leads to blame rather than problem solving.

Exhibit 8.1 **Some Common Bases for Attribution**

Basis	Explanation	Example
Projection	Assuming behavior is caused by the same factors that cause our own.	''G dresses well because he is trying to impress the boss.'' (That's why *I* wear what I do.)
Stereotyping	Assuming behavior caused by some trait supposed to be characteristic of a group to which the individual belongs.	''R voted against the proposal because he is Republican.'' (All Republicans are conservative.)
Attitudes	Assuming behavior is caused by some internal mental state.	''S failed the course because she had the wrong attitude from the start.''
Luck	Assuming success or failure is a matter of good or bad luck.	''A is a vice-president at 34 because she has had all the breaks.''

Understanding behavior is understanding its causes. While there are only two sets of causes—individual characteristics and environmental factors—the number of individual characteristics and environmental factors is large, and full knowledge of them is seldom available. In addition, our knowledge of the way they interact is limited. Nevertheless, our understanding has advanced far beyond the need to rely upon simple attribution when a fuller understanding is important.

The Basic Behavior Equation

The answer to what causes human behavior is expressed in the **Basic Behavior Equation,** $B = f(P \times E)$—that is, *behavior is caused by an interaction of the person with his or her environment.*

Individual characteristics are not the sole explanation for behavior. An individual's behavior changes with the environment (Art treats Ellen and his secretary differently). The environment is not the sole cause of behavior. Different people behave differently in the same environment (Ellen and Art's secretary treat him differently). *Any explanation that relies on only one or the other will be incomplete.*

Behavior is the *product* of the individual interacting with the environment. There is more than one relationship among these three variables, however. The environment can change the individual. For example, training programs (environment) are designed to provide employees with new skills and knowledge (personal characteristics). Individuals change the environment for themselves (by setting goals or gathering information) and for others (by providing incentives or improving technology). Thus, as a manager's skills in understanding behavior develop, he

Exhibit 8.2   A Dynamic View of the Interdependence of Behavior, Personal Characteristics, and the Environment

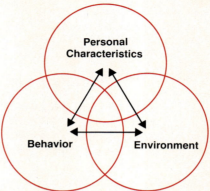

*Adapted from Tim R.V. Davis and Fred Luthans, "A Social Learning Approach to Organizational Behavior." *Academy of Management Review*, 1980, 5, 2, 281-290. page 283.

or she moves away from simplistic attributions to an awareness that personal characteristics, environmental factors, and behavior all influence each other. (Exhibit 8.2). The environment affects both behavior and personal characteristics; personal characteristics affect behavior; and behavior changes the environment.

There is a final point about the general problem of understanding human behavior. Each individual has a unique set of personal characteristics that are passed on from parents and changed or shaped by experiences. The uniqueness of individuals makes a manager's task of understanding behavior more complex. Fortunately, most people at work have a lot in common, such as the tendency to be influenced by reinforcement and extinction, as discussed in Chapter 6. Really skilled managers not only understand behavior in general, but can discern similarities and differences among those with whom they interact. How important is this skill? In the study of successful and unsuccessful executives described earlier, the ability to understand others' perspectives was the most obvious difference between the two groups. Only twenty-five percent of those who failed to reach the top were described as having special abilities with people; seventy-five percent of the successful executives were so described.

THE CAUSES OF HUMAN BEHAVIOR

Behavior is *any act that can be observed.* How people choose to behave and how well they perform are influenced by a wide variety of personal and environmental factors.

People are born with and develop personal characteristics that they bring with them from one environmental situation to the next. For example, personal characteristics relevant to the behavior of operating a computer console would include manual dexterity, eyesight, knowledge, experience, and interest. For the behavior

Exhibit 8.3   Personal Characteristics—Inherited and Learned

Inherited Characteristics	Learned Characteristics
Physiology	Personality
Sex	Attitudes
Intelligence	Values
Age	Perceptual Tendencies
Race	Skills
	Reinforcement History

of influencing subordinates, relevant personal characteristics would include personal appearance, voice, confidence, and knowledge of human behavior.

People acquire their personal characteristics in two ways. They are born with some that they *inherit* from their biological parents; they develop or *learn* characteristics from their experiences (see Exhibit 8.3).

Inherited Characteristics

Personal traits that people are born with are determined by the particular pattern of genes they get from their biological parents. These characteristics are the basic equipment with which each person begins life; however, certain inherited traits can be modified by environmental conditions: intelligence by training, and physiology by surgery and medication, for example.

In the past, managers have tended to pay a lot of attention to inherited characteristics in selection, placement, and evaluation, probably because traits such as sex, age, and race are easily identified and stereotyped. As we shall see, however, few of these traits are, in and of themselves, important determinants of performance in organizations.

Physical and Physiological Characteristics.   Such individual traits as height, body build, vision, dexterity, and strength *can* be and often *are* important factors in the performance of certain tasks or feats. Of all the inherited traits we discuss, they are the most significant. Besides their obvious relevance to tasks that require strength, stamina, and physical endurance, they affect behavior in ways that are less obvious. For example, students with uncorrected myopia (near sightedness) often sit in the front of a classroom to see the instructor and the chalkboard. Their poor eyesight directly affects their choice of seating. It also indirectly affects other behaviors, because sitting at the front also means sitting right in front of the teacher. Students who sit in the front are, thus, less likely to talk, eat, read, or sleep in class or to be absent, because such behaviors are more likely to be noticed.

Intelligence.   We designate learning abilities, adaptability, and various intellectual accomplishments as *intelligence*. Its physiological basis is the brain, but we are still learning how the brain affects intelligence. (There is evidence, for example, that the left side of the brain is related to types of human functioning different from the right side.)

Intelligence is usually measured by means of tests; there is abundant research relating such test scores to various behaviors. For example, more intelligent people are found to be less influenced by others. At the same time, they are usually more willing to listen to attempts to persuade them than are less intelligent people.[2] Not surprisingly, intelligence is an important factor in learning. However, it is not nearly as important in decision making.

Sex.   Sex is an inherited characteristic, but the number of known sex-linked differences in behavior is not very large, particularly in areas where physiology is not a critical factor. Many observed differences between the sexes can be attributed to learning. Many other presumed differences have not held up under the scrutiny of systematic research. For example, a recent review concluded "women, in general, do not differ from men, in general, in the ways they administer the management process."[3]

People act on the basis of their own perceptions of reality.

Most of the significant male-female differences that *have* been found in behavioral research are explained better by learned differences acquired at home and in school; female children were treated differently from male children. Child-rearing and educational practices encouraged and reinforced different interests, skills, and behavior patterns for males and females. The result has been sex-role stereotyping—different expectations for the behavior of men and women. Sex-role stereotyping is decreasing; men are nurses and women are jockeys. Women direct films, and men stay at home to raise children. Nevertheless, it is likely that social expectations will continue to produce some predictable differences between men and women for some time to come.

Age.   Age is a personal characteristic determined by one's date of birth. Its most obvious influence on behavior stems from the physical correlates of age. As people grow older, such faculties as coordination, strength, endurance, and reflex speed change, and related behaviors usually change as well.

The influence of age on behaviors that don't depend on physical abilities is less obvious, but has been extensively studied. For example, people generally reach the peak of their creative production between the ages of thirty and forty.[4]

Race.   Race is a genetically determined characteristic that offers a convenient opportunity to summarize our discussion of inherited traits.

Inherited characteristics produce certain differences among groups of people. Racial differences are usually associated with differences in skin color and certain structural factors such as body build or facial appearance, most of which are irrele-

Management in Action
Using Industrial Hygienists to Improve the Work Environment

Industrial hygienists are scientifically trained specialists who find and correct health hazards at work. Their numbers have increased dramatically in the past few years, as evidence of the effects of work environments on worker performance and health have increased. By using industrial hygienists to eliminate health hazards, employers can avoid liability claims and create environments that let employees do their best work.

We are all aware of the sensational cases of industrial hygiene, or its lack, such as the discovery of the effects of coal dust on the health of miners and of the effects of asbestos on workers in a variety of occupations. But industrial hygienists improve working conditions in many less spectacular cases every day. For example, a printing-plant worker complained of aches and pains that made his job difficult. An industrial hygienist corrected his problem simply by shortening the distance he had to reach in moving heavy catalogues from one place to another. Observation, attention to detail, and a knowledge of human anatomy provided the answer.

In another case, refinery workers at a silver mine became sick, suffered trembling hands and "crazy spells" from something in the air. The "something" was diagnosed as mercury poisoning. An industrial hygienist attributed the problem to mercury vapors released when ore containing mercury was heated in the refinery. By improving ventilation and keeping employees away from the refinery's furnace, management eliminated the problem.

Experts claim that small businesses have failed to make use of industrial hygienists, either out of ignorance or unwillingness to pay their high fees (typically $300 to $500 per day). However, small businesses now have access to a federally funded program that permits them to get this expertise from state agencies or universities free of charge. Frequently the solutions to the problems encountered are simple and inexpensive. For example, in one firm, tennis ball testers who squeezed tennis balls for firmness suffered a tendon disorder from clenching their hands at an uncomfortable angle. A hygienist changed this work procedure so that they squeezed balls only when their hands were in line with their wrists, and the tendon problem vanished. In another case, computer room employees were complaining of headaches, nausea, and tiredness. The cause was discovered to be a colorless, odorless gas seeping into the room from a water heater next door. The heater was producing carbon monoxide. It lacked oxygen because someone had blocked an air vent to keep the heater from warming the data-processing room. Once another vent was created, and insulation was added, the heater stopped producing carbon monoxide, and the complaints disappeared.

Source: "Industrial Hygienists Increase Firms' Output and Efficiency," *Wall Street Journal*, March 5, 1984, p. 33.

vant to most organizational activities. A few important differences can be directly associated with inherited factors. Blacks, for example, are especially prone to sickle-cell anemia.

Other than physiology and intelligence, however, inherited characteristics are not nearly as important a consideration for managers as they were once thought to be. Most of the differences that do exist can be traced to differences in the way people have been treated, raised, or expected to behave—that is, they are learned. Technology has even reduced the importance of many physiological differences. Visually handicapped, hearing impaired, and paraplegic people have proven to be capable and valuable employees in occupations to which they have previously been denied access.

In most occupations, age, sex, and race can no longer be considered as criteria in employee selection, placement, and training. By themselves, those traits are irrelevant. Unfortunately, some managers will continue to use them as criteria in making personnel decisions, despite evidence, laws, and policies to the contrary. Beyond moral and legal considerations, managers who discriminate on irrelevant criteria such as those are not managing well; they are systematically restricting the levels of ability in their organizations.

Learned Characteristics

Most of the characteristics that produce the enormous variation in human behavior are learned, not inherited. We acquire our attitudes and our values. We also learn behavior patterns. We are not born self confident, broad-minded, friendly, timid, or aggressive; we become that way. **Learning** is *a relatively permanent change in behavior resulting from interactions with the environment.*

Some knowledge is gained quickly. It usually takes only one experience to learn not to touch a hot burner. Most learning occurs more gradually. Information about what happens when we pursue certain values and not others accumulates slowly.

At any time, each of us is a complex and unique product of those interactions with the environment that we call *learning experiences*. Exactly what we learn depends upon what has been reinforced or rewarded, which, in turn, depends upon a variety of factors including:

1. our parents' values and expectations;
2. the values and norms of our culture and subculture;
3. the social conditions under which we grew up;
4. the physical environment in which we grew up.

What has been reinforced also depends upon the opportunities created or withheld by the inherited characteristics we possess. Team sports, for example, teach people how to cooperate and compete within prescribed rules. Children excluded from team sports because of their race, sex, or physiology can be at a disadvantage at work where those experiences can pay off.

There are many learned characteristics that affect behavior. We will briefly consider five groups: personality, attitudes, perceptions, skills, and reinforcement history.

Personality.   **Personality** is *the combination of particular behavior traits that makes each individual unique.* For practical purposes, it is the impression an individual makes upon others. He or she is usually described by terms such as *warm, friendly,* or *aggressive.*

There is research to suggest that tendencies to develop certain personality characteristics may be related to biological factors, but they are only tendencies. Whether a particular characteristic *actually* develops depends upon learning.

Personality traits are measured by specially designed tests. Some of these tests, like Rotter's *Internal-External Locus of Control Scale,* measure only a single trait. The Rotter scale asks respondents to choose which of two statements they believe (see Exhibit 8.4). The scale measures the degree to which the subjects believe that people control their own lives (that is, people get what they deserve), or that luck, fate, and other uncontrollable forces determine people's fates ("There will always be wars, no matter what people try to do about them.") Other personality tests, like the *Minnesota Multiphasic Personality Inventory (MMPI),* measure a number of traits and yield a profile. Among those traits measured by the MMPI are introversion/extraversion and dominance/submission.

There are a great many personality tests available, together with a considerable amount of research relating test scores or profiles to behavioral traits and tendencies. For example, people who are open-minded seem to be better able to work out bargaining agreements than those who are narrowminded.[5] People who are outgoing are more likely to become managers than are introverts.[6]

Exhibit 8.4   Sample Items from Rotter's Internal-External Locus of Control Scale

Respondents are asked to select which of each pair of statements they actually believe to be more true.

a. Many of the unhappy things in people's lives are partly due to bad luck.
b. People's misfortunes result from the mistakes they make.

a. Without the right breaks one cannot be an effective leader.
b. Capable people who fail to become leaders have not taken advantage of their opportunities.

a. Becoming a success is a matter of hard work, luck has little or nothing to do with it.
b. Getting a good job depends mainly on being in the right place at the right time.

a. Most people don't realize the extent to which their lives are controlled by accidental happenings.
b. There is really no such thing as "luck."

a. It is hard to know whether or not a person really likes you.
b. How many friends you have depends upon how nice a person you are.

a. With enough effort we can wipe out political corruption.
b. It is difficult for people to have much control over the things politicians do in office.

Source: Julian B. Rotter, "Generalized Expectancies for Internal versus External Control of Reinforcement," *Psychological Monographs,* Vol. 80, No. 1, Whole No. 609, 1966. Items from pp. 11–12.

Attitudes.   An **attitude** is *a relatively stable tendency to think, feel, and act in a certain manner toward some object.* People can have attitudes toward a behavior (working), an individual (a subordinate), or a group of people (unions).

The concept of attitude is widely used to explain behavior, but it is usually a weak explanation. That is because the only information we have about someone else's attitude comes from his or her behavior. For example, we may say that a subordinate's substandard work performance, disobedience to rules, and verbal grumbling is caused by a negative attitude toward work or the company. However, what is the basis for our belief that this subordinate has a negative attitude? He or she is observed performing poorly, violating rules, or complaining a lot. We have really not explained this behavior; we have only attached a label—"negative attitude"—to it, one of the attributes described in Exhibit 8.1.

Of course, there is an alternative to getting information about someone's attitude by observing his or her behavior. That alternative is to ask verbal or written questions about the attitude. Still, we know only about the attitudes of others from their behaviors. We are simply looking at the behavior of answering questions about an object instead of the behavior toward the object itself. The answers may be accurate, unintentionally slanted, or deliberately distorted. In short, all we get from an attitude questionnaire is what the person wishes to tell us.

Despite their inadequacies as measures of "true attitudes," attitude questionnaires do have their uses, particularly in uncovering problems or potential problems. If a job-satisfaction attitude questionnaire shows that 30 percent of the employees in a company express negative opinions about promotion opportunities, that is important information for management.

Perceptions.   A **perception** is *an individual's interpretation of the environment.* It is the result of a complex interaction of the perceptual processes of seeing, feeling, smelling, tasting, and hearing, other individual characteristics, features of the environment in which perception occurs, and qualities of the object of perception.

The individualized nature of perception cannot be overemphasized; people often perceive the same things differently. One employee may complain about a job assignment that another welcomes. A manager may perceive an employee's innocent suggestion as a complaint or threat. The words "What an unusual office!" may be perceived as a compliment, a meaningless social remark, or an insult.

Some differences in perception can be accounted for by inherited differences in sight, touch, smell, taste, and hearing. However, unless actual physical disability is involved, these differences alone cannot account for the wide variety of perceptual differences. Differences in past experiences with the object of perception are usually more important.

There are also certain systematic errors, or biases, called *perceptual tendencies,* that influence perception. Two of these, attribution and stereotyping, were discussed earlier. Some common tendencies that are learned over time are shown in Exhibit 8.5. A particular individual may be influenced by all, some, or none of these tendencies; they are common, but not universal.

Exhibit 8.5   Some Common Perceptual Tendencies

Tendency	Explanation	Example
Perceptual Readiness	Perceiving what a. we *want* to see b. we *expect* to see	a. Reading a test score of 71 as 77. b. Not noticing that a problem employee has improved.
Halo Effect	Tendency for evaluation of other characteristics to be affected by evaluation of a single characteristic. May be positive or negative.	Perceiving an unfriendly employee as a poor performer.
Implicit Personality Theory	Tendency to assume two traits are related. Observing that person has trait A leads to assumption about trait B.	Perceiving a very good-looking person as unintelligent: "beautiful but dumb."
Attribution	Leaping to conclusions about causes and effects.	Attributing extraordinary performance to luck.
Stereotyping	Perceiving traits believed to be typical of some *group* in an *individual* member of that group.	Expecting a sales representative to be fast-talking and hard-drinking.

The physical senses, attention, past experience, and learned perceptual tendencies combine to produce a person's perception of any particular object or event. Because so many factors are involved, there is considerable room for variation among people. The importance of this variation for understanding behavior lies in the fact that *people act on the basis of their own perceptions of reality.*

For example, a manager who perceives an employee's ability as limited will probably give him or her limited responsibility. A student who perceives a particular school subject as difficult is likely to put more time into studying it than into one perceived as easy (or avoid it altogether).

There has been substantial research about the existence and effects of perceptual differences on behavior in organizations. In one frequently cited study, five of six sales executives identified the most important problem in a management case as being in the area of sales. By contrast, only one of the five production executives who read the case perceived sales as a major issue.[7] Since people act on the basis of their own perceptions, we can be sure that the sales and production managers would have gone about solving the hypothetical case problem in quite different ways.

Skills.   A **skill** is *a learned ability to perform a specific task well.* It is a function of physiological characteristics, knowledge, and experience. Skill may be the single most important determinant in the performance of complex tasks such as solving calculus problems, negotiating contracts, or long-range planning.[8] People acquire skills through their own efforts and through formal and informal training. For example, both Ellen and Art could improve their techniques in understanding behavior through formal coursework or by reading and systematic observation of behavior.

Reinforcement History.   The **reinforcement history** of an individual *is made up of the pattern of positive, negative, and neutral outcomes he or she has experienced for each particular behavior.* It is that part of an individual's total past experience that is relevant to the behavior we are trying to understand. Suppose a store manager is interested in understanding why customers consistently prefer to be waited on by one particular sales clerk. One of the things the manager will look at is what generally happens to customers when this clerk waits on them. This is the reinforcement history of that behavior.

> *Learning to understand human behavior is like learning any other skill—it takes time, patience, and effort. It requires discipline to avoid jumping to conclusions about people. It involves analyzing both the personal and environmental factors that influence the behavior of a particular person at a particular time.*

As discussed in Chapter 6, there are three possible outcomes of any behavior. The outcome may be positive, or rewarding, in which case the behavior is reinforced, and the probability that it will be repeated is increased. The outcome may be negative, or punishing, in which case the behavior is not likely to be repeated. Finally, the outcome may be neutral, neither positive nor negative, in which case it becomes increasingly unlikely that the behavior will be repeated.

Of course, any behavior has many outcomes, some of which may be perceived as rewarding, some as punishing, and some as irrelevant. The *reinforcement history* of a behavior refers to whether the behavior has been *more* often rewarded, punished, or neither.

It is seldom possible to know much about someone else's reinforcement history of a certain behavior. The importance of the concept for understanding behavior lies in the fact that we do know one very important thing: *a behavior that persists has a history of reinforcement.* To the person concerned, the rewards of the behavior are greater than whatever punishments might also be associated with it. They are also greater than the rewards perceived to be associated with alternative behaviors. Consider the case of an employee who is chronically late for work and is criticized by her supervisor·every time. Perhaps her wages are also docked for the minutes she is not at work. Why does this behavior persist even though the employee is punished for it?

If we accept the fact that the employee must somehow be rewarded for being late, despite the way the situation appears to others, we can come closer to understanding the behavior. What might reward lateness? The employee may sleep late, miss rushhour traffic, have a good breakfast, or avoid unpleasant jobs associated with early arrival. Whatever the rewards, the important point is that it is *more rewarding* than being censured or being fined *is punishing.*

Summary: Personal Characteristics

The case of the late employee provides a way to emphasize the critical point about the influence of personal characteristics on behavior: It is the *combination* of characteristics that must be considered in understanding any particular behavior. Keep in mind that even people with similar perceptions of rewards and punishments and similar reinforcement histories may behave quite differently if other characteristics are different. Suppose the chronically late employee had few marketable skills and so was highly dependent on holding her current job. A threat about losing her job if she continued to be late might overcome the fact that she found the immediate outcomes of being late more rewarding than the immediate outcomes of being on time.

We could also speculate that the employee would behave differently if she placed a strong value on being well thought of by others or if she were a very ambitious person: being on time would be more rewarding. In short, such individual traits as age, skill level, values, and personality *modify* each other and other characteristics to produce behavior that would be unexpected from knowledge of only one characteristic. In addition, there is another set of factors to be considered that act in much the same way—environmental influences on behavior.

ENVIRONMENTAL FACTORS THAT INFLUENCE BEHAVIOR

The **environment** consists of *the relevant physical and social surroundings in which behavior takes place.* Note that the environment of relevance to understanding behavior has two parts—a physical part and a social part, as depicted in Exhibit 8.6. In both cases, what this environment looks like, or feels like depends upon a person's *perceptions.* For example, a manager who perceives dress standards as important will probably react to a subordinate's sloppy appearance, regardless of the attitude of peers.

The Physical Environment

Things that we can see, feel, smell, and hear compose the physical environment. Much of the influence of the physical environment on day-to-day behavior is obvious and straightforward. People talk loudly to be heard over the noise of machin-

Exhibit 8.6 Physical and Social Environment Factors

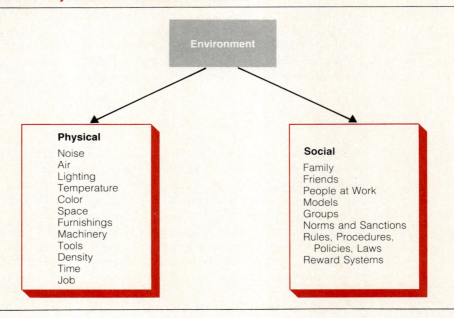

Environment

Physical

Noise
Air
Lighting
Temperature
Color
Space
Furnishings
Machinery
Tools
Density
Time
Job

Social

Family
Friends
People at Work
Models
Groups
Norms and Sanctions
Rules, Procedures,
    Policies, Laws
Reward Systems

ery, drive more cautiously on a rainy day than on a clear one, and adjust their golf swings to compensate for wind conditions.

Many influences of the physical environment on behavior are less obvious. Hot, crowded conditions decrease people's attraction to strangers.[9] Unpredictable and uncontrollable noise seems to have longterm as well as immediate effects on certain kinds of performance.[10]

At work, the physical environment includes noise, air, lighting, temperature, color, space, office furnishings, machinery, tools, and the number of other people around (density). It also includes the nature of the task to be performed (to be discussed in the next chapter).

The effects of the physical environment on performance have long been of interest to those who study organizations. The large amount of research has yielded considerable information for the design of work environments. It has also made it very clear that the physical environment affects behavior in ways that are not physical.

A recent study of the "open plan" office (low walls, or no walls, between employees) found that some employees were more productive and reported being more satisfied with the arrangement than with the traditional office plan. Others were less productive and less satisfied.[11] The difference stemmed partly from job requirements. For example, it is more difficult for some people to concentrate in an open-plan office. Part of the difference, however, stemmed from status considerations. Traditionally, a private office has meant higher status. Removing walls also removed the outward signs of this status.

The physical environment of an office can have an effect on the amount and quality of interaction among workers, and thus, their communication.

Clearly, the physical environment, like personal physical characteristics, affects behavior both directly and indirectly through its interaction with the various social factors.

The Social Environment

The social aspects of the environment have to do with the relationship between an individual and other individuals and groups. It consists of the individual's interactions with others and the multitude of norms, laws, and rules created by people to regulate the behavior of people.

The Presence of Others.   One important influence on behavior is simply the presence of other people. If people are together, there is the possibility that they are evaluating each other in some way. Thus, most people tend to take their feet off their desks, cover their mouths when they yawn, and refrain from singing the latest popular hit out loud when other people are around. More importantly, the presence of others tends to interfere with an individual's ability to produce newly learned responses. Therefore, employees learning new tasks require lots of practice before they're ready to perform them.

The presence of others can also act to change perceptions of a situation, and thus, behaviors. These changes have been studied extensively in emergency situations, beginning in the mid-1960s after thirty-three persons witnessed the murder of a young New York City woman without intervening. The research produced some interesting findings, including the fact that a victim of aggression is more likely to receive assistance when there is only *one* bystander than when there are several.[12] Many studies have found that assistance to others increases when someone else is observed helping or trying to help. In uncertain or novel situations, people tend to imitate the behavior of models.

The modeling of behavior is one of the more important general influences of other people on our own behavior. What others do serves as a guide when we are uncertain as to what behavior is appropriate. A new employee wonders how to address her new boss. Most likely, if others use the title "Mr.," she will follow suit. Is it all right to pad an expense account? If high-status members of an organization do so, others will model them. If they are scrupulously honest, others will be so also.

Group Membership.   A special case of the influence of other people on an individual's behavior occurs when the other people make up a group of which the individual is a member. Groups expect certain behaviors from their members, and outsiders expect certain behaviors from the members of certain groups. Both sets of expectations influence the behavior of the individuals in the groups.

When some group to which he or she belongs is particularly important to an individual, we say that group is a *reference group;* the individual identifies with the group. A reference group serves two purposes for an individual member: it serves as a standard for self-evaluation, and it serves as a source of opinions, values, and attitudes.

The substantial influence exerted by reference groups at work will be discussed in Chapter 9.

Norms.   *Informal, understood expectations about how to behave in a given situation* are called **norms.** Examples of such norms in our culture include going to the back of a line and waiting for your turn, avoiding conversations and staring in crowded elevators, or not being a show-off in class by answering more than one or two questions.

Note that none of the norms listed above are to be found anywhere as written rules for behavior. In fact, they look rather silly when put into writing. Nevertheless, most of us know, and follow, such norms in our daily behavior.

All social groups have norms. They exist in our society, in families, in friendship groups, in professions, and in all formal organizations including businesses, universities, hospitals, and prisons. They often directly affect productivity and promptness. Becoming familiar with the norms in any particular group is an important part of the process of *socialization,* to be discussed in Chapter 9.

Norms act to standardize a great variety of behaviors in a broad range of situations. Most of us abide by the norms of our various groups, even though the means for enforcing norms are as informal as the norms themselves. Conformity to norms is maintained by means of sanctions.

Groups expect certain behaviors from their members. An individual's status may be determined by things other than the person's role within the group.

Sanctions *are rewards for conforming to, and punishments for deviating from, the norms of any particular social group.* Acceptance as a group member is the most common reward, and ridicule a common punishment, used by work groups to control member behavior.

Rules and Laws.   When standards for behavior are formalized into written form, they become rules or laws. *Laws* govern all members of a society. There is, for example, a law against anyone stealing the property of others. *Rules* affect a particular segment of society, such as the members of a club or team, employees of an organization, customers or clients of a place of business, or visitors to a public place. Most hospitals have a rule forbidding visitors to smoke in certain wards, for example.

Unlike norms, laws and rules are expected to have good reasons behind them. As a result, reactions to a law or a rule are often quite different from reactions to norms. The same people who readily conform to *norms* about dress, for example, may condemn *rules* about dress (dress codes) as ridiculous or as a violation of their rights.

Most people tend to overestimate the influence of laws and rules on behavior and underestimate the influence of norms. In reality, norms are at least as important as laws and rules, and more so in some cases. In the first place, there are far more norms than either laws or rules. In the second place, there are virtually no laws or rules about some of our most frequent behaviors, such as the way we speak to or about others. It would probably be impossible to count the norms for such behavior.

Finally, norms affect the extent to which rules and laws are observed. The law says, for example, to drive fifty-five miles per hour on interstate highways. The norm, the speed "everybody" drives, is about sixty-two miles per hour. Most people are polite to their coworkers, for example, but it is doubtful that they are polite because of company rules. Chances of being formally punished for being rude are almost zero. Most workers are polite because norms support such behavior at work.

The Formal Reward System.   The varying relationships among norms, rules, and laws can be seen in all organizations. Of particular interest and importance is their relationship to an organization's *formal reward system*, the set of rules or standards that define behaviors to be formally rewarded. It is an important part of an organization's social environment, but organizations also have *norms* about the behaviors that will be rewarded.

Some of the norms in organizations support the formal reward system. Among themselves, for example, salespeople often measure success by *increases* in sales from month to month. If the formal reward system is based on total sales, the norms and standards support one another. Other norms operate in opposition to the formal system. Work group norms that restrict individual output for the perceived good of the group are a common example that will be discussed in the next chapter.

Summary: Environmental Factors

In this section, we have presented an overview of the factors in the physical and social environments that influence individual behavior. Understanding these influences may be somewhat easier than understanding how personal characteristics affect behavior, because such environmental factors as physical objects, laws, and norms exist where we can all see them or observe them at work.

UNDERSTANDING BEHAVIOR IN PERSPECTIVE

This chapter has covered a wide range of personal characteristics and environmental factors that combine to cause individual behavior.

Although understanding behavior is a complex process, most of us know far more than we use about the people whose behavior we may want to understand. For example, managers usually know the skills and physical characteristics of their subordinates. They work in about the same physical environment as those subordinates, and they know the policies, rules, and the formal reward system of the social environment. With a little thought, they can also identify the kinds of subordinate behaviors they reward, punish, or ignore.

The last statement deserves more attention. Managers are an extremely important part of their subordinates' environment. Not only do they exert control over the physical working environment, rules, procedures, norms, and reward systems, but they serve as highly visible models for subordinate behavior. Managers who want to be successful in understanding the behaviors of others need to understand their own behaviors as well. What are their relevant physical, intellectual, and emotional characteristics? What values, attitudes, and perceptions influence their behaviors? How do they react to the physical and social environment? What norms do they follow, what rewards do they seek, what punishments do they avoid? And who are their own models? Some corporations now require extensive periodic self-appraisals by managers so that they understand their own strengths, weaknesses, and behavioral tendencies. Managers who fail to do so, or who cannot demonstrate that they have learned from this selfunderstanding, are not considered promotable.

CHANGING BEHAVIOR

Understanding behavior is a general skill. Like all skills, it can serve a variety of purposes. For the manager, the potential strain of continually being required to deal with a wide variety of behaviors from peers, subordinates, superiors, and outsiders is substantial. Since it is almost always easier to handle things we understand than things we don't, some skill in understanding behavior can reduce this strain.

A second purpose served by understanding behavior is that it offers guidelines for *changing* behavior—one's own as well as that of others. Although this is an advanced topic in the study of organizational behavior, we can give you a preview by linking some basic principles to our current discussion.

Changing behavior requires changing some aspect of one or more of the personal or environmental factors causing it. With the exception of skills and knowledge, managers have little or no chance of making any significant alterations in the personal characteristics that influence behavior. Some, such as age or race, simply can't be changed. Others, such as attitudes and perceptions may vary over time as the individual interacts with the organizational environment. However, the direct influence of one person on such changes will usually be minimal, difficult to control, or both.

For the most part, managers can change factors in the physical environment. Moving one clerk's desk actually reduced the number of errors he was making by 92 percent in the first two weeks after the change!

Managers can also change many factors in the social environment. If retail store clerks are competing for customers (which usually causes negative customer reactions) to get sales commissions, the reward system might be changed to one based on equal percentages of total sales.

These examples, although brief, point up one fact—understanding behavior is a complex skill. The very source of its complexity opens up multiple channels for changing it. Because there are so many factors involved in producing behavior, there are many ways changes can be brought about. Even an apparently small or insignificant modification can have large or significant results on behavior.

The Bottom Line

Understanding behavior is a matter of fitting together as much knowledge about relevant personal and environmental factors as can be acquired. Skill in doing so makes day-to-day coping with the behaviors of others easier, and offers guidelines for changing one's own or others' behavior when necessary. In developing skills to understand behavior, managers should remember that:

1. The causes of an individual's behavior lie in an interaction between his or her personal characteristics and the physical and social environment. Armed with this awareness, managers will not be surprised when (a) a person's behavior is not the same in one situation as it is in the next, (b) two people react to the same situation differently, and (c) a change in the physical or social environment produces a change in behavior.
2. Because of individual differences, it is dangerous to assume that others will respond to the environment in the same way as the manager would. A manager who considers challenge and responsibility as rewards should not be surprised if others avoid them.
3. Work generally takes place in a social environment. Reward systems, group pressures, and high status models all have powerful impacts on work behavior. It is futile for a manager to insist on one form of behavior when the social environment creates strong pressures for another. For example, a manager who tells people to cooperate when reward systems, task designs, and group norms are competitive will be frustrated. The environment must be changed before behavior will change.
4. Managers who don't understand their own behavior are unlikely to understand others. A manager is an important part of his or her subordinates' environment. Those who are ignorant of their behavior and its impacts are ignorant of strong forces on their subordinates' behavior. Managers who recognize their own strengths, weaknesses, and behavioral tendencies have a great advantage in understanding others' behavior.

SUMMARY

Understanding behavior is a skill involving analysis of the personal characteristics and environmental factors that combine to cause the behavior. Personal characteristics are inseparable from the individual. Some, like sex, intelligence, and race, are biological. Others, like personality, attitudes, and values, are learned. By itself, any one characteristic is only a part of the total influence on behavior.

Personal characteristics interact with environmental factors to cause behavior. The familiar things that we can see, feel, smell, and hear make up the physical environment. The social environment consists of other people and the rules, laws, and social norms that they produce. Because of differences in perception, each individual sees the environment a little bit differently, and it is that perception that is the real environment for that individual.

REFERENCES AND NOTES

1. H. W. McCall, Jr. and M. M. Lombardo, "What Makes a Top Executive." *Psychology Today.* February 1953, pp. 26–31.
2. H. J. Reitz, *Behavior in Organizations*, Homewood, Ill.: Irwin, 1981. Chapter 16.
3. S. M. Donnell and J. Hall, "Men and Women as Managers: A Significant Case of No Significant Difference." *Organizational Dynamics*, 1980 (Spring), 60–77, p. 76.
4. H. C. Lehman, *Age and Achievement.* Princeton, N.J.: Princeton University Press, 1953.
5. *See* J. T. Tedeschi and S. Lindskold, *Social Psychology.* New York: Wiley, 1976., pp. 126–28 for a more complete discussion of this trait and its behavioral correlates.
6. D. Hellriegel, J. W. Slocum, and R. W. Woodman, *Organizational Behavior*, 3rd ed. St. Paul: West Publishing Co., 1983, p. 70.
7. D. C. Dearborn and H. A. Simon, "Selective Perception: A Note on the Departmental Identifications of Executives." *Sociometry*, 1958, 21, pp. 140–43.
8. Reitz, *op. cit.*, p. 78.
9. W. Griffith and R. Veitch, "Hot and Crowded: Influence of Population Density and Temperature on Interpersonal Affective Behavior." *Journal of Personality and Social Psychology*, 1971, 17, pp. 92–97.
10. B. Reim, D. C. Glass, and J. E. Singer, "Behavioral Consequences of Exposure to Uncontrollable and Unpredictable Noise." *Journal of Applied Psychology*, 1971, 1, pp. 44–56.
11. A. D. Szilagyi, W. E. Holland, and C. Oliver, "Keys to Success With Open Planned Offices." *Management Review*, 1979, 68, 8, 26–28, 38–41.
12. For a review of this line of research, *see* J. R. Macaulay and L. Berkowitz, eds., *Altruism and Helping Behavior.* New York: Academic Press, 1970.

SUGGESTED READINGS

Dobzhansky, T. *Mankind Evolving: The Evolution of the Human Species.* Yale University Press, 1962, pages 40–46. Also reprinted in W. Nord, ed., *Concepts and Controversy in Organizational Behavior.* Pacific Palisades, Ca.: Goodyear, 1972, 6–11. The article gives a very short but clear introduction to the issues involved in the distinction between inherited and learned personal characteristics.

Rosenthal, R. and L. Jacobson, *Pygmalion in the Classroom: Teacher Expectation and Pupils' Intellectual Ability.* New York: Holt, Rinehart, and Winston, 1968. This is a report of a classic demonstration of the mutual influence of a personal characteristic (intelligence) and a social environmental one (teachers' expectations).

Steele, F. I. "Physical Settings and Organizational Development." In W. L. French, C. H. Bell, Jr., and R. A. Zawacki, eds., *Organization Development: Theory, Practice, and Research.* Dallas: Business Publications, 1978, 308–15. This is one of the few sources available for introducing both the simple effects of the physical environment on work behavior and the more complex interaction of this environment with the organizational social system.

Zalkind, S. S. and T. W. Costello, "Perception: Some Recent Research and Implications for Administration." *Administrative Science Quarterly*, 1962, 7, 3, 218–32. Despite the fact that the research discussed is no longer recent, this article remains one of the best available in providing a summary of the factors influencing perception.

QUESTIONS FOR REVIEW AND DISCUSSION

1. What is an attribution and why can it be misleading?
2. Find an example of attribution in a newspaper or magazine. Is the basis for the attribution a personal characteristic, a factor in the physical environment, or a factor in the social environment? Explain briefly.
3. How do learned and inherited characteristics differ? Which are more important at work?
4. List all of the groups to which you belong. Place a check by those that you feel are *reference groups*. Give an example of a *norm* that influences the behavior of members of one of these groups.
5. List five ways in which other people can influence behavior at work.
6. For each of the following behaviors, note whether personal characteristics, the physical environment, or the social environment might be the *major* influence. Explain briefly.
    a. Total output of an assembly line.
    b. Amount of money donated toward fund to buy flowers for a sick co-worker.
    c. Number of good ideas for a new product generated by members of the research and development department.
7. What is a skill? How does it differ from intelligence?
8. What kinds of information would you need most if you were trying to understand the poor job performance of one of your subordinates? Divide your answer into personal characteristics, physical environment factors, and social environment factors.
9. What is modeling? When is it likely to affect behavior? How does it differ from the formal reward system?

Case *South Pacific Hotel**

The South Pacific is wholly owned by World Wide Enterprises. The hotel is located in the scenic area of a South Seas island, about fifteen minutes from the tourist district. The South Pacific is unique, since it is the only resort hotel on the island.

The hotel's clientele is made up of foreign dignitaries, government officials, movie stars, business executives, and other VIP's—including the President of the United States. Because the hotel's profits rely heavily on continuous patronage by VIP's, much emphasis is placed on maintaining an image of being the "in" vacationing spot. An occupancy rate of 70 percent is needed to break even on hotel operations.

Julie Kennedy, the hotel's public relations director, was initially employed to fill a secretarial position. She graduated from a finishing school on the East Coast and worked for several publishing companies. Since she has always been intrigued with the tourist industry, she selected hotel work as a career. At the age of thirty-seven, she has earned the reputation of being one of the top P.R. people in the Pacific islands.

Julie's motto has always been, "Never assume that anything is done." Whenever the general manager delegates work to other department heads, Julie always finds it necessary to examine their work if it affects public relations in any way. For example, if an important banquet is being planned, she approves the menu and inspects the silverware. Such interference usually results in friction with the banquet manager and the restaurant manager.

Although many of the managers resent Julie's interference, they have not brought their grievances to the general manager, since he is believed to favor the public-relations director.

The sales, banquet, and front-of-the-house managers have reached the point where they try to bypass Julie while doing their work. Rather than ask for her advice on publicity matters, the other managers prefer to rely on their own limited abilities. Therefore, Julie usually resorts to "snooping" tactics to see where her help is needed.

Occasionally, Julie has exchanged a few harsh words with some of the other managers in front of their subordinates. One such incident occurred at a hotel party. An assistant manager mistakenly seated his guests at tables Julie had reserved. Enraged, she called him an idiot in front of the employees servicing the banquet.

Although Julie usually riles a few tempers in the process of carrying out her duties as public relations director, she can always be depended on to get the job done. The local press and radio stations have always given the South Pacific preferential treatment because they have had favorable encounters with Julie. Many movie stars have extended invitations to Julie to visit them as their guests in Hollywood. One even went so far as to write a letter to the senior vice-president of World Wide Enterprises praising Julie's handling of public relations. In his reply, the senior vice-president said he considered Julie the best public relations manager in all of the World Wide Enterprises hotels.

Julie has received many job offers promising greater prestige and monetary compensation. However, she feels "at home" at the South Pacific. She will

*Adapted with permission from a case prepared for class discussion by Cyril P. Morgan, Washington State University.

probably be the public relations director at the hotel for many years, since she thrives on the glamour of her job. Although she has made many friends outside of the hotel, she has few friends among the other employees in the hotel.

The feelings of the other employees become evident if one sits in on a cafeteria conversation. Most of what is said about Julie is derogatory. The other employees view her as a busybody perfectionist who is impossible to work with. The employees often express their feelings to Julie's assistant. Although her assistant has some problems working with Julie, she still finds her job satisfying and feels that Julie is "a wonderful person to work for."

CASE QUESTIONS

1. Consider Julie's general behavior in the performance of her job.
   a. What do you know about Julie *as a person* that might explain her general behavior on the job?
   b. What about the *physical* environment of the South Pacific Hotel might influence Julie to behave this way?
   c. What about the *social* environment might influence her to behave this way?
2. Give one example from the case of Julie's violation of a general social *norm*.
3. Is Julie's *reinforcement history* for her "busybody behavior" generally positive or negative? Explain.
4. Give one example from the case of different individual perceptions of the same person, object, or event.
5. Julie perceives her job as "public relations," not "employee relations." Briefly explain to Julie how negative systems effects can make this a shortsighted viewpoint.

Report from the Field *Promoting Intergroup Cooperation*

Sharon Sines is Director of Fabrication for the Analog Division of Harris Corporation, a large high-technology manufacturer with worldwide markets. She is responsible for manufacturing five different product lines in the Analog Division, including semiconductor switches, amplifiers, and circuits.

Sharon describes some of the problems she routinely faces in trying to coordinate manufacturing with the engineering functions in her division.

"New products usually go through three stages. First, design engineers work on the concept, design, and layout of a product to fit a customer's specifications. Then production engineering takes over, working with the design engineers to figure out how we can manufacture this product efficiently. Finally, we get the product manufacturing specifications in fabrication and produce the required number of the specified products.

"Trying to plan and schedule manufacturing runs is very difficult, because it's hard to coordinate our operations with the design and production engineers. For one thing, the engineers are housed in a separate location about a quarter of a mile from the fabrication plant. They make their decisions in a comfortable, quiet office, away from the frenzy and action of fabrication.

"For another thing, their concept of time is entirely different from mine. Design engineers typically have 36 weeks to come up with a design; they work from 8 A.M. to 5 P.M.; they think in terms of weeks. Production engineers have 12 weeks to figure out how to make the product; they also work 8 to 5; they tend to think in terms of days. When we get a product, we're lucky to get 8 weeks to make a complete production run. At the same time we may be fabricating several other products. In fabrication we work 24 hours a day. We think in terms of hours.

"Let me give you an idea of the cost of this lack of coordination. At one point we had a year to develop a new product, which was to be introduced at an electronics show on the West Coast, but the design engineers ran into some problems. It took them more than the thirty-six weeks to come up with a workable prototype.

"Because there's no clear jurisdiction between design and production engineering, they have to work out any problems between them. So they got hung up, and pretty soon I had only five weeks, instead of eight, for fabrication. But that would have been OK; we're used to that kind of pressure.

"Unfortunately, they still couldn't resolve their problems. By the time we finally got the product specifications, we had only ten days, instead of eight weeks. We managed to meet the deadline all right, but at considerable cost. We basically had to drop everything we were doing, run lots of overtime, and use inefficient scheduling of machinery to get it done. The engineers never see any of this. They're already back on their eight-to-five schedule, working on another product. It's a continual problem that really plays havoc with my planning and scheduling."

Source: Personal interview, June 1983.

9 / Understanding Group Behavior

"Where've you guys been?" asked Ted, as he slid into the back seat of Terry's station wagon. "It's seven-fifteen already."

"Ignore him. He hasn't been fit to work with since he learned to tell time. In case you haven't noticed, it's precipitating precipitously and traffic is subsequently inextricably intertwined," replied Tom, as the car lurched off through the slush and snow.

"I love it when you talk dirty, Tom," jibed Tradd. "Does that mean we're gonna be late for the big meeting?"

"In words you can understand, yes," replied Tom. "I'm afraid the new boss is going to have to get used to the idea that the four T's do things their own way and that meeting before eight o'clock is not one of them."

"I imagine he's been clued in about us already. He had a long session with Charley last week; I'm sure Charley told him we were the best and brightest managers in the division," ventured Terry, as he expertly maneuvered the car around two stalled vehicles.

"My man! A driving fool, folks!" cried Tom, pounding Terry on the back. "With Terry at the helm, we'll get there or die trying!"

"If it's all the same to you, Terry, I'd prefer a less heroic trip to work. Besides, we can't die; we've got a new division head to break in today."

"OK, what have you guys heard about the new boss? Good guy or bad?" asked Terry.

"What I've heard so far isn't bad," offered Tom. "He's been with the company seven years, so he's no outsider. He's got a degree from a decent school—Midwest, I think—is married, has one kid, and another on the way."

"Sounds just like us. How'd he get to be division head?" asked Terry.

"The way I heard it," Tradd drawled, "he picked up the Beverly Lake project when Bert Owit dropped dead. He turned that loser into a winner, and the brass was impressed."

"Were impressed," corrected Tom. "I swear, you illiterates will never succeed without my help."

"Well, if he's the one who masterminded that Beverly Lake project, then I are impressed too," offered Terry, as Tom winced. "I know a couple people on that project. I remember that Marie Eland said the guy who took it over did a super job."

"Marie? She's good people," said Ted. "Down-to-earth. Smart. Hard-working. If she admires the guy, that counts for a lot with me.''

"Next thing, you guys'll have him walking on water,'' observed Tradd drily. "I don't know him, and I don't trust anybody I don't know. I say we make him prove himself before we jump on his bandwagon.''

"Ah, come on Tradd,'' chided Tom. "You Southerners haven't trusted a Yankee since Bull Run. Let's give this guy a break. He sounds OK to me.''

"For once I agree with Tom,'' said Terry. "Everything I've heard is good.''

"I think Terry's right,'' agreed Ted. "Let's give him the benefit of the doubt. If he turns out to be a jerk, we can always withdraw our support. We've done it before.''

"OK, you guys,'' Tradd relented. "I'll go along for now. The last thing the division needs is trouble with the division head. We've got to start making some more money. I've got a family to feed and a new car to buy.''

"Don't we all?''

You will recall from the previous chapter that a group, especially a reference group, exerts considerable influence on its members' behaviors. Groups are an important part of an individual's social environment. In this chapter, we shift emphasis to the group itself and to the factors that determine group performance and influence.

GROUPS AND THE MANAGER

A **group** is *two or more people who interact with one another and share common goals, values, or interests.* Tom, Ted, Terry, and Tradd, the young managers who call themselves "the Four T's" work together, car-pool together, and share common work and family interests. They are a group. Groups of all sizes, compositions, and purposes are to be found in any organization, and managers often work *with* them and *in* them. For example, a manager must deal with groups:

1. when the manager is part of, or responsible for, a decision-making group, such as a committee;
2. when the manager's subordinates are, or must be, formed into teams to accomplish a job;
3. when the manager is part of a policy-making group; or
4. when some of the manager's subordinates have formed a strong informal group that has substantial influence on the behavior of its members (such as the four T's).

As these examples suggest, groups in organizations may be formed deliberately or spontaneously. In either case, they can have impacts on the success of a manager as well as on general organizational effectiveness. This impact can be either positive or negative, as the story in Exhibit 9.1 illustrates. Clearly, there are times when groups can make or break an organization. More often, their behavior simply makes things go more or less smoothly, a sufficient reason for acquiring and using knowledge of the factors that determine group behavior.

Exhibit 9.1   The Impact of Groups on Organizational Functioning

One spring in a midwestern American city, a small influential group of workers in a food processing plant led its coworkers out of the plant on a wildcat strike. They were protesting management's decision to limit pay raises to 7 percent. For five days the pickets successfully shut down the plant. Thousands of pounds of unprocessed food began to spoil. On the third day, warm rains began to fall throughout the upper Midwest, melting record amounts of snow and ice. On the fifth day, flood warnings were issued for the area. On the sixth day, as the threatened flood became imminent, the group summoned all workers back to the plant site. There they worked virtually nonstop for two days moving supplies, sandbagging, and preparing the plant for the flood. Because of their efforts, the plant escaped serious damage and was back in operation two days after the flood subsided. Company officials estimated that the workers' efforts saved the company more than twenty-five times the cost of the strike.

Source: L. N. Jewell and H. J. Reitz, *Group Effectiveness in Organizations*. Glenview, Ill.: Scott Foresman and Company, 1981, p. 2.

Groups in organizations come to exist in different ways. *Formal groups* are deliberately established on a temporary or permanent basis to accomplish a task. Committees, teams, and other such groups may be created by an authorized member of an organization, or they may be called for by the organization's structure.

Informal groups come together spontaneously on the basis of common interests, mutual convenience, or simple attraction of the members for one another. Car pools, bowling teams, "lunch bunches" or cliques are examples.

The membership of informal groups in organizations depends a great deal on the physical location of people, the nature of their work, and their schedules. Thus, informal groups often arise among people, like the four young managers, at the same level in an organization, since these people are more likely to have interests in common and opportunities to interact.

There are some important differences between formal and informal groups. Membership in informal groups is voluntary, while membership in formal groups may not be. For example, many university departments require that recommendations for faculty promotion and tenure be made only by current full professors with tenure. Thus, position, rather than interest, determines membership in that group.

Another difference between formal and informal groups has to do with the reason they are formed. Formal groups have a task that is determined, at least in a general way, by the person or policy that formed the group. Informal groups may set themselves tasks, but members may get together just to enjoy one another's company.

DETERMINANTS OF GROUP BEHAVIOR

The analysis of group behavior is not fundamentally different from the analysis of individual behavior. The same personal and environmental variables are involved. As in the last chapter, our discussion will be built around these factors.

Group Composition Characteristics Affecting Group Behavior

The basic unit of the group is the individual member. Every group consists of some number of individuals, each of whom has his or her own unique combination of inherited and learned characteristics. However, a group is more than the sum of its individual parts, because the members *interact* with one another. These interactions produce the differences that make each group unique. For example, a committee comprised of Terry, Tom, Tradd, and Marie will be different from a group composed of the four T's. An early study in group problem solving, for example, found clear differences in the amount of problem-related activity *among groups*, as well as *among the members* of each particular group. Each group responded to the problems in a way that was different from the other groups.[1]

It would be impossible to list the specific characteristics a group might have, because the possibilities are limitless. However, there are three aspects of any group that affect group behavior. These are the relative homogeneity or heterogeneity of the group, the stability of its membership, and its size.

Homogeneity or Heterogeneity.   The extent to which members of a group have similar or different individual characteristics determines the group's *homogeneity* (member similarity) or *heterogeneity* (member differences). Since all individuals have unique combinations of characteristics, no group can be perfectly homogeneous. On the other hand, some members will share certain characteristics, so no group will be perfectly heterogeneous. Thus, the terms are relative. The four T's form a homogeneous group. They are all young male managers, college-educated, with wives and children, who live in the same area.

Outside of classrooms and juries, few groups have random membership. Similarity on important characteristics such as interests, attitudes, personal backgrounds, or vocations has long been recognized as a major factor in the formation of informal groups.[2] Formal groups also may consist of members with important similarities, such as the same field of interest or the same position in the organization. However, formal groups may be formed with a deliberate eye to heterogeneity. Varied backgrounds, interests, knowledge, and personal characteristics have proven helpful to problem-solving groups.

There is a fairly large body of literature about the effects on group behavior of similarities and differences among people. Some of the more consistent conclusions are:

1. There is generally more conformity in mixed-sex groups than in same-sex groups.[3]
2. Variations in ability levels produce variations in problem-solving approaches that gives heterogeneous groups a slight edge with respect to flexibility and creativity.[4]
3. Task performance, in general, seems to be slightly better when groups are relatively heterogeneous but group members tend to like the homogeneous groups better.[5]

The size and composition of a group are factors in its effectiveness.

Stability of Membership.   A second important characteristic of group composition is the extent to which group membership remains constant. *A group that regularly changes its membership* is called an **open group.** A fraternity or sorority, for example, is a relatively open group. Each spring, some members graduate, and each fall some members join.

A group with a stable membership is a **closed group.** New members are added only when old ones move away, retire, or die. The Supreme Court of the United States is a closed group. So are most boards of directors.

The extent to which a group is open or closed affects a variety of its behaviors:

1. A relatively open group is more likely to have, and to tolerate, a wider range of opinions. This diversity tends to give open groups a broader frame of reference than closed groups.
2. It is more difficult for a new member to have any influence in a closed group than in a more open one. It usually takes some time before a new member of a closed group acquires sufficient status to have any weight given to his or her opinion.[6]
3. Closed groups generally have well-established interaction patterns, or ways of working together, and they spend little or no time getting organized for any particular activity. By contrast, the shifting membership of open groups tends to keep them off balance; the same kinds of organizational issues keep arising. Such issues include the designation of a leader, the division of work, and the choice of direction.

In organizations, a few groups, such as the board of directors or an informal friendship clique, are relatively closed. Most groups, however, are more open as an indirect result of turnover, transfer, and organizational expansion. As we have seen, there are possible advantages to both groups.

Group Size.   The size of a group is one of the easier aspects of its composition to measure, and so there has been considerable research in this area. Among the more generalized findings are:

1. Very small groups have fewer resources (ideas, experiences, and approaches) for problem-solving than do larger groups. Other things being equal, the number of creative ideas or problem solutions tend to vary directly with the size of the group.
2. Communication among members in larger groups is more difficult than in smaller groups. Opportunities for each member to participate in a group discussion decrease as the group becomes larger, and so the discussion will more likely be dominated by a few members.[7]
3. As groups get larger, subgroups are more likely to form, and the strength of the bond holding the original group together (group cohesiveness) is reduced.
4. Group size affects leadership. Even when no formal provision is made for selecting a leader, the probability that some member of the group will assume leadership increases directly with group size. The truly leaderless group is probably impossible once a group has more than four members.

When you read the *Management in Action* feature for this chapter, note that these three characteristics—homogeneity, stability, and size—are usually carefully controlled by organizations that use quality-circle groups to solve problems. Groups are homogeneous (drawn from the same work area or holding similar jobs); they are stable in the short run, but new volunteers are rotated into the circle about once a year; they are usually kept to seven or eight members. The homogeneity of interests makes it easier for them to find problems that are of concern and interest to all members; their stability lends itself to efficient use of time, while rotating in new members helps bring in fresh ideas and perspectives; their small size makes them manageable and permits all members to participate in discussions.

Managers who wish to increase their skills in understanding behavior can draw a number of inferences from these key group characteristics, summarized in Exhibit 9.2. For example, a manager with few subordinates may be able to forge them into a cohesive group; a manager with many subordinates can expect a number of subgroups to form which may unite only at crucial times, if at all.

Environmental Factors Affecting Group Behavior

Much of the influence of the environment on group behavior, as on individual behavior, is direct. However, individual differences among members in their *perceptions* of the physical or social environment can cause problems for groups that don't exist for individuals.

This can be illustrated by the story of a man who came home from a condominium owners' meeting. The meeting had been called to decide whether to build more tennis courts. When his teenage son eagerly inquired if they'd be getting new courts, the man replied, "Oh, we never got around to that. But the vote on

Management in Action
Using Groups to Improve Quality

Quality circles are groups of workers who meet regularly to discuss work problems (particularly in product quality), to determine causes of those problems, recommend solutions, and take appropriate actions. Quality circles originated in the United States, but Japanese industry is largely responsible for their development and popularity.

American industry, impressed by the excellence of many Japanese products, has adopted the quality-circle concept to improve worker commitment to quality and to take advantage of worker expertise in solving problems related to work. Among those companies using some form of quality-circle techniques are J. C. Penney, Uniroyal, Ampex, Armstrong Cork, Firestone, R. J. Reynolds, Bendix, 3M, Hughes Aircraft, General Motors, Ford, Westinghouse, General Electric, Bank of America, Memorex, Foremost Foods, Polaroid, and Crucible Steel. Recently their use has expanded to service organizations, hospitals, accounting, engineering, and other nonindustrial firms in both this country and Japan.

Although the process varies from company to company, a typical quality circle is a voluntary group from the same work area or people who do similar work. The size of groups may vary from three to fifteen or more, but seven or eight is considered ideal for maintaining cohesiveness and enabling each member to contribute. A supervisor usually leads the group, which meets for an hour or so once a week to discuss problems. Problems may be identified by the group as a whole, or by a single member, by the supervisor, by management, or by staff personnel, like quality-control experts.

Groups usually decide which problems to work on and often call for outside assistance when problems exceed their expertise. If the solution is something they can implement themselves, then they do so. If the solution requires resources or changes that must be approved by management, the group makes a formal presentation to solicit its approval and support.

Honeywell assigned the problem of reducing the cost of an electronics product in order to win a government contract that was being sought by a number of highly competitive firms. The quality circle suggested a way to automate a manufacturing process that improved costs by twenty percent and enabled Honeywell to win the contract. Lockheed credited nearly three million dollars in savings to fifteen circles in their first two years of operation. In one situation, a quality circle helped reduce rejects from twenty-five per thousand products to six per thousand. Other documented success stories include bank employees who cut the time in half for processing commercial customers' accounts and insurance-company employees who cut absenteeism in half.

Sources: D. L. Dewar, *The Quality Circle Guide to Participation Management* (Englewood Cliffs, N. J.: Prentice-Hall, 1980; E. G. Yager, "The Quality Control Circle Explosion," *Training and Development Journal*, April 1981, pp. 98–105.

Exhibit 9.2   Some Key Characteristics of Groups

Characteristics	Effects
Heterogeneity vs. Homogeneity	More flexibility More creativity More satisfaction More cohesiveness
Open, changing membership vs. Closed, stable membership	More tolerant Broader frame of reference Shorter time horizons Quicker to organize Little influence for new members Longer time horizons
Few members vs. Many members	More cohesiveness Better communications More satisfaction More creative ideas More domination by individuals More likely to have *a* leader

the temperature of the room was twenty-three too hot, thirty-one comfortable, and sixteen too cold." In this case, different perceptions of the physical environment diverted the group from its task accomplishment.

The environment can also affect the way group members interact. We will consider briefly four aspects of a group's environment not yet discussed—spatial arrangements, time, nature of the task, and reward systems.

Spatial Arrangements.   The arrangement of the space in which a group interacts can have important, but easily overlooked effects on group behavior. If a group meets around a table, the shape of the table will affect communication. If the table is long and narrow, group members at opposite ends will have difficulty talking to one another. As shown in Exhibit 9.3, people tend to communicate with those across the table or immediately on either side. If the group continues to meet around the long narrow table, cliques may form among those at opposite ends. If the group is a decision-making group, this splintering can make it considerably more difficult to reach a decision. Arrangements, like a round table, which permit all members to see and communicate with each other, easily promote good communication and thus better decision making.

Time.   Both research and observation suggest that groups under perceived time pressures interact differently from the way they interact when there are no such pressures. Like individuals, groups are inclined to attach more weight to negative information than to positive information when making a decision under time pres-

Exhibit 9.3   Influence of the Physical Environment on Group Processes

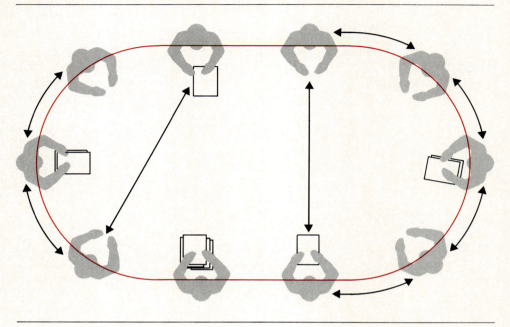

sures.[8] Thus, if a group must decide quickly whether to advertise a product on radio or television, the greater cost of television advertising may carry more weight than its visual qualities.

Time pressures can also affect whether the members of a group cooperate with each other. Cooperation is a more complex behavior than competition, requiring more communication, understanding of others' positions, and mutual adjustment. Time pressures make it more difficult to do all the things necessary to cooperate; therefore, competition is more likely, particularly when members feel they do not share equally in the group's outcomes. A group pressured to make a decision will find it difficult to sit quietly and listen to each other. Members are more likely to compete with each other in making suggestions and influencing the group.

Exhibit 9.4   Key Characteristics of a Group's External Environment

Characteristics	Effects
Spatial Arrangements	Can promote or hinder group formation and communications
Time Pressure	More weight given to negative information in decision making; less cooperation; more competition
Nature of Task	Interdependent tasks promote communication and cooperation
Reward Systems	Shared rewards promote communication, satisfaction with group, and cooperation
	Differential rewards based on relative performance promote competition

A group is effective when its members function as a team to accomplish their task through the use of the available resources.

Nature of the Task.   When a group wants, or is expected, to accomplish a task, the nature of that task is part of the physical environment. The task may be to solve a problem, to assemble a machine, to sell a thousand tickets, or to win a football game. Each has special characteristics that influence group behavior.

If the task is *new* or *difficult*, the group may have to spend more time discussing it and dividing up the labor according to skills. There may also be less group socializing and a greater tendency for conflict to develop over the performance of the task.

The nature of the task can also affect communications and cooperation within the group. Certain tasks, such as group decision making and problem solving, team sports, construction, research and development, and surgery, are *interdependent*—group members depend on each other to accomplish them. The nature of these tasks demands communication and cooperation. Other tasks, such as sales activities, piecework, crafts, and individual sports, are *independent*—group members can perform their roles without regard for or aid from others. The nature of these tasks demands relatively little communication and cooperation.

Reward Systems.   Group members are subject to the same norms and laws of society and to the same rules and policies of organizations as individuals. Thus, much of the discussion of the social environment and its informal reward systems for individuals in the last chapter also applies to groups. However, we need to look further into formal reward systems by focusing on three ways members of a group can be rewarded.

Group members can be rewarded *independently* of the group. This is quite common in informal groups consisting of members from a variety of levels, jobs, or locations within an organization. The rewards offered by the organization to members of such groups are unrelated to their group memberships. The salaries of the four T's depend on their individual performances. The group is not formally reorganized or rewarded.

Group members can be rewarded *individually.* When the members of a formal group (or an informal group whose members all work together) are rewarded on an individual merit basis, the rewards are individual. They do not depend on group performance.

Differential reward systems based on relative performance promote *competition.* In such systems there are limited rewards and the more one group member gets, the less the others get. Or the reward may be "winner take all," as when a bonus is given to the most productive salesperson.

Group members can be rewarded on a *group basis.* This reward system, in which individual rewards are shared evenly among group members, encourages *cooperation.*

Failure to appreciate the influence of a reward system upon cooperative behavior leads to failure to understand why group members won't cooperate with each other. If the formal rewards are irrelevant to cooperation or encourage competition, there is nothing at all mysterious about a lack of cooperation.

A group is more than the sum of its individual parts, because the members interact with one another. These interactions produce the differences that make each group unique.

Few reward systems in organizations are purely cooperative or competitive, but the extent to which a system is more one or the other has a number of effects on group behavior. Members of cooperatively organized groups show a more even distribution of participation in the group, more friendliness, and greater mutual understanding of communications than do members of competitively organized groups.[9]

In general, members of cooperative groups report greater satisfaction with the group, but individual differences can be strong. Some people find competition very rewarding and cooperation rather limiting.[10]

Whether or not cooperation or competition is more effective for accomplishing a task depends on the nature of the task. For an orchestra to be successful at a performance, cooperation is required. For the Lion's Club to raise a large amount of money in its annual campaign to help those who are blind, competition is more appropriate.

The findings above relate to groups for which the *formal* reward system encourages cooperation or competition. However, groups often turn formal reward systems around. For example, a competitive reward system (such as piecework) can be changed to a cooperative reward system by the group. Instead of trying to out-produce one another for greater rewards, all workers may produce about the same to reduce effort and promote group solidarity. This process is called *work restriction*.

Groups also have their own sets of rewards and punishments, and these may be more important to group members than those offered by the organization. For example, a nurse may find it more rewarding to stay with friends on one shift than to transfer to another shift where the pay is higher.

The capacity to create and use their own goals and reward systems is one reason groups are such a powerful force in organizations.

The implications of these environmental effects on group behavior are numerous. Managers can design group environments that are consistent with the task. If the nature of the group's task is interdependent, such as decision making, construction, or assembly, the manager can promote communication and cooperation by setting up the work area to encourage face-to-face interaction among all members. By planning ahead, a manager can avoid time pressures that inhibit cooperation. Shared reward systems can avoid competition. On the other hand, if tasks are independent and members are competitive, a manager can spend less time worrying about physical arrangements and use time pressures and differential rewards to promote competition. Sales contests with bonuses for relative performance over a given time period (a trip to Hawaii to the salesperson with the most new customers in thirty days) are common examples.

The Group's Internal Social Environment

The particular goals and reward systems of a group are an important part of the internal social environment unique to that group. No other group has one that is quite the same. At least four other aspects of this social environment are critical to the group's behavior—roles, communication patterns, group cohesiveness, and group norms.

Roles.   A **role** is *a shared set of expectations about the behavior of an individual in a certain position.* Two major types of roles in a group are *leader roles* and *follower roles.* There are typically two leader roles. The *task-directive leader* gets the group organized and gives it direction. The *group-maintenance leader*, on the other hand, looks after the interpersonal relations within the group. Leadership will be discussed in more detail in the next chapter.

Follower roles, as well as leader roles, also differ. Some followers play a *submissive role;* they do what they are told with no questions asked. Others play a *devil's advocate role;* they question everything to be sure the reasoning is sound. Still others play *expert roles, comic roles*, or *scapegoat roles.* A scapegoat, of course, is the "official" person to blame when things go wrong.

The different roles in a group are not always played by the same members, nor does each group have all these roles.

In the anecdote, Terry played a task-directive role, Tom played comic and group-maintenance roles, Tradd was a devil's advocate, and Ted was submissive.

Some roles in groups are more likely to shift from one member to another. Generally, the least stable role is the expert role. Most members of a group have expertise in some area. Peacemaker and comic roles, by contrast, tend to be stable since being able to successfully resolve conflicts or make people laugh are less common skills.

Although some roles tend to shift, one characteristic of a well-established group is that members know, in general, what roles each will play. These shared expectations produce an important balance in the group, which can be disrupted should the group suddenly lose a member who has played an important role, such as a leader role or the expert or scapegoat.

> *Cooperation is a more complex behavior than competition, requiring more communication, understanding of others' positions, and mutual adjustment.*

The number and kinds of roles that exist in a group, and the way these roles are carried out, have important effects on all aspects of group behavior. Decisions, for example, can suffer if there is no devil's advocate to question assumptions and push for the exploration of alternatives.[11] If group-maintenance or peacemaker roles are unfilled or unsuccessfully carried out, conflict can disrupt the group. Task accomplishment can be jeopardized if too many members play comic roles—everyone has a good time, but nothing much gets done.

In general, groups function most effectively when the important roles are filled and carried out in ways that meet the shared expectations of the group's members. Some of these roles may be assigned; most are usually assumed by group members with the appropriate attributes or skills. Whether assigned or assumed, however, roles sometimes cause problems that affect the performance of the individual members and of the group. These problems are called role conflicts.

Three types of role conflicts in groups are presented in Exhibit 9.5. All three influence group behavior, but intrarole conflict, disagreements about how a particular role should be carried out, probably has the greatest negative impact. Such conflicts are likely to arise over the performance of the leader role.

Communication Patterns. For managers, communication is an especially important skill to which we devote an entire chapter later in this section. In this chapter we are concerned less with individual communication effectiveness and more with the influence of communication patterns within a group on group behavior.

Communication is *the process by which group members exchange information to accomplish the group's tasks and activities.* There are many ways to carry out this process, however, and groups develop *patterns* that are particular to

Exhibit 9.5   Types and Sources of Role Conflict

Type	Source	Example
Intrapersonal	Clash within an individual between expected behavior and values.	Conflict between the necessity of laying off surplus workers and a belief in guaranteed work.
Interrole	Clash within an individual between behavior expected in one role and that expected in a different role.	Conflict between having to work overtime and weekends (work role) and spending time with spouse and children (family role).
Intrarole	Disagreement among members of the relevant group as to the appropriate behaviors for a role.	Conflict between different subordinates' expectations of how manager (leader role) should behave—dignified and aloof, or down to earth.

themselves. The typical pattern of communication becomes an important part of the group's social environment.

The most important feature of a group's communication is **distribution,** *the extent to which the members can participate equally in that communication.* Distribution can range from one member dominating group interaction (centralized) to every member participating equally (decentralized). In centralized communication, all communications pass through one or relatively few members of the group. In decentralized communication, all members can and do communicate directly with each other.

Whatever the typical communication pattern in a group might be, it affects both group success and member satisfaction. For example, research demonstrates that member satisfaction with a group is increased when their communications are relatively decentralized. On the other hand, when the group has a relatively simple task to perform, this pattern of communication is far less efficient than a more centralized one, which is quicker to organize, makes fewer errors, and wastes less time.[12]

The distribution of communication has also been found to affect group decision making. One reason organizations use groups to make certain kinds of decisions is that groups bring more perspectives, knowledge, and experiences to the problem. However, if one or a few members dominate the group discussion, this greater range of resources is not utilized. In such cases, the deliberate imposition of rules to balance participation has often improved significantly the quality of the group's eventual decision.[13]

The group's communication pattern affects individual members. In centralized networks, those who occupy the most central positions (who can freely communicate with other members or through whom communications must flow) tend to be more satisfied and more likely to play a leadership role in the group. Those who control the flow of information in the group have the power.

Group Cohesiveness.   The bond holding a group together is called *group cohesiveness;* it is one of the most important aspects of a group's social environment. **Group cohesiveness** is *the degree to which members of a group are attracted to, and want to stay in, the group.* We speak of *more* or *less* cohesive groups; a *noncohesive* group could not exist.

Greater group cohesiveness comes about in a variety of ways. In general, groups whose members find one another likable and attractive, and groups that are difficult to enter, tend to be more cohesive than other groups. Groups that must be organized cooperatively to accomplish their tasks also tend to be more cohesive, as do groups that face some outside threat that cannot be easily escaped. It has often been noted, for example, how much stronger formal tenant or neighborhood associations become when faced by some outside threat such as a disinterested landlord or a new highway.

The effects of group cohesiveness on group behavior have been well documented.[14] Among these effects are:

1. more communication among members of the group;
2. a more favorable evaluation of group members by one another;
3. more expressions of hostility toward outsiders or other groups;
4. more influence attempts and more yielding to influence among members of the group.

Group cohesiveness also has important effects on task performance. Evidence from a large body of research is consistent: *more cohesive groups do whatever they set out to do more effectively than less cohesive groups.* Remember, for example, the success of the wildcat strikers (Exhibit 9.1) in first shutting down and then saving the plant. Only a highly cohesive group could have accomplished two such divergent goals in such a short time.

The fact that more cohesive groups can achieve their goals more effectively than less cohesive groups does not mean that they are necessarily more productive. As the wildcat strikers illustrate, such groups will be more productive only *if* their goals and those of the organization coincide; if, however, the goals are counterproductive (such as work restriction), more cohesive groups will be less productive.

Group Norms.   Chapter 8 discussed the influence of unwritten standards for behavior, or norms, on individual behavior. Subcultures, organizations, and formal and informal groups develop their own norms. Recently, engineers working for a large technologically oriented company provided examples of norms from work groups to which they belonged. Responses included the following:

1. Never, NEVER wear company neckties!
2. Complain about managers, even when you really like them.

3. Put the group first. Give up a date if it means backing out of something the group has planned.
4. Never directly compare salaries. Salary discussions must be vague and deal with satisfaction, not amount.
5. If you invite some members of the group to a party, invite them all, even if you don't really like them.

Norms serve a variety of functions for groups. They help to present a particular image of the group to outsiders (by not wearing company neckties), suppress status differences (by not comparing salaries) and the formation of subgroups (by inviting everyone to a party), and provide a common ground for group discussions (by complaining about managers). Taken together, they promote group solidarity.

Few groups will tolerate a member's persistent deviation from group norms, because such deviance threatens group unity. Evidence suggests that persistent deviation by a member will eventually result in his or her rejection from the group. Usually, however, this rejection occurs only after intensive, persistent efforts to bring the individual involved back into line with group norms.[15]

Groups also have their own sets of rewards and punishments, and these may be more important to group members than those offered by the organization.

In a sense, conformity to group norms is a price paid by an individual for admission to and acceptance in a group. If the group is very important to an individual (a reference group), this price will be paid even if it harms his or her own best interests. Conformity to work restriction norms under a piece-rate pay system, for example, causes faster workers to earn less pay than if they ignored the group norm.

The influence of group norms on behavior is twofold. First, since group norms are about behavior standards, there is a direct influence on what the group does. If there is a strong group norm for quality workmanship, for example, then work will be performed at a high level of quality; if speed is the norm, quality may be sacrificed.

Second, since conformity to norms is important to maintaining the group, some of its behavior is directed toward achieving that conformity. Thus, a group will spend time discussing the behavior it desires and the associated values, attitudes, and sanctions. As mentioned earlier, the group will also spend time trying to bring nonconformists back into line.

Exhibit 9.6 summarizes the key characteristics of a group's internal social environment. Managers can learn a great deal about groups simply by careful observation. Communication and conformity patterns, norms, sanctions, roles, and hostility toward outsiders are not difficult to determine if the observer knows what to look for. Understanding these characteristics enables a manager to deal more effectively in and with such groups.

Exhibit 9.6   Key Characteristics of Group's Internal Environment

Characteristic	Effects	Examples
Communication patterns	Individual and group satisfaction Group efficiency Distribution of power in group	When a manager must approve all subordinates' communications without outsiders, the manager's power is increased; subordinates' satisfaction decreases.
Cohesiveness	Communications Hostility toward outsiders Influence on members Goal achievement	When a manager gets his or her group united in the pursuit of a goal, they will influence each other to achieve that goal.
Norms	Promote group identity and cohesiveness Increase conformity and influence	A group norm of zero defects promotes its identity as a high-quality producer and increases its cohesiveness.

The Bottom Line

A manager must not only deal with people as individuals, but as members of groups. Some managers pretend groups don't exist. It doesn't work. In striving to be a successful manager, remember that:

1. Informal groups exist and will flourish within, across, and in spite of formal groups. Learn who belongs to what groups, what roles they play, and what the norms are. That information will be useful in understanding group behavior.
2. Groups can be powerful tools. They can accomplish more and exert more influence than any individual. Win the support of influential members of a group and you win the group. A manager whose subordinates form a group that is committed to his or her goals is free to plan and organize work. Most of the direction and all of the control can be carried out by the group itself.
3. By the same token, a manager opposed by a cohesive group faces a formidable foe. Managers can influence such groups, but usually at great cost, and the group wins at least as often as the manager. Don't unite the group against you. It's better to have a less cohesive group than a group banded together against you.
4. To the extent possible, create and structure groups to fit their tasks. In assigning people to groups, consider not only expertise and experience of the individuals, but heterogeneity, stability, and size. Structure communications and reward systems to promote cooperation or competition, whichever happens to be appropriate for the task.
5. If you are the leader of a group, remember that it is a role *in* the group. Leaders who elevate themselves above the rest of the members may find that they have effectively removed themselves from the group and destroyed their own role.

Exhibit 9.7   Group Behavior as a Function of the Group's Interaction with Its Environment

Environment

Physical Environment:
Spacial Arrangements
Time
Nature of Task

Social Environment:
Other People and Groups
External Laws, Rules, Norms
Reward Systems

Group

Composition:
Characteristics of Members
Homogeneity–Heterogeneity
Stability of Membership
Group Size

Internal Social Environment:
Roles
Communication Patterns
Cohesiveness
Norms

Group Behavior

Communications	Interpersonal Relations
Influence	Task Performance
Decision Making	Goal Achievement

SUMMARY

A group is two or more people who perceive themselves as a group and interact with one another for some purpose. Formal groups are established by authorized personnel to accomplish some task. Informal groups are formed on the basis of common interests, convenience, or liking.

Exhibit 9.7 summarizes the key characteristics of groups and their environments. As with individuals, group behavior is a result of interactions between personal characteristics and environmental factors. The major difference is that personal characteristics include not only characteristics of the individual members, but those of the group which develop from the interactions of its members.

A manager who is interested in changing group behavior has the same two choices as one interested in changing individual behavior—modify the personal characteristics or the environmental ones.

Altering personal characteristics is somewhat easier for groups than for individuals, because the group itself can be effectively changed by adding or subtracting members. It can be made relatively more heterogeneous or homogeneous, larger or smaller, or sometimes broken up entirely. Remember, however, that the group may see the manager who takes such liberties with its membership as an outside threat; since this will increase group cohesiveness, the group may simply become stronger and more determined to persist in the undesired behavior or to resist further managerial influence.

As with an individual, the most effective strategies for changing the behavior of a group involve altering the group's physical or social environment. Changing from a cooperative to a competitive reward system, or vice versa, can complement a group's task.

It is also possible to change a group's internal social environment, especially if the group is a formal one. Appointing or replacing a leader and establishing rules or policies about group interaction are two ways to bring about such changes.

QUESTIONS FOR REVIEW AND DISCUSSION

1. What are the functions of reference groups?
2. Give at least two reasons why a manager must have some skill in understanding the behavior of groups.
3. How do open and closed groups differ?
4. Briefly discuss the meaning of the statement: A group is more than the sum of its parts.
5. What factors promote cohesiveness? What ones discourage it?
6. Describe the typical communication patterns in your class according to the dimensions discussed in this chapter.
7. How do norms promote cohesiveness? How does cohesiveness affect norms?
8. Suppose you are the manager of a large assembly department. Despite your threats, the members of a small informal group continue to play practical jokes and disrupt the work of those around them. Given what you know about groups,
   a. why do you think this behavior persists despite your threats?
   b. how could you effectively change this behavior?
9. What is the relationship between the group's reward system and the nature of its task?
10. Describe work restriction as a control process in a group, using the terms discussed in Chapter 7.

REFERENCES AND NOTES

1. L. R. Hoffman and C. G. Smith, "Some Factors Affecting the Behaviors of Members of Problem-Solving Groups." *Sociometry*, 1960, 23, 273–91.
2. H. J. Lott and B. E. Lott, "Group Cohesiveness as Interpersonal Attraction: A Review of Relationships with Antecedent and Consequent Variables." *Psychological Bulletin*, 1965, 64, 259–302.
3. See the review by M. B. Shaw, *Group Dynamics: The Psychology of Small Group Behavior*, 2nd ed. New York: McGraw-Hill, 1976.
4. P. R. Laughlin and L. G. Branch, "Individual vs. Tetradic Performance on a Complementary Task as a Function of Initial Ability Level." *Organizational Behavior and Human Performance*, 1972, 8, 201–16.
5. See, for example, R. Hall, "Interpersonal Compatibility and Workgroup Performance." *Journal of Applied Behavioral Science*, 1975, 2, 210–19.

6.   R. C. Ziller, "Toward a Theory of Open and Closed Groups." *Psychological Bulletin*, 1965, 64, 164–82.

7.   J. R. Hackman and N. Vidmar, "Effects of Size and Task Type on Group Performance and Member Reactions." *Sociometry*, 1970, 33, 37–54.

8.   P. Wright, "The Harassed Decision-Maker: Time Pressures, Distractions, and the Use of Evidence." *Journal of Applied Psychology*, 1974, 59, 5, 555–61.

9.   These findings have emerged consistently from both the original and the follow-up research of M. Deutsch, "An Experimental Study of the Effects of Cooperation and Competition Upon Group Processes." *Human Relations*, 1949, 2, 199–232.

10.   D. J. Cherrington, "Satisfaction in Competitive Conditions." *Organizational Behavior and Human Performance*, 1973, 10, 47–71.

11.   I. L. Janis, *Victims of Groupthink*. Atlanta: Houghton Mifflin, 1972.

12.   A review of this research may be found in M. E. Shaw, *Group Dynamics: The Psychology of Small Group Behavior*, 2nd ed., New York: McGraw-Hill, 1976.

13.   See A. L. Delbecq, A. H. Van de Ven, and D. H. Gustafson, *Group Techniques for Program Planning: A Guide to Nominal Group and Delphi Processes*. Glenview, Ill.: Scott, Foresman and Company, 1976.

14.   For a more complete summary of the causes and effects of group cohesiveness, see H. J. Reitz, *Behavior in Organizations*, rev. ed. Homewood, Ill.: Irwin, 1981, 293–300.

15.   The classic reference in this area is S. Schachter, "Deviation, Rejection, and Communication." *Journal of Abnormal and Social Psychology*, 1951, 46, 190–207.

SUGGESTED READINGS

Jewell, L. N. and H. J. Reitz, *Group Effectiveness in Organizations*. Glenview, Ill.: Scott, Foresman and Company, 1981. There is a short, but comprehensive, treatment of the material covered in this chapter by the authors of this text.

Lytle, D. H. "A Narrative." In W. G. Bennis, E. H. Schein, F. I. Steele, and D. E. Berlew, eds., *Interpersonal Dynamics*, rev. ed., Homewood, Ill.: Dorsey Press, 1968, 454–61. *A Narrative* is a short story about the influence of reference groups on behavior that most students will find easy to read and enjoyable.

Ritti, R. R. and G. R. Funkhouser, "Better the Devil You Know . . . " in *The Ropes to Skip and the Ropes to Know: Studies in Organizational Behavior*. Columbus, Ohio: GRID, Inc., 1977, 49–52. The fictionalized account of some issues involved in picking the "best people" for a formal group illustrates the role of group cohesiveness.

Roy, D. F., "Banana Time: Job Satisfaction and Informal Interaction." *Human Organization*, 1960, 18, 4. This is a classic reading illustrating the role of the informal clique as a source of support and satisfaction for workers with routine, repetitive jobs. Note especially the description of group communication patterns.

Thompson, V. A., "Dramaturgy." Chapter 7 of *Modern Organization*, The University of Alabama Press, 1977. Reprinted in J. M. Shafritz and P. H. Whitbeck, eds., *Classics of Organization Theory*. Oak Park, Ill.: Moore, 1978, 252–59. A sociologist's analogy of the "boss role" in an organization combined with the drama of the theater makes entertaining and thoughtful reading.

Case Group Number Three

The professor in the Behavior Factors in Organizations course opened the first day of class by giving an overview of the course requirements and objectives . . . . the class of some twenty students would be broken down into several small groups of four or five members each to work primarily as a unit in analyzing cases and submitting reports based on this analysis.

The second class meeting was devoted to the formation of task groups within the class. Group 3 originated with Bob and Bill mutually agreeing to be in the same group. They looked around the room for students to join them and chose to ask Paul, a mutual friend from the previous quarter. Paul accepted the invitation and joined the group at the next class session. Bill urged Bob, "Hurry up, and ask that girl over there before someone else does." Complying with Bob's request, Leslie joined the two original members. Larry, the fifth member, abruptly joined the group without invitation and with the remark, "Well, I guess I'm in this group."

The Members of Group Number Three

Bill: Age 28, Air Force veteran, major undecided, married
Larry: Age 25, Air Force veteran, works full-time, management major, married
Paul: Age 24, Army veteran, works two parttime jobs, management major, married
Leslie: Age 22, works parttime, management major, divorced
Bob: Age 20, management major, single

The first project the group encountered revolved around a case in which a decision had to be made on whether an engineer should or should not accept a management position. At the first group meeting, only three members were present. Larry, Bob, and Paul agreed at this time that the engineer should not accept the promotion. They decided to present this opinion to the other members of the group. With this, the meeting ended.

The next meeting followed a regularly scheduled class. All five members met in the university cafeteria. The three presented their opinion to the group and agreement followed that the engineer would be foolish to accept the promotion.

The group proceeded to answer other questions that were included with the project. They agreed on all the questions except one, "Is this a 'real problem?' Can he have his cake and eat it too?" Larry felt strongly that "he should be able to work on the bench and supervise too." He added, "In the service, we had an NCO who was not afraid to get his hands dirty with bench work, and he was the most highly respected supervisor we had."

Bill just as emphatically responded, "You cannot be on the bench and manage at the same time. You just cannot be a manager and a good guy too!"

The other members supported Bill's point of view. Paul suggested that Larry write a minority opinion and submit it with the report. Larry agreed and the meeting was concluded.

Before the reports were turned in, the professor asked each group to present its ideas, recommendations, and conclusions to the rest of the class for comments. During the discussion that followed, it became obvious that Group 3 had come to a conclusion contrary to

Source: This case is an abbreviated form of the case of the same name written as a basis for class discussion under the supervision of D. R. Kenerson, University of South Florida.

that of the rest of the class. Other group leaders attacked the viewpoint. Bill looked at his fellow group members and exclaimed, "Too bad. They're all wrong," and proceeded to argue in defense of his group's conclusions. He supported the consensus of his group's decision by reading supporting statements from the group's paper.

At the following class meeting, the papers were returned. Group 3 received an "A." They discovered that all the other groups had received either a "B" or a "B + ." At the end of class, one classmate from a different group approached Bill saying, "We'll meet you in the hall with chains!"

CASE QUESTIONS

1. Is Group Three a formal or an informal group? Explain.
2. Is Group Three an open or a closed group? Explain.
3. List as many characteristics as you can on which Group Three is *relatively homogeneous*. On what characteristics is it *relatively heterogeneous?*
4. Give an example and briefly explain how time and the nature of the task affected the behavior of Group Three.
5. Was Group Three operating under a cooperative or a competitive formal reward system? How would you characterize its *internal* reward system?
6. How would you rate Group Three's cohesiveness at the end of the case? Which of the factors that tend to increase group cohesiveness do you think were operating? Which of the effects of cohesiveness do you see in the case?

10/Power, Influence, and Leadership

Art Conway felt pretty good. He had talked over his decision with his wife, and she agreed it was the thing to do—meet with Ellen James and clear the air. After all, Ellen was his boss, was successful, seemed to know her way around. If anyone could help, it was she.

"Ellen," Art began, "I've been doing a good bit of self-examination since our run-in last month, and I'd like your input—candid, no holds barred."

"OK, Art, I don't know any other way to deal with people," admitted Ellen.

"Well, I know we've had some disagreements, but I trust your judgment and respect your honesty. You've been telling me lately that I lack leadership ability. I want you to help me improve, if you think I can."

Ellen leaned forward, "Wrong, Art. If I felt that you lacked the ability, I wouldn't bother with you. You've got the ability; what gets me upset sometimes is that I don't see you using it. You're just not exercising enough positive influence on your group. They're drifting, Art, and so are you."

"I feel that too. But I've never seen myself as a natural leader."

"You don't have to be. I'm certainly not," replied Ellen. "But what I am is goal-oriented, and I use whatever influence I can muster to achieve those goals—both for the organization and for myself. To me, that's what leadership is, not a personal trait, but simply the process of moving a group of people toward some goals. Like right now. My goal for this division is a twenty-percent annual growth in profits, and we'll get it, too, despite the economy."

"You know, I believe you when you say that. If I went to my people with a goal

like that, I don't think they'd buy it," Art mused.

"If not, it'd be because they sensed you didn't buy it either. You can't expect your people to believe in something that you don't. Credibility is a key to influence, Art, and a very delicate one. If people think you're conning them, you'll lose all your credibility. By the way, I think you've taken the first big step to improvement already. Having the guts to evaluate yourself and lay it out for me suggests that you're willing to change. What else have you come up with in your self-analysis?"

"I tried to analyze my strengths and weaknesses vis-a-vis my department. Strengths? First of all, I've got authority. You've made it clear from the start that I'm in charge, and you've never undermined that authority. Second, I've got some expertise and experience. I've done a lot of the stuff my people do, done it well, and they know it.

"Weaknesses? There's not a lot I can do to reward people officially. Bonuses and promotions are hard to come by in our section, and what else is there besides a pat on the back? I've never been comfortable using criticism or *punishment, and I think some people sense that and take advantage. Finally, I lack magnetism, or charisma, or whatever it is that causes people to give up their lives, or at least their lunch hours, for you. Most of the people like me, but do they respect or admire me? I doubt it. So what can I do?"*

"You're right on target, Art," observed Ellen. "That's just about how I see you right now, although you've got more going for you than you think. Whether you know it or not, you're talking about power. That's what it's all about, and I'm going to show you how to get it and use it effectively."

In this chapter we come to one of the most fascinating topics in the study of management—power. Power is probably most often seen as something that comes with certain positions or jobs, and which can be, and often is, abused. A broader understanding of power shows it to be a resource which almost everyone has in some measure. Like all personal skills and resources, it can be put to uses labeled either "good" or "bad" by others.

In her discussion with Art Conway, Ellen James may have exaggerated a bit. Power is not what it's *all* about, at least not for most managers. True, some get turned on by it, so that acquiring power becomes an end in itself. But for the successful manager, power is simply another tool. It is one of the ways managers use to get things done through people. In this chapter, we'll discuss power, influence, and leadership, show how they are related, and describe their usefulness to successful managers.

INFLUENCE AND POWER

Influence is *the process by which managers affect others' behavior.* **Power** is *the ability to exert influence.* Managers cannot exert influence without *some* kind of power, whether it be credibility, charisma, or coercion. That's what Ellen James meant when she said, "Power is what it's all about." Managers can, however, fail to exert influence by not using the power they have, which was one of Ellen's criticisms of Art. Despite his authority and expertise, he let his people stray from their objectives.

When Ellen and Art began to work on improving Art's leadership, their analyses inevitably turned to power. **Leadership** is simply a type of influence, the *influence an individual exerts over a group.* We will discuss this important type of influence later in the chapter, but first, like Ellen and Art, we'll start with the basics.

A manager's job is to plan, organize, direct, and control the behavior of others to accomplish organizational goals. His or her success (and the accomplishment of personal goals) depends entirely on the extent to which these "others" help or hinder; as one author notes, " . . . while it is theoretically possible that all of these people . . . would automatically act in just the manner that a manager wants and needs, such is almost never the case in reality. All the people on whom a manager is dependent have limited time, energy, and talent, for which there are competing demands."[1]

How does a manager get a sufficient part of the time, energy, and talent of the others on whom he or she is dependent? The answer is by exerting influence, which requires power.

Types of Power

In general, there are only five types of power;[2] any influence is based on one, or some combination, of these types.

Reward power is *the ability to influence others by controlling things they want, such as money, acceptance, praise, promotions, and status.* For example, Ellen influenced Art to persist in his self-evaluation by recognizing and praising his effort.

Coercive power is *the ability to influence others by controlling experiences they find unpleasant or aversive, such as pain, ridicule, penalties, rejection, or the withholding of a reward.* A work clique may influence a member to work more slowly by threatening to exclude that member from the group.

Expert power is *the ability to influence others through the possession of knowledge or skills that are useful to others.* Ellen's expertise as a successful executive influenced Art to seek her advice about his own management skills.

Referent power is *the ability to influence others through the possession of characteristics or traits others find attractive, such as status, money, physical beauty, or fame.* Art felt he had little referent power over his group; he felt they liked him but neither respected nor admired him. The advertisement shown in Exhibit 10.1 uses the identification with a famous athlete to influence people to contribute to a cause.

Legitimate power is *the ability to influence others by holding a position which tradition or society endows with the right to influence.* For example, Art, as the appointed head of his department, has legitimate power over his subordinates. Fortunately for Art, Ellen has not undermined his authority despite his problems. She deals with Art, and lets him deal with his people.

Everyone in an organization, not just those in high positions, has power. A secretary may be the only one who can get the information the boss needs (expert power); an assembly-line worker may get favored treatment because he is attractive or charming (referent power); a maintenance worker can give quicker and better service to some than to others (reward power); or a receptionist can deny others access to the boss (coercive power).[3]

The complexity of power relationships in an organization is a fascinating area of study on its own. However, in this chapter, we are focusing on *power as a resource* for the individual manager. It is well to keep in mind, however, that this influence is not one-sided; subordinates do have power over supervisors.[4] They lack authority, but they may have referent power or expertise. They can withhold effort to punish a supervisor or exert effort as a reward. Power is seldom unilateral.

Exhibit 10.1   Using Referent Power to Influence Donors

"Join our team to help beat MS."
. . . Steve Garvey, Chairman, National MS Sports Committee

Athletes vs. MS

A Manager's Power

The fundamental source of a manager's power, legitimate power, is often called *authority*. There are two reasons why authority often appears to be the most critical source of power in organizations. First, there is a wide range of behaviors about which few people care enough to question a manager's authority. This range of behaviors has been called the *zone of indifference*; that is, others are indifferent about doing things in this range the manager's way or their own way. Since the manager has authority, and they have, at least, implicitly agreed to accept this authority by being a member of the organization, they do it the manager's way.

A second reason that legitimate power seems to be so effective is that it is usually accompanied by reward and coercive power. Most managers, for example, have some reward power over subordinates, such as giving or recommending raises, promotions, bonuses, good schedules, and so on. They also have coercive power, because they are able to make unpleasant assignments, withhold rewards, or criticize subordinates. If these managers are also seen as highly attractive (referent power) or knowledgeable (expert power), their abilities to influence the behavior of others will be substantially increased.[5]

It is not easy to learn to acquire power that goes beyond authority. Classical research into power motivation suggests that a desire to be strong and influential is important,[6] but obviously, desire alone is not enough, or more people would be more successful in influencing others.

> *Influence is the process by which managers affect others' behavior. Power is the ability to exert influence. Leadership is simply a type of influence, the influence an individual exerts over a group.*

One reason that it is difficult to acquire power is that power is highly dependent upon the perceptions of others. Managers who want to have expert, referent, reward, or coercive power, must be perceived as knowledgeable, attractive in some sense, or in control of rewards and punishments and likely to use them.

This leads to an important conclusion: *Power is dependent not only upon a manager's resources but upon the perceptions of those the manager seeks to influence.* To be successful, managers must exert more influence than can be derived from authority alone. Managers who fail to use their expertise, who are stingy with rewards, or who are perceived as unlikely to reprimand or criticize will simply not be influential enough to be successful. Managers who avoid using power are a disappointment to their subordinates. Research indicates that employee morale is higher when managers have and use power than when they shun power in an effort to be liked.[7]

Influence from the Manager's Perspective[8]

Any attempt at influence involves two parties, the one who is exerting influence, referred to as the *agent* of influence, and the one who is being influenced, called the *target*. Either the agent or the target can be an individual, a group, or an organization.

Managers themselves are both the agents and targets of influence. They influence, and are influenced by, the organization, groups of subordinates and peers, and individuals at all levels. There can be three outcomes when the manager acts as the agent of influence:

Sometimes *nothing happens*. The influence attempt is not recognized or is ignored. For example, in Chapter 8, Art Conway's secretary ignored his request to check with him before going home.

Other times *an undesired change occurs*. The person who the manager attempts to influence recognizes the attempt and changes his or her behavior, but not as desired. For example, Art might have responded to Ellen's criticism by avoiding her or sulking.

Still other times *the desired change occurs*. The influence attempt is recognized, and the change desired by the manager occurs. Art responded to Ellen's in-

A marine recruit generally has a great deal of dependence on the drill sergeant, increasing the influence of the sergeant over the recruit.

struction to "get his act together" by recognizing his weaknesses and coming to her for help.

Obviously, a manager who attempts to influence others wants to avoid outcomes one and two. The first wastes time, requiring the manager to make another attempt. The second also requires another attempt, but this result may be more serious than the first. Such a response may suggest hostility or the opening gambit in a power struggle. As a general rule, the second outcome suggests that something about the relationship of those involved needs attention.

Influence from the Target's Perspective

Since a response to an influence attempt is a behavior, that response (like all behaviors) will be the result of personal characteristics of the target interacting with the environment in which the influence attempt occurs.

Social psychologists have long been interested in the personal characteristics that make any individual likely to yield to or resist influence. Certain traits, such as self-esteem and intelligence, have been found to be related to someone's tendency to be influenced. In general, however, factors in the environment, especially in the social environment, appear to be more important. Among these factors are:

1. *The relationship between the parties.* The greater the target's dependence on the agent, the more likely the target will yield. Subordinates with few or no alternative job prospects are more influenced than those with other options.
2. *The balance of power between the parties.* Power is relative. A vice-president can influence a foreman through authority alone; a vice-president needs other power to influence another vice-president.
3. *The uncertainty of the target.* When circumstances make the target uncertain about what behavior is most appropriate, the target is susceptible to influence. In such cases, referent power is especially effective. People tend to imitate, in uncertain or novel situations, the behavior of high status or successful models—one reason that the military places great value on commanders who remain calm in the stress of battle.
4. *The behavior of others.* Targets are much more likely to comply with influence attempts when everyone else is doing so. However, if one or more people ignore the attempt or rebel, a target is much less likely to be influenced.
5. *The perceived rewards and costs of yielding.* Obviously, rewards affect the success of influence. But so do costs. Making it expensive for a target to yield, such as causing him or her to lose face with subordinates or peers, makes influence attempts less successful. A manager who forces a subordinate to change his or her mind in public through coercion or authority invites rebellion.

If the target of an influence attempt does yield and make the desired change, the influence attempt has been successful, but may or may not be permanent.

Internalization Versus Compliance

The difference between influence attempts that change behavior permanently and those that do not is the difference between internalization and compliance.

Internalization is *a relatively permanent change in behavior as the result of an influence attempt.* The most important characteristic of internalization is that little further effort is required on the part of the agent to maintain the change in behavior; this outcome of influence has been called *true change.*

Compliance is *a temporary change in behavior as the result of an influence attempt.* The most important characteristic of compliance is that continued surveillance and influence attempts are necessary to maintain the change; this outcome of influence has been called *surface change.* There is no way to distinguish it from true change simply by observing what happens after an influence attempt. The only real test is whether the behavior change persists over time or in situations when there is no possibility that the agent will observe it.

Although we cannot know simply by looking whether an observed change in behavior has been internalized, we do know that there is a relationship between the type of power on which influence is based and the outcome. Influence based on reward or coercive power is *more likely* to result in compliance. Influence based on expert or referent power is *more likely* to result in internalization. In-

Management in Action
Strategies to Influence Others

David Kipnis and Stuart Schmidt studied different strategies managers use to influence their subordinates and their own superiors. Based on their discussions and observations of managers, they identified seven basic strategies:

Manager's Preferences in Influence Strategies

	When Influencing Superiors	When Influencing Subordinates
Most Preferred	Reason	Reason
	Coalition	Assertiveness
	Friendliness	Friendliness
	Bargaining	Coalition
	Assertiveness	Bargaining
Least Preferred	Higher Authority	Higher Authority
		Sanctions

Reason. Managers use facts and data to support their positions. Logic and argumentative tactics are also involved. ("You ought to support our project because it will earn the highest return on investment.")

Friendliness. Goodwill is created with those people managers want to influence by flattering them, and managing other's impressions to create a favorable image. ("I'm asking you to help because you're the only one smart enough to understand the problem.")

Coalitions. Gaining the support of others in the organization helps managers exert influence. ("Several of us feel the same way about this.")

Bargaining. Managers negotiate and exchange benefits or favors with those they influence. ("If you'll help us out on this one, we'll forget about that debt you owe us.")

Assertiveness. Managers use a direct and forceful approach to insist on getting their way. ("This is what I want done and this is the way you're going to do it.")

Higher authority. By gaining the support of superiors, managers can back up their demands or requests. ("I've got the support of the executive committee for what I propose to do.")

Sanctions. Rewards and punishments are used to influence others. ("Either you do it my way, or you can look for another job.")

Together with colleagues in Australia and England, Kipnis and Stuart studied lower-level managers in those two countries and the United States to determine the strategies managers preferred to use and the conditions they preferred. They found that, in all three countries, managers preferred using reason to using higher authority and sanctions, but their preferences for other strategies depended upon the target of influence—superiors or subordinates.

Managers with a great deal of expertise rely mainly on reason to influence others. Inexperienced managers are likely to use any of the above strategies without regard for their own positions or those of their targets.

Source: D. Kipnis, S. M. Schmidt, C. Waffin-Smith, and I. Wilkinson, "Patterns of Managerial Influence: Shotgun Managers, Tacticians, and Bystanders." *Organizational Dynamics*, Winter 1984, pp. 58–67.

Exhibit 10.2   Power Bases and Successful Influence

Reward Power	Coercive Power	Expert Power	Referent Power
Control over positive outcomes	Control over negative outcomes	Control over useful information	Possession of attractive traits

Legitimate Power
Position in social structure

Compliance
Continued influence necessary to maintain change

Internalization
Little additional influence necessary to maintain change

*From L.N. Jewell and H.J. Reitz, *Group Effectiveness in Organizations.* Glenview, Ill.: Scott, Foresman, 1981.

fluence based on legitimate power (authority) can go either way, depending on the agent's other powers. These relationships are diagrammed in Exhibit 10.2.

While internalization is more efficient and may be more personally satisfying to a manager, it is also more difficult to achieve in organizations. Fortunately for the manager who wishes to become a more effective influence agent, it frequently makes no practical difference whether change is real or surface. There is a wide range of behaviors for which compliance is perfectly satisfactory, such as compliance with dress codes, operating procedures, company rules, and safety regulations.

Where the difference between internalization and compliance becomes more critical is in the realm of such basic dimensions of behavior as effort, commitment to the organization, and ethics. It is simply impossible to monitor behaviors associated with effort, commitment, and ethics well enough for compliance to be an adequate form of influence.

Compliance will not be a sufficient form of influence over those who occupy boundary roles in the organization. A ***boundary role*** is *a position that requires its occupant to spend a great deal of time outside the organization.* Outside salespeople, service representatives, labor negotiators, public-relations specialists, foreign diplomats, news correspondents, and undercover agents have boundary roles. The nature of their jobs makes observation of their activities extremely difficult. Without observation, compliance cannot work. Boundary-role occupants who have not internalized organizational values and policies are more likely to sell out the organization.

The ability to successfully influence others to internalize changes is often cited as the hallmark of a true leader. However, leadership is considerably more complex, and individuals who can consistently influence others successfully are rare, owing to the enormous variations in superior, coworker, and subordinate characteristics as described in the two previous chapters. In most organizations, internalization is a gradual process. It results from selection, training, socialization, and rewards, as well as direct personal influence.

Effective Influence and the Skillful Use of Power

Effective influence consists of changing behavior; the means for doing this, as explained earlier, is power. *Power is a resource, but the use of power is a skill.* Part of that skill lies in communicating influence attempts, a subject to be discussed in the following chapter. Another part of that skill, however, lies in recognizing the costs and benefits associated with the forms of power and using the more "expensive" forms only when necessary.

From the standpoint of the manager, the least expensive form of power to use is referent power. When others do what you wish because they like you, want to be like you, believe there is prestige in being accepted by you, and so on, it costs you little or nothing. Of course, acquiring referent power is not without expense. With the exception of those rare individuals who seem to have natural charisma, referent power in organizations tends to stem from achievement, success, and recognition. These take effort, even if the use of the associated referent power does not.

At the other extreme is coercive power, the most expensive form of power to use. Threats and punishments can damage or destroy relationships, give rise to resistance for the sake of resistance, or lead to retaliation. There are also psychological costs to the user of coercive power; most of us like ourselves better when we can get things done some other way.

The cost of using reward power is the cost associated with using up a limited resource. Most managers control only a limited number of tangible rewards such as raises, promotions, and desirable job assignments. Social rewards, such as praise and acceptance are unlimited, but become ineffective if overused.

Expert power can also be used up. To be effective, the agent's knowledge must be perceived to be greater than the knowledge of the target. As that expertise is shared, knowledge becomes equalized and expert power is reduced. At the same time, however, referent power usually increases.

The relative costs of the various power bases suggest that the long-term, skillful use of power is a balancing act. The aim is to influence others successfully without incurring exorbitant costs or running out of resources. Although the acquisition and use of power is a relatively complex subject, even our limited discussion suggests three guidelines to help accomplish this balance:

1. Use referent power freely if you have it.
2. Use coercive power as little as possible.
3. Take steps to offset the use of rewards and expert power by acquiring additional resources. Taking advantage of employee-development or continuing education opportunities (increased expert power) and work to move up in the organizational hierarchy (increased legitimate and reward power).

Exhibit 10.3 lists the various power bases, their advantages, and disadvantages.

LEADERSHIP

Leadership may be the most discussed topic in management. It predates even the intense ongoing interest in motivation to which it is, of course, related. The question of what makes a leader has been debated almost endlessly.

In these debates, the words *leader* and *leadership* are used in many ways. The basic confusion stems from the fact that both words are used to refer to three different things—personal characteristics, position, and behavior.

Leader and *leadership* can refer to such *personal attributes* as energy, extraversion, commitment to a cause, and charisma. Behind these words often lurks a belief that leaders are born, not developed. One article on leadership, for example, asks whether "the talent for leadership has abruptly disappeared from the American genes."[9]

A leadership *position* is a role in a social unit, a job which someone inherits, or to which someone is appointed or elected. Business organizations have presidents and managers. Countries have presidents and prime ministers. Armed forces have generals and admirals. Hospitals have administrators. All of these are leadership positions; they exist independently of the person or persons who fill them.

The use of the words *leader* and *leadership* to refer to *behavior* is relatively common, but it is not always consistent. Sometimes the words refer to the behavior of someone in a position of leadership, and in that case, they are usually used to *evaluate* the behavior of that person. Thus, we get phrases such as "a weak leader" or "a true leader." Sometimes the terms refer to the behavior of people who are not in formal leadership positions. Delighted parents hear that their child is "a real leader on the playground." Supervisors write on performance appraisals that an employee "shows considerable leadership."

We will concentrate on *leadership as behavior.* Back in Chapter 1 we described a manager's job as a set of roles—interpersonal, informational, and decision making. The first interpersonal role was that of **leader:** *one who influences his or her group.* **Leadership** is *the behavior a manager uses to influence a group.*

Further, we will focus on *formal, appointed, or elected leaders* while not denying the importance of all of those people who are influential in their own domains, even though they hold no formal position. These informal, or *emergent,*[10] leaders are important to the functioning of their own groups and can be a critical factor in the success or failure of formal leaders. You will study informal leadership in detail in organizational behavior courses.

Why Organizations Need Leadership

Most organizations are deliberately designed to operate independently of the particular individuals in them and to regulate the activities of whatever members the organizations happen to have at any given time. Why, then, doesn't the organizational system simply "roll on unchanged and unchanging in social space?"[11]

The authors of this quotation discuss four reasons why more than their structures are needed to keep organizations functioning:

Exhibit 10.3   Types of Power and Influence: Their Advantages and Drawbacks

	What They Can Influence	Advantages	Drawbacks
Face-to-Face Methods: Exercise obligation-based power. (legitimate power)	Behavior within zone that the other perceives as legitimate in light of the obligation.	Quick. Requires no outlay of tangible resources.	If the request is outside the acceptable zone, it will fail; if it is too far outside, others might see it as illegitimate.
Exercise power based on perceived expertise. (expert power)	Attitudes and behavior within the zone of perceived expertise.	Quick. Requires no outlay of tangible resources.	If the request is outside the acceptable zone, it will fail; if it is too far outside, others might see it as illegitimate.
Exercise power based on identification with a manager. (referent power)	Attitudes and behavior that are not in conflict with the ideals that underlie the identification.	Quick. Requires no expenditure of limited resources.	Restricted to influence attempts that are not in conflict with the ideals that underlie the identification.
Exercise power based on perceived dependence for rewards. (reward power)	Wide range of behavior that can be monitored.	Quick. Can often succeed when other methods fail.	Repeated influence attempts encourage the other to gain power over the influencer.
Coercively exercise power based on perceived dependence. (coercive power)	Wide range of behavior that can be easily monitored.	Quick. Can often succeed when other methods fail.	Invites retaliation. Very risky. Promotes avoidance, subterfuge.
Use persuasion (internalization)	Very wide range of attitudes and behavior.	Can produce internalized motivation.	Can be very time-consuming. Requires other person to listen.
Combine these methods.	Depends on the exact combination.	Can be more potent and less risky than using a single method.	More costly than using a single method.
Environmental Methods: Manipulate the other's environment by using any or all of the face-to-face methods.	Wide range of behavior and attitudes.	Can succeed when face-to-face methods fail.	Can be time-consuming. Is complex to implement. Is very risky, especially if used frequently.
Change the forces that continuously act on the individual:	Wide range of behavior and attitudes on a continuous basis.	Has continuous influence, not just a one-shot effect. Can have a very powerful impact.	Often requires a considerable power outlay to achieve.

Source: Reprinted by permission of the Harvard Business Review. An exhibit from "Power, Dependence, and Effective Management," by John P. Kotter (July/August 1977). Copyright © 1977 by the President and Fellows of Harvard College; all rights reserved.

1. No structure is ever complete or sufficient. It is not possible to regulate all aspects of organizational functioning completely.
2. External conditions change and the organization's dependence on its external environment requires that it change too if it is to function effectively.
3. Internal conditions change; the organization expands, contracts, changes direction, and so on.
4. An organization is staffed by human beings whose individual characteristics put continual stress on its structure.

It seems clear that organizations require some things beyond structure if they are to survive and prosper. One of these is the leadership exerted by managers to influence groups in achieving organizational goals.

What Makes Effective Leadership?

Part of the confusion about leadership in general, and leadership in organizations in particular, is simply confusion about what leaders do or should do. A recent informal survey showed that leaders are expected to:

make decisions

cope with crises

define and solve problems

develop, take care of, and inspire
   subordinates

set a good example

find and acquire resources

set the "tone" of the organization

facilitate group efforts

communicate organizational policy and
   goals to subordinates

instigate and manage change

serve as an information center

help subordinates with their problems

"sell" ideas and decisions to those who
   must be persuaded

see that the job gets done

represent the organization to outsiders.

What this list tells us most clearly is that there is enormous variation in what people believe someone in a leadership position is *supposed* to do. However, the great majority of these responsibilities can be divided into two categories—behavior concerned with *the accomplishment of the group's tasks and goals,* and behavior concerned with *the welfare of the group and its members.*

This simple model, depicted in Exhibit 10.4, makes it possible to distinguish levels of leadership effectiveness. A leader who promotes neither the group's welfare nor the accomplishment of its tasks is an ineffective leader. Ineffective leaders include both those who do nothing and those who use their position only to promote themselves, usually at the expense of their subordinates.

More effective are those leaders who either increase the group's task performance and goal achievement or promote the group's welfare. Leaders whose behavior is mainly concerned with task performance and goal accomplishment are

Exhibit 10.4   A Two-Dimensional Model of Leader Behavior

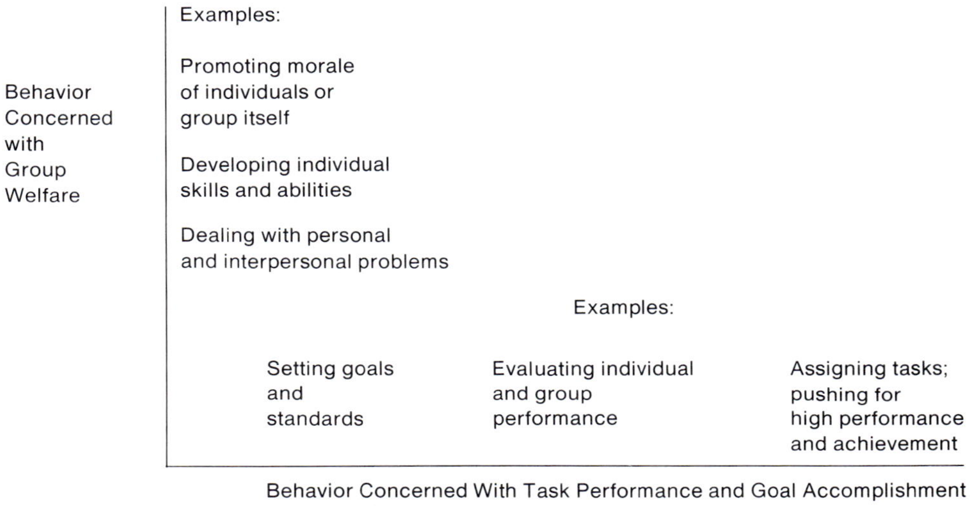

Behavior
Concerned
with
Group
Welfare

Examples:

Promoting morale
of individuals or
group itself

Developing individual
skills and abilities

Dealing with personal
and interpersonal problems

Examples:

Setting goals and standards	Evaluating individual and group performance	Assigning tasks; pushing for high performance and achievement

Behavior Concerned With Task Performance and Goal Accomplishment

often referred to as *task-oriented* leaders. They attend to the group's welfare only when internal problems threaten its performance. Leaders whose behavior is mainly concerned with the welfare of the group and its members are often referred to as *country-club* leaders. They attend to the group's task and goals only when forced by crises, time pressures, or other threats.

The most effective leaders are those that promote both task and goal accomplishment and group welfare. Managers do not *have* to choose between these two sets of activities; there may be times when one is more important than the other, but they are not antithetical.

Because organizations are more experienced in measuring task performance and goal accomplishments than they are in measuring group welfare, you are more likely to encounter task-oriented leaders than either country-club or do-nothing leaders. Do-nothing leaders eventually lose their positions, unless political forces support them. Country-club leaders tend to be more underevaluated than task-oriented leaders, because organizations tend to measure their contributions poorly, if at all.

Leaders who successfully promote both goal accomplishment and group welfare are likely to be successful as well as effective. Their concerns for group welfare provides them with strong and loyal support that can overcome many obstacles managers encounter during their careers. The need for both concerns is demonstrated by the study of successful and unsuccessful executives described in Chapter 8. Among the four basic reasons for the failure of the unsuccessful executives to reach the top were these two:

1. Deficiencies eventually matter. If talented enough, a person can get by with insensitivity at lower levels, but not at higher ones, where subordinates and peers are powerful and intelligent. Those who are charming but not knowledgeable find that the job gets too complex to get by on interpersonal skills alone.
2. Success goes to their heads. After being told how good they are for so long, some executives simply lose their humility and become cold and arrogant. Once this happens, their information sources begin to dry up and people no longer wish to work with them.[12]

A formal position of leadership makes the holder of the position *responsible* for accomplishing its defined functions. Leaders are expected to get things done, to make it work, whatever "it" may be. To do so, they are dependent on a large number of other people, either to actually do what must be done or to provide the information, resources, and support for what must be done. In either case, leaders must influence. To restate the matter simply, it is possible to have power and influence without being an effective leader, but it is not possible to be an effective leader without power and influence.

Determinants of Leader Behavior

By this time, it will not come as any surprise to you to hear that the behavior of anyone in a leadership position is determined jointly by his or her personal characteristics and the physical and social environments. The history of leadership theory has seen emphasis on one, then the other, of these two factors. Quite recently, the two have finally begun to receive equal emphasis.

Personal Characteristics of the Leader.   For about the first half of this century, the study of leadership was dominated by the study of the personal characteristics of the leader. Initially, people believed that effective leaders were simply different from other people, particularly in terms of physical characteristics, intelligence, or personality characteristics. However, the search for these traits was unsuccessful.[13] *Trait theory* failed because there were just too many exceptions. Some effective leaders were tall, outgoing, college-educated, or came from prominent families. Others were short, reserved, had little or no formal education, or came from families of humble origins.

The failure of trait theory increased determination to find one best way for leaders to behave. Reminiscent of the one-best-way approaches to management described in Chapter 2, this research tried to determine if task-oriented leadership was more effective than group welfare-oriented leadership,[14] or if democratic leaders were more effective than autocratic leaders.[15] Like other one-best-way approaches, this attempt also failed. In some cases task-oriented leadership was more effective; in others it was not. In some cases democratic leadership was more effective; in others it was not.

The Environment of the Leader. As it became apparent that research could uncover no one best way to lead, attention turned toward a contingency approach, discussed in Chapter 2. Perhaps some ways of leading were better in some situations than others. Those who took up the search looked to a leader's environment.

> *The most effective way for a leader to behave depends upon the characteristics of the group, the group's task, and the distribution and extent of power and authority.*

The first contingency theory of leadership effectiveness was developed by Fred S. Fiedler.[16] Fiedler systematically studied a wide range of groups and leaders—land surveying teams, decision-making and problem-solving groups, small cooperative corporations, service stations, steel fabricating departments, basketball teams, tank and aircraft crews. His research uncovered three key factors that determined the relative effectiveness of different types of leaders:

1. Leader-member relations—whether the leader and the group got along well together. Good leader-member relations are as much a function of group characteristics as they are of leader characteristics.
2. Nature of the group's task—whether the task was relatively structured or unstructured. Structured tasks can be evaluated objectively, can have clearly understood goals, can have a small number of correct solutions, and a handful of ways to be accomplished.
3. Position power of the leader—whether the leader's position was strong or weak relative to the group. The position powers are legitimate, reward, and coercive—they are a function of the leader's position rather than of the leader personally.

Fiedler combined these three variables into eight different combinations, as depicted in Exhibit 10.5. In comparing the relative effectiveness of groups and leaders across these eight situations, Fiedler found that in situations I, II, III, VII, and VIII, leaders who valued task success had more productive groups than leaders who valued interpersonal success. In situations IV, V, and VI, leaders who valued interpersonal success had higher performing groups than their more task-oriented peers.[17]

Encouraged by this support for a contingency approach, Robert J. House developed another model called the Path-Goal Theory.[18] The Path-Goal Theory argues that, consistent with the motivation models described in Chapter 8, a leader can best promote group performance and satisfaction by using rewards as goals contingent upon good performance, and by helping the group understand what paths they must follow to achieve their goals. The Path-Goal Theory is a contingency approach; it states that the behaviors most likely to clarify paths to group goals depend on the situation. The factors identified as crucial in determining the relative effectiveness of different leader behaviors include:

Exhibit 10.5   Fiedler's Classification of Leadership Situations

Leader member relations	Good				Poor		
Task structure	High		Low		High		Low
Position power	Strong	Weak	Strong	Weak	Strong	Weak	Strong	Weak
	I	II	III	IV	V	VI	VII	VIII

Very favorable ◄─────────────────────────► Very unfavorable

Source: F.E. Fiedler, *A Theory of Leadership Effectiveness*. New York: McGraw-Hill, 1967. Used by permission of McGraw-Hill Book Company.

1. Characteristics of the group members—their abilities, needs, and motives;
2. The nature of the group's task—routine or nonroutine; intrinsically satisfying or not;
3. The formal authority system of the organization—many policies, rules, and regulations or few policies, rules, and regulations.

These factors are not greatly different from those proposed by Fiedler's model. The path-goal theory proposes, however, that the most effective leader behavior complements the situation. If the task is routine and the authority system strong, skilled subordinates will resent and not respond well to task-oriented, directive leadership. However, when tasks are ambiguous, or policies unclear, task-oriented leadership will be effective. When the situation is one that is stressful, frustrating, or dissatisfying to subordinates, then leadership supportive of their welfare is more effective.

Fiedler's contingency model and House's path-goal theory both indicate support for a contingency approach to leadership effectiveness. The most effective way for a leader to behave depends upon the characteristics of the group, the group's task, and the distribution and extent of power and authority. Unfortunately, research on these models does not yet allow us to make specific statements about exactly which leader behaviors will produce what effects. Research on Fiedler's model has concentrated on group productivity and ignored goal achievement and group welfare; research on House's theory has been more consistent in demonstrating the effects of leader behavior on subordinate satisfaction than on productivity and goal achievement. We have a lot to learn about leadership effectiveness.

Limitations on Leadership

So much emphasis is placed on leadership that it is easy to forget that management and leadership are not the same thing. All leaders are not managers. And the leader role is only one of many roles managers play. Being an effective leader is an ob-

Exhibit 10.6   Substitutes for Leadership

	Relationship-oriented supportive leadership	Task-oriented instrumental leadership
1. Subordinate characteristics		
a. Ability		Substitute
b. "Professional" orientation	Substitute	Substitute
c. Closely knit, cohesive work groups	Substitute	Substitute
2. Task characteristics		
a. Unambiguous and routine		Substitute
b. Provides direct feedback concerning accomplishment		Substitute
c. Intrinsically satisfying	Substitute	

Source: Adapted with modifications from "Substitutes for Leadership: Their Meaning and Measurement" by S. Kerr & J. M. Jermier, *Organizational Behavior and Human Performance*, 1978, *22*, 375–403.

vious asset for any manager who wants to be successful; but many managers make up for leadership deficiencies by emphasizing their strengths in other areas—in planning or organizing, in communicating or staffing.

In addition, certain characteristics of the group or its tasks can reduce the need for certain kinds of leadership. These "substitutes for leadership" are depicted in Exhibit 10.6.[19]

For example, a cohesive group will often take care of its own welfare and that of its members, with little direction from the leader. Tasks that are clear, routine, and provide performance feedback require less task-oriented leadership. Identification of these substitutes for leadership is consistent with the contingency approach. The situation helps determine not only what kinds of leadership will be most effective, but how much. A manager who finds that the group and its tasks require little direct, personal leadership is free to concentrate on other roles.

The Bottom Line

In attempting to lead or otherwise successfully influence subordinates, peers, and superiors in an organization, keep in mind that:

1. There are five different bases of power. New managers typically start with some legitimate power, a little reward power, and virtually no expertise relative to their more experienced subordinates and peers. Take time to increase your different bases of power and understand those you want to influence before attempting to "throw your weight around." Initially, you will have less weight than you think.

2. Subordinates expect you to exert influence over them. They also expect you to exert influence over your superiors and peers, to keep them off your subordinates' backs, and to provide subordinates with resources and information. Upward influence will increase your referent power, and thus increase your influence over subordinates.

3. Targets can react to influence attempts by ignoring, rebelling against, or complying with them. A successful manager has a high rate of compliance for his or her influence attempts. A manager who tries to exert a lot of influence without regard for likely outcomes can erode his or her power base. Be aware of circumstances which will affect the likely outcomes of your influence attempts. If practical, arrange situations to increase the likelihood of compliance and decrease the chances of rebellion.

4. Leadership is a complex form of influence. Effective leaders fit their behavior to the situation. Therefore, effective leaders need to be aware of their own behavior and characteristics, and alert to key characteristics of the group, its task, and the situation. You may not have the time or the inclination to be sensitive to all these factors. However, you don't have to be perfect. First, leadership is only a part of a manager's job. Second, some leadership, even if not perfectly appropriate, is better than none. Third, not all leadership has to come from the formal leader. Certain characteristics of the situation may reduce the need for some types of leadership. Other people in the group may provide leadership. If they do, and they are effective in helping you achieve your goals, don't view them as a threat, but as assets in helping you manage successfully.

SUMMARY

Exerting influence is a critical managerial skill. Managers get things done through people. Therefore, successful managers are influential, with peers and superiors as well as with subordinates.

Influence requires power, which comes in many forms. Reward, coercive, and legitimate power stem from the manager's position in the organization. Expert and referent power are personal powers managers use to augment their positions. All types of power are relative: their effectiveness depends upon the characteristics of those whom the manager is attempting to influence.

Leadership is a special form of influence; the influence an individual exerts over a group. Leadership is one of many roles managers play. It consists of basically two classes of behaviors—those that promote task performance and goal achievement, and those that promote individual and group welfare. The effectiveness of different kinds of leader behaviors depends upon characteristics of the group and its members, the group's task, and power and authority.

QUESTIONS FOR REVIEW AND DISCUSSION

1. As a new manager out of business school, what kinds of power would you expect to have *vis-a-vis* your subordinates? What sources of power would be particularly weak?
2. What kinds of power would a group of experienced subordinates have over a new manager?
3. What are five possible outcomes for a manager trying to pressure subordinates

into greater productivity through coercion? What might be done to avoid rebellious outcomes?

4. What would be the most effective source of power over boundary-role occupants? The least effective? Why?
5. Evaluate the assertion, "Leaders are born, not made."
6. What kinds of problems are task-oriented leaders likely to have? Under what conditions might task-oriented leadership be effective?
7. What kinds of problems are "country-club" leaders likely to have? Under what conditions might they be most successful?
8. According to contingency theory, what kinds of people make the most effective leaders? Why?
9. Suggest some substitutes for leadership for the following situations:
    a. an operating room team during surgery
    b. a scientific group working on the development of a new product
    c. an athletic team in competition
    d. a military unit in combat
    e. a sales force facing stiff competition

REFERENCES AND NOTES

1. J. P. Kotter, "Power, Dependence, and Effective Management." *Harvard Business Review*, 1977, 55, 4, 125–36, quotation from page 127.
2. The following is the classic power typology of J. R. P. French and B. Raven, "The Bases of Social Power." In D. Cartwright and A. Zander, eds., *Group Dynamics: Research and Theory*. New York: Harper & Row, 1968, Chapter 20.
3. A sample of recent research with this typology is A. T. Cobb, "Informal Influence in Formal Organizations: Perceived Sources of Power Among Work Unit Peers." *Academy of Management Journal*, 1980, 23, 1, 155–61.
4. *See*, for example, N. C. Hill and P. H. Thompson, "Managing Your Manager: The Effective Subordinate." *Exchange*, 1978 (Fall-Winter).
5. A. S. Tannenbaum, "Control in Organizations." *Administrative Science Quarterly*, 1962, 7, 236–57.
6. The pioneer research in this area is that of D. C. McClelland and Associates. See *The Achieving Society*. New York: Van Nostrand, 1961.
7. D. C. McClelland and D. H. Burnham, "Power Is the Great Motivator." *Harvard Business Review*, 1976, 54, 2, 100–110.
8. This discussion is adapted from L. N. Jewell and H. J. Reitz, *Group Effectiveness in Organizations*. Glenview, Ill.: Scott, Foresman and Company, 1981, Chapter 4.
9. "A Cry For Leadership." *Time*, August 6, 1979, 25.
10. See E. P. Hollander, "Emergent Leadership and Social Influence." In L. Petrullo and B. M. Bass, eds., *Leadership and Interpersonal Behavior*. New York: Holt, Rinehart, and Winston, 1961, 30–47.
11. D. Katz and R. L. Kahn, *The Social Psychology of Organizations*, 2nd. ed., New York: Wiley, 1978, p. 530.

12. M. W. McCall, Jr. and M. M. Lombardo, "What Makes a Top Executive?" *Psychology Today*, February 1983, p. 29.

13. A review of this research may be found in C. S. Gibb, "Leadership." In G. Lindzey and E. Aronson, eds., *The Handbook of Social Psychology*, 2nd. ed., Vol. 4. Reading, Mass.: Addison-Wesley, 1969, pp. 205–82.

14. The original report of the research using the terms *employee-centered* and *production-centered* is D. Katz, N. Maccoby, and N. C. Morse, *Productivity, Supervision, and Morale in an Office Situation.* Ann Arbor, Mich.: University of Michigan, 1950. Another group of researchers reached similar conclusions but called the styles *showing consideration* and *initiating structure.* See J. K. Hemphill, *Leader Behavior Description.* Columbus, Ohio: Ohio State University, 1950. Both sets of terms describe the same general kinds of leader behavior and both are in common use today.

15. The research that gave this approach its impetus is reported in K. Lewin, R. Lippitt, and R. K. White, "Patterns of Aggressive Behavior in Experimentally Created 'Social Climates'." *Journal of Social Psychology*, 1939, 10, 2, 271–99.

16. F. E. Fiedler, "Engineer the Job to Fit the Manager." *Harvard Business Review*, 1965, 43, 5, 115–22.

17. For a recent review of this research, see M. J. Strube and J. E. Garcia, "A Meta-Analytic Investigation of Fiedler's Contingency Model of Leadership Effectiveness." *Psychological Bulletin*, 1981, 90, 307–21.

18. R. J. House, "A Path-Goal Theory of Leader Effectiveness." *Administrative Science Quarterly*, 1971, 16, 1, 19–30.

19. S. Kerr and J. Jermier, "Substitutes for Leadership: Their Meaning and Measurement." *Organizational Behavior and Human Performance*, 1978, 22, 3, 375–403.

SUGGESTED READINGS

Gellerman, S., "Supervision: Substance and Style" *Harvard Business Review*, 1976 (March-April), 54, 2, 89–99. The author observed and recorded the activities of twelve supervisors in a large food processing plant to determine the relative impact of *what* is done in such a position (substance) versus *how* it is done (style). Material was later used for supervisory training.

Hollander, E. P. and J. W. Julian, "Contemporary Trends in the Analysis of Leadership Processes." *Psychological Bulletin*, 1969, 71, 5, 387–97. This classic reference remains a useful summary of research in the leadership area over the first two-thirds of this century.

McMurry, R. N., "Power and the Ambitious Executive." *Harvard Business Review*, 1973 (Nov.-Dec.), 51, 6, 140–65. On the basis of thirty years of observation, the author presents eight strategies for the manager or executive to use in acquiring sufficient power to hold the job and get things done.

Menzies, H. D., "The Ten Toughest Bosses." *Fortune*, 1980 (April), 62–72. This article gives an interesting look at "old style" bosses in a modern world.

Case Tracking the Great Persuader

It was countdown to roll call in Congress, and the vote on the tax bill in the House, according to all predictions, was going to be close. The White House knew that a little salesmanship was in order, and so the Great Persuader went to work. After it was over and Ronald Reagan had once again stunned the House leadership by picking up 48 Democratic votes for his bill, the President insisted: "There hasn't been any arm twisting of any kind." Shucks, no. But there are ways, all sorts of ways . . .

Three days before the House vote, the President invited 15 pivotal Democrats to Camp David for an all-American afternoon of hot dogs, hamburgers and homily. Among them was Glenn English, a fourth-term Congressman from Oklahoma. Reagan followed up the hamburger with a hand-written note to "Dear Glenn," promising to veto any bills that would authorize a windfall-profits tax on natural gas. English later showed the note to colleagues of his with natural gas interests among their constituents. They, like English, voted Reagan's way.

Everyone likes to shuffle his feet in the Oval Office. Reagan invited a score of Congressmen to visit him there on Monday, and 43 more on Tuesday. Some came alone, others in groups of six or seven. After Democrat Ralph Hall of Texas affirmed his commitment to his party's bill, the President followed their chat with a telephone call to a radio talk show in Hall's district. So many constituents called Hall's office afterward that he begged party leaders to release him from his commitment to the leadership bill. When it came time to vote, Hall backed the President.

Armed with a list of Congressmen and their pet projects, the President spent hours on the phone. "What can I do to help you make up your mind?" he would ask the reluctant Democratic dragoons. Angry about windfall oil taxes? Worried about Cuban refugees? Just tell me what you want. Reagan won New York Congressman Mario Biaggi's backing when he promised to support legislation that would preserve minimum Social Security benefits for the truly "needy."

A few days before his TV address, Reagan called Texas Democrat Charles Stenholm into the Oval Office to ask for his support. Stenholm agreed and pointed out that one way the President could win some Southern Democrats would be to stop opposing a peanut-crop allotment scheme. Taking his advice, Reagan later assured the ten-man Georgia delegation that the matter was not peanuts to him. When former President (and sometime Peanut Farmer) Jimmy Carter called Congressman Bo Ginn, it was too late. Carter was Ginn's 405th caller that day—and only the fifth to support the Democratic bill. Ginn and seven other Georgians had decided to back Reagan.

What is good for General Motors may be good for the country, after all. Reagan invited more than 200 business leaders to the White House on Monday to push his program. Executives of GM made calls to Congressmen, and Dow Chemical urged its employees to contact their Representatives. At the heart of the corporate effort was the "No Name Group," a little-known gathering of Washington lobbyists for the Chamber of

By Ellie McGrath. Reported by Douglas Brew and Hays Gorey / Washington.
Source: *Time*, August 10, 1981, page 14.

Commerce and similar business associations. At their weekly breakfast at the Sheraton Carlton Hotel, the lobbyists had been supplied by the White House with the names of 43 Democratic Congressmen whose votes might be winnable. No Name was ready. Since the Chamber of Commerce is a presence in cities and towns of any size, the wires started humming in critical congressional districts. Result: 29 of the 43 targeted Democrats supported the President. Admits David Franasiak, director of tax policy for the U.S. Chamber of Commerce: "It was the business community working for its best interests."

DoALL Company, a Chicago-area machine tool distributor with nationwide offices, hired the Eastern Onion Singing Telegrams Company of Bethesda, Md., to bring its message to 74 undecided Congressmen. DoALL's local branches had been hurt by the business slump, and they favor the President's tax plan. Their ditty, sung to the tune of The Yankee Doodle Boy, concluded: "You'll have a job for every man / So just say 'Aye' / Don't be a slob / Someday you might have Rea-

gan's job / So please vote for Reagan's tax-cut plan." Six singers, dressed in top hats and tuxedos, invaded three congressional office buildings Wednesday morning, armed with kazoos and cymbal-playing mechanical monkeys. Only Bonzo was missing. Some Congressmen, however, were not amused. Los Angeles Democrat Edward Roybal, 65, took to the House floor that afternoon to denounce the stunt. Said he: "We are dealing with serious economic issues, and some of our loyal opposition seems to think it is time to send in the clowns."

It worked beautifully against Jimmy Carter. When all else fails, the Republican trump card is television, as practiced by Ronald Reagan. During his 22-minute speech to the nation, the President told the American people to keep those cards and letters coming in to their Congressmen. Although the hot dogs at Camp David did not convert Maryland Democrat Beverly Byron, a thousand calls to her after the speech did. She, like so many others, went the President's way after a nudge from the voters.

CASE QUESTIONS

1. The news article, used in this chapter instead of a traditional case, describes some events in one of Ronald Reagan's "salesmanship campaigns." In terms of this chapter, Reagan was trying to influence the behavior of a large group of people.
   a. What was the behavior he wished to influence?
   b. What was the outcome of the influence attempt that he desired?
2. Give one example from the article of Reagan's use of each of the following:
   a. reward power.
   b. referent power.
3. To what extent do you think it was important to Reagan that his influence attempts result in internalization versus compliance?
4. On the basis of the article, give two examples of Reagan's understanding of the suggestions in this chapter for acquiring power that goes beyond authority.

Report from the Field *Making a Nonroutine Decision*

Carol Littge is assistant controller for Water and Air Research, Inc., a small, scientific engineering research firm that specializes in environmental consulting. Carol, the only MBA on an otherwise science-educated management team, was given the assignment of recommending a computer-based information system that could process the company's growing financial transactions.

"The first thing I did was to go to the library and check out some books on the process of implementing computer-based information systems in organizations. This helped me become aware of many of the problems and pitfalls, such as failing to account for the needs of the people using the system.

"The second thing I did was to learn our current financial system, both by talking to the people who worked with it and by studying our books and ledgers. My first real decision in this whole process was to concentrate on finding the software or programs that could best handle our system, and then to worry about finding a computer that could handle that software.

"The third step in my information-gathering phase was to go back to top management to find out what kinds of plans they had in mind for our computer system, both now and in the future. Talking with them and with some of our engineers who would be potential users of the system led me to conclude that we'd need a system that was expandable, flexible, and easily accessible by several people, including people working out in the field.

"Finally I felt prepared enough to start talking to vendors. I started by contacting local vendors of computer software, and quickly learned to avoid salespeople and go directly to the general manager, who was often the only person really knowledgeable about software and programming. I got the idea of using a consultant familiar with software to help direct my search. My boss approved of the idea, and also suggested that I go to one of the professional groups to which we belonged, the American Consulting Engineers' Council. ACEC had been gathering data from its members on systems that they were using. That information gave me the names of other vendors who, in turn, sent me information on their systems.

"While waiting for all this new information to come in, I started to generate a list of criteria by which to evaluate the systems, such as the ability to integrate financial and cost accounting, to generate employee productivity and project management reports, speed, cost, compatibility with different hardware systems, and estimated time to install and get operational. The consultant was useful in this area, both in establishing criteria and in evaluating different systems. He was particularly helpful in getting through to manufacturers of software, who usually will not deal directly with end-users.

"Finally I narrowed the choices down to six systems that met our standards. I made up several charts comparing and describing these systems and took them before the board for about two hours one day, and together we narrowed the list down to two. The board approved my work and gave me another thirty days to make a final recommendation.

Source: Personal Interview, October 1983.

11 / Communications and Management Information Systems

Tradd reread the memo as he waited for his secretary to put his call through:

To: All Managers Level 3 and Higher
From: EDP Systems
Subject Computer Security

Effective 1 March we will implement ACF2 for all EDP systems to promote system integrity and access control. Familiarization meetings will be held biweekly in 2412A from 1700–1800 Fridays commencing 11 January.

He shook his head as his secretary reported, "Mr. McKee is on the line."

"Thanks," Tradd replied. "Terry? Tradd. Listen, which one of your computers wrote that memo on computer security? I'm sure I'd be all for promoting 'system integrity' and 'access control' if I knew what they were. What's going on?"

"You liked that memo, huh? Our section head prides himself on keeping all memos to fifty words or less," answered Terry.

"Oh? I figured this guy ACF2 wrote it. Must be some relation to R2D2, right?"

Terry laughed. "Wrong. ACF2 is a new security program developed by some firm outside Chicago. 'System integrity' prevents a user from gaining access to unauthorized parts of the system. Keeps nosy guys like you from discovering company secrets like my incredible salary."

"OK. I buy that—but why the big deal? What's behind it?" Tradd asked.

"Just between you and me, we've had some problems. We're pretty sure somebody has used the system to get technical information that was sold to one of our competitors. We also suspect possible embezzlement; a small amount, but some funds disappeared from a few accounts."

"Sounds interesting. You'll have to fill me in this weekend. Gotta go. My section head is on the way to my office. Thanks, Terry.

Tradd went to meet his section head. "What's up, K.V.? Want some coffee? Let me clear a chair off so you can sit down."

"Thanks, Tradd. No coffee. Did you get that memo on the new computer security system?" the section head asked.

"Yeah, I did. I was just talking to a friend of mine in EDP to find out what it was all about. Didn't sound like anything that would affect us; something to do with protection against espionage and embezzlement."

"There's more to it than that, Tradd. For example, access control."

"You mean giving each user a password to operate the system?" asked Tradd. "That's nothing new."

"It is under ACF2," K.V. responded. "Each user would make up a password and could change it as often as necessary."

"No kidding? That'd solve the problem of somebody stealing your password all right," observed Tradd. "But still, meeting every other Friday at five P.M. What if I just send one of my people to take notes and fill me in?"

"No dice, Tradd," K.V. replied, getting ready to leave. "I know it's inconvenient, but it's important. Be there."

Managers thrive on information. Having the right knowledge at the right time makes decision making easier. It's a great source of power; it can give a manager or an organization a competitive edge.

Planning, organizing, directing, and controlling all depend on accurate and timely information. Operating in the uncertain, fast-moving, and dynamic environment of today, poorly informed managers must either guess or procrastinate. Either alternative is dangerous.

Small wonder, then, that most managers spend the majority of their time communicating—receiving or sending information—with others. Three of the ten roles described in Chapter 1 deal directly with communications. The manager monitors and disseminates information and acts as spokesperson for the unit. The other seven, involving interpersonal and decision-making skills, also depend heavily upon communications.

This chapter concentrates on the two types of communications skills demanded of successful managers: the ability to receive and transmit information on a personal basis, and the management of formal information systems.

TYPES OF COMMUNICATIONS

Communication is *the process of exchanging information*. In the anecdote introducing this chapter, information was exchanged by the EDP Department, Terry, Tradd, and K.V. Some communication was written; most was oral, as is typical in organizations. Managers spend far more time in face-to-face meetings or on the phone than they do writing or reading.

Most managers prefer oral to written communication. First, it is easier to convey certain aspects of a message—its urgency, for example—by the spoken (and shouted) word. Second, talking is more naturally suited to *two-way* communication that permits the receiver of a message to seek immediate clarification from the sender, and that permits both receiver and sender to give off and observe responses to the communication in process.

For example, K.V. was able to determine Tradd's response to the message about the EDP system changes, and Tradd was able to get feedback about his attendance at the meetings. When Tradd explored the possibility of sending a substitute, K.V. said, "Be there." The message was immediately clear.

By contrast, written communications, such as the memo from EDP, tend to be *one-way* communications. The receiver has little or no opportunity to respond directly to the sender of the message. One-way communications tend to be quicker, but less accurate and effective, than two-way communications (See Exhibit 11.1).

Managers rely on both formal and informal communications. *Formal* communications are governed by organizational policy, structure, or job descriptions. Most, like the EDP memo, are written, although some are oral. *Informal* communications are not regulated; they develop from the interactions of the people who fill various roles in the organization. Tradd's phone call to Terry is an example of informal communication. They exchanged work-related information to clarify a formal communication. Because they are friends, they frequently exchange work-related information orally to clarify a formal, written communication. Colleagues who dislike each other or who have more formal relationships tend to restrict their communications to formal methods.

Frequently informal communications develop into a system referred to as the organizational *grapevine*, a network that operates with extraordinary efficiency to transmit information throughout an organization before it is formally announced.[1] Not all members of an organization are part of a grapevine, membership in which is usually based on friendship and access to information. Only a small minority of members actually receive and pass on information; these are key people in an organization's informal communications system.

EFFECTIVE COMMUNICATIONS

People are inclined to evaluate communications by a simple criterion: if the receiver gets the message, the communication was effective. Actually, communications, particularly in organizations, may have several objectives beyond the mere transmission of information to a receiver. For managers, communications are effective only when they achieve their intended purposes.

Purposes of Communication

All communication attempts have one or more of four basic purposes. We will discuss these purposes separately, but remember that any particular communication attempt may serve more than one purpose.

Conveying Information.   The *transmission* of information is the simplest use of the communication process, because no specific action is expected or required of the receiver. *Information* here includes ideas, opinions, feelings, and gossip, as well as facts. For example, the information Terry passed on to Tradd about espionage and embezzlement was interesting, but Terry's only intent was to provide information, nothing more.

Exhibit 11.1   One-Way vs. Two-Way Communication

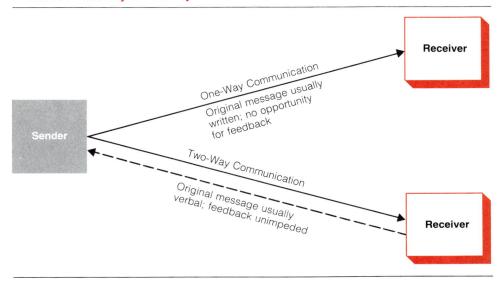

When the purpose of the communication attempt is only to convey information, the communication is effective if the receiver gets the message, and understands it. If the sender of the information expects the receiver to take some specific action, the purpose of the communication falls into another category.

Commanding or Instructing.   These messages tell receivers to do something, to stop doing something, or how to do something. The communication is effective only if the receiver complies.

Downward communication in organizations (from higher to lower levels) is frequently intended to command or instruct. Such communication typically stresses policies, rules, practices, and job instructions. K.V.'s instruction to Tradd about the EDP meetings ("Be there.") is a clear example. If Tradd indeed shows up, the communication is effective.

Influencing or Persuading.   The purpose of communication that influences or persuades is to bring about a *voluntary* change in the receiver's behavior. These communications often occur when the sender lacks authority to command or instruct. Many communications between peers, or between subordinate and superior, fall into this category. Tradd's suggestion to K.V. to send a subordinate to the EDP meetings did not persuade K.V.; the communication was ineffective.

Communication to influence or persuade is not always so obvious. The memo from EDP, appearing only to convey information, also suggested that managers attend the familiarization meetings. The memo, by itself, was ineffective, because it was unclear and one-way.

Exhibit 11.2 Purpose and Effectiveness of Communication

Purpose of Communication	Successful Outcome
To Convey Information	Receiver receives and understands information
To Command or Instruct	Receiver carries out command or follows instructions
To Influence or Persuade	Receiver's behavior is voluntarily modified in the desired direction
To Clarify Relationships	Receiver interacts with sender consistent with sender's perception of their relationship

Clarifying Relationships. Attempting to clarify authority, status, or social relationships is the most complex purpose of communication. The sender not only transmits what he or she believes to be a fact about a relationship, but has definite expectations about what the receiver should do with this fact. If receivers do not agree, the communication is not effective.

Messages intended to clarify relationships are often disguised. The senior executive who tells a junior executive, "Bring that display down to my office, will you, Sam?" may be making clear the hierarchy in the relationship, especially if Sam has shown signs of stepping out of bounds. Many of these communications are nonverbal. For example, military protocol dictates that a senior officer is the first to enter a vehicle and the last to leave it, but the last to arrive at an official function and the first to leave. When Tradd interrupted his call to Terry, rose to greet K.V., offered to get coffee and clear off a chair, he was communicating a subordinate-to-superior relationship. K.V.'s acceptance reinforced the message that K.V. is Tradd's superior in the organizational hierarchy. The communications were effective.

Outcomes of Communication

The four basic purposes of communication and their successful outcomes are shown in Exhibit 11.2. However, there are at least four other outcomes for each purpose:

1. Nothing relevant may happen.
2. The purpose may be accomplished.
3. An undesired effect may occur.
4. Some combination of (2) and (3) may occur.

To illustrate the differences among the four outcomes, consider the memo from EDP. One purpose of this communication was to influence or persuade managers to attend the familiarization meetings. Four outcomes are possible:

Two-way communication can be face-to-face, by telephone, or by computer-based MIS.

1. No one mentions the memo and no managers attend the meetings.
2. Many or all level-three managers and above attend the meetings.
3. Several managers complain about the memo to company executives, and others confront EDP personnel with accusations of empire building.
4. Both (2) and (3) occur.

Both (2) and (4) represent effective communication *for the purpose of influencing or persuading managers to attend the meetings.* However, the last outcome is less attractive because it includes an undesired side effect.

With improved communication skills, the EDP section head might find a way to communicate that does not produce negative reactions. This is why we make a distinction between communication *effectiveness* and communication *skill.*

COMMUNICATION SKILLS

Communication skills are *means of achieving the intended purpose with the intended receiver(s) with a minimum of undesired side effects.* Communication, like all skills, is a matter of degree. It is impossible to avoid all the undesired side effects all the time. Skilled communicators simply cause fewer of them.

Exhibit 11.3   Skills Used in Successful Communications

Sender Skills	Receiver Skills
Knowing when to communicate	Listening
Choosing the receiver of the message	Understanding the interpersonal
Choosing the form of communication	aspects of communication
Timing the communication	
Expressing the message clearly	
Understanding the interpersonal aspects of communication	

Communication is also multidimensional. It requires knowing when to communicate, choosing the receiver of the message, choosing the form of communication, timing the communication, expressing the message clearly, understanding the interpersonal aspects of communication, and listening. These skills, and how to improve them, are the focus of this section.

Knowing When to Communicate

Knowing when to communicate is an important communication skill for a manager, precisely because so much of a manager's time is spent communicating.

Identifying Opportunities and Needs.   One result of the enormous volume of communication required of a manager is that it becomes very difficult to detect situations where more or better communication might be useful. Identifying such situations involves three activities:

1. Seeking out direct feedback when feedback from the results of actions is too slow or indicates communication problems. A series of botched orders in one company, for example, were traced to the poor handwriting of the person writing the orders. The clerk *thought* he could read the writing; results clearly indicated he couldn't.
2. Watching out for blocked or inefficient formal communication channels. If a particular employee always goes around the immediate supervisor with reports and problems, there is a blocked channel. If it takes a week to get paperwork from one department to another, there is an inefficient channel.
3. Initiating unrequired communication to give or receive information that might increase either performance or satisfaction. Resistance to change can be reduced by keeping those affected by it informed of the reasons and plans for the change and the consequences to be expected.[2] Unrequired communication may also be solicited simply to receive feedback.

When Not to Communicate. Communication often becomes an end in itself. As one manager admitted, "I'm a communication junkie. I can't seem to stop. I even write memos to my wife." Subordinates of other "communication junkies" have noted. "My supervisor is a master of the art of stating the obvious. He's constantly explaining stuff to me that I already know or could figure out with no trouble. Maybe he just thinks I'm dumb." Or, "My boss sends me a dozen memos a week on everything from articles I should read to a reminder of my secretary's birthday. Most of them aren't very important, but I have to read them all, in case. I hate to think how much time he wastes writing them and I waste reading them."

Moving from a disorganized state to an organized one requires limiting communications among members of the system.[3] Unrestrained and inappropriate communication wastes time and can interfere with relationships. Knowing when to communicate is part of the skill of communicating, but knowing when *not* to communicate can be equally effective.

Choosing the Receiver of the Message

A marketing manager about to test a new product must decide what segment of the market will receive the promotional material. A vice-president concerned about a plant's poor safety record must decide whether to communicate these concerns to the plant clinic, the supervisors, or the employees directly, or simply to the next person in the chain of command.

A useful rule of thumb for identifying the appropriate receiver of a message is send it to a receiver from whom the desired response is both *possible and appropriate*. The two do not necessarily go together. Tradd could undoubtedly draft a memo to K.V., but it would be inappropriate for K.V. to instruct Tradd to do so, because drafting memos is the secretary's job.

Identifying the appropriate receiver for a communication involves knowing the informal organization structure as well as the formal. In most organizations, certain individuals play key roles in informal communications. They serve as major links between a group or department and the rest of the organization or outsiders. Often referred to as "gatekeepers" of information, these individuals regulate the flow of new and useful technical information between their groups and the environment.[4]

Choosing a Form of Communication

There are dozens of ways a sender transmits a message, but most can be placed into one of three categories. *Oral communication*, or speech, may take place face-to-face or by some electronic means, such as telephone, radio, television, or audio recordings. Managers prefer oral communications.[5] *Written communication* includes all forms of communication that are physically separated from the sender and his or her voice. Letters, memos, computer printouts, signs, and books are familiar examples. *Nonverbal communication* consists of *body language*, such as gestures, posture and facial expressions, as well as *paralanguage*—voice tone, quality and pitch, the pacing of speech, and the use of pauses. It also includes *signals* about status or intentions that are revealed by speech, decisions, and actions.

In many situations, the communication form is determined by the type of message, organizational policy, or by the fact that someone else initiated it. When there is a choice, there are at least two important questions to ask: Who is the intended receiver of the message, and what is the purpose of the message?

Adapting the Form to the Intended Receiver.   Knowing who the receiver of a communication is going to be is important, because it offers clues to the form of communication most likely to be understood. Three receiver characteristics are especially important.

Ability. People with poor reading skills or little or no command of English present problems in choosing an appropriate form for the communication.

Experience. A manager who routinely deals with others orally may pay more attention to oral messages. In like manner, a computer programmer may be more receptive to written messages.

Preference. Some managers routinely reject attempts to communicate noncritical information orally. Others dislike written communication. Knowing such preferences can improve relationships as well as communication effectiveness.

> *Communication is the process of exchanging information. Whatever the purpose or the message, communication is an interaction that requires interpersonal skills.*

It is difficult to overestimate the importance of recognizing the ability and preferences of those to whom a manager is communicating. Recent evidence suggests that many employees have a strong preference for oral communication because of a basic disability: they cannot read or write. The International Reading Association estimates that 20 million English-speaking, native-born American adults have trouble on the job because they read or write poorly. The *Wall Street Journal* cited the plight of a manager in a supermarket who, although he was a high school graduate, could only read at a third-grade level.[6] When forced to produce memos or reports, he went home and dictated the information to his wife. If he was given something to read, he put it off until he got home. Small and large businesses alike are beginning to recognize the proportions of this problem of employee illiteracy and its effects on productivity and safety. In the short run, they are simplifying written messages and backing them up with oral and nonverbal communications such as signs. In the long run some are working to improve employee reading skills through training and education, while others are including literacy tests in their selection processes.

Identifying the Purpose of the Message.   All forms of communication have strengths and weaknesses, but some are more useful than others for particular purposes. The great strength of written communication is its permanence. A memo, report, or letter can be reread and saved for future reference. Thus, this form tends to work well for a communication whose purpose is to inform.

Oral communication, while not permanent, does usually allow for instant feedback to determine whether the message is being received as intended. This makes it especially effective for messages intended to influence or persuade. For example, in one study, face-to-face comments by former students about certain courses were found to have much greater impact on the course choices of prospective psychology students than the same information in the form of printed numerical course evaluations.[7]

Interestingly enough, many managers prefer oral to written communication, not only because of its persuasiveness, but because they are wary of being held accountable for what they put in writing. For some managers, the relative permanence of written communication creates a liability they want to avoid.

Timing the Communication

Appropriate timing—sending the message when the receiver is likely to be able to attend to it and to make the desired response—involves knowing what to look for and what to avoid.

Among the conditions that should warn the sender of a message that "now is not the time" are noisy, crowded, or rushed physical surroundings, deep involvement of the receiver in a task, problem, or conversation, distracting personal situations such as illness, worry, or anger, and inappropriate social environment.

In addition to a calm environment and a receptive listener, a salient message helps ensure a communication's effectiveness. *Salient* means *standing out.* The best way to be sure a message stands out is to be sure it arrives as closely as possible to the time when it will have meaning for the receiver.

Most of us receive messages that lack salience fairly often. The first day of each new term, professors communicate information about course content, policies, and requirements in great detail, only to be asked about the typing of term papers or the date of the next test. The professors are ignoring salience. Details of assignments become salient only as these activities get close enough to require planning and execution.

Timing communications to ensure salience is not always easy. Knowledge of the receiver helps, as does *repetition.* For example, a manager who learns extensive building remodeling will begin in six months might immediately pass this information along to the personnel involved. Later, instructions to develop plans for carrying on work during the upheaval may be given. Still later, influence or persuasion may be directed toward those who failed to submit plans. This can be followed, if necessary, by a command, the ultimate in salience—DO IT NOW!

Exhibit 11.4   Unclear Communication About Improved Communications

In an effort to improve their written communications, hundreds of corporations are simplifying the language used in their documents—from corporate policy manuals to interoffice memos. Major law firms are training young lawyers to write clear legal drafts. Thirty-four states have legislated standards for clear language in insurance policies. The Internal Revenue Service strives to simplify tax forms every year. Yet much remains to be done, as witnessed by this document quoted by Edwin Newman in his book *A Civil Tongue.*

Western Institute of Aviation
A Concept

"Aviation services and their impact now have great dimensions. With appreciation of the facts—including that only great things can have great faults and that perfection takes some time—oversimplification can be misleading. Improved communications are vital if aviation is to attain the full measure of its possible greatness.

"We trust, that by joining together the many specialists groups who make the system work—who have treated technical problems as opportunities—and who have achieved, for a majority of people, a quality of service that tends to satiate the recipients to a point approaching apathy, we may treat the opposition so as not to inflame the anti-aviation enthusiasts, but to convert them.

"Toward finding better ways to work out our problems, we offer the Western Institute for Aviation for broadening the base of understanding, evolving a means of lifting up our eyes and objectives and, hopefully, realizing our mutual interdependence in optimizing aviation services to people through the synergism of our efforts."

Source: From E. Newman, *A Civil Tongue* (Indianapolis: Bobbs-Merrill Co., Inc. 1976), pp. 103–104.

Expressing the Message Clearly

In evaluating business-school graduates today, executives tend to give them high marks on quantitative abilities, but low marks on their abilities to speak and write clearly. Executives place considerably less value on the length and scholarship of presentations than do academicians. The time pressures most managers face lead them to prefer messages that are short and clear.

Clear expression is not as easy as it seems. Because people are shy, afraid, want to impress others, are trying to be polite, or have a limited vocabulary, they often cloud their messages.

There are at least five guidelines for developing clarity:

1. Use language that will be understood by the receiver. Avoid technical terms or jargon, (see Exhibit 11.4) and choose an appropriate level for the audience. This can be tricky. Using big words and fancy sentences may offend some people, but so may talking down to them. Treading this sometimes fine line takes practice, feedback, and time.
2. Be as direct as possible. Noting, "These accounts need some attention," may not get them attended to. Most people prefer being asked to do things nicely, but directly.
3. Don't assume too much about the prior knowledge or opinions of the receiver. Research suggests that there is usually a general gap in information and

understanding between superiors and subordinates.[8] This gap applies to work expectations, perceptions of authority, and bases for evaluating others, as well as more objective facts. While some gap is to be expected, and strengthens distinctions between work roles, it can also interfere with communication.

4. Keep the message as brief as possible. In addition to the other considerations, it is more likely that a written message will be clear if it is read in its entirety. Organizations are busy places. People lack both time and inclination to wade through ten pages when four would do. At Procter & Gamble, for example, executives expect written memoranda to be confined to one page.

5. Reinforce the message with action. Evidence suggests that if a message conveyed by behavior contradicts the message conveyed by words, it is the behavior that is usually believed.[9] Telling a subordinate about your "open door" policy while ushering that subordinate *out* the door will only create confusion and doubt.

Understanding the Interpersonal Aspects of Communication

Whatever the purpose or the message, communication is an interaction that requires interpersonal skills. Three important ones are openness, trust, and avoidance of defensiveness.

Openness.   **Openness** is *the desire to communicate with others and to send honest messages, as well as the desire to receive messages from others, even when those messages are unfavorable.*

Willingness to communicate and receptivity to honesty create an open climate. A manager must be attentive consistently to interactions with others. Most people are more willing to *talk*, as well as to *listen*, to someone who is open to communication; managers who are open will convey and receive more information.

Openness in communication also affects employees' perceptions of the work situation. For example, employees report greater job satisfaction when they perceive open communication between subordinate and supervisor. Furthermore, supervisors who are perceived as open are also perceived as better supervisors.[10]

Trust in the sender increases the credibility of a message; trust in the receiver affects the willingness of others to communicate honestly or at all. Establishing this climate takes time to nurture and is easily destroyed.

Both trust and openness are critical when the sender of a message has less authority than the receiver. Without them, the power imbalance can lead to a distortion of messages.

Defensiveness.   When the receiver of a communication behaves defensively, he or she responds to what may be behind the message, rather than to the message itself. An innocent question like, "Have you seen that computer printout I was working on before I went to lunch?" may be responded to by, "Well, *I* certainly didn't take it."

Exhibit 11.5   Guidelines for Giving Performance Feedback

Be Descriptive, Not Evaluative

Focus on behavior or the results of behavior, not on the receiver as a person.

''Sales are down for the third month in a row.''
instead of
''You seem to have forgotten everything you know about selling lately.''

Be Specific and Practical, Not General and Useless

Feedback is intended to help the receiver keep doing the things that are effective and change the behaviors that aren't. General feedback is not very helpful either way.

''This report is well organized, contains useful information, and is brief and to the point.''
instead of
''Good report, Kim.''

Be Provisional, Not Absolute

Performance feedback reflects the perceptions of one person about the performance of another. Avoid presenting perceptions as if they were established facts.

''It seems to me that you have difficulty getting others to listen to your ideas.''
instead of
''Nobody listens to you.''

Avoiding or reducing defensiveness is partly a matter of developing communication skills. It also depends on expressing oneself in a nonthreatening manner. This skill is particularly critical when giving feedback to others about their performances. (Guidelines for reducing or avoiding defensiveness in this situation are presented in Exhibit 11.5.) Reducing defensiveness helps ensure that the feedback will get through. Also, when the receiver believes the feedback is useful, relevant, and open to discussion, undesired side effects are far less likely.

Listening

A recent survey of business executives highlighted the importance placed on the communication skills of business-school graduates. In this survey, respondents from small, medium, and large companies ranked written and oral communication skills as more important than leadership, problem-solving, or any other skill except one. In their opinion, the most important skill for a new business graduate to have was listening.[11]

Listening, of course, is a receiver skill. It involves both hearing and understanding. Hearing requires paying attention. Usually listeners do not pay attention because they are thinking about something else, often about what they will say when the speaker stops.

If the message is simple, hearing may be all that is necessary. However, when several messages, some in disguised form, are sent at one time, understanding requires active listening. The active listener tries to perceive things as the speaker perceives them. If this effort is successful, active listening leads to empathy, understanding *with* a person as well as *about* a person.

The major barrier to empathy is judgmental listening, listening that approves or disapproves, rather than trying to understand. To see the difference between empathy and judgmental listening, consider the following conversation:

Tradd: I saw this article in a magazine the other day about new ways to set up work schedules. Might be worth looking into.

Terry: You can't really believe that magazine stuff would work around here?

K.V.: Actually, I think our scheduling works pretty well the way it is, but it sounds like that article really got you interested.

Notice that K.V. expressed doubt about applying something from a magazine to the work situation, just as Terry did. However, K.V. expressed doubt in personal, provisional terms, not in judgmental terms. To listen with empathy does not always mean to agree.

Developing skill in active listening takes practice, but success is easy to measure. A listener has understood a complete message if he or she can restate the ideas and feelings of the sender to the sender's satisfaction.

MANAGEMENT INFORMATION SYSTEMS

Up to this point we have discussed both the written and oral communications managers use to receive and send information effectively. We have described techniques successful managers have used for decades. But today's managers need more than basic written-and-oral-communications skills to handle the mass of data that is available to them. They need to understand and use management information systems.

A **management information system (MIS)** is *the systematic management of information for managers, usually centered around computer technology to permit rapid and accurate processing, storage, and retrieval of information.* The information consists of any data useful to managers. Successful administrators manage their MIS, whereas unsuccessful ones often are managed by them.

The purpose of MIS is to provide managers with useful information at a reasonable cost. "Reasonable" cost suggests that the costs of information are evaluated in terms of usefulness. Corporations routinely spend millions of dollars to develop and maintain MIS. In 1981 a group of Japanese financial and academic institutions paid $4.5 million for 2 percent of the stock of Genentech Corporation just to get access to information about genetic engineering.[12]

Although $4.5 million might seem a high cost for an opportunity to get information (stock ownership does not entitle them to products or technology), any information the Japanese can obtain has great utility, given the potential of genetic engineering. Japan had over 100 companies and research institutes working in the area in 1981, spending $217 million in the process. By those standards, a few million dollars for some fast information is definitely worthwhile.

The most useful information for a manager is that which is relevant, accurate, precise, timely, and complete. Relevant information is applicable to the situation. A manager who needs credit information on a demanding customer needs to know about the payment of bills, not the preferences in order quantities. Inaccurate information is not only worthless but potentially dangerous. If the manager gets an overly optimistic credit report, thousands of dollars may be lost to bad debts. Precise information reduces uncertainty; ambiguous information heightens it.[13] A report that the customer "appears to pay reasonably quickly most of the time" is less useful than "customer pays eighty percent of payables in thirty days." Complete information tells a manager everything necessary to make a decision. Having an up-

---

Listening involves both hearing and understanding.

---

to-date credit history on a customer will enable the manager to make a timely, confident decision. A credit history that does not include the last few months increases uncertainty and lowers confidence. Finally, relevant, accurate, precise, complete information is of little use to a manager who gets it too late. The credit manager who learns about a customer's poor credit rating *after* approving a big order will not be satisfied with the information system that provided it.

The Functions of Management Information Systems

Management information systems carry out several functions while providing managers relevant, accurate, precise, timely, and complete information. These include acquiring, organizing, and storing data; retrieving and processing it; and transmitting, displaying, and disposing of information after its use.[14] These functions, depicted in Exhibit 11.6, do not necessarily have to occur in this order. Processing, for example, may take place at any time (or several times) between acquisition and disposal.

An MIS must acquire data before processing it. If data are unavailable, irrelevant, or inaccurate, there is little an MIS can do. Once it has acquired data, an MIS systematically organizes them to make them easier to store, process, or use. Information is usually temporarily stored at different stages of its processing, and thus must be located and retrieved. Fast, accurate retrieval is a major asset for those who must make quick decisions.

Data processing may require the use of experts or sophisticated machines to increase the information value of the data. The system then transmits the information to those who need it and displays it for their use. Afterwards, the information may be disposed of or stored for future use.

Consider the processing of student records at a typical college or university. The system acquires data from the students themselves (personal data and registration) and others (transcripts from high school, course schedules from the registrar's

Exhibit 11.6   The Functioning of an Information System

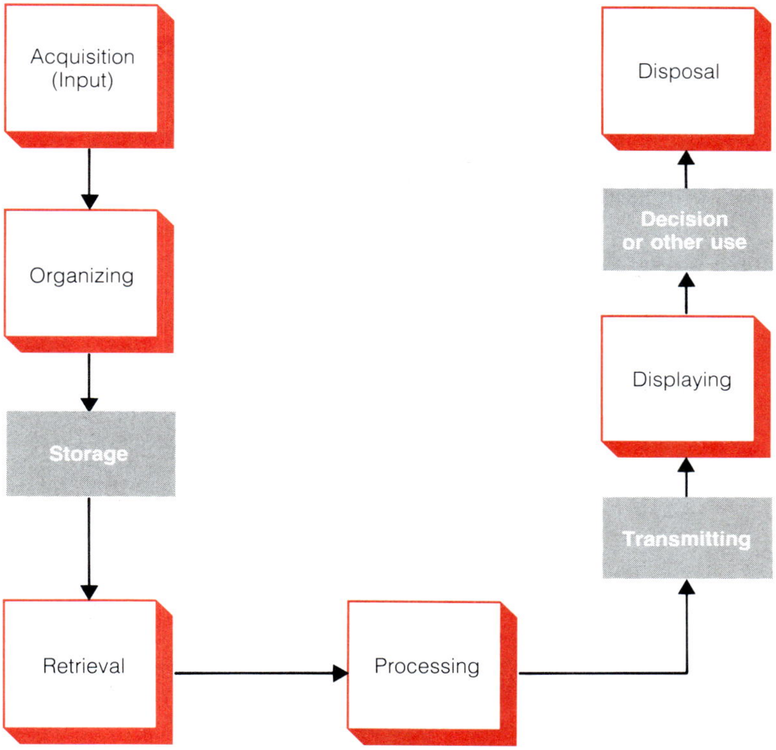

office, grades from instructors). These data are organized by student, by semester, or by quarter into a file and then stored for updating or decision making.

When the system acquires information that needs processing (a course dropped or added, grades received, address changed), the file is retrieved. Processing may consist of changing information (schedules or addresses) or changing computations (grade-point averages).

The system itself may signal the need for a decision or action (grade average below standards, unpaid tuition or parking fines, impending graduation) which it transmits to the appropriate user. Or an administrator may call for a file for review or decision.

MIS may display information in many ways. Printouts are the most common, but electronic display devices are increasingly popular; they are quicker, the same information can be used by several people at one time, and storage and disposal are easier and cheaper.

Management Information Systems Today

A number of forces are combining to increase the sophistication and forms of information systems today. One is simply the mass of data most managers confront today. Information-overload is bad and getting worse. One survey of American corporations found that three of every four managers and executives report their paperwork has increased by moderate to great amounts.[15]

The costs of handling paper are moving us away from the traditional types of information systems. Government regulations and laws which increase the demand for documentation and reporting are having similar economic effects. In 1981, American businesses produced an estimated 325 billion documents. That figure increases more than twenty percent each year.

At the same time, continuing miniaturization of components has increased the power and decreased the size and cost of computer technology. Managers in the future will have access to more information and information-processing at lower costs.

Finally, appliances and devices are becoming more "intelligent." They can make decisions and carry out activities that heretofore have been done only by humans. For example, modern copying machines not only make copies; they collate, staple, sort, organize, and keep track of their work.

Each of these trends has had an impact on current information systems technology, which today is dominated by computers.

Computer-Based MIS

The first computer system used in business activities was introduced thirty years ago. Since then, the use of computers in management information systems has grown dramatically. Although computers were originally intended to serve scientists and engineers, three times as many business people today use computer-based information systems and services.[16] Between 1975 and 1981, the number of computer systems in operation in the United States jumped from less than two hundred thousand to over one million. Businesses of every size and in every field from aerospace to trash removal depend on computer-based information systems for transaction processing, control, and decision making.

The elements of a computer-based system are hardware, software, procedures, and people. These elements interact to acquire, store, transform, and distribute data and information. **Hardware** denotes *the machines and equipment that process data.* **Software** refers to *the programs that control the operation of the computer's computation and processing activities.* **Procedures** are *those activities prescribed by the user which govern the use of hardware and software.* The *people* who interact with hardware, software, and procedures include operators, engineers, programmers, analysts, and, of course, managers and others who are users of the system.

The information-processing industry has done a remarkable job of increasing the demand for, and use of, better and more sophisticated products. The costs of

Management in Action
Should Managers Use Computers?

On the left is an excerpt from a Wall Street Journal *article and on the right is the response it engendered. The controversy still goes on.*

Real men don't eat quiche. Real women don't pump gas. And real managers don't use computer terminals.

Ray Moritz, vice-president of service for Computervision, one of the highest of the high tech companies says that even after 20 years in the computer business he wouldn't touch one of the things. He has no need for one. Many of Mr. Moritz's subordinates must use computers, but as a manager he must manage his complete function. He understands that even in the computer age, management skills are what produce results through others—not flashy displays.

Managers still must do fundamental things like manage the people who produce the results that pay the light bills. Sure computers are useful. In some cases they are indispensable tools. But the key word is tool, i.e., something a laborer uses to produce results.

If you need information that a computer can supply, let someone with the time and talent filter it for you.

Instant information in the hands of a manager is actually dangerous. Let those as far down in the organization as possible have the instant information. Let them react and do what must be done and then pass on the results. Give them a chance to use their lead time to take appropriate action.

Your article can only be described as "outrageous" by anyone who has any level of computer literacy. Even if executives choose not to have a computer or a terminal in their office, it is absolutely essential that effective managers know what computers can do for them personally and for their business.

Information is the cornerstone of effective decision making. Effective leaders in all segments of business and government strive to obtain the information they need to make good decisions. When it is accurate, timely, and available, the quality of decisions improve dramatically.

Once managers realize that the information they need may be available to them in minutes, when and where they want it, they are no longer content with waiting until the right people can be contacted, meetings are scheduled, reports are generated and presentations prepared. The personal computer or the remote terminal changes the way executives and managers do business—and changes it for the better. Today's technology allows executives to make effective use of the tool without having to build it, repair it, or understand its inner workings.

JAY M. SEDLIK
Executive Vice President
National Training Systems Inc.

Source: J. Falvey, "Real Managers Don't Use Computer Terminals," *Wall Street Journal*, Feb. 7, 1983. p. 16.

Source: Letters to the Editor, *Wall Street Journal*, Feb. 16, 1983, p. 25.

Virginia Electric and Power Company uses this computer-directed energy management system to control eighteen power stations from one central operations room.

computing have been reduced by an average of twenty percent per year for the last twenty years. This amazing feat, coupled with the rising costs of paper-based systems, has made computers an attractive way of accomplishing more and more tasks. At the same time, cost and size reductions have made computers available to more and more users.

If these trends continue, every manager is likely to have his or her own computer-based information system on the desk. The so-called "executive work station" will be composed of a keyboard and video screen, along with electronic mail, telecopiers, and similar devices. The system will permit the manager to communicate all over the world, to retrieve, store, and process information without ever leaving the office.[17] This trend has created considerable controversy.

Computer-based management information systems today serve a variety of functions for managers, such as transaction processing, information reporting, decision support, and decision making. In each of these functions, MIS permit the manager to work more productively and effectively in a complex and dynamic environment (See Exhibit 11.7).

Most organizations engage in large numbers of transactions every day, from hiring employees to receiving inventory to making sales. Each transaction must be processed and recorded for future actions and decisions. Managers depend on the speed and accuracy of MIS to keep up the pace. MIS also provide reports on organizational activities and status for managers and government agencies. Automating reporting systems such as cost accounting, inventory status, and payroll taxes, save considerable time and money.

Exhibit 11.7   Managers and Computers: Results of a Poll of Middle Managers

Managers Depend on Computers to Help Them in Their Jobs...

Q. Does computer access have an impact in these areas?

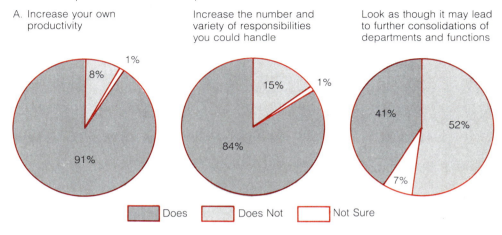

A. Increase your own productivity

Increase the number and variety of responsibilities you could handle

Look as though it may lead to further consolidations of departments and functions

Does   Does Not   Not Sure

But Not Many Have Mastered Operation of the Machines

Q. Have you taken formal computer training paid for by you or your company?

A. Paid for yourself   Company paid for   Never took computer training

Source: *Business Week*, April 25, 1983, p. 64.

The use of MIS to support management decision making by providing information and performing analysis is enjoying rapid growth. The large memory units and rapid computational capabilities make computers ideal support systems for decision making, as demonstrated vividly whenever NASA launches a manned space vehicle.

While computer-assisted decision making is growing, the use of computers to actually make final decisions is in its infancy. The major benefit of programmed decision making is that it gives managers more time to spend on nonprogrammable decisions. In some instances, the speed and reliability of computerized decision making makes it an attractive alternative to human systems. In the airline industry, gate agents use computers to assign passenger seats; the agent types information about requests into the system, which in turn supplies the seat assignment. Some airlines use computers to make fuel purchase and allocation decisions; one airline reported saving $500,000 per month. A computerized landing system, developed to use in bad weather or nonroutine circumstances, now makes and executes all aircraft control decisions that pilots normally made.

Why Managers Don't Use MIS More

Given that MIS provides managers with more powerful, accurate, timely, and less costly information than ever before, it is surprising that its use is not much greater. One of the bottlenecks has been the slow development of software: the demand for people to write software is so great that in 1981, 92 percent of all computer users couldn't find enough programmers to staff their systems.[18] The other bottleneck is management itself—the reluctance of many managers to exploit this valuable tool.

> *Why do some defense strategists support building the MX missile at a cost of about $40 billion? Not entirely because of its military efficacy, but also because of what a commitment to such a system might signal the Soviet Union about U.S. resolve.*
> Source: Frank Tippett, "Why So Much is Beyond Words." *Time*, July 13, 1981.

In his book *Why Information Systems Fail*, MIS expert and consultant Henry Lucas says, "All our experience suggests that the primary cause for system failure has been organizational behavior problems."[19] That is, software and hardware aside, systems fail because of some failure in the human element. As a result, the people who must use the hardware and software fear it, distrust it, misuse it, don't understand it, are overwhelmed by it, or simply don't use it.

Lucas systematically studied MIS problems in 16 companies, including 2266 users, over a four-year period. The major conclusion was that systems failed because too much attention was focused on technology and not enough on users.

His experience with these problems has led Lucas to suggest a number of actions to prevent them. The major prescription is for managers, users, and MIS specialists to work together in designing the system.

1. Involve the user in systems design. If users initiate systems, they will be committed to them.
2. Don't overload users. Avoid sending them irrelevant data.
3. Design flexible systems to fit differences in user requirements and capabilities.
4. Include training in the design of the system. The more people trained, the more the system will be used.
5. After installation, be sure the system operates according to specifications. Monitor user reactions and make adjustments to the system accordingly.

When top management does not actively support MIS, or when managers are inadequately briefed about its uses and functions, it is likely to fail. Unless effort is made to reduce the fear or hostility of some managers, MIS will not perform effectively. Systems that are frequently designed without closely consulting users and potential users are likely to fail. MIS will change and disrupt normal routines. It can be the source of interdepartmental conflict. Unless these disruptions are planned for, MIS is likely to fail.

The Bottom Line

Every managerial role requires information and communications. Communicating and using information successfully requires you to:

1. Understand the purpose of your communication—to inform, persuade, command, or clarify. Use two-way communications whenever possible to enable you to determine whether your communication achieved its purpose.
2. Know when to communicate. Choose the receiver and the form of the message intelligently, and time the communication to achieve the desired impact on the receiver. Be direct, clear, and brief.
3. Pay attention when receiving messages. Make an effort to see things from the sender's perspective. Withhold evaluation until you know you understand the message. Don't violate privacy or confidences.
4. Be proactive in learning how to use management information systems. Developing successful MIS means more than buying hardware. It means planning, setting objectives, and eliciting the support of and training users. Sytems designed with users in mind are more likely to succeed.
5. Protect your information systems because information is a valuable and powerful commodity. Be actively involved in establishing security and ensuring that it is effectively carried out.

SUMMARY

Communication is the process of exchanging information, an essential commodity for managing organizations. Managers communicate through both formal and informal networks, using one-way and two-way communications. They prefer oral to written communications.

All communication aims at conveying information, commanding or instructing, influencing or persuading, or clarifying relationships. If the communication accomplishes the purpose, it is effective. If it does so with a minimum of undesired side effects, it is skillful.

Communication skills include knowing when to communicate, choosing the appropriate receiver of a message, choosing the form of the communication, timing the communication, expressing the message clearly, dealing with interpersonal aspects of communication, and listening.

The major function of MIS for managers is in recording and processing transactions. The reporting of information remains as yet a secondary function. The use of computer-based decision support systems is growing, and may ultimately prove to be the biggest benefit of MIS.

Faced with a dynamic, complex, uncertain environment, managers today need information that is accurate, specific, relevant, timely, and complete. Management information systems help managers fulfill those needs by carrying out a variety of functions from acquiring data to disposing of it. Managers use MIS today for recording, reporting, and decision making.

Over the last two decades, computer-based information systems have enjoyed phenomenal growth. Major breakthroughs in hardware technology have expanded computer power and lowered costs. This growth has been due primarily to advances in hardware systems. The demand for competent MIS personnel continues to far exceed the supply. The major bottleneck in MIS growth is software, the development of which heavily depends on human programmers.

QUESTIONS FOR REVIEW AND DISCUSSION

1. What does the complaint, "We have a real lack of communication around here," usually mean in an organization?
2. Describe the primary purpose of each of the following communication attempts in terms discussed in this chapter. Which skill is most obviously lacking in each?
   a. Firing an employee by putting a written notice in his or her pay envelope.
   b. Asking the boss for a more expensive piece of equipment than is currently in use a week after the following year's budget request has gone in.
   c. Telling a subordinate that you want "action, not excuses," when he or she tries to explain why certain work instructions were not followed.
3. What are the elements of an information system? What function do they generally serve?
4. What functions does a MIS perform in the process of transforming data or information?
5. What are the main advantages of electronic information systems over paper systems? Are they relevant to small businesses as well as large ones?
6. Compare formal and informal information systems. What are the limitations of informal systems?

REFERENCES AND NOTES

1. H. Sutton and L. W. Porter, "A Study of the Grapevine in a Governmental Organization," *Personal Psychology*, 1968, 21, pp. 223–30.
2. E. F. Huse, *Organization Development and Change*, 2nd ed. St. Paul: West, 1980, pp. 118–23.
3. D. Katz and R. L. Kahn, *The Social Psychology of Organizations*, 2nd ed. New York: Wiley, 1978, p. 430.
4. H. J. Reitz, *Behavior in Organizations*, rev. ed. Homewood, Ill.: Irwin, 1981, pp. 333–34.
5. H. Mintzberg, *The Nature of Managerial Work*. Englewood Cliffs, N.J.: Prentice-Hall, 1980, p. 38.

6. D. Machalara, "For Americans Unable to Read Well, Life Is a Series of Small Crises," *Wall Street Journal*, Jan. 17, 1984, p. 1.

7. E. Borgida and R. E. Nisbett, "The Differential Impact of Abstract vs. Concrete Information on Decisions." *Journal of Applied Psychology*, 1977, 7, 3, pp. 258–71.

8. F. M. Jablin, "Superior-Subordinate Communication: The State of the Art." *Psychological Bulletin*, 1979, 86, 6, pp. 1201–22.

9. *See* A. Mehrabian, *Silent Messages.* Belmont, Ca.: Wadesworth, 1977.

10. F. M. Jablin, "Message Response and 'Openness' in Superior-Subordinate Communication." In B. D. Ruben, ed., *Communication Yearbook II.* New Brunswick, N.J.: Transaction Books, 1978.

11. M. G. Prentice, "An Empirical Search for a Relevant Management Curriculum," *Collegiate News and Views*, Winter, 1983–84, pp. 25–29.

12. M. Kanabayashi and H. Lancaster, "Japan's Aggressive Move in Biotechnology Worries U.S. Firms Fearful of Losing Lead," *Wall Street Journal*, October 9, 1981, p. 29.

13. G. E. Nichols, "On the Nature of Management Information," in V. T. Dock, V. P. Luchsinger, and W. R. Cornette, *MIS: A Managerial Perspective* (Chicago: SRA, 1977), pp. 71–79.

14. These functions represent a synthesis of those activities described in R. M. Landau, *Information Resources Management*, (New York: AMACON, 1980), Chapter 2, and J. A. Seun, *Information Systems in Management*, (Belmont, California: Wadsworth Publishing Co., 1978), Chapter 1.

15. C. Jouzaitis, "Execs Buried by Information Overload," *Chicago Tribune*, February 7, 1983, Sec. 4, p. 10.

16. *Wall Street Journal*, September 3, 1981, p. 1.

17. "Information Systems: The Management Challenge," *Eastern Review*, October 1981, pp. 53–70.

18. "Missing Computer Software," *Business Week*, September 1, 1980, pp. 46–53.

19. H. C. Lucas, Jr. *Why Information Systems Fail* (New York: Columbia University Press, 1975).

SUGGESTED READINGS

Archer, D. and Akert, R. M. "How Well Do You Read Body Language?" *Psychology Today*, 1977, 68–69, 72, 119–120. This is an interesting illustrated report of research into the difficulties of clear nonverbal communication.

Dock, V. T., V. P. Luchsinger, and W. R. Cornette, *MIS: A Managerial Perspective* (Chicago: SRA, 1977). This collection of articles written by professionals in MIS covers a broad range of topics of interest to managers using MIS.

Lucas, H. C., Jr. *Why Information Systems Fail* (New York: Columbia University Press, 1975). Based on the author's own research and that of others in the field, this book analyzes the failures of MIS and why failures are likely to occur.

Malone, P. B. III, "Humor: A Double-Edged Tool for Today's Manager?" *Academy of Management Review*, 1980, 5, 3, 357–60. This author suggests that humor, as well as clarity, may be useful and important to skillful managerial communication.

CASE The Great Majestic Company

Robert Hoffman, the manager of the Great Majestic Lodge, was sitting at his desk and debating what he would say and what action he would take at a meeting with his bellmen, which was scheduled to begin in two hours. He had just weathered a stormy encounter with Mr. Tomblin, the general manager of the Great Majestic Company.

Mr. Tomblin was visibly upset by an action taken by the bellmen at Great Majestic Lodge three weeks ago. At the end of the explosive meeting, Mr. Tomblin roared, "Bob, I don't care if you fire the whole damn bunch! I want you to do something about this right now!"

Great Majestic Lodge was located in a popular park in the western United States. It was rather remote, yet offered all of the modern conveniences featured at any fine metropolitan hotel. Because of its size and accommodations, the lodge was a favorite spot for large, organized tours.

The bellmen at the Great Majestic Lodge were directly responsible to the lodge manager, Mr. Hoffman. They were college students who, before being chosen for the bellman position, had worked for the company at least three summers. A total of seven were chosen on the basis of their past work performance, loyalty, and ability to work with the public. Mr. Tomblin, the general manager, chose the bellmen himself.

The bellmen had the responsibility of placing the tour luggage in the guests' rooms as soon as the bus arrived. The front desk provided them with a list of guests' names and assigned cottage numbers.

On the morning of departure, the guests left their packed bags in their rooms while they went to breakfast. The bellmen picked up the bags, counted them, and then loaded them on the bus.

As payment for the service rendered by the bellmen, the tour directors paid fifty cents per bag. This was the standard gratuity paid by all tours. It was considered a tip, but it was included in the tour expenses by each company.

The Jones Transportation Agency had a reputation throughout the area of being fair and equitable with their gratuities. However, one of their tour directors, Mr. Sirkin, did not live up to the company's reputation. On a visit to the Great Majestic Lodge, Mr. Sirkin had not given a tip, even though the bellmen knew their service to Mr. Sirkin had been very good.

Mr. Sirkin's tour also stayed at several other nearby resorts. Several of the Majestic Lodge bellmen knew the bellmen at the other lodges and in discussing the situation, discovered that Mr. Sirkin had neglected the tip at each of the other lodges. It was apparent that Mr. Sirkin had made a profit of more than $180 on his four-day tour through the region.

Upon hearing of Sirkin's actions, the Majestic Lodge bellmen decided that some action had to be taken. They immediately ruled out telling Mr. Hoffman. On previous occasions when there had been a problem, Mr. Hoffman had done very little to alleviate the situation.

Roger Sikes, a first-year bellman and a business undergraduate, suggested that a letter be written directly to the president of Jones Transportation Company. He felt that the company would appreciate knowing one of their tour directors had misused company funds. After some discussion, the other

Source: Abridged from "The Great Majestic Company" by J. B. Ritchie and P. Thompson in *Organization and People*, 2nd ed. St. Paul: West, 1980, 222–25.

bellmen present agreed. Sikes prepared a detailed letter, which told the Jones president the details of the Sirkin incident. The bellmen didn't expect to recover the money from the tour, but they felt that this was the appropriate action to take.

Three weeks after the bellmen's letter had been mailed to the Jones Transportation Company, Mr. Tomblin was thumbing through his morning mail. He noticed a letter from his good friend Grant Cole, the president of the Jones Transportation Company. Mr. Tomblin opened this letter first. Mr. Cole had written that there was a problem at the Great Majestic Lodge and he thought Mr. Tomblin should be made aware of it. He enclosed the letter from the bellmen and suggested that, if the bellmen had any problems with any Jones directors in the future, it might be wise for them to speak to Mr. Tomblin before action was taken.

Mr. Tomblin was enraged.

CASE QUESTIONS

1. Was Mr. Tomblin's communication to Robert Hoffman in the opening paragraph of the case formal or informal communication? Explain briefly. What was the purpose of the communication? Do you think it was accomplished? Why or why not?
2. Consider the bellmen's letter to Grant Cole. Was it an effective communication? Explain briefly. Was it skillful? If not, which skill would you say the bellmen *primarily* lacked? Explain briefly.
3. What do you think was the purpose, or purposes, behind Mr. Cole choosing to send a letter to his good friend Mr. Tomblin about the bellmen's behavior? Explain your answer.
4. Do you have any evidence in the case pertaining to Robert Hoffman's skill as a communicator? Explain briefly.

12 / Decision-Making Skills And Operations Management Techniques

Jim Ambercrombie paused on his way back to his office, then walked over to Yvonne's desk. He watched quietly as she finished entering a set of data into her desktop computer. As she sat back to reach for a manual, she noticed him for the first time.

"I should be through updating the files in about twenty minutes, Jim," she offered. "I'll bring everything down to your office by 10:30 at the latest."

"Fine and dandy, Yvonne," Jim replied. "See you then."

Jim sauntered back to his office, feeling fairly smug. Putting the inventory-control system on the computer had been a big step in freeing up his time. As purchasing manager, Jim was responsible for buying and maintaining inventories of hundreds of different items. Now eighty percent of those items were controlled by a computer program that provided Jim with weekly reports indicating what needed to be purchased, when, and in what quantities. In effect, the computer now made the majority of the routine purchasing decisions.

As Jim approached his office, his secretary signalled that he had a phone call. "Ambercrombie," he said, picking up his phone and shrugging off his jacket.

"Jim? Frank Marbach here. I've got some bad news. We lost a truck today. It had your shipment of cartons on it."

"Whaddya mean 'lost it,' Frank?"

"I mean 'lost it'—in the river. Tim Lubow hit a patch of ice on the bridge by the airport and went right through the guard rail about ten yards from shore.

"Jesus, Frank. How's Tim? He's a good man."

"He's been better, but he'll survive. Broke a few ribs is all. Managed to swim to shore. Only a few feet of water there anyhow."

"He's lucky," observed Jim. "Was the truck totalled?"

"I'm sure it was," replied Frank, "but I don't know about the shipment. There was no fire, so if the thing stayed watertight, we might be able to salvage some of it. I'm on my way out there now, but I wanted to alert you right away."

"Yeah, OK; thanks, Frank," said Jim. "Listen, get back to me as soon as you know something. I think we'd better go ahead and assume that most of it will be lost. You'd better initiate a replacement order, at least in the number 10 boxes for right now. We can't afford to run out of those, and they've got the longest lead time."

"Will do, Jim. Another ten thousand number 10's. I'll be back to you as soon as possible with a report on the status of the shipment and a delivery date for the boxes," said Frank.

"OK, Frank. Thanks for calling. I'd better get to work."

Jim hung up the phone and reached for a pad of paper. He buzzed his secretary and told her to have Yvonne come to his office immediately.

These are the kinds of decisions you can't computerize, thought Jim. The lead time on some of those supplies was three to four weeks, and Jim wasn't sure if he had three weeks' inventory in stock. He began to write:

Frank's early warning gave Jim some breathing room, but not much. He knew he'd have to make some decisions before the day was out. If the shipment was a total loss, he'd either have to pick up some substitute boxes from another supplier or try to get by with existing inventory. They could not afford to run out; production and sales depended on purchasing to maintain inventory. However, ordering from another supplier would be an expensive safeguard. Frank's company gave the best prices, and somebody else would realize Jim was in a bind.

He needed more information. He had some time, but not a lot. He'd get as much information as he could by four P.M.; then he'd have to act. If you learned one thing in this business, he thought; it was that you couldn't wait until you had all the information. Every decision had some uncertainty and entailed some risk. You had to make the best decision you could with the information available when the time came. You hoped that it was good enough, or if not, that it could be fixed. One thing was sure: he and Yvonne would earn their salaries today.

Many people believe that managing is decision making.[1] While we know that managers play many roles other than decision maker, this skill is critical to good planning, organizing, directing, and controlling.

Managers, like Jim Ambercrombie, make scores of decisions every day. Some, probably most, of their decisions are routine, like most of those Jim has to make. When decisions are routine, managers can establish routine methods for making them. In some cases, rules and criteria can be programmed, as Jim has done with inventory control.

Managers make other decisions in response to unusual or novel situations for which rules do not exist. Like Jim's problem regarding the wrecked shipment, out-of-the-ordinary questions must get the personal and concentrated attention of decision makers, who must exercise insight and judgment to solve them.[2]

All decisions involve choosing between two or more alternatives. Each routine purchasing decision Jim faces provides many alternatives involving suppliers, prices, and quantities to purchase. The uncommon decision he faces involves only two alternatives—ordering from another supplier, or waiting to get more information about damages. Sometimes a decision maker has only the choices of acting or doing nothing.

In the first section of this chapter, we will look at factors that affect decision making. By understanding these factors, you will have a better idea of your own strengths and weaknesses and the way they are affected by factors in the environment. In the second section, we will look specifically at skills involved in various stages of the decision-making process and consider ways to develop them. Finally, we will look at some operations management techniques that are used to improve organizational decision making today.

FACTORS THAT AFFECT DECISION MAKING

Like all behaviors, any decision-making process is the result of an interaction between the characteristics of the individual and the surrounding physical and social environments. We will look briefly at each of these factors to provide a background for our discussion of decision-making skills.

The Decision Maker

An individual brings all of the inherited and learned characteristics discussed in Chapter 8 to the decision-making process. A person's perception may have important effects on interpreting information. Self-esteem affects confidence and the amount of effort that is put into making decisions. Two characteristics have received particular attention in the study of decision making—cognitive limits and decision-making style.

Cognitive Limits and Decision Making.   Surprisingly, little hard evidence can be found for the commonsense notion that more intelligent people should make better decisions than less intelligent people.[3] What seems to be more relevant is the way in which people use their **cognitive limits,** *the amount of information an individual can deal with at one time.* More intelligent people may be able to deal with relatively more information, but all individuals, whatever their intelligence, can not deal with information overload.

Managers, like everyone else, may overlook, oversimplify, and use habit, tradition, or impulse as thinking shortcuts in an effort to avoid being overwhelmed by incoming information. Obviously, the more of this they do, the more likely it is that their decision making will suffer.

It is possible to reduce these unprofitable responses, but to do so one must be aware of them. Daniel Katz and Robert Kahn have noted, "We often neglect cognitive limitations and ascribe errors in human judgment to motivational factors such as wishful thinking. We may be using emotional predisposition as an explanation for faulty conclusions when the difficulty is one of cognitive functioning."[4]

This comment is especially important in the context of a discussion of decision-making skills. Training and practice will help overcome some of the negative effects of cognitive limits on decision making.

Decision-Making Styles.   A **decision-making style** is *an information-processing pattern characteristic of an individual decision maker.* It comes about through an interaction of intelligence, personality, and reinforcement history.

M. J. Driver and A. J. Rowe have proposed two fundamental dimensions along which these styles vary—complexity, or amount of information used, and focus, or

Exhibit 12.1   Decision-Making Styles

Complexity: Amount of Information Used

Moderately Low | High

		Decisive	Hierarchic
Focus: Number of Alternatives Developed	One	**Decisive** Example: Harry S Truman	**Hierarchic** Example: Richard M Nixon
	Many	**Flexible** Example: Franklin D Roosevelt	**Integrative** Example: Adlai Stevenson

Source: M. J. Driver and A. J. Rowe, "Decision-Making Styles: A New Approach to Management Decision Making." In G. L. Cooper, ed., *Behavioral Problems in Organizations.* Englewood Cliffs, N. J.: Prentice-Hall, Inc., 1979, p. 151.

number of alternatives developed.[5] These two dimensions form a matrix of four decision-making styles: decisive, flexible, hierarchic, and integrative (Exhibit 12.1).

The decisive decision maker looks for just enough information to identify a satisfactory alternative; this style is action-oriented. The flexible decision maker shows a preference for having a number of options by generating a number of alternatives from which to choose. The hierarchial decision maker searches for and evaluates a great deal of information about a small number of alternatives; the hierarchial style is information-oriented. An integrative decision maker is intellectually oriented; he or she gathers information and generates several alternatives before deciding.

Driver and Rowe suggest that every individual has a dominant and a back up style. Better decisions are made if at least one of a decision maker's styles fits the requirements of a situation. For example, if the situation calls for creative problem solving, an integrative decision maker, who uses a great deal of information and generates several alternatives, will be more effective than a decisive decision maker. This, of course, is a contingency theory; the "best style" is the one that fits the particular situation.

Other aspects of a decision-making situation that affect the agreement between that situation and individual decision style include the complexity of the relevant information, time pressures, responsibility, planning demands, the organization's reward system, and the decision styles of peers. With so many factors involved, it seems clear that no one style is best, and managers with an opportunity to develop a full range of decision styles and strategies are likely to be more effective than those who are limited in approach.[6]

The Physical Environment

As discussed in Chapter 9, the nature of the task helps shape the physical environment for any behavior. In order to study the relationship between aspects of decision-making behavior and the nature of the decision to be made, one must be able to describe types of decisions. A number of ways have been suggested, based on such criteria as how often the decision must be made, how much creativity is required, to what extent the decision can be programmed (made according to some set strategy or rule), and how much uncertainty (as to alternatives and consequences) is involved.

All decisions involve choosing between two or more alternatives.

A particularly useful but simple system developed by E. F. Harrison for classifying management decisions is presented in Exhibit 12.2.[7] Category I decisions are routine decisions for which a best alternative can be computed, like the typical purchasing decisions Jim Ambercrombie faces. Examples of other Category I decisions would include retail pricing, sequencing work operations, and financial investing. Category II decisions are unusual decisions, requiring more judgment and innovation, such as Jim's handling of the wrecked shipment, creating an advertising campaign to market a new product, filling a vacancy at the executive level, or selecting the location for a new plant.

This classification system offers some guidelines for decision making in organizations:

1. Treating Category I decisions as if they were Category II decisions is a waste of organizational resources. Category I decisions can be programmed efficiently. Category II decisions require concentrated effort and time.
2. In organizations of any size, most Category I decisions can be handled competently by individuals at the middle or operating levels of management, using decision rules approved at higher levels.
3. Some decision-making steps, such as setting objectives, can be omitted for the relatively simple Category I decisions, but Category II decisions require the full process.
4. Nonroutine, Category II decisions generate significantly more conflict between decision makers than routine, Category I decisions.[8]

The Social Environment

Nowhere is the influence on behavior of the social environment clearer than in the decision-making process. The number of social forces that affect how a decision maker acquires information, how good the information is, how it is used, and what alternatives are feasible is impressive. A manager must deal with three sets of social forces.

1. Human—attitudes and values, status and power relationships, the informal communication network
2. Organizational—precedents, structure, climate, reward system
3. Environmental—the economy, market conditions, politics, government restraints, opportunities

Exhibit 12.2   A Categorization of Decision Characteristics

	Category I Decisions	Category II Decisions
Classifications	Programmable, routine, generic, computational, negotiated, and compromise	Nonprogrammable, unique, judgmental, creative, adaptive, innovative, and inspirational
Structure	Proceduralized; predictable; certainty regarding cause/effect relationships; recurring; within existing technologies; well-defined information channels; definite decision criteria; outcome preferences may be certain or uncertain	Novel, unstructured, consequential, elusive, and complex; uncertain cause/effect relationships; nonrecurring; information channels undefined; incomplete knowledge; decision criteria may be unknown; outcome preferences may be certain or uncertain
Strategy	Reliance upon rules and principles; habitual reactions; prefabricated response; uniform processing; computational techniques; accepted methods for handling	Reliance on judgment, intuition, and creativity; individual processing; heuristic problem-solving techniques; rules of thumb; general problem-solving processes

Source: E. F. Harrison, *The Managerial Decision-Making Process*. Boston: Houghton Mifflin, 1981, p. 14.

The net effect of these forces is to place social limits on the decision making process. Certain alternatives cannot be chosen, even though they meet the objectives, because they are judged by the social environment to be inappropriate, unethical, or illegal. For example, consider the constraints on an executive who must decide what to do with a "burned-out" manager who is making costly mistakes in the performance of daily operations. Some of the alternatives are to pension the employee off with full pay, give him or her glowing recommendations in hopes of a transfer, termination, or a leave of absence for rehabilitation. Each alternative will solve the problem; the manager will be out of the way. However, the organizational social environment calls the first alternative inappropriate (it would set an undesired precedent) and the second unethical. The broader social environment limits the executive's alternatives to the third and fourth.

In a fanciful view of decision making, an objective decision maker operates in a perfect world, using perfect information to identify all possible alternative choices, predicting the outcomes of each choice, ranking the alternatives in the order in which they are most likely to meet the objectives of the decision, and choosing the alternative that maximizes those objectives.

In reality, perfect information is seldom available. Even if it were, managers would not have enough time to collect it or use it because of their cognitive limits. Furthermore, the limits placed by the social environment on the aspects of the decision process usually prevent the decision maker from maximizing gains.

While perfect rationality is a useful model of how decision making *should* proceed, a picture of how it *does* proceed shows a decision maker with individual cognitive limits, perceptual biases, values, and habits. Within these limitations, managers collect what information they can in the time available, extract from it some possible alternative courses of action, and choose one that will satisfy major objectives.[9] Personal, social, time, and information factors all place limits on managers' abilities to maximize objectives. This decision maker is operating with **bounded rationality,** *that managerial decision making affected by imperfect information, social constraints, and cognitive limits.* Using bounded rationality, a manager seldom, if ever, *maximizes* (finds the optimal answer) but instead *satisfices* (chooses a satisfactory alternative).

Why do managers satisfice rather than maximize? First, there are problems of social constraints and cognitive limits already discussed. Second, information changes with time, so managers can never be sure they have all the necessary information. Third, time pressures restrict the amount of effort a manager can put into any given decision. In addition, managers tend to be action-oriented. They prefer *doing* to *analyzing.* Finally, Category II decisions do not lend themselves to maximizing because of their complexities, novelties, or qualitative natures.

Interestingly enough, this imperfect process seems to work. In their book describing what are generally considered America's best-run companies—IBM, 3M, Texas Instruments, Digital, McDonald's, Procter & Gamble, for example—Thomas Peters and Robert Waterman find a consistent bias toward action.[10] Problems and opportunities are analyzed and studied carefully, but analyses and reports are neither exhaustive nor exhausting. Big problems are broken into manageable chunks, attacked, and acted upon. An axiom by which these companies operate would seem to be "Do it, fix it, try it." That is, identify a problem, gather a reasonable amount of information, analyze it, find a good solution, then implement it. If it doesn't work, fix it. Experimentation—trying something to see how it works—is preferred to inaction and endless analysis. Chase Manhattan Bank accomplished a major, successful adjustment of its retail operations in just this fashion. One regional manager tried some new ideas and when he was successful, others followed suit. McDonald's introduced their breakfast menu in the same way.

Decision making in organizations is pulling in two directions today. Managers retain their action biases, but would like to do better jobs of analyses. To a certain extent, management information systems can help overcome cognitive limits and improve imperfect information. Social constraints that limit alternatives will always be there, though their forms and contents change as values and customs change. We will discuss these constraints in some detail in Chapter 18.

THE DECISION-MAKING PROCESS

At various stages in the decision-making process, certain skills can help managers do a better job of making decisions, whatever their styles or strategies. The steps in that process are shown in Exhibit 12.3.

Initiating the Process

Just as the first step in communicating is knowing when to communicate, so, the first step in decision making is knowing when to start the process. Often this step requires no particular skill. In organizations, many decisions are a routine part of

Exhibit 12.3   Steps in the Decision-Making Process

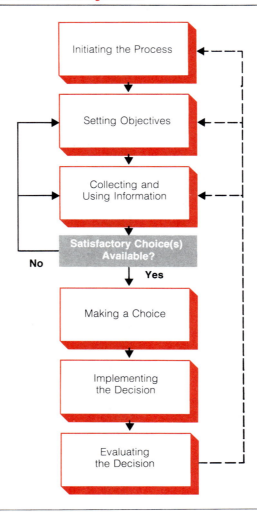

the work day, others are requested by superiors, peers, or subordinates, and some simply arise out of the immediate pressures of the situation. But some decision-making needs and opportunities are not so obvious. Identifying problems that many not be immediately obvious can be particularly difficult.

Identifying Problems.   A **problem** is *an obstacle to a goal.* Many so-called problems in organizations are only *pseudo-problems,* conditions or behaviors that are annoying, but aren't really standing in the way of anything. For example, a manager might prefer more space and nicer furniture for his or her employees, but lack of these things is not necessarily a problem; it may not be interfering with either work accomplishment or employee morale.

Most real organizational problems take time to identify, formulate, and solve. Increased skill in identifying and formulating problems makes more time available for solving them, because less time is wasted on pseudo-problems. Basically, identifying and formulating problems is a three-step process:

1. observing a discrepancy between what is happening and what is necessary or desirable if a goal is to be accomplished;
2. discovering what is standing between the current state and the desired or necessary state (identifying the problem);
3. determining if the desired or necessary state will more likely be reached if the obstacle is removed.

Despite the seeming simplicity of the process, it often goes astray. Partly this is because decision makers get sidetracked by pseudo-problems; partly it is because they tend to go about the process backwards. Many managers begin with a preconceived notion that a problem exists and then look for evidence to support that notion. Others begin with some desired course of action and look for a problem to justify it. This backwards approach has been described as "solutions looking for issues to which they might be an answer, and decision makers looking for work."[11]

Solving problems by starting with solutions often reflects one-best-way thinking. For example, the belief that "better communication" is the answer to all problems may be so strong that it is assumed "poor communication" must be reducing effective performance, even though no problem has been observed.

Deciding Not to Decide.   One often-overlooked aspect of decision-making skill involves knowing when to leave a decision unmade. Recognizing when the best decision is no decision is one way to avoid wasting time. Skillful managers decide not to decide for:

1. *problems that will take care of themselves* unless the cost of leaving them alone exceeds the cost of intervening. For example, it is probably not worth the time to decide what to do about a frequently absent, time-card employee who has given notice that she is leaving. She doesn't get paid if she isn't at work, and the wheels for a replacement have already been set in motion.
2. *pseudo-problems.* You may not like your boss' habit of "touring" your department every afternoon, or the fact that one worker insists on using the same machine every day. However, unless this behavior significantly interferes with the health, safety, or performance of someone, it isn't worth your time.
3. *problems that probably can't be solved.* Such problems are likely to stem from external laws and regulations, discussed in Chapter 18. For example, a particular safety regulation may stand in the way of performing a task efficiently, but there may be no way to solve this problem short of violating the law or risking injury.

Setting Objectives

Decisions are made to meet objectives. The more clearly the purpose can be stated, the more likely it is that a decision can be made to accomplish it. As explained in Chapter 5, specific goals work better than vague ones. This is as true in decision making as it is in motivation.

Sometimes setting a specific decision goal is easy, particularly when the decision isn't seen as very critical. The objective may be simply to get the decision made. In another case, things are not so clear, and it is tempting to be vague and worry about the details later. To say that the objective is "to solve a problem" is true, but it doesn't offer much guidance.

Whatever the nature of the decision, objectives are generally more useful if they are *specific*, *measurable*, and *realistic*. Consider, for example, a manager who is facing a problem of absenteeism. "I've got to do something about this absenteeism," is not a very specific objective. If the objective is stated, "I want to cut out absenteeism," it is specific and measurable, but hardly realistic. "Reduce absenteeism in six months" is probably realistic and can be measured, but it is not specific. "I want to make a decision that will reduce absenteeism by ten percent over the next six months," is a specific, measurable, *and* realistic objective.

> *In reality, a decision maker has individual cognitive limits, perceptual biases, values, and habits. Within these limits, the decision maker collects what information there is in the time available, extracts from it some possible alternative courses of action, and chooses one that will satisfy major objectives.*

Defining the criteria for a decision means determining ahead of time an answer to the question: How will I know if I've made a good decision? There are basic criteria for any good decision.

The first criterion is *effectiveness*. Is the decision likely to meet some or all of the objectives? Deciding to fire anyone who is absent from work twice in the same month, for example, will most likely reduce absenteeism by ten percent in six months.

The second is *feasibility*. Can the decision be implemented? No matter how well a decision meets the objective(s), if it cannot be carried out, it is not a good decision. Under most circumstances, the decision to fire anyone absent twice in a month would not be feasible because of union contracts prohibiting such a penalty.

Next, the manager must consider *timeliness*. Will the effects of the decision be felt in time? Toy manufacturers, like Mattel, must make decisions in April and May on toys they plan to promote during the Christmas season, in order to provide enough lead time for production and promotion.

Cost-effectiveness is the fourth criterion. Will the outcomes of the action directed by the decision be worth the cost? In the long run, most profit-making organizations expect that decisions will be cost-effective. In the short run, however, decisions that are expensive to implement are often tolerated. For example, in the wake of the Tylenol scare in 1982, Johnson & Johnson spent over $100 million in removing the product from stores, creating an expensive tamper proof package, and getting Tylenol back on the market. The short-term losses were tolerated to salvage customers and, eventually, to regain the long-term market share.

Collecting and Using Information

Although the acquisition, use, and distribution of information were discussed in detail in Chapter 11, we are concerned here with knowing what information is needed and how to use it to make decisions.

Knowing What Information Is Needed.[12]   To carry through a complete decision-making process, a decision-maker needs *basic information*, such as the alternatives from which to choose, possible future conditions in which alternatives may have to function, and criteria used to evaluate each alternative. In addition, the decision maker would need *important information*, such as the probability that a particular future condition will occur, and the relative importance attached to each criterion. Finally, *complete information* would include performance data such as payoffs for each alternative and constraints that limit alternatives. These requirements are summarized in Exhibit 12.4 with an example of staff overload. The manager must make a decision in order to solve the problem of having too few people and too much work.

The example assumes that the manager has already collected the information from the manager's own perceptions of the situation, knowledge of organizational policies and workings, other parts of the organization, and sources outside of the organization. Whatever its source, it is not as complete, detailed, or solid as the manager wishes. The manager does not know whether the current increased work load will continue. Neither is it certain that a particular permanent employee will fit in better than a particular temporary one.

The uncertainty that accompanies most decision making is frustrating; it is the gap between the information available and perfect information. There is a natural tendency to try to reduce uncertainty by prolonging the information-collecting process. At some point, however, the decision maker must move on and do the best he or she can with the information available.

Knowing When to Stop Collecting.   Some of the information required for decision making is relatively easy to get. Other information can only be obtained with great effort. Some may simply not be available. At what point does the decision maker stop pursuing information?

Theoretically, the answer is straightforward: *stop collecting information when the costs of obtaining it outweigh the benefits of having it.* For example, the time it takes to check each supplier's price for a specific part is probably more costly than the possible savings of finding the least expensive source, unless it is known in advance that there is a very large variation.

Exhibit 12.4   Information Needed to Make a Decision About Staff Overload

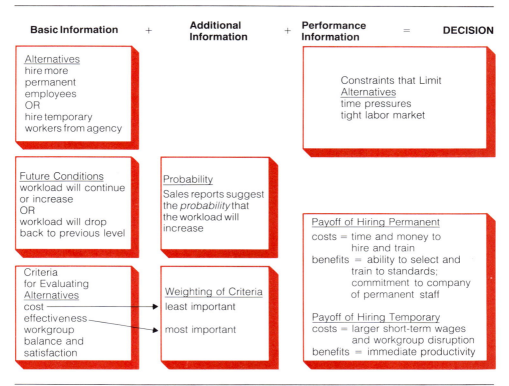

| Basic Information | + | Additional Information | + | Performance Information | = | DECISION |

Basic Information

Alternatives
hire more
permanent
employees
OR
hire temporary
workers from agency

Performance Information

Constraints that Limit
Alternatives
time pressures
tight labor market

Basic Information

Future Conditions
workload will continue
or increase
OR
workload will drop
back to previous level

Additional Information

Probability
Sales reports suggest
the *probability* that
the workload will
increase

Performance Information

Payoff of Hiring Permanent
costs = time and money to
hire and train
benefits = ability to select and
train to standards;
commitment to company
of permanent staff

Payoff of Hiring Temporary
costs = larger short-term wages
and workgroup disruption
benefits = immediate productivity

Basic Information

Criteria
for Evaluating
Alternatives
cost
effectiveness
workgroup
balance and
satisfaction

Additional Information

Weighting of Criteria
least important

most important

Improved methods of collecting, storing, and communicating information in recent years suggest a corollary to the cost-benefit rule: *stop collecting information when the costs of having it outweigh the benefits.* Too much information can be as harmful as too little. The decision maker can feel overwhelmed and focus on the least important or most dramatic information, or just shortcircuit the entire process to get it over with.

It is often difficult to assess the relative costs and benefits of collecting information. However, there are warning signals that too much time is being devoted to this phase of the process: searching for information to support a decision that has already been made, rather than for information to help make the decision; using the search for more information as an excuse to avoid making the decision; making the process of collecting information an end in itself, or more interesting than the original task.

Using the Information.   The purpose of collecting information is to use it to find and evaluate alternatives from which to make a choice. Therefore, it is necessary for the decision maker to make some sense out of the information—to get it into an organized form so that its meaning can be evaluated.

Exhibit 12.5 A Decision Tree

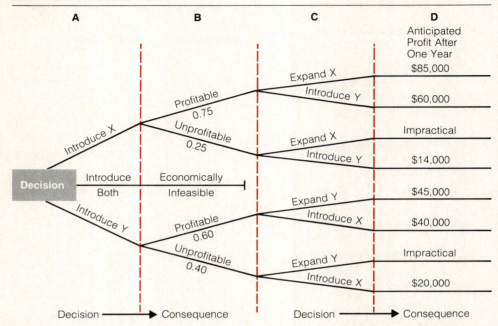

	A	B	C	D

Anticipated Profit After One Year

Expand X — $85,000
Introduce Y — $60,000

Profitable 0.75

Introduce X

Unprofitable 0.25

Expand X — Impractical
Introduce Y — $14,000

Decision

Introduce Both — Economically Infeasible — $45,000

Introduce Y

Profitable 0.60

Expand Y — $45,000
Introduce X — $40,000

Unprofitable 0.40

Expand Y — Impractical
Introduce X — $20,000

Decision → Consequence   Decision → Consequence

*Adapted from R. Kreitner, *Management: A Problem-Solving Process*. Boston: Houghton Mifflin Company, 1983, page 268.

At this point in the decision-making process a variety of decision-making techniques are especially useful. Some specialized techniques, such as queuing theory, linear programming, and payoff tables, are discussed at the end of this chapter. Now we shall use a more general one, the decision tree, to illustrate the role such techniques can play in ordering and evaluating information.

Exhibit 12.5 shows a simple decision tree developed by a manager faced with making a decision about marketing two new products, X and Y. The company cannot afford to introduce both at once, so the manager must decide which product to introduce first, and whether to introduce the second one at all.

A. Basic Information
   1. Alternatives: Columns A and C
   2. Future Conditions: Column B (profitable or unprofitable)
   3. Criterion: Profit
B. Additional Important Information
   4. Probability: Column B (where 0 = impossible, 1.0 = absolutely certain)
   5. Weighting of criteria: Not necessary here; profit is the sole criterion
C. Performance Information
   6. Payoffs: Column D
   7. Constraints: Can't introduce both at once

Some decisions can be made without the added pressure of time constraints, while others must be made immediately.

In a decision tree, each possible sequence of decisions and consequences is shown by a different branch. Collectively, these branches allow for the arrangement of the information required for making a decision. All the elements outlined in Exhibit 12.4 can be seen in Exhibit 12.5.

This decision tree is a simple one, but the technique can be expanded to handle very complex situations, especially with the aid of computer-based management information systems. Knowing how to use such aids is an important decision-making skill.

Making a Choice

The moment of choice is the high point in the decision-making process. Arriving at this point with a clearly winning alternative, such as that shown on the top branch of the decision tree in Exhibit 12.5, is exhilarating. Unfortunately, it is also rare. One of the following conditions is far more likely:

1. Two or more equally attractive alternatives will accomplish the objectives.
2. No single alternative will accomplish the objectives.
3. Unwanted side effects are associated with all of the alternatives that meet the objectives.
4. None of the alternatives will accomplish the objectives.[13]

When a manager does the best job he or she can and arrives at the moment of choice to face one of these conditions, there are any number of courses of action. If two or more alternatives are equally attractive, one can flip a coin. However, this rarely occurs; some factor, no matter how trivial, usually tips the balance.[14] Often it is the manager's personal preference.

If no single alternative will accomplish the decision objectives, the choice may be to combine several alternatives. For example, the manager faced with a decision whether to hire permanent or temporary workers could hire temporaries while recruiting and training permanent workers.

The condition in which the only decision alternatives that meet the objectives have unwanted side effects requires skill on the part of the decision maker. For example, worker resistance to having temporary workers in well-established social work groups may be strong. In this case, the manager must make a series of decisions: Is this side effect likely to be a problem? If so, can it be solved? If so, do the benefits of hiring temporaries outweigh the dissatisfaction among workers?

When the alternatives that will meet an objective have side effects that are too costly, or when no alternative will meet the objective, it is time to revise the objectives or go back to an earlier step in the decision-making process.

Implementing the Decision

At least three personal skills and resources are necessary to implement a decision in an organization, once it has been made. Assuming that the decision is feasible (that is, that the resources are available), a manager will need communication skills, timing, and power.

Those involved in implementing the decision must understand what they are to do. If the decision involves any substantial change from current practice, implementation is also easier if those affected by the decision understand what is to be done and why. The skills involved in these communications were discussed in Chapter 11. Trust and an open-communication climate are especially important in decisions that affect people who were not included in the decision making process.

Implementation is more likely to be effective if it is timed to fit in with existing operating procedures. For example, a change in work procedure can be implemented more smoothly during a slack period than during a busy one. Good timing also involves knowing how much lead time is required and allowing for it, if possible.

There is more to implementing a decision than giving directions and waiting for them to be carried out. It is often necessary to persuade others about the situation. Sometimes these others must formally approve the decision; other times they need only support, or at least not hinder it. To persuade or influence others about a decision takes power, as discussed in Chapter 10. Most managers prefer to use reason, but other types of influence are frequently necessary.

Management in Action
Some Ways Managers Deal With Time-Wasters

Some executives find that they have to retreat to the corporate library to make decisions. Some hide out in an abandoned office, or in the company bathroom. And most become adept at telling white lies.

These are a few of the many strategies managers adopt to cope with a familiar nuisance: the things and people that interrupt work or waste time. The telephone ranks high among culprits. It can ring too often, or bring to the busy executive's ear misdirected or longwinded callers.

People are nearly as annoying, it seems. They're late for appointments or pitch an idea or product for too long. They often don't know when to leave.

Managers meet such problems with varying degrees of patience, resentment, and ingenuity. There's also room for a philosophical attitude, such as that of Michael Tomczek, a product-marketing manager for Commodore International: "Einstein was right—time is relative. If you don't do something in the next five minutes and nobody dies, it can always be done in the next five minutes."

But any five minutes may bring another summons from the telephone. For many managers, the first line of defense is the call-screening secretary, whose tenure may depend on mastering the white lie.

Not every nuisance comes from outside the company. William M. Carpenter, a senior vice-president of Tenneco Inc. in Houston, says one of the biggest time-wasters is having to set up appointments to see other Tenneco executives, so the company encourages executives to drop in on each other, Mr. Carpenter says. But partly as a result of that policy, if he has "any serious writing to do, when I can't be interrupted, I generally do it at home in the evening."

In the advertising business, "the occasional time-waster is not a very high price to pay for the interaction you need," according to Ruth Salevouris, executive account director at N. W. Ayer. But if things get too hectic she hangs outside her closed door a needlepoint sign that reads, "Leave Me Alone. I'm Having a Crisis."

Salesmen are a major interruption for managers. Gary Allen, executive vice-president of Flagship National Bank of Miami, says salesmen "always say 'can I talk to you for just a moment.' Those are some of the longest moments I've ever endured."

Above all, "it's a case of measuring priorities," says Morton Handel, senior vice-president for finance of Coleco Industries Inc. "Running the business is the main priority," he says, "but we try to be responsive."

Source: "Managers Use a Variety of Tactics Against Time-Wasters, Nuisances," *Wall Street Journal*, February 9, 1983, p. 27.

The implementation phase is crucial. No decision, no matter how brilliant, is of value until it is implemented. An average decision well executed is superior to a brilliant decision no one implements. A major problem with relying on outside consultants is that, while they may make excellent recommendations, they often leave before implementation, without gaining the support needed to carry out the recommendations. The frequent result is an expensive, excellent, unused decision.

Evaluating the Decision

Implementing a decision in organizations is seldom a tidy process. Operations may need to be reordered or personnel redirected. Unforeseen systems effects may have to be dealt with. Such complications do not mean that the decision was a poor one. They merely reflect the uncertainty under which decisions are made. Therefore, the extent to which the decision is meeting objectives without undesired side effects should be evaluated.

Possibly the most difficult aspect of evaluating a decision is recognizing that it is not working and acting before the full impact of the failure is felt. Negative consequences are not always serious, but they can be. The decision to diversify into computers, for example, eventually resulted in a $490 million loss for the National Broadcasting Corporation; they could not compete with specialists like IBM, Digital, and Burroughs.

> *Defining the criteria for a decision means determining ahead of time an answer to the question: How will I know if I've made a good decision?*

There are basically two reasons why a decision turns into a disaster: inadequate or inaccurate assumptions were made when there was uncertainty in the information, or the decision maker's skills in making or implementing a choice were not adequate. Unfortunately for decision makers, this distinction is not always made. When a decision goes wrong, especially an important one, the decision maker is the obvious scapegoat. Looking for a scapegoat accomplishes little in the long run; failure should be a clear call to improve skill in problem identification.

Evaluating a decision is a matter of comparing results with objectives. If things turn out exactly as planned, attention can be turned to other matters. If problems arise, it is time either to make implementation adjustments or to repeat the decision making process, as shown by the dashed line in Exhibit 12.3.

It is important to remember that in business, there is a definite bias toward action, as opposed to endless analysis. Decisions need to be made when people are interested enough in the problems to implement their conclusions. The philosophy is espoused succintly by an executive at Cadbury's, "Ready. Fire. Aim." In other words, make the decision, implement it, learn from the mistakes, and make it better. Do it; fix it; try it.

ALTERNATIVES TO INDIVIDUAL DECISION MAKING

We have been discussing decision making as an activity performed by individuals. However, many decisions in organizations are made by small groups. When teams or task forces make decisions, the process is *group decision making.* If everyone affected by the decision participates, the process is *participative decision making.*

Group Decision Making

Decision making by formal and informal groups is an especially strong norm in many companies such as Hewlett Packard, Emerson Electric, Exxon, and Harris Corporation. At 3M, several hundred groups of four to ten people make decisions about new products. TI has some nine thousand small groups looking at productivity problems. Group decision making is a fact of modern organizational life.

Group decision making is based on two assumptions: that groups make better decisions than individuals, and that it is easier to implement decisions made by groups.[14]

Quality of Group Decisions. Research into group decision making generally supports the assumption that groups make better decisions than individuals but only under the following conditions:

1. The decision to be made is appropriate to group analysis. Groups make better decisions if the decision is of moderate difficulty, and if the work can be divided. For example, a group could well make a decision about a new plant site. Information about the factors to be considered could easily be collected by various group members and assembled at the appropriate time. In addition, the decision should be neither so easy that an individual could do it as well nor so difficult that a group is likely to have trouble reaching a consensus.
2. The group is small enough to be efficient and is mixed with respect to member characteristics, experience, interests, and so on. Four to ten members is the range in most organizations, with groups of seven members providing the norm. As was explained in Chapter 9, large groups tend to split up into factions, which can hinder group decision making. As was also explained, heterogeneous groups generally perform tasks better than homogeneous groups, other things being equal. This is especially true in group decision making; individual differences are the major source of the success of groups in decision making.
3. Group interaction allows for the use of the resources of all the members. Two heads are not better than one if one dominates the discussion. In general, free and open communication is more likely if the group is organized cooperatively, status differences are not too large, the group is relatively cohesive, and group leaders actively encourage the free expression of ideas, including minority viewpoints, and discourage the premature evaluation of ideas.

4. Group goals are consistent with the goals of those who will evaluate the decision. In Chapter 9 we discussed the fact that group goals may not be the same as the goals others have for the group. We also noted that highly cohesive groups are more likely to accomplish their goals. A special problem with the qqality of group decisions can arise if a group is an extremely cohesive one with the primary goal of presenting a united front to outsiders, rather than making good decisions. The resulting behavior has been called *groupthink*, "deterioration of mental efficiency, reality testing, and moral judgment that results from in-group pressures."[15] Not all highly cohesive groups are afflicted by groupthink, but a high level of cohesiveness makes this behavior possible.

This list of conditions for good group decision making makes clear that the manager who works with such groups has more control over some factors than others. If the manager is not also the group's leader, control can be quite limited. However, it is possible to establish rules for group interaction that will substitute for manager control and make it more likely that a good decision will result.

> *Any decision involves some action alternatives, some chance of solving a problem, and a set of possible outcomes.*

One way to overcome some common obstacles to full communication in decision-making groups is the *Nominal Group Technique*. This technique, shown in Exhibit 12.6, structures group interaction, helping to offset problems like individual domination and groupthink. Research suggests that the decisions of groups that use this technique are often superior to those from other groups.[16] There is evidence that more effort is made to implement decisions made by structured groups.[17]

Acceptance of Group Decisions.   A good decision is not worth much if it does not get the support required for implementation. Research generally supports the assumption that people are more satisfied with decisions they or their representatives have had a part in making. Another reason organizations have turned increasingly to the use of groups to make decisions is the belief that the decision is more likely to be accepted than one made by an individual. This acceptance, in turn, is believed to lead to more effective implementation.

Participative Decision Making

Participative decision making occurs when those affected by or implementing a decision participate in making the decision. Proponents of participative decision making argue that it enhances employee morale and increases their acceptance of decisions. Critics contend that the process wastes time, does not result in better decisions, and avoids managerial responsibility.

There is little doubt that participative decision making takes more time than unilateral decision making. There is only scant evidence about the relative quality

Exhibit 12.6   The Nominal Group Technique

1. The group meets face to face, but each member is given the problem in writing. He or she silently evaluates and writes down suggestions.
2. Each member in turn presents one suggestion to the group. There is no discussion until all ideas have been presented; they are simply recorded on a flip chart or chalkboard.
3. The group discusses the suggestions to clarify, elaborate, and evaluate them.
4. Each individual ranks the suggestions anonymously in writing.
5. The group decision is determined to be the suggestion with the highest group ranking.

Source: A. L. Delbecq, A. H. Van de Ven, and D. H. Gustafson, *Group Techniques for Program Planning: A Guide to Nominal Group and Delphi Processes.* Glenview, Ill.: Scott, Foresman and Company, 1975.

of the process. Two studies looked at participative decisions about employee absenteeism. In one case, the participative decision was more effective than one made by management alone in reducing absenteeism; in the other, it was not.[18]

Allowing employees to participate in decisions affecting them *does* increase morale and acceptance. Several companies now permit employees to participate in determinations of salaries and bonuses. The evidence suggests that not only does this participation improve attendance, reduce turnover, and enhance morale, but that the employees are highly responsible in making the decision.

Participative decision making appears to be gaining popularity in industry. Further impetus comes from the current fascination with Japanese management practices, fostered by Japan's phenomenal industrial success. That interest has focused on, among other things, the commitment to worker participation in operational decisions.

One particular Japanese technique being adopted by many Western firms is the quality circle as discussed in Chapter 9. In large Japanese companies great emphasis is placed on work groups, which tend to be relatively autonomous and highly competitive. Quality Circles are formed within these groups to pinpoint and solve particular problems, typically dealing with quality control. The technique, as adopted in the West, provides for autonomous work groups to consider specific job problems and execute decisions to solve them.

OPERATIONS MANAGEMENT TECHNIQUES

In the past thirty years a number of quantitative decision-making techniques have been developed, many of which have been adopted and applied by managers today. Most of them evolved from the special concerns of operation managers, who manage the production of goods and services. However, these techniques are now regarded as useful for managers in most organizations. Purchasing, inventory, and quality-control techniques are as relevant for restaurants and department stores as they are for appliance manufacturers. Scheduling and forecasting are no less useful to airlines, trucking companies, hospitals, and military units than they are to clothing and toy manufacturers. Breakeven analysis and facilities location are used by fast-food franchises, the entertainment industry, and governments, as well as oil and gas companies.

All of these techniques improve operational efficiency through some mathematical analysis of the costs and benefits of alternative uses of resources. Each technique tends to be applicable to a particular class of problems, such as resource allocation, material handling, scheduling and sequencing, and the location of facilities and machinery. Two of the more commonly used techniques are expected value and breakeven analysis.

Expected Value Analysis

To illustrate expected value, a technique commonly used to deal with decision making under uncertainty, let us consider the plight of John French, manager of an automobile-assembly plant. One day, while touring the assembly line, he discovers that the drivers door on several cars fails to close when slammed shut. As he ponders the situation, some questions come to mind, highlighting his uncertainties: How big is this problem? Does it extend to all the cars being produced that day, or only a few? Does it indicate a minor assembly flaw, or a major defect in materials? If he shuts the line down, how long will it take to find the problem? If he lets the line run, how many defective cars will have to be pulled off for additional work?

John can answer none of these questions with absolute certainty. He can make reasonable estimates, but he is *sure* about none.

Any decision involves *some action alternatives*, *some chance of solving a problem*, and a set of possible *outcomes*. A manager may be uncertain about the cost or time that an action will take, about the likelihood that the action will be successful in solving the problem, about what outcomes will occur or what their payoffs will be.

John French's situation reflects uncertainty in each of these areas. Let us assume that Mr. French's objective is to produce quality cars. His problem is defective doors. One alternative is to shut down the line until the source of the defect is found and corrected. Mr. French cannot be certain how much this action will cost. He feels fairly certain that it will correct the problem, but is uncertain how long it will take. One of the outcomes of shutting down the line is falling behind the production schedule of sixty cars per hour, but how far behind is also uncertain.

A second alternative is to let the line run and hope that the defective doors do not indicate a serious long-term production flaw. French cannot be certain that this action will enable him to meet both his quality and productivity objectives. Correcting the defective doors, if the line is allowed to run, will take time and money. How much depends upon how long the defect continues.

Ultimately, John's decision hinges on an unknown—whether the source of the defect is temporary or long-term. If it is of short duration, the better (least costly) alternative is to permit the line to run and to repair the defective doors. If the source of the defect is serious, it will be better to shut down the line rather than allow defective cars to pile up.

Fortunately for Mr. French, and all managers who deal with uncertainty, operation-management scientists have developed a number of techniques to aid their decision processes. All of these techniques involve using the concept of probability to help quantify uncertainty.

Even though John French is uncertain about the nature of his production-line problem, he is not totally ignorant of its nature. His experience and historical data on the processes in the plant will enable him to make some "educated guesses" about the nature and seriousness of the problem.

Let us suppose that the data indicates that, over the past year, similar problems have occurred ten times. Eight of these times the problem was short-term. The line was able to continue running without serious delay because of the small numbers of defects. Twice, however, the line had to be shut down. Historically, then, eighty percent of the time, such problems turned out to be short-term (eight out of ten); twenty percent of the time they turned out to be more serious (two out of ten).

Based on these data, Mr. French might assume that the chances of the current problem being a serious one are also 2 out of 10. His *subjective probability* (educated guess about the possibility of some event taking place) is 2/10 or .2. His subjective probability that the problem is not serious, then, is $1 - 0.2$ or 0.8.

Nothing happens until a decision is implemented.

Mr. French can now use these probabilities to help with his decision by employing the **expected-value technique,** based on the principle that *decision makers who are uncertain about some aspects of a problem should choose that alternative action which has the highest expected value.* The principle states that, over the long run, a decision maker who consistently chooses those alternatives with the highest expected value will do better than those decision makers who do not.

Determining the expected value of an alternative is easy, once the decision maker (DM) has the data. Mr. French, for example, is interested in keeping costs down. He wants to select that alternative that will yield the lowest possible costs. Suppose that the past year's data revealed the following:

Action	Conditions	Costs
Shutting down line	short-term problem	$250,000
Shutting down line	long-term problem	$300,000
Letting line run	short-term problem	$ 5,000
Letting line run	long-term problem	$500,000

Shutting down the line is always expensive, because workers must be paid regardless. Letting the line run when the problem is long-term is most expensive, because the line must eventually be shut down to correct the problem and a great deal of rework must be done.

Mr. French can use these data to construct a *payoff matrix.* Such a matrix enables the DM to compare the expected outcomes of each alternative given the different conditions about which he is uncertain.

A payoff matrix usually lists the alternative actions down the left side and the possible conditions across the top. In Exhibit 12.7, the two actions and the two conditions are so listed. The expected costs of each action for each condition are shown inside the matrix.

Exhibit 12.7   Payoff Matrix

	Conditions and Probabilities of Occurrence	
Action	$P = .8$	$P = .2$
Alternatives	Short-Term Problem	Long-Term Problem
Shut down line	$250,000	$300,000
Let line run	$ 5000	$500,000

The payoff matrix depicted in Exhibit 12.7 is used to calculate the expected value table (Exhibit 12.8). The DM multiplies the payoffs under each condition by the subjective probability for that condition.

Exhibit 12.8 depicts the average costs that Mr. French can expect to incur under either strategy over a period of time. If he shut the line down 10 times, for example, he would expect 8 of those times to be short-term and 2 times to be long-term. The expected costs of shutting down the line would be 8 × $250,000 + 2 × $300,000 = $2,600,000 ÷ 10 = $260,000 average cost per shut down. The expected costs of letting the line run over 10 similar situations would be 8 × $5,000 + 2 × $500,000 = $1,040,000 ÷ 10 = $104,000 average cost.

The expected value or cost of any alternative is simply the sum of its conditional payoffs. Thus, the expected cost of shutting down the line is $200,000 + $60,000 = $260,000. The expected cost of letting the line run is $4,000 + $100,000 = $104,000. Since Mr. French's objective is to keep costs down, his preferred alternative is to let the line run.

This simple technique can be used to help managers choose among action alternatives in uncertain situations. The steps are as follows:

1. Assign probabilities to each possible condition (p).
2. Assign realistic costs to each action alternative under each condition (P).
3. Multiply each cost or payoff times the appropriate probability (Pxp).
4. For each action alternative, add up the appropriate Pxp figures to get its expected value (cost).
5. Choose that alternative with the highest expected value or the lowest expected cost.

Breakeven Analysis

Managers generally undertake a project or investment because they expect to get more out of it than they put into it. They expect to "make a profit"—either in dollars, goodwill, greater efficiency, or some other resource. Breakeven analysis is a useful tool that can help them decide whether a project or investment is worthwhile. They can calculate whether an investment will generate enough revenues to offset its costs, and if so, when it will start to generate profits.

The **breakeven point** for a project or investment is *that point at which accumulated payoffs or revenues finally equal accumulated costs.* Before that point, costs exceed payoffs. After that point, payoffs exceed costs; the investment generates a "profit."

Exhibit 12.8   Table of Expected Costs

Action Alternatives	Conditions		Expected Costs
	Short-Term Problem	Long-Term Problem	
Shut down line	$200,000 (250,000 × .8)	$ 60,000 (300,000 × .2)	$260,000
Let line run	$ 4000 (5000 × .8)	$100,000 (500,000 × .2)	$104,000

Breakeven analysis requires information about costs and payoffs (or revenues). Costs and payoffs are usually calculated in terms of money, although any resource or commodity to which numbers can be attached may be used. The only requirement is that the same measure of units be used for all calculations in a given breakeven analysis. For example, if costs are measured in terms of hours or personnel, then payoffs or revenues must be measured in the same way.

In our discussion we will use dollars as the unit of measure, since it is the most common unit employed. A manager performing a breakeven analysis needs the following information:

1. *Fixed costs:* those costs that will occur regardless of the level of output or activity. These may include real estate, machinery, administration, and other overhead costs.
2. *Variable Costs:* those costs that will vary with the level of output or activity. In a manufacturing operation, they include the direct labor and material costs associated with each unit produced.
3. *Revenue per unit:* the price at which the product or service is sold. The breakeven point is the number of units of output that must be produced and sold to generate enough revenues to meet total costs. Total costs (TC) are simply the sum of fixed costs (FC) and total variable costs (TVC):

$$TC = FC + TVC$$

Total variable costs equal the number of units produced (n) multiplied by the variable costs per unit (VC).

$$TVC = nVC$$

Total revenues (TR) are the price per unit (P) multiplied by the number of units produced (n).

$$TR = nP$$

Cost accounting will supply information on fixed and variable costs. Armed with these figures and the price per unit, a manager can calculate the breakeven point either by using algebra or by constructing a graph.

Using algebra, the manager finds that number of units (n) for which total revenues produced (TR) equals total costs (TC). We know that $TR = nP$ and $TC = FC + n\,VC$. Therefore, when

$$TR = TC$$
$$\text{then } nP = FC + nVC$$
$$\text{and } nP - nVC = FC; \text{ or}$$
$$n\,[P - VC] = FC$$

Solving this equation for n, the manager determines that

$$n = \frac{FC}{P - VC}.$$

In other words, the breakeven point equals fixed costs divided by the amount by which the price of a product exceeds its variable costs.

Suppose that the manager of a record company wants to calculate the breakeven point for a new album. Cost accounting tells the manager that fixed costs for the album (studio costs, wages of musicians and technicians, jacket design, and promotion costs) will be $900,000. Variable costs (direct materials and labor for each record and album cover, plus royalties per record for recording star, composer, and lyricist) are $3.50. The price which the record company gets from distribution is $5.00 per album. With this information, the manager determines the breakeven point using the formula

$$n = \frac{FC}{P - VC} = \frac{\$900{,}000}{\$5 - \$3.50}$$

$$n = \frac{\$900{,}000}{\$1.50} = 600{,}000.$$

Breakeven analysis and market research will help the manager decide how attractive this recording project is. If market research suggests that the album "can't miss" achieving gold record status (one million copies sold), the manager can look forward to profits on every album sold after the 600,000 mark is reached:

$$\text{Minimum expected profits} = (\$5 - 3.50) \times (1{,}000{,}000 - 600{,}000)$$
$$= \$600{,}000.$$

If expected sales are less than the breakeven point, the manager will anticipate losses.

One simple fact is apparent from breakeven analysis. If the revenue per unit does not exceed the variable cost per unit, there will be no profits, only losses. No matter how large n becomes, TR will never equal TC.

Other Popular Operations Management Methods

In addition to expected value and breakeven analysis, managers currently use a number of other quantitative techniques derived from operations management. Linear programming helps managers decide how to allocate resources among alternatives in order to best achieve some objective such as maximum profit or minimum cost. Using computer programs performing linear programming functions, managers can make decisions about:

the mix of ingredients to use in food processing to minimize costs subject to constraints in quality, taste, and availability;

the allocation of financial resources to investments to maximize returns subject to constraints such as diversification, liquidity, and taxes;

the routing of sales calls and trash collection to minimize costs subject to constraints of time, clients, customers, and transportation difficulties.

Methods such as economic-order quantity and materials-requirement planning mathematically determine when and how much material to order to minimize total costs. Queueing theory helps managers schedule and sequence operations under conditions of uncertainty. Applications of this theory are particularly useful for managers of service establishments, such as banks and transportation companies. The transportation method uses a form of linear programming to help managers determine locations for warehouses or shipping facilities, for determining best transportation routes, or for calculating shipping routes. We will leave the detailed discussion of these and similar techniques to more specialized texts.

The Bottom Line

From a manager's perspective, there are two key factors in decision making—numbers and time. Most managers must make scores of decisions every day, usually under some time pressures. To cope with these pressures, while at the same time making good decisions, is an important skill. It is therefore useful to:

1. distinguish between important and trivial decisions, programmed and unusual decisions. Establish routines and delegate decision making to give yourself time to deal with important nonroutine decisions.
2. have clear objectives. Goals help identify problems and set criteria for evaluating alternatives. Remember: a problem is an obstacle to a goal. Without clear goals, problems will be harder to identify.
3. group decision making and participative decision making are aids that you should use when appropriate. Not only can using these techniques relieve you of some of the work, but the group will find these decisions more acceptable and satisfying. Group decision making can be used when there is sufficient time, when the task can be reasonably divided up, when the group shares the relevant organizational goals, and has access to the necessary information. In deciding whether to use participative techniques, use these three rules of thumb.

If the primary criterion by which a decision alternative will be judged is its acceptability to those it will affect, it is probably a good idea to involve those others in the process.

If the primary criterion by which a decision alternative will be judged is the extent to which it meets stated objectives, involvement of others should depend upon the extent to which they can contribute useful knowledge and expertise.

If time is a major constraint in the decision-making process, the decision is probably more appropriate for an individual, as groups almost always take more time than individuals.

SUMMARY

Decision making is a much-used managerial skill that is affected both by the manager's characteristics and the physical and social environment. As a result, managers are constrained by their own limits, and by rules, policies, norms, and time

Many corporations use quality circles for group decision making.

pressures from making perfect decisions. Managers typically make decisions with less information and more uncertainty than they would prefer.

Decision making doesn't begin until someone recognizes the necessity for a decision. Managers have to be able to recognize problems and opportunities. Having clear objectives makes this task easier. Objectives also make it easier to evaluate alternatives, which must meet the criteria of feasibility and timeliness as well as effectiveness.

Skillful decision makers know what information they need. They use other people and good MIS to keep that information available. They also know when to stop collecting information and make the decision. Making the actual choice among alternatives can be done by the manager alone, as part of a group, with the advice of a group, or with some sort of participation by those who will be affected by the decision. Other decision-making aids include a number of quantitative techniques that can simplify decision making when economic criteria are paramount.

Although many techniques have evolved to improve the analytical side of decision making, it is important to remember that nothing happens until a decision is implemented. Managers today are still action-oriented. Rather than agonize over problems, they are likely to look for a workable solution, implement it, and improve it as needed.

QUESTIONS FOR REVIEW AND DISCUSSION

1. Describe your own dominant decision-making style in terms of the categories in Exhibit 12.1.
2. What functions do goals play in the decision-making process?
3. Give some examples of how bounded discretion might affect your behavior when you start looking for a job.

4. When should a decision maker stop the search for more information?
5. Distinguish between group decision making and participative decision making.
6. Assume that you have had the same position for six years. You like the work, find it challenging, and have turned down several opportunities to be promoted to work that looks less interesting. How would you respond to a friend who told you your problem was you had no ambition?
7. If you were a manager of a family-style restaurant, which of the following decisions would you make alone and which would you involve employees in? Explain your answers briefly.
   a. The menu
   b. Hours of operation
   c. Individual employee schedules
8. For what kinds of problems would quantitative decision-making techniques be most appropriate? Least appropriate?

REFERENCES AND NOTES

1. The most famous proponent of this view is H. A. Simon. See *The New Science of Management Decision.* Englewood Cliffs, N. J.: Prentice-Hall, 1960.
2. D. C. Feldman and H. J. Arnold, *Managing Individual and Group Behavior in Organizations.* New York: McGraw-Hill, 1983, pp. 333–34.
3. H. J. Reitz, *Behavior in Organizations,* rev. ed. Homewood, Ill.: Irwin, 1981, Chapter 6.
4. D. Katz and R. L. Kahn, *The Social Psychology of Organizations,* 2nd ed. New York: Wiley, 1978, p. 508.
5. M. J. Driver and A. J. Rowe, "Decision-Making Styles: A New Approach to Management Decision Making." In G. L. Cooper, ed., *Behavioral Problems in Organizations.* Englewood Clifs, N. J.: Prentice-Hall, 1979, Chapter 6.
6. *See* W. Taggart and D. Robey, "Minds and Managers: On the Dual Nature of Human Information Processing and Management." *Academy of Management Review,* 1981, 6, 2, 187–95.
7. E. F. Harrison, *The Managerial Decision-Making Process.* Boston: Houghton Mifflin, 1975, Chapter 1.
8. D. S. Cochran and D. D. White, "Intraorganizational Conflict in the Hospital Purchasing Decision-Making Process." *Academy of Management Journal,* 1981, 24, 2, 324–33.
9. These contrasting models of decision making were first put forth by H. A. Simon in *Models of Man,* New York: Wiley, 1957.
10. T. J. Peters and R. H. Waterman, Jr. *In Search of Excellence.* New York: Harper and Row, 1982.
11. M. D. Cohen, J. G. March, and J. P. Olsen, "A Garbage Can Model of Organizational Choice." *Administrative Science Quarterly,* 1977, 17, 1, 1–25, p. 1.

12. From G. P. Huber, *Managerial Decision Making.* Glenview, Ill.: Scott, Foresman and Company, 1980, p. 30–40.

13. Adapted from E. F. Harrison, *The Managerial Decision-Making Process.* Boston: Houghton Mifflin, 1975, p. 35–36.

14. *See* T. V. Bonoma and G. Zaltman, *Psychology for Management.* Boston: Kent, 1981, p. 60–62.

15. I. L. Janis, *Victims of Groupthink.* Atlanta: Houghton Mifflin, 1972, p. 9.

16. J. J. Sullivan, "An Experimental Study of a Method for Improving the Effectiveness of the Nominal Group Technique." Unpublished Ph.D. Dissertation, University of Florida, College of Business, 1978.

17. S. E. White, J. E. Dittrich, and J. R. Lang, "The Effects of Group Decision-Making Process and Problem-Situation Complexity on Implementation Attempts." *Administrative Science Quarterly,* 1980, 25, 3, 428–40.

18. J. Bragg and I. Andrews, "Participative Decision-Making: An Experimental Study in a Hospital." *Journal of Applied Behavioral Science,* 1973, 9, 6, 727–35. Also, R. M. Powell and J. L. Schlacter, "Participative Management: A Panacea?" *Academy of Management Journal,* 1971, 14, 2, 165–73.

19. G. D. Jenkins, Jr. and E. E. Lawler, "Impact of Employee Participation in Pay Plan Development." *Organizational Behavior and Human Performance,* 1981, 28, pp. 111–28.

SUGGESTED READINGS

Cabot, A. V. and D. L. Harnett, *An Introduction to Management Science* (Reading, Mass: Addison-Wesley, 1977). This is an introductory level book that covers both basic quantitative decision-making techniques and more sophisticated techniques such as nonlinear optimization and dynamic programming.

Harris, R. D. and R. F. Gonzalez, *The Operations Manager: Role, Problems, Techniques* (St. Paul: West Publishing Co., 1981). The authors take a managerial approach to operations management. Rather than being organized around techniques, it describes the role and functions of modern operations managers, problems they face, and techniques they use.

Harvey, J. B. "The Abilene Paradox: The Management of Agreement." *Organizational Dynamics,* 1974, 3, 1, 63–80. Conflict management is a subject that has been thoroughly explored, but this article takes a look at the less frequently examined subject of the problems created when an organization has difficulty obtaining agreement in decision making.

Maier, N. R. F. "Assets and Liabilities in Group Problem Solving: The Need for an Integrative Function." *Psychological Bulletin,* 1974, 74, 239–49. This is probably the most frequently quoted article in the group decision-making literature. Maier's discussion of the role of a leader in an effective decision-making group should be especially helpful to the student or new manager.

Shuler, C. O. "How Good Are Decision Makers?" *Business Horizons,* 1975, April, p. 89–93. This is an interesting discussion of the difficulties of evaluating good managerial decision-making using the analogy of a baseball player's batting average.

Case California Paper Company

The toughest immediate decision facing Wes Palmer, general manager of the hardboard division of California Paper Company, when he returned from a three-week vacation was what to do about George Sherman, the general superintendent. Sherman, a few days after Wes left on vacation, had gotten the company into serious trouble with the state pollution commission. The manufacturing vice-president had immediately reported this to Wes by long-distance telephone. He said, "I don't want to fire Sherman in your absence. You will have to decide what to do yourself when you get back. It's your problem. But if you keep him and he gets us into another jam, I'll fire you."

George Sherman had been associated with Wes Palmer and the California Paper Company in one capacity or another for six years. He was about fifty years old, of less than medium height, thin and siry. He was a mechanical engineer with a bachelor's degree from the University of Illinois.

At frequent intervals, George Sherman had shown a positive talent for getting into trouble himself or causing trouble for others. As he looked back, Wes could remember at least one unpleasant incident each year in which George had been involved.

Toward the end of the fourth year, George got the company into really serious trouble with the state pollution commission, which had been uneasy for some time about pulp discharge from the hardboard mill. The commission's engineers frequently set up test screens in the rivers below the mill to determine whether the pulp content was so high as to endanger the fish life therein. The commission had served notice on the company during the third year of mill operation that they would require it to put in a pulp impounding pond if the existing pollution level was exceeded in the future by any substantial amount.

One day while George was walking through the mill, he suddenly decided that he wanted a chest containing waste pulp cleaned. He immediately told a workman to dump the whole chest of waste pulp directly into the river, without putting it through the effluent screen as usual. This was in definite violation of explicit instructions.

The concentrated discharge of pulp from the emptied chest rammed into a test screen which the state fisheries department had recently set up to keep fish out of a series of irrigation ditches fed by the river. The screen broke and the fisheries department protested to the pollution commission. California Paper narrowly averted issuance of a shut-down order. A few weeks later, the commission instructed the company to start work immediately on a pulp-impounding pond. This cost $200,000.

George first denied having anything to do with the dumping. Wes then confronted him with the man who had actually performed the dumping operation. George then said: "OK, I told him to." Wes was so angry that he didn't trust himself to speak. Instead he walked away, just to cool off.

Now, while Wes was on vacation, a waste pulp chest had been dumped directly into the river again. George was not directly responsible on this occasion. As general superintendent, he could be

Source: "California Paper Company" by A. Grimshaw and J. W. Hennessey in their *Organizational Behavior: Cases and Readings.* New York: McGraw Hill, 1960.

held responsible, however, for not making certain that direct dumping never happened again.

The fish screen was smashed for a second time. The pollution commission's resident engineer immediately called on the manufacturing vice-president, who then conducted his own investigation. He found the employee who had dumped the chest. This man told him that he had washed out the chest's contents through the screen into the impounding pond. When he thought the chest was empty, he had pulled the plug. It was not

completely empty, however, and the residue had gone directly into the river.

In response to further questioning by the vice-president, the employee said that George had told him, "You needn't bother to keep the gate from the chests to the river locked when you're emptying chests into the impounding pond."

The vice-president confronted George with the facts he had just unearthed. George admitted telling the employee that he didn't have to make sure the gate was locked again before beginning the chest-dumping operation.

CASE QUESTIONS

1. At the beginning of the case, the manufacturing vice-president says to Wes Palmer, "It's your problem." Exactly how is George Sherman a problem for Palmer? Be specific in terms of the definition of a problem given in this chapter.
2. Give one example of California Paper's decision making being affected by *bounded discretion.*
3. Evaluate George Sherman's decision in the fourth year to get a waste pulp chest cleaned by dumping it into the river against instructions by the criteria of effectiveness, feasibility, timeliness, and cost-effectiveness.
4. Is the information *uncertainty* Wes Palmer faces with respect to the decision to fire Sherman or keep him high, medium, or low? Explain briefly.
5. List out the major costs and benefits you see to keeping George Sherman or firing him.

Report from the Field Managing A Creative Enterprise

For John Martin, creativity is a way of life. His business produces some of America's premier sports art and portraiture of sports figures. John Martin Studios was selected to create the covers for the 1980 and 1981 World Series programs. His studio has painted murals for a number of universities including Michigan, Kansas, South Carolina, and LSU, depicting great athletes or sports events in their histories.

"We generally face two kinds of creative problems in our business," Martin explains. "One is illustration—trying to get across an idea without reference to a specific individual or event. For example, I did the art work for a big advertising campaign for the Kansas City Chiefs of the NFL, concentrating on the fans and their involvement in the game rather than on the players. Doing the cover for the 1980 World Series gave us a similar problem. The client didn't want a specific event or player, but an illustration that described what the World Series was all about.

"The second type of problem we face is depicting a real person or famous event. For example, we created murals for the University of Michigan Sports Hall of Fame and for the University of Kansas All-Americans' Room. In both cases we had to figure out how to portray specific individuals performing in their particular sport or event in a way that expressed their uniqueness.

"My approach to either type is the same. First, we research the problem. I read everything I can find about the athlete or event, pore over pictures or films that may be available, and interview fans and athletes themselves. Then we do thumbnail sketches—as many as seventy-five for the World Series covers—until I find something that truly expresses the idea, athlete, or event. Once I know we've got it, then we do the detail work, the color, and so on.

"Let me give you a specific case. LSU hired us to create paintings of great moments in its sports history—Billy Cannon's punt return to beat Ole Miss, and so on. One event they wanted was Bert Jones' last second, winning touchdown pass that beat Mississippi 17–16 in 1972.

"A lot had been written about that game, so I had that to start with, but the only available pictures didn't show much, and the only film they could provide was a grainy 8mm film taken from high up in the press box.

"So I decided the only way to get a true perspective on the event was to go to Baton Rouge, the site of that game. I spent one afternoon looking over the field, trying to visualize the play and trying to figure out how to capture the moment in a single picture. It occurred to me that a good angle would be from the end zone, catching the receiver close up with the quarterback in the background.

"That night I returned to the stadium to watch LSU play Indiana University. I discovered that it was possible to get not only the receiver and the quarterback into the picture, but the scoreboard at the opposite end of the stadium as well.

"Anyway, the painting was a success, but it was the hard work we put into preparation, immersing ourselves in the event and the environment, that made the creative part of it come to life."

Source: Personal Interview, October 1983.

13/Creativity and Innovation

Dawn crept in over the marsh. Slowly but steadily, black outlines took on color and form, making it possible to distinguish water from land. Somewhere a flock of geese lifted off the water, their clamoring increasing as they gained altitude enroute to their feeding grounds.

In the boat Henry breathed in the cold air contentedly as he scanned the sky for ducks. God, how I love it, he thought to himself. Dawn, the cold, the water, the isolation, the anticipation—the perfect antidote to the pressures and demands of the job. He loved his job, but sometimes "getting away from it all" was not only rewarding but . . .

Suddenly he stiffened. "See something, Hank?" whispered Willy, his best agent and a frequent hunting partner.

"No, just had an idea, that's all," replied Henry.

"We're supposed to be hunting, not thinking," admonished Willy. "Get your mind off work."

Funny, thought Henry, my mind was off work when the idea struck me. I've been worrying about it and talking about

it and thinking about it for weeks, and suddenly, out here in the middle of the marsh, it comes to me—the perfect incentive for the agency's sales drive.

Henry was general manager for the Minneapolis agency of a large life insurance company. While the agency was only the tenth largest, this year it had a chance to lead the company in total sales.

With only three months left, Henry had been searching for some incentive to get the extra effort, time, cooperation—and creativity—needed to sell large policies. Large policies in the $500,000 and over range required teamwork and creativity. Each program had to be tailored to the individual client's needs and preferences, which required hard work and insight.

Since the first-quarter figures had been released, Henry had been intrigued by the notion of winning the interagency competition. Commissions, pride, and his own encouragement had provided sufficient incentive to keep his agency in the race through September, but Henry had felt that something special and different was needed to boost the efforts during the final three months.

And now he had it. He knew about what it would take in fourth-quarter sales to finish first. Monday morning he would make his pitch to the whole agency. If they met that figure, he would take them all—agents, estate planners, secretaries— to New Orleans for the Super Bowl in January. And each member of the agency would be permitted to take a guest.

It was the perfect incentive for a lot of reasons. First of all, many of the staff were football fans, and followed professional football avidly. Even for those who weren't fans, a chance to leave Minnesota's winter for a few days in New Orleans would be a powerful

inducement. They'd stay at the Royal Orleans in the French Quarter, where fine restaurants and fascinating shops would provide plenty to do besides the game itself. The agency would pay for tickets, plane fare, hotel accommodations, and meals. Henry knew that he could get a good price from a travel agency specializing in Super Bowl trips. And the expense would be worth it if they could meet the sales goal.

The more he thought about it, the more excited he became. Everyone would realize what a generous incentive it was. That would help make it work. He knew they'd be excited, and the television and media hype about the football season, playoffs, and Super Bowl would keep them excited and continually aware of what could await them. People would encourage and help each other out, because they'd all share in the reward. Henry himself would be in there doing whatever he could to help them—he wanted to make the trip as badly as they would.

All that remained was to try out his idea on Willy, who had long served as a sounding board for Henry's ideas. Henry respected his judgment, particularly when it concerned the agents. If Willy bought it, it was a good idea. And this time Henry felt he knew what Willy's reaction would be.

We usually think of organizational creativity and innovation in terms of developing new products or technology. No wonder: innovative products and processes are important. They enable businesses to maintain or increase market shares and profitability; they make it possible to survive in highly competitive markets. They enable organizations to function more efficiently, safely, and at lower costs, and increase the quality and availability of products to the consuming public.

But creativity and innovation are not qualities limited to scientists and engineers usually associated with technological advancement. In organizations today, creativity and innovation mean the conception and application of new, useful ideas by anyone in the organization, including managers. The story that introduced this chapter involves creativity at two levels. The insurance agents need to be creative in order to design and sell large policies; Henry needs an innovative incentive to enhance his agency's effort and creativity for the next three months. Henry and his agents need to be no less innovative than the scientists and engineers who worked on the Eagle project described in Chapter 8.

In recent years, much has been made of the apparent decline in innovation in American business.[1] Foreign competition has taken over and made strong inroads in formerly American-dominated markets such as steel, shipbuilding, and electronics. The number of patents granted to American citizens has dropped by twenty percent. Productivity, which used to increase at a steady two to three percent per year, has declined.

The responsibility for the decline of creativity and innovation in this country is laid at many doors. Although the federal government funds a great deal of research, it promulgates high taxes and regulations which discourage investment in innovation. Inflation and the energy problems have been other causes of decline in innovation, although both seem to be diminishing.

But managers themselves must shoulder some of the responsibility as well. Many executives fail to understand creativity, fail to be inventive themselves, and fail to stimulate and manage innovation in their organizations. One study by the consulting firm of Moye, Allen, and Hamilton, Inc. highlighted this problem.[2] It found that many American industries were misusing their creative people and failing to exploit new technology. The lack of understanding of the basic creative processes, inability to communicate with imaginative, innovative people, and unwillingness to take short-term risks had thwarted this potential in their organizations.

Make no mistake about it: creativity can be stimulated and managed. Technical and nontechnical people can be innovative, and their managers can be as well. In this chapter we will describe individual and organizational creativity to provide some ideas about the process.

MANAGING FOR CREATIVITY AND INNOVATION

The incentives for organizations to foster and manage innovation are significant. Successful innovators outperform noninnovators both in profits and in growth. For example, a study of American companies in steel and petroleum found that, in both industries, successful innovators grew much faster than noninnovators in every time interval studied.[3] A successful innovation increased a firm's annual growth rate by figures ranging from four to thirteen percent.

With such incentives, most organizations try to be innovative. Not all are successful, however. Out of every ten products that research and development produce, five fail in product and market testing, and only two become commercially successful. Managers have come to realize that successful innovation requires more than finding and hiring creative people. Managers themselves have a lot to do with successful innovation.

Planning

Can creativity and innovation be planned? Chief executives of innovative firms say that it can; and given that innovative ideas often take years to reach the implementation stage, the kind of planning needed is often long-range.

Planning can assist innovation in two ways. First, when managers establish long-range goals and objectives, such as market shares, numbers of innovations, and target areas, they give direction and focus to the creative individuals and groups in the organization. For example, DuPont is beginning to look for more innovation in the special-products end of its business. Its long-range plans call for life sciences, electronics, and specialty fibers and plastics to bring in fifty-five percent of its revenues, almost quadrupling the current revenue production.[4] Meeting these goals will require considerable creative effort.

Secondly, good plans also provide for the needed resources. They should provide the organization with creative people and see to it that these people have sufficient resources to meet the objectives. Consistent with its objectives, DuPont plans to double its research and development (R & D) investment in special products. It has already assembled a staff of ten scientists who are seeking ways to restructure living cells as a means of mass-producing specific microorganisms.

By setting objectives, the manager indicates to creative people what they should be working on. The planning process makes it possible for innovators to alert top management to potentially successful prototypes and to the kinds of resources needed. Provision of these resources establishes management's commitment to the objectives. Scientists and engineers who see R & D objectives backed up by resources will be less hesitant to commit themselves to risky, long-term projects.

The President of Emery Air Freight, John C. Emery, Jr., established the following objective for 1990: "The Emery high-speed logistics system of tomorrow . . . will provide a total and complete service that will allow shippers anywhere and everywhere to select the best combination of transportation services from a single company."[5] That objective will serve as the basis for long-range planning and resource allocation for Emery for several years. The number of creative and innovative ideas demanded by such an objective are great, but Emery has provided the focus and direction for that effort.

Organizing

Organizing for innovation requires a balance between too much and too little formal structure. Innovative enterprises do require organizational structure, if for no other reason than to reduce the instability and uncertainty that surrounds creative effort.

The amount of uncertainty varies with the type of activity, as shown in Exhibit 13.1. Basic research, such as genetic engineering, holds the greatest uncertainty, whereas minor technical improvements hold the least. Excessive uncertainty inhibits creativity. Individuals working on highly uncertain projects who must also worry about changes in job assignments, supervisors, policies, or resource allocations will not work to their potential.

On the other hand, excessive formalization of rules, policies, and structure can likewise inhibit the creative process.[6] Creative people need to be able to communicate with each other freely. In addition, they need to be able to communicate important breakthroughs or special requests to top management quickly. For this reason, innovative organizations tend to favor relatively flat organizational structures, to reduce the number of levels of organizational hierarchy between the in-

Exhibit 13.1   Degree of Uncertainty Associated with Types of Innovation

Degree of Uncertainty	Type of Innovation
True uncertainty	Fundamental research Fundamental invention
Very high degree of uncertainty	Radical product innovations Radical process innovations outside firm
High degree of uncertainty	Major product innovations Radical process innovations in own establishment or system
Moderate uncertainty	New 'generations' of established products
Little uncertainty	Licensed innovation Imitation of product innovations Modification of products and processes Early adoption of established process
Very little uncertainty	New 'model' Product differentiation Agency for established product innovation Late adoption of established process innovation in own establishment Minor technical improvements

Source: C. Freeman, *The Economics of Industrial Innovation*, (Penguin Books, London, 1974) p. 226.

novators and top management. Matrix organization, a structure used by many high technology companies, will be described later in this chapter.

Using Market Research

According to an estimate by Booz, Allen, and Hamilton, only one of every five products of research and development becomes a commercial success. The high costs of research activities in the face of such odds make good market research an important managerial activity for firms that intend their products for the marketplace.

Market research may provide the necessary stimulus by identifying a consumer demand which the organization can seek to meet. For example, it has recently indicated a rapid change in the clientele of small computer stores.[7] Originally these stores catered to hobbyists who needed help in setting up or building their own systems. In the past few years, however, customers have become more interested in already assembled computers. In addition, the small-business market has developed, as both professionals and entrepreneurs have found uses for small computers. Now business and professional sales account for two thirds of computer-store sales. This change in clientele required new product packages and new ways of providing customer services. Stores had to differentiate among their clientele. Many stores run by very competent technical people didn't respond to the changing market fast enough and failed.

Market research can also find potential uses for new products or discover different customer requirements which may require modifications in product design and engineering. Field research may be used to uncover potential customers for a new product and to evaluate the size and nature of its market. When a product is judged to be commercially marketable, research will assist sales managers in determining how and to whom the product can most profitably be sold.

Institutionalizing Innovation

Successful innovators don't always stay successful. Success often leads to complacency, and firms became content to exploit past successes without pushing for new ones. Even big, highly advanced corporations like TRW and DuPont have suddenly found themselves losing their creative edges.

To maintain their innovative processes, some firms are moving to "institutionalize" them. That is, they design policies and structures which continue to monitor the company's creativity. The intent is to maintain the search for new markets, to set new goals to stimulate and direct innovation, and to look for new opportunities.

Texas Instruments institutionalized its innovative processes by bringing creative technical people into corporate strategy and planning.[8] Its Objectives, Strategies, and Tactics (OST) system combined the capabilities of different businesses, technologies, and specialties by bringing together research, engineering, and corporate managers to work on projects and decision-making committees. OST had three effects: First, it brought together the research orientation of the company and its product-profit emphasis. Second, it eventually made the whole organization aware of the goals and perspectives of top management. Third, it focused the attention of senior management on R & D while training junior managers in this approach to managing innovation.

Though the system took years to implement, TI felt that it successfully decentralized the innovation process. At the same time, the organization learned how to continue its innovative processes effectively and efficiently. OST helped to bring about the delicate balance between standardization, coordination, and decentralization on which organizational innovation thrives.

MANAGING CREATIVE INDIVIDUALS

Research about creativity indicates that fear, anxiety, and defensiveness impede creative behavior. Managers who create or promote these reactions are going to interfere with innovation. Stressing the consequences of failure promotes fear of failure; inconsistent directives or lack of stability promotes anxiety and defensiveness. Managers who allow creative people little or no time to expose themselves to new ideas are depriving them of the ingredients necessary for creative insights.

On the other hand, reinforcement, goals and deadlines, and autonomy can promote creative behavior. Managers who identify and reward creative output increase the likelihood that it will recur. Clear goals provide incentives and direction for creative thinking. Research and experience reveal that realistic deadlines also serve to energize creative effort in every field from music to space exploration.

Creativity and innovation certainly paid off for Chris Haney, John Haney, and Scott Abbott.

The story that introduced this chapter illustrates how an innovative manager will stimulate intense, creative effort among his employees. Henry's plan for his agency emphasizes a clear goal (leading the company in total annual sales) and a deadline (December 31st). He spent a great deal of time searching for and finding an incentive to augment the reinforcement provided by commissions, pride, and praise. At the same time, he allows his people sufficient autonomy, making himself available for assistance without being intrusive.

Decentralization helps provide the freedom and autonomy which boost organizational innovation. Freedom does not, however, mean freedom from budget constraints. It is not necessary to give creative people "a blank check." A study of 567 successful technological innovations found that two thirds of them cost less than $100,000, while only 12 cost more than $1 million.[9] Modest budgets can yield innovative ideas when those budgets fund directed efforts managed by people who know enough about the process to assist, rather than interfere with it.

An effective manager must be able to identify and understand creative people and to develop originality in the organization. Researchers have studied creative individuals to find characteristics indicative of creative potential and to learn how they work. This information helps managers recognize and develop this behavior.

Characteristics of Creative Individuals

It is not as easy to link creative potential to other individual characteristics, as was once hoped. Contrary to popular thought, creative people are not necessarily more intelligent. Neither are they more likely to suffer from mental problems, contrary to the old adage about "a fine line between genius and madness."

Age, however, *is* one characteristic strongly associated with creative output. Studies of the creative achievements of men and women in the arts and sciences reveal that their greatest productivity occurs between the ages of 30 and 40. For chemists, mathematicians, physicists, and inventors, their peak occurred between the ages of 30 to 34. For example, Thomas Edison who invented the electric light, the phonograph, the movie camera, the microphone, and the stock ticker, and is responsible for the whole field of electronics in general, held 1,093 patents.[10] Although Edison's inventing career spanned sixty years, he obtained one fourth of his patents between the ages of 33 to 36.

Some studies have found that creative people change jobs more than average; others have found that they identify less strongly with the organization than their less creative colleagues. Creative people tend to be nonconformists, but they are not necessarily revolutionary. Their high turnover and nonconformity can be explained by the same characteristic, a tendency to identify so strongly with their work that they pay less attention to rules, norms, or organizational loyalty.

Studies of creative people have often focused on their personality characteristics. A series of conferences supported by the National Science Foundation to identify creative scientific talent produced a list of traits which several studies had found characteristic of productive scientists. This list is reproduced in Exhibit 13.2.

Testing for Creative Potential

As the preceding section suggests, identifying creative individuals by looking for certain characteristics is not very easy. We know that intelligence is not a very good predictor. Although we know when peak creativity is likely to occur, that doesn't tell us much. We know that certain personality traits are characteristic of creatively productive individuals, but these are hard to measure.

Exhibit 13.2   Characteristics of Productive Scientists

1. A high degree of autonomy, self-sufficiency, self-direction
2. A preference for mental manipulations involving things rather than people: a somewhat distant or detached attitude in interpersonal relations, and a preference for intellectually challenging situations rather than socially challenging ones
3. High ego strength and emotional stability
4. A liking for method, precision, exactness
5. A preference for such defense mechanisms as repression and isolation in dealing with affect and instinctual energies
6. A high degree of personal dominance but a dislike of personally toned controversy
7. A high degree of control of impulse, amounting almost to overcontrol: relatively little talkativeness, gregariousness, impulsiveness
8. A liking for abstract thinking, with considerable tolerance of cognitive ambiguity
9. Marked independence of judgment, rejection of group pressures toward conformity in thinking
10. Superior general intelligence
11. An early, very broad interest in intellectual activities
12. A drive toward comprehensiveness and elegance in explanation
13. A special interest in the kind of ''wagering'' which involves pitting oneself against uncertain circumstances in which one's own effort can be the deciding factor

Source: Calvin W. Taylor and Frank Barron, *Scientific Creativity: Its Recognition and Development* (Huntington, N.Y.: Robert E. Krieger Publishing Co., 1975) pp. 385–86.

Because of these drawbacks, researchers have worked to develop more direct methods of identifying creativity. The tests they have developed measure verbal and nonverbal abilities which have been found to be related to creativity. One of the most popular is the Remote Associates Test, which is a short, easily administered verbal test (See Exhibit 13.3). Basically, each item provides the subject with three words. The subjects' task is to find a fourth word which links the three words. For example, try to find a word which links the three words *dew, fumble,* and *eye.* (The linking word is *drop.*)

Many other tests are more complex than the Remote Associates Test. A number of them require the individual to write stories or to think of new uses for common objects or new ways of doing things. The *Journal of Creative Behavior* periodically lists tests available for creativity; there are currently more than seventy listed.

Developing Creative Behavior

One of the results of creativity testing has been the discovery that most people have creative potential, but few of them use it. This discovery led to the idea of trying to help "ordinary" people develop their creativity potential and learn how to use it.

Most attempts to develop adult creativity come in the form of workshops. Participants learn about the creative process and how it might apply to them. They are given tests, and go through exercises designed to teach them to think in different ways. Seminar leaders help participants express their creativity. (Research has found that a great deal of creativity is frustrated by a lack of means for expression.)

> *Creativity and innovation are not qualities limited to scientists and engineers. In organizations today, creativity and innovation mean the conception and application of new, useful ideas by anyone in the organization, including managers.*

These programs have been surprisingly successful. Engineers and business managers have scored higher on creativity tests and have thought of more innovative ideas subsequent to participating in these seminars. In one study, middle managers from a large department store chain were randomly assigned to two groups. One group served as a control; the other participated in creativity training involving testing, lectures, and exercises. After the program, both groups' creativity was measured by tests and by supervisory ratings. Both measures found the training group to rate as significantly more creative than the control group. Subsequent programs with two additional middle management groups and fifty-two merchandise managers yielded similar results: training improved creativity.[11]

Creativity training has been an useful tool for some time. General Motors, for example, first introduced a program in the 1960s and found that it significantly increased both the number and dollar value of profitable ideas generated by automo-

Exhibit 13.3   Sample Questions from the Remote Associates Test of Creativity

REMOTE ASSOCIATES TEST
FORM 3
Sarnoff A. Mednick
Martha T. Mednick
The University of Michigan

INSTRUCTIONS. In this test you are presented with three words and asked to find a fourth word which is *related* to *all three*. Write this word in the space to the right.

For example, what word do you think is related to these three?

| A | cookies | sixteen | heart | _____ |

The answer in this case is "sweet." Cookies are sweet; sweet is part of the phrase "sweet sixteen," and part of the word "sweetheart."

Here is another example:

| B | poke | go | molasses | _____ |

You should have written "slow" in the space provided. "Slow poke," "go slow," "slow as molasses." As you can see, the fourth word may be related to the other three for various reasons.

Try these next two:

| C | surprise | line | birthday | _____ |
| D | base | snow | dance | _____ |

Source: S. A. Mednick and M. T. Mednick, "The Associative Basis of the Creative Process," Cooperative Research Project No. 1073, The University of Michigan, 1965.

tive engineers. Helping people understand their creative potential and its use is an effective way to develop organizational creativity.

THE CREATIVE PROCESS

One of the keys to understanding creativity is to understand the process through which it occurs. Studies of famous individuals in the arts and sciences, and observations of creativity at work, have identified four phases in the process: preparation, incubation, insight, and verification.[12]

It is important that managers understand the nature of the creative process and its different phases: Managers who want their organizations to be innovative need to know what the process is in order to help it along. Managers who must be innovative can understand how to enhance their own creative processes.

Preparation

Like virtually everything worthwhile, creativity requires hard work. Contrary to popular belief, creative ideas don't emerge in a vacuum. Rather, they are the result of a lot of effort by an individual or a group working on a problem.

Motivation.   We learned in Chapter 6 that motivation and effort go hand in hand. This suggests that creativity is motivated.

A problem to solve, a challenge to meet, a goal to achieve, an attractive reward to obtain are all capable of generating the effort which creativity demands. Scientific breakthroughs and innovative ideas are not the products of idle individuals. Studies of creativity in all fields, whether industry, health, sports, or music, support this finding. Meeting the challenge of foreign competition, finding a cure for cancer, striving to be a champion, or shooting for a platinum record directs individual and group effort toward making a better videodisc player, finding a link between cancer and pollution, inventing a new defense, or writing a new song. The story that introduced Chapter 8 described the motivation of many of the key people working on Digital's Eagle project. Though their incentives were different, all were strong.

Exposure.   *Exposure* means *the immersion of oneself in information and experience.* It requires seeking out and absorbing information from a variety of sources, being open to new ideas and new ways of doing things. For scientists, exposure means reading; talking to others in the same or different fields; and experimenting. For managers, it may mean listening to employees, customers, and suppliers; talking to and listening to other managers; and observing what's going on.

American managers have recently started looking at Japanese factories in hopes of getting new ideas about implementing technology. Japan Air Lines alone handled fifty tours of steel, automobile, and electronics industries by American businesses in 1981.[13] Particularly popular are the Ohgishima steel mill of Nippon Kokkan, said to be the world's most advanced, and the Yamazaki Machinery Wales in Nagoya, where robots do everything except bring in raw materials and carry away finished products.

Obviously, exposure implies openness—listening to and not prematurely disposing of new or strange products, processes, or ideas. Exhibit 13.4 provides some examples of what can be lost by rejecting something out-of-hand.

Work.   Motivated individuals who have been exposed to new information then must do a great deal of work. Much of it is experimental, trying out new ideas, changing or discarding them. Some of it is simply practicing. Most authors write for a certain number of hours every day; musical composers spend hours at the piano; innovative football coaches spend hours looking at films to design new plays; researchers run experiments and collect data; managers sketch out solutions to problems and discuss them with knowledgable coworkers. Often creative people virtually saturate themselves with information as preparation for a creative breakthrough.

Incubation

Incubation can be described as *a period of relaxation which follows the hard work of preparation and often precedes a breakthrough.* It often occurs when an individual who has been struggling with a problem stops to relax or to do some-

Exhibit 13.4 Examples of the Hazards of Rejecting Something Out of Hand

Oops

An irate banker demanded that Alexander Graham Bell remove "that toy" from his office. That toy was the telephone. A Hollywood producer scrawled a curt rejection note on a manuscript that became "Gone with the Wind." Henry Ford's largest original investor sold all his stock in 1906. Roebuck sold out to Sears for $25,000 in 1895. Today, Sears may sell $25,000 worth of goods in 16 seconds. The next time somebody offers you an idea that leaves you cold, put it on the back burner. It might warm up.

thing completely different. Some say that incubation allows the subconscious mind to absorb and work on the information obtained during the preparation phase. Others say that relaxation simply allows the creative person to restore energy needed for breakthrough.

It is difficult to know what happens during incubation. To all appearances, the creative person ceases visible effort or does something entirely different for a while. In many cases, incubation occurs during sleep.

For examples of the incubation processes, we turn to the reflections of creative individuals. The brilliant mathematician Henri Poincaré recalled that two of his greatest discoveries occurred after spending some time as a reserve in the military and after a long journey.[14] The famed psysiologist Walter Bradford Cannon reported that, "According to my experience a period of wakefulness at night has often been the most profitable time in the twenty-four hours."[15] Eric Heimholtz, the great German physicist, told of similar experiences, "So far as I am concerned, they (inspirations) have never come to me when my mind was fatigued or when I was at my working table."[16] For Heimholtz, original ideas came after a good night's sleep.

How long does incubation take? In some instances, as little as a few hours. In others, weeks, months, or years. A study of the creative process in artists revealed wide variations, as demonstrated by these quotes:[17]

"I almost always carry an idea around a while in my mind before I start to work. It keeps coming back several times while I am doing other things."

Management in Action
Creative Entrepreneurs

Creative and innovative individuals are often noted for the frequency with which they change jobs. Their relatively high turnover rates can be attributed to several things, among which are an impatience with organizational policies or personalities that they see as inhibiting their work, and a pervasive restlessness that leads them to seek new challenges. One way many creative people eventually respond to these tendencies is to start their own companies. As entrepreneurs, they feel independent of intrusions on their work and able to create their own challenges.

Josef Sedelmaier spent twelve years as an art director for three different major advertising firms—Young & Rubicam, Leo Burnett, and J. Walter Thompson—before he set up his own production company. Sedelmaier Productions operates out of Chicago, despite the fact that most companies that produce commercials are based in New York or Los Angeles. Mr. Sedelmaier stays in Chicago because he likes it, and says he doesn't care about socializing with people in the business, a major reason that others live in New York or Los Angeles. "I want people to come to me because of my work, not because I know the right people or where to go to dinner," he explains.

Mr. Sedelmaier's commercials are known for a sense of style, victimization of characters, and broad comedy. His six years of ads for Federal Express—"When it absolutely, positively, has to get there the next morning"—are cred-

ited with moving that company from an also-ran to number one in the field of small-package delivery. He has used a man vaporized by a lightning bolt to sell life insurance, a passive thirteen-year-old to sell shower massages, and a woman throwing a coffee pot to sell Mr. Coffee.

His independence and success allows Mr. Sedelmaier to charge $7500 a day to produce a commercial, and to take only jobs that give him control over the shooting, directing, writing, and editing, an amount of control unusual in the business. Perhaps his biggest success to date has been his series of ads for Wendy's, where his "Where's the beef?" ads quickly became a phenomenon and made an elderly woman, Clara Peller, into a celebrity.

J. William Poduska helped found Prime Computer, Inc., designed and developed its computers, and headed its engineering staff for years. Twelve years later he started his own company, Apollo Computer, to make minicomputers designed for engineers designing products and scientists doing complex calculations. He describes the experience as "the most fun I've ever had over an extended period. It's like being on a rocket with the fuse lit."

Phil Villers had worked for five high-technology companies by the time he was thirty-four. Then he started Computervision, based on his ideas about computer-automated design. Its success made him a millionaire but he left that company in 1980 to start Automatix, entering the field of robotics.

Sources: T. Lewin, "An Ad Man's Distinct Style," *The New York Times*, March 6, 1984, pp. 29, 32; W. M. Bulkeley, "The Attractions of Starting a New Venture Prove Irresistible to Some Entrepreneurs," *The Wall Street Journal*, June 9, 1981, p. 56.

"I incubate an idea for periods of two or three weeks. It may be for a month or more if I am not working on it."

"I usually carry an idea around in my mind. . . . It recurs from time to time and lasts a couple of weeks."

"I incubate an idea, as color and movement might interest one. It lasts a week only."

Insight

However it works and however long it lasts, successful incubation leads to **insight,** *the creative breakthrough for which the individual has been searching.* Insight occurs when the person first becomes aware of a new and valuable idea, association, or solution.

Some creative individuals report a flash of inspiration; others report that the idea dawns upon them slowly, or in bits and pieces. Most, however, agree that insight comes without great effort, during or following a period of relaxation (incubation), which in turn had been preceded by hard work (preparation).

Insight is frequently an experience of emotion and excitement, as the individual realizes the potential value of the new idea. Scientists and artists who have experienced a breakthrough frequently cannot wait to share it with others. One can imagine Archimedes leaping from his bath shouting, "Eureka!" upon grasping the principle of the displacement of water.

Especially creative people often discern a pattern to their own insightful processes. For some, they occur at a particular time of day. For others, they are more likely to occur in certain places, or during or after particular activities. Many creative people experience insights upon waking from sleep, and keep materials by their beds to allow the recording of these ideas as soon as possible. Many managers report that they do their most creative work at home, away from the hectic environment of the office. In the opening anecdote, Henry's insight occurred in a boat.

Verification

Insight, when it occurs, is only an idea. Its creative value remains to be tested. During the verification phase, the creative person tests an idea for its value and applicability: How does it look? Does it work? How does it sound? Will it sell?

In the research and development laboratory, verification may take a long time. The lab may be required to run hundreds of experiments to test the new process or product, to make corrections and adjustments, and to refine it. In medicine, a thorough verification process may take years, as researchers look for conditions under which the breakthrough will or won't work, the types of patients who can most be helped, and possible side effects of the treatment.

In some cases, verification may be relatively easy. The musician records, the artist paints or performs, the novelist writes, and all submit their products for evaluation by critics. In Henry's case, his longtime friend, Willy, served as a trusted critic.

Many insights require refinement. Some fail to meet the tests of application or criticism and are discarded. Some must be demonstrated time and time again. Ultimately, verification confirms that the insight is new and useful. When the creative product is part of an organizational effort, verification begins to involve organizational members other than the originator of the idea.

Exhibit 13.5 summarizes the four basic steps in the creative process. In the opening anecdote, the creative process began with Henry's motivation to find a powerful incentive for his agency. He talked and listened to his staff and consulted other managers to get some ideas. He thought and worried about the problem for several weeks. His motivation, exposure, and work were the preparatory steps.

Getting away from it all served as an incubation stage. Henry relaxed and avoided the distractions of work, while he subconsciously thought about the problem. When the insight occurred, after preparation and during incubation, he was ready for it. All that was left was verification, first with Willy, and then with the rest of his staff on Monday.

THE CREATIVE PROCESS IN THE ORGANIZATION

The individual creative process described above can occur whether the individual is working alone or as part of an organizational effort. In an innovative organization, the individual process becomes part of the organizational process. The organization can provide the incentives and resources needed for preparation, and further assistance during verification.

Exhibit 13.5   The Creative Process

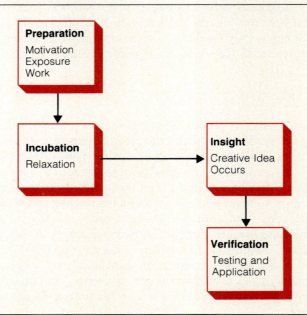

Initiation

Innovation in organizations can be initiated in one of two basic ways.[18] An *idea-based* innovation is one in which someone starts with an idea, then looks for ways to use it. Idea-based innovations often result from basic research. In a typical case a laboratory discovers a new process or material which prompts the organization to find ways to exploit it. DuPont's venture into office copying-machines was an idea-based innovation. The company's research laboratories invented chromium dioxide, a unique magnetic material. In trying to find ways to use the new material, DuPont's Central Research Department evolved a method for using the material in a process for copying (thermomagnetic recording). From that process came the concept of a new copying machine, which was found to be technically and commercially feasible. The project launched DuPont's entry into the field.[19]

A *problem-based* innovation is one in which the process begins by searching for a solution to a problem. The problem may range from attempting to replace a scarce material, to trying to improve a costly production process, to figuring out how to meet a market opportunity or demand. Henry's idea was problem-based—looking for a unique incentive.

Research suggests that the majority of organizational innovations are problem-based. They occur as a result of a search process initiated by some problem, opportunity, or demand. One study examined 600 innovations generated by 121 companies in five manufacturing industries. These innovations were rated as the most important and successful innovations experienced by the five industries. The study found that three out of every four innovations had been initiated either by a market opportunity or a production problem.[20]

Reliance on problem-based rather than idea-based innovation is a deliberate strategy for many companies. As the president of Texas Instruments, Patrick Haggerty, described TI's successful silicon transistor and pocket radio ventures, "It's what we *set out* to do; we *set out* to make a silicon transistor; we *set out* to make a pocket radio."[21] TI felt that innovation was too important to be left to chance. Its strategy was to set goals for research and development, and then find ways to solve the problems.

Obviously, if an organization is concerned with marketing its innovations, searching for ways to satisfy market demands is an attractive strategy. Most of the tremendous efforts being made today in energy and energy-related fields can be classified as problem-based: How can one reduce the need for foreign oil? How can nuclear energy be made safer? How can solar energy be harnessed and exploited? How can oil be produced from shale without ruining the landscape and using too much precious water?

Development

Whether idea-based or problem-based, an innovation enters the developmental phase sometime during or after verification. When the individual or group responsible for the idea has verified that it works, the organization begins to develop the idea into some useful product or process.

Generally, development has two goals: to find ways to make the product feasible and economical, and to find out how it can best be exploited. The first goal is usually the responsibility of the product-design and engineering department. In many cases, those research and development people most closely associated with the original idea will work closely with product-design and engineering to develop the product or process. Simon Ramo, a director of TRW, Inc., and a student of the innovative process, advocates such a relationship: Most often the closest relationship is needed between those who are providing basic knowledge and conceptions and those who are trying to apply them in detail to achieve specific performance and physical characteristics of the product.[22]

If the idea evolves into a production or manufacturing process, then production-design and engineering also work on the problem of how best to exploit it. For example, the process used to extract natural gas liquids (such as propane) from the earth was for many years inefficient. Typically only thirty to thirty-five percent of the available liquid was being extracted from each well. However, Mitchell Energy and Development Corporation of Houston hired an innovative thinker named Bruce Withers to work on the problem.[23] Withers was familiar with cryogenic technology, which can cool natural gases to minus 140 degrees Farenheit. Working with Mitchell's gas production people, Withers applied that technology to portable gas-processing plants and enabled Mitchell Energy to extract up to 90 percent of the available liquid from a gas stream. As a result, between 1979 and 1981, Mitchell's operating earnings from gas processing quadrupled. As a Houston natural gas consultant put it, "They [Mitchell] got an innovative thinker when they hired Withers, and really beat everybody to the punch with cryogenics."[24]

Implementation

Once an organization confirms that an idea is both commercially feasible and exploitable, it moves into the implementation stage. In this phase, the organization begins to integrate production ideas into its ongoing processes, and to produce and market new products.

This last stage is often the most difficult. The initiation and development phases require creative people and technological resources. The last phase requires organizational skills, and human and financial resources. There are scores of organizations which lack the organizational and financial skills needed to exploit their ideas. Either the ideas die, or other organizations acquire and exploit them.

Matrix Organization.   A major problem facing an organization with a fully developed idea in a competitive environment is how to maintain its competitive advantage. Usually this means moving into full implementation as soon as possible, because organizational secrets have a way of getting to the competition very quickly. An organizational device adopted by many firms to speed up this process is the matrix organization.[25] Among firms using matrix organization are General Electric, Citibank, Dow Chemical, and Texas Instruments.

A **matrix organization** is *one that employs dual-command responsibilities: subordinates report to two superiors rather than to a single one.* Exhibit 13.6 describes a typical matrix organization. One command responsibility is organized by *function:* marketing personnel report to the marketing manager, manufacturing personnel report to the manufacturing manager, and so on, just as in a traditional organization. Functional command is shown by vertical lines. However, this organization has a second command responsibility, organized around *major projects,* each of which involves personnel from the various functions.

It is important that managers understand the nature of the creative process and its different phases. Managers who want their organizations to be innovative need to know what the process is in order to help it along. Managers who need to be innovative themselves can understand how to enhance their own creative processes.

Project command is shown by horizontal lines. Thus, engineers working on the Delta project report to both the engineering manager and the Delta project manager. Accountants working on the Gamma project report to both the accounting manager and the Gamma project manager.

Companies that use matrix organizations are usually those that deal in high technology or new products in a competitive environment. The matrix structure permits flexibility and balanced decision making to meet both product and market demands, but it results in increased complexity. Matrix organization enables a company to focus its human resources on developing and implementing a given product or process. At the same time, these individuals retain their membership in and identification with the functional departments from which they were drawn. For example, when a new product idea begins to look commercially feasible, a project team may be assembled to bring it through the final stages of development and into implementation. The project director may have people from R & D, product design and engineering, marketing, finance, and the legal department working on this project. Some of these people may work full-time on the project for several months or even years; others, like finance and legal experts, may be involved for only a short time.

The matrix organization is often described as a product type of organization superimposed on a functional organization chart. As you might expect, this type of organization is complex and not without its problems.[26] One major problem arises because a team member has more than one boss, the project manager to whom he or she is assigned temporarily and the functional manager to whom he or she is assigned permanently. When projects are big, or extend for long periods, power struggles may develop over responsibilities and resources. Because of these conflicts, decision making may be slowed down.

High-technology firms which have developed experience in matrix management are experimenting with methods for making it work more smoothly. For example, Ebasco Services, Inc., a large energy engineering and consulting firm, has developed an approach to minimize some of the conflict and confusion.[27] First,

Exhibit 13.6   An Example of a Matrix Organization

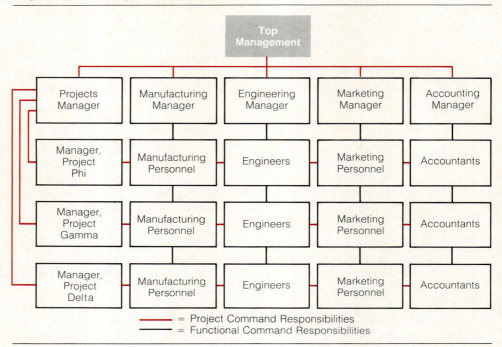

— = Project Command Responsibilities
━ = Functional Command Responsibilities

Ebasco runs formal seminars to explain the system to employees. It has a dual performance-evaluation program which ensures that project personnel are evaluated by both their project and functional supervisors, and a computerized career-tracking program to assure employees that they won't get lost. Finally, trained "facilitators" are used to help resolve conflicts among project personnel and between project and functional managers. These steps are being adopted by other matrix organizations in hopes of making the method less troublesome.

Patents.   A traditional part of the transition from development to implementation has been a thorough effort to obtain patents on new products or processes. A patent is a legal device which guarantees the rights of the individual or organization creating an idea. A patent is supposed to allow the creator to keep others from exploiting the innovation.

In the last several years, however, the value of patents as protection devices has declined.[28] The federal government's efforts to prevent monopolies have made the acquisition of strong patents difficult, costly, and time consuming. Corporate lawyers have helped product engineers find ways to copy products or processes without infringing on patent laws. Finally, most innovations today involve several patented ideas, not all of which belong to one organization. Thus, patent rights are exchanged, or bought, or otherwise traded in complex transactions. While patenting is still a way of protecting ideas, the only real protection is to get as much as possible out of the idea as soon as possible.

Exhibit 13.7 shows how the individual and organization creative processes interconnect. The organization provides incentives and resources, including information, to individuals and groups who need this material for the preparation phase. As an insight is refined and tested, the organization provides resources to verify the insight's usefulness and then takes over the development and implementation, sometimes with the continued help of the original innovator.

RESEARCH AND DEVELOPMENT ACTIVITIES TODAY

Most manufacturing firms today carry on some level of research and development, ranging from simple attempts to improve manufacturing techniques to long-range projects aimed at developing entirely new classes of products. Managers usually recognize two classes of innovative activities: **product innovation,** which is *developing something new that can be marketed,* and **process innovation,** which is *developing a new way of making products or carrying out activities.*

Exhibit 13.7   *The Individual and Organizational Creative Processes*

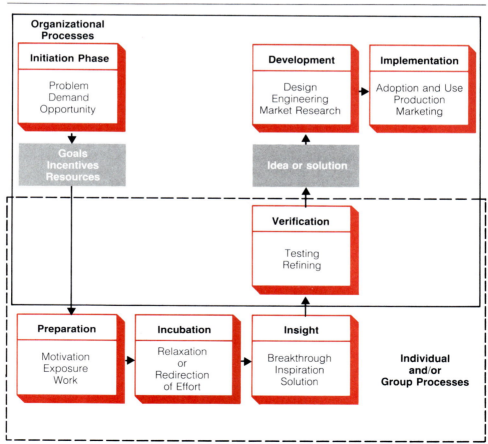

Both product and process innovation are important. New products enable an organization to maintain or increase market shares. They are generally more profitable than old products. As depicted in Exhibit 13.8, the profitability of a new product, once it has caught on, remains high until competition or other new products begin to make inroads in the market.

Process innovation enables the organization to function more efficiently or more safely (and thus at lower costs). It also helps increase product quality and availability, making the organization's products more attractive and marketable.

At present, two major competitive battles for consumer dollars involve product and process innovations. The product innovation battle is over the video-disk and audio-disk markets. Sony (Japan), Philip's (Holland), and Zenith and GE (United States) are competing for an estimated multimillion dollar annual market.[29] The process innovation battle is over the cable television market, as different groups vie for new ways to get entertainment and sports programming into the home.[30] No one can confidently predict the size of this market, but it is clear that the new process technology has the potential for completely revolutionizing sports and entertainment in this country. In the latter case, the basic product, a sports event, a movie, or a television show, hasn't changed, but the process by which it is delivered has been revolutionized.

The *formal, systematic search for new knowledge* is called **research.** One type of research is produced by scientific communities such as those in universities. The purpose of this *pure* research is often simply the generation of new knowledge. The researchers and their sponsoring organizations are frequently content to leave the application of their research up to others.

Directed research is carried on by organizations whose ultimate aim is to solve problems or create or improve products or processes. Research sponsored and car-

Exhibit 13.8   Typical Life Cycle of a New Product

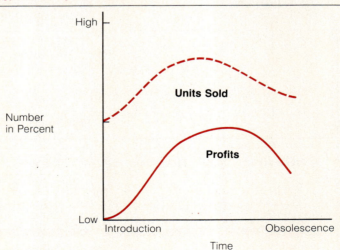

Adapted from *Sales Forecasting* (New York: The Conference Board, 1978), pp. 11–12.

One example of an innovative idea in search of a market is the underground storage concept. In Kansas City, a group of limestone caves have been turned into the country's largest underground industrial complex. The major attraction is that the air in these caves stays at a steady fifty-eight degrees Farenheit and is not at all damp. Energy bills for storage here are ninety percent less than above ground, and the potential space is enormous. Market research efforts to find customers who could benefit from this idea have been quite successful. Fruit and vegetables, and meat and dairy products are stored by the carloads for short periods. Manufacturers can store imported goods duty-free, as the area has been given foreign trade-zone status. This move enabled the storage center to warehouse machinery from Europe, shoes from Korea, and wines from France. The most exotic use thus far is an experimental trout farm, which found the cave to provide the optimal growth temperature for trout. The farm is attempting to produce a million pounds of fish monthly in these caves to sell to the supermarkets which store their groceries there.

Source: ''Kansas City Businesses Move Underground to Stay Cool, Ease Expansion, Save Rent,'' *Wall Street Journal*, June 26, 1981, p. 17.

ried out by the National Cancer Society and the National Law Enforcement Association is ultimately intended to help in the fights against disease and crime. Research carried out by oil and automobile companies, the entertainment media, and most government organizations is intended to further knowledge in a particular area in hopes of improving products or processes. Directed research can be classified by its organizational purpose into three types.[31]

Research in Support of Established Activities

Much research is aimed at maintaining, improving, or expanding current products and processes; developing new products to replace or extend a current product line; as well as improving current products or developing new processes for making established products. Research aimed at increasing the fuel efficiency of automobiles, improving the flavor of foods, enhancing the care and comfort of hospital patients, and revising a book fits into these categories.

Exploratory Research

Some research activities are aimed at new scientific discoveries in areas which are related to the sponsoring organization's central interests. *Exploratory* or *basic* research is high-risk. If it pays off at all, the payoffs are usually in the future. When organizations are forced to cut back on research funds during tight financial periods, this research is often the first to be cut.

Exploratory research, however, can have enormous payoffs. Creating an entirely new product or process often enables an organization to solve a major problem or to get a huge competitive advantage. Basic research in DuPont's chemical laboratories created a whole industry (synthetic fibers) with annual sales of over $20 billion.[32] Other DuPont discoveries revolutionized the gunpowder and plastics industries.

Spurred on by foreign competition, many American industries are beginning to realize that cutting back on basic research is shortsighted. Even though commercial applications may be ten or more years down the road, companies are making big commitments to exploratory research.[33] For example, Raytheon scientists are experimenting with high-frequency millimeter radio waves. It is hoped that these closely packed waves will carry more energy and information than conventional radio waves. General Motors plans to increase its basic research five-fold by the end of the decade. Exxon scientists are using electron microscopes to study the nature of industrial catalytic reactions. Monsanto, whose labs created agricultural chemicals, is analyzing the effects of herbicides at the molecular level. Using high-pressure liquid chromatography and studying light waves enables Monsanto scientists to separate plant molecules from herbicide molecules, leading to a detailed understanding of herbicidal effects. General Electric is studying the side-effects of continuing microminiaturization of integrated electronic circuits. United Technologies is experimenting with composite materials which may one day replace exotic metal alloys made of scarce materials. Recent scientific successes such as gene-splicing and Voyager's probe of Saturn have helped create an environment in which government and industry are excited about future possibilities of basic research.

New Venture Development

When exploratory research results in scientific discoveries with potential new product or process applications, *new venture development* begins. Market and engineering research take over to determine whether products or processes can actually be developed from the discovery, whether they can be successfully marketed, and whether any projects are commercially feasible.

Exhibit 13.9 Types of Organizational Research

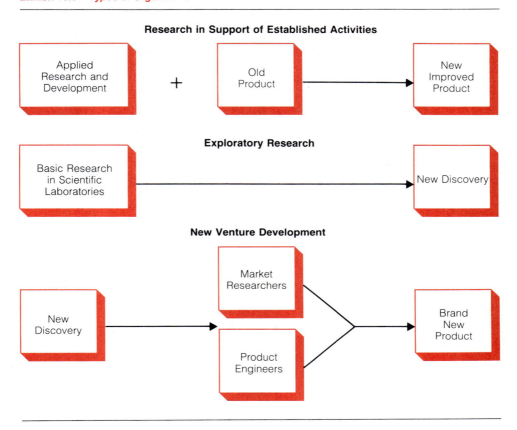

Research in Support of Established Activities

Exploratory Research

New Venture Development

For example, Flow Laboratories, Inc., wanted to develop a biological fuel cell. Researchers discovered that a major problem was insuring a sufficient supply of uncontaminated human and animal tissue cells. They subsequently found a way of collecting and storing tissues which was superior to any methods known.[34] When Flow Laboratories realized it had a novel process with commercial potential, producing uncontaminated tissue for sale to other research labs, a new venture was started. Market research found a sizeable demand for uncontaminated human tissue. Technical research devised a way to speed up the production process. Within four years, Flow Laboratories was supplying tissue culture products and services to one half of American and Canadian markets. Within ten years, it had become one of the world's leading suppliers of living cells. A successful piece of exploratory research had led to research in a new venture which wound up being enormously successful.

The three classes of purposeful research are illustrated in Exhibit 13.9. Some organizations are involved in all three types of research.

The Silverdome, home of the Detroit Lions, is constructed of a material created by NASA in 1967 when it was looking for a new fabric for astronaut suits.

The Bottom Line

Few organizations will survive in a world of changing economics, scarce resources, and fierce competition without being creative and innovative. Managers who seek to manage creativity or to manage creatively can follow these guidelines:

1. It takes more than simply hiring creative people to promote creativity. Managers have a lot to do with how creatively their subordinates perform.
2. Creativity begins with incentive. Give people goals, ideas, and opportunities. Creative people need autonomy, but should not be ignored. They respond well to deadlines and pressures, as do most talented people.
3. Provide a reasonably stable environment for creativity. Be tolerant of experimentation. Stress the consequences of success, not of failure.
4. Learn to recognize the different stages of the creative process in yourself and others. Encourage the kind of open communication that stimulates new ideas. Departmental boundaries may inhibit the free exchange of good ideas.
5. Be prepared to exploit creativity and innovation. They can be planned and organized for. Making sure that creative people have the resources they need is a first basic step.

SUMMARY

The creative process experienced by individuals and groups seems to follow a four-stage process: Preparation involves the motivation to create, exposure to information and ideas, and hard work. Incubation is a period of relaxation or reduction of effort which frequently precedes creative insight. Insight, often an exhilarating or emotional experience, occurs when the individual is first aware of the new idea or solution. Verification is the process by which the new idea is tested or refined to make it more workable.

The creative process in the organization begins with the incentive to innovate. This initiation phase may be started by an idea, a goal, an opportunity, a threat, or a demand. It leads to the individual and/or group creative process, which results in a verified idea or product. This output is further developed by the organization through product design and engineering. In the case of marketable products, implementation includes market research and patent protection. New organization structures, such as the matrix organization, are often required to manage large or continued innovative efforts.

The search for individuals to do creative work has identified only a few traits characteristic of creative individuals. Selection therefore relies on creativity tests and/or past evidence of creative behavior. Creativity training-programs have been developed which can increase creative thinking and activity.

Managing creativity requires more than the acquisition of creative talent. Planning for innovation involves setting goals and objectives, and acquiring the necessary human, financial, and material resources. Organizing requires a balance between enough structure to provide stability, and enough decentralization to provide autonomy and uninhibited communication. Because of the high failure rate of new products, market research is an integral part of managing innovation.

Research and experience provide some guidelines for those who manage creative people. Managers who identify and reinforce creative behavior, who set goals and incentives for innovation, and who allow creative individuals sufficient freedom and autonomy, increase the likelihood that innovation will occur.

At a different level, governmental policies which increase business risks or create greater uncertainty about research and development activities inhibit organizational creativity and innovation.[39] Governmental regulations which permit some freedom and tax policies which provide incentives for investment, will increase the level of research and development and stimulate growth.

QUESTIONS FOR REVIEW AND DISCUSSION

1. How do product and process innovation help organizations?
2. Why is exploratory research considered a high risk? Why are its potential benefits often not realized?
3. How does new venture development evolve from exploratory research? What is its purpose?
4. Compare idea- and problem-based innovation. In what sort of industries or organizations would each be typically found?
5. What are the goals of development and implementation innovation? What implications do these have for interdepartmental communication and interaction, and organizational structure?
6. What are the advantages of a matrix organization structure? What are its disadvantages? How would you feel about working in such a structure?
7. How has the usefulness of patents changed in recent years? Besides the effect that government and corporate lawyers have had in these changes, what role has technology played in this process?

8. What do the characteristics of creativity, and especially its lack of correlation with intelligence, imply for the selection process of organizations?
9. How can managers foster innovation and creativity? Compare the roles of a CEO and a middle manager.
10. How does market research function in an organization's innovative endeavors?

REFERENCES AND NOTES

1. "The Sad State of Innovation," *Time*, October 20, 1979, pp. 70–72.
2. "Poll Suggests U.S. Industry Mismanaging Technology," *Wall Street Journal*, September 3, 1981, p. 25.
3. W. E. McMillan, "The Two-Factor Conceptualization of Creativity Stimulation," *Journal of Creative Behavior*, vol. 11 (Fourth Quarter 1977), p. 287.
4. "DuPont: Seeking a Future in Biosciences, *Business Week*, November 24, 1980, pp. 86–98.
5. E. A. Gee and C. Tyler, *Managing Innovation* (New York: John Wiley & Sons, 1976), p. 155.
6. Zaltman, D., and Holbeck, *Innovations and Organizations*, pp. 138–43.
7. "Computer Stores Must Adapt to Changing Customer Needs." *Wall Street Journal*, July 6, 1981, p. 15.
8. M. Jelinek, *Institutionalizing Innovation*, Chapters 4 and 5.
9. Much of this material is based on H. J. Reitz, *Behavior in Organizations*, pp. 183–89.
10. "The Quintessential Innovator," *Time*, October 22, 1979, p. 72.
11. I. Burstiner, "Creative Management Training for Department Store Middle Managers: An Evaluation," *Journal of Creative Behavior*, vol. 11 (Second Quarter 1977), pp. 105–8.
12. H. J. Reitz, *Behavior in Organizations*, rev. ed. (Homewood; Illinois: R. D. Irwin, Inc., 1981), Chapter 7.
13. "Japanese Factories are Points of Interest to Foreign Tourists Studying Technology," *Wall Street Journal*, September 3, 1981, p. 44.
14. G. Wallas, "Stages in the Creative Process," in A. Rothenburg and C. R. Hausman, eds., *The Creativity Question* (Durham, N.C.: Duke University Press, 1976) pp. 69–73.
15. W. B. Cannon, "The Role of Hunches in Scientific Thought" in Rothenburg and Hausman, *The Creativity Question*, p. 64.
16. Cannon, op. cit., p. 66.
17. C. Patrick, "Creative Thought in Artists." In Rothenburg and Hausman, *The Creativity Direction*, pp. 76–77.
18. G. Zaltman, R. Duncan, and J. Holbek, *Innovations and Organizations* (New York: Wiley-Interscience, 1973), Chapter 2.
19. Gee and Tyler, *Managing Innovation*, pp. 132–38.
20. D. G. Marquis, "The Anatomy of Successful Innovation," in *Managing Advancing Technology*, vol. 1 (New York: American Management Association, 1972). Chapter 3.

21. M. Jelinek, *Institutionalizing Innovation* (New York: Praeger Publishers, 1979), p. 79.
22. S. Ramo, *The Management of Innovative Technological Corporations* (New York: Wiley-Interscience, 1980), p. 194.
23. "Mitchell Energy: Pumping up Profits with Portable Natural Gas Processors," *Business Week*, July 20, 1981, pp. 134–39.
24. op. cit., p. 134.
25. J. R. Galbraith, "Matrix Organization Designs" in J.A. Litterer, ed. *Organizations: Structure and Behavior*, 3rd ed. (New York: John Wiley & Sons, 1980) pp. 144–54.
26. S. Davis and P. Lawrence, "Problems of Matrix Management," *Harvard Business Review*, May-June, 1978, pp. 131–42.
27. "How Ebasco Makes the Matrix Method Work," *Business Week*, June 15, 1981, pp. 126–31.
28. S. Ramo, *The Management of Innovative Technological Firms*, pp. 200–4.
29. "Phillips: An Electronics Giant Rearms to Fight Japan," *Business Week*, March 30, 1981, pp. 86–100.
30. "Monopoly Pays Off in the Business of Sports," *Business Week*, October 13, 1980, pp. 147–52.
31. Gee and Tyler, *Managing Innovation*, Chapter 9.
32. "DuPont: Seeking a Future in Biosciences," *Business Week*, November 24, 1980, pp. 86–98.
33. "Many Firms Increase Basic Research Outlays After Years of Neglect," *Wall Street Journal*, September 3, 1981, p. 1.
34. Gee and Tyler, *Managing Innovation*, Chapter 9.
38. D.G. Marquis, "The Anatomy of Successful Innovation," op. cit.
39. A. S. Marcus, "Policy Uncertainty and Technological Innovation," *Academy of Management Review*, vol. 6, 1981, pp. 443–48.

SUGGESTED READINGS

E. A. Gee and C. Tyler, *Managing Innovation* (New York: John Wiley & Sons, 1976). This book traces the innovative process in an organization from ideas to patents. Authored by a vice-president of DuPont and a management consultant, the book illustrates the innovation process by cases in which the authors were personally involved.

M. Jelinek, *Institutionalizing Innovation* (New York: Praeger Publishers, Inc., 1979). The author describes and analyzes a system developed and used by Texas Instruments to manage innovation.

S. Ramo, *The Management of Innovative Technological Corporations* (New York: John Wiley & Sons, 1980). Written by a director of TRW, Inc., this book is designed for technical and business students who plan to work in technological corporations. It includes discussion of the economic, financial, manufacturing, and marketing aspects of technological innovation.

C. W. Taylor and F. Barron, *Scientific Creativity: Its Recognition and Development* (Huntington, N.Y.: Robert E. Krieger Publishing Co., 1975). This is a collection of thirty papers from three conferences on identifying creative scientific talent. It includes measuring creativity, individual traits, environmental conditions, and creative processes.

Case *Fired For Moonlighting*

Five key employees of General Electronic's Brasstown plant, which employs about 1300 persons producing and assembling printed circuit boards for computers and military equipment, were fired in late January, after company officials discovered they were starting their own business. A spokesman for the company said it learned of the group's activities on Tuesday of last week and took action to terminate their employment on Thursday.

"Company policy does not allow employees to be involved in business that could be in conflict or competition with General Electronic," said Mark Stone, manager of central operations and acting vice-president for operations. He added that many of General Electronic's employees have parttime jobs on the side, "but these five people did not ask us or do this in the open. They chartered their company more than three months ago under the name of Advanced Board Circuitries, Inc., with Dale Garfield as president and the other four persons as either officers or founders of the new company."

Upon being interviewed, Dale Garfield, a six-year employee who had formerly been unit manager over engineering and production of printed circuit boards at General Electronic, said it was "self-preservation" that kept them from revealing their plans to General Electronic while working weekends and evenings on the building that houses their embryonic company and while installing equipment. He said it was "challenge" as much as anything that had provided the drive to start their own

company. "We have no animosity toward General Electronic whatsoever. Every company has the prerogative to manage as it sees fit. We have no ax to grind," he stated emphatically. Garfield said his group even hoped to have a working relationship with General Electronic, possibly supplying circuit boards to the plant's assembly lines. If this worked out, the new company would be more of a supplier than a competitor to General Electronic, he believed.

Mr. Stone was careful to point out that "there is nothing illegal here as far as we know and, as far as we can determine, no business was siphoned off from General Electronic. It is," added Stone, "an unpleasant situation."

Garfield said, "We sweated blood to make that Brasstown plant one of the best in the country. But we, too, have a desire to have the best circuit-board shop in the country. Maybe not the biggest, but the best."

There was no indication from Stone of any dissatisfaction with the on-the-job performance of any of the five people who had been fired. Indeed, they were viewed as key employees by the company.

On the charter of Advanced Board Circuitries, Inc., a Brasstown attorney was listed as resident agent. When contacted and asked about the firing of the people for moonlighting, he said that he had advised the group of former General Electronic employees "to make no statements concerning either their position or General Electronic's position."

Source: J. Champion and J. James, *Critical Incidents in Management*, Homewood, Ill.: Richard D. Irwin, 1980, pp. 112–13.

CASE QUESTIONS

1. Under what category of research would you classify the circuit boards that Advanced Board Circuitries plans to make?
2. To what extent could patents benefit either General Electronics or Advanced Board Circuitries in this situation?
3. From what you know about creative individuals, why do you suppose these five people left the security of General Electronics to start their own company?
4. What could General Electronics do to decrease the likelihood that other key employees might leave to join Advanced Board Circuitries or to start their own company?

4/What Defines the Manager's World?

Part 4 describes the characteristics that define the manager's world today—the structure, policies, and resources that the organization provides; the social environment in which it functions; and the stress and time pressures inherent in managing.

14/Organizational Structure and Design describes different types of organizational structures and the relationships among the work roles in those structures. It shows the power, control, and flexibility with which managers operate.

15/Policy discusses the role of policy in channeling and integrating effort toward organizational goals. It defines the roles of various levels of management in the policy process and offers suggestions for avoiding some of the more common policy problems managers encounter.

16/Budgets looks at the budgeting process and its role in defining and controlling the use of financial resources. The importance of budgeting in planning, organizing, and controlling work, and the different types of budgets managers commonly use are highlighted. The chapter points out ways to avoid common pitfalls in using budgets.

17/Staffing covers the processes and the activities that provide managers with the human resources they need. It examines recruitment, selection, and placement techniques, and the special role of government regulation. Managers need to use the tools of orientation, training, development, and performance appraisal to maintain and enhance their organizations' human resources.

18/Social Responsibility, Governments, and Unions examines the organization as part of the larger society, focusing on the relationships between unions, governments, and the organization. How a manager functions as a member of society, and the social responsibilities, both within and outside the organization itself, is of particular interest.

19/Stress and Time concentrates on two general characteristics of the managerial job today—stress and time pressures. Causes and effects of stress, and ways to alleviate its more harmful effects, are presented. The chapter focuses on the particular role of time pressure as a cause of stress and suggests methods successful managers use to manage time efficiently and effectively.

14 / Organizational Structure

Clyde Forrester, the director of manufacturing, looked at his watch. "Well, it's eight o'clock. Unless anyone has anything worthwhile to add, we're adjourned. We've got a lot of product to get out today." Amidst scraping chairs and loud voices, the room emptied quickly.

Left alone, Mario shook his head. How does he do it, he wondered. He finishes every production meeting at precisely eight o'clock. By 8:01 every manager in the meeting is out on the production floor, and Forrester is on the phone. Then there are the constant series of phone calls and visits from and to the several manufacturing managers which don't stop until everyone goes home, which might not be until six or seven at night.

The organization and activity reminded Mario of a military operation. Conversations were brief and to the point. Everyone had a specific job to do and did it. Things were tightly controlled, yet hectic. "Organized chaos" was the way someone described it. Mario had been in the manufacturing division for four weeks now, but still marveled at the way things ran.

As part of his management training program, Mario was spending three months in each of the functional departments of the company. His first tour had been in finance and accounting, where the climate could best be described as quiet, orderly, and formal. The vice-president there had a staff of five, and three supervisors who reported directly to him. Each supervisor managed from fifteen to twenty people, each of whom carried out routine assignments every day.

Since everyone in finance and accounting seemed to know what to do, Mario observed little direct supervision. Instead of giving orders and making job assignments, supervisors clarified questions and coordinated activities. The head of the department spent much more time with the staff than with the supervisors who reported to him. Mario couldn't remember a single crisis and only one occasion when anyone other than the department head and the staff had worked overtime.

From finance and accounting Mario had moved to research and development (R & D). In contrast, life in the R & D department was informal, loosely structured, and irregular. The organization of the department was hard to identify. Mario knew there was a director and five or six project leaders. Everyone else seemed to be on an equal footing, interacting with everyone and anyone, including the director, on an informal and spontaneous basis. At least one person served as the leader on two projects; a number of the staff appeared to be involved in more than one project.

Although each project leader held a scheduled meeting once a week, which the R & D director frequently (but not always) attended, most meetings seemed to be between two or three people and were instigated by the staff rather than their leaders. Where the finance and accounting personnel invariably reported for work at eight o'clock and left at five o'clock, R & D people came and went at all hours. He had known some project members who spent three or four consecutive days at the plant without ever going home, and then vanished for a long weekend of equal duration. When he came to work at eight, Mario frequently found people who had been at work for hours. Occasionally, these same people went home for lunch and didn't return until the next day.

As best he could determine, the manufacturing section had several levels of supervision. Each foreman supervised from five to nine people. Foremen reported to supervisors, who in turn reported to managers; the managers answered to other managers, who communicated directly to the director of manufacturing. The director had a large staff of specialists, who in turn had staffs of three or four people. Everyone had his or her own field of interest, requiring a great deal of coordination by the various levels of supervision. People spoke in terms of hours, rarely days. Workers seldom knew what they'd be doing from one day to the next. Supervisors gave a lot of orders and directions, were constantly in motion, and were involved in a lot of meetings.

The amazing thing to Mario about all these styles was that each one worked.

Every department was organized and run differently from the others, and the differences were obvious to anyone who spent as little time at the company as a single day. Yet each department did its job and did it well. The company prospered, and the corporate executives with whom he had come in contact all had spoken highly of every department's contributions. Mario wondered if the differences reflected differences in the philosophies and personalities of the heads, or whether there was more to it than that. Whatever the reason, it appeared that there was no one best way to structure a department, at least not in this company.

Like many other young managers, Mario is gaining experience in different functional areas of a firm through on-the-job training. One of the things Mario has learned is that these functional areas differ in the ways they operate, as well as in the tasks they perform. To Mario, each of these areas has a unique climate. Some of the differences are because of the nature of each area's work; some are because of the natures of the key individuals operating in each area. Some of the differences are a function of the way each department is structured. In a sense, the structure of an organization is a lot like the climate of a geographical area: natives and visitors do not see the climate directly, but they feel it and notice its effects. They adjust their behavior to operate effectively within that climate.

Unlike climate, however, the structure of a department or organization is designed by management to achieve certain objectives. It can be modified or even completely altered as missions, goals, personnel, or technologies change. Whatever its form, structure defines a considerable part of every manager's job. It affects, among other things, a manager's power, control, communications, decision making, and flexibility. A given structure will make it easier to do some things and more difficult to do others. Therefore, successful managers understand structure, how to use it to achieve their objectives, how to work within (and sometimes around) it, and when and how to change it.

THE PURPOSES OF ORGANIZATIONAL STRUCTURE

Any organization of more than a few people harbors the potential for considerable complexity and uncertainty. The manufacturing area in which Mario finds himself employs 125 people. The head of the area is responsible for all of them and their work. The number of possible different relationships the head of manufacturing can have with 124 other employees is 1.3×10^{39}. Obviously, he needs to organize and control all those people and all that work, as Chapters 4 and 7 pointed out. Organization structure is a major tool in organizing, controlling, and coordinating work. It substantially reduces uncertainty and complexity, easing the work of both managers and their subordinates. The **structure of an organization** *describes and defines the work roles and the relationships between these roles that enable its members to accomplish goals efficiently and effectively.*

Work roles are *the behaviors expected by the organization.*[1] For example, the role of a management trainee, like Mario, is to assist the department head and to learn as much as possible about the process, technology, and management of each department to which he or she is assigned. The role of the head of the manufacturing is to plan, organize, direct, and control the the manufacture of products in specified quantities, qualities, and prices. Defining work roles helps reduce uncertainty by assigning each member certain responsibilities toward the accomplishment of organizational goals. No individual is responsible for everything; each individual is responsible for only a part of the whole.

Organization structure defines **work relationships** as *specific lines of communication and authority*. Each individual has a limited number of people with whom to communicate information. Those who have direct authority over each work role, and the subordinates over whom each supervisor or manager has responsibility, are clearly defined. For example, the structure of Mario's organization specifies that management trainees are responsible to the department head to whom they are assigned and to the director of management training for their assign-

Exhibit 14.1   A Simplified Organization Chart for a Manufacturing Plant

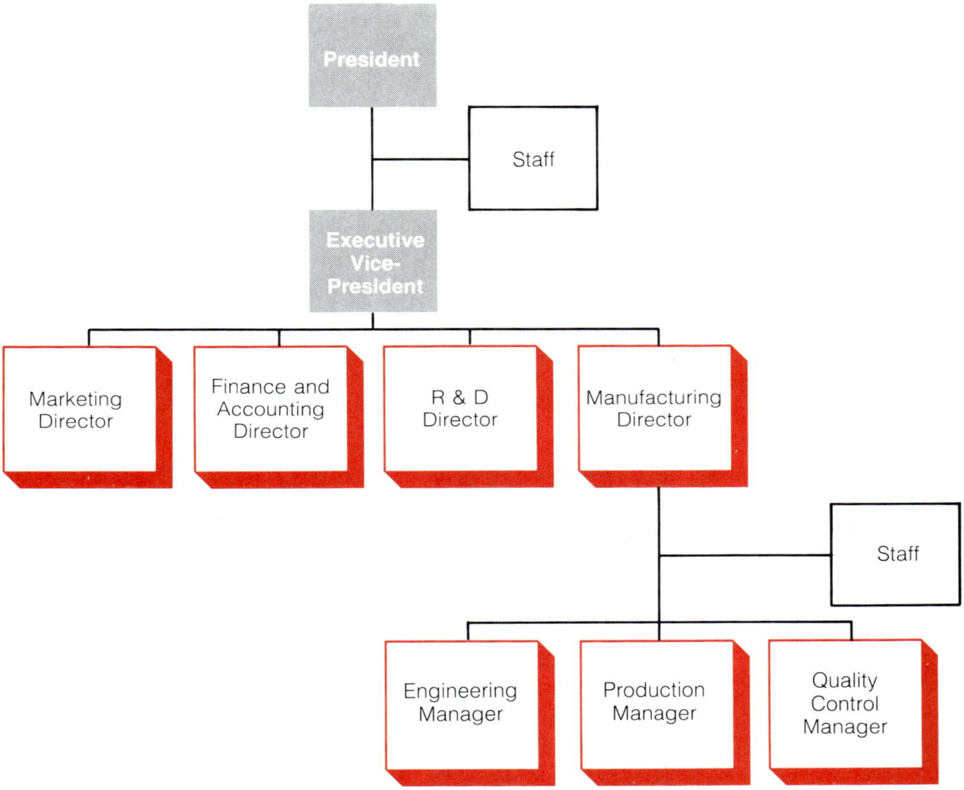

ments. Any supervisory responsibilities that a trainee may get are temporary, assigned only by the department head. Thus, Mario cannot use legitimate power (Chapter 10) unless the department head authorizes it. He can still influence people via charisma or expertise, for example, but the organization structure gives him no formal authority or responsibility.

Organizational structure is usually described in graphic fashion by an **organization chart,** *a visual means of depicting work roles and relationships between them.* The chart provides a picture of the intended, or designed, patterns in which work is organized (as described in Chapter 4). Exhibit 14.1 provides a simplified organizational chart for Mario's company. It shows that the manufacturing head has three managers plus his staff (to which management trainees like Mario are assigned) reporting directly to him.

Chapter 4 describes the process of organizing as dividing up the work (specializing) and then coordinating it. An organization chart shows both the division of labor and its coordination. The horizontal dimension depicts division of labor. Exhibit 14.1 shows that the work of Mario's company is divided into marketing, finance and accounting, R & D, and manufacturing. It also reveals that the work of manufacturing is divided into engineering, production, and quality control. The vertical dimension describes lines of authority, sometimes called the *chain of command.* In Exhibit 14.1 the managers of engineering, production, and quality control, along with the staff personnel, all report directly to the director of manufacturing. The directors of manufacturing, R & D, finance and accounting, and marketing all report directly to the executive vice-president.

> *In a sense, the structure of an organization is a lot like the climate of a geographical area: natives and visitors do not see the climate directly, but they feel it and notice its effects. They adjust their behavior to operate effectively within that climate.*

An organization chart is the official blueprint of the organization. That does not mean that it accurately depicts *all* of the roles and relationships that actually operate. Informal groups develop, and individuals exercise charisma, expertise, and other "unofficial" forms of power. This "informal organization" sometimes indicates that the formal organization has weaknesses and problems resulting, perhaps, from changes in the organizational goals, strategies, or personnel.

Nevertheless, an organization's structure, no matter how loose, is not a frill—it is a necessity. Without it an organization ceases to be an organization, because it is no longer organized. This structure should help accomplish organizational objectives, clarify task performance, facilitate communication, reduce gaps and overlaps in assigned duties, make clear the career paths available to individuals, and facilitate ongoing organizational development.[2] Persistent deviations from formal organizational structure suggest the existing structure may not be fulfilling one or more of its purposes. Members of the organization may be modifying the formal structure to better meet their job requirements. Formal communication lines are often ignored because they are too restrictive, too slow, or simply inadequate.

Deviations from formal organizational structure can also suggest poor matches between role duties and personal characteristics. A position of authority as shown on an organizational chart may be regarded by others as a "figurehead position," because the person who holds that job does not or cannot exert the required influence. For example, a "lame-duck" President often has little real power and performs only ceremonial functions until the new President is sworn in.

Whether deviations from the formal organizational structure require action depends upon whether the actual role-behavior of the informal organization blocks the accomplishment of organizational goals. Such diagnosis falls within the area usually called organizational development; the formal structure of an organization is used as a baseline. In fact, the concept of informal organization does not have any meaning without the comparable concept of a formal organization.

CHARACTERISTICS OF ORGANIZATIONAL STRUCTURE

Structure defines roles and specifies relationships. It therefore affects much of what managers and their subordinates do, particularly in the areas of communications, authority and responsibility, control, and decision making. In a way, structure is like the geography of an area, and an organization chart is a map. While it is possible for a visitor to blunder his way through unfamiliar territory without a map or knowledge of the geography, most people will function much more effectively with both. Understanding the characteristics of organization structure and the implications for what managers do is a prudent step toward success.

In general, people speak of "the structure" of an organization, although most, like Mario's, have different substructures within different departments, divisions, or other subsystems. There also tend to be structural differences among the three main levels of an organization—*operative* (those employees engaged in performing the basic product or service tasks), *middle management*, and *top management* (or executives). However, none of these differences change the fact than an organization has an overall structure. Varied substructures merely lead us to describe this overall structure in a way that is different from the description of an organization where there are similar structures among levels.

Any organizational structure can be described along four dimensions—complexity, configuration, centralization, and formalization.[3] Keep in mind, however, that an organization's structure is made up of a combination of all of these dimensions.

Complexity

Structural complexity is *the degree of role specialization within an organization.* Complexity is the result of differentiation among groups of work roles. This differentiation occurs both vertically and horizontally, making complexity a function of both vertical and horizontal differentiation.

Vertical Differentiation.   Vertical differentiation distinguishes between groups of work roles on the basis of authority and responsibility. A distinction between management and operative employees, for example, between a foreman and his subordinates, is vertical differentiation at its simplest. If management is further differentiated into levels, such as president, executive vice-president, department heads, managers, and supervisors, as in Mario's company, the structure is even more complex. A relatively complex vertical differentiation of a hypothetical business school is shown in Exhibit 14.2. In this figure, there are six groups of authority-responsibility roles: dean, associate dean, department chairperson, associate chairperson, student coordinator, and professor, all at different levels of vertical differentiation.

Exhibit 14.2   Vertical Differentiation in a College of Business

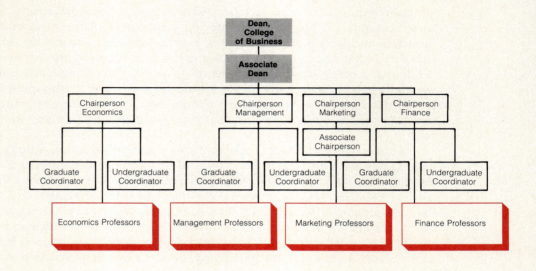

Horizontal Differentiation.   Horizontal differentiation distinguishes between groups of work roles that are at the same vertical level in the organization based on the work performed. Thus, horizontal differentiation, called departmentalization, creates the familiar department, unit, or division within an organization. There are three common ways to differentiate between groups of work roles.

Functional differentiation is also called *process* or *skill* grouping. Work roles are grouped according to commonality of function. Simple functional differentiations are shown in both Exhibits 14.1 and 14.2. The functions represented in 14.1 are marketing, finance, R & D, and manufacturing; in 14.2 they are economics, management, marketing, and finance.

Functional grouping is the oldest, and probably still the most common, form of horizontal differentiation. It offers the advantages of clear task assignments, knowledgeable coworkers, and efficient use of skilled personnel and machinery. Coordinating within functional units is relatively easy; everyone understands, at least generally, the work of everyone else. Many universities, mass-production manufacturing firms, and retail outlets are differentiated this way.

The major disadvantage of functional grouping is that no one group has responsibility for the final product or service. Within functional groups there is little understanding of the task as a whole, and pressure to coordinate functions is increased at the top of the organization.

Product differentiation is also called *divisional, market,* or *purpose* grouping. Tasks are grouped around specific products, customers, or geographic locations. General Electric pioneered this form of differentiation in the early 1950s, and it is widely used in diversified consumer-goods organizations. Instead of having one

Exhibit 14.3   Complexity: Product Differentiation in a Forest Products Company

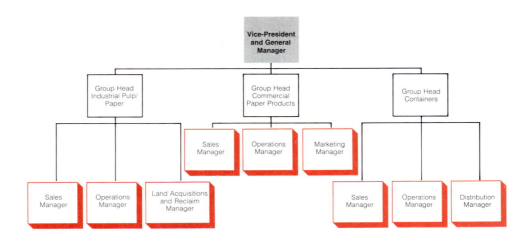

manufacturing department, one engineering department, or one planning department, manufacturing, engineering, and planning personnel are found in each separate product group (see Exhibit 14.3).

Product grouping has advantages and disadvantages different from functional grouping. Each product group usually has responsibility for its final product or service. Because it groups together people with different skills and interests, the product grouping can be flexible and adaptable to market conditions. At the same time, internal coordination is more difficult; not everyone understands the work of others. In addition, product grouping can create expensive duplication of skills and equipment for the organization as a whole.

Matrix differentiation, which we described in Chapter 13, probably originated in the aerospace industry in the early 1950s. The increasingly specialized requirements of aircraft purchasers led to more specialized research and development efforts within the same company. Gradually, these groupings evolved into a recognizable organizational structure.

Essentially, the matrix grouping is achieved by dividing the same basic product into different product groups and overlaying it. The general functional grouping of the organization as a whole to produce a simultaneous product-function grouping. An example of this matrix differentiation is shown in Exhibit 14.4.

The matrix organization can have the advantages of both product and function groupings (that is, it can be both flexible and easy to coordinate); it has been used successfully by many organizations including Shell Oil, Texas Instruments, Corning Glass, and Lockheed Aircraft Corporation. Its most frequently cited disadvantage is that it violates the old unity-of-command, "one man, one boss," principle. For example, a salesperson in Exhibit 14.4 may be responsible to the sales

Exhibit 14.4 Complexity: Matrix Differentiation in an Interior Design Firm

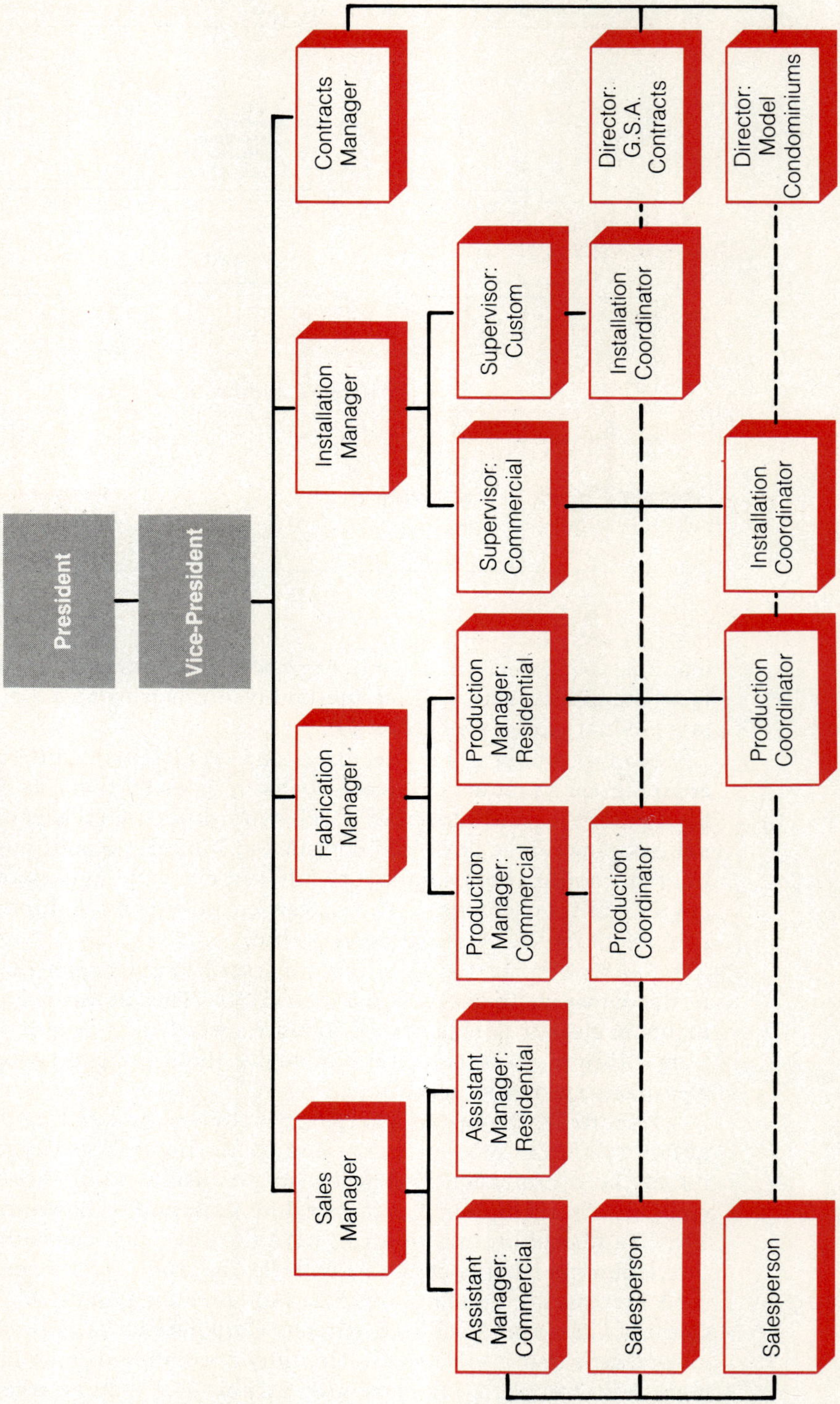

manager and to the director of model condominiums. This is by no means the only problem with this difficult structure,[4] but many believe that the matrix design will be commonplace in the future.

Consistent with the principle that structure follows strategy, organizations often change structures as they grow and develop. Typically, a new organization will have a simple structure: one level of management and a few workers each of whom do many tasks—generalists rather than specialists. As the business grows, specialization is needed, which in turn requires coordination. The organization takes on a functional structure with more levels of management.

With continued growth, the structure may change again. In technologically oriented industries, like aerospace, or those tailoring their products or services to individual customer requirements, like advertising, matrix structures may appear. If the company develops overseas, it often evolves a division structure, with an overseas division handling the marketing and personnel requirements of overseas business. When the overseas division gets big enough (sales rivaling the largest domestic division), the structure will change again, probably incorporating divisions based on geographic areas of the world. Each division will have its own functional areas tailored to the opportunities and demands of the area it serves.[5]

Line and Staff

A simple organization will have few departments (horizontal differentiation) and a simple management-operative distinction (vertical differentiation). A more complex one will have more levels of management and more departments. Still more complexity is introduced by the **line-staff distinction,** *a horizontal division of labor within the vertical authority and responsibility division.*

Most managers are line because they are directly in the line of authority-responsibility relationships that make up the vertical differentiation of an organization. Personnel whose jobs are to provide assistance or special expertise to management, rather than being directly involved in the organization's product or service, are *staff*. Examples are research assistants, data processing specialists, lawyers, members of the organization's personnel department, and personal assistants like Mario. On an organization chart, they typically appear to one side of the main body of roles in the organization.

A simple line-staff organization chart was shown in Exhibit 14.1. The president and each of the vice-presidents have a staff who are directly responsible to their immediate superiors, their only formal authority-link to the organization. Typically, they recommend action to their superiors, who authorize its execution.

Configuration

Configuration is *the shape of an organization's structure.* This shape is largely determined by decisions about managerial division of labor (vertical differentiation), but complexity is not the only determinant of configuration. The number of subordinates assigned to each manager is also a factor. Thus, the primary determinants of configuration are the traditional structural issues with which the classical organizational theorists were concerned—hierarchy and span of control.

The **hierarchy,** or *chain of command,* of an organization is produced by differentiations between the formal authority and responsibility of the various management roles. *Authority and responsibility increase as one moves from lower to higher managerial levels in the hierarchy* **(the scalar principle).** Each person higher in the chain has authority over and responsibility for the work of those below him or her.

Span of control is *the number of subordinates for whom someone has responsibility.* This number, along with the number of levels of management, determines the basic configuration of the organizational structure. If an organization is characterized by large spans of control and few levels, the resulting configuration is relatively flat. Smaller spans of control and more levels create a relatively tall configuration. Examples of these two configurations are shown in Exhibit 14.5

> An organization's structure, no matter how loose, is not a frill—it is a necessity. Without it an organization ceases to be an organization, because it is no longer organized.

Both tall and flat structural configurations have advantages and disadvantages. A flatter structure reduces the costs of supervision, but this structure may be inefficient if managers have to control too many people. It takes more time for information and decisions to get through a tall structure, but this disadvantage is offset by the large amount of time spent resolving differences in a flatter one.

In determining the relative configuration of an organization, one should consider the nature of the work performed by subordinates; the ability and expertise of subordinates; the geographical dispersal of subordinates; and the ability and expertise of the supervisors. When subordinates are capable, and perform similar or easily observed tasks in the same area, one supervisor can coordinate the work of many. A flatter structure is possible. When a lot of coordination is needed, and work is diverse, the ratio of supervisors to subordinates increases. For example, a study of one hundred British firms found that mass-production industries, like the automobile industry (lots of low-skill workers and job specialization requiring coordination), had much flatter structures than industries with skilled workers who custom-designed their products, like the machine-tool industry.[6]

Centralization

Centralization of structure is *the extent to which decisions are made or controlled by those at the top, or power center, of the organization.* In other words, centralization refers to the level at which *important* (not all) organizational decisions are made. Centralization ranges from completely centralized decision making (all decisions made at the center, or top, of the organization) to completely de-

Exhibit 14.5   Examples of Tall and Flat Configuration

A National Manufacturer and Distributor of Cosmetics

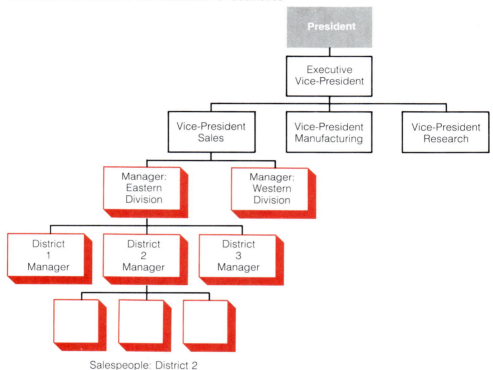

Salespeople: District 2

A Branch Banking Firm

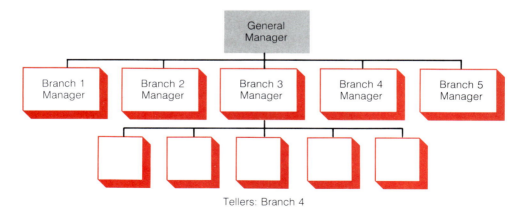

Tellers: Branch 4

centralized decision making (all decisions made in the part of the organization involved). The majority of organizations fall somewhere between these two extremes.

Centralization and decentralization are often confused with other characteristics of organizations. Decentralization is not the same as physical dispersion, in which a single organization has plants or branches in several different locations. The United States Foreign Service, for example, has embassies and consulates all over the globe, but its decision-making process is basically centralized. Ambassadors are often recalled to Washington when important decisions about their host countries are being made.

> *The more successful organizations are those whose structures are compatible with their goals and traditions, their key individuals, the environments in which they operate, and their major forms of technology.*

Neither is centralization the same as authoritarian decision making, nor is decentralization the same as democratic decision making. Centralization-decentralization reflects *where* decisions are made in an organization; authoritarianism-democracy refers to the *number of people* involved in making a decision. A manager in a decentralized organization can make a decision just as unilaterally as a manager in a centralized one, while a particular ambassador may exert considerable influence over a decision that is made in the State Department in Washington.

As is true with both complexity and configuration, centralized or decentralized structure is not a simple one. It involves consideration of individual limits, the information-processing capacity of the organization, and personal accountability/motivation of organizational members.

There is little doubt that centralized decision making offers the tightest means of organizational coordination. At the same time, it may be difficult to move the information required to the central location quickly enough. Flexibility is reduced and opportunities may be lost. Many also believe that centralized decision making reduces the motivation of managers who must always live with the decisions of others. In general, decentralization works better when superiors have confidence in the decision-making competence of subordinates, information can be transmitted quickly through the organization, and decisions made in one area have little effect on other parts of the organization.[7] Burger King and McDonald's are good examples of large, decentralized organizations that rely on regional offices rather than corporate headquarters to make most important decisions.

Formalization

Formalization of organizational structure refers to *the degree to which work behavior is regulated*. As a *structural* characteristic, formalization does not refer to individual manager behavior, but to those organizationally prescribed

Management in Action
Changing Organizations' Structures to Fit New Situations

An organization's structure tends to become rigid, and this lack of flexibility often keeps the organization from changing goals or exploiting opportunities. Large organizations, in particular, are viewed as having unyielding structures which protect the interests of powerful individuals.

But even large organizations can change their structures when necessary. It has taken John Hanley, the chief executive officer of Monsanto, almost ten years to shift that company's emphasis from commodity chemical business toward the manufacture of patented products.

Along the way, Monsanto has built up considerable financial resources (four hundred million dollars in cash and marketable securities), while divesting itself of unprofitable or marginally profitable businesses. Reorganizations can be expensive (Monsanto wrote off one hundred seventy-five million dollars in five years in shifting away from industrial chemicals, which accounted for thirty-two percent of their sales in 1982, as compared with fifty-three percent ten years earlier).

Monsanto's new structure has reduced the number of operating companies from five to four and redistributed the responsibilities of its executives. Richard Mahoney, Monsanto's president, described the changes as "much more than drawing boxes" on an organization chart. Howard Schneiderman, senior vice-president for research and development, says the company is working to develop products that come from human ingenuity and innovation as opposed to those that come from huge amounts of capital investment.

To accommodate the shift from traditional business to the development and marketing of patented products, Monsanto's new structure groups areas of emphasis, including a nutrition-chemicals division, an agricultural products company, and an industrial chemical unit. Such a structure is consistent with the complex/decentralized configuration discussed in this chapter. Monsanto plans to shift its capital spending from expanding plants to building research facilities. The company has more than doubled its expenditures for research and development over the past five years, and plans to continue that trend through the 1980s.

This reorganization does not mean that Monsanto will ignore its traditional business, such as detergents and phosphates. But even there, R&D will receive greater emphasis as the reorganization reinforces Monsanto's shift to patented products.

Source: D. P. Garino, "Monsanto Slowly but Deliberately Shifts Emphasis to Research, Patented Products," *Wall Street Journal*, January 13, 1983, p. 33.

rules, job descriptions, and work-flow regulators designed to produce standardization. Dress codes seek to standardize dress; order forms standardize sales requests; training programs are geared to bring skills to a standard level. Controls of various kinds are used to enforce and maintain such formalization mechanisms (see Chapter 7). Generally, formalization will be strongest where work is routine and repetitive, so it tends to be greater at the operative level of an organization.

Much has been written about negative worker reactions to formalization in organizations. Some say that formalization stifles creativity, stunts individual growth, and produces worker alienation and "petty bureaucrats." On the other hand, positive reactions have also been noted. In one recent study of R & D divisions in four industries, formalization was actually associated with *reduced* worker alienation, because it decreased uncertainty about work-role performance expectations and increased identification with the organization.[8] Formalization aids planning, and also provides a basis for the equitable treatment of employees and customers. For example, promotion based on seniority and performance evaluations is both formalized and equitable. In Chapter 6, equity was an important aspect of rewards.

STRUCTURAL PROFILES

The four dimensions of organizational structure are inseparable. Vertical specialization, one measure of complexity, has a direct influence on hierarchy, one measure of configuration. If we are to appreciate the structure of an organization, we must consider it as a whole.

A **structural profile** *depicts the approximate location of an organization on the four structural dimensions at a given point in time.*[9] The structural profile of a typical university is shown in Exhibit 14.6. Such an organization tends to have a complex structure (many departments) and a configuration that is relatively flat (a department chairperson responsible for fifteen to twenty-five faculty members).

Decisions about graduation requirements, number of courses to be offered, and salary ranges are usually made centrally. Personnel assignments, the nature of the offered courses, and textbook orders are usually decentralized. On balance, this produces a slight tendency toward centralization. Formalization tends to be strong except in actual classroom conduct for which academic freedom is the norm.

The structural profile of an organization is an indicator of the way it feels to be in that organization. In the anecdote at the beginning of this chapter, Mario detected a different atmosphere in each of the three departments in which he worked. Finance and accounting felt calm and orderly; R & D was informal and exciting; manufacturing was organized chaos. When employees generally agree about the way it feels to work in an organization, the organization is said to have a particular *climate.*[10]

Employees at Ringling Brothers describe the climate there as informal, but disciplined; like a family. The climate at the Bloom Agency is said to be one of informal, creative tension. At the Killington, Vermont Ski Resort, it's logical, no-nonsense, hard work.[11] In general, the farther to the right an organization's structural profile lies on a chart like Exhibit 14.7, the less positively employees perceive its climate to be. They feel more positively about organizations that are less complex and less formalized, flatter, and more decentralized.

THE DESIGN OF ORGANIZATIONS

We have suggested that the structure of an organization is designed to meet the organization's objectives. Although organization structures can evolve, purposeful design can result in superior structure and better organizational performance. Decision makers design the structure of an organization to integrate the organization's goals or purposes, the patterns of division-of-labor and coordination, and the people who will do the work. In designing or redesigning an organization, managers take a contingency approach; there is no one-best design. What is best depends upon several key factors, including the organization's goals, technology, environment, its size, and key individuals.

Organizational Goals and Purpose

An organization's products or services, the markets it serves, and overall objectives (profit; service; growth; survival) immediately affect design decisions. The organizational structure of a French restaurant will be more centralized and formalized than that of a fast-food restaurant because the products are different (large selection, cooked to order vs. limited selection, ready-to-eat) as are the services (elegant dining vs. inexpensive, fast meals) and operational objectives (smaller volume but higher profit margins vs. high volume, lower margins).

Exhibit 14.6   Structural Profile of a Typical University

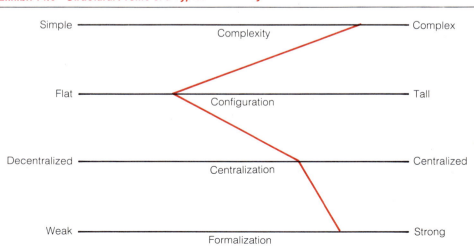

Technology

Technology is *the processes used by the organization to transform inputs into outputs.* Most organizations use different technologies in different areas. For example, hospitals use machines for billing, but their main technology remains human. Doctors, nurses, and technicians are the primary means for improving the health of the patient "inputs."

As with the organization environment, there should be some match between structure and technology. For example, span of control can be larger if the predominant technology is a machinery, mass-production one (such as that used by Ford Motor Company) than if the technology is based on unit production (such as that used by Rolls Royce Ltd).

Environment

Important environmental characteristics to consider in design decisions include the environment's complexity (a concept similar to structure complexity), stability, market diversity, and social and economic favorableness. Organizations that operate in a stable environment experience little fluctuation in supply and demand patterns, and few knowledge explosions or technological breakthroughs. Their environments are relatively predictable, allowing for more long-term planning. Markets that create these stable environments usually want consistent quality rather

Exhibit 14.7   Factors that Affect Organization Design

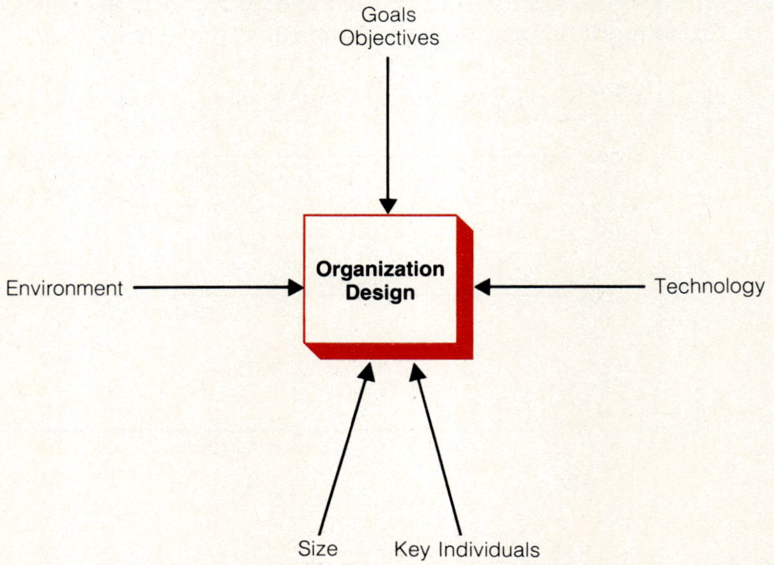

than innovation and flexibility. Therefore, an organization with such a market environment will probably be more successful with a more formalized structure, as this usually creates greater standardization.

Size

Initially, goals and available resources determine the size of an organization in a general way, and size exerts a separate influence on structure. If the organization must start small, for example, it is more likely to be toward the left of our organizational profile depicted in Exhibit 14.7.

Organizations that are successful usually grow. Since success is at least partially the result of a well-designed structure, we get something of a paradox: a structure appropriate for one size both aids organizational effectiveness and is a factor in causing the organization to outgrow its structure.

The influence of size on workable organizational structure partially explains why so much of the organizational-design activity is really redesign. Organizations face different problems at different stages of growth, and managers must reevaluate the structure if the structure is to continue to be effective.[12]

Key Individuals

The roles of those at the top of an organization are another design variable in determining its structure. One author has suggested that the degree of influence management has over an organization's markets and technology is an important aspect of organizational design.[13] Undoubtedly, both the preferences and influence of key individuals affect structure. This influence serves to remind us what a general contingency approach sometimes makes easy to forget—situational factors are not entirely beyond an organization's control. It can usually set limits on size, and choose from a range of technologies and geographical locations.

Despite good reasons for basing organization design on factors like goals, environment, and technology, too many organizations rely on history and tradition in making structural decisions. New organizations tend to imitate the structure of existing ones, which in turn are reluctant to depart from traditional structures despite changes in goals, environment, and technology. Until recently, for example, American automobile manufacturers modeled new plants after Henry Ford's assembly-line concept. Companies eventually began to break from tradition out of frustration with productivity, quality, costs, and morale, and began to use "new factories" that increased worker control and responsibility, and that emphasized teams rather than individuals.[14]

Exhibit 14.7 summarizes the factors that should affect an organization's design. Understanding *why* an organization is structured a particular way, as well as *how* it is structured, makes it easier for a manager to work with, modify, or work around that structure.[15]

The Bottom Line

Few of you will design organizations, or modify their structures, until you have had years of managerial experience. But each of you will work within an organizational structure that will influence your work in several ways. Anticipating the effects of certain structural characteristics will enable you to manage more effectively.

1. Centralization limits the amount of information available to a manager who is not at the center of the decision-making process. Centralized organizations channel information to decision centers; useful information may simply pass you by if it concerns an area for which you have no formal decision-making responsibility. Therefore, if your organization is centralized, you'll have to seek out information rather than wait for it to come to you. Establishing good informal sources of information is a key toward being "in the know" in such organizations.
2. The differentiation that is characteristic of highly complex organizations may find you trying to communicate with someone in another part of the organization whose background, training, job, and time frame are different from yours. It will require sensitivity to these differences so you can communicate effectively with such people. In complex organizations, not everyone "speaks the same language." You will have to understand your audience to communicate well.
3. Formalization in an organization tends to limit a manager's authority. Complexity limits the scope of authority of any manager who isn't near the top of the organization. If you want to wield a lot of personal influence, stay away from formalized , complex organizations, at least in the early stages of your career.
4. Finally, highly centralized, formalized, and tall organizations tend to inhibit creativity, because they narrow individual perspectives. They also reduce the opportunity and incentive for coming up with new ideas. On the other hand, structural complexity and decentralization encourage creativity. If creativity and innovation are among your strengths, look for organizations with complex, decentralized structures.

SUMMARY

The structure of an organization defines its work roles and the formally established authority and communication relationships among those roles. This structure can be described in terms of four dimensions—complexity, configuration, centralization, and formalization. Complexity is the pattern of specialized role grouping in the organization. Configuration is determined by the number of levels of management hierarchy and the size of the span of control that is typical of the organization. Centralization of structure refers to the formal location of decision making, and formalization to the degree to which work behavior is regulated by rules, policies, and job descriptions.

Work roles and the communication relationships in those roles are defined by an organization's structure and influence the behavior of the people in an organization and their perception of the climate.

These four dimensions influence both the behavior of those in the organization and their perceptions of the organizational climate. An organizational profile shows the organization's location along each of the four structural dimensions: simple-complex, wide-flat, decentralized-centralized, and weak formalization-strong formalization.

Organizational design is the process of making decisions about the location of a particular organization on each of the dimensions. These decisions are influenced by the goals and the traditions associated with these goals, the organization's size, its key individuals, the environment in which it operates, and its major form of technology. The more successful organizations are those whose structures are compatible with these factors.

QUESTIONS FOR REVIEW AND DISCUSSION

1. Is it necessary to know the particular individuals who work for an organization to understand its structure? Why or why not?
2. What is the difference between complexity and formalization?
3. Which of the four dimensions of organizational structure is *least* clear from looking at an organization chart? Explain your answer.
4. What is centralization? When it is appropriate? When is it particularly inappropriate?
5. Within the overall structure of this college or university, would each of the following individuals be considered line or staff?
   a. someone who works in the library
   b. the professor of this class
   c. the president of the school
   d. someone who works in the registrar's office
6. How is departmentalization related to division of labor and coordination?
7. Draw a structural profile of the organization for which you work, or one with which you are familiar. If necessary, interview a friend or relative who works. Briefly explain why you drew it as you did; you may use examples in your explanation.
8. Draw a profile of the kind of structure you would prefer to work in.
9. Give at least one example not in the text of a way each of the four structural dimensions discussed might affect the way a manager does his or her job.

REFERENCES AND NOTES

1. The concept of *role* is also applied to smaller social and work groups, as in the "devil's advocate" and "peacemaker" role discussed in Chapter 9. In this chapter we are focusing on formal work roles.
2. B. J. Hodge and W. P. Anthony, *Organization Theory: An Environmental Approach.* Boston: Allyn and Bacon, 1969, p. 1.
3. This scheme is based on that of R. H. Miles, *Macro Organizational Behavior.* Santa Monica, Ca.: Goodyear, 1980, 23–25.
4. *See*, for example, S. M. Davis and P. R. Lawrence, "Problems of Matrix Organizations." *Harvard Business Review*, 1978 (May-June), 131–42.
5. J. R. Galbraith, *Organization Design.* Reading, Mass.: Addison-Wesley, 1977, pp. 90–91.
6. J. Woodward, *Industrial Organization: Theory and Practice*, Oxford, England: Oxford University Press, 1965.
7. H. Stieglitz, "On Concepts of Corporate Structure: Economic Determinants of Organization." *The Conference Board Record*, 1974 (February), 7–13.
8. D. W. Organ and C. N. Greene, "The Effects of Formalization on Professional Involvement: A Compensatory Process Approach." *Administrative Science Quarterly*, 1981, 26, 2, 237–52.

9. An interesting discussion of how structure changes over time is to be found in S. Ranson, B. Hinings, and R. Greenwood, "The Structuring of Organizational Structures." *Administrative Science Quarterly*, 1980, 25, 1, 1–17.

10. A classic review is that of L. R. James and A. P. Jones, "Organizational Climate: A Review of Theory and Research." *Psychological Bulletin*, 1974, 81, 1096–1112.

11. Descriptions of these organizations may be found in "King of the Mountain" and "Managing the Right Side of the Brain," *Inc.* December 1982, pp. 76–91.

12. *See* L. E. Greiner, "Evolution and Revolution as Organizations Grow." *Harvard Business Review*, 1972 (July-August), 37–46.

13. R. A. Pitts, "Toward a Contingency Theory of Multibusiness Organization Design." *Academy of Management Review*, 1980, 5, 2, 203–10.

14. *See* D. Katz and R. L. Kahn for a full discussion of early "new factory" experiments, such as those of Saab and Volvo. *The Social Psychology of Organizations*, 2nd ed. New York: John Wiley and Sons, 1978, Chapter 20.

15. A good review of this literature is to be found in D. R. Dalton, W. D. Todor, M. J. Spendolini, G. J. Fielding, and L. W. Porter, "Organizational Structure and Performance: A Critical Review." *Academy of Management Review*, 1980, 5, 1, 49–64.

SUGGESTED READINGS

Burns, T. and Stalker, G. M. "Mechanistic and Organic Systems of Management." In John F. Veiga and John N. Yanouzas, eds., *The Dynamics of Organization Theory: Gaining a Macro Perspective*. St. Paul, Minn.: West Publishing Co., 1979, 109–14. Excerpts from the authors' classic works compare the extremes of organizational structure and climate, and outline the conditions under which each is appropriate. Burns and Stalker were in the vanguard of the contingency approach: "The beginning of administrative wisdom is the awareness that there is no one optimum type of management system" (page 114).

Kotter, John P. "Managing External Dependence." *Academy of Management Review*, 1979, 4, 1, 87–92. The systems view of organizations has led to considerable research on the relationship between an organization and its external environment. This article reviews studies relevant to four strategies for dealing with an organization's dependency on external factors.

Ross, Joel E. and Murdick, Robert G. "People, Productivity, and Organizational Structure." *Personnel*, 1973 (September-October), 8–18. This article presents a simple overview of the ongoing structure issues of the 1970s and 1980s.

Thompson, Victor A. "Bureaucracy and Bureaupathology." In Bernard L. Hinton and H. Joseph Reitz, eds., *Groups and Organizations: Integrated Readings in the Analysis of Social Behavior*. Belmont, Ca.: Wadsworth Publishing Company, 1971, 462–75. A leading sociologist discusses the reactions of those who work in or deal with the bureaucratic structure. This work is noteworthy for its balanced perspective on a topic that is frequently approached in an emotional and biased manner.

Case Winthrop Hospital

Winthrop Hospital is located in a medium-sized suburban community. A general hospital, it serves a large portion of the surrounding area and is usually operating at, near, or sometimes beyond, its capacity. Each floor of the hospital has its own particular structure with regard to the nurses who staff it. This formalized hierarchy runs from the supervisor (who must be a registered nurse), to registered nurses (RNs), licensed practical nurses (LPNs), students and nurses' aides. Professionally, there are some duties that are supposed to be performed only by the RNs; these are spelled out in the hospital manual. In practice, however, the LPNs do much of the work that is supposed to be done by the RNs. Through time the work done by the RNs and the LPNs has meshed so thoroughly that one just does the work without thinking of whose job it is supposed to be. The hospital is normally so crowded that, even with everyone performing all types of work, there never seems to be enough time or enough help.

The procedural manual at Winthrop Hospital was first used in 1947 and has not been revised. Everyone connected with the hospital realizes that it is extremely outdated, and actual practice varies so greatly that it has no similarity to what is prescribed in the manual. Even the courses that the student nurses take teach things entirely different from what is prescribed in Winthrop's manual.

The vacation privileges for nurses at the hospital show extreme differences for the different types of nurse. RNs receive two weeks' vacation after nine months on the job, whereas LPNs must be on the staff for ten years before receiving their second week of vacation. The LPNs believe this to be extremely unfair and have

been trying to have the privileges somewhat more equalized. Their efforts have met with little cooperation and no success. The hospital superiors have simply told them that the terms for vacation are those stated in the hospital manual.

Some of the individual nurses at Winthrop are beginning to take matters into their own hands. The LPNs on the fourth floor of the hospital decided that if they couldn't have the extra vacation because of what was written in the manual, then they would follow the manual in all phases and go strictly according to the book. Difficulties surfaced as soon as the LPNs began to behave in this manner. The RNs now seemed to have more work than they could handle adequately, and the LPNs were just as busy doing solely their "prescribed" duties. The same amount of effort put forth previously was being exerted, but less was being accomplished, because of the need to jump around from place to place and job to job in order to work strictly according to the book. The LPNs' practice of going by the book brought about hostile feelings among both groups of nurses and among the doctors who had to work on the floor. The conflicts led to a lower degree of care than the patients had been receiving.

The RNs now complained to the hospital superiors more vehemently than ever about being understaffed. They felt that they simply needed more RNs on every floor on every shift to meet what was required of them. The shortage was especially acute at nights, when unfamiliarity with individual patients often led to mixups in the treatments.

The ill feelings led to arguments among the nurses. The LPNs felt that they were always doing more work than

Source: Thomas Kolakowski; reprinted from S. J. Carroll, F. T. Paine, and J. B. Miner, *The Management Process: Cases and Readings.* New York: Macmillian Publishing Co., 1973.

the RNs, that they spent more time with the patients, because the RNs had more to do at the desk, and that they knew more about treatments, because they more often accompanied doctors on their rounds. They now voiced these opinions. The RNs argued superiority on the basis of a longer period of formal training.

All these factors combined to bring about a tremendous drop in morale and a marked decrease in efficiency, and the conflict was in danger of spreading to other floors in the hospital.

CASE QUESTIONS

1. What are the work roles described in the case?
2. Using the information provided, draw an organization chart of one floor of Winthrop Hospital. Assume that there are 3 RNs plus one supervisor and 5 LPNs per floor. The other work roles may be omitted from the chart.
3. Is the formal horizontal (task) differentiation at Winthrop Hospital primarily functional, product, or a matrix? Explain your answer briefly.
4. Is the formal decision-making structure at Winthrop primarily centralized or decentralized? Give an example to support your answer.
5. What is the primary difference between the formal structure on a Winthrop floor and the informal organization described at the beginning of the case. Which of the four structural dimensions discussed in this chapter was most clearly involved?

15 / Policy

"Two rib sandwiches with hot sauce and two ales," the man behind the counter called out.

"I'll get it, Rita," said Jim. Rising from the table he walked to the counter and returned with two cold bottles of ale and two plates piled high with barbequed pork ribs covered with a thick, dark sauce.

"Now look, Jim," began Rita.

Jim interrupted with a wry smile. "I know, I know, you insist on paying for lunch and all that. Ordinarily I'd be happy to let you outfight me for the check! After all, you're my boss, and you're making a lot more money than I am. But today I need your help. Consider this lunch a small bribe."

"Fair enough," grinned Rita. "You talk and I'll listen. Wow—this sauce is hot! But it's too good not to eat."

"That's part of my plan. If you don't help me out, I'll let you eat your way to an ulcer," said Jim, reaching for his glass.

"It's about my turnover problem, Rita," Jim began. "I know that last year's figures showed my section with a thirty percent higher-than-average rate. Well, we're halfway through this year, and it's still bad. Turnover hurts morale; it hurts our ability to function effectively as a section; and I'm the one getting the ulcer."

"I know we decided during your last performance review that it wasn't you or the pay or fringe benefits that were the problem," acknowledged Rita.

"Well, I've now got a pretty good idea about what's been happening. I've been holding exit interviews with everyone who quit over the last six months, and I even went to see three people who left last year. I'm convinced that personnel policy, in a complex way, is behind all this."

"Policy? How?" asked Rita, reaching

for another napkin. "And don't talk with your hands full of ribs."

Jim put the ribs down and continued. "Here's the deal. Say we have normal turnover. That means I lose five or six people every six months. In a small section like mine, a personnel shortage is tough. You don't have many people to pick up the slack. So when it takes personnel six weeks to get me a replacement, it means that the people who are left in my section are consistently doing their own jobs plus the jobs of the vacant positions. Add to that the occasional absentee, and you've got a severe case of people being consistently overworked—not because their own jobs are too demanding, but because we're always operating shorthanded.

"Now I'll tell you where policy comes in. Since the company merger two years ago, personnel policy has been tough. First, I can't start the paperwork requesting them to post a job until the person who is quitting has actually gone, even though I get two weeks' notice. Then, a job-opening has to be advertised for a week before personnel will start interviewing. I can't hire until a week after interviewing begins, and if none of the first batch of interviewees are hired, they won't readvertise the job for eight days.

"As a result, when I do get replacements, they have to learn the jobs on their own instead of being trained by the old employees, like we used to do. If that isn't bad enough, I always have to wait at least five weeks after I initiate a request before I even get to interview a replacement. When I talked to personnel about it,

they just said it's part of the corporation's cost-reduction policy—cutting the fat out of personnel costs by stretching out the replacement time.

"But the effect of that policy on my group is demoralizing—turnover leads to unfilled positions, which leads to greater pressures, which leads to more turnover. Something's got to be done, and I don't know what. After all, it's policy. It's out of my hands."

Jim's story is true, and it reflects the feelings of many lower- and middle-level supervisors towards company policy:

"Policies are rules dreamed up by somebody upstairs to take care of problems we don't have anymore."

"A policy is a guideline you need to get around a problem created by another policy."

"Policies are only around when you don't need them."

These frustrations are widespread. One researcher asked accountants and engineers to describe an instance when they felt particularly upset about work, in order to discover what factors frustrated them. Among the factors mentioned were supervisors, working conditions, relationships with fellow workers, and pay. But the most frequently mentioned source of dissatisfaction and frustration was company policy.[1]

At worst, policies are necessary evils. At best, they serve to channel and integrate organizational effort toward overall goals. In this chapter we'll look at some of what is best, and worst, about policy.

POLICY DEFINED AND DEFENDED

A **policy** is *a guideline established to provide direction to organizational effort and to bring consistency to organizational decisions and actions.*[2] Policies can be very broad or quite specific. When W. Michael Blumenthal became Chief Executive Officer of Burroughs Organization in late 1980, he instituted a number of policy changes.[3] The changes were intended to reverse a year-long decline in earnings and ultimately to restore Burroughs to its former successes (it had averaged twenty-percent annual increases in profits in the 1970s).

One broad policy change was to decentralize marketing and product development. This policy complemented Burroughs' plan to expand its small-computer product-line and its efforts in the area of office automation.

A more specific policy change dealt with Burroughs' financial management. Blumenthal, a former United States Secretary of the Treasury, wanted his managers to handle their assets more effectively. To that end, he established a financial-management policy which reduced management's concern with return on sales. Instead, the policy concentrated efforts on return on assets, which was only two percent in 1980, compared with eight percent for NCR and thirteen percent for IBM, Burroughs' main competitors.

> *At worst, policies are necessary evils. At best, they serve to channel and integrate organizational effort toward overall goals.*

To help distinguish *levels* of policy, we'll use the term **overall policy** to mean *broad guidelines that affect organizational activities in general.* A company adopts overall policy to guide and direct the organization, as a whole, toward complementing its strategy, or long-term plan. Burroughs' adopted a policy of decentralization to implement its strategy of expansion. Note that this policy dealt with organizational structure. As we pointed out in Chapter 14, structure follows strategy. In this case, Burroughs developed a strategy, then decided on a structure to help carry out that strategy, and established an overall policy to bring about that structural change.

We'll use the term **operational policy** to mean *those stated guidelines that channel and direct activities in any department, division, or other subsystem of the organization.* Burroughs' financial-management policy is an operational policy; so is the personnel policy about which Jim complained to Rita in the introductory anecdote. Both policies affect subsystems of the organization. The relationships among strategy, overall policy, and operational policy are depicted in Exhibit 15.1.

In Defense of Policy

As we discussed in Chapters 4 and 7, organizational success requires coordination of the efforts, decisions, and actions of each and all its members. Some coordination comes from goals, such as profitability or market share; some coordination is provided by individual or group incentives for accomplishments, such as improving productivity, safety, or efficiency; some coordination comes from standardization, such as using standard parts, layouts, or procedures; and some coordination comes from policies, which can be thought of as a means for standardizing decisions and actions, particularly at the managerial and supervisory levels.

Every manager or supervisor is capable of making decisions and doing things in a wide variety of ways. For example, suppose a district manager of a medium-sized corporation is trying to hire several new college graduates as management trainees. The issues faced by such a manager are numerous. "What kinds of salary offers should I make? What about trying to recruit females or minorities? Can I pay moving expenses? Should I make better offers to more qualified applicants? Can I invite them to visit the home office? Can I pay their expenses (and those of their spouse) for such a visit? What can I promise them about promotions, raises, and training opportunities over their first eighteen months with the company?"

Exhibit 15.1   The Relationships Among Strategy, Overall Policy, and Operational Policies

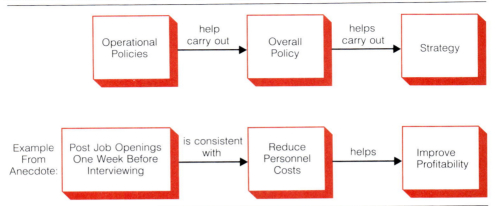

Most organizations have a personnel policy to cover each of these questions and to reduce that manager's uncertainty. Each policy would serve as a guideline, to make it easier for the manager to make the necessary decisions. The policies would be designed to coordinate decisions with overall company policy, strategy, and objectives, and to make the decisions consistent throughout the organization.

Coordination.   Assume that the company for which the district manager is hiring has a strategic plan that involves consolidation rather than growth. The plan emphasizes overall policies of holding down costs, tightening budgets, and eliminating nonprofitable product lines and programs. Operational policies in personnel have changed to become consistent with that strategy. There is a standard salary offer for all management trainees. The most qualified applicants may be offered an expense-paid trip for only themselves to the home office, but no flexibility in salary offers is permitted. Trainees are expected to become productive fast; after six weeks' on-the-job training, they will be given supervisory responsibility. By the end of eighteen months, the top twenty-five percent will be promoted, the bottom fifty percent will be terminated, and the remaining twenty-five percent will be given another year to prove themselves.

The new personnel policies influence not only the district manager's decisions about what kinds of offers and promises to make, but also what kind of people to look for: people who are competitive, who don't demand a great deal of security, and who are eager to get to work and prove their worth.

One hiring policy that hasn't changed during the consolidation has to do with female and minority hiring practices. The company has an affirmative-action policy which states that all hiring will be coordinated with the district affirmative-action officer. This officer helps the manager find and interview qualified female and minority applicants.

In this company, personnel hiring policy acts as a type of feedforward control to bring the hundreds of hiring decisions made by middle management into line with corporate strategy about consolidation and cost-cutting. Without these policies, thousands of dollars would have been spent on hiring and training new managers, most of whom would have taken a couple of years to become productive.

Of course, the district managers who are doing the hiring may not like the policy. Lack of flexibility in offers may make their jobs more difficult; instead of "buying" outstanding graduates, they have to "sell" them on the long-term or nonmonetary advantages of joining the company. Restrictive policies often have that effect. Managers feel not only guided by such a policy, but often frustrated by it. Managers commonly lament, "It ties my hands."

Consistency. On the other hand, most managers recognize the purpose of policy and accept it as something they must learn to live with. In many cases, in fact, policies are developed because managers demand them. Frustrated by inconsistencies in the way their peers or superiors deal with a common situation, they appeal to policy-setting levels of management to provide guidelines which will reduce the inconsistencies. For example, consider a manager who uses reprimands and suspensions as methods for dealing with employees who are frequently late. Will this manager encounter resistance to such discipline if other managers are ignoring excessive lateness? Asking for a policy directive is a way for that manager to avoid being labeled as unfair and to get other managers to discipline lateness. It promotes equity and reduces uncertainty for managers and employees alike.

Policy as a Control Process

It is probably easiest to understand the policy-making process if we think of policy primarily as part of the control function. Chapter 7 defined control as keeping something within acceptable limits. Organizations require control because the individuals, processes, and resources which comprise them are highly variable. Policy is simply one way that organizations can reduce variability to manageable limits. In this respect, policy is like job design, performance standards, and organizational structure.

We can look at policy as a standard against which decisions and actions are compared. If a decision or action is consistent with policy, no corrective action is necessary. If a decision or action is inconsistent with policy, corrective action is taken. It may include overturning the decision, sending the decision back to its originator for revision, or remedying the action. In some cases the individual or group who violated the policy may be reprimanded or disciplined. In other cases, exceptions to the policy may be granted under unusual conditions.

Exhibit 15.2 depicts policy as a control process much like that described in Chapter 7. A policy, whether overall or operational, is established and communicated to those whose decisions and actions it affects. Their decisions and actions are then compared with the policy. If they are consistent, the policy is affirmed. If they are not consistent, action is taken. Occasionally that action includes re-examining the policy to see if it should be revised.

The policy process has two unique criteria which are essential for it to function successfully as a control process: timeliness and clear communication.

Exhibit 15.2   Policy as a Control Process

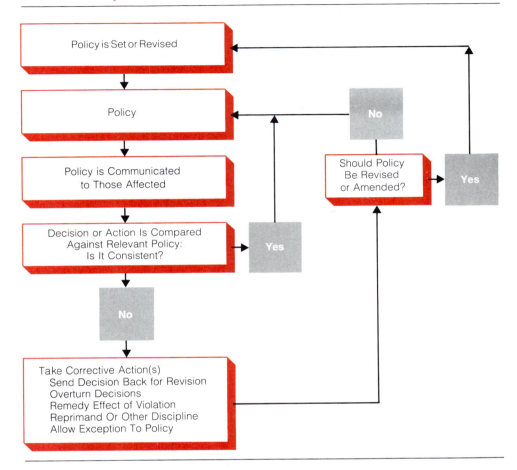

Timeliness.   First of all, policies tend to affect a great many people. That means that, in order to be effective, a policy must be communicated to those people affected, in time for them to carry it out. In order to "carry it out" they must understand it and they must have the time and resources to implement it.

Faced with huge sales costs, because of steadily increasing costs of travel, many companies have made policy decisions restricting the travel of their sales personnel. To implement this policy and still sell effectively, sales managers need time and resources to develop alternative methods of contacting customers. Temporary exceptions may be required to deal with important customers, who might feel slighted by substituting telephone calls and letters for personal visits. Failure to develop and communicate policy in time for those affected to implement it effectively is a major reason for resistance to company policy.

Clear Communication. Even more basic than the timeliness of policy is the extent to which it is communicated, and communicated clearly, to those affected by it. Ignorance may be no excuse, but it is often a reason for the failure to carry out policy.

Policy is typically set at the highest levels of an organization, division, or department, yet it often affects people several levels below. As we discussed in the chapter on communications, communicating up and down an organization's hierarchy is very difficult. As the number of levels that information must pass through increases, so does the number of people who get involved in transmitting it. This increases the chances for faulty information.

Three problems may occur during the transmission of policy from higher to lower levels. First, the information may fail to reach those for whom it's intended. Second, the message may become garbled. Third, as in the introductory anecdote, the reason for the policy does not reach those who must live with it. The first two problems result in policy not being implemented. The third leads lower-level employees to conclude that policy makers are capricious, ignorant, or uncaring about the problems that their policies create.

Thus, we can conclude that to make the correct or appropriate policy decision is only half the battle. An uncommunicated or poorly communicated policy will be no more effective than a poor one. Two specialists in business policy make the point that, "To communicate [a policy] requires as much trouble and time as to conceive it."[4]

THE POLICY MAKERS

We have defined policy as a stated guideline that provides direction to organizational efforts and brings consistency to organizational decisions and actions. At the very top of the organization, the chief executive officer (CEO) and his or her closest advisors formulate overall goals and strategy which serve as the bases for overall organizational policy. Heads of divisions, plants, or departments, in turn, set operational policies to complement overall policy and strategy.

The Role of the CEO

Overall organizational policy and strategy tend to be the province of the chief executive officer (CEO) and his or her closest advisors, who may include the board of directors. One of the foremost writers in the field of management, Peter Drucker, identifies six tasks that are the major responsibility of the CEO.[5] These include building and maintaining the human organization, assuring proper relationships between top management and other organizations and agencies, performing ceremonial functions, and being prepared to exert leadership in time of crisis. But the number-one task on his list of CEO responsibilities is setting overall policy and strategy. The responsibility for overall policy is so clearly the CEO's that when he or she does not carry it out effectively, the organization can flounder.

The position demands the perspective of a generalist rather than a specialist. Indeed, business-school courses, and texts which deal with policy, encourage students to forgo the specialist perspective developed by their course work. Instead, they are urged to make decisions on the basis of all the relevant areas in which they have been educated—accounting, finance, marketing, production, economics, behavorial science, and quantitative analysis.

> *Organizational success requires coordination of the effort, decisions, and actions of each and all its members. Some of this coordination comes from an organization's policies, which can be thought of as a means for standardizing decisions and actions, particularly at the managerial and supervisory levels.*

Nevertheless, most CEOs retain some specialist perspective which is reflected in their policies and strategies.[6] In Chapter 1 we described the policy changes wrought by Ken O. Curtis at Denny's, Inc. Curtis' background in accounting has influenced his policies, which include tightening control, emphasizing cost-reduction, and savings. Edgar Bronfman, CEO of Seagram Co. Ltd., the world's biggest producer of distilled spirits and wines, has an intense interest in marketing. He told his subordinates, "When they talk about marketing at the Harvard Business School, I want them to mention Seagram first."[7] Emphasizing marketing was a major change for Seagram; indeed, for the whole industry. To implement this policy Bronfman hired Philip Beekman as president. Beekman had been president of Colgate-Palmolive International, the highly market-oriented, consumer-products corporation. Other changes consistent with a market-oriented policy have included doubling Seagram's advertising budget, hiring more high-level consumer marketers, and paying more heed to market research.

The Role of the Lower-Level Manager

Once overall goals, strategy, and policy are established, lower-level policy can develop to guide operating-level decisions. Unfortunately, the most insightful or best-conceived policy can only be effective if it is carried out. When the chief of police initiates a policy that police will fire their weapons only when it is essential in protecting life, it is up to each individual officer to carry out that policy. When the head of the Internal Revenue Service develops a policy that emphasizes the pursuit of smaller taxpayers, it is up to the individual agents to carry it out. When a production manager establishes a zero-defects policy, it is up to the individual managers and supervisors to see that it is executed.

All lower-level managers must implement policy. To do so successfully, they must be aware of, understand, and accept the policies, and have sufficient resources to carry them out. New policies, or policy changes, can strain or exceed the resources of those managers, as Jim complained to Rita in the introductory anecdote. Lower-level managers usually hope that policy makers will recognize this fact of organizational life and make provision for the necessary resources.

Unfortunately, policy makers are not always that farsighted. One consumer-products division of a large corporation decentralized access to its computers. Unfortunately, the peak demands of the users tended to overlap. This overlap created big backlogs, driving the systems manager "up the wall." No wonder a common complaint made by middle- and lower-level managers about policy is, "They don't seem to understand the problems I've got down here."

THE POLICY-MAKING PROCESS

The resource problem suggests that managers should be aware of and knowledgeable about company policy. They should likewise be able to provide input for policy-making processes at the stage where the need for additional resources is being considered. A typical policy-making process follows the format outlined in Exhibit 15.3.

Exhibit 15.3 breaks the policy-making process down into four parts. These are the appraisal phase, the selection phase, the implementation phase, and the evaluation and control phase.

Appraisal

In the appraisal phase, policy makers explore the organization's environment. They try to uncover or anticipate threats to be avoided (such as harmful legislation or resource shortages) or opportunities to be exploited. Threats or opportunities can originate anywhere in the organization's environment—from competitive, technological, social, governmental, or resource factors. For example, changes in policies of *Newsweek's* major advertisers, and increased competition from cable television, prompted William Broyles, when he was the magazine's editor-in-chief, to adopt policies increasing feature stories and deemphasizing certain types of government news.[8]

The appraisal phase also includes examining the organization's strengths and weaknesses, including those of its resources. Identifying internal weaknesses may generate policies; changes covering the acquisition of managerial talent often come from internal audits which reveal actual or potential weaknesses in management. For some organizations, this means changing from a policy of promotion from within to a policy of hiring higher-level managers away from other companies.

The internal-appraisal phase provides managers with their first opportunities to introduce information about their own resource base into the policy-making process. Unfortunately, the information they provide is not always accurate. Some managers underestimate their resources in hopes of obtaining an increased allocation. Worse yet, some managers overestimate their resources, either out of fear of

Exhibit 15.3   The Policy-Making Process

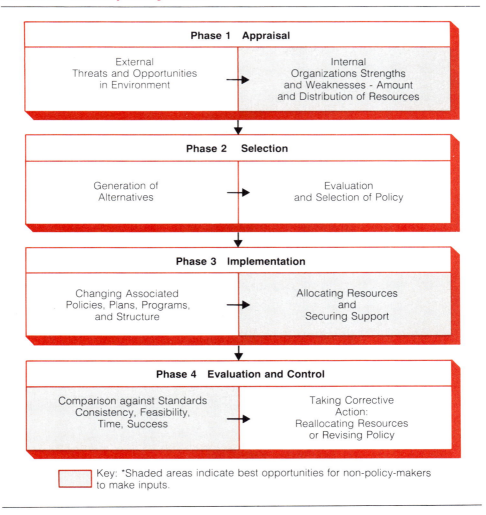

Phase 1   Appraisal

External
Threats and Opportunities
in Environment

Internal
Organizations Strengths
and Weaknesses - Amount
and Distribution of Resources

Phase 2   Selection

Generation of
Alternatives

Evaluation
and Selection of Policy

Phase 3   Implementation

Changing Associated
Policies, Plans, Programs,
and Structure

Allocating Resources
and
Securing Support

Phase 4   Evaluation and Control

Comparison against Standards
Consistency, Feasibility,
Time, Success

Taking Corrective
Action:
Reallocating Resources
or Revising Policy

Key: *Shaded areas indicate best opportunities for non-policy-makers to make inputs.

disapproval or in hopes that they will increase their chances of being called on to carry out new policies. The armed forces routinely carry out internal appraisals conducted by inspection teams from headquarters. The purpose is to appraise the readiness of personnel and equipment. However, pressures to pass the inspection is great, regardless of its intent. As a result, officers and NCOs often "beg, borrow, or steal" enough equipment for the duration of the inspection to meet standards. Rather than admit they are short-handed or lack equipment, they fool the inspecting team. Consequently, the inspector's appraisal of the state of readiness of military units is often dangerously overestimated. This, in turn, can lead to the military's taking on objectives for which they are ill-prepared.

Management in Action
Financial Control and Resource Acquisition

The *control* of capital is generally carried out by a system of budgets, audits, and internal control policies. One example of a financial control policy comes from Best Western International, Inc., the affiliation of hotel owners.

Best Western is a nonprofit association; its members have banded together to improve their ability to compete with the big hotel chains. Under Robert Hazzard, their CEO in 1980, Best Western Hotels had undergone a period of heavy spending, promotion, and centralized decision making which increased the association's share of American room occupancy from five percent in 1974 to eleven percent in 1980. But untamed heavy spending in the face of declining travel in 1980 led to members' dissatisfaction with Mr. Hazzard's policies. He left in November 1980, followed by charges of financial irresponsibility.

Under the new CEO, Best Western financial control policies have changed. One notable change has been to require program managers to report directly to the governing board of members anytime they exceed any three-month budget by ten percent or more. This policy has had an effect on these managers. One of them confided that, before the change, budgets were ignored. "I always thought any budget was a bottomless pit." Backing up policies with action makes them more effective.

Policies governing the *acquisition of resources* shape the decisions and actions of those whose job it is to provide the organization with the materials, technology, and information needed to produce its goods or services. One major example of acquisition policy is provided by Mobil Corporation. For years Mobil's board of directors was dominated by refining, marketing, and finance specialists. Drilling and exploration took a back seat to purchasing existing reserves as a means of acquisition. In the 1970s, however, Mobil changed its acquisition policy in an attempt to reduce its dependency on Mideast oil. It promoted a strong policy of drilling and exploration in the western hemisphere. The effects of this policy change included reorganizing the company and centralizing drilling decisions. Mobil doubled its drilling rights (to 100 million acres), and upgraded its exploration technology. This major policy decision affected thousands of other decisions and actions over the years.

It took several years for the Mobil policy change to pay off. But in 1979 a major oil field was discovered in Hibernia, off the coast of Newfoundland. Mobil's share of that find is estimated at four hundred million barrels of oil. Other successes include oil and gas reserves in Wyoming, Mobile Bay, Georges Bank and Sable Island off the United States' East Coast.

Sources: "Best Western: Ready to Put On the Brakes." *Business Week*, February 23, 1981, pp. 62–70; "Mobil's Successful Oil Exploration," *Business Week*, October 13, 1980, pp. 112–18.

Selection

In the selection phase, policy makers consider alternatives and choose a policy from among them. (The process of selection was discussed in greater detail in the chapter on decision-making skills.) Remember, however, that decision makers seldom *optimize*, or choose the one-best policy offer, having carefully considered all possible alternatives. More typically, they satisfice; that is, they examine a limited number of alternatives, compare them against some minimum criteria, and pick one that satisfies these minimum criteria.

Once a set of satisfactory alternatives has been identified, the criteria by which the actual policy is chosen may vary from policy maker to policy maker. It is safe to say, however, that a policy which requires little change from the *status quo* will stand a good chance of adoption.

Consider the plight of a well-known entertainment center. The center caters to people of all ages, yet maintains a policy of hiring only nineteen to twenty-four-year-olds for positions dealing with the public—managing rides, selling concessions and tickets, and providing information. The center plans to expand its facilities and, consequently, to increase its labor force. However, projections indicate that the supply of nineteen to twenty-four-year-olds will be insufficient to meet the labor demands. One policy alternative is to increase the range of ages to seventeen to twenty-six. A second is to hire senior citizens, who are in great supply in the area. Both alternatives will satisfy the criterion of increasing the labor supply enough to meet the center's requirements.

The policy more likely to be adopted is the one closer to current policy—expanding the current age range to seventeen to twenty-six. This choice is more likely even though the other alternative might increase the labor supply by one hundred fifty percent rather than by thirty percent. The tendency to choose policies that are close to existing policies has been called *disjointed incrementalism*—making policy by marginal comparisons. This is one of the reasons that policy tends to change very slowly.

Implementation

During the implementation phase, changes in other policies, plans, programs, and structure are made, if necessary, to accommodate the new policy. This systems-effect of policy making, first discussed in Chapter 2, is another reason that policy tends to change slowly and incrementally.

A drastic change in policy often requires major changes in other policies, plans, and programs. If, for example, the entertainment center, described earlier, changed its staffing policy from hiring nineteen to twenty-four-year-olds to hiring senior citizens, how many other changes would have to be made to implement this policy? There would be alterations in the promotion and retirement policies, work schedules, job descriptions, and even uniforms. Recruiting and selection procedures would change as well. The benefits of the new policy might easily outweigh the effort and cost of the changes required to implement it; however, the very thought of all those potentially related changes makes many policy makers very cautious about changing existing policies.

During the implementation phase communication about the new policy intensifies, and human, financial, and other resources are allocated to make the policy work. This is the second and last opportunity for managers affected by the new policy to make their resource requirements known. It may be too late to stave off the policy since a choice has already been made, but it is time for affected managers to demand the resources they require.

During this phase, policy makers often "sell" their policies to subordinates, expressing confidence that the policies will be carried out. At the same time, they avoid committing additional resources. The manager who fails to speak out during the implementation phase may find it increasingly difficult later on.

> *To make the correct or appropriate policy decision is only half the battle. An uncommunicated or poorly communicated policy will be no more effective than a poor one.*

There have been numerous suggestions that setting a policy does not guarantee its implementation. One study of educational policies found a number of problems that interfered with the actual performance of stated policies. Chief among these problems were lack of key-personnel commitment and even resistance from those whose efforts were most required.[9] Another study, this time of government organizations, attempted to discover what factors influenced the extent of policy implementation.[10] The policies examined stemmed from the Equal Opportunity Employment Act and the Alcoholic Rehabilitation Act. EEO policies provide equal-employment opportunities for all citizens. Alcoholic-rehabilitation policies provide guidelines for detecting and dealing with drinking problems at work. These policies required the support and cooperation of the managers who would have to implement them, but represented additional responsibility, not substitutions for old policies.

Structured interviews were conducted with several hundred managers in nine departments of the federal government such as Agriculture, Commerce, and Treasury, to find out what affected the implementation of these two sets of policies. The results indicated that managers who perceived their performances as important for future promotions, who worked in larger organizations, and to whom top-level management had emphasized these policies, were most receptive to implementing them, while managers who felt themselves already overloaded were less receptive.

Most importantly, when top management emphasized the policies, insured that their managers were familiar with them, and provided needed resources, managers were receptive, and policies were implemented.

The implications are fairly clear: Merely stating a policy does not insure its enactment. As Exhibit 15.4 points out policy makers can increase effectiveness by making their managers familiar with the policy, helping them understand its purpose, emphasizing the support of top management, evaluating and rewarding its implementation, and reducing work overload and strain on managers' resources.[11]

Exhibit 15.4   Guidelines For Managers In Implementing Policy

For Managers Who Make Policy	For Managers Who Carry Out Policy
1. Explain the nature and purpose of policy to those it affects.	1. Understand the nature and purpose of the policy.
2. Emphasize top management support.	2. Assess its impact on responsibilities and resources.
3. Relieve strain on managers and their resources.	3. Bargain for needed revisions or additional resources *before* it goes into effect.
4. Evaluate and reward its implementation.	

Implications for managers who must implement policy are also clear: They should assess the impact of policy changes on their areas of responsibility and make the case for revision or additional resources as quickly as possible. This suggests that managers keep themselves well informed about the strengths, weaknesses, and resource needs of their organizations.

Evaluation and Control

By the time a policy moves through the implementation phase into evaluation and control, top management is usually committed to it. Ideally, the policy will be reviewed on a regular basis to monitor its intended and unintended effects. In practice, however, there will be a stronger tendency to look for evidence that the policy is working. Evidence to the contrary is likely to be discounted by comments such as, "We've got to give it more time. You've got to expect some initial problems and setbacks."

While any policy takes time to work, short-term problems are still problems. Managers like Jim who are policy implementers have their work cut out for them once the evaluation phase begins. They are going to have to speak out forcefully, as he was trying to do with Rita, to get any corrective action. The most likely response to negative feedback at this stage is to ignore it or to adopt a position of wait-and-see. The least likely response is to revise the policy. It is more probable that consistent negative feedback about problems will elicit a greater commitment of resources in an attempt to correct, rather than revise, policy.

One has only to recount the history of American foreign policy for evidence that policy, once implemented, is not easily deterred. American positions toward North Korea in 1950, Cuba in 1961, and Vietnam in 1964 all provide abundant evidence of problems either ignored or eliciting greater commitment of resources rather than revisions of policy. The policy toward Iran in 1979 failed to change despite growing evidence that the Shah was on his way out. Instead, the United States increased its support and commitment of resources to his regime until the actual overthrow of his government proved the failure of their policy.

In summary, the role of non-policy makers in the policy process is limited. They are seldom invited to provide input before policy is set. Afterward, the job of providing useful feedback is difficult. This is particularly true when policy makers are encouraged to progress from being relatively open during the appraisal stage to increasingly committed as the policy is being carried out and evaluated.[12] For a middle- or lower-level manager to convince committed policy makers that they have made errors may be the most difficult of all managerial tasks.

OPERATIONAL POLICIES AND THEIR EFFECTS

Thus far we have focused primarily on overall policy, made by the chief executive officer or administrative head of an organization. Overall policy is typically long-range and is formulated from a generalist, rather than a specialist, perspective.

More specialized policies tend to be made more frequently, often at lower levels of the organization. Like overall policy, they coordinate decisions and actions with other policies and plans and provide consistency within the unit or area for which they are intended.

Many operational policies are developed as guidelines for a specific organizational function such as finance, marketing, or production.

Financial Policies

The function of finance is to make sure that the organization has sufficient monetary resources. Sufficient means, broadly speaking, enough for the organization to acquire and operate the other resources (land, labor, materials, equipment) needed to achieve its objectives. Therefore, financial policies are developed to guide the acquisition, management, and control of funds.

One of the fundamental policy-decisions that any company makes deals with the *acquisition of capital.* Is it going to acquire capital by borrowing or by selling stock? A policy of borrowing will subject the company to policy restrictions imposed by the lender to protect its investment. A policy of stock-funding will subject the company to policy restrictions imposed by the Securities and Exchange Commissions and by the stockholders themselves.

A company which changed its financial policy is Hughes Tool Co., founded by Howard Hughes, Sr.[13] In 1972 the company earned $10.3 million on sales of $94.5 million. At that time it manufactured and marketed only two products, drill bits for cutting into rock and tool joints for oil drilling. No funding was available to develop new products. Then Howard Hughes, Jr., changed the financial policy to allow the company to go public—to sell common stock. Sufficient cash was raised from the sale of stock to allow Hughes Tool to diversify its product line and to acquire other businesses. The success of these policy changes was reflected in a tenfold increase in the company's earnings and sales.

The *management of capital* generates policies designed to maximize the return on capital once acquired. Financial policies which have great impact on nonfinancial managers include those stating a minimum-expected return on investment for projects that will be internally funded. During periods of high interest rates, such policies restrict business activity; financial managers can earn from fifteen to twenty percent on low-risk, outside investments. Therefore, the policy of maximizing expected return on investment leads to a short-term policy requiring a fifteen percent return on internally funded projects, a difficult achievement. Thus, very few projects are funded.

Marketing Policies

The functions of marketing are to determine what consumers want, and to move goods and services from the producer to the consumer. Thus, marketing policies can be developed to serve as guidelines for decisions and actions involving market research and product development, sales, and delivery. Coppertone, the leading producer of sun-care products had relied, for twenty-five years, on its basic suntan lotion, promoted by "Little Miss Coppertone" and her dog urging the public, "Tan, don't burn." But the late 1970s found Coppertone facing increasing competition from Sea and Ski, Hawaiian Tropic, and Bain de Soleil, prompting the company to embark on a three-year program of consumer research.

Based on its research findings, Coppertone changed its policy by diversifying the product line and changing the advertising. It created four new sun-care products—a line for facial care, a water-resistant sunscreen, and two oils less greasy than the original Coppertone. In 1980 Coppertone introduced these products with a $5 million advertising campaign on TV, radio, in magazines and buses, as well as its traditional billboards. Coppertone targeted its audience (twelve- to twenty-four-year-old females), sponsored sweepstakes, and gave away cars to promote its new products, adding the slogan, "the savage tan." These policy changes enabled Coppertone to maintain its market leadership, despite new and heavy competition.[14]

Sales policies probably come to the attention of the general public more than most organizational policies, because they are often advertised as a means of attracting customers. In an attempt to restore public confidence and to get the public to buy its products after its much-publicized flirtation with bankruptcy, Chrysler Corporation instituted a policy of rebates on new car purchases in the winter of 1980–81.[15] The policy was designed to increase sales at the expense of profits. The rebate policy was costly (an estimated $106 million in the first six months), but it enabled Chrysler to meet its sales objectives for the first time in a long time. In one year, Chrysler's share of the domestic car market jumped from 9.9 percent to 12.5 percent.

Policies concerning post-sales decisions and actions provide guidelines for everything from delivery to refunds. All of us have encountered such policies in dealing with retail-sales organizations. Most telephone companies have service-call and delivery policies promising service on a particular date, but not at a particular time of day. Most clothing stores have refund policies, accepting returned merchandise only with a sales receipt and only within fifteen days of the sale.

Post-sales policies are carefully developed to help store managers and other personnel deal with scores of different customer requests in a consistent and cost-efficient manner. These policies, when clearly and publicly stated, also serve to guide

Because Kraft, Inc. believes in providing high-quality products and services to meet its customers' needs, Kraft employs home economists to perform a variety of functions including developing and testing new products and recipes.

the decisions and actions of customers. Some may choose not to patronize a store with a restrictive return-policy but may buy from a store with a liberal return-policy, even though its prices are higher.

Production Policies

The function of production is to convert resources into goods and services. Manufacturing companies convert raw materials into physical products such as consumer goods, machinery, and equipment; service organizations convert resources into transportation, entertainment, and health. Whether it delivers goods or services, every organization develops policies to guide the conversion of its resources into products.

Policies are needed to insure that resources are used in ways consistent with organizational goals. In profit-seeking organizations, these policies can often be developed in a manner consistent with some financial policy which will promote a high return on investment. Not-for-profit organizations have no such rational remedies handy, and most develop policies consistent with other values. Hospitals are often faced with greater demands for resources than they can supply. A myriad of policies develop to assist medical administrators and staff in making decisions consistently and quickly. For example, each hospital has only so many beds, so policies are developed to promote the efficient use of available beds consistent with good medical practices. In the past, new mothers might spend a week in the hospital after delivery, before returning home. Today, most hospitals have a policy of discharging uncomplicated deliveries within seventy-two hours. Similarly, policies are created to help personnel decide which patients or physicians get priority in using scarce resources such as operating rooms, intensive-care units, and special-treatment facilities.

We usually think that policies governing the conversion of resources into outputs are derived from hard financial data. This is not always so. A far-reaching policy decision being looked at throughout American industry today deals with the involvement of workers in production decisions. The predominant policy for the last fifty years has been described as one in which "workers work and managers think." In the past few years, however, several large companies have changed that policy in response to today's work force, which is younger and better educated than ever, and productivity and wage gains, which have become stagnant.

Xerox has adopted a policy of pushing decisions to ever-lower levels of the organizational hierarchy. This policy is encouraged by Xerox President David Kearns, who circulates a videotape throughout the corporation in which he pledges "that management of this company at all levels will listen to you and put your ideas to work."[16] The new policy has affected decisions and actions of managers and nonmanagers throughout the corporation. Groups of people from the same level of different departments and different levels in the same department work together to solve problems and suggest improvements. Union leaders have endorsed the policy, and both foremen and hourly workers have been trained to provide input. The intent of the policy is to foster decisions and actions which involve workers and management in each others' and the corporation's success, to share information and gains, and to increase job security and weather unexpected setbacks.

Research and Development Policies

As was explained in Chapter 13, the function of research and development is to provide the organization with new products or services to market and new or improved technology for producing them. Before World War II, research and development activities were formally recognized by relatively few companies. Today most organizations support R & D in some form. It is absolutely critical in the semiconductor, automotive, data-processing, and pharmaceutical industries, to name a few.

One major policy decision in any organization is the amount of capital that should be invested in research and development activities. Although there is abundant evidence that research investments pay off handsomely, many American businesses remain reluctant to make major commitments. Managers, impatient for short-term payoffs, seem to believe that the demand for their existing products is inexhaustible.[17]

R & D spending policies have been critical in television-set manufacturing. The United States, long the leader in technology, saw its leadership erode as long-term Japanese research began to pay off. In ten years the number of American color-TV makers dropped from twenty-five to fourteen, and eight of the survivors were taken over by foreign companies, mostly Japanese. Zenith changed its R & D policy in an attempt to regain leadership. As technology permitting giant-screen TV developed, Zenith embarked on a costly, long-term program to develop an attractive set which produced a sharp picture. When Zenith introduced its model in mid-1981, it had a unique product. Unlike Sony, its chief rival, Zenith's model had a rear projector, and unlike other rear-projection models, Zenith's forty-five-inch screen was completely hidden in its cabinet until the set was turned on. The potential market is now estimated at five hundred thousand sets annually.[18]

> By the time policy moves to the evaluation and control phase, commitment is usually so strong at the top of the organization that middle managers have little influence on the process.

A second guideline for most R & D policy decisions is the amount of emphasis that should be placed on applied versus basic research as discussed in Chapter 13. Applied research has a specific product or process objective as its target, while basic research is simply an attempt by scientists to learn more about processes or technology, without necessarily having any specific applications in mind. Polaroid and Xerox are two companies which capitalized on basic research in the past. The current example is Genentech, a company formed to do basic research on genetic engineering. At the time Genentech went public, no one knew if there would ever be any marketable applications for the products of its research. Yet the idea of genetic engineering excited the public enough to bid up its common stock from the initial ten-dollar offering price to a high of eighty-seven dollars within a short time.

In applied research, policies usually help determine the kinds of projects which will be funded. That is, how much available funding shall be applied to satisfying an existing demand, and how much shall be applied toward developing ideas which then must be sold? Although people believe that companies create products which nobody wants and then market them to a gullible public, actually eighty percent of applied research is directed toward satisfying an existing demand.[19] Relatively little research monies are expended to develop ideas which have little or no demand.

Personnel Policies

The personnel function is to provide the organization with sufficient quantity and quality of human resources to accomplish its objectives, as will be discussed further in the next chapter. As such, personnel policies (or human-resource management policies, as they are now often called) affect every individual in every organization. We will describe three types of personnel policies—disciplinary (see Exhibit 15.5), hiring, and appraisal.

Exhibit 15.5   Patterns of Disciplinary Policies For Various Offenses

Disciplinary policies are designed to guide the actions of managers dealing with violations of company regulations and procedures. In recent years, legal suits brought by disciplined employees, unions, and/or government agencies have led to increasingly more restrictive policies governing employee discipline.

For many managers, terminating a chronic offender has become such a costly and tedious procedure that firing has become an impractical solution. Firing an employee becomes an alternative, not for poor performance, but only for documented violations of specific rules, such as possession of narcotics or firearms, fighting, theft, or sabotage. The table below describes the relative frequency of policies governing the use of warnings, suspensions, or dismissals enforced by 160 companies responding to a government survey.

Type of Offense	First Offense			Second Offense			Third Offense			Fourth Offense		
Attendance Problems	W	S	D	W	S	D	W	S	D	W	S	D
Unexcused absence	84	21	3	60	28	3	13	47	26	2	11	52
Chronic absenteeism	88	3	2	55	32	4	8	44	38	1	4	50
Unexcused/excessive lateness	92	1	0	68	24	1	20	53	21	4	12	55
On-the-job Behavior Problems												
Intoxication at work	28	33	36	8	22	32	2	5	22	1	0	7
Insubordination	36	28	34	9	22	35	1	8	22	0	1	7
Fighting	16	25	54	4	9	30	1	1	11	0	0	2
Failure to use safety devices	81	2	2	46	31	6	12	30	32	4	8	27
Failure to report injuries	6	10	46	1	2	12	0	1	3	0	0	1
Dishonesty and Related Problems												
Theft	2	6	90	1	0	9	0	0	1	0	0	0
Falsifying employment application	6	0	88	1	1	2	0	0	1	0	0	0
Willfull damage to company property	17	17	64	4	11	21	0	2	13	0	0	4

W = Warning; S = Suspension; D = Discharge

Source: Personnel Policies Forum, Employee Conduct and Discipline, PPF Survey # 102 (Washington, D.C.: Bureau of National Affairs, Inc., August 1973), p. 6.

Hiring policies, like the ones Jim and Rita discussed in the opening anecdote, are developed to guide the thousands of decisions made in the acquisition of human resources. Some of these policies are heavily influenced by federal and state legislation. For example, the Equal Employment Opportunity Commission, designed to promote equal opportunities in employment for all Americans, influences recruitment, interviewing, testing, and selection procedures throughout most organizations. Many organizations have created a position for someone to do nothing but interpret company personnel policies in light of EEOC guidelines. In some organizations, the minority affairs, or affirmative-action officer helps set policies specifically designed to increase percentages of minority and female employees in certain areas.

Policies which are current and fully communicated to employees can become influential in reinforcing control.

For some managers, these policies have been helpful ways to assist them in their efforts to bring females and minorities into their work force. Other managers have viewed these policies as severely restricting their freedom of operation. Regardless of their views, all managers are affected.

Performance appraisal, as described in Chapters 6 and 9, is used both to make decisions about employees (promotions, transfers, retention, salaries) and as feedback to help employees develop their skills and careers. Some of the policy decisions which affect this important managerial activity influence the methods used to rate performance, the frequency with which evaluations are carried out, and the ways in which appraisals are used.

General Electric provides an example of policies which affect performance appraisal.[20] GE's program, called *Work Planning and Review*, evolved out of dissatisfaction with the traditional appraisal policies which were found to affect neither the performance nor the satisfaction of GE workers. The policies of *Work Planning and Review* include the following:

1. Appraisal will be based on the employee's accomplishment of goals mutually set by the employee and his or her superior.
2. Discussions of performance between supervisor and employee will occur frequently, rather than once or twice a year.
3. Discussions about salary will be separate and independent from performance-evaluation sessions.
4. Managers and supervisors will receive training in performance-appraisal techniques and procedures.

These basic policies had a dramatic effect on appraisal decisions and actions of all managers and supervisors at General Electric.

The Bottom Line

As a new manager, your primary responsibilities will include implementing rather than setting policy. To do so successfully, remember that:

1. You may have to be assertive to find out what policies apply in a specific situation. When you learn the policy, find out its purpose as well. The purpose will help you make an informed judgment in how to implement the policy and how closely to follow it.
2. When you hear that a new policy is being developed that might affect you, find out what it is and how it will affect you. If it's going to help, actively support it. If it's not, suggest improvements. If it's going to strain your resources, let your immediate superior know *before* the policy becomes final. Remember that it's much easier to change a policy before it's enacted than after.
3. Explain policies and policy changes to subordinates whom they affect. That means explaining the reasons for the policy as well as how it is to be executed.
4. Policies are guidelines intended to reduce uncertainty and increase consistency. If a policy instead increases uncertainty and/or inconsistency, get it clarified. People who set policy need feedback on its effects from those who must implement it.
5. When you get the opportunity to create your own policies, remember that no policy is effective unless it is carried out. To carry out policy, subordinates need to understand it and have sufficient resources. Make sure they do.

SUMMARY

A policy is a guideline established by an organization to influence the decisions and actions of its members. Policies serve to coordinate decisions and actions with overall strategy and other policies. They also help make managerial and supervisory decisions consistent with each other, although often at the cost of reducing managerial flexibility.

Policy can be thought of as part of the organization's control systems. Actions and decisions are compared with relevant policies. If they are inconsistent with policy, corrective action is taken either to make them consistent or to remedy the effects of the violation. Special problems arise, however, in using policies as controls. Because policies are often set at the top of the organization and carried out at the bottom, communicating policy directives in a clear, timely, and effective manner is usually difficult.

Overall organizational policy is the responsibility of the chief executive officer. Experience shows that when the CEO fails to set or communicate policy, the rest of the organization flounders. However, no organization can rely solely on the CEO for all policy decisions. It is up to the rest of the organization to contribute to the policy-making process, to provide feedback about its feasibility and effectiveness, and ultimately to implement policy. To successfully implement policy, managers need to be aware that it exists, understand and accept it, and have sufficient resources to carry it out. It is often up to the managers themselves to acquire these necessities.

To carry out their roles effectively, managers should understand their organization's policy-making processes. Typically, the process begins with an appraisal of the organization's strengths and weaknesses *vis-a-vis* perceived threats or opportunities in the environment. This phase provides managers with an opportunity to make inputs about their own resource needs. The second phase is selection, in which one policy is selected from a set of alternatives.

In the implementation phase, the policy is communicated throughout the organization, and resources are allocated to implement it. This is the last opportunity managers have to make their resource requirements known. By the time policy moves to the evaluation and control phase, commitment is usually so strong at the top of the organization that middle managers have little influence on the process.

QUESTIONS FOR REVIEW AND DISCUSSION

1. What is the role of policies within organizations? How can policy be seen as part of the control function?
2. What factors cause managers to 'satisfice' rather than 'optimize' in policy choosing?
3. What determines the degree of success a policy will have in implementation? How can the probability of success be increased?
4. How can the level of interest rates affect financial policies in terms of the acquisition and management of funds?
5. How has the development of production policies changed within organizations in the past years?
6. How and why have organizations changed their policies towards research and development?
7. Discuss the advantages and disadvantages of having lower-level managers involved in overall policy decisions.
8. What are the disadvantages of having the CEO be the sole architect of policy? Are there any advantages? If so, what are they?

REFERENCES AND NOTES

1. F. Herzberg, *Work and the Nature of Man* (New York: World Publishing Co., 1966).
2. This definition is consistent with that offered by G. A. Steiner and J. B. Miner, *Management Policy and Strategy* (New York: MacMillan Publishing Co., Inc., 1977), Chapter 2.
3. "The Long Road Back for Burroughs," *Business Week*, May 18, 1981, pp. 119–20.
4. C. R. Christensen, K. R. Andrews and J. L. Bauer, *Business Policy: Text and Cases*, 3rd ed. (Homewood, Ill: Richard D. Irwin, 1973), p. 29.
5. P. F. Drucker, *Management: Tasks, Responsibilities, Practices* (New York: Harper & Row, 1974), pp. 611 ff.
6. D. Zand, "Reviewing the Policy Process," *California Management Review*, Fall 1978, pp. 35–46.

7. "What Edgar Bronfman Wants at Seagram," *Business Week*, April 27, 1981, p. 136.
8. D. Machalaba, "New Editor Shifts Newsweek's Emphasis and Stirs Up Staff, Trying to Gain on Time," *Wall Street Journal*, February 17, 1983, p. 29.
9. N. Gross, S. Giaquinta, and M. Bernstein, *Implementing Organizational Innovations*, (New York: Basic Books, 1971).
10. J. Stevens, J. Beyer, and H. Trice, "Managerial Receptivity and Implementation of Policies," *Journal of Management*, Vol. 6, No. 1, 1980, pp. 33–54.
11. *Ibid.*, "Managerial Receptivity;" p. 51.
12. B. Staw and J. Ross, "Commitment to a Policy Division: A Multitheoretical Perspective," *Administrative Science Quarterly*, March 1978, Vol. 23, pp. 40–64.
13. "Hughes Tool: Once Unleashed, It Grows Into a Very Profitable Giant," *Business Week*, October 13, 1980, pp. 106–11.
14. "Sun Care Product War Heats Up." *Marketing Communications*, July, 1980, pp. 21–25, 83.
15. "What is Fueling Chrysler's Comeback?" *Business Week*, June 1, 1981, p. 40.
16. "The New Industrial Relations," *Business Week*, May 11, 1981, pp. 84–98 (quote from p. 89).
17. G. Starling, *The Changing Environment of Business* (Belmont, Calif.: Wadsworth Publishing Co., 1980), p. 428.
18. "A Fine Tuning for a Big Screen TV," *Business Week*, June 8, 1981, p. 94.
19. D. G. Marquis, "The Anatomy of Successful Innovations," in *Managing Advancing Technology*, 2 vols. (New York: American Management Association, 1972), vol. 1, Chapter 3.
20. R. L. Mathis and J. H. Jackson, *Personnel: Contemporary Perspectives and Applications*, 2nd ed. (St. Paul: West Public Co., 1979), pp. 309–10.

SUGGESTED READINGS

Hofer, C. W. and Schendel, D. *Strategy Formulation: Analytical Concepts* (St. Paul: West Publishing Co., 1978). The focus is on how strategies *should be* formulated rather than how they *are* formulated. The concept of strategy is defined and descriptions of various analytical concepts, models, and techniques useful for the formulation of strategy are presented.

Lindblom, C. E. "The Science of Muddling Through," *Public Administration Review*, Spring 1959, pp. 79–88. The article analyzes the decision-making processes of public administrators. It contrasts the processes with more scientific or rational approaches.

Tushman, M. L. and Moore, W. C. *Readings in the Management of Innovation* (Boston: Pitman Publishing Co., 1982). Section III, "Setting Strategy and Direction for Innovation," consists of six diverse articles on forecasting, policy, and strategy for technological innovation.

Zand, D. "Reviewing the Policy Process," *California Management Review*, Fall 1978, pp. 35–46. The author presents three models of the policy process. The third, a problem-solving model, can be used by the manager or planner to analyze his or her organization's policy process.

Case Chiefland Memorial Hospital

Mr. James A. Grover, retired land developer and financier, is the current president of Chiefland Memorial Hospital Board of Trustees. Chiefland Memorial is a 200-bed voluntary short-term general hospital serving an area of approximately 50,000 persons. Mr. Grover has just begun a meeting with the administrator of the hospital, Mr. Edward M. Hoffman. The purpose of the meeting is to seek an acceptable solution to an apparent conflict-of-authority problem within the hospital between Hoffman and the Chief of Surgery, Dr. Lacy Young.

The problem was brought to Mr. Grover's attention by Dr. Young during a golf match between the two men. Dr. Young had challenged Mr. Grover to the golf match at the Chiefland Golf and Country Club, but it turned out that this was only an excuse for Dr. Young to discuss a hospital problem with Mr. Grover.

The problem that concerned Dr. Young involved the operating-room supervisor, Geraldine Werther, R.N. Ms. Werther schedules the hospital's operating suite in accordance with policies that she "believes" to have been established by the hospital's administration. One source of irritation to the surgeons is her attitude that maximum utilization must be made of the hospital's operating rooms if hospital costs are to be reduced. She therefore schedules in such a way that operating-room idle time is minimized. Surgeons complain that the operative schedule often does not permit them sufficient time to complete a surgical procedure in the manner they think desirable. More often than not, insufficient time is allowed between operations for effective preparation of the operating room for the next procedure. Such scheduling, the surgical staff maintains, contributes to low-quality patient care. Furthermore, some of the surgeons have complained that Ms. Werther shows favoritism in her scheduling, allowing some doctors more use of the operating suite than others.

The situation reached a crisis when Dr. Young, following an explosive confrontation with Ms. Werther, told her he was firing her. Ms. Werther then made an appeal to the hospital administrator, who in turn informed Dr. Young that discharge of nurses was an administrative prerogative. In effect, Dr. Young was told he did not have authority to fire Ms. Werther. Dr. Young asserted that he did have authority over any issue affecting medical practice and good patient care in Chiefland Hospital. He considered this a medical problem and threatened to take the matter to the hospital's board of trustees.

As the meeting between Mr. Grover and Mr. Hoffman began, Mr. Hoffman explained his position on the problem. He stressed the point that a hospital administrator is legally responsible for patient care in the hospital. He also contended that quality patient-care cannot be achieved unless the board of trustees authorizes the administrator to make decisions, develop programs, formulate policies, and implement procedures. While listening to Mr. Hoffman, Mr. Grover recalled the position belligerently taken by Dr. Young, who had contended that surgical and medical doctors holding staff privileges at Chiefland would never allow a "layman" to make decisions impinging on medical practice. Young also had said that Hoffman should be told to restrict his activities to fund-raising, financing, maintenance, housekeeping—administrative problems rather than medical problems. Dr. Young had then requested *that Mr. Grover clarify in a definitive manner the lines of authority at Chiefland Memorial.*

As Mr. Grover ended his meeting with Mr. Hoffman, the severity of the problem was unmistakably clear to him, but the solution remained quite unclear. Grover knew a decision was required—and soon.

CASE QUESTIONS

1. What policy or policies are the issue in this case?
2. What policy would Dr. Young like to have in effect?
3. What policy would Mr. Hoffman like to have in effect?
4. Who is responsible for setting and enforcing policy at this level?
5. What were the likely causes of this conflict over authority?

16 / Budgets

The tall, young woman strode briskly through the door marked Barrett & Grinne, CPA. "I'm Leigh Phillips. I'm here to see Marianne Barrett, please."

"Oh, yes, Ms. Phillips, Ms. Barrett asked me to give you this and to tell you she'll be available in a few minutes, if you have questions," the receptionist smiled brightly. "We have an empty office if you'd like some privacy."

"Thanks, but this will be fine," responded Leigh, taking a chair in the waiting room and opening the file marked Readily Available Books, Inc.—Financial Statements. Her eyes went immediately to the bottom line in the profit-and-loss statement. There it was, in black (not red, thank goodness) and white: net profit after taxes—$8350.

Leigh sat back in her chair, pleased and excited. She'd done it, actually turned a profit in her second year of operation! All those months of work and worry seemed well worth it now. She was going to make it!

Only two and a half years ago Leigh had left a good job to start her own business, financed by a generous inheritance from her grandparents' estate. Her parents had argued that she should invest the money and keep her job, but she'd always wanted to run her own business, and she was too impatient to wait. When the small bookstore she had frequented for years went out of business, she moved in, convinced that proper management could make it a very profitable enterprise.

Initially, Leigh had done everything herself, except remodeling, which she supervised. She ordered the books, kept inventory, arranged displays, and made sales. She opened the store every morning at ten o'clock and didn't leave until ten o'clock at night. She saw, heard, and experienced everything that went on in the store, ordered books when supply was low and money available, rearranged displays when time permitted, offered discounts on old stock when things were slow. She made her decisions and exercised control based on observation. She kept her own financial records and, at the end of the year when she added up her gross revenues, deducted the costs of goods sold, adjusted her inventory, and applied her gross profit against her overhead of rent, utilities, and her own salary, she found that she had lost $6000. She had been somewhat disappointed, but it hadn't been a total disaster; she had determined to break even her second year.

Her business improved with experience, as did her operating efficiency. She hired an assistant. Volume began to increase. She determined the rate of improvement by using the previous year's records as a control standard. Her revenues in June were thirty percent better than those of the previous June. Inventory was higher, but so was its turnover. Each month she compared the gross margin per dollar-of-sales to that of the previous year and the previous month. Historical records enabled her to define more precisely the relationships among inputs and outputs. They provided clues which helped her make decisions about future actions and changes, resulting in a net profit.

And now, Leigh thought the bookstore had become successful enough for her to expand facilities and personnel. She wanted to set some goals, but she also wanted to know if those goals were realistic, and if she could afford them. That was why she had hired a CPA to prepare her financial statement—to improve her financial analysis and planning for the future.

At that point the door opened, and Marianne Barrett walked out of her office, said goodbye to her previous client, and ushered Leigh inside.

"Congratulations, Leigh, you had a good year. Any questions?" Marianne asked as they took their seats.

"Not about these figures, but about future ones. Frankly, I'm ambitious. I've got some goals and plans for expansion, and I want your advice. I may need to borrow some money, and I don't want to

get in over my head. What do I do first?"

"In a word," replied her CPA, "budget. First of all, let's start with revenues. I want you to set a realistic sales figure for next year, based on your expansion plans. From that figure we'll devise monthly sales figures, costs of goods sold, and average inventory levels. We'll use those figures to determine expected cash flow, after we consider inflation, salaries, and other overhead. This will give us the data we need to figure out roughly how much capital you'll need to finance your plans. If that looks realistic, then you can take it to the bank, or whomever you're looking to for a loan. If not, we'll make adjustments until it looks right."

Leigh Phillip's experience as owner-manager of Readily Available Books, Inc. shows the evolutionary aspects of the budgeting process in new organizations. Managers, like Leigh, usually begin with a rough idea of the financial resources they'll need for the first year or two. Initially, most of their decisions about finances are based on observation: Is inventory too low? Is there enough money to buy another machine? Can we meet the payroll? After a year or so, they begin to use historical records as they accumulate; their experiences permit them to anticipate cash flow, seasonal variations in demand, and other forces that affect finances. Eventually, they turn to budgeting, an important managerial tool for both planning and control.

A **budget** is *a formal statement of the financial resources to be used for an organization's planned activities for a given period of time.* Among the items included in the bookstore manager's budget for the coming year, we might find:

Sales (net of returns)			$200,000
Cost of Goods Sold:			
Purchases	$105,000		
Less: Ending Inventory	15,000		
Plus: Beginning Inventory	10,000	$100,000	
Wages and Salaries		40,000	140,000
Gross Profit			$60,000
Overhead: Rent	$24,000		
Utilities	6,000		
Taxes	5,000		35,000
Net Profit before Taxes			$ 25,000

The above figures represent a ***fixed budget,*** which is a *budget based on one level of activity*—in this case, $200,000 in net sales. (Later in this chapter we will discuss flexible budgets and other more sophisticated forms of budgeting.) A budget can be used both for planning and control. It translates plans into financial terms and provides a standard against which performance can be measured.

THE FUNCTIONS OF BUDGETS

Budgets are guidelines. Managers learn to live within them and to use them to plan, organize, and control, but budgets have costs. *Resources, plans, and programs that are cut back to meet a budget* are ***opportunity costs.*** *The time, information, and resources used to derive budgets* are the ***direct costs of budgeting.*** Managers and administrators in some organizations spend weeks or months on the budget process. Organizations are willing to endure these costs because they believe that budgets serve functions that more than offset their costs.

Planning

Chapter 3 argued that planning enables managers to have the resources necessary to carry out their missions at the appropriate time. Planning means more than setting objectives and determining what needs to be done to meet those objectives. Planning also means identifying the resources required and insuring that they are available at the proper time.

Whatever those resources are, they will have a cost. Personnel, machinery, information, equipment, expertise, and buildings all require financial expenditures. Therefore, in order to insure that these resources will be available to carry out plans, a manager needs to be sure of one particular resource: sufficient financial support to acquire them, which financial policies, like those described in Chapter 15, are designed to do. Establishing a budget tells managers how much the activities they planned for will cost. It indicates whether their plans are feasible. For example, suppose a public television station's planned activities for the year are budgeted at $500,000 based on the manager's estimates of support as follows:

Initial Funding Budget

State government	$160,000
University funding	150,000
Corporation for Public Broadcasting	110,000
Private donations	80,000
	$500,000

Because the budget does not exceed expected funding, the budget is financially realistic.

Subsequently, however, the federal government, which funds the Corporation for Public Broadcasting, revises its budget figures. In an effort to reduce taxes, the administration reduces the budgets of many of its programs and agencies, including the Corporation for Public Broadcasting (CPB). CPB notifies the station that it will be forced to reduce its funding from $110,000 to $50,000. Now the station budget exceeds expected funding by $60,000. The station manager quickly discovers that no additional funding from the state or university is possible; these institutions are experiencing their own financial problems. The most optimistic estimate for increases in private donations is 15 percent to $92,000. This leaves the budget $48,000 over expected revenues.

Revised Funding Budget

State government	$160,000
University funding	150,000
CPB	50,000
Private donations	92,000
	$452,000

Unless other funds can be found, the station will have to revise its plans in ways that will allow it to live within its budget. Programs and/or staffing will most likely have to be cut. The budget allows the manager to prepare for that likelihood.

Organizing

Budgets are a concrete means of communicating and coordinating plans and activities, key elements in organizing work, as discussed in Chapter 4. Top management usually initiates the process. It sends to lower-level managers a set of figures, objectives, and assumptions about the upcoming budget year. Lower-level managers then prepare their own preliminary budgets, based on top management's figures and their own plans. They can coordinate their plans with the master budget.

Lower managers turn back their preliminary budgets to their superiors. This step allows the communication of their plans for the budget period to those who must do the coordination. Managers often must negotiate with their superiors before their budgets are approved. Eventually, all budgets throughout the organization have been communicated, negotiated, and coordinated. The process reduces duplication of effort (for example, two departments trying to purchase the same expensive piece of equipment that both can easily share). It also coordinates use of resources. A unit manager can arrange the spending of his or her subunits to meet

A budget is a formal statement of financial resources allocated for planned activities.

the predicted cash flow of his or her department, as the manager of the public television station did. In this way, the manager can avoid running short of funds sometime during the fiscal year.

Controlling

Budgeting is an observable management function; managers are evaluated on the way they carry out their budgeting activities. Do they submit timely, realistic budgets which are consistent with overall objectives and higher-level budgets? Do they stay within their budgets, or do they routinely exceed them, having to ask for revisions? In times of high interest-rates, a manager's ability to stay within his or her budget is greatly valued, because it keeps costs down. Organizations exceeding their budgets usually have to look for additional funds, and the cost of those additional funds will be substantial.

Although budgets are typically established for a one-year period, they may be broken down into quarterly or monthly figures for control purposes. In this way actual performance can be compared against budgeted performance more frequently, and corrective action taken more quickly. For example, the public television station stages four fund-raising drives each year to acquire private donations. The budget for the following year calls for $92,000 in private donations, about $23,000 per quarter. If the first two-months' donations are only $12,000, something must be done quickly to increase revenues or reduce expenditures. Management may decide to stage an additional fund-raising drive or they may decide to cut back on programming as a means of reducing expenses. The early warning provided by the budgetary process makes a flexible response possible. Uncertainty is reduced, making corrective action easier.

THE BUDGETING CYCLE

Translating the organization's plans and activities into financial figures provides a basis for beginning the budgeting process. Almost all organizations begin with some estimate of their financial receipts for the year, just as Leigh's CPA instructed her to do.

Estimating Revenues

For a business firm the budgeting process begins with the sales forecast. For example, Avco CEO Ray B. Mundt forecast sales revenues of $130 million in fiscal 1984 for its paper-products division. His 1984 forecast was 80 percent higher than 1983 sales figures; much of the increase was forecasted to come from seven office-products distributors Avco had just acquired.[1] Avco then used that $130 million forecast to project the level of activities needed to support it and the financial resources available, some of which undoubtedly budgeted for new acquisitions.

Nonbusiness organizations, likewise, try to estimate the funds they will receive. A county hospital will estimate the funds it will receive from patient fees, private donations, county, state, and federal governments, and concessions such as parking and cafeterias. A local, state, or federal government will estimate total receipts from the various taxes it levies, fines it collects, and sales or transfer payments from other government agencies. A women's health center estimated its yearly funding as follows:

Patient fees	$350,000
United Fund	50,000
Private donations	75,000
	$475,000

The total estimated receipts were then used by the center to establish its budgets for programs, operations, personnel, and fund-raising activities.

For most of these organizations, forecasts of funds received are objectives as well as estimates. Top management, often, but not always, in consultation with lower-level managers, establishes objectives for those segments of the revenue budget over which it has some control. In a relatively stable business, top management will use previous years' sales figures (historical records) to start. Projections of economic conditions, estimates of competition, and their own planned innovations in products or marketing will be used to set what they hope are realistic but challenging objectives.

Individual Unit Budgets

A small business like Readily Available Books will prepare only one budget. In larger operations, once top management has initiated the process, each individual unit, including every division, department, center, and program, prepares its own preliminary budget. Typically, a unit will start with last year's budget and actual performance figures. The unit will make adjustments for changes in planned activities and financial considerations such as interest rates and inflation. The objectives and estimated receipts established by top management may affect the unit's budget setting as well.

> *Organizations are willing to endure the costs of budgeting, because they believe that budgets serve functions that more than offset their costs.*

Large organizations may employ staff personnel as specialists to assist line managers in setting their budgets. These specialists understand the assumptions on which management's figures are based, and how they should affect the unit's budget. For example, an automobile dealership may set a ten percent sales revenue increase as its goal for the next budget year. The service department needs to know how much of that increase is supposed to come from the number of cars sold, and how much from inflation. A budget specialist can point out that if the increase is due solely to inflation, the service department can figure that it will repair about the same number of cars as last year, and base its budget on that level of activity. If, on the other hand, the dealership plans to increase the units sold in order to hold prices down, the service department will have more cars to work on. This increased level of activity will be an important factor to consider in preparing the department's new budget.

Let's assume that last year's key figures for the service department are those in Exhibit 16.1.

For the next year, the service department manager starts with a budgeted new-car sales figure of 1100 cars—a 10-percent increase. The dealership management advises the department head they're assuming an 8-percent inflation rate. With this information and last year's figures, the service manager starts to prepare next year's budget.

First, the manager estimates that the department will service 4100 cars, about 5 percent more than last year. That figure, together with the 1100 new cars, is a volume that can be handled with 10 full-time employees. The local demand for good mechanics means that the workers should get raises in order to keep them. Therefore, the manager figures the labor costs at $215,000 for 10 employees, about 7 percent higher than was budgeted for 10 employees last year. Parts will be higher than last year, due to greater volume and higher prices. The estimated parts-costs are $110,000. The purchase of some new painting equipment would enable the department to eliminate much of the subcontracting. A capital expenditure of $20,000 for that equipment will save $10,000 per year in subcontracting. Finally, utility rate increases will result in a 5-percent increase in overhead, to $65,000. The service manager submits a preliminary budget reflecting these figures (Exhibit 16.2). The preliminary budget calls for a 7-percent increase in cars serviced and a 16-percent increase in expenditures.

Reviewing Preliminary Budgets

After each unit has prepared its own budget, it sends that budget either to higher-level management or, in large organizations, to the budgeting department for review. The budget department's function is to analyze each budget in detail. It determines whether budgeted figures are realistic. It looks for errors in logic, omitted items, or faulty mathematics. Errors or unrealistic items are specified and discussed with the originating department. Eventually, each unit's budget is sent to top management with the budget department's recommendations for approval or adjustment.

If the total of the budgets exceeds the overall budget, as is usually the case, then top management must decide how to allocate its finances among the various units. The criteria range from strictly financial (which allocations will yield the greatest expected return), to strictly political (which allocations will yield the greatest support for top management), and may include considerations of equity (which units deserve to have their turns at special projects or programs). At this stage of the budgetary process, unit managers are often asked to justify their budgets in front of top management or its representatives. For many managers, the success of their arguments will affect the scope of their operations for an entire year or longer. Suppose the service department's request for $20,000 for additional equipment is questioned. If the service manager can convince top management to fund this capital expense (an endeavor requiring influence and communication skills as well as financial data), subcontracting can be virtually eliminated. This gives the manager greater control over the quality and speed of service. It also paves the way for future capital expenditure requests, if this one proves worthwhile.

Exhibit 16.1   Westshore Auto Service Department

	Budgeted	Actual
New Cars Serviced	1000	940
Other Cars Serviced	4000	3910
Average Number of Employees	10	9
Labor Costs	$200,000	$186,000
Parts Cost	100,000	92,300
Subcontracting	20,000	20,800
Overhead (Insurance, Utilities, Rent, Taxes)	60,000	62,000
TOTAL	$380,000	$361,100

Exhibit 16.2   Westshore Auto Service Department Preliminary Budget

	Last Year Actual	This Year Budget
New Cars Serviced	940	1100
Other Cars Serviced	3910	4100
Average Number of Employees	9	10
Labor Costs	$186,000	$215,000
Parts Cost	92,300	110,000
Capital Expense	—	20,000
Subcontracting	20,800	10,000
Overhead	62,000	65,000
TOTAL	$361,100	$420,000

Evaluating Performance Against Budget

As the budget period begins, revenues are taken in, money is spent, and plans are enacted. Each week, month, or quarter provides management with actual figures to compare against budgeted figures. Annual budgets have been broken down into detailed weekly or monthly figures. These data enable management to evaluate performance, the progress of plans, and to determine whether and what kinds of corrective action should be taken.

The combined figures for the first three months for Westshore's service department are shown in Exhibit 16.3. These figures enable Westshore management to evaluate how well the service department is performing with respect to its budget and to decide what, if any, corrective action should be taken.

At first glance, performance doesn't look so good. The service department has spent $12,000, or about 10 percent more than its budget for the first three months. However, the department has serviced 130 cars more than budgeted, so the average-cost per car serviced ($70.37) is only slightly higher than budgeted ($68.03). Most of the increase can be attributed to higher labor costs. The service manager failed to hire a new mechanic, and so has had to pay a lot of overtime to the nine current mechanics and use more subcontracting to keep up with the additional volume.

Since management of the dealership anticipates that the increased volume will persist for several more months, the service manager is directed to hire a new mechanic immediately to improve service and cut down on overhead. If the dealership had, instead, anticipated a downturn in business, it is possible that it would have taken no corrective action. In this way we can see how detailed budgets provide flexibility to the control process.

Budget Revision

As we have seen, a budget is a financial statement projected into the future. It is typically based on historical records, and its final form depends upon plans, forecasts, and assumptions about the future.

Exhibit 16.3   Quarterly Budget Report Westshore Auto Service Department

	Budget	Actual	Variance
New Cars Serviced	320	400	+80
Other Cars Serviced	900	950	+50
Average Number of Employees	10	9	−1
Labor Costs	$55,000	$ 62,000	$ +7,000
Parts Cost	25,000	28,000	+3,000
Capital Expense	—	—	—
Subcontracting	3,000	5,000	+2,000
Overhead	16,000	16,000	—
TOTAL	$99,000	$111,000	$+12,000

If the future turns out to be different from the predictions (and it usually does), managers must adjust. If sales of one product fail to meet expectations, sales in other areas must be increased; if utility costs rise faster than expected, cuts must be made in other expenses. Living within a budget means adapting to changes in order to meet the overall budget.

However, some unforeseen changes may make it practically impossible for a manager to meet his or her budget. Disasters such as fires, floods or explosions, or unexpected shortages of raw materials may wreak havoc with budgets. Boycotts, wars, strikes, or abrupt changes in policy by top management may directly or indirectly make budgets impossible to live with. In such cases the affected managers can appeal to the budget committee or to top management for revisions. These changes are generally not granted easily; if they were, managers would have less incentive to anticipate and plan for the future.

The 1981 Major League Baseball players' strike is a good example of an anticipated disruption. The owners and managers of the twenty-six teams had two budgets, one based on playing a full season, the second based on a strike. Anticipating the probability of a strike, the owners took out an insurance policy that would pay each club $100,000 per day, enough to meet its expenses under the strike budget. The strike budget did not have to account for such major expenses as player salaries and travel, but did have to cover salaries of managers and coaches, office expenses, and upkeep of the parks. Anticipating the disruption and preparing a second budget enabled the owners to remain solvent despite huge losses in revenue incurred by the strike.

Exhibit 16.4 presents an overview of the budgeting process used by most organizations which may be governed by organizational policy. Top management, usually, but not always, consulting with lower level managers, sets objectives and estimates revenues. It then forwards these figures, together with assumptions and deadlines for budgets, to unit managers. Each unit manager prepares his or her budget, based on past-performance records and top management's data, then sends it back through the organizational hierarchy. These budgets are reviewed by superiors and/or the organization's budget committee or department, then sent to top management with recommendations for approval or revision. After final approval, budgets are enacted and used as means of evaluation and control. Occasionally, budgets may be revised if unforeseen problems make them impractical.

Exhibit 16.4   Major Steps in the Budgeting Process

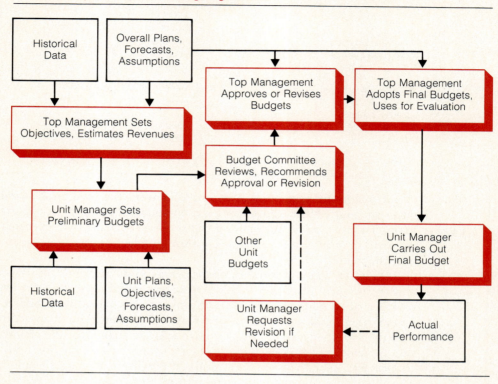

RESPONSIBILITY CENTERS

As explained above, each unit is responsible for preparing its own preliminary budget. How does an organization identify, for budgeting purposes, an organizational unit? What kinds of things should an organizational unit be responsible for budgeting?

Responsibility accounting is *a process that makes managers more responsible for those budget activities over which they have some control.*[2] It identifies and traces budget activities to the individual manager who is primarily responsible for making decisions about them. Thus, marketing departments are responsible for sales revenues and certain costs directly associated with sales (advertising, delivery, bad debts), but are not directly responsible for profits, since the marketing manager does not have primary responsibility for production and inventory costs. Likewise, a production department is not responsible for sales revenues or profits, but for costs which are primarily under the influence of the production manager. Although marketing and production need to coordinate many of their activities, their cost responsibilities are their own.

The intent of responsibility centers is to exercise control where it should be exercised and yet allow managers the freedom to make decisions that they should make. For example, marketing managers can make decisions affecting sales revenues and costs without worrying unduly about effects on production budgets, which are assessed at a higher level in the organization. There are several types of responsibility centers in budgeting. The most common are investment centers, profit centers, revenue centers, and expense centers.

Investment Centers

An **investment center,** *a large unit in which the parent organization has invested a great deal of capital,* has considerable control over its objectives, revenues, costs, and the use of the investment. It is responsible to the parent organization for earning a certain return on that investment, calculated as: revenue less expenses divided by investment in assets. Thus, an investment center that had income of $5 million and expenses of $3 million on assets of $10 million would have return-on-investment (ROI) of 20 percent.

Industrial conglomerates, such as Litton Industries and Avco, are often organized as a group of investment centers, such as foreign investments, high technology products, entertainment, and financial. Each investment group is given a capital budget and a target ROI for control and evaluation.

Profit Centers

A **profit center** is *a unit which has little control over how it invests its capital, but great control over resources and costs.* It generally does not have the investment flexibility which an investment center have. For example, it generally cannot buy or sell other firms. For the parent organization, the profit center's job is to produce the greatest profits possible year-in and year-out while maintaining the value of its assets.

Profit centers are commonly found in large decentralized business organizations. Retail chains like Sears, for example, may treat each store as a profit center. The store's budget objective is to maximize profits. General Motors is based on a profit-center concept. Each of the major divisions—Chevrolet, Buick-Oldsmobile-Pontiac, Cadillac, and GM Truck—is a profit center trying to maximize revenues and minimize costs.

Revenue Centers

A **revenue center** is *an organizational unit that has very little control over costs while being largely responsible for marketing outputs.* Its utility to an organization lies in its effectiveness in generating revenues and increasing turnover of the goods or services produced by the organization.

The sales and marketing departments of business firms are often designated as revenue centers. Sales budgets are generated for each center, both in the amounts of various products or services to be sold and in total dollar volume. These centers, in turn, establish sales budgets for each subunit and individual salesperson.

For example, an insurance agency may have three revenue centers—life insurance, casualty insurance, and estate insurance. Each of these groups has a sales budget, and each insurance agent has his or her own sales goal for the year. Insurance agencies and other firms, where the costs of selling are a relatively low percentage of sales price and/or gross-profit margins are high, are likely users of the revenue-center concept in budgeting. However, as the costs of personal selling increase, due to increased travel costs and sales salaries, many firms are preparing expense budgets for their revenue centers as well.

Expense Centers

Some organizational units are necessary but value of their outputs is extremely hard to calculate. Their managers control expenses, but control over outputs is vague, imprecise, or infrequent. Examples of such units would be administrative centers (that is, home or regional offices), service units (housekeeping, legal), and research and development. They are often designated as expense centers.

Budgets are a concrete means of communicating and coordinating plans and activities, key elements in organizing work.

An **expense center** is *a unit where the budget is based on estimates of what it will cost to provide a given level of service or activity.* Some of these costs are *engineered* costs, which can be predetermined. These include reliably estimated costs like direct labor (janitors, clerks, research assistants) and materials (brooms, typing paper, calculators). Other costs are *discretionary;* they cannot be calculated reliably before the budget period begins, but are incurred at the unit manager's discretion. For example, the President of the United States is allocated a certain amount of discretionary funds each year in the budget which he can use for certain projects. An R & D manager will have a discretionary budget to use to exploit a promising line of research which may develop during the year.

These four types of responsibility centers—investment, profit, revenue, and expense—are all in wide use. Whether an organization designates a unit as an investment or a profit center depends on its particular circumstances and the philosophy of its top management. The tendency, however, seems to be toward making managers who were once responsible for only revenues or expenses accountable for both, and for converting profit centers into investment centers. The high costs of capital have increased the extent to which managers are being held accountable for its use.

Management in Action
Using Sales Forecasts to Initiate the Budget Process

Few people expected Continental Airlines to have a future to budget for in 1984. A 1982 merger with Texas International Airlines in an attempt to compete with airline-industry giants proved disastrous; Continental filed for bankruptcy in September of 1983. But negotiations with creditors and unions allowed Continental to try again—at a more modest level. The airline changed its strategy to concentrate on fewer markets, principally to and from Houston or Denver, offering frequent flights at unrestricted low fares.

The new strategy helped Continental fill 65 percent of its seats in early 1984, 10 points higher than its rivals. By March 1 the airline was operating at 75 percent of its prebankruptcy capacity. Executives expected to be operating at 95 percent of that capacity by July 1. Based on that figure, the company forecast 1984 sales revenues at $1 billion, compared to $1.1 billion in 1983. But Continental's new strategy made it possible for the airline to break even at only 60 to 65 percent of capacity. Its chairman, Frank Lorenzo, forecast pretax earnings of $30 million for 1984, compared to a loss of $218 million in 1983.

The favorable earnings forecast enabled Continental to include in its budget two very important items. First was the payment on forty percent of its debt, keeping its creditors happy and increasing their inclination to continue backing the company's financial needs. The second was raises for most employees, keeping them satisfied enough to continue with the airline rather than leaving in search of better pay.

Continental's 1984 budget reflected its austere financial practices made necessary by its 1983 failure. In order to meet its goals of flying more passengers than any other airline in the markets it serves, the company had to continue its policy of unrestricted low fares. Low fares, in turn, required low costs. After being empowered to do so by the terms of the bankruptcy filing, Lorenzo unilaterally eliminated inefficient work rules and drastically cut overhead and labor rates. His 1984 payroll was budgeted to carry only 9000 employees in 1984, compared to 12,000 in 1983. This reduction in personnel enabled Continental to budget labor costs for 1984 at only 20 percent of operating costs, down from 35 percent in 1983. Costs per available-seat mile were projected at $6.5 for the summer of 1984, 30 percent lower than its competitors' forecasted costs.

Despite the modest new strategies, the airline's ability to meet its budget depended on certain factors beyond its control. If its competitors could reduce their costs to meet Continental's, its projected revenues would suffer. Philip J. Bakes, the company's executive vice-president, admitted that its cost advantage would not last indefinitely.

Source: "The Trying Times for Continental Aren't Over Yet," *Business Week*, March 19, 1984, pp. 44–46.

Exhibit 16.5   A Variable Budget for Westshore Auto Service Department

	Budget A	Budget B	Budget C
New Cars Serviced	1000	1100	1210
Other Cars Serviced	3700	4100	4510
Average Number of Employees	9	10	11
Labor Costs	$193,500	$215,000	$236,500
Parts Costs	99,000	110,000	121,000
Capital Expense	20,000	20,000	20,000
Subcontracting	10,000	10,000	10,500
Overhead	65,000	65,000	65,000
TOTAL	$387,500	$420,000	$453,000

TYPES OF BUDGETS

Regardless of the type of responsibility centers they manage, managers will use and be responsible for a number of budgetary controls. We will describe several types of budgetary and financial controls commonly encountered today.[3]

Fixed vs. Variable Budgets

A *fixed budget* is *one that assumes that a given level of activity will occur, generating a predictable amount of revenues and/or costs.* Fixed budgets are generally used by organizations when they first evolve from budgeting based on historical records to budgetary control and planning.

Fixed budgets are relatively simple to devise. Unfortunately, they are often off-target, because predictions and assumptions are too high or low. They then must be revised, sometimes hastily, to reflect the new unanticipated levels of activity. Such revisions are troublesome, time-consuming, and often not well-thought out.

Variable or flexible budgets are an alternative to fixed budgets. They are a more sophisticated form of budget which evolved because of the problems resulting from irrevocable forecasts. A *variable budget* is *one that sets out a different set of budget figures for each of a number of different levels of activity.* For example, the service manager at Westshore Auto may prepare three different budgets (see Exhibit 16.5) reflecting the best cost estimates associated with three possible levels of business. Some of the items in this budget are *variable costs,* costs that vary directly with the level of activity being performed, such as raw materials and direct labor. In Exhibit 16.5, labor costs and parts costs are variable costs.

Fixed costs do not vary with the level of activity. For a given budget period these costs can be expected to remain the same whatever the actual activity level. Rent, insurance, utilities, telephone, licenses, and certain taxes are common examples of fixed costs. In Exhibit 16.5 overhead costs for the service department are fixed at $65,000.

Semivariable costs remain the same through certain levels of activity, but eventually increase when the level of activity gets high enough. Managerial and administrative costs are often semivariable. For example, Westshore Auto could probably get along with one service manager until the volume of cars serviced reached 7000, at which point the service manager would need an assistant. In Exhibit 16.5, subcontracting is a semifixed cost.

Special Approaches to Budgeting

In the last several years, special approaches to budgeting have developed. The two most used approaches originated to deal with special problems involved in governmental budgets.

PPBS. The **Planning-Programming-Budgeting System** is *a five-step program designed to provide greater budgetary control over governmental programs.*[4] It is attractive to institutions which find themselves responsible for funding large numbers of diverse continuing programs, which often result in great duplication of efforts and services, but are difficult to control through normal annual budget procedures.

PPBS increases the responsibility of program managers. First, it requires them to demonstrate the contributions of their programs to the overall goals of the parent organization or agency. Second, it forces them to carry out long-range financial planning and to identify possible application of other programs' activities.

> *A budget is a financial statement projected into the future. It is typically based on historical records, and its final form depends upon plans, forecasts, and assumptions about the future.*

The first step in PPBS is to define overall organizational objectives. Each program manager demonstrates how his or her program contributes to these overall organizational objectives. Then, each program manager estimates the total cost of that program for the next several years into the future. Next, top management searches for and compares alternative ways of accomplishing stated programs. Finally, information generated in the first four steps is used in the regular budgeting process.

When PPBS works, it saves money. It reduces duplication of effort among programs and identifies programs that no longer promote overall objectives. It forces managers to look for less costly or more effective alternatives to current program activities. Finally, it exposes programs which, in the long run, might end up costing much more than anyone anticipated, such as the B-1 bomber and the Social Security programs.

Zero-Base Budgeting. Zero-base budgeting[5] is designed to attack the problem of self-perpetuating programs. In large organizations, particularly governmental agencies, once a program gets into a budget and gets funded it is difficult to eliminate. Budget planners have so much to do in evaluating new proposals and programs that those from previous budgets get approved with little or no scrutiny. This can obviously result in many programs outliving their usefulness.

In zero-base budgeting, each manager is forced to assume that his or her base budget is zero. The manager cannot assume that prior programs and activities will automatically be renewed. Instead, the manager must describe, justify, and set priorities for each separate element of the preliminary budget.

The major step for the manager is to prepare *decision packages* which encompass all the unit's planned activities for the coming budget period. Each package describes the activity, its benefits, its costs, possible alternatives, and the costs to the organization of not funding it. The manager then ranks all these activities in order of their importance. Top management, armed with this information from all unit managers, allocates resources accordingly.

POTENTIAL BUDGET PITFALLS

Most of the preceding discussion about budgets has described them in very rational terms. They are guidelines designed to improve organizational planning, coordination, communication, and control. They enable managers to avoid unpleasant surprises (like running out of cash). They help reduce redundancy and inefficiency.

One might assume that managers wholeheartedly accepted the budgeting concept and used it to increase organizational effectiveness. Experience and research has shown, however, that some managers encounter problems with budgets that their more successful colleagues avoid.

Pitfalls in Planning

Budgets force managers to plan. In order to determine what financial resources they need for the next budget period, managers must set some objectives and determine the level of activities they plan to operate for that period.

Unfortunately, some managers emphasize short-run budgets at the expense of the long run. In order to meet this year's budget, managers are tempted to do things which will cost more in the long run. They defer maintenance, which saves costs this year but results in reduced lives for machinery and equipment. They put off hiring and training workers, which may leave them short-handed in the future. They sell off assets, which must later be replaced at higher costs.

Some managers try to "beat" the budget system by overstating their needs. If their experiences have been that preliminary budgets are always cut by ten percent, they may add ten percent to their estimated costs. This tactic enables them to survive the budget cuts with all activities fully funded. Overstating expected costs (or understating expected revenues) is one way managers can make themselves look good—in the short run. Such tactics make it easy for them to meet their budgets. Unfortunately, these tactics create problems for planning because they force planners to work with erroneous data. In the long run, emphasizing short-term budgets and overstating needs reduces efficiency.

Managers must plan in order to develop a budget.

Pitfalls in Organizing and Communicating

Budgets require a great deal of communication between higher and lower level managers. Lower level managers get an opportunity to find out about overall organizational goals, assumptions, forecasts, and priorities. Top managers have opportunities to review the goals and plans of organizational units and to coordinate their activities. Both parties have opportunities to discuss, justify, and argue their various points of view in front of each other. In these ways, budgets enhance communication and coordination.

At the same time, managers may see themselves vying with one another for limited organizational resources. This is particularly true where preliminary budgets are frequently cut. They look on the budget process as "the battle for the budget" and often call it just that. They view their task as trying to wrest as much money as possible from the clutches of top management at the expense of rival department heads. The classic example of these forces at work is the annual federal budget.

Sprinkled liberally throughout the comments of legislators, agency heads, and budget planners during the federal budget process, one finds words like, *heartless cuts, outright defiance, like amputating your own leg, bullheaded, targets, we won't roll over and play dead, preemptive strike, foolish gamble, deliberate sabotage,* and *escapism budgeting.*[6] None of these phrases are inclined to increase communication or coordination.

The competitive nature of many budget processes can lead to attempts by management to keep secret the outcomes of the process. Budgets are supposed to reduce uncertainty, but secrecy increases it. As a result, many managers spend a lot of time and effort trying to find out how other units fared and how well their own units did in comparison. These covert information systems usually result in managers overestimating the success of their rivals and increasing their own dissatisfaction.[7]

Pitfalls in Controlling and Evaluation

Budgets provide top management with a relatively objective means of evaluating managerial performance—how close did a manager's unit come to meeting its budgeted activity levels, expenses, and revenues. They also act as standards for control purposes at all levels. Failure to meet budget targets is a signal for corrective action.

Managers are willing to use budgets for planning, coordination, and control, but the use of budgets as a means for evaluation may create resistance. Many managers resist evaluation, particularly if they feel they have insufficient control over performance or standards.

Another managerial tendency working against overall evaluation and control objectives is the tendency to "spend to budget."[8] Managers who find themselves in the last few weeks of a budget period with unspent allocations often go on a spending spree. They reason that failure to spend all they were allocated will cause budget-planners to cut their requests for next year. When many managers feel this way, a great deal of money can be wasted. It is not uncommon at the end of a budget year to find managers and their secretaries pouring through equipment catalogues looking for things to buy.

Avoiding Budget Pitfalls

We have shown that budgeting can be a powerful managerial tool for planning, organizing, and control. We have also seen that lower level managers may view a budget as more of a constraint than a guideline. Some of their reactions work to offset budgeting's positive effects. Many of these problems can be avoided by increasing participation in the budget process and providing incentives for budget performance.

Participation.   One of the implications to be drawn from research on budgets and their effects has to do with the participation of lower level managers in the process. Budgets which are set more or less autonomously by top management run the risk that lower-level managers will resist or fail to understand them. One study of nineteen manufacturing plants looked at some characteristics of the budget process and their effects on lower level managers. The study found that the more managers participated in the budget setting process, the more likely they were to have met their budget goals.[9]

Companies have also found that enlisting the aid of nonmanagers in budget activities can lead to greater efficiencies. B. F. Goodrich sought the help of managers and rank-and-file workers in reducing their budget for paperwork. Their target was more than 2.5 million pages of computerized reports Goodrich generated annually. As a result, paperwork was reduced by an average of 80,000 pages per month. In six months, paper costs were reduced 17 percent. Other large companies who have emphasized greater employee participation in budget problems include Holiday Inns, Grumman, and Honeywell.[10]

Incentives For Budget Performance. A manager who exceeds costs is likely to receive a negative evaluation. A manager who spends less than his or her budget may have next year's requests cut. In the study of nineteen manufacturing plants described earlier, managers who viewed the budgetary process as punitive were less likely to meet their budget goals.[11]

The American Productivity Center in Houston urges companies to reward cost-saving and coming in under budget. Some companies have responded by giving high performance appraisals to managers who spend less than budgets. Others provide monetary incentives to employees for cost-reduction activities and ideas.[12] Holiday Inns gave special T-shirts to employees in units that reduced telephone costs more than ten percent and sweatshirts or umbrellas for twenty-percent reductions. As a result, they have been able to eliminate two of their forty WATTS lines.

One advertising executive proposed returning as a bonus to employees ten percent of unused budgets. If a department spent $50,000 less than its annual budget, the employees would receive a $5000 bonus to be divided equally among them.[13] The potential for huge savings is there, if it can be tapped. In 1977, a Congressman returned to the federal government $439,000 in unspent funds from his budget. One suspects that similar savings are available in government and industry alike, given sufficient incentive.

The Bottom Line

Budgets are essential tools for successful managers at all levels. They reduce uncertainty, facilitate planning, improve communication, coordination, and control. To make the best use of budgets

1. Learn about the different types of budgets your organization uses and the reasons for them. Find out how the budgeting process works, who participates, and when it takes place.
2. Become actively involved in budgets that affect your area. Start planning your own budget and discuss it with your immediate superior just before the formal process starts.
3. Try to anticipate the long-term effects of short-term budget decisions. If you must overspend, be able to explain the long-term benefits of short-term budget overruns. If you underspend your budget, point out the efficiencies that enabled you to do so.
4. In establishing your own budget, involve key subordinates in the process. Provide incentives for good budget performance. Use the process as a tool for increasing communication and coordination.

SUMMARY

A budget is a formal statement of financial resources to be used, during a given time period, for an organization's planned activities. Budgets not only aid in planning, but force different levels of management to communicate their plans and objectives. This communication makes it easier for top management to coordinate the diverse activities under its authority. Budgets are also used as control devices, as a means for evaluating managerial performance.

Top management usually initiates the budget process. It sets goals and objectives, and estimates total revenues based on certain assumptions and forecasts. The figures are then sent to individual units, together with deadlines for the budget process. Individual-unit managers then prepare their own budgets based on top management's figures and their own goals and plans.

The preliminary budgets prepared by unit managers are generally reviewed by a budget committee, which evaluates the accuracy and feasibility of each budget and the extent to which it fits in with overall plans. The budgets may be revised, or passed on to top management for approval or revision. The final budgets are then enacted and used for evaluation and control. Revision after enactment is possible, but is usually reserved for adjustments to unforeseen occurrences such as strikes, disasters, or shortages.

To increase managerial responsibility for budget activities they control, organizations often create responsibility centers. Expense centers are responsible for holding down costs, while revenue centers are given sales or receipts targets. Profit centers are expected to increase revenues and hold down costs. Investments centers try to maximize return on investment.

Research and practice suggest that organizations encourage and support the participation of managers and nonmanagers in the budget process. Managers who do participate are more likely to understand their budgets and to meet their budget goals. Incentives for cutting costs and underspending budgets have been found to be effective means for improving budget performance in organizations.

QUESTIONS FOR REVIEW AND DISCUSSION

1. What functions do budgets perform for organizations?
2. How do organizations without budgets achieve these functions?
3. What role does top management play in the budget process?
4. What roles do individual unit managers play in the budget process?
5. What are the advantages of variable or flexible budgets over fixed budgets?
6. Why are the budget-setting processes of government so rife with conflict?
7. What would happen if governments had no budgets?
8. What are the differences between PPBS and zero-base budgeting approaches? In what ways might they complement each other?
9. As a lower level manager, what would be your greatest concerns about your organization's budgeting process?

10. As a top manager, what would be your most serious problems about budgeting?
11. What budgeting concepts might be useful in ''managing'' your activities outside of work?

REFERENCES AND NOTES

1. ''Avco Standard: Getting out of Manufacturing to Become a Big-Time Distributor,'' *Business Week*, March 26, 1984, pp. 126–28.
2. C. T. Horngren, *Cost Accounting: A Managerial Emphasis*, 4th ed. (Englewood Cliffs, N.J.: Prentice-Hall, Inc., 1977), pp. 156–60.
3. C. Gillespie, *Standard and Direct Costing* (Englewood Cliffs, N.J.: Prentice-Hall, Inc., 1962).
4. J. M. Shafritz and A. C. Hyde, *Classics of Public Administration* (Oak Park, Ill: Moore Publishing Co., 1978), Section VIII, ''The Budgetary Process,'' pp. 249–67 and pp. 332–46.
5. L. M. Cheek, ''Zero Base Budgeting in Washington,'' *Business Horizons*, June 1978, p. 24; ''Symposium on Budgeting in an Era of Resource Scarcity,'' *Public Administration Review*, November/December 1978, pp. 510–44.
6. ''Rep. Perkins Looks For Ways to Save Social Programs His Panel Must Cut,'' *Wall Street Journal*, May 29, 1981, p. 27; ''Outcome of Complex Budget Battle Could Alter Course of Government,'' *Wall Street Journal*, June 9, 1981, p. 35.
7. H. Tosi, ''The Human Effects of Budgeting Systems on Management,'' *MSU Business Topics*, No. 22 (Autumn, 1974), pp. 53–63.
8. J. H. Feegan, ''Spending For Its Own Sake: Time For a Change,'' *S.A.M. Advanced Management Journal*, Autumn 1980, pp. 16–20.
9. I. Kerris, ''Effects of Budgetary Goal Characteristics on Managerial Attitudes and Performance,'' *The Accounting Review*, Vol. 54, 4, October 1979, pp. 707–21.
10. ''Bosses Enlist Workers in Cost-Cutting Battles,'' *Wall Street Journal*, May 28, 1981, p. 27.
11. I. Kerris, ''Effects of Budgetary Goal Characteristics,'' p. 716.
12. ''Bosses Enlist Workers,'' *Wall Street Journal. op. cit.*
13. J. H. Feegan, ''Spending For Its Own Sake,'' p. 19.

SUGGESTED READINGS

Gillespie, C. *Standard and Direct Costing* (Englewood Cliffs, N.J.: Prentice-Hall, 1962). This book explains three fundamental methods of operating standard costs and how to apply standard costs to direct costing. It is written for both students and managers.

Horngren, C. T. *Cost Accounting: A Managerial Emphasis*, 5th ed. (Englewood Cliffs, N.J.: Prentice-Hall, 1981). This is an excellent managerial accounting book that describes and explains budgets and the budgeting process.

Robertson, J. C. *Auditing* (Dallas: Business Publications, 1979). The author describes and explains the reasons for and processes of auditing and internal control.

Case Supervisory Performance In the Budget Department

The ZD Company is a large prime contractor in the defense and aircraft industry. The company is noted for its ability to develop advanced products and has grown rapidly in the past twenty years.

In April Richard Larson, supervisor of the overhead budget department, resigned to take a position as a management consultant. He had been dissatisfied for some time because top management had refused to implement a number of his ideas they regarded as too "radical" for effective financial management. However, the department had functioned satisfactorily under his supervision.

About a week after Larson's resignation was made known, Fred Taylor was appointed as his successor. Fred Taylor, age thirty-six, had been with the company for eight years and had compiled an outstanding record as a Project Ajax budget supervisor. Project Ajax was a much-publicized aerospace project that was being phased out due to its being near completion. Taylor had an M.S. degree in accounting, and before joining the ZD Company, he had worked several years for a large national CPA firm as an auditor.

While working on the Ajax space project, Taylor had been well liked by his subordinates who were all in their early or mid-twenties and recently graduated from college. His relations with higher-level management in various company divisions and within the space project were also reported to be good. Taylor had worked on the Ajax project from its inception, being the only budget supervisor assigned to it in the beginning. As the project grew, additional personnel were assigned to it under his supervision.

In his new capacity as supervisor of overhead budgets, Taylor directly supervised three senior analysts, each of whom had one analyst reporting to him or her. The organization of the department is shown in Exhibit 1. Taylor reported to Charles Dickson, manager of budgets. The function of the overhead budget department was to prepare and administer the overhead budgets for the entire company. Detailed budgets were negotiated and prepared quarterly for each overhead department. Long-range budgets for periods as long as five years were also prepared whenever changing business conditions necessitated a revised long-range plan. The administration of the budgets consisted of the regular preparation of variance reports to top management and numerous ad hoc analyses to determine the immediate effect of operational changes on overhead rates. The overhead account structure was very complex, and the analysts in this group were required to have a strong accounting background. This department, along with its counterpart, direct budgets, acted as a service group for company management and was a major source of analytical cost information for the entire company.

The three senior analysts in the overhead budget department, George Lewis, Mary Warren, and Bob Monroe, were all about the same age as Taylor and had approximately equal or longer service with the company. They had been on their respective jobs for several years and had performed satisfactorily. They reacted negatively to Taylor's promotion. Each openly expressed dissatisfaction to Mr. Dickson, contending that any of them

Source: R. L. Hilgert, S. H. Schoen, and J. W. Towle, *Cases and Policies in Human Resources Management,* 3rd ed. (Boston: Houghton-Mifflin, 1978), pp 150–52.

Exhibit 1

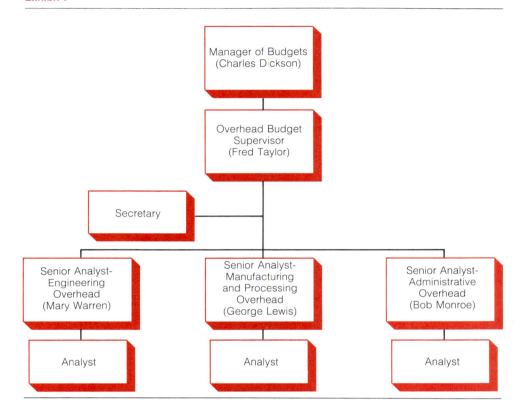

could have taken over the job. Dickson, who had a long-standing reputation as a strict authoritarian, dismissed their complaints and was quoted by Lewis as saying, ''That's the way it is—take it or leave it.'' Shortly thereafter Monroe left the company, openly declaring that his reason for doing so was Taylor's promotion and Dickson's reaction to his complaints. Monroe's responsibilities were then shifted to Mary Warren, and a new man was hired to work for Ms. Warren to absorb the additional duties. The new man was a recent college graduate. Warren's grade classification and salary remained the same.

Shortly thereafter, in August, the department was engaged in negotiations with various divisions of the company for overhead budgets for the October-December quarter, and the work was not proceeding satisfactorily. Negotiations were progressing slowly and still not completed after three weeks had passed. It was critical to the issuance of approved budgets that the negotiations be completed on time because a series of lengthy calculations had to be performed after the total divisional budgets were resolved. The first proposed budgets that had Taylor's approval for issuance were rejected by the controller—Dickson's superior—as being unsatisfactory, and negotiations were reopened. Warren and Lewis were obviously not pressing to complete the job. Lewis told Mr. Dickson *in an informal conversation that he would "be damned" if he was going to push himself just to make Taylor look good.*

The problem was complicated by the fact that on several occasions during the preceding weeks, various members of the department had been diverted from their normal budget work for special assignments. These assignments were largely to compile special data reports for top management. As a result Fred Taylor requested that his department members be placed on paid overtime for several Saturdays, but the request was refused by Dickson.[1] Mr. Dickson believed that the budget departments should set a company example in keeping overtime to a minimum, and he rarely authorized it.

As a result, Taylor went directly to Dickson to review with him the present situation that had by this time become critical. The following discussion took place.

Taylor: We can't hope to have the quarterly budgets on time unless I can work at least four people this Saturday and next Saturday.

Dickson: Tell your people it's their responsibility to get the work done and to come in here on their own time.

Taylor: I can't do that when some of the time was put in on special jobs requested by you.

Dickson: We always handled these things before without falling down the crack. I think your help is slowing down on you to make you look bad. They all want your job, you know.

Taylor: I don't think you're far off, but what can I do about it?

Dickson: Don't ask me. I gave you the job. I expect you to do it. If they won't work for you, find a few other people, and you can fire the whole bunch with my blessing. But I expect results, not a lot of overtime.

Taylor was well aware that firing people was not the answer, so he proceeded to continue operations as in the past. The quarterly budget for October-December was eventually approved and issued three weeks late. Subsequent budgeting operations of similar nature also were in difficulties and behind schedule, and Dickson increased the pressure on Taylor to "start getting the job done." Taylor responded that he had successfully supervised five hich-caliber young employees in his previous position, and he was puzzled by his present problems and worried about Dickson's comments.

[1] It was company policy to pay salaried employees for overtime when such overtime was requested by their supervisors.

CASE QUESTIONS

1. Describe the budgeting cycle used by ZD Company.
2. What is the role of the overhead budget department in ZD Company's budgeting process? '
3. What are some possible effects of the overhead budgets for the fourth quarter being three weeks late?
4. Do you agree with Mr. Dickson's argument for refusing overtime for the overhead budget department?

Report from the Field Developing Policy

The Annual Report for Texas Commerce Bancshares for 1983 attributes a great deal of its financial success to an aggressive business development program. Texas Commerce is widely perceived as being the best managed bank in the state.

Stephen D. Bunten, president of Provident Bancorp, Inc. of Dallas, describes the policies that formed the foundation of Texas Commerce's current business development program.

"Texas Commerce emerged from a merger in 1967 in bad shape. Management had grown old, innovation was discouraged, and customers were defecting. The bank had retained its tradition of tight credit control, but had little else to attract either customers or investors.

"Before I had been with the bank a year, I was put in charge of the National Division, which serviced all nonenergy accounts outside of Harris County. My predecessors had run the division out of their hip pockets and were usually unaware of the whereabouts of their business development officers. Reports of visits made to customers or potential customers were seldom completed at the time of the contact and were rarely reviewed by management. Preparation for trips was haphazard, and no system existed for informing other departments in the bank about developments and information that might be useful to them.

"In order to gain control of my subordinates' activities, I established a policy requiring that all trips be planned *six months* in advance, and that the purpose be clear and justifiable to me. This policy eliminated the majority of trips to visit in-laws in St. Louis, and it caused a great deal of soul-searching before trip schedules were submitted. The policy further required my business development officers to submit specific itineraries one month prior to any trip, and no trip could be made without my prior approval. Actually, I could not stop my employees from taking unauthorized trips short of firing them, but the threat of not having the expense account approved greatly facilitated the implementation of the policy. Finally, after the trips were made, expense claims were to be submitted within two days of the end of the trip, and reports of the calls were to be delivered to me within two weeks. I discovered that a call report is an excellent way to evaluate performance and to see how the market is reacting, since the calling officer was obliged to report bad news as well as good.

"The advent of multibank holding companies increased the value of these policies, since we soon owned banks far from Houston. Most of these banks had no national call program, but they needed one, since their customers included national names such as Sears, IBM, and Penney's. By advising each bank of the planned trip well in advance, and by sending a copy of pertinent call reports after the contact, we were able to serve as a central business development group for all of the banks, which now number sixty-four.

Source: Personal Interview, April 1984.

17 / Staffing

In an interview about the management and development of people, Edson W. Spencer, the CEO and chairman of Honeywell, and Fosten A. Boyle, Honeywell's vice-president of employee relations, discussed their perspectives on Honeywell's staffing for the 1980s and 1990s.

Spencer: About six years ago, we senior managers sat back and said: "What kind of people are we going to need in the 1980s and 1990s to manage this business? What are we going to have to do to attract them? What kind of motivation and desires are they going to have? What differences are there between their motivations and the motivations that we all have? We are all products of World War II, the job boom, and the years immediately after that, when getting work was fairly easy. Most of us in senior management are in our mid-40s and 50s. And we suddenly realized that the people we will need are, first, going to have to be trained differently; they will have backgrounds in computer science, mathematics, and engineering. And we'll need a whole new raft of skills to deal with the type of products in our high-technology business.

    The second thing we realized is that we are going to shovel a lot of software. We are moving from a hardware to software company. We're moving from an electro-mechanical or mechanical type of product to an electronic product. We're moving throughout the whole business into computer- or micro-processor-driven systems with all the software implications that goes with it. So we will require very differ-

Edson W. Spencer

ent skills. The old skills of the mechanical engineer, assembly-line worker, and tool-and-die maker are always going to be there, but they are going to be less important in the total picture. Well, then, suddenly somebody said, "Gee, you know those people we're going to have to recruit are like our kids; more college-educated, having more finely tuned skills, probably brighter, and many more women will be competing for top jobs." Then we considered what our kids are interested in: They're much more mobile, for example; they may have less loyalty to companies and more loyalty to the quality of life that they want to live. They may want to live in the South-

and keep them because their desires and motivations are so different than ours were when we were their age.

Boyle: I think we're going to have a difficult time in the 1980s getting the kind of people that Ed is talking about—that is, people who will really make a contribution in a more competitive, world-based economy. This is because if you look, for example, at electrical engineers—one of the prime technical skills we need—I think about 14,000 electrical engineers graduated in 1969. Then the number of electrical engineer graduates actually went down in the early 1970s, and this past year the number rose back to about 14,000. So we are dealing with a static supply, and with the end of the baby boom hitting the colleges; in a few years we will be fighting over not a static supply, but a decreased supply.

Spencer: The implication is that we will need a growth business that is going to grow faster than the slow-moving averages I talked about, so Honeywell looks like a place where there is opportunity. But we are also going to have to be a place where people are going to want to work, where people will like their work, and where they will want to come and stay with with us.

west or the mountains and less in the industrial heartland of the country. So we decided that we'd better start changing the way we deal with people in the company—otherwise we wouldn't be able to attract them

Source: "Conversation with Edson W. Spencer and Fosten A. Boyle," *Organizational Dynamics*, Spring 1983, pp. 21–45 © 1983 AMACON Periodicals Division, American Management Association.

In previous chapters in this section we have discussed the organization's structure, policy, and financial resources as they define and shape the manager's world. Each of these factors is important, but because management is, by definition, getting things done through people, none is as important as human resources, the people with whom the manager has to work.

The introductory discussion between the two Honeywell executives highlights the function of **staffing** an organization—*providing the human resources needed to accomplish an organization's goals*. The changes in Honeywell's products, from electromechanical hardware to electronics and software, will bring about changes in the human-resources skills that Honeywell will need, both at the operative and the managerial levels. The company will have to choose different kinds of employees, and it will have to do different things to attract and keep these people in a competitive labor market.

If these two executives are correct in their assessments, and make the kinds of changes that enable Honeywell to attract talented people, managing at Honeywell will be considerably easier and more productive than if they are wrong. They ways an organization staffs its positions, and its success in doing so, have major implications for its managers.

AN OVERVIEW

In this chapter we focus on the staffing function and its many activities that, in the end, determine the quality of the human resources managers have to accomplish their objectives. A wide variety of organizational activities go into staffing an organization, but all have the same goal that the Honeywell executives aimed for—to attract and keep good employees.

An overview of the staffing process is diagrammed in Exhibit 17.1. The first two activities are *preliminary;* before an organization attempts to staff positions, it analyzes the work to be done, forecasts staffing requirements, and plans the next activities. The next three activities are *directly* related to staffing—recruiting, screening and selection, and placement. The remaining activities—orientation and socialization, performance appraisal, and employee development—are *support* and *follow-up* activities. Of these, the last two provide information for assessing an organization's requirements. Thus, they provide feedback for the planning and forecasting activities.

PRELIMINARY STAFFING ACTIVITIES

Job analysis is the basis for determining what kinds of abilities, skills, knowledge, and general characteristics are required by an organization's work roles. Staff planning and forecasting, together with information about current and expected vacancies, provide the basis for determining which combinations of individual characteristics are needed, and when.

Job Analysis

Job analysis is *the breakdown of an individual work role into its component tasks.* The process determines what activities and skills are necessary for a specific job. Factors such as personality characteristics and attitudes are not relevant; it is the job, not the person, that is being analyzed.

Exhibit 17.1   The Staffing Process

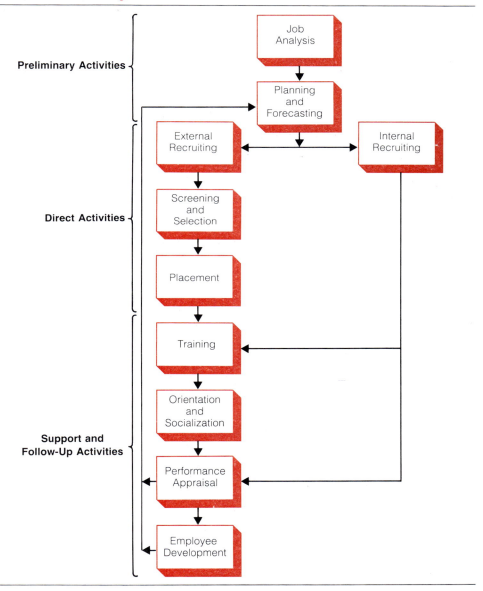

There is a variety of job-analysis methods commonly is use. (One of these methods, the Requisite Task Attributes approach, was discussed in Chapter 4.) Each method has the same purpose—the *systematic* differentiation of one job from another in terms of work activities and behaviors; machines, tools, or other work aids used; the products made or the services performed; and skills and knowledge required.

The outcome of the process of job analysis is a **job description,** *an organized, factual statement of the duties and responsibilities of a particular work role.* It tells what is done, how it is done, and why it is done. This information allows the job analyst to write a **job specification,** *a statement of the skills, abilities, physical characteristics, and education required to perform a job.*

The job specification is the basis for staffing. It describes the kind of person needed to fill a particular work role. Because it is a detailed, specific statement based on an analysis of the work to be performed, it allows for a realistic assessment of the employee skills and aptitudes required. This helps avoid hiring people who cannot learn to do the job, as well as people who are overqualified and likely to find the job boring and unsatisfying.

Job specifications, based on job analysis, tell an organization what kinds of characteristics are required to perform given jobs satisfactorily. Job analysis, then, is a basic activity; information should be available before hiring is necessary.

Job analysis, and the resulting job description and job specification, is easier for some positions than for others. Managerial work has been especially difficult to analyze because of the wide variety of activities and skills it requires. Even when jobs are not so complex, formal analysis can be time consuming and expensive; many organizations concentrate their efforts on critical areas or those requiring large numbers of personnel. Small organizations are often less formal in job analysis, description, and specification, tending to concentrate their staffing resources on direct and support activities.

However, the investment of time and effort in this first preliminary step produces job descriptions and job specifications that are extremely valuable tools, as seen in Exhibit 17.2. For example, the quality of job descriptions has been critical to the settlement of numerous equal-pay court cases.[1]

Forecasting and Planning

Determining when hiring is necessary is done on an "as needed" basis in some organizations. When an employee is terminated, retires, takes a leave of absence, or simply quits, wheels are set in motion for a replacement. A more complete staffing program, however, includes activities aimed at forecasting future hiring requirements, a program of *human resource planning,* as it is called at Honeywell and elsewhere.

There is a variety of methods available for this estimation, all based on a comparison of projected employee demand (from the organization) with projected employee supply (from both within and without the organization). The conversation between the Honeywell executives centers around their estimates for the 1980s and 90's. Such planning requires three kinds of information.

1. The *base rate of turnover* for a particular job, unit, or organization. The **base turnover rate** is *an estimate of the average number of jobs that must be filled in any given time period, even if nothing else changes.* It is voluntary turnover that occurs for personal reasons, such as retirement, relocation, or dis-

Exhibit 17.2   Job Analysis and Staffing Activities

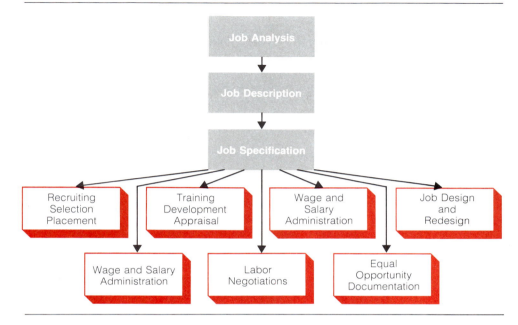

satisfaction with the job or company, concerns Honeywell's CEO expresses in describing the future work force as "more mobile, . . . less loyalty to companies and more loyalty to the quality of life."

The base rate can be estimated by examining the appropriate turnover records for a period of one to five years. Figures collected over shorter periods are often biased by seasonal factors, or short-lived phenomena. For example, turnover might be unusually high in one six-month period if a new plant offering higher wages opened nearby.

Because they have been consistently found to be related to voluntary turnover, many organizations use pay, fringe benefits, and good working conditions to combat job dissatisfaction.[2] As the CEO puts it, "Honeywell [is] going to have to be a place where people are going to want to work, and where they will want to come and stay with us." However, in most organizations some undesirable jobs exist, particularly at the entry level. It is seldom possible to reduce turnover in such jobs beyond a certain level, and a realistic base turnover-rate will reflect this.

2. *Anticipated changes* in the number of work roles or the type of worker characteristics required. Factors that call for such changes include expansion or cutbacks, mergers, schedule changes, product diversification, changes in technology, changes in market or economic conditions, and equal employment opportunity pressures. The Honeywell executives anticipate changes in technology and products to be major factors affecting future staffing requirements.

Together, anticipated changes in staffing requirements and base turnover rates allow for an estimate of *demand*—the total number and type of jobs to be filled in the forecast period. Anticipated changes are offset or added to by base turnover-rates. Fewer new employees will be needed in a two-year expansion period, for example, if the base turnover-rate is low than if it is high.

3. *An assessment of supply*—that is, of the extent to which the number and kind of people to fill jobs will be available. The basic question is if the right number of people with the right kinds of skills be available when the time comes. A complete human-resources planning program looks both inside and outside the organization for the answer.

Educational trends, population data, and industry trends will affect an organization's future labor requirements. For example, Honeywell's vice-president sees all three making a human resource—electrical engineers—scarce. Numbers of electrical engineers graduating from college have been no greater than they were fifteen years ago, despite increasing demands for their talents from the fast growing computer industry. Combined with population data indicating fewer college students in the 80s and 90s, these figures indicate a shortage of electrical engineers, meaning fierce competition among companies and higher salaries for engineers.

Once they have used such information to estimate *outside* labor supply, most organizations add to it an assessment of *inside* supply, which includes information on performance appraisals, special skills, enrollment in training or education programs, age of workers, time in current position, and career ambitions for existing employees. If this inside assessment is done formally, it is called a personnel inventory.

DIRECT STAFFING ACTIVITIES

In this section, we will examine those staffing activities that are directly related to the goal of filling work roles—recruiting, screening and selection, and placement. Keep in mind that these activities are easier, less costly, and more effective if the preliminary steps of job analysis, forecasting, and human-resource planning are carried out.

Recruiting

There are two places to look for people to fill jobs—within the ranks of current employees or outside the organization. The objective is to find some number of individuals both qualified and willing to accept a particular job.

Internal Recruiting. Internal recruiting is the identification of employees within the company who are willing and able to be promoted or transferred to another job. Internal recruiting is usually less expensive than outside recruiting. In addition, first-hand data about skills and past performance are available. Finally, promotion from within can have certain motivational qualities. For those employ-

Recruiting is what an organization does to attract job candidates who have the skills, abilities, and motivation to help it accomplish its goals.

ees who want to move up in the organizational ranks, or "sideways" to a preferred job at the same level, a policy of internal recruiting may be expected to increase effort and commitment. Part of the strong commitment Japanese workers have for their companies is because of a strong tradition of internal promotion in Japanese industry.

Internal recruiting may be carried out in a variety of ways. A general announcement may be posted, and anyone interested may then apply for it. In other cases, those responsible for filling a job may approach potential candidates directly. Sometimes, word just seems to get around that a vacancy is coming up.

However it is handled, the success of internal recruiting is heavily dependent on the effectiveness of past hiring practices, training, development, and performance-appraisal methods. Thus, a complete staffing plan builds in policies and practices that support the ongoing development of a promotable and flexible work force.

Trends seem to indicate that organizations are looking increasingly to internal sources for job candidates, especially at the management and executive levels. Since its acquisition by Pillsbury Company in 1979, all of the executive positions in Green Giant Company that have opened up have been filled by promotion from within.[3]

Management in Action
Involving Current Employees in Recruiting Efforts

It may pay to know someone when looking for a job, but at corporations nationwide it could be worth more to know someone looking for a job. Firms are paying up to $1,000 to employees who can recommend the right person for a position.

Offering the bonuses can put a big dent in the cost of recruiting workers through advertisements or head hunting agencies. And many executives say they place a great deal of confidence in their employees' suggestions, assuming the workers would be too embarrassed to recommend a dud.

"You really can't argue with its effectiveness," says William Baney, manager of resource development at an RCA Corp. facility in Cherry Hill, N.J. The program at the company's government systems division began five years ago when RCA was looking for scientists and engineers.

At least 100 division employees have been hired through the program in three years, Baney says. Employees are paid $1,000 for each recommendation that results in a hiring. Smaller prizes also are awarded, and the company is thinking of conducting a drawing for a personal computer.

But that is nothing compared to what the company saves. Baney estimates that costs associated with hiring a new engineer or scientist in the division total $9,000 once advertising, employment agency fees, visits and relocation expenses are considered.

At Wang Laboratories Inc. in Lowell Mass., one division hired 43 employees through a similar program in the last half of 1983, and all passed the 30- to 90-day probation period.

"The response has been extremely enthusiastic," says Jula Davenport, a Wang spokeswoman.

Several divisions at Wang pay $300 to $500 for each employee who is hired through the program and who passes the probation period. Wang also is looking at other bonuses, such as vacations, dinners and jogging suits.

Company officials say that the program, which began several years ago, boosts the self-esteem of employees who recommend new hires.

And they say they save on relocation costs—in addition to other expenses associated with the recruitment of desirable employees—because the new workers live near the company.

Mutual of Omaha, the Nebraska-based insurance company, finds the program gives the corporation an edge in recruiting sales agents who contract with the company to sell its insurance.

With a high turnover rate among the 10,000 sales agents, says Thomas O'Connor, "there's a real competition going on for the agents out there."

The philosophy behind the program is that successful agents are probably likely to bring in successful agents. Some of out best agents have been found through the program," O'Connor says.

Source: P. Brownstein, "Recommend a Worker, Get a Bonus." Associated Press, March 25, 1984.

External Recruiting.   Promotions and transfers will not remove all necessity for outside recruiting; the jobs that promoted or transferred employees leave must be filled. If followed consistently, a policy of internal promotion generates a steady number of vacancies at lower organizational levels.

Hiring experienced people from outside may avoid the costs of training promoted employees. In certain situations, these training costs may be higher than the benefits of promoting from within. In addition, external recruiting is an important source of new ideas and perspectives for an organization. This "new blood" can be especially important at upper levels, if the organization is to remain flexible and responsive to its environment.

> *Job analysis is the basis for determining what kinds of abilities, skills, knowledge, and general characteristics are required by an organization's work roles. Staff planning and forecasting, together with information about current and expected vacancies, provide the basis for determining which combinations of individual characteristics are needed, and when.*

For whatever reason it occurs, external recruiting can be carried out generally or directly. General recruiting is the practice of making job opportunities public, in some manner, and then screening everyone who applies. Common examples include "Help Wanted" signs outside a place of business or newspaper, television, or radio advertisements.

General recruiting often produces a large response, but many of those who apply may be unsuitable. An employment agency can be helpful in screening, but certain of their own internal policies can reduce the effectiveness of this screening. Private agencies, for example, are paid their fees when an applicant is actually hired. In the short run, therefore, they lose little by sending out marginally qualified applicants.

Direct recruiting is the practice of going directly to sources of likely candidates, usually educational institutions, union halls, and professional societies. Some organizations formalize this recruiting through internship and work-study programs. The Cooperative Education Plan, begun in 1906 at The University of Cincinnati, currently has over 30,000 companies and 200,000 students participating. Under this plan, students go to school full-time for part of the year and work full-time for the sponsoring organization the remainder of the year.

Most organizations use some combination of internal, external, general, and direct recruiting. In addition, some job applicants show up without any recruiting effort. Current employees tell family and friends, or applicants simply walk in looking for a job. Studies of the relationship between the recruiting source and employee success and tenure usually find general recruiting, especially newspaper ads, to be the least effective, probably because of the limited information they provide.[4] There is also evidence that absenteeism is higher among newspaper-recruited employees than among those recruited from other sources.[5]

While most organizations manage to recruit sufficient numbers of qualified applicants from some source to meet their staffing requirements, an increasing number are running into difficulties. Recruiters for the all-volunteer armed-forces, for example, often say they get the numbers, but not the quality, of recruits they need.[6] Other organizations simply cannot recruit sufficient numbers; a recent article cited some 100,000 vacancies in American hospitals.[7] Recruiting problems in other industries are described in Exhibit 17.3.

The fact that some organizations cannot recruit the number and type of applicants they need points up the fact that recruiting is only one part of staffing. The Army, for example, mounts one of the more impressive recruiting campaigns around, but continues to be plagued by a poor image and an inability to compete with civilian pay-rates.

Unsuccessful recruiting also emphasizes the role the environment of an organization plays in its staffing. Economic and social conditions, government regulations, work force mobility, and geographical and competitive conditions all affect the supply of available applicants. For example, the nursing shortage is partially the result of social changes that have increased other career opportunities for women.

Screening and Selection

The recruiting phase provides applicants the basis for screening; screening, in turn, provides candidates for selection.

Types of Screening.   *The process of separating qualified from unqualified (or less qualified) job applicants* is called **screening.** In order to do this, screeners must be able to identify, for each job, what is meant by "qualified." They can determine these qualifications from a good job analysis and a job specification.

Once the required characteristics for a job are determined, screeners must find a way to identify the individuals who possess them. They use screening devices, methods such as application data, interviews, and tests, for assessing employee characteristics and determining which candidates are job-qualified.

The familiar application form is usually the first screening device used in most organizations. Because the information provided is often used to reject job applicants, we have seen increasingly strict government regulations of the kinds of questions that can be asked. The general rule is: If you can't prove the response is relevant to job success, an application question cannot be used for screening. Self-incriminatory information, such as a prison record, for example, cannot be required. Other questions *may* be asked, however, so long as the response is voluntary and used only for research or documentation purposes. An applicant may be asked his or her race, for example, so that compliance with equal opportunity employment laws may be maintained.

The most common form of screening device has always been the employment interview. Unfortunately, while interviewing as it is usually practiced is a poor screening device, few, if any, organizations are willing to give it up.

The generally poor results from interviews are largely because of their subjectivity. A study of interviewing in the life-insurance industry illustrates the problem. In that study, one hundred interviewers were asked to judge whether certain items of information taken from employment interviews made an applicant more or less qualified for a job. Interviewer disagreement was substantial. Half of the in-

Exhibit 17.3   Recruiting Problems

Jobs Go Begging

Ever shifting and complex, the U.S. economy cannot precisely match people and jobs even in the best of times, let alone now when sluggishness and slowdown have reduced overall employer demand for workers. This predicament shows up clearly in Labor Department statistics. In October, for example, 110,000 jobs went unfilled, even while the unemployment rate rose.

Nearly all the openings were for blue-collar and clerical employees, those tracked most consistently by the Labor Department, using figures supplied by employment offices in all 50 states. Thus the Government's figures exclude many white-collar professional jobs that are not listed with such offices, and the number of open jobs is actually higher than reported.

About 67,000 of the openings were in clerical and sales positions, and 49,000 were in the service sector. In greatest demand were auto mechanics, clerk typists, restaurant cooks, materials handlers, secretaries and waitresses. The job openings knew no geographic bounds; employment in those fields was generally available throughout the U.S.

In October, 643 arc welder's jobs paying $4.11 to $9.88 an hour went unfilled, as did 315 jobs for electronics technicians, 1,279 openings for insurance sales agents and 532 slots for machinists at $4.16 to $9.80 an hour.

The upstate New York city of Binghamton showed a 25% increase in available jobs because defense-related industries in the area have won new Government contracts, while the thriving Texas cities of Fort Worth, Longview and Midland had 15% increases because of greater petroleum activity and a construction boom. Even depressed Detroit, burdened with an estimated 112,000 laid-off auto workers, had openings for practical nurses, receptionists, security guards, machinists and production assemblers. Jobs for construction workers were mainly available in such Sunbelt cities as Phoenix, Greenville, N.C., Houston and Tampa.

The American economy in the late 1980s is expected to have even more severe problems of worker shortages in some key industries. A Labor Department study shows that while the U.S. will need far fewer shoe repairmen, gas station operators and postal clerks by 1990, it will be looking for increased numbers of computer programmers, computer systems analysts and home health aides.

terviewers said they would look more favorably at an applicant who reported being active in groups outside of work; the other half of the interviewers would no longer consider such an applicant for the job.[8]

Despite the flaws of the traditional interview, proponents argue that it is the only way to get a complete picture of an applicant. Many feel that certain job requirements, such as conversational skill, cannot be evaluated any other way. Some believe that alternative methods are too expensive, and others state flatly that they want to see those whom they are hiring.

Fortunately, research on interviewing has found a number of ways to make the process more useful and less subjective. Evidence suggests that interviews are better screening-devices when the interview is *structured* (covers a predetermined set of topics); the interview is *supplemented* with other pieces of information, such as tests and reference checks; the interviewer is *informed* and understands the nature of the jobs for which applicants are being screened; and the interviewer has been *trained* in effective interviewing techniques.[9]

Because almost all managers interview job candidates from time to time, interviewing skills are worth developing. In particular, training can help avoid placing too much emphasis on first impressions, overestimating applicants who appear to be like the interviewer, and giving more weight to negative than to positive information.

> *There are two places to look for people to fill jobs—within the ranks of current employees or outside the organization. The objective is to find some number of individuals both qualified and willing to accept a particular job.*

Improvements in the conduct of employment interviews may also increase the chances that a manager will be able to *hire* desired applicants. Studies suggest that the behavior of the interviewer is an important factor in an applicant's decision to accept a job offer.[10]

A **test** is *a standardized procedure for measuring one or more individual characteristics.* Tests are based on the assumption that people differ significantly in intelligence, manual dexterity, and mathematical ability. The use of tests as screening devices is based on the assumption that there is a direct and important relationship between the possession of these traits and certain job behaviors.

Screening tests come in all varieties, including interest, intelligence, aptitude, and personality tests. These tests may require written or oral responses, or a physical demonstration of skills and abilities. They may be used singly or in batteries, given individually or in groups.[11] Four examples of physical aptitude tests that are administered individually are shown in Exhibit 17.4.

Whatever test is used, government regulations, as well as practical considerations, require that it be *valid;* that scores on the test can be shown to have a relationship to measures of job behavior, such as supervisory ratings of performance, production figures, absenteeism, and turnover.

Validating a test is a time-consuming and expensive process. Finding satisfactory criteria can be a major problem. It is relatively easy for some jobs, such as that of typist, but difficult for jobs on which good performance is less well defined. The criteria problem is believed by many to be the most difficult problem in screening and selection.

Even when good performance criteria are available, the characteristic is only one of a large number of factors affecting job behavior. Nevertheless, even a weak prediction can improve the selection decision. An applicant who makes a high score on a dexterity test is more likely to do well at assembling watches than one whose test results read "All Thumbs!"

Although the misuse of testing by some organizations has tarnished its reputation, the effective use of valid tests in selection should not be underestimated. The conclusions of 515 validation studies of the General Aptitude Test Battery (GATB) carried out by the U. S. Employment Service indicate that cognitive, perceptual, and psychomotor abilities are valid predictors of job proficiency for all 12,000 jobs

Exhibit 17.4   Some Aptitude Screening Tests

(a) *Pyramid Puzzle.* The pyramid problem involves moving the blocks to a designated post without placing a larger block on a smaller one. Demonstrates problem solving. (b) *Steadiness Tester — groove type.* Calibrated. Sides are electrified to activate buzzer or electric counter if user's hands are unsteady and sides are touched. (c) *Steadiness Tester — hole type.* Conventional hole type with terminals for completing electric circuit to activate buzzer or counter if sides are touched. (d) *Tapping Board.* Stainless steel metal plates at each end complete circuit when stylus contacts each successive plate. Number of taps within designated period are counted, to measure rapidity of hand movements. (All equipment made by Lafayette Instrument Co.)

Source: N.R.F. Maier and G.C. Verser, *Psychology in Industrial Organizations,* 5th ed. (Boston: Houghton Mifflin, 1982), p. 226.

in the Dictionary of Occupational Titles. Further, experts estimate that optimal use of the test (for example, placing more weight on cognitive ability and less on psychomotor ability for more complex jobs) could save billions of dollars for the federal government as an employer, and result in substantial savings in administrative costs, turnover, and productivity even for small organizations.[12]

Other screening devices range from physical and psychiatric examinations, handwriting analysis and group interviews, to polygraph (lie-detector) tests. All of these methods are currently being used, although their validity and, in some cases, their legality is in question. For example, polygraphs have already been outlawed as screening devices in at least ten states.

Selection.   After candidates are screened, selection begins. **Selection** is *the decision to offer a job to a particular person.* In general, this decision is improved by having information from a variety of validated screening methods. Unfortunately, it can be difficult to combine such information in a meaningful way. An applicant may do well on the tests, but poorly in an interview (or vice-versa). He or she may have extensive experience, but unenthusiastic references (or the other way around).

How is mixed information from a variety of screening sources to be summed up into a "yes" or "no" decision? The most rigorous approach to this problem is to devise some system of weighting the various pieces of information. Even then, however, the selection decision usually is based partly on the information available and partly on individual judgment. For this reason, many believe that there has been too much emphasis on developing sophisticated screening devices and too little emphasis on training those who use them.

Legal Implications of Screening and Selection.   Equal-Employment-Opportunity (EEO) guidelines and court rulings have had a substantial effect on screening procedures and have served to reinforce principles of good screening procedures and selection.

For the Equal Employment Opportunity Commission (EEOC), the key word with respect to the use of screening devices for making personnel decisions and for the success of organizational staffing is *validity*. In short, government regulations have generally been in the best interest of the staffing function with respect to screening. The effects of these regulations on hiring practices are discussed in detail in Chapter 18.

As Exhibit 17.5 suggests, changes associated with the EEO Revolution have been substantial. At the same time, organizations are beginning to rebel against government interference in their traditional right to hire the employees they want. Sears, Roebuck and Company, for example, actually sued the federal government over this issue.[13] The suit was dismissed in Federal Court, emphasizing the government's determination to enforce equal employment opportunity but the fact that it was filed at all makes it clear that the issues are real, serious, and persistent.

Placement

The core of the staffing process is placement, the activity that actually places specific people in specific work roles. How important is placement? Consider the following statement by Roger Martin, chairman of the fifth largest industrial corporation in France:

Q. *As a chairman of a national corporation with more than 100,000 employees, what do you consider your most important function?*
A. *I think it is to choose good people and to put them in the right places.*[14]

A ***placement*** is *a job assignment*. Most textbooks have little to say about this staffing activity, probably because most applicants are screened and selected for a particular role in the organization. In that case, the selection decision *is* the placement decision.

However, there are a number of exceptions to the general practice of hiring for particular jobs. In large organizations, or unionized plants, general hiring may be done for a variety of entry-level jobs. Hiring may be done to fill several similar jobs in different parts of the organization, as electrical engineers are hired at Honeywell. Finally, organizations may hire trainees to fill entry-level management positions, placing them in specific jobs based on the nature and success of their training experiences.

The importance of placement, as distinct from screening, is often underrated. When an individual has been hired, he or she becomes part of the human re-

Exhibit 17.5   Staffing and the EEO Revolution

Nurse, airline flight attendant, telephone operator: You probably picture women in these jobs, but in recent years men have begun to fill them, too.

Ironically, such new employment opportunities for men are a result of the women's movement, since laws that prohibit job discrimination apply to both sexes and changing attitudes have freed men to consider a wider range of careers.

After only one college course in nursing, Fred Goldman of Danbury, Connecticut, knew that he had found his life's work. "I'm a burly guy, and my size is an advantage," he says. "Male nurses are in demand to deal with agitated patients in psychiatric wards and emergency rooms."

Although the percentage of men in his field remains small (3.5 percent), the trend is definitely upward. In 1971 the Bureau of Labor Statistics reported 16,000 male nurses; by 1980 that number had almost tripled.

NEW JOBS FOR MEN

sources of an organization. Poor placement-decisions waste these resources, as well as the resources expended in recruiting, screening, and selecting. For example, some organizations make placement decisions based on simply filling the job that has been open the longest or that has the more immediate need. If the employee doesn't work out, it is difficult to determine whether the screening devices were inaccurate or the placement was inappropriate.

Support and Follow-Up Activities

Once employees have been selected and placed in work roles, support and follow-up staffing activities are used to enhance performances. These include training, orientation and socialization, performance appraisal, and employee development.

Training.   **Training** is *the process of turning abilities and general knowledge into the skills and particular knowledge required to do a particular job.* In this section, we are concerned with initial job training. Retraining, remedial training, skill upgrading, and more general continuing-education training are considered employee-development activities.

Initial training for any job may be given on the job and/or off the job. There are four basic approaches which may be used alone, or in some combination.

The most common way to train employees is *on the job*. The new employee is placed directly into the work role and taught how to perform its duties by his or her immediate supervisor, coworkers, or both. Occasionally, outsiders perform on-the-job training. The J. I. Case Company, for example, sends factory teams to job sites to train new owners and operators of its heavy-range construction equipment. Such training is particularly valuable to small businesses with few training resources.

Sometimes trainees are guided in the acquisition and practice of job skills in a protected environment *away from the job site* by experienced trainers. Honeywell Corporation, for example, has a multimedia, individually paced program for trainees who will eventually maintain its R4140 safety control device. The program includes live instruction and supervised practice in job performance.

Many organizations use *special courses* for various types of training. In some cases, these courses are run by the company, such as Denny's Restaurant ten-week manager-training course. In other cases, trainees are sent to courses offered by outside institutions. Managers to be sent to other countries, for example, may take language courses at universities or special language schools.

The usual *apprenticeship* program combines on-the-job training with classroom or special-course training. In this country it is usually a union-affiliated program for a craft, such as electrician, plumber, and carpenter. The outcome is usually some form of certification or licensing, called *journeyman status*. Both entry to the apprenticeship program and its content are regulated by the union and subject to fair-employment-practice regulations.

Whatever the location, level, or method of training, certain conditions are associated with the likelihood of success. Research suggests that effective training provides content and organization that are meaningful to trainees; active involvement on the parts of trainees; practice and repetition; feedback as to progress; reinforcement of desired behaviors; and a way to assist the transfer of the training to the actual job if the training is done elsewhere. Note the similarity of these characteristics to the management principles described in Chapters 5 and 6. Good direction enhances training; good training facilitates direction.

An evaluation of the more common training methods according to the criteria listed above is shown in Exhibit 17.6.

Orientation and Socialization. Both orientation and socialization are intended to help a new employee fit into, or feel at home in, an organization. **Orientation** is *a process designed to acquaint new employees with rules, regulations, policies, and operating procedures of the organization.* This information is often given in the form of an employee handbook, which includes where and when to clock in, what to do in case of accident or illness, and when work breaks occur.

Some organizations, recognizing that employees often do not read such material, have formal orientation programs. Carolina Power and Light, for example, has a thirty-minute slide-and-tape program that covers what new construction-craft employees need to know. A complete orientation program will cover most of the questions new employees have about the organization and its personnel policies. Such

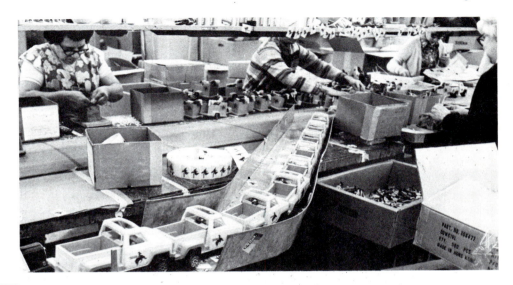

The old skills of the assembly-line worker will always be necessary, but they will be less important in the high-technology world of today, according to E. W. Spencer.

programs usually include a brief history of the organization, its products, services, and mission; a listing of rules and regulations for both routine and nonroutine occurences; a description of employee benefits such as vacation policy and eligibility for stock options.

Many organizations leave employee orientation largely in the hands of immediate supervisors. Unfortunately, some managers take this responsibility lightly, volunteering little information unless prompted. Despite evidence that good orientation programs contribute to the morale and early productivity of new employees, it is often left to the employees themselves to "learn the ropes."

Socialization includes ". . . *all those processes by which an individual acquires the attitudes, values, and norms necessary to function as a member of a social unit.*"[15]

Orientation is a first step in the broader socialization process. Generally, socialization is a gradual, informal process that transforms a newcomer into an insider. However, some companies build in mechanisms to help this process. McDonald's, for example, assigns coaches, or "buddies," to help minorities and lower-level managers get acclimated.

The role of immediate supervisors and higher executives in employee socialization cannot be overestimated. Because superiors are in positions of power and status, their behavior provides employees with models to follow. The CEO of Honeywell recognizes this impact by his response to a question about human relations in the company:

I think it depends on those of us in senior management and whether the chief executive can maintain a nonpolitical, open, easy environment between himself and the people who work for him. Those who work for him, who are smart and

Exhibit 17.6   Evaluation of Popular Training Methods

	Motivation: Active Participation of Learner	Reinforcement: Feedback of Knowledge of Results	Stimulus: Meaningful Organization of Materials	Responses: Practice and Repetition	Stimulus-Response Conditions Most Favorable for Transfer
On-the-job techniques					
Job-instruction training	Yes	Sometimes	Yes	Yes	Yes
Apprentice training	Yes	Sometimes	?	Sometimes	Yes
Internships and assistantships	Yes	Sometimes	?	Sometimes	Yes
Job rotation	Yes	No	?	Sometimes	Yes
Junior board	Yes	Sometimes	Sometimes	Sometimes	Yes
Coaching	Yes	Yes	Sometimes	Sometimes	Yes
Off-the-job techniques					
Vestibule	Yes	Sometimes	Yes	Yes	Sometimes
Lecture	No	No	Yes	No	No
Special study	Yes	No	Yes	?	No
Films	No	No	Yes	No	No
Television	No	No	Yes	No	No
Conference or discussion	Yes	Sometimes	Sometimes	Sometimes	No
Case study	Yes	Sometimes	Sometimes	Sometimes	Sometimes
Role playing	Yes	Sometimes	No	Sometimes	Sometimes
Simulation	Yes	Sometimes	Sometimes	Sometimes	Sometimes
Programmed instruction	Yes	Yes	Yes	Yes	No
Laboratory training	Yes	Yes	No	Yes	Sometimes
Programmed group exercises	Yes	Yes	Yes	Sometimes	Sometimes

Source: *Training in Industry: The Management of Learning*, by B. M. Bass and J. A. Vaughan. Copyright © 1966 by Wadsworth Publishing Company, Inc. Reprinted by permission of the publisher, Brooks/Cole Publishing Company, Monterey, California.

observant, and who agree on the concepts (if they disagree differences are talked out), are going to transmit that in the way they deal with the people who report to them, and it's going to go on down through the organization that way. It's probably a lot easier for a forty-year-old executive to do that than it is for a sixty-year-old executive. And there are some of our senior management who struggle with this, but recognize it and push it in their organizations. There are others, though, who just can't adapt to it, so the process doesn't go at the same rate of speed throughout the whole organization.[16]

As his vice-president of employee relations puts it:

People really measure you in terms of what your actions are and what you do, not what you say, so senior management has to set the tone. In a larger organization there are some symbols that you use.[17]

In any organization, these symbols include rites and rituals, rewards and promotions, privileges, and tokens of respect.

Much of an employee's socialization occurs informally. He or she learns by observing the behavior of supervisors and coworkers, and by paying attention to the consequences of behavior. For example, a new manager will learn by observation what kinds of dress standards are enforced for different work roles (coat and tie when interacting with executives or outsiders, shirtsleeves otherwise) and what work hours are normal (working late on weekdays, but rarely on weekends).

Rites and rituals of the organization are part of the socialization process as well. Ceremonies that recognize special achievements, promotions, or long service provide valuable information about the importance (or unimportance) of alternative activities. In one major university each college selects a faculty member as "Teacher of the Year" and awards the recipient $100 at a regular meeting of the faculty senate. In a sister university, similarly selected teachers receive awards ranging from $2000 to $3000 at an elaborate banquet, hosted by the university president. The relative value of teaching in these two institutions is not lost on their young faculty members.

Performance Appraisal. Performance appraisal, as a control process, was discussed in Chapter 7. Here we will look at it as the major coordinating staffing-activity. Performance appraisal fills this role because it is both a feedback and a feedforward mechanism for the organization's staffing function. It feeds back information about the success of recruiting, screening, selection, placement, and training; it feeds forward the information required for human-resource planning and individual employee development. Performance appraisal is also a vital part of documenting fair-promotion practices.

A performance appraisal measures the extent to which an employee's work meets or exceeds certain standards. Like many other kinds of measurement, care-

> *Staffing provides the manager with the human resources needed to get the job done.*

fully constructed measures are important determinants of performance appraisal success. In addition, the way an appraisal form is used is equally important. Ignorance of its proper use, carelessness, and intended or unintended bias can make even a good performance appraisal worthless.

Because performance appraisal is both important and vulnerable to problems arising from the way in which it is carried out, there has been a great deal of research in this area. Results suggest that performance appraisal, in general, will be better when job *behaviors*, rather than *traits* of "loyalty," or "attitude" are evaluated; raters are trained in how to use the performance appraisal instrument and how to avoid common types of bias; and several raters and several methods of appraisal are used.[18]

Involving those to be evaluated in designing the methods by which they will be evaluated can help overcome employee resistance and provide new insights into areas of performance previously overlooked or overestimated. For example, evaluation of city and county employees, like clerks and safety personnel, used to be done by a direct supervisor filling out a general form. Today many local governments involve employees, supervisors, and members of the public in establishing appraisal methods and forms. Employees are judged by the public and their coworkers, as well as by their supervisors, using both rating forms and objective criteria (numbers of calls answered, clients served, and so forth). The result has been both improved appraisal and greater satisfaction with the appraisal system.

Employee Development.   Employee development is *the process of increasing individual potential for job success and career achievement.* In contrast to job training, which is usually standardized, employee development is individualized training designed to build strengths and flexibility, and reduce or remove obstacles to success.

Today organizations use a variety of employee-development activities. Many use *skill development* in the form of remedial or refresher training, or skill upgrading. Eckerd Drugs, for example, sends its pharmacists to regular certified courses each month to keep them aware of the latest developments in the field.

Employee development can also include *general educational development*. The practice of offsetting all, or some portion, of the cost of a degree in business is now fairly widespread. Some programs are quite specific. Gulf Oil began a collaborative program with Chatham College in 1979, specifically to assist promising women employees in furthering their educations. Large organizations sometimes conduct their own educational development, particularly of managers and executives.

Finally, a variety of employee development activities are focused on *personal development*. These are not directly related to job duties but are intended to help employees deal with issues and problems that might get in the way of their work. Examples of such programs are personal and financial counseling, physical fitness, and alcoholic treatment.

Any employee-development program will be more effective if it follows the general principles for effective training outlined earlier. There are, however, at least two aspects of effective employee-development that are unique. First, the appropriate standard for evaluating such a program is the extent to which it helps individuals progress toward development goals. It should not be possible for an employee to "fail" a development activity. Next, development, unlike training, is the primary responsibility of the individual employee. The organization can only supply the resources; it cannot force growth on people who do not want it. Managers and executives can encourage and reward development. Beyond that, they can set examples by openly working to develop their own talents and skills.

The Bottom Line

Staffing provides the manager with the human resources needed to get the job done. When managers provide information about jobs, make decisions about filling jobs with people, evaluate employee performance, and recommend and encourage staff training and development, they affect the quality of those resources and, ultimately, their own successes. From this perspective, you as a manager should:

1. Get involved in staffing decisions. Grumbling about "the kinds of people personnel sends me" has never corrected staffing problems nor earned respect. If other people recruit, select, and place employees for you, make sure they know and understand your staffing requirements. Update job descriptions and provide those who make staffing decisions with feedback about their decisions.

2. If you do your own hiring, make sure you know what you are looking for. Be able to define success for each job and to recognize its critical characteristics. Be realistic in describing the job to prospective employees. Give them enough information to make informed decisions about their own suitabilities. If you hide something about a job from candidates, they will eventually resent it.
3. Work with those responsible for training and development to identify useful employee skills that can be upgraded or learned. Don't send employees to programs simply "for additional training." You and they should have specific training goals in mind before you agree to their participation. Few things are more damaging to an employee's morale than being sent off for training without knowing why, or returning from training with new skills nobody values.
4. Develop your own skills in performance appraisal. This may require reading, practice, and training, if available. It is a critical task that most managers perform inadequately because they lack training and experience.
5. Don't underestimate the importance of good staffing. Do all you can to see that competent, qualified personnel are placed in positions that use their talents. Once they are there, see that they are encouraged and rewarded. Help them develop their talents, remembering that your own behavior as a manager provides the clearest example for your subordinates.

SUMMARY

Staffing is filling work roles with people. The nine basic staffing activities begin with job analysis, the process of analyzing a job in terms of its component tasks. The resulting job descriptions and job specifications can be used for a broad range of purposes, and made human resource planning possible.

Staff planning and forecasting provide the information for determining staffing needs by estimating future staff demand and comparing this with projected supply. A personnel inventory helps determine the portion of the supply that may be recruited from within the organization. The balance must be obtained by direct or indirect external recruiting.

Once recruited, applicants are screened to segregate qualified from non-qualified applicants. On the basis of information obtained from some combination of screening devices, such as interviews, tests, or application data, a selection decision is made. When there is more than one possible job for a selected applicant, there is also a placement decision to be made.

Training may follow placement, but often precedes it. Employee training can be carried out on or off the job, with on-the-job training being the most common. In general, training that actively involves the trainee, provides frequent feedback, and reinforces desired behavior is more effective.

Socialization implies a broad range of processes, including training, that gradually transform an organizational newcomer to an insider. There is some evidence that unsuccessful socialization is associated with increased turnover.

The major coordinating staffing-activity is performance appraisal. This process feeds back information about the success of recruiting, screening, selection, placement, and training. It also feeds forward information for human-resource planning and employee development.

Employee development covers a variety of activities to increase individual growth and career achievement. It differs from initial job training, which emphasizes the requirements of the job, in its emphasis on individual strengths and weaknesses.

Knowledge of all these issues involved in a complete staffing program can be of direct use to the manager who is given formal responsibility for some staffing activity. It can also be useful on an informal basis to solve staffing problems.

QUESTIONS FOR REVIEW AND DISCUSSION

1. Interview another student about the "job" of student. Write a job description listing the tasks (behaviors) required by this job. Then write a job specification, listing the characteristics required to be a successful student. Be specific. Remember that such information must often be used in organizations by people who have little familiarity with the job in question.
2. What is the difference between screening and selection?
3. Interview someone you know who has a full-time, nonmanagerial job about the training he or she received from the organization. Briefly describe this training and evaluate it in terms of our criteria for effective training.
4. How does performance appraisal affect training?
5. What connection can you see between employee-development programs and motivation, as it was discussed in Chapter 6?
6. How does training differ from development?
7. Suggest at least two criteria for making a placement decision when there are several possible jobs for a newly hired individual.
8. What can job analysis do for training? for appraisal?
9. Affirmative-action programs are formal attempts to hire and promote members of groups that have suffered unfair discrimination. What kinds of effects might such a program have on recruiting, training, and performance appraisal?

REFERENCES AND NOTES

1. G. Wendt, "Should Courts Write Your Job Descriptions?" *Personnel Journal*, 1977, 55, 9, p. 450.
2. A review of the role of job dissatisfaction and other factors in turnover may be found in W. B. Mobley, R. W. Griffeth, H. H. Hand, and B. M. Meglino, "Review and Conceptual Analysis of the Employee Turnover Process." *Psychological Bulletin*, 1979, 86, 3, pp. 494–522.
3. J. Curley, "More Companies Look Within for Job Managers." *Wall Street Journal*, October 28, 1980.
4. P. J. Decker and E. T. Cornelius, III. "A Note on Recruiting Sources and Job Survival Rates." *Journal of Applied Psychology*, 1979, 69, pp. 463–64.

5. J. A. Breaugh, "Relationships Between Recruiting Sources and Employee Performance, Absenteeism, and Work Attitudes." *Academy of Management Journal*, 1981, 1, pp. 142–47.
6. "Patriotism is No Longer Enough." *Time*, June 9, 1980, pp. 32–33.
7. "Florence Nightengale Wants You!" *Time*, August 24, 1981, p. 37.
8. E. D. Mayfield and R. E. Carlson, "Selection Interview Decisions: First Results from a Long-Term Research Project." Personnel Psychology, 1966, 19, 1, pp. 55–56.
9. L. N. Jewell, *Industrial/Organizational Psychology for the Eighties.* (St. Paul: West Publishing Co., 1985, in press).
10. *See* N. Schmitt and B. W. Coyle, "Applicant Decisions in the Employment Interview." *Journal of Applied Psychology*, 1976, 61, pp. 184–92.
11. The most complete source of information about commercially available screening tests is the regularly updated *Mental Measurements Yearbook*, edited by O. K. Buros, Highland Park, N.J.: Gryphon Press.
12. J. E. Hunter, "Dimensionality, Generalizability, Utility, and Fairness of the General Aptitude Test Battery (GATB)," paper presented to the American Psychological Association, August 15, 1982.
13. L. J. Tell, "EEOC's Secret Struggle with Sears." *Business and Society Review*, 1979 (Summer), 30, pp. 29–34.
14. "Distinguished Speakers," *Sloan*, Summer 1983, p. 18.
15. H. J. Reitz, *Behavior in Organizations*, 2nd ed. Homewood, Ill.: Irwin, 1981, p. 458.
16. "Conversation with E. W. Spencer and F. A. Boyle," *Organizational Dynamics*, Spring 1983, American Periodicals Division-American Management Associations, p. 27.
17. *op.cit.* p. 28.
18. More extensive coverage of these issues can be found in chapters 3–5 of G. P. Latham and K. N. Wexley, *Increasing Productivity Through Performance Appraisal.* Reading, Mass.: Addison-Wesley, 1981.

SUGGESTED READINGS

Meyer, H. E., "The Science of Telling Executives How They're Doing." *Fortune*, 1974 (January), pp. 102–12. The author gives a short history of performance appraisal with examples of methods used by a variety of American organizations. Although the article is focused on executives, the points are generally applicable.

Ritti, C. R. and G. R. Funkhouser, *The Ropes to Skip and the Ropes to Know: Studies in Organizational Behavior.* Columbus, Ohio: GRID, Inc., 1977. This is a readable, enjoyable, effective treatment of organizational socialization.

Schneider, B., *Staffing Organizations.* Pacific Palisades, Ca.: Goodyear Publishing Company, 1976. The student can use this book as a short supplemental source for several of the topics covered in this chapter. It is particularly strong on testing.

Wareham, J., "How to Judge an Executive Candidate." *Across the Board*, 1980 (October), pp. 26–35. Most students will enjoy this discussion of the kinds of information that the interview can provide and how to get it without running afoul of the EEOC. Again, the discussion has general applicability despite the title.

Case *Dr. Shibata Has Resigned!*

Todd Daniels was stunned when he read the short interoffice memorandum:

August 7

To: Todd Daniels
From: I. O. Shibata
Subject: Resignation

Please accept my resignation effective August 31. Although I do not have another position at the moment, I cannot continue working in a climate which is not conducive to creativity. It is very unfortunate that this company equates ability in direct proportion to seniority.

With regret,
I. O. Shibata

cc R. Moore

Dr. Shibata has resigned! That thought refused to leave his mind as he continued to sort through the many routine pieces of correspondence which were on his desk. Why? Why should Shibata quit so suddenly? What did he mean about ability and seniority?

Normally, Daniels would be far less concerned over a resignation, but Shibata would be a significant loss. The thirty-nine-year-old researcher had only been with the company for fourteen months but already had made several major technical contributions. Two of his concepts were already incorporated in new product designs being readied for production.

Shibata, with a Ph.D. in Electronic Engineering, was respected nationally for his theoretical papers and presentations to the American Society of Electronic Physics and other professional organiza-

tions. He had two patents to his credit and a stable, creative work background.

Daniels himself had originally approved hiring Shibata. It was just over a year ago when the company was attempting to move into the design and manufacture of a new line of sophisticated computer peripheral equipment. Shibata was hired to provide the extra bit of talent to ensure that these new products would be technically superior to all existing competition. Until now, Shibata had been doing just that and, apparently, from outward appearances at least, happy with his work and the company.

Damn, thought Daniels. If a problem was developing, why hadn't Moore taken care of it before? Why do these things end up on my desk when it's often too late for corrective action?

Most of the mail was routine and Daniels was down to the last few pieces. Then a closed envelope marked Confidential caught his eye and he opened it.

August 5

To: Todd Daniels
From: Roger Moore
Subject: Sam Fischer

Sam Fischer continues to cause problems for me. I respect the fact that he is one of our most senior employees in terms of length of employment. He is certainly one of our most loyal employees. But he is having constant blowups with Dr. Shibata and Dr. Mason on technical matters.

Sam is a fair technical man, but no match for those two. Both Shi-

Source: Abridged from "Dr. Shibata Has Resigned! In R. D. Joyce, *Encounters in Organizational Behavior: Problem Situations.* New York: Pergamon Press, Inc., 1972, pp. 106–9.

bata and Mason are annoyed with his antiquated ideas and methodologies, and I could lose one or both of them because of it.

Under other circumstances I would transfer the man. But you know how highly Martin Masters regards him. Martin still thinks of him as "Mr. Research" in this company, even though he hasn't come up with anything significant in years.

Could you please inform Martin of the seriousness of the problem, in a diplomatic way of course, before I take some kind of action?

(Note: Mr. Masters is Todd Daniels' superior. Mr. Daniels is Roger Moore's immediate superior, and Mr. Moore is the immediate superior of Mason, Fischer, Shibata, and others.)

CASE QUESTIONS

1. Dr. Shibata's letter of resignation suggests a problem in at least one of the nine basic personnel activities discussed in this chapter. What is the activity and what does Shibata see as the main problem?
2. Roger Moore's memo to Todd Daniels suggests another problem with the way the company performs one of the nine personnel activities. What might have been done to avoid the Sam Fischer problem? Is it too late?
3. What special problems will Todd Daniels face in terms of staffing activities if he has to replace Shibata? Your answer should be directed to one or more of the nine activities discussed in this chapter.
4. On the basis of the facts in the case, how would you describe the role that job analysis played in recruiting Shibata? Do you see any connection between this and Shibata's resignation? Explain your answer briefly.

18 / Social Responsibility, Government, and Unions

Suzanne was just leaving her office as the telephone rang. "Roberts here," she said, dumping a stack of computer printouts back on her desk.

"Mrs. Roberts?" a voice asked. "Mr. Carmichael wondered if you'd come up to his office for a few minutes? He said to bring your notes on the memo you sent him last Friday."

"Right away," replied Suzanne, hanging up the phone and picking up a file marked Driver Safety Memo.

As she waited for the elevator to the fifth floor, she wondered at the speed with which she had gotten a response to her memo. She had only talked with Mr. Carmichael, the director of the Regional Transit Authority, twice since she had been hired six months ago. Her memo to him had been inspired by some recent

data she had been analyzing, which indicated a sharp rise in complaints from the public about the speeding and reckless driving of the Authority's bus drivers. The memo was simply an information item, and she had expected no response at all. So Carmichael's request to see her less than a week later was a pleasant surprise. Big companies can respond quickly to problems, she thought happily.

Mr. Carmichael's greeting was businesslike, but cordial. He waved her to a chair, then got right to the point. "About your memo on Friday. First of all, I liked the style—brief, informative, to the point. Most of the young people around here have to learn that if you can't get my attention in one page, you can't get it at all. But you're different. You got it right

the first time, and I'm impressed."

Suzanne nodded and said a prayer of thanks for the instructor who had helped her make the transition from academic writing (elegant, wordy) to business writing (streamlined, functional).

"Your data show a clear and significant upward trend in both written and phoned-in complaints. Any other evidence?" he asked.

"Yes, sir. Traffic citations are up, too, though the increase is not as significant," she replied.

"What about accidents?" he asked.

"Accident reports show no discernable increase in number, hours lost, or estimated costs—yet," Suzanne replied.

"What do you mean, 'Yet'?"

"Well, if our drivers are, in fact, speeding more and driving more recklessly, it's only a matter of time before they have more accidents," she offered.

"Not necessarily," he countered. "We've got good drivers, most of them highly experienced, with good driving records. We get rid of people who have accidents. Nevertheless, your report disturbs me. I'll get a memo out to all drivers today telling them, in effect, to cool it for a while."

Sensing the meeting was over, Suzanne rose to leave, then hesitated.

"Something else?" Mr. Carmichael asked. Suzanne thought for a few seconds, then decided to press her luck. "Actually, yes. I prepared another memo over the weekend just in case you felt the driver problem was important."

"It is," he affirmed. "What's it say?"

"It outlines a program to change driver habits, reduce reckless driving, and increase compliance with speed limits," she answered.

Mr. Carmichael stared for a few seconds. Finally, he sighed. "Sit down, Ms. Roberts. Let me explain to you a few simple facts of life about urban

transportation. We exist to serve the riding public. We compete against all other forms of transportation, including cars, bicycles, motorcycles, and horses, I suppose. People ride on buses because they can't drive, because it's cheaper and only somewhat less convenient than other ways, or to avoid parking problems. They stop riding buses when buses are slow or late, infrequently scheduled, or fares make it cheaper to drive.

"To meet their demands for frequent, fast, and cheap service, our drivers have to meet tight schedules, even—no, especially—during rush hours. If they obeyed all traffic laws and speed limits during those times, they'd wind up fifteen to twenty minutes off schedule. Then you'd really see complaints from the public—which would reach the ears of the mayor and city council—which would threaten our jobs or our subsidies.

"Therefore, we provide incentives to drivers who meet their schedules. Sometimes they get a little enthusiastic, like now, and we have to tell them to slack off for a while. It's bad public-relations to get too many complaints or tickets.

"But what about the danger of accidents?" Suzanne persisted.

"We don't encourage our drivers to be reckless. Anyone who has an accident is suspended, regardless of cause. Two accidents and he or she is out, transferred to other duties, unless circumstances suggest otherwise. But to serve the public's demands for fast, frequent, efficient, cheap service, we increase the number of trips each driver makes per day."

"But one bad accident," she began.

"Ms. Roberts," he interrupted, *"look at your data. When was our last 'bad' accident? Six years ago? We carry insurance. Our drivers get better every year. Our rates go down. If the insurance company's satisfied, so are we."*

"Yes, sir," she replied, and again stood up to leave. As she turned to go, he looked up from his next stack of papers and stopped her.

"Ms. Roberts? Keep up the good work. And show your colleagues how to write a memo—short, direct, and to the point. Save time—everybody's; that's what it's all about."

Up to this point in Part 4 we have defined and described the manager's world in terms of the organization itself, its policies and structures, its financial and human resources. We have described its impact on the manager's job.

In this chapter we will look at the environment, the larger system of which an organization is a part. While not denying the importance of the physical environment such as the climate and material resources, we will concentrate on an organization's social environment. In particular we will look at the limits placed on an organization and its managers by unions and government agencies, and its responsibilities as a member of society.

The Regional Transit Authority, in this story, is interdependent with various parts of its environment. Federal, state, and local government regulate its fares and operations. They also permit its operation as a monopoly in public transportation. State and local government provide operating subsidies from tax revenues; the public provides taxes and riders who pay fares; unions provide drivers and negotiate their pay and working conditions. Sometimes the interests of these different segments of the environment conflict with each other; in the story, traffic laws control speed while the riding public's demand for cheap service encourages it. It is usually left to the manager to strike a balance among the conflicting demands and constraints of the environment.

INTERDEPENDENCY OF ORGANIZATIONS AND SOCIETY

A systems view of organizations emphasizes the interdependence of the various parts, or subsystems, of the organization. It also highlights an organization's dependence on its external environment for resources, such as labor and materials, and markets for its products or services. These are, at the same time, both opportunities for and limits placed on organizational inputs and outputs.

The environment also places constraints on policies and day-to-day activities. They put demands that would have been unheard of seventy-five years ago on today's organizations. These demands arose initially because organizations did not

Exhibit 18.1 The Organization and Its Environment

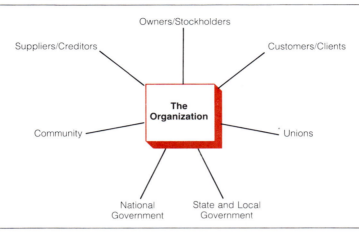

assume sufficient responsibility for the people who worked for them, consumed their products or services, or lived in the changed environments they created. Pressures to be concerned with the effects of their activities and decisions on society in general, and workers in particular, have been growing throughout this century. They came first from unions; now they also come from state, local, and federal governments, consumer advocate groups, environmentalists, and a variety of groups interested in specific aspects of worker welfare. (See Exhibit 18.1)

The question of whether organizations and their managers should accept part of the responsibility for the welfare of citizens and the environment is no longer open to debate. It is generally recognized that they have a certain degree of accountability for their actions, because they are members of the societies that tolerate their existence. When *an organization's responsibilities to others are legally formalized by outsiders,* they are called **institutionalized constraints.** *The broader, less formalized accountability to consumers, the environment, and general social welfare* is usually referred to as **corporate social responsibility.** These two issues form the subject matter of this chapter.

CORPORATE SOCIAL RESPONSIBILITY

Corporate social responsibility includes all those claims made on an organization by the interest groups represented in Exhibit 18.1: the community, suppliers and creditors, owners and stockholders, customers and clients, unions and governments. In addition to these segments of the organization's environment, corporate social responsibility has come to include the interests of the organization's employees. In many cases, their interests are represented by unions. However, only one third of the American labor force is unionized, so the interests of employees are often a separate issue.

In this section we will discuss the responsibilities of an organization to five groups that lay claim to consideration in its activities and decisions: customers/

clients; suppliers/creditors; owners/stockholders; the community; and employees. In later sections we will discuss, in more detail, the relationships between organizations and governments and unions. In the introductory story, the director of the RTA explained to Suzanne the pressures he felt from its customers, while she argued for the concerns of the community. Their conflicting interests affected another concerned group, the drivers themselves, whose welfare both Suzanne and the director had overlooked: they were under pressures which induced them to violate traffic laws.

Responsibility to Workers

Among those responsibilities organizations now may be expected to bear for employees are providing for equitable pay, satisfaction, opportunity, and a healthy work environment. The term *quality of working life* has received considerable attention in both academia and business, as concerns with mental and physical health problems, drug abuse, and other stress-induced outcomes have grown. Stress and its outcomes will be specifically discussed in the next chapter; we should point out here, however, that many organizations are redesigning jobs and creating work environments that will improve the quality of working life for their employees. Leaders in this area include Cummins Engine, General Motors, Nabisco, and Shell Oil.[1]

Concern for employee health has been particularly visible in the past few years. It has been estimated that one in four workers in this country may run a risk of illness because of past exposure to dangerous materials on the job. Companies are now providing regular medical checkups for their employees and sponsoring fitness, diet, and antismoking campaigns to improve employee health. One of the more extensive programs is run by Pittsburgh Corning Corporation, which spends hundreds of thousands of dollars a year on checkups for 1074 employees and retirees who worked for the company when it made asbestos pipe covering.[2]

Responsibility to Customers and Clients

Most of us realize that consumer protection has become a big issue in recent years. A considerable amount of this protection has become institutionalized in the form of legislation, such as consumer safety laws, truth-in-advertising laws, and various "disclosure laws," such as statements of interest rates on retail charge accounts and listings of ingredients on foods and drugs.

From a corporate social-responsibility viewpoint, the obligations of organizations to customers and clients do not end with compliance to laws. There are additional responsibilities.

First, there is continued self-initiated monitoring and research of products for possible safety hazards. A few years ago, Corning Glass initiated a mass voluntary, recall program. Its target was a popular line of ceramic coffee pots, the handles of which had been found to detach without warning. While Corning could have merely issued information about this hazard, it went a step further. Merchandise incentives were offered to customers who returned the lids from the potentially dangerous items.

Companies also have provisions for back-up services to confused or dissatisfied customers. Polaroid Corporation, for example, prints a customer-service telephone number on every product, and will take toll-free calls to answer any questions. Other companies offer no-questions-asked refunds in exchange for feedback about the source of dissatisfaction with the product.

Finally, organizations try to provide advance explanations of services, costs, and risks. Those who provide professional services are being increasingly pressured to take the mystery out of their activities. The "Put yourself in my hands; I'm the doctor" mystique is under severe attack. Patients are now demanding rights to make certain treatment-related decisions themselves, as well as asking for full disclosure of the hows and whys of treatment, and risks, if any.

Responsibility to Suppliers and Creditors

An organization is responsible to those who supply materials and financial resources for its products and services. There are really two issues here. One is the definition of an appropriate behavior *toward* suppliers and creditors, which includes payment for goods and services rendered; fair consideration of bids; and the use of supplies and credit in a legal manner. The other issue is the definition of ethical behavior.

Payoffs and kickbacks are not new phenomena in organizations. Neither are personal gifts to "oil the wheels of commerce." But with the increasing internationalization of business, bribery on a large scale seems to have become a major problem. It has also taken on a new complexity. Bethlehem Steel, for example, recently pleaded guilty to a conspiracy in which about $1 million was smuggled into the United States from Switzerland. Approximately half of this money, most in cash, was paid to shipowners and agents in return for ship repair trade for Bethlehem ship yards.

Responsibility to Owners and Shareholders

The responsibility of an organization and its managers to its owners is the oldest recognized form of corporate, social responsibility. It is usually seen in monetary terms—a responsibility to provide a satisfactory return on shareholder investments. In recent years, the responsibility for protecting the owners of a company from financial harm and rewarding shareholders for their investment in this company has begun to conflict with other social responsibilities. Money spent on public-service advertising and information programs; sponsorship of public television, local orchestras, ballet companies, and theater groups; donations for such activities as removing litter from parks or highways; provision of libraries, gymnasiums, and other recreational facilities for employees; and voluntary environmental projects

The Rouse Company has pioneered retail shopping places that include major downtown redevelopments, such as this blend of old and new buildings with restored commerce flourishing along New York's East River.

such as reforestation or urban renewal is money that is not available for distribution to owners and shareholders.

From the perspective of the organization as part of the larger system of society, there is really no clash between its responsibility to its owners and to other aspects of its social environment. Fulfilling what the public sees as its social responsibilities is becoming increasingly necessary to organizational survival. This is especially true in areas, like oil companies and retailing operations such as Sears and J. C. Penney, where potential customers see fewer and fewer real differences in quality or service.

Responsibility to the Community

The question of the social responsibility of an organization to its community is really a question of the extent of business' responsibility for such broad social problems as urban blight, unemployment, pollution, inflation, and even declining moral standards. To date, this is the least institutionalized aspect of corporate social responsibility. Most efforts are entirely voluntary. For example, Delta Airlines finds other work for employees unable to perform their usual jobs, instead of dismissing them or laying them off during slack periods. Procter & Gamble, attacking a different social issue, has withdrawn advertising from some fifty television programs in a recent one-year period because of the excessive sex and violence on these programs. Finally, a Toronto merchant and restauranteur bought and restored an historical theater slated for demolition. The theater is now a center of cultural activity in the city.

No one would say that the actions of Delta, Procter & Gamble, or the Toronto businessman were without self-interest. However, that is precisely the rationale of the claims laid to organizations by the social environment. Social responsibility is everybody's business because it serves everyone's interests. The well-being of our country's senior citizens, for example, affects each and every one of us sooner or later. (See Exhibit 18.2.)

SOCIAL RESPONSIBILITY AND THE MANAGER

Of necessity, our discussion of the relationship between organizations and their social environments is simplified. However, it requires only a brief consideration of the dilemmas posed by conflicting institutionalized regulations and moral obligations to put the matter into a more realistic perspective.

1. Higher quality goods (responsibility to consumers) cost more to produce (reduced profits for owners, higher costs to consumers).
2. Better compensation programs (responsibility to workers) result in higher prices (high costs to consumers, fewer able to buy product or service).
3. Compliance with laws to make up for past employment discrimination (responsibility to women and minorities) takes job opportunities away from white males who need them (denial of equal opportunity to one segment of the population).

INSTITUTIONALIZED CONSTRAINTS

Of the five major interest groups to which organizations are obligated, two are organized sufficiently to be discussed separately: workers, who are represented by unions, and the community, represented by local, state, and federal governments. Because governments predate unions and are a more pervasive force in management, we will discuss them first.

Impact of Regulation

Although governments have always been an important part of organization's environments, their impact on organizational functioning has grown dramatically since World War II. Regulations are established and enforced at all levels of government, from local pollution ordinances to federal antitrust laws, and are widely diffused through a bewildering variety of agencies and court rulings. It can take considerable detective work just to figure out exactly what regulations apply to a particular organization in a given situation and what it must do to be in compliance.

One effect has been to increase the size and power of corporate legal departments, which grew by an estimated fifty percent in the early 1980s. In 1984, one out of every five lawyers in the United States worked directly for a corporation! Their advice is no longer limited to dealing with existing problems. According to

Exhibit 18.2   Community Social Responsibility: A New Way to Help Senior Citizens

Property Rich, Cash Poor

On paper, Ruth Boe, 72, is a wealthy woman. Since she bought her modest six-room house near San Francisco in 1950, its value has surged from $10,500 to $139,000. But interest payments on her savings, plus a monthly $395.50 Social Security check, are not enough to pay for her rising food, utility and repair bills. Desperate and disheartened, Boe feared that if her savings became depleted, she could be forced to sell her home in order to raise enough money to live.

Last month the Crocker National Bank solved Boe's cash problem. The mechanism: a reverse mortgage, meaning in essence a loan against the value of her house. For the next six years, she will receive a monthly payment of $746.50. Then at the end of that period, she can sell the home in order to pay back the money or she may be able to take out an additional loan, provided that her home has continued to increase in value. Says Boe hap-

Ruth Boe at home in Fairfax

pily: "I urgently needed the money. It's my home, and I love it. I'd have been sick if I had to leave."

The loan was arranged by the San Francisco–area Reverse Annuity Mortgage Program, a pilot project sponsored by the Ford and San Francisco Foundations and the Federal Home Loan Bank Board to help elderly homeowners who are property rich but cash poor. Nearly 60% of Americans 65 or older own their homes, free of mortgage debt. The value of that property is estimated to be some $500 billion.

Consumers are expected to welcome the loans once they become more widely available; at present, though, some are taking a wait-and-see attitude because of high interest rates. Bankers say they support the program's social goals, but they question whether the program will become a real money-maker. Banks earn very little on the loans in the early years, since their value is rather small. The sponsors, though, hope that banks will learn how to make a profit on the loans and help retired people unlock the wealth stored in their homes.

Martin G. McGuinn, general cousel for Mellon National Corporation, "We are providing counsel in management decisions from beginning to end."[3]

Government Regulation

State and Local Government Regulation.   State and local governments solely regulate zoning, building codes, fire regulations, taxes, insurance provisions, waste disposal, hours of operation, employment of minors, serving of alcoholic beverages, and bonding of service personnel. Other areas may be subject to dual regulation, such as state regulation of employee health and safety, which is subject to federal approval.

Because state and local regulation is so business- and location-specific, it is difficult to make general statements about the limits it places on the individual manager. We can point out, however, that since most organizations are licensed for operation by the state, city, or county in which they are located, these regulations are important.

General Federal Regulation.   Like state and local regulation, federal prescriptions for organizations are extensive, depending on the nature of the business. The Internal Revenue Service promulgates financial limits for all organizations. Banks, and savings and loan institutions, have the interest rates they can charge or pay regulated via policies set by the Federal Reserve Bank; and since the Wall Street crash of 1929, buying and selling of stocks and securities have also been regulated. There are minimum wage laws and regulations about prices. All airline fares, for example, must have government approval, although airlines are no longer subject to controls on competition.

There are regulations to protect the environment from industrial exploitation and pollution, and regulations to protect consumers from dangerous products and fraudulent claims. A controversial rule requiring used-car dealers to disclose what mechanical inspections they have made on cars offered for sale to the public is one of the latest efforts in consumer-protection.[4]

The few examples in the paragraphs above are meant only to suggest the nature and scope of federal constraints on organizational functioning. In the remainder of this section, we will focus on the areas of federal regulation that probably have the greatest impact on the manager's day-to-day activities—equal opportunity and health and safety. Both fall into the category of protective controls.

Equal-Employment-Opportunity (EEO) Regulation. Few kinds of institutionalized, external constraints have caused the confusion, frustration, and distress of those relating to organizational personnel practices. At least a dozen federal laws are involved, and it seems that hardly a week goes by without the appearance of a new case or court ruling that must be implemented. Amidst this confusion, it helps to remember this one fact: *The primary goal of equal-employment-opportunity legislation is the prevention of unlawful discrimination.*

> *The individual manager may expect to deal with ethical problems created by situations arising out of conflicting claims for social responsibility on organizations. Developing a strong set of personal ethics before confronting these issues will make such decisions considerably easier.*

It is often supposed that the purpose of government regulation of organizational personnel practices is to prevent *discrimination*. That is not true. The purpose is to prevent *unlawful* discrimination.

In the true sense of the word, organizations have no choice but to discriminate. They cannot hire every person who applies for a job. They cannot promote and give big raises and bonuses to all of those they do hire. They must find some way to distinguish, or discriminate, the more qualified job applicants from the less qualified, and the better performers from the poorer ones. The intent of EEO laws is to see that this discrimination is lawful; that it is carried out on the basis of job-related characteristics such as skills, ability, knowledge, experience, and performance.

When discrimination among job applicants or employees is on the basis of characteristics not related to job behavior, or keeps out a disproportionate number of some group (such as women or blacks), it is unlawful. Suppose that a manager is hiring a truck loader. The loading process is automated, but loading goes more quickly and efficiently if the loader is able to shift heavy boxes and make position adjustments. Thus, strength is a job-related characteristic.

A manager could interview only men for this job. After all, men, in general, are stronger than women, in general. However, if the manager follows this policy, he or she is hiring on the basis of sex, not strength. Therefore, the manager is clearly guilty of unlawful discrimination.

To avoid the possible problems stemming from using sex as a screening device for the job of truck loader, the manager decides to use a strength test. Since many of the items to be loaded weigh as much as 250 pounds, the manager decides to hire only those applicants who can lift such a box. Following this procedure, he hires over the next year, approximately one quarter of the men and one of the fifty women who apply for the job.

However, unless the manager can prove that the ability to lift 250 pounds is the *best* way to select people strong enough to load trucks quickly and efficiently, he or she may still be guilty of unlawful discrimination. The screening test keeps out a disproportionate number of women who apply. In legal terms, it has adverse impact.

Adverse impact occurs *when a personnel practice systematically excludes a disproportionate number of some employee or applicant group from selection, promotion, or other employment opportunity.* This dimension is measured by *selection ratio.* In the example of the truck loader, the selection ratio for male applicants was one out of four applicants (1:4); that for female applicants was one out of fifty (1:50). In general, this is an adverse impact since there is more than a 20-percent difference between the relevant selection ratios. Thus, to avoid adverse impact, the ratio for women in our example would have to be raised to approximately 1:5.

Lawful discrimination is discrimination that is *valid* (based on job-related characteristics) and *free of adverse impact.* All other bases constitute unlawful discrimination. Intent, or lack of it, has proved almost impossible to document, but effects can be demonstrated by statistics such as the selection ratio.

There are some twelve federal acts and executive orders related to EEO. Of these, the main pillar is Title VII of the Civil Rights Act of 1964, as amended by the Equal Opportunity Act of 1972. **Title VII** *prohibits discrimination on the basis of race, creed, nationality, color, and sex in all terms and conditions of employment.* "Terms and conditions of employment" include hiring, promotion, special training, and similar opportunities. (Discrimination on the basis of age was specifically made unlawful by the Age Discrimination in Employment Act.)

Title VII and the related EEO legislation are administered and enforced by the Equal Employment Opportunity Commission (EEOC). Either the Commission or an individual (or group) may bring charges against an organization if reasonable cause can be demonstrated. *Reasonable cause* here means a suspicion of discrimination founded on circumstances sufficiently strong to cause a reasonable person to believe the charge is true. A portion of a claim of discrimination on the basis of age is shown in Exhibit 18.3.

As we have noted, intent to discriminate is almost impossible to prove. Therefore, most charges rest on whether the effect of a practice is unlawful discrimination. If it is shown to be so, the EEOC is empowered to require the organization to do any, or all, of the following, depending on the case:

1. Reinstate, or admit, the individual (or group) to the job, organization, training, or other, opportunity.
2. Make restitution for lost opportunities in the form of back pay.
3. Pay all attorney fees associated with the case.
4. Develop a mandatory affirmative action program for the group to which the individual(s) bringing the suit belongs.

An affirmative-action plan (AAP) has goals, means, and timetables for recruiting and promoting members of groups that are underrepresented in a particular

Exhibit 18.3 Partial Reproduction of an Age Discrimination Complaint

30 Jul 1980

From: Secretary of the Navy
To: Mr. William S.
Via: Commanding Officer,

Subj: Discrimination complaint; decision on

Encl: (1) Copy of Complaints Examiner's report
       (2) Copy of hearing transcript

1. The complete case record concerning your complaint of discrimination based on age (over forty), including the findings and recommended decision of the Complaints Examiner, has been carefully reviewed. Copies of the Complaints Examiner's report and the hearing transcript are forwarded as enclosures (1) and (2).

2. You allege that because of your age you were not selected for the position of Supply Management Trainee, GS-5 (various series), advertised in Announcement No. 45 (73), a position for which you applied and for which you were found to be highly qualified.

3. Your complaint was initially rejected as untimely by your employer whose action was affirmed by Civil Service Commission's Appeals Review Board. You then sought relief in an appropriate U.S. District Court and were successful. On 5 November 1976 the court issued an order remanding your complaint to your employer for further processing.

4. Your complaint was thereupon referred for investigation. Following the conclusion of that process and after submission of the Investigative Report, a copy of which was furnished you, you were issued a notice of proposed disposition of your complaint reflecting a finding of no discrimination. The issuance of the proposed disposition was preceded by a discussion between you and the Commanding Officer, on 28 November 1977, held in an unsuccessful attempt to resolve the issues causing your dissatisfaction and underlying your complaint. The proposed disposition was not to your liking and by letter of 20 December 1977 you requested that a hearing of your complaint be held.

5. A Complaints Examiner of the Civil Service Commission's Federal Employee Appeals Authority was appointed and a hearing was scheduled for 31 January 1978. By letter dated 18 January 1978 your representative asked that the scheduled hearing be postponed until early March. The Complaints Examiner thereupon remanded the case file to your employer who, on 1 February 1978, forwarded the case file to this Office for a decision based on the then existing record.

The Commission ruled in favor of the employee making the complaint.

---

job, organization, trade, or industry. It is, then, a strategy for compensating for *past* unfair personnel practices. EEO, by contrast, is aimed at preventing *future* unlawful discrimination.

Underrepresentation occurs when there is a large discrepancy between the numbers of some group available for a job and the numbers hired for or promoted to it. Women, for example, make up approximately 42 percent of the American work force, but only 5 percent of all upper-level managers and administrators earning over $20,000 a year; they are underrepresented in upper management.

An AAP may be completely voluntary, part of a voluntary settlement of a case, or ordered by the EEOC as part of a claims settlement. However, other legislation does specify certain organizations that must develop and implement written AAPs, even if no charges have been brought against them. Executive Order #4 (Revised), issued by the Office of Federal Contract Compliance Programs, requires organizations of a certain size, doing business with the federal government in excess of certain yearly amounts, to submit plans for hiring, developing, and promoting women and minorities.[4] The Rehabilitation Act and the Vietnam Era Veterans Readjustment Assistance Act extend this requirement to the handicapped and to veterans of the armed forces who served during the conflict in Vietnam.

In many ways, the impact of EEO regulations is similar to the limits imposed by unionization. Both require certain practices and prohibit others, but for the individual manager, compliance also means he or she must remember these constraints in the course of daily planning, organizing, directing, and controlling. Looking briefly at the implications of a labor force analysis for the directing function and a review of research for the controlling function shows why. Forecasts for the 1980s indicate that more women, more imigrant workers, and fewer workers over fifty-five years of age will be in the labor force.[5] These trends, combined with the effects of EEO regulations, suggest that it will become even more difficult to make general assumptions about the rewards that should be given to workers. Individual differences will continue to be important, but there must be an added consideration of changes in the general composition of the work force, one which the white male will no longer dominate (See Exhibit 18.4).

A recent review of the relevant research found that sex bias in performance appraisal does indeed exist to a significant degree. Furthermore, it affects some evaluation situations more than others; women in jobs traditionally held by men are particularly subject to such bias.[6] Since one effect of EEO is to place increasing numbers of women in such jobs, the use of performance appraisal in controlling will require more attention if a manager is to be both effective and in compliance with the law.

The claims of various segments of an organization's environment that are not yet formalized are usually referred to as social responsibility.

Managers of the future may expect to face related issues that were not even mentioned a few years ago. One of these issues is sexual harassment.

The Civil Rights Act of 1964 was amended in 1980 to make sexual harassment in the workplace illegal. Guidelines issued by the EEOC outlaw any requests for sexual favors, unwelcome sexual advances, or verbal or physical conduct of a sexual nature if *any* of the following conditions exist: submission to such conduct is either an explicit or an implicit condition of employment; employment decisions affecting an individual are made on the basis of submission to, or rejection of, such conduct; or such conduct creates an offensive work environment or interferes with an individual's work performance.

Many women are reluctant to accuse someone of sexual harassment. It is also very difficult to prove, even if an accusation is made. However, there is no doubt that things are changing. Recently, for example, the director of a popular state recreation-area was asked to resign his $38,000-a-year post after a female tour guide filed a sexual harassment charge against him. Such cases are becoming more frequent.

Issues such as this one make it clear that, as a society, we are at least considering the goal of fair- and equal-employment opportunity for all. Impressive gains

Exhibit 18.4   Increasing Percentages of Women Now Occupying Traditionally Male-Dominated Jobs

Occupation	Percentage of Jobs Held by Women 1970–71	1980–81
Engineer	1%	4%
Lawyer, judge	4	14
Medical doctor	9	22
Manager	19	31
Insurance adjuster	26	58*
Postmaster, mail superintendent	32	44
Personnel, labor relations	33	47
Bill collector	37	63*

*Other occupations in which women outnumber men are real estate agent; photographic process worker; checker, examiner, and inspector; production-line assembler.

Sources: F. J. Prial, "Women Are in Majority in Six Major Jobs," *N.Y. Times News Service,* May 14, 1982; "U.S. Women Control Almost 33% of Management Jobs," *Associated Press,* April 11, 1984.

have been made in a relatively short period of time. Both the spirit and the letter of EEO laws require a manager to make personnel decisions on the basis of an employee's ability to do the job rather than on the basis of the manager's personal feelings. Fortunately, this works to everyone's advantage.

Employee Health and Safety Regulations.   There is little agreement about the actual number of work-related illnesses, accidents, and deaths that occur each year, but no one disputes that the number is too high by any standards. All cost money, time, and psychological distress; human beings suffer and so do organizations.

Prior to 1969, when the Coal Mine Health and Safety Act was passed, the primary responsibility for health and safety was placed on the individual. Employees were expected to be careful and to see their doctors regularly. Exposure to the hazards of particular jobs, such as coal mining, were believed to be a matter of individual choice.

The comprehensive Occupational Health and Safety Act (OSHA), passed in 1970, shifted the main formal responsibility for employee health and safety from the individual to the employer. Organizations were expected to create and maintain a healthful and safe work environment for all employees. This responsibility included designing jobs for maximum safety, providing and maintaining safety equipment, and eliminating or reducing such hazards as air pollution, noise, extremes in temperature, and overcrowding (see Exhibit 18.5).

OSHA, passed only after a great deal of legislative haggling, has broad powers. With some exceptions, all private employers who do any business affecting interstate commerce are required to provide a work environment free from obvious and recognized hazards, and comply with the safety provisions of OSHA. To comply with these provisions, employers must also submit to OSHA inspections, and keep records of work-related illnesses, accidents, and deaths, which are then submitted annually to OSHA. Exhibit 18.6 shows the form to be used in the required annual summary.

Battle Building Over 'Right to Know' Laws Regarding Toxic Items Used by Workers

By Frank Allen

Staff Reporter of The Wall Street Journal

Over the past couple of years, small bands of people have gathered briefly outside city halls and state capital buildings, wearing surgical masks and carrying placards that say "We need to know."

The demonstrators represent an alliance of factory workers, disabled people, environmentalists, lawyers, union organizers, firefighters, police and other people who show increasing political savvy. What they seek are laws requiring businesses to disclose to their employees and the public the names and potential health hazards of any toxic substances the employees use on the job.

New York, California, Michigan and five other states already have such "right-to-know" laws, as do Philadelphia, Cincinnati and Pennsauken, N.J. Similar measures are pending in about 20 state legislatures. Some unions have vowed to seek such legislation in every state, a prospect that alarms chemical makers and other businesses.

"We're going to introduce a bill in another East Coast state on Jan. 18," says Michael J. Smith, research director for the International Association of Fire Fighters. "But I won't say which state. We don't want to give the chemical companies a chance to get lined up against it before then."

New Jersey Battle

The fight already brewing over such a bill in New Jersey promises to be a vigorous test. The state has one of the largest concentrations of chemical manufacturing in the world and, according to the Environmental Protection Agency, 65 of the worst hazardous waste sites in the country.

Chemical makers believe the law would be costly for them and would endanger trade secrets. They see the New Jersey contest as a turning point that provides an opportunity to weaken the right-to-know movement. But labor unions and other groups, helped by sympathy for victims of such occupational ailments as asbestosis, are rallying to support the New Jersey legislation.

"What we are most interested in is labeling the chemicals in the work place," says James Lanard, an attorney who works for the New Jersey Environmental Lobby. "Without labeling, workers have no way of knowing what precautions to take."

Injured and disabled workers often relate their experiences at legislative hearings. Some say they unwittingly inhaled toxic fumes or suffered eye damage from toxic smoke. Others tell of burns and blisters from unlabeled or mislabeled acids.

"For some of us, it's already too late," says Thaddeus Kowalski, a 54-year old resident of Manville, N.J., who retired with full disability at age 38 after working 20 years in an asbestos factory. "This town is just loaded with asbestosis victims, even though a lot of them never worked in the plant."

Most right-to-know laws require companies to provide employees with information sheets that describe certain toxic substances used on the job, the symptoms of exposure and the procedures to take in emergencies. The New Jersey bill, still being revised in committee, also would require companies to make information sheets about these substances available to the public, particularly in communities where the materials are being used.

It's difficult to say how extensive toxic-exposure problems in the work place have become. Based on an 18-state survey, the Bureau of Labor Statistics estimates that 44,000 U.S. employees filed worker's compensation claims in 1980 for

> *"The large chemical companies aren't the ones this bill is aimed at," says a Du Pont worker about the New Jersey bill. "We worry about the little plants and the nonunion plants."*

occupational injuries and illnesses of which chemicals were the source. The bureau says these claims represent less than 2% of all claims for occupational injuries and illnesses filed that year.

But other workers who also were hurt or sick in 1980 because of exposure to chemicals probably didn't file claims, the bureau says. Besides, some illnesses stemming from exposure to toxics go undetected for years, and the cause itself often isn't easy to isolate.

Many manufacturers have excellent programs for informing employees about hazardous substances and training them in safe usage. "The large chemical companies aren't the ones this bill is aimed at," says Charles Morris, a Du Pont Co. pipe fitter who belongs to the New Jersey Right-to-Know Coalition. "We worry about the little plants and the nonunion plants. Why shouldn't everyone be entitled to get this information?"

Exhibit 18.6   OSHA Summary Reporting Form

Injury and Illness Category		Fatalities	Lost Workday Cases			Nonfatal Cases Without Lost Workdays*	
			Number of Cases	Number of Cases Involving Permanent Transfer to Another Job or Termination of Employment	Number of Lost Workdays	Number of Cases	Number of Cases Involving Transfer to Another Job or Termination of Employment
Code 1	Category 2	3	4	5	6	7	8
10	Occupational Injuries						
	Occupational Illnesses						
21	Occupational Skin Diseases or Disorders						
22	Dust Diseases of the Lungs (Pneumoconioses)						
23	Respiratory Conditions due to Toxic Agents						
24	Poisoning (Systemic Effects of Toxic Materials)						
25	Disorders due to Physical Agents (Other than Toxic Materials)						
26	Disorders due to Repeated Trauma						
29	All Other Occupational Illnesses						
	Total — Occupational Illnesses (21-29)						
	Total — Occupational Injuries and Illnesses						

*Nonfatal Cases Without Lost Workdays—Cases resulting in: medical treatment beyond first aid, diagnosis of occupational illness, loss of consciousness, restriction of work or motion, or transfer to another job (without lost workdays).

Source: Occupational Safety and Health Administration.

OSHA is administered by the U.S. Department of Labor. Its inspectors respond to requests for inspection from employers, employees, or union officials. It also initiates its own inspections, but a court ruling in the late 1970s dictates that these inspections must be accompanied by a court-issued authorization.

If an organization is found guilty of a violation, OSHA may levy fines or close the place of business if there is extreme hazard. The Justice Department is also considering the possibility of criminal charges against employers who consistently flout OSHA provisions.

Management in Action
Corporate Social-Responsibility Projects at Control Data

BLOOMINGTON, Minn.—A few years back, Control Data Corp. had what it thought was a bright idea for helping ex-convicts. To make it easier for them to find and hold down jobs, a Control Data subsidiary began financing used cars at low rates for former inmates.

But the Wheels Program didn't work out as planned. Some of the ex-cons took the cars and vanished forever. The former inmate hired to run the program pocketed some of the money for himself. Before the company's auditors caught on, 34 autos and some $137,000 were missing.

If you think that was the end of the program, though, think again. After shelving it for a while, Control Data plans to give it another try—with a few more safeguards, of course.

"Cars for Cons," as some wags at the company call it, is vintage Control Data—a venture that most corporations would view skeptically but that Control Data embraces zealously under its self-proclaimed mission of "addressing society's major unmet needs as profitable business opportunities."

Control Data is one of the most eccentric—admirers say visionary—corporations in America. Founded 25 years ago, it has grown into a computer and financial-services giant that earned $170.6 million on revenue of $4.2 billion in 1981. It makes one of the fastest super-computers in the world. Its peripheral computer products are so advanced that other computer companies use them.

But it also is a company that, largely because of the whims of William C. Norris, its founder and chairman, dabbles in numerous ventures that perennially lose money. Control Data grows vegetables hydroponically on rooftops, imports products such as Yugoslavian wine, draws up urban-renewal plans and provides health care on Indian reservations. And over the past 20 years, it has poured more than $900 million into a computer-education project that has yet to show a penny of profit, while newcomers in the field already are making money.

As unusual as they sound, Control Data says, these projects are positioning the company for prosperity for years to come and showing corporate America how to solve social problems. But for the foreseeable future, critics respond, they are a drag on corporate profits.

But the 71-year-old Mr. Norris, a short, white-haired man who relishes his reputation as a maverick, couldn't care less what the critics say. In his view of the future, Mr. Norris sees nothing less than a new role for private enterprise: Corporations, not government, increasingly will take the lead in finding new ways to solve unemployment, rehabilitate criminals, redevelop inner cities and improve schools.

Source: L. Ingrassia, "Seeking to Aid Society, Control Data Takes on Many Novel Ventures," *Wall Street Journal*, December 22, 1982, pp. 1, 10.

As with union agreements and equal-employment-opportunity regulations, the individual manager is required to be aware of external regulations regarding employee health and safety, and to operate within these guidelines. This is no easy task. The original OSHA standards cover several hundred pages of fine print, and yearly updates can be twice that length. Few managers have either the time or the inclination to monitor compliance to such intimidating volumes of regulations. The fact remains, however, that they are responsible for enforcement. Planning and organizing must be guided by safety, as well as by efficiency and effectiveness, even in the small things. If company standard-issue ladders have a maximum OSHA safety rating of 225 pounds, for example, a 270-pound employee should not be allowed on it, even if that employee is the most skilled person available for the particular task.

An obvious requirement of directing is that the goals set do not prejudice the health and safety of employees. Particular attention should be paid to deadlines or quotas that may encourage overexertion or safety shortcuts, such as those experienced by the bus drivers of the RTA in the story that introduced this chapter.

One of the more debated issues with respect to safety and the directing function of management is the wisdom of implementing specific incentive programs for employee safety. The idea behind the practice is sound; if safety is the desired behavior, reward it. This was the kind of program Suzanne had proposed for the RTA bus drivers.

A typical safety incentive program gives some form of award for accident-free work days or an award to the organizational unit with the fewest accidents in some period of time. Proponents say the practice is a valuable follow-up to safety education. Detractors say it encourages failure to report accidents. Some believe that incentives more powerful than typical safety awards are required to make any real improvement. The experience at Parson's Pine Products in Oregon suggests that strong incentives can work dramatically. Parson's offered to distribute to employees any refund from the state's industrial accident fund. As a result, the firm's accident bill dropped from over $28,000 to under $3000 in one year. Refunds amounted to almost $1000 per employee.[7]

The controlling function of management is affected by health and safety regulations, both in general and in particular. It is necessary to have controls to see that the OSHA regulations are being followed. Larger organizations often institute a direct control system in the form of safety departments. These departments set policy and rules for compliance, make regular inspections of the work environment, investigate accidents, and undertake safety training programs. In smaller companies, it is usually the individual manager who operates these controls.

Total federal regulation of health- and safety-related aspects of organizational functioning is only about a decade old, and many feel it is premature to judge its effectiveness. Others are not so hesitant and say flatly that OSHA's standards are unrealistic, and enforcement is impossible.

The evidence with respect to OSHA's effectiveness to date in reducing work-related injuries, deaths, and illnesses is mixed. There has not been any overall decline in the problem; in fact, there appears to have been an increase in the number of injuries and the number of workdays lost because of injury and poor health in the years since 1970. On the other hand, there have been marked improvements in

Exhibit 18.7   A Statement on Social Responsibility by a Bank Holding Company

''The organization's seventeen banks are important factors in the growth and development of the primary trade territory encompassed by the Corporation. Boatmen's commitment is to operate sound progressive banks that make a constructive contribution to the economic well-being of their respective communities. This commitment takes other forms as well; in the support of responsible government, in the contribution of time and talent as well as money to civic and charitable organizations and in the support of the arts and of other cultural and educational institutions. In addition, members of the staff provide active leadership in their communities through volunteer support for schools, hospitals and welfare agencies and for various cultural and performing arts organizations.

''While responsible organizations like Boatmen's have always accepted their social and civic responsibility, public concern has led to the adoption in recent years of numerous laws and regulations involving such matters as the health and safety of employees, protection of community environment, energy conservation and equal employment and housing opportunity and others. Compliance with these laws and regulations is monitored by banking regulatory authorities and others. In all examinations to date, no Boatmen's bank has been criticized for failing to live up to the spirit of the legislation.''

Source: *Boatmen's Bancshares, Inc. Annual Report, 1982,* p. 15.

some areas. One widely quoted study, for example, attributes a thirty-percent decrease in accidents in the meat packing industry to tough OSHA regulations.[8]

Whatever its direct effectiveness, there is no doubt that industry has become more aware of safety issues since the passage of OSHA. In fact, the desire to avoid the inconvenience and red tape of a hassle with OSHA may turn out to be as great a boost to safety as the actual regulations, which are admittedly often trivial.

Some evidence that OSHA may be accomplishing its ends indirectly is to be found in the increased state activity in the area of safety since the passage of the Act. OSHA provides a mechanism whereby states can assume control of their own safety programs, and an increasing number are doing so, despite the stringent requirements. The traditional belief that states can do things better than the federal government appears to have been borne out in at least one instance. Injuries in California dropped fourteen percent following its approved state safety-inspection program, despite a seven-percent average national increase in the same period.[9]

Federal safety regulations, like more general personnel practices legislation, are in transition. OSHA is trying to make its standards more comprehensible and eliminate some of its less critical requirements. Unions have become involved in these issues, and further changes may be expected from the outcomes of union-management litigation and bargaining over health and safety measures (See Exhibit 18.7).

UNIONS

The history of labor organization in this country goes back more than two hundred years, although unions were illegal and viewed as criminal conspiracies for several decades. Companies could, and often did, exploit workers through low pay, harsh working conditions, and absolute managerial control. Then, in 1842, Chief Justice Shaw of Massachusetts ruled that formation of a union in and of itself was not a crime. The way was cleared for organized labor, but both government and industry remained basically hostile for another half-century.

Unions and their activities can have a great effect on a manager's job.

An Historical Overview

It was not until 1926 that the first pro-labor legislation, the Railway Labor Act, was passed in the United States. Subsequent legislation, culminating in the 1935 Labor Relations Act (Wagner Act), firmly established collective bargaining as a fact of American organizational life. Organizations began to concede some of their control over their employees.

The Wagner Act was followed by a series of challenges to union conduct that culminated in the Taft-Hartley Act of 1947. Taft-Hartley identified, and specifically prohibited, certain unfair union-practices, including the closed shop, the practice of employing only union members.

Together, the Wagner and Taft-Hartley Acts laid the legal foundation for union activity in the private sector. In 1961, President John F. Kennedy issued Executive Order #10988, which extended the right to organize to employees of the federal government. As of this writing, somewhat less than one third of the American work force is represented by unions.

Labor Relations

The specific area in the field of management that formally deals with the relations between unions and management is called *labor relations*, or *industrial relations*. It focuses on the contract bargaining process, negotiation strategies and issues, and contract administration. It can also include the study of union behavior, trends in labor militancy, or bargaining issues.

A manager may not be involved directly in labor relations, but what happens in this area has a great effect on his or her job. Relationships with union subordinates may be strained during periods of contract negotiation, for example. If negotiations break down and a strike occurs, goals and plans may require extensive revision.[10]

Despite the importance and interest, the focus of this section is not on the processes of labor relations. These are advanced topics in the field of management. Instead, we will look more generally at the boundaries placed on the activities of management by unionization. As used here, **unionized organization** means *any organization in which any union has the legal right to bargain for any segment of the work force.*

Planning.   As discussed in Chapter 3, formulating a plan is preceded by setting goals, evaluating resources, and forecasting. A manager in a union organization will find it necessary to incorporate into the decisions made at each of these stages the relevant aspects of a union-contract agreement, if the resulting plan is to be feasible.

To illustrate union-contract influence on planning, we will consider a manager who is planning for production increases to meet a projected increase in sales. *Setting a goal*—a numerical target—for the production increase will be affected by contract stipulations regarding overtime and production methods. *Evaluating resources* may include resolving union constraints on hiring new workers or transferring current ones.

Forecasting requires the manager to predict, as best he or she can, future conditions that might affect a plan. Among the union-related factors that might affect a production increase plan are upcoming contract talks, or current cost-of-living adjustment (COLA) wage provisions that will increase the costs of production as inflation rises over the forecast period.

Although managers in union organizations clearly have constraints on planning that do not exist in other organizations, they also have greater certainty in areas covered by the agreement. Wages, for example, can be figured into the plan with considerable accuracy for the contract period.

Organizing.   The extent to which union agreements affect organizing—deciding what jobs will be done and who will do them—varies. In the extreme, union control can be substantial. In 1979, for example, the Brotherhood of Railway and Airline Clerks won the right to a guaranteed five years of pay for certain employees whose jobs were abolished.[11] Such a provision makes reorganizing or job redesign a potentially expensive undertaking indeed.

The BRAC settlement with the Norfolk and Western Railway is extreme, but it does underscore the strong interest unions have traditionally shown in work organization. Contracts frequently prohibit split shifts, job switching, or alterations in job descriptions or task technology without union consent. Establishing new jobs may require going through a process of negotiating, whether the jobs fall within the bargaining unit. A sample union organizing provision is shown in Exhibit 18.8.

Possibly the clearest message to managers in union organizations is to organize carefully the first time and try to build in flexibility to meet anticipated changes in

Exhibit 18.8   A Union Contract Provision That Affects Organizing

The Blacksmith will do only Blacksmith work as long as there is any Blacksmith work on the plant. In the event there is no Blacksmith work, the Blacksmith will be allowed to perform such Boilermaker and Rigger work that he is able to do in the Central Shops Building. If a Blacksmith job comes up while the Blacksmith is doing Boilermaker and Rigger work, he will be put on this Blacksmith work immediately. In no case will the Blacksmith perform Boilermaker or Rigger work in the Blacksmith Shop.

Source: Article XIV of the June 2, 1964 Agreement Between Ethyl Corporation and Allied Oil Workers; Baton Rouge, Louisiana (page 135).

requirements. In general, union opposition to management-organizing activities tends to be opposition to *change.*

Directing.   The directing function of management consists of guiding the efforts of employees toward the accomplishment of organizational goals. Some of the implications of a union agreement for goal setting were mentioned earlier. Here we will briefly examine its impact on guiding and influencing employee effort.

It is the role of a union to establish, through negotiation with management, the rewards to which its workers will be entitled. This usually includes job security, time off, and desirable job assignments, as well as basic compensation and benefits. Promotions may also be under union control, particularly promotion by seniority.

Union involvement in employee wage, promotion, and benefit policies has considerably altered the manager's ability to link performance to rewards. With the best intentions, unions have made it difficult for managers to reward good performance rather than punish poor performance. Under most union agreements, monetary rewards are automatic, unless performance falls below some minimal standard.

Collective bargaining has also made it difficult, or at least risky, to do anything voluntarily for employees; that is, to give them benefits not in the union contract. The "Past Practices Doctrine" has been widely interpreted to formally bind management to any regular practice beneficial to workers, even if it is voluntarily given. Thus, the firm that gives each employee a Christmas ham every year when times are good is likely to be stuck with the practice even when times are not so good. Discontinuing the gift may be possible only if the union agrees to let the company do so.

Controlling.   The influence that union contracts have on management controls varies, but typical labor agreements establish the right of unions to monitor certain management controls over employee behavior. Recently, for example, unions have been arguing for the right to approve certain aspects of performance appraisal.[12]

As representatives of an organization's workers, unions also exercise control over certain management actions. The most familiar example is the grievance procedure—a control over arbitrary, unfair, or illegal actions by management toward employees. A **grievance procedure** is *a formal series of steps by which an em-*

Exhibit 18.9   Controlling: The Grievance Procedure

Section 1.   Any individual employee or group of employees shall have the right to present grievances to the Company and to have such grievances adjusted. . . .

Any complaint or problem which an employee has not been able to adjust with his supervisor, with or without a steward, if it involves the interpretation and application of any of the terms of this Agreement, shall be presented in the following manner:

Step 1.   The grievance may be taken up with the General Foreman or his representative by a steward of the Union in the steward's defined area. The General Foreman shall answer the grievance in writing within two (2) days after it is so presented.

Step 2.   If the grievance is not satisfactorily adjusted under Step 1 hereof it shall be referred to the appropriate committeeman by the steward who may appeal it to the Superintendent or his representative in the department where the grievance arose. A decision in writing shall be made within three (3) days after presentation.

Step 3.   If the grievance has not been satisfactorily adjusted under Step 2 hereof, it may be referred to the Employee Relations Manager of the particular Division by the Bargaining Committee at the next scheduled meeting of the Bargaining Committee and the Employee Relations Manager or his representative. The Employee Relations Manager or his duly authorized representative shall render a decision in writing within five (5) days after adjournment of the meeting. . . .

Step 4.   Any grievance not satisfactorily adjusted in Step 3 hereof may be appealed to the Company's Labor Relations Committee. A hearing shall be scheduled in five (5) days and an answer shall be given in writing within five (5) days after the close of the hearing. The President of the Local Union, the Chairman of the Bargaining Committee and not more than two representatives of the International Union may be present and participate in the meeting provided for in this step.

Section 2.   A decision rendered on a grievance in Step Four of said Grievance Procedure shall be final and binding upon all parties and the grievance deemed settled in accordance with such decision. . . .*

*Unless an appeal is made. Appeal procedures are also determined by the Agreement.

Source: Article VIII of the November 14, 1963 Agreement between Martin Company (a Division of The Martin-Marietta Corporation) and the International Union, United Automobile, Aerospace and Agricultural Implement Workers of America (UAW-AFL-CIO). Pages 28–29.

ployee can protest a management action. Common sources of grievances are layoffs, disciplinary action for rule violation, orders to perform tasks outside the job description, and alleged management retaliation for union activity. A portion of one formally established grievance procedure is shown in Exhibit 18.9.

Unions in Perspective

The relationship between labor unions and management has traditionally been an antagonistic one. Recently, a seventeen-year battle between J. P. Stevens and Company and the Amalgamated Clothing and Textile Workers Union finally ended when the company signed its first labor contracts. The struggle to unionize is estimated to have cost both sides as much as ten million dollars.[13]

Some believe the adversary relationship between management and labor is necessary and proper. According to the late Eric Hofer, "Our sole protection lies in keeping the division between management and labor obvious and matter-of-fact.

We want management to manage the best it can, and workers to protect their interests the best they can."[14]

Others are of the opinion that a hard and fast division between management and labor hurts everyone involved, and that it is in management's interests to look out for workers' interests. Specifically, poor management-labor relations are thought to be seriously undermining the ability of American industry to compete with foreign industry.[15]

A recent analysis of industrial relations in this country cites the increase of quality circles as some evidence that unions and management are beginning to reevaluate their traditional adversary positions.[16] A quality circle, as discussed in earlier chapters, is a committee of workers that analyzes and solves production-quality problems. This, of course, traditionally has been a management function. At the same time, unions are beginning to concede costly work rules to improve worker productivity.

Whatever changes may be coming in union-management relations, the fact remains that union representatives have the legal right to bargain for their members and managers have a legal responsibility to uphold the management end of the resulting agreement. This means working within the boundaries of the contract. However, to do this it is necessary to understand the contract itself. Lack of knowledge can make planning less effective and can lead to trouble for managers who try to organize, direct, or control outside contractual limits. Ignorance of these limits, like ignorance of the law, is not an acceptable excuse for violation.

The Bottom Line

Organizations operate in, and are part of, complex social systems. Society and the interest groups that comprise it play an increasing role in defining the real world in which every manager must function. Pretending that the organization is autonomous and ignoring the claims or interests of outside groups are no longer feasible alternatives.

1. Learn about the unions in your industry, their history and development. If your company is unionized, study the union contract. Develop good relations with union representatives *before* you are required to deal with them.
2. Find out about those government regulations that particularly apply to your company. If there are local, state, or federal inspectors on site, get to know them. They are good sources of information and ideas.
3. Develop and practice a set of personal ethics, so that you will be prepared to deal with dilemmas when they occur. You may, for example, confidently expect to be confronted by one or more of these issues early in your career: conflicts between customer/client service and organizational policy; conflicts between organizational practices and fair employment or health and safety regulations; unethical conduct by peers or superiors.

Dealing with situations like these will not be easy. No matter how strong your ethical principles or how well developed your sense of social responsibility, the fact that your career advancement, or even your job, may ride on what you can do can considerably complicate the issue. Beyond these issues, as a manager you will have many opportunities to use your position and influence to promote your own personal interests and biases; whether or not you avoid this temptation is up to you.

Deciding what is ethical is often difficult. Three questions which can help you make that distinction are as follows:

1. Can I affirm that I am subordinating my personal interests to the interests of the company?
2. Am I placing my duty to society above my duty to the company and above my personal interests?
3. Have I revealed the facts of any situation where my private interests conflict with those of the company, or the company's with those of society?[17]

It will not necessarily be easy for you to reply "yes" to all of those questions in any particular situation. That fact illustrates the challenge of being socially responsible as a manager in today's complex world.

SUMMARY

Organizations are dependent upon their environments for resources and markets. They are also subject to claims from various segments of their environments for responses to the welfare and concerns of a variety of others in their policies and day-to-day activities. Some of these claims have formal or legal status; these are institutionalized constraints on managerial activities. Other claims, not yet formalized, are usually referred to as social responsibility.

The two most common and important forms of institutionalized constraints on most organizations are government regulations and union contracts. Management in a union organization is subject to limits over and above those in other organizations. Contracts vary considerably, but an agreement with a legally elected union compels management to operate within certain prescribed boundaries.

State and local regulation of companies varies considerably from location to location, but in most cases it is very broad. Since the license to operate a business is issued at this level, these regulations are of considerable importance.

Federal regulation of organizations is complex and places numerous constraints on functioning. A manager may expect to encounter at least two sets of these regulations every day—those concerning personnel practices, in general, and employee health and safety, in particular. General personnel practices are regulated by equal-employment-opportunity (EEO) laws, which are interpreted and enforced by the Equal Opportunity Employment Commission (EEOC). These laws have two goals. One is abolishing unlawful discrimination—discrimination based on characteristics that are *not* job related—in personnel practices. The other goal is compensating for past unfair discrimination, by such means as quota systems and affirmative-action plans.

Rigorous governmental regulation of employee health and safety is slightly over a decade old. The main piece of relevant legislation is the Occupational Health and Safety Act (OSHA) passed in 1970. OSHA requires employers to main-

Everybody's interests are served when an organization uses its financial and human resources to improve the community in which it does business.

tain a healthy and safe working environment and to comply with its extensive regulations.

Noninstitutionalized claims on what organizations do and how they do it come from customers and clients, suppliers and creditors, owners and shareholders, and the community-at-large. The broadest concept of an organization's responsibility to such groups ranges from individual ethical behavior to a commitment of organizational resources to attack urban blight, hunger, and unemployment. Such a concept sets up claims which are often conflicting.

The individual manager may expect to deal with ethical problems created by situations arising out of conflicting claims for social responsibility on organizations. He or she will also meet more personal, ethical issues in the course of day-to-day decision making. Developing a strong set of personal ethics before confronting these issues will make such decisions considerably easier.

QUESTIONS FOR REVIEW AND DISCUSSION

1. One provision of a now-expired, labor agreement states: "Except in an emergency, employees reporting for work at their scheduled time shall be paid from such time even though they do not actually start to work until later." Which of the four management functions do you think this provision primarily affects? Briefly explain.
2. What is the difference between equal opportunity and affirmative action?
3. Which of the following bases for selection would probably be considered unlawful on the basis of *job-relatedness?* (You may assume that none have adverse impact.) Briefly explain your answers.
   a. Ten years' experience for an executive position
   b. Two years or more of college for a salesperson in an exclusive men's shop
   c. Height restrictions for aircraft flight attendants
   d. Unmarried status for a traveling fund-raiser
4. When does discrimination become illegal? When is it legal to discriminate?
5. List the aspects of employee health and safety that you believe should be the primary responsibility of
   a. the organization.
   b. the manager.
   c. the individual employee.
6. Using magazines, television, newspapers, radio, or other sources, find five examples of corporate social responsibility. For each, specify
   a. what the organization is doing;
   b. the group toward whom the action is directed; and
   c. whether the responsibility represented by the action has been institutionalized.
7. Write a paragraph explaining why you either agree or disagree with the following statement: "There is no point to teaching business ethics in school, because when the student gets out, he or she will be only one person and won't be able to make any difference in a corrupt organization."

REFERENCES AND NOTES

1. A. D. Szilagyi, Jr., *Management and Performance*, 2d ed. Glenview, Ill.: Scott, Foresman and Company, 1984, p. 654.
2. J. S. Lublin, "Occupational Diseases Receive More Scrutiny Since the Manville Case," *Wall Street Journal*, December 20, 1982, p. 1.
3. "New Corporate Powerhouse: The Legal Department." *Business Week*, April 9, 1984, pp. 66–71.
4. Originally, this requirement covered firms with at least 50 employees and $50,000 per year in government contracts. Under the Reagan administration, these figures became 250 employees and government contracts worth at least $1 million a year.

5. D. Q. Mills, "Human Resources in the 1980s." *Harvard Business Review*, 1979, 57, 4, pp. 154–62.
6. V. F. Nieva and B. A. Gutek, "Sex Effects on Evaluation." *Academy of Management Review*, 1980, 5, 2, pp. 267–76.
7. "How to Earn Well Pay." *Business Week*, June 12, 1978.
8. L. Ettkin and J. B. Chapman, "Is OSHA Effective in Reducing Industrial Injuries?" *Labor Law Journal*, 1975, (July), pp. 236–49.
9. "The Overhaul that Could Give OSHA Effective Life Under Reagan." *Business Week*, January 19, 1981.
10. For a complete discussion of the various effects of strikes on organizational functioning, *see* W. Imberman, "Strikes Cost More Than You Think." *Harvard Business Review*, 1979 (May-June), pp. 133–38.
11. "The Maverick Leader Who Bested the N & W." *Business Week*, January 22, 1979, pp. 27–28.
12. "NRLB Urges Supreme Court to Allow Union to See Results of Employment Examinations." *The Chronicle of Higher Education*, November 13, 1978, p. 11.
13. G. Bronson and J. H. Birnbaum, "Labor Milestone: How the Textile Union Finally Wins Contracts at J. P. Stevens Plants." *Wall Street Journal*, October 20, 1980.
14. E. Hofer, "Workingman and Management," in *The Ordeal of Change*. New York: Harper & Row, 1963.
15. D. R. Sease and U. C. Lehner, "Steel Blues: Poor Labor Relations at U.S. Steelmakers Cut Ability to Compete." *Wall Street Journal*, April 7, 1981.
16. "The New Industrial Relations." A *Business Week* Special Report, May 11, 1981, pp. 84–98, quote from p. 86.
17. R. W. Austin, "Code of Conduct for Executives," *Harvard Business Review*, 1961, 39, 5, 53, 53–61, p. 69.

SUGGESTED READINGS

Anderson, H. J., *Primer of Equal Employment Opportunity*. Washington, D.C.: The Bureau of National Affairs, 1978. This is a useful basic summary reference of EEO legislation and related rulings to that date.

Brett, J. M., "Why Employees Want Unions." *Organizational Dynamics*, 1980 (Spring), 47–59. Brett explores the reasons for and implications of worker beliefs that they are better off if they act collectively.

Ford, D. L., Jr. "Cultural Differences in Organizational Behavior." In J. B. Ritchie and P. Thompson, eds., *Organization and People: Readings, Cases, and Exercises in Organizational Behavior*, 2nd ed. St. Paul, Minn.: West, 1980, 388–99. This article explores black-white cultural differences and the implications for organizational functioning.

Greenwood, W. T., "Components of a Social Audit of the Corporation." In W. T. Greenwood, ed. *Issues in Business and Society*, 3rd ed. Boston: Houghton Mifflin Co., 1977, 592–603. Greenwood discusses the measurement of business social performance; an appendix presents a social audit form that covers all of the areas discussed in this chapter.

Case *Reverse Discrimination?*

Arthur Ruggerio, an unskilled laborer, had been out of work for five months. While he had been collecting unemployment insurance he had been actively seeking any kind of work. One day he read in the newspaper that Thomsen & Thomsen, Inc., had been awarded a federal grant to set up a hard-core-unemployed training program for assistant machinists. Feeling that he might qualify, Arthur hurried over to the firm's personnel department and submitted an application for the program. After having an interview and taking an intelligence test and a vocational-interest test, he was told that the company would be in touch with him. A week later he received a letter telling him to report to the personnel department. Arthur arrived at the scheduled time and was asked to join the other program applicants in the conference room. He went in, sat down, and waited patiently. As he sat there, he suddenly realized that he was the only white person in the room. The other twenty were either black or Puerto Rican.

A few minutes later, the personnel director, Mr. Arnold Francis, entered the room. He began speaking almost immediately.

"Good morning, gentlemen. Welcome to Thomsen & Thomsen, Inc. I am happy to inform you that based on your interviews and test scores, you twenty-one men have been selected for our unemployed training program. The program will last ten weeks, in which time you will become acquainted with the history and philosophy of our firm in addition to receiving training as a machinist assistant. During this training period you will be paid $2.95 an hour. Then, upon successful completion of this program,

you will be given a permanent position in our company as a full-fledged machinist assistant at $3.35 an hour. We realize that you may know nothing about machines, but don't let that frighten you. You will be taught everything you need to know. Now, before turning you over to my assistant, Mr. Friedrick, I would like to emphasize that this company is truly interested in you. We will try to assist you in every way. If you have any problems, please call them to our attention. At this point Mr. Friedrick is going to take you on a tour of our facilities. Have a good ten weeks."

Throughout the tour and that evening, Arthur kept thinking how fortunate he was to have this opportunity. Here was a chance for a full-time, steady job, just what he had always wanted. He was determined to do his best. By 7:45 A.M. the next day, Arthur was at the plant waiting for the program to begin. It was scheduled to start at 8 A.M. but did not get going until about 8:45 A.M. because of six or seven stragglers. In fact, four of the new trainees did not show up until after lunch and, as Arthur learned later, they made it then only because Mr. Friedrick personally went to get them.

At the end of the first week of training Arthur was very pleased with his progress. For example, several times the instructors singled him out for his ability. There was little doubt that Arthur was one of the top trainees in terms of both intelligence and drive.

While Arthur was reading the Sunday paper he came across a story of Thomsen & Thomsen's training program. The president of the firm, Fred Thomsen, was quoted as saying, "We are pleased with the first week of this program. Both

Source: F. Luthans, R. M. Hodgetts, and K. R. Thompson, *Social Issues in Business*, 3d. ed. (New York: McMillan Publishing Co. Inc., 1980), pp. 127–29.

our black and Puerto Rican trainees are showing tremendous interest in the program and we are certainly glad to be able to provide them this opportunity. Of course, none of this would have been possible without the assistance of the federal government. They provided us with enough funds for a program to train twenty hard-core unemployables.''

On Monday morning, soon after the first session had begun, Arthur was told to go downstairs and see Mr. Francis in personnel. When he entered the office, he noticed Mr. Friedrick was sitting quietly in the corner. ''Come in and sit down, Arthur,'' said Mr. Francis. ''The reason I've asked to see you is that I'm afraid I have to convey some bad news. Although we have asked for more, the federal government only approved funds for twenty trainees for our program. We are going to have to drop one man. After much deliberation, we decided since you have the best chance of securing

employment elsewhere, we are going to drop you from the program. Now, we realize that you've been out of work for five months and jobs are scarce. However, I've been authorized to give you a check for $200, a sort of severance payment. It's a little something to tide you over until you can get another job.'' Mr. Francis then shook Arthur's hand, wished him luck, and showed him out.

Arthur was both shocked and disappointed. However, after a couple of hours he regained his composure. Then he cashed the $200 check at a local bank, kept $20 for spending money, put the balance in a savings account, walked to the office of the Equal Employment Opportunity Commission and filed a formal complaint charging discrimination on the basis of color. ''Because I was white,'' he told an EEOC official, ''I was dropped from the program. This is discrimination and I am entitled to be reinstated. I demand my rights.''

CASE QUESTIONS

1. Do you feel Arthur was discriminated against on the basis of color? Was the firm justified in dropping him from the program?
2. How would you explain the $200 check given to Arthur? What is your interpretation of the company's action? What do you think about the way Arthur handled the money?
3. What would you have done if you were Arthur and had been dropped from the program?
4. How does this case relate to social responsibility? Be philosophical and specific in your answer.

19/Stress and Time

Jill Morris is a senior in college, majoring in finance and accounting. Her academic program is quite rigorous, with great emphasis on quantitative analytical techniques and regular, time-consuming, written homework assignments.

Jill is also a member of the university women's gymnastics team. During the fall semester, the gymnasts work out three to four hours a day, six days per week, refining their skills and developing the routines they will use in competition. In the spring semester, in addition to working out regularly every day, the gymnastics team competes several times. They usually have ten meets, followed by conference, regional, and national events.

During the spring semester, Jill feels that she has almost no free time: she is either in class, studying, working out, traveling to a meet, or competing. Yet, she says, "I seem to feel much better about myself then, even though I'm much busier. First of all, it's always fun to start competing after all those months of preparation. We have a good group of

girls on the team, and we all support each other a lot, particularly during travel and competition. Some of the girls are really funny and help us break the tension while we're waiting to compete or when one of us misses one of our tricks or happens to fall during a routine.

"Not only that, but I tend to do a lot better in my courses during the spring term than I do in the fall. I take about the same number of hours both semesters, but I usually make A's and B's in the spring and B's and C's in the fall."

David Moser, a recent graduate of Jill's university, is currently working in his first managerial position, supervising a small data-processing operation in a relatively large consumer-products company. David was promoted to his present job from a management training program, is regarded as ambitious, bright, and hard-working.

David feels that his immediate supervisor, a man about fifty years old, is "really a nice guy." David describes him as someone who never seems to get angry and never openly criticizes his employees. When asked whether his boss ever behaved autocratically, David laughs and says, "Hardly! He seldom, if ever, gives many directions, and basically lets us figure everything out for ourselves. It's funny—sometimes I really get frustrated because I really want us to do things, to get ahead, to have an impact. But he's just so easy-going. Everything about my job seems to be vague: how much authority I have, what my responsibilities are, what our department's objectives are.

"I can't seem to get my boss to clarify anything for me. I don't really know if I'm getting anywhere or accomplishing anything. And I'm afraid it's getting to me. I know I'm becoming more and more irritable, both at work and at home. My boss and my wife both tell me to take it easier, but I'm not like that. I really want to achieve something. Instead, I find myself taking longer and longer lunch hours, and I've started having a drink or two at lunch, something I vowed I'd never do. I've taken up smoking again, a habit that I thought I'd left behind forever in my sophomore year in college."

George Harris, who had graduated with an engineering degree some ten years before David, was promoted to a supervisory position about a year ago. George loves engineering, and was convinced he could do a good job in supervising other engineers because, as he put it, "I've been down there in the trenches with those guys. I know what they have to put up with from management and I'm going to be different."

For a few months George lived up to his own expectations. But then, as he put it, "The paperwork began to take its toll. I just couldn't seem to keep up with all the reports and still find time to stay on top of all the engineering work. Looking back on it, in my zeal to be different and better, I got in over my head. I accepted every request from my engineers and every additional assignment from my own boss. I found myself working longer and longer hours, but falling further and further behind. I felt like I was working for everybody but myself, and not accomplishing the important things I wanted to do.

"My behavior at home got weird, too. I didn't seem to have much energy left to do anything—me, who always had three or four projects going at once. I lost interest in recreational activities and just sat around the house in the evenings watching television or daydreaming. On weekends, instead of going sailing or cycling, I began sleeping till noon."

All three individuals faced different situations. Jill, a student and gymnast, felt better and performed better during her busiest terms. David, after his promotion, began drinking and smoking. George became a supervisor, couldn't keep up the work, and became depressed. What do Jill, David, and George have in common? Stress.

Stress is *a set of physiological and psychological changes in an individual reacting to certain changes in the environment.* These changes result from a situation which the individual perceives as being *uncertain,* but with *important outcomes.*[1] These can range from social situations, like a blind date, to work situations, like a new assignment, to life-threatening situations, like being assaulted.

Stress comes in many forms and has many causes. However, individuals differ in their abilities to cope with stress. They also differ in the ways they react to it. In this chapter, we will describe stress, its forms and causes, and what managers can do to help themselves and their employees deal with it.

A MODEL OF STRESS

Exhibit 19.1 depicts a model of stress from a managerial viewpoint. Stress is caused by *changes in the environment,* called **stressors,** *that are perceived as threatening or demanding.* Stress itself is the set of physiological and psychological

Exhibit 19.1   A Model of Stress

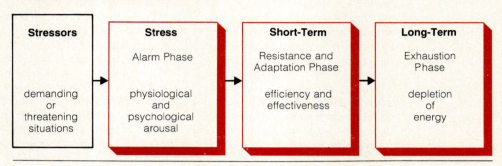

changes that occur in response to stressors. The *outcomes* of stress are broken down into *short-term* and *long-term* effects on health and job performance.

Stress begins with changes in the environment, changes that the individual perceives as important and which increase his or her uncertainty. These changes produce stressful situations that we will refer to as stressors. For Jill it was the spring semester and the demands upon her time from classes and gymnastics. For David it was the new job and the ambiguity of his boss. For George it was a promotion and the increasing amount of paperwork it required.

The physical and psychological reactions that we call stress prepare the individual to deal with stressors by heightening awareness and mobilizing the body. This is the *alarm* phase of stress.[2] Certain hormones are released that increase heart and breathing rates. Metabolism increases and digestion stops. Blood pressure goes up as more blood is pumped to the skeletal muscles. The individual becomes more alert. Physically and psychologically, the individual is ready for action.

The short-term effects of stress, called the *resistance and adaptation* phase, are generally beneficial. In this phase, the body is working at high efficiency, enabling individuals to deal with crises or emergencies. They can make decisions quickly, stay awake for long hours, adapt to extremes of cold, heat or noise, or perform great feats of strength or skill.

Unfortunately, the long-term effects of stress are not so beneficial. The physiological and psychological changes that enable people to deal with stressors in the short run tend to consume physical and psychological energy. If the stressor persists, the individual eventually comes to the *exhaustion* phase of stress, in which his or her reserves of energy and strength are used up.

There needs to be some relief from stress. This requires rest, relaxation, and nourishment. Without relief, an individual can become exhausted; the body and mind give out, defenses are lowered, and he or she becomes susceptible to disease, injury, mistakes, or collapse. Exhaustion happens differently to different people. Some become mentally exhausted first; others become physically exhausted.

Each individual differs in his or her tolerance for stress. Some, like Jill, can cope with the stress of time pressures for long periods and perform better because of increased alertness and energy. Others, like David, experience stress from long periods of ambiguity and uncertainty, and they become irritable. They may seek temporary relief through drugs or alcohol. Still others, like George, are overwhelmed by changes in work or home life. They have not learned to cope with the situation, although they try. They become depressed, apathetic, uninterested.

There are a number of symptoms that tell us that a person may be approaching his or her limits. *Physiological* symptoms of stress may include high blood pressure, increased rates of breathing and heartbeat, and frequent migraine headaches (disabling headaches accompanied by dizziness, loss of vision and/or nausea). *Psychological* symptoms may appear as substitutes for overt action. David, for example, may feel uncomfortable about a confrontation with his boss who, after all, is a nice guy. So David becomes irritable. He may feel persecuted, or get angry over unimportant matters. He may express dissatisfaction, or become very negative about his work or life. All of these are safer substitutes for fighting the agent of stress directly.

Other psychological symptoms can be seen as substitutes for escape. A person experiences stress in a job, in school, or as part of a family, yet believes that physically running away is not an option. He or she will therefore respond with a safer substitute, such as apathy or resignation. The overstressed person may become forgetful or unable to concentrate. He or she may indulge in flights of fantasy. Anxiety and uncertainty about whom to trust are common symptoms. Finally, like George, the individual may become depressed and uninterested in anything.

A third set of stress symptoms are *behavioral*. Persons experiencing stress may suddenly change their appearances or dress. They may lose their appetites, change their smoking or drinking habits, or experience a sudden weight gain or loss. They may begin to procrastinate or find it difficult to make decisions.

Any of these symptoms may suggest that a person is reaching his or her tolerance limits for stress. But stress can be either good or bad for a person. Its effects depend upon the *amount* of stress induced and upon the *individual's ability to tolerate* stress and cope with the situation.

Managers need to understand stress because it affects them and the people with whom they work. In the short run, or at moderate levels, stress can increase efficiency. In the long run, or at excessive levels, stress can produce serious negative outcomes for both the health and performance of people at work. Understanding the causes and effects of stress, and factors that can alleviate it, enables managers to manage their own stress and that of their subordinates.

SOURCES OF STRESS

Stress of some sort is likely to occur whenever a person is facing an uncertain situation that has important outcomes. Such situations are common in the business world where there is an enormous amount of pressure to perform more and more activities in less and less time. Added to this is the constant competition for power and position. A manager must identify the sources of stress and develop strategies to deal with them.

Demands, Constraints, and Opportunities

The Chinese word for *crisis* is written by combining the symbols for the words *danger* and *opportunity*—two very different concepts. Just so, three very different environmental forces—demands, constraints, and opportunities—can generate the uncertainty and sense of urgency which lead to stress.[3]

We don't find it difficult to think of demands as creating stress. When something is demanded of an individual, it means that person is under pressure to do it or suffer serious consequences. When an instructor demands a fifty-page term paper, or a job demands constant attention to detail, or inflation demands earning more and more money just to keep up, people experience stress which enables them to deal with those demands.

Likewise, all of us face *constraints* which make it more difficult to meet demands or to do what we want to do. Time constraints and the demands of other courses make the fifty-page paper more difficult. Union and government regulations limit the ways managers go about their jobs. Policies and budgets act as internal constraints on members of all organizations. Whenever constraints make it more difficult for people to carry out their functions, their uncertainty is increased, and stress is a common result. For some, it may increase their effectiveness. For others, it may have the opposite effect.

What many people don't realize is that *opportunities* can be stressful as well. An opportunity is simply a chance to do something new or different. The uncertainty of the outcome may lead to stress. An individual suddenly presented with the opportunity to get a new client, to move to a new city, to enter a new relationship, or to take on a new job is likely to feel stress. "Can I do it?" "Will I enjoy it?" "Will I do it?" The stress of opportunities can be exhilarating, while the stress of demands and constraints can be frustrating.

Ambiguous or Conflicting Roles

As previously defined, a role is a set of expectations about the way someone is to behave in a particular social position or situation. In a sense, roles are demands—demands that we or others place on our behavior.

At work, most people like to have some idea of what their roles are. When their jobs are not well-defined, when they don't know what they are supposed to do, they can experience stress. Most students have experienced stress at one time or another when an instructor has failed to make clear his or her expectations. In the story that began this chapter David Moser felt stressed because he couldn't get a definition of his job from his boss. The goals, line of authority, and responsibilities were unclear. David is not alone. One national survey estimated that one third of the American labor force experienced stress from a lack of clear information about their jobs.[4]

When an individual confronts conflicting expectations about what he or she is supposed to do, stress can result. Role conflict comes in many forms, as we discussed in Chapter 9. For example, a manager may be expected to cut budgets by laying off good employees. Older employees may expect the manager to dismiss younger workers, while younger workers may demand that layoffs be shared equally. The time that the manager spends working on the budget will interfere with time spent with his or her family. Whatever the type of role conflict, stress is a likely outcome.

Overwork and Underwork

We are all familiar with the stereotype of the overworked executive: too much to do, too little time to do it in. This is as true for the small business executive as it is for those in big business. Anyone whose job-demands exceed his or her time and talents can be overworked and experience stress. In one of the anecdotes that began this chapter, George Harris was swamped by his new job. He couldn't keep up with the demands of his workers, his boss, and his paperwork.

A study of government employees demonstrated that excessive work-demands lead to harmful stress. Employees who were most overworked (had most visitors, phone calls, and other interruptions) were compared with those who were not overworked. The overworked employees were found to have higher levels of serum cholestrol and higher heart rates—clear signs of overstress.[5]

On the other hand, jobs that create no challenge and have few demands can also be stressful. Boring, meaningless, or insignificant jobs are constraints for people who would like to get something more out of their work. Someone who feels that he is being underutilized in his job will be frustrated. Managers who get kicked up-stairs to meaningless positions, workers whose jobs have been stripped of challenge and meaning by technology, employees who suddenly find themselves retired, all may feel underutilized and therefore feel stress.

For most people, being unemployed is the ultimate case of being underworked. It is no coincidence that suicide rates are so high among the unemployed in a society that places great emphasis on an individual's work. In one study of suicides in New England, over fifty percent of the males were unemployed at the time of their suicides.[6]

Other Occupational Hazards

Certain occupations and certain occupational characteristics are inherently stressful, such as those involving great responsibility and varied working conditions.

Responsibility. Jobs which create a great deal of responsibility for their occupants are obviously stressful. We only have to look at the appearances of American presidents for evidence.

Particularly when the occupant has only limited control over the outcomes does he or she experience great amounts of stress, as the outcomes are relatively uncertain. Psychiatrists feel responsible for their patients' emotional and behavioral problems. Yet the patients' families, jobs, and the patients themselves have more influence over these than the psychiatrists. Air traffic controllers are responsible for the lives and safety of thousands of passengers each day. Yet pilots, mechanics, and weather have influence on ultimate passenger safety which is beyond the controllers' domain. Managers are responsible for tasks and people, yet forces beyond their control like governments, unions, and competitors have a great deal to say about ultimate outcomes.

Perhaps even more frustrating is the job that combines great pressures and responsibilities with little authority, where decision making is highly centralized. Army commanders in Vietnam were frustrated by the many tactical decisions that were being made in Washington, rather than by the combat commanders themselves. The colonel who led the attempted rescue of the American hostages in Iran was frustrated because the President was making battlefield decisions.

> *Managers need to understand stress because it affects them and the people with whom they work. In the short run, stress can increase efficiency. In the long run, or at excessive levels, stress can produce serious negative outcomes for both the health and performance of people at work.*

Research in other organizations reveals that high pressure jobs combining little authority with monotonous, repetitive tasks, such as assembly line work, may be the most stressful of all. A study of working men in the United States and Sweden examined the relationship between job characteristics and mental strain. The researchers found that workers whose jobs combined high pressure with low authority suffered the highest rates of depression and exhaustion.[7]

Working Conditions.   In Chapter 8 we described some of the psychological effects of the physical and social environment in which work is performed. Jobs which are physically or psychologically uncomfortable, or those which are actually dangerous, are stressful. Extreme temperatures or noise; overcrowding; bad lighting; lack of privacy (one of the hazards of being rich and famous); air pollution; radiation and toxic chemicals; and safety hazards are conditions which may be potentially stress-producing.

Research in job-related stress has enabled us to identify a number of jobs whose occupants are particularly likely to experience stress: physicians, welfare workers, air traffic controllers, psychiatrists, dentists, health technicians, waiters and waitresses, nurses, paramedics, assembly line operators, musicians, public relations officials, dishwashers, warehouse workers, nurses aides, managers, sea pilots, and certain clerical workers.[8]

The fact that clerical work is a high stress occupation may seem surprising. Yet the monotony of the work, which is often accomplished under time pressures, and the lack of authority lead to the observation that clerical workers "suffer from the second-highest rate of psychological stress for 132 occupations," according to the president of Working Women. A National Institute for Occupational Safety and Health study of electronic video display terminal (VDT) users found "higher levels of job stress than had ever been observed on assembly lines." Typical physical problems reported by VDT users are eyestrain, back and neck pain, changes in color perception, and nausea.[9]

It is also interesting to note that seven of the eighteen high-stress occupations are in health-related areas. Being responsible for people's health and lives is a high-pressured and uncertain job.

EFFECTS OF STRESS

Stress mobilizes the body to fight or flee. Defenses are up, awareness is heightened. The individual is prepared to deal with or to escape the stressful situation. There are, however, more specific effects of stress which are of particular interest to managers. Some of these effects are directly related to performance; others have to do with physical and psychological health.

Effects on Job Performance

Stress at work is common, because work situations are frequently characterized by uncertainty and importance.

Task Effectiveness and Efficiency. For most people, moderate amounts of stress enable them to work at high levels of efficiency and effectiveness. Prolonged periods of stress or too much stress at one time, can cause efficiency and effectiveness to fall off rapidly.[10] George, for example, functioned well for the first weeks of his new supervisory job. Then he fell apart.

The general relationship between stress and task performance is described in Exhibit 19.2. Low levels of stress (point *A*) usually indicate that the individual is not being challenged by the task; he or she is coasting along. At point *B*, something happens to increase stress. The task changes, becomes more uncertain, important, or more difficult. The individual's body responds to the challenge with increased alertness and energy. Performance improves to point *C*.

If the challenge is successfully met and overcome within the individual's tolerance levels, stress is reduced naturally. The individual returns to the state of comparative relaxation. If the stress increases and the task becomes too difficult (point *D*), exhaustion sets in and performance falls off rapidly.

For example, at point *A* George Harris has not yet been promoted. He is still a technician, doing his job well, but only occasionally challenged by his work. At point B he is promoted to supervisor. It's a new job, a big change, with increased demands and new responsibilities. For a while, George copes. He works harder than ever, accepts more responsibility. His performance increases to *C*. But C is as far as he can go; his individual limit in supervisory ability and/or tolerance for stress. At

Exhibit 19.2   Task Demands, Stress, and Task Performance

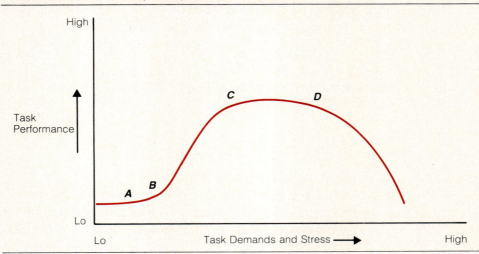

D, the job has become too much for him, and his performance has begun to dete-riorate. Stress, which was at first functional, has eventually beaten George down. He becomes depressed, withdrawn, and apathetic at home. It is only a matter of time before he falls apart at work, unless something happens to relieve his stress.

Absenteeism, Turnover, and Dissatisfaction.   One of the key factors in the satisfaction of working people is the *quality of their working life*[11]—their psycho-logical well-being at work. People who are under great stress at work perceive the quality of their working life as low. They are unhappy and dissatisfied.

They express their dissatisfaction by griping a lot, expressing negative feelings when asked, "bad-mouthing" the organization, or by becoming apathetic; they may even resort to sabotage.

One way to deal with stress at work is to flee—that is, to quit. High-stress jobs tend to have high turnover rates. Turnover in some jobs which are highly demand-ing, dangerous, physically uncomfortable, or any combination thereof can be very high. Turnover rates among canners and packers sometimes exceeds two hundred percent. In one metropolitan police force turnover exceeded 120 percent over a four-year period. In that case, pay was relatively good, but officers who quit said it was low relative to the stressful nature of the job.[12]

For those who can't quit, who have no alternatives to their stressful jobs, ab-senteeism is a "safe" method of fleeing. When demands and constraints at work produce high stress, both absenteeism and turnover increase, as depicted in Exhibit 19.3. In 1981, some 12,000 American air controllers went on strike. They sought pay increases and reduced work weeks to compensate for the stressful nature of their jobs.

Exhibit 19.3   Relationships Between Stress and Turnover and Absenteeism

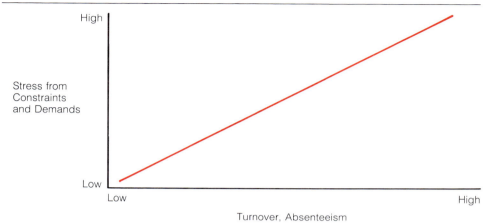

Source: Adapted from A. R. Brief, R. S. Schuler, & M. Van Sell, *Managing Job Stress* (Boston: Little, Brown, 1981). p.57.

Stress and Health

Too much stress leads to exhaustion of the body's physical and emotional resources.

Stressful situations are a constant part of our lives. Work is stressful. Modern living is stressful. We live with anxieties over cancer, nuclear war, crime on the streets. It is impossible to escape stress completely, and its effects build up over time. The additive nature of stress increases the likelihood that it will have damaging effects on the health of people today.[13]

Stress-Related Diseases.   The bodies of normal, healthy human beings have built-in defense mechanisms which fight off disease. As we have said, the bodies of individuals experiencing great stress become exhausted, and the defense mechanisms no longer do the job. That individual becomes susceptible to disease.

The particular type of disease to which a person experiencing stress is likely to succumb depends, of course, on the individual and his or her environment. Nevertheless, researchers have linked stress to any number of diseases. Some are mild, like headaches, colds, and flu. Diarrhea, cramps, gas, and constipation are all digestive distresses which may be stress-produced.

Other types of disease which have been linked to stress are not so mild. Most people know that stress can produce ulcers and other severe stomach problems. There is less well-known evidence that cancer may have a stress-derived component. One theory is that stress reduces the body's natural defenses against cancer-producing viruses.[14]

Evidence that stress is a major factor in heart disease continues to grow.[15] Stress can lead to high blood pressure and excessive production of serum cholestrol.

In the long run, coronary heart disease can be the unhappy result. Both individually and collectively, coronary heart disease is a serious problem. One out of every five male Americans will suffer a heart attack before he reaches the age of 65, and half of all heart attacks are fatal.[16]

The Abuse of Alcohol, Tobacco, and Other Drugs.   Drugs can often provide temporary relief from some tensions. They are a way of "fleeing" stress. Many experts, in fact, believe that drug abuse is really a form of self-medication for stress.[17]

Unfortunately, the temporary relief provided by drugs does not compensate for any long-term harm which may follow. Alcohol depresses the central nervous system. Regular abuse can lead to bleeding ulcers, cirrhosis of the liver, and alcoholism. Tobacco is a stimulant, depressant, and tranquilizer. Its abuse can lead to emphyzema, heart disease, or lung cancer.

The effects of other kinds of drug abuse are too lengthy and complicated for this book, because the effects are different for each type of drug. One thing is clear: a drug only masks stress; it does not solve the problems which are causing it. Using drugs too often leads to absenteeism, tardiness, erratic job performance, and excessive mistakes.

> *Stress prepares us to fight or flee. Stress can come from overwork, underwork, or ambiguity. Demands, constraints, or opportunities can be sources of stress. Stress is additive.*

The costs at work are staggering. One researcher estimated that drug abuse costs industry between $20 and $30 billion annually, with $10 billion of that resulting from lost worktime from alcoholism alone.[18] Given that an estimated 5 million workers are alcoholics, the costs are not surprising.

Accidents and Injuries.   Because of the efforts of government and industry to make work safer, accidents and injuries are not the problems they used to be. Today fifty times as many workers suffer from heart disease as die in industrial accidents. Yet accidents and injuries do occur at work under conditions which should be safe. Individuals experiencing stress become exhausted, and their judgments and coordination may suffer. Under continual time pressures, an employee may overlook or ignore safety procedures, and people and property suffer as a result.

In summary, in moderate amounts or over short periods, stress can be energizing and lead to higher levels of work effectiveness and efficiency. But excessive stress exhausts the body's physical and emotional resources. Performance drops off. Dissatisfaction, absenteeism, and turnover increase. Employees, turning to alcohol or other drugs for temporary relief, may become susceptible to disease or injury. In the long run, stress can kill.

The Chief of Motivation and Stress Research for the National Institute for Occupational Safety and Health sums up stress at work as follows:

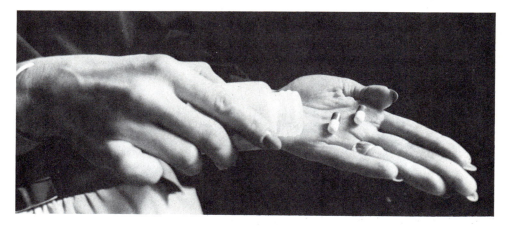

Although drugs often provide temporary relief from some tensions, they only mask the symptoms of stress; they do not solve the problems that are causing it.

Stress affects all workers to some extent and some more than others. In addition to the stresses the individual experiences in his or her private life, the job itself can induce certain "set-up" stress levels, which bring the worker close to the danger point. Then, all it takes is some precipitating event or problem, and the person gets pushed beyond the limits of adaptation, and he or she simply breaks down.[19]

MANAGING STRESS

In the past few years stress has become a popular topic for researchers and practitioners alike. Scores of books and articles have been published, and seminars on stress management are offered throughout the country. Advice on how to deal with stress is abundant. We will look at this advice from two perspectives: what individuals can do for themselves, and what managers can do for their employees.

What Managers Can Do for Themselves

In the introductory story, Jill handled her stress well. David and George did not. What could they have done to increase their ability to deal with job stress?

In planning ways to deal with stress, managers, such as David and George, can build upon a few key pieces of information: stress prepares us to fight or flee. Stress can come from overwork, underwork, or ambiguity. Demands, constraints, or opportunities can be sources of stress. Stress is additive. Each individual has a particular tolerance level for stress.

Management in Action
Stress at the Top

If you hate stress, steer clear of small businesses. People who own them complain of stress more than twice as much as those who run giant corporations.

Over forty percent of top executives sometimes lie awake at night, thinking about business problems. But fewer than one in five thinks he or she would be happier in a less stressful job.

Those are some of the findings of a Gallup Organization poll of business leaders conducted for the *Wall Street Journal*. It shows that highly placed executives and business owners commonly feel stress, and that they have developed a great range of techniques to cope with it.

Gallup found that forty-nine percent of the small-business proprietors it polled consider stress either a major problem, or somewhat of a problem, compared with only thirty-three percent of the executives who headed medium-sized companies, and only nineteen percent of those who led big corporations.

Of executives who do complain of stress, a disproportionate number are young. In medium-sized companies, for instance, forty-eight percent of the chiefs under forty-five find stress a problem, compared with only twenty-nine percent among those forty-five or older. "As you grow older, you learn to handle stress and don't feel it," says the chairman of a manufacturing concern. The president of a beverage concern adds, "I'm less strained at fifty-four than at thirty-five, I've had to work on it."

Business leaders also think the amount of stress in jobs varies substantially according to the industry or specialty. For instance, most executives—seventy-four percent at big companies, seventy-three percent at medium-sized and sixty-two percent at small ones—think commodity-trading involves a great deal of stress. More than two in five executives think the advertising business is stressful.

Percentage of Executives at Large Companies and Their Specific Business Areas of Stress

Commodity Trading	74%
Advertising	42
Investment Banking	21
High Technology	15
Legal Profession	7
Insurance	6

A much smaller number—seven percent at big companies, fourteen percent at the medium-sized and twenty-six percent of small ones—think the legal profession has a great deal of stress. An even smaller number think there is great stress in the insurance industry.

In business generally, many executives notice physical effects of stress. A large number—forty-one percent at big companies, fifty-two percent at medium-sized and forty percent at small companies—say they sometimes or often lie awake at night or wake up thinking about work problems.

Source: Roger Ricklefs, "Many Executives Complain of Stress, But Few Want Less-Pressured Jobs," *Wall Street Journal*, September 29, 1982, p. 35.

Maintain Physical Fitness. Physically fit individuals seem to tolerate more stress and become exhausted less quickly. The first step is to have a complete physical examination. The physician will look for physiological symptoms such as high blood pressure and cholesterol levels. The physician will also evaluate diet, smoking and drinking habits, job and family data to help determine susceptibility to stress. Together, the physician and manager can work out a program of physical fitness, including exercise, to help the manager deal with stress.

Deal with Stressors. Rather than worrying over problems, managers can learn to deal with them directly. David could have insisted on more structure from his boss. For problems which cannot be directly attacked, like George's, suggestions include making a list of problems and then writing down some possible actions. Some action, even identifying problems and writing them down, seems to be better than no action in reducing stress.

Avoid Excess Stress. Managers who are realistic about their own capabilities and learn to say "no" can avoid excessive stress. The temptation to take on more than one can handle is often great, a temptation to which George succumbed. The rewards (a fast promotion, for example) are sometimes powerful, but the costs may be high as well. Programs to eliminate or reduce demands which are particularly stressful provide another strategy. Delegating responsibility is a common way for managers to reduce their own job demands, one that would have considerably alleviated George's stress.

Relax. Relaxation in various forms can be thought of as ways of giving the body an opportunity to recover from stress. "Getting away from the job" may mean leaving work at the office instead of taking it home at night, or going away for a weekend or vacation. Relaxation training has become a popular antidote for many managers who learn to relax in a few minutes' undisturbed privacy while at work (See Exhibit 19.4). Meditation and other forms of deep relaxation have been found to be effective in reducing blood pressure and cholesterol levels of professionals and executives.[20]

Develop and Maintain Personal Relationships. Social support at work and away from work can help alleviate some of the negative effects of stress. While it is not clear how these relationships alleviate stress, they do seem to help.[21] Perhaps having someone to talk to about stressful situations helps individuals cope with stress.

The "loneliness at the top" that is characteristic of many top executive jobs make them particularly susceptible to the long-term effects of stress, if they do not provide themselves with some means of social support either on or off the job. According to Harry Levinson of the Levinson Institute, which provides clinical services for managers and executives, these people see themselves as being very powerful, and yet still susceptible to uncontrollable events such as energy crises, wars, strikes, and natural disasters. The sense of helplessness that such events bring is very difficult for them to cope with.[22] A pivotal reason why undue stress may cause

Exhibit 19.4   Relaxation Techniques in Stress Management

Most professionals in stress management recommend some form of relaxation technique in their programs. There are any number of ways to relieve the tension that is symptomatic of stress. They all involve both body and mind, and they all are directed at "letting go." Suggested techniques include meditation, prayer, yoga, deep breathing, guided imagery, stretching, progressive muscle relaxation, and even yawning.

One increasingly popular technique is autogenics, in which an individual learns to control involuntary responses such as heartbeat and brainwaves through the use of an oscilloscope which monitors those responses. The data from this device, often referred to as "biofeedback," enables the individual to observe the effectiveness of such activities as repeating and meditating .

these strong people to collapse is the isolation of the job. They fear appearing mortal, confide in no one, and have no one to lean on or even talk to when the crisis hits. The key to avoiding such problems for future executives is to develop a social support network of friends and family in the early stages of a career and to maintain it as their success and responsibilities grow. It would also be useful for young managers to develop good relationships with their own immediate superiors. Because the boss is an important source of job definition and workload, a good relationship enables managers to negotiate and clarify assignments and responsibilities. Both David and George could have profited from such a relationship.

What Managers Can Do for Their Subordinates

The preceding paragraphs suggest that managers can have a lot to do with employee stress. There are, in fact, several actions managers can take to keep stress or its effects at manageable levels for their subordinates.

Promote Employee Awareness and Fitness. Employees can control a significant amount of their own stress, if they are aware of its sources and symptoms. At stress-management training sessions employees can learn to evaluate themselves, their jobs, and their lives in terms of stress tolerance and potential. Exhibits 19.5 and 19.6 provide examples of stress evaluation questionnaires. Medical checkups, physical fitness programs, and relaxation training are part of stress-management education in both business and nonbusiness organizations today.

Facilitate Social Support. We have already emphasized social support as a means for helping executives and managers cope with job stress. There is growing

In order to minimize the negative effects of stress, individuals can participate in a program of regular exercise and health maintenance.

evidence that interacting with peers, family, and friends helps workers of all kinds deal with stress at work. Social support from supervisors and coworkers has been found to relieve both anxiety and emotional exhaustion of people working on dangerous jobs. Social support from family and coworkers has been found to significantly moderate the effects of stress for hospital nurses.

Among both blue-collar and white-collar workers, those with supportive friends, colleagues, and families show fewer symptoms of stress than isolated coworkers. Managers can work to change job schedules and physical layouts that isolate people. They can provide encouragement and ways for workers to interact with one another either during or after work.

Evaluate the Design and Flow of Work. Some stressors at work are immediately obvious. Dangerous working conditions, extremes of temperature or noise, and long or erratic work schedules are often easily remedied. In one case, the stress from severe noise levels caused parts inspectors to misinterpret written directions and to run tests incorrectly. When management finally recognized the problem, the inspectors were provided with ear protection devices that alleviated the situation. Once managers are made aware of the costs connected with job stress, the costs of job redesign described in Chapter 4 can seem relatively small. Boring, repetitive jobs in harsh working environments (automotive plants, steel foundries) are being made less stressful by the introduction of robots to replace or aid humans. Managers can reduce the stress of ambiguity and uncertainty in many jobs simply by better communication. Goal setting and management-by-objectives can help.

Exhibit 19.5   A Stress-Evaluation Questionnaire

Meter Reading (at the start of each phrase)		Phrases
left	right	
_____	_____	1. I feel quite quiet.
_____	_____	2. I am beginning to feel quite relaxed.
_____	_____	3. My feet feel heavy and relaxed.
_____	_____	4. My ankles, my knees & my hips feel heavy, relaxed & comfortable.
_____	_____	5. My solar plexus, & the whole central portion of my body, feel relaxed and quiet.
_____	_____	6. My hands, my arms & my shoulders, feel heavy, relaxed and comfortable.
_____	_____	7. My neck, my jaws & my forehead feel relaxed. They feel comfortable and smooth.
_____	_____	8. My whole body feels quiet, heavy, comfortable & relaxed.
_____	_____	9. Continue alone for a minute.
_____	_____	10. I am quite relaxed.
_____	_____	11. My arms and hands are heavy and warm.
_____	_____	12. I feel quite quiet.
_____	_____	13. My whole body is relaxed and my hands are warm, relaxed & warm.
_____	_____	14. My hands are warm.
_____	_____	15. Warmth is flowing into my hands, they are warm, warm.
_____	_____	16. I can feel the warmth flowing down my arms into my hands.
_____	_____	17. My hands are warm, relaxed and warm.
_____	_____	18. Continue alone for a minute.
_____	_____	19. My whole body feels quiet, comfortable & relaxed.
_____	_____	20. My mind is quiet.
_____	_____	21. I withdraw my thoughts from the surroundings and I feel serene & still.
_____	_____	22. My thoughts are turned inward and I am at ease.
_____	_____	23. Deep within my mind I can visualize & experience myself as relaxed, comfortable & still.
_____	_____	24. I am alert, but in an easy, quiet, inward-turned way.
_____	_____	25. My mind is calm and quiet.
_____	_____	26. I feel an inward quietness.
_____	_____	27. Continue alone for a minute.
_____	_____	28. The relaxation and reverie is now concluded and the whole body is reactivated with a deep breath and the following phrases: ''I feel life and energy flowing through my legs, hips, solar plexus, chest, arms & hands, neck & head . . . The energy makes me feel light and alive.'' Stretch.

Source: L. A. Longfellow, *Stress, The American Addiction: How To Break The Habit,* Lecture Theatre, Inc., Phoenix, AZ 85029.

Some researchers hope that managers will be able someday to design a job to match an employee's stress tolerance. To do so would require assessing the stress potential of each job and the stress tolerance of each employee. As of yet, we can't do either reliably enough:

Until industry is able to rate its jobs in terms of the type and magnitude of stressors in each job and job situation, there is little scientific basis for selective employment and placement of "vulnerable" individuals. It should be added that con-

Exhibit 19.6   Stress Diagnostic Survey

The following questionnaire is designed to provide you with an indication of the extent to which various individual level stressors are sources of stress to you. For each item you should indicate the frequency with which the condition described is a source of stress. Next to each item write the appropriate number (1–7) which best describes how frequently the condition is a source of stress.

Write *1* if the condition is *never* a source of stress.　　Write *5* if it is *often* a source of stress.
Write *2* if it is *rarely* a source of stress.　　　　　　　Write *6* if it is *usually* a source of stress.
Write *3* if it is *occasionally* a source of stress.　　　　Write *7* if it is *always* a source of stress.
Write *4* if it is *sometimes* a source of stress.

		Answer
1.	My job duties and work objectives are unclear to me.	_____
2.	I work on unnecessary tasks or projects.	_____
3.	I have to take work home in the evenings or on weekends to stay caught up.	_____
4.	The demands for work quality made upon me are unreasonable.	_____
5.	I lack the proper opportunities to advance in this organization.	_____
6.	I am held accountable for the development of other employees.	_____
7.	I am unclear about whom I report to and/or who reports to me.	_____
8.	I get caught in the middle between my supervisors and my subordinates.	_____
9.	I spend too much time in unimportant meetings that take me away from my work.	_____
10.	My assigned tasks are sometimes too difficult and/or complex.	_____
11.	If I want to get promoted I have to look for a job with another organization.	_____
12.	I am responsible for counseling with my subordinates and/or helping them solve their problems.	_____
13.	I lack the authority to carry out my job responsibilities.	_____
14.	The formal chain of command is not adhered to.	_____
15.	I am responsible for an unmanageable number of projects or assignments at the same time.	_____
16.	Tasks seem to be getting more and more complex.	_____
17.	I am hurting my career progress by staying with this organization.	_____
18.	I take action or make decisions that affect the safety or well-being of others.	_____
19.	I do not fully understand what is expected of me.	_____
20.	I do things on the job that are accepted by one person and not by others.	_____
21.	I simply have more work to do than can be done in an ordinary day.	_____
22.	The organization expects more of me than my skills and/or abilities provide.	_____
23.	I have few opportunities to grow and learn new knowledge and skills in my job.	_____
24.	My responsibilities in this organization are more for *people* than for *things*.	_____
25.	I do not understand the part my job plays in meeting overall organizational objectives.	_____
26.	I receive conflicting requests from two or more people.	_____
27.	I feel that I just don't have time to take an occasional break.	_____
28.	I have insufficient training and/or experience to discharge my duties properly.	_____

Source: Reprinted by permission of STress RESearch Systems.

siderable work needs to be done in measuring individuals in terms of the type and magnitude of stressors with which they are able to cope.[23]

TIME AS A SOURCE OF STRESS

Time pressures are the most common sources of stress in all occupations. Managers have only so much time to get things done; they face deadlines for completing projects, making decisions, acting. Finally, they have only so many years in which to develop and enhance their careers.

Every popular book on stress management emphasizes the importance of getting control of time, rather than letting time get control. *Stress and the Manager,* for instance, lists twenty-five rules for low-stress living such as, "Make time your ally, not your master." Among the list of fifteen rules for low-stress working the author advises, "Rate your work by order of importance and manage your time effectively."[24] By examining the nature of a manager's work, we can derive some suggestions for managing time effectively.

Wasting Time

A manager's job is busy, varied, random, and often filled with minor crises. Managers spend most of their time interacting with a wide variety of other people, usually face-to-face. They are often involved in several projects at a time, and are faced with random interruptions. By its very nature, the job of managing has the potential for a great amount of time-wasting, and time is the one thing all managers, from the president to the newest supervisor, share equally. Every manager has 168 hours per week in which to live and work. Those who manage these hours more effectively are generally more satisfied and less stressed—and they have more nonwork time to enjoy.

Studies of managers in a variety of settings have uncovered a long list of time-wasters. Wasting time doesn't necessarily mean loafing; it means spending too much time doing things which are relatively unimportant, leaving little or no time to do important things.

Exhibit 19.7 lists over thirty time-wasters identified by a diverse population of male and female business executives, military officers, religious leaders, and college presidents.

The "Too Much or Too Many" list in Exhibit 19.7 suggests things on which managers spend more time than they think worthwhile. The "Too Little or Too Few" list suggests things which cause them to spend too much time on the "Too Much or Too Many" list. The "Too Late" list generally suggests that managers waste time because they fall prey to others' priorities; other people make the manager wait.

The idea that managers spend too much time on relatively unimportant activities has been derived from the **Pareto Principle** which states that *eighty per-*

Exhibit 19.7   Time-Wasters Identified by Managers

Too Much or Too Many	Too Little or Too Few	Too Late
Coffee Breaks	Authority	Cancellations
Committee Work	Clear Objectives	Information
Community Affairs	Competent Personnel	Decisions
Correspondence	Delegation	Procrastination
Crises	Feedback	Waiting for Others
Demands from Peers	Information	
Junk Mail	Planning	
Meetings	Priorities	
Questionnaires	Routine Procedures	
Red Tape	Self-Discipline	
Reports		
Routine		
Socializing		
Subordinate Problems		
Telephone Calls		
Travel		
Visitors		

Source: Compiled from R. A. McKenzie, *The Time Trap* (New York: McGraw-Hill Book Co., 1972) and N. Stuart, *The Effective Woman Manager* (New York: Wiley-Intersource, 1978).

cent of the results of one's job come from only twenty percent of the tasks. If this is true, then it follows that most individuals spend eighty percent of their time on activities which account for only twenty percent of the results of their jobs.[25] For example, sales representatives may spend eighty percent of their time on clients who account for only twenty percent of their sales; teachers may spend eighty percent of their time on twenty percent of their students; production managers may spend eighty percent of their time on twenty percent of their products.

People whose time management is as inefficient as the Pareto Principle suggests have only twenty percent of their time left to deal with those activities which account for eighty percent of their results. Their ineffective management of time leads to hasty, often ill-informed decisions and actions about that part of their work which is most important. The sales representative who spends little time with his best customers is in for a rude awakening when someone else who realizes their value gets their business. The manager bogged down in routine and minor crises misses the once-in-a-decade opportunity.

Managing Time

The nature of managerial work, the time wasters identified by managers, and the Pareto Principle give some clues about time management.

Assessing the Use of Time.   The first step a manager can take to get control of time is to find out how he or she actually spends it. Studies have shown that managers are notoriously poor judges of how they actually spend their time. They overestimate the amount of uncommitted time they have, and underestimate the amount of time they waste. They also place most blame of their time-wasting on others, failing to realize how much time-wasting they are responsible for themselves.

A manager must get control of time.

Accurate assessment usually requires the use of a *time log* for a week or two. A time log (see Exhibit 19.8) breaks the day into short intervals of fifteen minutes or so. The manager records each activity as he or she carries it out throughout the day. At the end of a week or two, the manager records how much time was spent in each of several categories, such as the activities done, the people involved, and the site (own office, other's office, plant, home). The categories are up to the individual manager, depending upon information he or she wants (see Exhibit 19.8).

Planning the Use of Time.   Once managers have completed an analysis of their own time, they are usually shocked enough to take action. Getting control of their time means learning how to spend it effectively, devoting more time to those activities which are more important. This can be done by a *establishing priorities.*

One suggestion is listing everything that has to be done on a specific day and then separating the tasks into three categories.[26] Category A contains the highest priority items. These must be done, and should include only those activities of the greatest importance, such as spending some time planning for a major reorganization, dealing with an important client, or getting a key piece of information. Category B items are less important but still should be worked on that day. Category C items are those which are least important and can be put off. The manager then identifies all activities that the manager can delegate to someone else.

The list of activity priorities and appointments can be combined into a *daily work plan*, such as shown in Exhibit 19.9. In this plan, both phone calls and activities other than appointments are arranged in order of their priorities. The cardinal rule for following a daily work plan such as this is to complete all A priorities before going to B priorities; complete all B priorities before going to C priorities. This helps the manager resist the temptation to do lots of easy, low-priority items first, leaving no time for the most important activities. If something has to be left for another day, it is better to put off the least important items.

Controlling Time.   One of the problems that managers frequently encounter is lack of sufficient uninterrupted periods of time to work on important projects such as planning and organizing. In Chapter 1 we described a study which found that executives experienced only about one uninterrupted thirty-minute period in a typical week—not much time for executive-type thinking.

Managers can regain control over their time in several ways. One is by meeting whenever possible in someone else's office, so that they can leave as soon as

Exhibit 19.8 A Manager's Daily Time Log and Weekly Summary

Time Log and Analysis   Date: _____

Time	Activity	Type	Who	Where
7:30	Commute	Travel	Alone	Car
7:45	"	"/Reflecting	"	"
8:00	"	"	"	"
8:15	Meeting	Unscheduled	Elizabeth E.	My office
8:30	Meeting	Scheduled	Staff	My office
8:45	"	"	"	"
9:00	"	"	"	"
9:15	Plant Tour	Inspection	Stephanie M.	Plant floor
9:30	"	"	"	"
9:45	Meeting	Unsched.	Govt. Inspector	Plant floor
10:00	Interruption	Long Distance Phone	Customer	David's office
4:45	Meeting	Sched.	Finance Comm.	VP's office
5:00	"	"	"	"
5:15	"	"	"	"
5:30	"	"	"	"
7:45	Drive to dinner	Travel	Customers	Car
8:00	Dinner	Social/Meeting	Customers, Chris M. and Cathy S.	Four Winds
8:15	→	→	→	→
8:30				
8:45				
9:00				
9:15				
9:30	Drive home	Travel	Alone	→
9:45				
10:00				Car

Time Allocation Summary (in hours)   Week of February 9-13

Type of Activity		With Whom	
Scheduled Meetings	20 hours	Alone	17 hours
Unscheduled Meetings	13	Peers	12
Telephone	6	Subordinates	18
Reading	12	Superiors	12
Writing	5	Others in Plant	3
Reflecting	3	Customers	11
Waiting	5	Suppliers	3
Socializing	7	Community	2
Inspecting	7	Government	4
Interruptions	4	Others	—
Others	1		

Place of Activity

Own Office	20 hours
Other's Office	17
Plant Floor	8
During Travel	12
Home	15
Restaurant	9
Other	1

Exhibit 19.9   An Example of a Daily Work Plan

Daily Organizer   Date: _June 20_

To Phone: To Do:

Person	Regarding	Priority
JT	Order	B
CN	Shipment	A
LLC	Construct	A
MN	Replace JD	B
SSN	Travel 6/14	B
RS	Union	C
WC	Lunch	C

Task	Priority
Finish Contract	A
Work on Budget	A
Find Shipment	A/D
Hire Sec'y.	C
Check new machines	B
Arrange trip	B/D
Info. for P. Meeting	A/D

Appointments:

When	Person and Place	Time
9	DF- office	15 m
10	F Comer - Office	1 hr
11:30	CPA- his office	30 m
12:15	Jerry - Ed's	1 hr
2:15	Affirm Act. Ofc.	20 m
4:30	Secy - Ofc	30 m
8:00	Don- Joseph's	2 hr

To Follow Up:

Cartons Arrive
BC progress

Source: Adapted from Helen Reynolds and Mary E. Tramel, *Executive Time Management* (Englewood Cliffs, N.J.: Prentice Hall, Inc., 1979), p.16.

their business is finished. Another is to start meetings on time without waiting for late-comers. The idea is to let late-comers adjust their schedules rather than everyone else adjusting theirs. A third is to set aside a block of time to work on an important project without interruption. This may require ignoring the telephone, being protected by an aggressive secretary, or hiding out. Whatever it takes is worth it.

Delegating Tasks. Managers who are "overworked" usually are doing too many things. A manager can delegate some of these tasks to subordinates. The benefits are twofold. First, a manager who delegates frees up time to work on high-priority projects with potential for high payoffs. Second, a manager who delegates is helping subordinates develop skills and knowledge, and preparing them for advancement.

The daily work plan depicted in Exhibit 19.9 shows several tasks the manager has decided to delegate to a subordinate. Half of the tasks delegated are B or C priorities, leaving the manager free to work on the highest priority items. Two management consultants suggest delegation of the following tasks:

1. Duties that can be assigned on a temporary basis
2. Fact-finding assignments
3. Preparation of rough drafts of written material, such as reports, resumes, policies, procedures, and so forth
4. Problem analysis and possible solutions
5. Routine tasks
6. Collection of data for reports and/or presentations
7. Tasks that will challenge the subordinate
8. Tasks to test the subordinate's ability in a specific area of responsibility
9. Small units of work assignments from the manager's responsibilities and functions.[27]

The Bottom Line

Because managing involves uncertainty and time pressures, stress is a part of every manager's job, and those of his or her subordinates. There are several guidelines that managers can follow to reduce the effects of stress in their organizations:

1. Promote an awareness of the symptoms and causes of stress so that employees can better understand and protect themselves against excessive stress. Encourage them to have regular medical checkups (and do so yourself).
2. Identify stressors in your environment and devise ways to cope with them.
3. Be on the lookout for alcohol and drug abuse, increase in errors, accidents, or illness as signs of increased stress.
4. Because uncertainty and anxiety are major factors in stressful situations, try to improve communications with superiors and subordinates. By reducing uncertainty for yourself and your subordinates, you are alleviating stress.
5. Find ways to relax. Then use them—frequently.
6. Build a support system, people whom you can trust to listen to your problems and crises, who will be supportive and encouraging.
7. Make it possible for subordinates to develop their own support systems at work. Don't design work to make people social isolates.
8. Control your use of time. Set goals and list priorities. Work on important matters before trivial ones. Delegate work to subordinates. Don't let others waste your time.

SUMMARY

Stress is a set of physiological and psychological changes that a person experiences in reaction to certain changes in the environment. A stressful situation is usually one in which the individual experiences uncertainty about important outcomes.

An individual experiencing stress can proceed through three phases. In the alarm phase, the individual becomes more alert and aware. The body secretes important hormones and blood pressure increases. In the resistance and adaptation phase, the body and senses are ready for action. The individual can work at a high level of energy to meet the stressful situation. In the exhaustion phase, the individual's energy resources are depleted. The body's defenses are reduced, and the individual is highly vulnerable. As the individual approaches the exhaustion phases, certain physical and behavioral changes may occur.

Stress affects both health and job performance. Mild stress can provide the energy needed for superior job performance. Excess or prolonged stress will eventually cause performance to deteriorate. Too much stress is a major factor in many diseases, particularly coronary heart disease. Excess stress also shares the blame for the abuse of alcohol and other drugs, and contributes to accidents and injuries.

In organizational settings, individuals experience stress as a result of ambiguous jobs or conflicting roles, from being either overworked or underutilized. Finally, working conditions which are excessively uncomfortable or dangerous are stressful.

Managers should be capable of dealing with stress both for themselves and for their employees. Awareness of the relationship between stress and physical fitness is a first step. Relaxation techniques and social-support systems can help people survive stressful work. Reducing ambiguities and conflicts at work, and trying to match work loads to individual capabilities, can remove many sources of stress.

Time is frequently a factor in organizational stress; the nature of managerial work makes the manager's job particularly susceptible to time-wasting and stress. Managers can reduce stress by actively taking steps to gain control of their time, by systematically assessing time allocation and planning its use, setting and following priorities, and delegating tasks to subordinates.

QUESTIONS FOR REVIEW AND DISCUSSION

1. What characteristics do stressful jobs have in common? How can stress affect behavior?
2. How has the role of stress in our lives changed over time? What are the implications of this for workers today? Do you think they are good or bad? Why?
3. What types of demands and constraints might cause middle managers to feel stress?
4. What types of demands and constraints might cause an assembly-line worker to feel stress?

5. Evaluate: "Managers in highly structured organizations feel more stress than managers in loosely structured organizations, because they are faced with more constraints in their work."
6. Evaluate: "Easy work is good for one's health."
7. What are the purposes of stress-management programs? What is their focus in trying to reduce stress?
8. How can managers relieve stress for their subordinates? What problems might they encounter in trying to do so? How can company policies affect their attempts?
9. What are the problems that managers might encounter while trying to control their time? How can managers overcome these problems?
10. Just at the busiest time of the season, you find yourself with a difficult project, the results of which may influence your promotion. You are considering delegating it to a recently acquired bright and eager MBA, because you would like to test her potential and because you have relatives coming to visit for a month and are already flooded with work. What factors should you consider in making your decision? What is your decision, and why?

REFERENCES AND NOTES

1. H. J. Reitz, *Behavior in Organizations*, rev. ed. (Homewood, Ill.: Richard D. Irwin, 1981), p. 231.
2. The discussion of the three phases of stress is taken from *Coping with Stress* (Hartford, Conn.: Keyword Publications, Inc. 1977).
3. R. S. Schuler, "Definition and Conceptualization of Stress in Organizations," *Organizational Behavior and Human Performance*, vol. 25 (1980), pp. 4.
4. R. L. Kahn, et. al., *Organizational Stress: Studies in Role Conflict and Ambiguity* (New York: John Wiley & Sons, 1964).
5. R. D. Caplan, "Organizational Stress and Individual Strain," reported in D. Katz and R. Kahn, *The Social Psychology of Organizations*, 2nd ed. (New York: John Wiley & Sons, 1978), p. 598.
6. D. E. Sanborn III, C. J. Sanborn, and P. Cuibolic, Sr., "Occupation and Suicide," *Diseases of the Nervous System*, vol. 35 (January 1974), pp. 7–12.
7. R. A. Karasek, "Job Demands, Job Decision Latitude, and Mental Strain: Implications for Job Redesign," *Administrative Science Quarterly*, vol. 24 (1979), pp. 285–308.
8. This list is taken from Brief, et al., *Managing Job Stress*, pp. 77–78; and Reitz, *Behavior in Organizations*, p. 246.
9. G. Baker, M. D. "Stress and Electronic Video Display Terminal Operators," *Gainsville Sun*, January 19, 1982, p. 11D.
10. J. E. McGrath, "Stress and Behavior in Organizations," in *Handbook of Industrial and Organizational Psychology*, M. D. Dunette, ed. (Chicago: Rand McNally, 1976), pp. 1351–95.
11. A. P. Brief, R. S. Schuler, and M. Van Sell, *Managing Job Stress* (Boston: Little, Brown & Co., 1981), Chapter 2.

12. J. Gaines and J. M. Jermier, "Emotional Exhaustion in a High Stress Organization," *Academy of Management Journal*, 1983, 26, pp. 567–86.
13. H. Selye, *The Stress of Life*, rev. ed. (New York: McGraw-Hill Book Co., 1956).
14. K. Albrecht, *Stress and the Manager* (Englewood Cliffs, N.J.: Prentice-Hall, 1979), p. 33.
15. M. T. Matteson and J. M. Ivancevich, "Organizational Stressors and Heart Disease: A Research Model." *Academy of Management Review*, vol. 4 (1979), pp. 347–57.
16. Albrecht, *Stress and the Manager*, p. 33.
17. C. L. Bete, *What Everyone Should Know About Stress* (South Dearfield, Mass: Channing L. Bete Co., 1981), p. 12.
18. J. W. Schuier, *Behavioral Sciences Newsletter*, May, 1977.
19. Dr. M. Smith, cited in Albrecht, *Stress and the Manager*, p. 43.
20. E. Roskies, M. Sperak, A. Sukis, C. Cohen, and S. Gilman, "Changing the Coronary—Prone (Type A) Behavioral Pattern in a Non-Clinical Population," *Journal of Behavioral Medicine*, 1978, 1, pp. 201–16.
21. J. Newman and T. Becker, "Personal and Organizational Strategies for Handling Job Stress," *Personal Psychology*, Spring, 1979, pp. 1–38.
22. "It's Lonely—and Stressful—at the Top," *Chicago Tribune*, January 7, 1983, Section 4, p. 11.
23. A. A. McLean, *Work Stress* (Reading, Mass.: Addison-Wesley, 1979).
24. R. A. MacKenzie, *The Time Trap* (New York: McGraw-Hill Book Co., 1972); N. Steward, *The Effective Woman Manager* (New York: Wiley-Interscience, 1978).
25. A. Lakein, *How to Get Control of Time and Your Life* (New York: Signet Books, 1973).
26. H. Reynolds and M. E. Tramel, *Executive Time Management*, (Englewood Cliffs, N.J.: Prentice Hall, 1979).
27. Reynolds and Tramel, *Executive Time Management*, pp. 136–37.

SUGGESTED READINGS

K. Albrecht, *Stress and the Manager*, (Englewood Cliffs, N.J.: Prentice-Hall, 1979). A practically-oriented approach to stress management, this book is written to be read and used by managers.

A. P. Brief, R. S. Schuler, and M. Van Sell, *Managing Job Stress*, (Boston: Little, Brown & Co., 1981). This is a more academically oriented look at stress, its effects, and its management. The book heavily referenced, with a topical bibliography.

R. A. Mackenzie, *The Time Trap.* (New York: McGraw-Hill Book Co., 1972). This is a how-to book written for managers and supervisors by the president of a management consultant firm.

H. Reynolds and M. E. Tramel, *Executive Time Management*, (Englewood Cliffs, N.J.: Prentice-Hall, 1979). The authors have written a practical book oriented toward the executive and professional level.

Case: *No Response from Monitor Twenty-three*

Loudspeaker: IGNITION MINUS FORTY-FIVE MINUTES . . .

Paul Keller tripped the sequence switches at control monitor 23 in accordance with the countdown instruction book just to his left. All hydraulic systems were functioning normally in the second stage of the spacecraft booster at checkpoint 1 minus forty-five. Keller automatically snapped his master control switch to GREEN and knew that his electronic impulse along with hundreds of others from similar consoles within the Cape Kennedy complex signaled continuation of the countdown.

Free momentarily from data input, Keller leaned back in his chair, stretched his arms above his head and then rubbed the back of his neck. The monitor lights on console 23 glowed routinely.

It used to be an incredible challenge, fantastically interesting work at the very fringe of man's knowledge about himself and his universe. Keller recalled his first day in Brevard County, Florida, with his wife and young daughter. How happy they were that day. Here was the future, the good life . . . forever. And Keller was going to be part of that fantastic, utopian future . . .

Loudspeaker: IGNITION MINUS THIRTY-FIVE MINUTES . . .

Keller panicked! His mind had wandered momentarily and he lost his place in the countdown instructions. Seconds later he found the correct place and tripped the proper sequence of switches for checkpoint 1 minus thirty-five. No problem. Keller snapped master control to GREEN and wiped his brow. He knew he was late reporting and would hear about it later.

Damn!, he thought. I used to know countdown cold for seven systems monitors without countdown instructions. But now . . . you're slipping Keller . . . you're slipping, he thought. Shaking his head, Keller reassured himself that he was overly tired today . . . just tired.

Loudspeaker: IGNITION MINUS THIRTY MINUTES . . .

Keller completed the reporting sequence for checkpoint 1 minus thirty, took one long last drag on his cigarette, and squashed it out in the crowded ashtray. Utopia? Hell! It was one big rat-race and getting bigger all the time. Keller recalled how he once naively felt that his problems with Naomi would disappear after they left Minneapolis and came to the Cape with the space program. Now, ten thousand arguments later, Keller knew there was no escape . . .

"Only one can of beer left. Naomi? One stinking lousy can of beer, cold lunchmeat and potato salad? Is that all a man gets after twelve hours of mental exhaustion?"

"Oh, shut up, Paul! I'm so sick of you playing Mr. Important. You get leftovers because I never know when you're coming home . . . your daughter hardly knows you . . . and you treat us like nobodies . . . incidental to your great personal contribution to the Space Age."

"Don't knock it, Naomi. That job is plenty important to me, to the Team, and it gets you everything you've ever wanted . . . more! Between this house and the boat, we're up to our ears in debt."

"Now don't try to pin our money

Source: R. D. Joyce, *Encounters in Organizational Behavior: Problem Situations* (New York: Pergamon Press, 1977) pp. 168–71.

problems on me, Paul Keller. You're the one who has to have all the same goodies as the scientists earning twice your salary. Face it, Paul. You're just a button-pushing technician regardless of how fancy a title they give you. You can be replaced Paul. You can be replaced by any S.O.B. who can read and punch buttons!''

Loudspeaker: IGNITION MINUS TWENTY-FIVE MINUTES . . .

A red light blinked ominously indicating a potential hydraulic fluid leak in a subsystem seven of stage two. Keller felt his heartbeat and pulse rate increase. Rule 1 . . . report malfunction immediately and stop the count. Keller punched POTENTIAL ABORT on the master control.

Loudspeaker: THE COUNT IS STOPPED AT IGNITION MINUS TWENTY-FOUR MINUTES SEVENTEEN SECONDS.

Keller fumbled with the countdown instructions. Any POTENTIAL ABORT required a cross check to separate an actual malfunction from sporadic signal error. Keller began to perspire nervously as he initiated standard cross check procedures.

"Monitor 23, this is Control. Have you got an actual abort, Paul?" The voice in the headset was cool, but impatient. "Decision required in thirty seconds."

"I know, I know," Keller mumbled. "I'm cross checking right now."

Keller felt the silence closing in around him. Cross check one proved inconclusive. Keller automatically followed detailed instructions for cross check two.

"Do you need help, Keller?" asked the voice in the headset.

"No, I'm O.K."

Keller continued cross check two.

"Decision required," demanded the voice in the headset. "Dependent systems must be deactivated in fifteen seconds."

Keller read and re-read the console

data. It looked like a sporadic error signal . . . the system appeared to be in order . . .

"Decision required," demanded the voice in the headset.

"Continue count," blurted Keller at last. "Subsystem seven fully operational." Keller slumped back in his chair.

Loudspeaker: THE COUNT IS RESUMED AT IGNITION MINUS TWENTY-FOUR MINUTES SEVENTEEN SECONDS.

Keller knew that within an hour after lift off, Barksdale would call him in for a personal conference. "What's wrong lately, Paul?" he would say. "Is there anything I can help with? You seem so tense lately." But he wouldn't really want to listen. Barksdale was the kind of person who read weakness into any personal problems and demanded that they be purged from the mind the moment his men checked out their consoles.

More likely Barksdale would demand that Keller make endless practice runs on cross check procedures while he stood nearby . . . watching and noting any errors . . . while the pressure grew and grew . . .

Today's performance was surely the kiss of death for any wage increase too. That was another of Barksdale's methods of obtaining flawless performance . . . which would surely lead to another scene with Naomi . . .
and another sleepless night . . .
and more of those nagging stomach pains . . .
and yet another imperfect performance for Barksdale . . .

Loudspeaker: IGNITION MINUS TWENTY MINUTES . . .

The monitor lights at console twenty-three blinked routinely.

"Keller," said the voice in the earphone. "Report, please."

"Control, this Wallace at monitor twenty-four. I don't believe Keller is *feeling well. Better send someone to cover fast!*

Loudspeaker: THE COUNT IS STOPPED AT NINETEEN MINUTES THIRTY-THREE SECONDS.

"This is Control. Wallace. Assistance has been dispatched and the count is on temporary hold. What seems to be wrong with Keller?"

"Control, this is Wallace. I don't know. His eyes are open and fixed on the monitor but he won't respond to my questions. It could be a seizure or . . . a stroke."

CASE QUESTIONS

1. Identify the possible sources of stress for Keller.
2. Could this problem have been detected earlier? Could the outcome have been avoided? If so, how?
3. What is the supervisor's proper role in this case? Should he attempt counseling?

5 / What's Ahead?

Part 5 provides a brief look at the future for students who decide to embark on a career in management. It describes the opportunities and challenges offered by three types of managerial careers.

20 / Entrepreneurship and Small Business *discusses the attractions and requirements of entrepreneurship—managing one's own business. It outlines the required skills, knowledge, resources, and individual traits characteristic of successful entrepreneurship. How to set up a small business and how to find sources of assistance for this career alternative are discussed.*

21 / International Management *covers the field of international business and management. Managers today can find themselves in three types of international positions: working for a domestic company in a foreign country, working for a foreign company in a foreign country, or working for a foreign company in the home country. The chapter describes the special roles played by international managers and the particular areas in which international management differs from domestic management.*

22 / Managing as a Career *discusses the opportunities of traditional managerial careers. It describes the processes by which organizations recruit, select, evaluate, train, and develop young managers. Some particular problems faced during the early stages of managerial careers and the dual–career couple are highlighted. The chapter covers the kinds of compensation managers can expect and concludes by describing some particular challenges managers will face in the future.*

20/Entrepreneurship and Small Business

Crack! The ball seemed to explode off the bat, still rising as it cleared the left-field fence 330 feet away—just foul. Jerry Daniel shook his head as the umpire threw him a new ball. I've had it, he thought. When some 18-year-old rookie can hit my best pitch that far, foul or not, it's time to think about getting an honest job.

He checked the scoreboard as he worked-up the new ball in a rite that had more effect on the pitcher than on the ball. Time to settle down and get out of here. Two out, bottom of the ninth, protecting a one-run lead with two runners in scoring position. Challenging the rookie with a fastball on a one-and-two count was pure macho, and it had almost cost him the game.

Composed now, he stepped back on the rubber, leaned toward home plate, and squinted against the harsh Arizona sun for the catcher's sign. The runners took cautious leads as he came to the set position, hands at his belt. It was a good pitch, a curveball low and away. With two strikes already, the batter had to swing. Whack! Another line drive, this time to right field, but the first baseman lunged to his left and speared the ball as it went by. Had the ball been a few inches closer to the line, the game would have ended differently.

Jerry accepted the ritual handshakes of his teammates and headed for the shower. Thirty minutes later, in the cool confines of his hotel room, he finally relaxed, as his roommate tossed him an ice-cold beer.

''Mike,'' he announced as he popped the tab from the can, ''you ever think about what you're gonna do when you give up this game?''

''Not really. I'll probably still be trying to finish my degree. Why?''

''I dunno. I guess the way that kid hit me today made me think that my baseball career is nearing an end. He mashed my best two pitches.''

''Man, you're only twenty-four! You've got time to make it,'' Mike rejoined.

''I know, but I gave myself five years to make the major leagues. This is my fifth year, I finished my college degree last winter, and after today—well—I can't see myself surviving another cut. Besides, I've got plans.''

''Like what?'' asked Mike.

''I want to go into business for myself. A guy back home and I have talked about it since high school. We've both saved up some money, and believe it or not, I'm still something of a local hero back there. That could help us get financing.

''What kind of business are you thinking about?'' asked Mike.

"We're not sure, but something to do with young people. Andy—that's the guy back home—is really creative, and we've always worked well together. We've talked about a fancy skating rink, a bowling alley with old-time movies, or a restaurant with games and slide shows."

"I thought you worked as an accountant or something in the off-season. I figured you'd wind up working for some CPA firm or corporation," offered Mike.

"No way. Five years in baseball has convinced me I want no part of big business. Too many rules and policies; too long to get to the top; too many people making decisions for me.

"I want to be my own boss. I want to make things happen without worrying about how it looks or who takes offense. Besides," Jerry added with a knowing wink, *"you'll never get rich working for somebody else. Being an entrepreneur—that's where the big bucks are."*

Like many other people, Jerry Daniel feels somewhat frustrated in his job. In the twilight of a short and mediocre career in professional baseball, Jerry returns to his other dream, being an entrepreneur. Entrepreneurship, starting and managing an independent business, is an important alternative to the more traditional management positions we have discussed in this book. It is an alternative attractive to a lot of people for its challenge, autonomy, and potential gains, which are still available in this country, despite big business and big government.

One of the many success stories that make entrepreneurship an attractive alternative is that of Xavier Roberts, an entrepreneur in every sense of the word, an individual who went from rags to riches on the strengths of his own talent, vision, and drive.

A few years ago Xavier Roberts was an unknown artist working in the hills of northern Georgia, a poor mountain boy with talent, ideas, and ambition. He was the creator of Little People, soft dolls that he induced customers to adopt (not buy) for $125 to $1000 each by referring to them as "babies," complete with formal adoption papers.

Three years later his drive and ambition, coupled with a receptive market, made him president, chief designer, and major stockholder of Appalachian Artworks, Inc., which produced ninety thousand "babies" in those three years. His company employs three hundred workers to supply Little People for stores in all fifty states, Canada, and Europe. Mr. Roberts built his own business, ran it his own way, had the satisfaction of seeing his creations featured on television programs and in national magazines. The fruits of his labor include four cars (two Mercedes, an MG, and a silver Jaguar with built-in picnic tables) and a house "like nothing anybody ever saw this side of Southern California."[1]

Few entrepreneurs have the sort of one-of-a-kind idea that made Xavier Roberts famous. Not all are financially successful, whatever their field of business. But stories like his continue to inspire men and women like Jerry to risk going out on their own in search of independence and wealth.

ENTREPRENEURS AND SMALL BUSINESS

The word *entrepreneur* is borrowed from the French language to denote a person who strikes out on his or her own to deliver a product or service for profit. More formally, an **entrepreneur** is *one who creates, manages, assumes the risks, and enjoys the profits of a business enterprise.* Because most entrepreneurs, like Xavier Roberts and Jerry, start small, the terms *small business* and *entrepreneurship* often appear together. A small business is one that employs fewer than five hundred workers.

The Role of Small Business in the American Economy

In sheer numbers of enterprises and workers, small business is indeed the "backbone of the economy." In Florida, the small-business capital of the nation, ninety-nine percent of its corporations are classified as small businesses, averaging only thirteen employees. Entrepreneurs start a new Florida business every three minutes, or some fourteen thousand per month![2]

Although giant corporations attract the greatest publicity because of their individual impacts, political clout, and nationwide advertising, small businesses comprise ninety-five percent of all American companies, some fourteen million in all. As a group, small businesses account for over fifty percent of the labor force, create almost two thirds of all *new* jobs, and generate about forty-three percent of the total gross national product. And they are continuing to grow.

In a country whose business is business, small firms are bellweathers of the economy. Often the hardest hit during recessions, they are also the first to recover when good times return. In one seven-year period of recovery, small businesses added six million new jobs to the economy. Their flexibility enables them to make a substantial contribution to creativity and innovation. A National Science Foundation study concluded that smaller companies produce twenty-four times more innovations per research-dollar than large firms.[3] As Chapter 13 pointed out, big budgets are no guarantee of high creativity. The structure and energy required to run big companies often interfere with creative output.

The importance of small business to the American economy does not mean that success is easy for such firms. Inflation, high interest rates, and government regulations hit them proportionally harder than the giant companies, and many of them fail. During the first week of October, 1981, for example, 468 small U.S. companies went out of business. In 1982, an estimated 25,000 went bankrupt before the economy began to recover in 1983.[4]

The relatively greater vulnerability of small businesses has led to an increasing tendency for the owners of such firms to band together to provide assistance for one another and to pressure the Federal government for outside help and support. There are also a growing number of publications, workshops, and college courses for those who have, or want to have, their own businesses. Approximately one hundred fifty colleges and universities now offer entrepreneurship courses, for example

Exhibit 20.1   Extension Courses in Small Business and Entrepreneurship

---

Small Business Management

Course information: (415) 642-4231

Courses of related interest:

Marketing Your Small Business Through the Media, page 44

Restaurant Management, page 44

Forming Your Own Bank, page 39

Small Business Management I
X 443.1 (3) (Business Administration)

Evening class. The object of this course is to stimulate entrepreneurship by providing a working knowledge of the practical business and legal tools needed to start a business or to expand or improve one. Topics include negotiating commercial leases, cash-flow budgeting, small business accounting, acquisition of capital, and evaluating the advantages of the sole proprietorship, partnership, and corporate forms of conducting business.

BUDD E. MacKENZIE, J.D., M.B.A., Attorney

SAN FRANCISCO: 10 sessions, Sept. 21 to Oct. 21; Tues. and Thurs., 7-10 pm; UC Extension Center, 55 Laguna St.; $120 (edp 158188)

How to Become a Consultant
(.6 ceu)

What are the opportunities and pitfalls inherent in starting and operating a consulting firm? What are the techniques necessary to establish a firm? A step-by-step approach shows participants how to analyze their ability to act as consultants. Topics include how to find clients and get contracts; fees; how to build a consulting reputation and a support network and client base; and how to set up a consulting practice *while continuing existing employment.*

MICHAEL W. POGGENBURG, J.D., management consultant who has conducted many courses on this subject

SAN FRANCISCO: 1 day, Oct. 30; Sat., 9 am-4:30 pm; UC Extension Center, 55 Laguna St.; $70, including program materials and box lunch (edp 168146)

Effective Listening **can help you improve an essential skill in working with people; see page 37.**

Entrepreneurs & Business Owners

How to Write a Proposal and Get a Business Loan
(.6 ceu)

This seminar is designed to enable participants to research, prepare, and present a small-business loan proposal and business plan, or a venture-capital funding proposal, to financial institutions or government financing agencies—e.g., the Small Business Administration. It covers the essential elements of the state-of-the-art debt or equity funding proposal: preparation of financial statements; preparation of a business plan that includes marketing plans, management plans, financial planning, debt or equity structure, etc.; the politics of capital funds acquisition; language and writing; and related topics. Potential funding sources and their requirements and interests also are discussed.

SAN FRANCISCO: 1 day, Sept. 25; Sat., 9 am-4:30 pm; UC Extension Center, 55 Laguna St.; $75 individuals, $115 couples, including program materials and box lunch (edp 198333)

How to Raise Money for Your Business (.6 ceu)

The objective of this seminar is to provide the information needed to plan a systematic course of action that will lead to financing for a business project. Emphasis is on the characteristics, interests, and funding requirements of various debt and equity financial institutions, including banks, venture-capital firms, local development corporations, private individuals, and federal and state financing agencies; preparing documents and forms; the gamesmanship of securing business financing; and strategy development for the solicitation of financing.

SAN FRANCISCO: 1 day, Oct. 9; Sat., 9 am-4:30 pm; UC Extension Center, 55 Laguna St.; $75 individuals, $115 couples, including program materials and box lunch (edp 198341)

Instructor for both seminars

JOHN Q. JOHNSON received his M.B.A. from the Wharton School of Finance and Commerce and was president of his own consulting firm, specializing in financial and management services to small and medium-size businesses throughout California. Currently he is an author and freelance writer.

Supervisory Training & Management Development

Course information: (415) 642-4231

Courses of related interest:

Cross-Cultural Communication, page 37

Courses for Non-Native Speakers of English, page 67

Effective Supervision: Principles and Methods
X 451.4 (3) (Business Administration)

Evening class. Effective supervisors improve the productivity, attitudes, and skills of their workers. This class helps you to learn principles and practical techniques you can use to improve your supervisory ability in specific problem areas. Topics include the roles and responsibilities of supervisors; planning, defining tasks, establishing standards and controls; decision-making techniques; how to delegate effectively; key communication skills; improving motivation and morale; employee selection, training, and performance evaluation; counseling and discipline; training your subordinates; leadership techniques; self-evaluation and improvement.

San Francisco section

ROBERT GARDNER, M.A., Director of Personnel, Transamerica Airlines

SAN FRANCISCO: 10 sessions, Sept. 28 to Nov. 30; Tues., 7-10 pm; UC Extension Center, 55 Laguna St.; $120 (edp 158519)

Berkeley section

BOB EDDY, M.S., Training Program Designer, Bechtel Corp.

BERKELEY: 10 sessions, Sept. 30 to Dec. 9 (no meeting Nov. 25); Thurs., 7-10 pm; 126 Barrows Hall, UC campus; $120 (edp 158527)

The Process of Interviewing and Hiring
(.6 ceu)

What should you look for when you talk with job applicants? How many times have you misjudged someone? How can you find out what you need to know, even if it is hidden beneath the surface of polite conversation? Is there a scientific method of interviewing and evaluating job applicants, or should it be done intuitively? What are you legally entitled to ask?

(see Exhibit 20.1). Conferences, such as the International Symposium on Small Business that bring together people interested in this aspect of business, have also become popular.

Entrepreneurship is a vital part of the American economy. A variety of forces make it difficult to be successful as an entrepreneur, but there are an increasing number of counterforces to help make it possible. For the individual, the decision to take this path rests on his or her own assessment of the relative rewards and costs.

Owning and managing your own business is an alternative to working for someone else. For Jerry Daniel, the freedom to put his ideas to work and the ability to make things happen added to the attraction. For others, the inducement may be independence, power and influence, job satisfaction, financial gain, or job security.

In a country whose business is business, small firms are bellweathers of the economy. Often hardest hit during recessions, they are also the first to recover when good times return.

Financial gain, of course, is a major reward of successful entrepreneurship. The founder of Atari Corporation, for example, started with $500 and sold the company four years later for $28 million; the giant Weight Watchers enterprise began as a self-help group around a kitchen table; Apple Company (personal computers) had storybook success when it went from a garage workshop to sales of $100 million in four years. Exhibit 20.2 describes similar successes on a smaller scale.

Cinderella stories such as these inspire thousands each year to try to achieve similar success. Yet the rewards of entrepreneurship, whether astounding or modest, don't come without difficulty. In their early days there may be stress and fatigue, financial insecurity, and long work hours that leave little or no time for other interests. Most successful entrepreneurs have no doubts that the rewards are greater than the costs, but the fact remains that the word *sacrifice* is often heard when the topic is owning your own business. Nevertheless, more than a thousand new business ventures are started each day in this country. The balance of this chapter will examine the skills and resources necessary for those who decide to join that number.

What It Takes To Be an Entrepreneur

The difference between being a manager in someone else's company and being the owner/creator of your own company lies in degree of responsibility and scope of activity. To be the manager of your own business takes the same skills, knowledge, and resources required to be a manager in someone else's company—plus. You may expect to perform a wider range of activities and to deal with a far greater number of people; the demands on your personal resources will be increased accordingly.

Skills, Knowledge, and Resources.   The activities of the entrepreneur, at least in the early stages, include all of the usual manager functions, plus those typically handled by executives or staff personnel in the larger organization. The responsibility for the structure of the organization, organizational policy, personnel functions, marketing, and accounting, as well as for the day-to-day running of the busi-

Exhibit 20.2   Recent Entrepreneurial Success Stories

#6 CompuShop; computer-store retailer; Richardson, Tex.

As the market for personal computers has exploded, CompuShop, a computer retailing chain based in Richardson, Tex., has resisted the temptation of going after rapid growth through national franchising. Instead, the company, which has opened 18 stores in the past five years, believes that owning its retail outlets, though they demand precious capital, is a better way to go. The corporate staff takes care of advertising, accounting, and purchasing for all the outlets. "The only things the people at the stores have to do is sell computers and service customers," says Warren Winger, founder and chairman.

In early 1977, Winger, now 40, had been a manager for General Electric Information Services, marketing its computer time-sharing services, when he read an article in *The Wall Street Journal* on the incipient market for personal computers. In three months—just before the first Apple II models became available on the market—Winger had his first store in northern Dallas.

While Dallas, Houston, and Chicago are CompuShop's major markets today—a Denver store opened last August—Winger says that by mid-1985 the company will have 100 stores and be in new markets. The expansion, he claims, could be financed internally; the company projects its return on equity will increase 80% per year.

Specializing in Apple and IBM personal computers, CompuShop saw 1981 sales rise around 65%, to $8.4 million. But Winger anticipates increasingly stiff competition from national retailers like Sears, Roebuck & Co. and retail outlets owned by computer manufacturers. To meet these challenges, CompuShop is tightening quality standards throughout the chain and building a strong management organization. For instance, it recently hired a veteran Sears executive who had helped launch the giant retailer's new business systems centers. Explains Winger: "There isn't anyone who knows retailing and service better than Sears."—*B.G.P.*

Dan LeKander's wife is in the driver's seat.

#87 Corvette America Inc.; manufacturer and distributor of Corvette automobile parts; Boalsburg, Pa.

For Dan LeKander, it was a lucky accident. In 1974, LeKander wrecked his 1966 Corvette.

"I was going to rebuild the car," he remembers, "but I got discouraged and advertised the parts for sale." Some parts he sold, others he swapped. By the end of the year he had $6,000 in cash, $4,000 worth of parts, and an idea. The idea became, in 1977, Corvette America Inc., a Boalsburg, Pa.–based manufacturer and nationwide wholesaler and retail distributor of Corvette parts and accessories with almost $3 million in sales for fiscal 1981.

A huge market and a strict credit policy have been responsible for LeKander's success. There are more than 500,000 Corvette owners in the United States today. Rather than selling them the parts most dealers supply, LeKander, 37, concentrates on high-profit-margin items—such custom accessories as car covers, aluminum wheels, and interior parts. Retail customers, who account for 70% of his business, can order by credit card or COD. LeKander's 600 wholesale customers are denied credit as well; instead he encourages them to keep $10,000 on account by offering a discount price.

The business has grown some 1,220% in five years, from one man in a garage to a 35-person staff. Now LeKander plans to promote his wife, Peggy, to the company presidency and spend his time fishing and working on a 150-page catalog for the company. He still owns a Corvette himself, but in the business it will be Peggy in the driver's seat.—*C.H.*

Paul Munsen is carefully attentive to the concerns of his special group of customers.

#245 Munsen's Discovery Enterprises Ltd.; chartering and leasing tours; Hinsdale, Ill.

When 23-year-old Paul M. Munsen set up a company in 1974, he planned to market low-cost, group motor coach tours to students and organizations. But within a year he discovered that there was more gold in another market: the golden-agers. Although the number of senior citizens was growing rapidly, there were no companies that had developed tour programs to meet the special needs of the group. "The Discovery Experience" was born, limited to men and women over 55 years of age.

Everything about Discovery tours has been calculated with the needs of the group in mind—even the travel brochure is printed in boldface type for easy reading. Trips are carefully planned, with travel time never more than 2½ hours without a stop. Long walks and steep steps at attractions are kept to a minimum. One price covers virtually everything—meals, hotels, attractions, and trips—so that seniors on a budget get no unwelcome surprises.

Such attention to detail has paid off. Over the last five years sales have climbed 563%, to nearly $8 million in 1981. Careful planning has been the hallmark of Munsen's growth. In 1980, Munsen purchased his own fleet of buses, buying the Illinois company from which he had originally leased his coaches, thus ensuring the quality of equipment. Later that year, he bought a bus company in Florida. Traditionally the business in the Midwest is slow in the winter and busy in summer and fall, while the business pattern in Florida is reversed. By having two companies, Discovery can get maximum use of its equipment and ensure a smooth, rather than seasonal, cash flow. In addition, the company has opened a commuter operation and a company offering one-day coach tours, both of which further increase utilization of equipment and generate income. Gross sales for the entire system are expected to hit the $11 million mark this year.—*R.C.W.*

The articles in this section were researched and written by INC. *staff members Curtis Hartman, Robert A. Mamis, Bruce G. Posner, and Robert C. Wood.*

ness is the entrepreneur's. The wider scope of activities also means dealing personally with a greater variety of people. Entrepreneurs must try to understand, communicate with, and influence more than bosses, coworkers, and subordinates. Customers or clients, suppliers, bankers, lawyers, accountants, and representatives of insurance companies, unions, advertising media, and various local, state, and federal government agencies will all claim time, attention, and skills.

Given the great demands of entrepreneurship, there is considerable interest in the personal characteristics of those who undertake such a task. For people like Jerry Daniel, part of deciding to be an entrepreneur is deciding if they have what it takes.

Personal Characteristics.   To many, entrepreneurship is more than a collection of activities; it is a composite of personal traits often described as a spirit. Among the traits frequently cited as characteristics of that spirit are self confidence, courage, intensity, practicality, tolerance for uncertainty, persistence, imagination, creativity, and resiliency. Studies have found that successful entrepreneurs are likely to have had another entrepreneur in the family, have been an immigrant, have had a paper route as a young person, or excelled at individual sports, but lacked interest in team sports.[5]

Attempts to identify the traits that make a successful entrepreneur have much in common with research on the trait theory of leadership discussed in Chapter 10. Entrepreneurs, like leaders, vary. No match of personal characteristics or background with those of successful small-business leaders will guarantee success. Only experience will show whether someone indeed has what it takes. In fact, one writer says bluntly, "If you even have to ask yourself that question, then you probably *don't* have the stuff."[6]

SETTING UP A SMALL BUSINESS

One chapter is not enough space to provide instructions for setting up an independent business, but it can provide an outline of the steps involved, the issues an entrepreneur will face, and some of the decisions that will have to be made.

Setting Goals

Both business and personal goals should be considered before establishing a company. Personal goals are those that attracted Jerry Daniel—being one's own boss, putting ideas into action, being solely responsible for success (or failure), and so on. Business goals are those discussed in Chapters 3 and 5, determining what is to be accomplished and in what time period.

All entrepreneurs begin with personal goals. Unfortunately, many people struggle longer than they might have to before they realize that business goals are important as well. As the owner of one small graphics company said, "I left the firm I was with to start my own company, because I believed I was compromising my principles at my old firm by working on projects that I knew were awful. I quickly found out, in my own company, that taking only work that met my standards was a sure path to starvation. Now my goal is to become financially secure enough to do *mostly* what I like."

A hard-line adherence to nonfinancial personal goals without concern for the market place is fine for those who have an independent source of financial support. A more realistic strategy is to incorporate business and personal goals into as specific and measurable a hierarchy as possible. A general model might look something like that shown in Exhibit 20.3

Determining Feasibility

Most people know that they should do a feasibility study before embarking on a business venture, but what does this mean and what does it include? **Feasibility** means *doing what can be done with the resources available in a given period of time.*

Determining if one has the resources to accomplish personal and business goals is a matter of collecting information about a sufficient demand, or potential demand for proposed products or services to meet income goals (income sales) and obtaining sufficient resources to set up shop and operate long enough to capture the necessary market (expenses).

Sales. Experts recommend some average of optimistic, most likely, and pessimistic sales forecasts when determining demand for a product or service. This information comes from a variety of sources, including published market information, analysis of sales of similar existing firms, surveys, and analysis of existing and likely competition.

Expenses. In determining whether it is possible to go into business and stay there long enough to capture the projected share of the market, it is necessary to estimate start-up and ongoing (fixed and variable) costs. **Start-up costs** are *the costs of acquiring and modifying (if necessary) a place of business, utility deposits, inventory, office equipment, licenses and legal fees, and advertising and promotion.*

Fixed, ongoing expenses are *utilities, rent or mortgage payments, interest on loans (if any), insurance, and vehicle maintenance.* A major item often overlooked includes living expenses for the entrepreneur (and family). Typical variable expenses include payroll and advertising. A sample estimate of sales, expenses, and profit is shown in Exhibit 20.4.

Capital. Part of the purpose of a feasibility study is to demonstrate that the enterprise in question will be a profitable concern within some reasonable period of time. In general, entrepreneurs can not expect this to occur immediately. Sale estimates for the first year are generally lower than those of subsequent years, and expenses, because of start-up costs, are somewhat higher. This usually produces more expenses than sales, which increases the minimum amount of capital required to get started.

Exhibit 20.3   *Integrating Personal and Business Goals: An Example*

Year 1	Business goal	Break even
	Personal goal	Get established, become known
Year 2	Business goal	Make a profit
	Personal goal	Establish reputation for quality
Year 3	Business goal	Maintain profit
	Personal goal	Turn down work that is particularly unpleasant
Year 4	Business goal	Make twice last year's profit
	Personal goal	Increase the amount of interesting or exciting work
Long-term	Business goal	No financial worries
Long-term	Personal goal	Accept only work that is pleasant, interesting, or highly profitable

Some firms, such as the ones represented in Exhibit 20.2, have reason to expect sales to exceed expenses, even in the first year. These firms still need starting capital. Even for such a fortunate enterprise, **cash flow**—*the amount of money coming in relative to the amount going out*—will be negative for some months. Most of the small-business owners that we interviewed told us that they do not expect to collect on billings for sixty days, and are prepared to wait ninety days.

Arranging Financing

Opinions vary about the amount of capital required to start a business. If there is good reason to expect profits in the first year, enough money to get started and to meet operating expenses for three months may be sufficient, but this is extremely risky. For most businesses, a long-standing rule of thumb has been to have enough capital to see the business through the first year. Even this may not be enough, and may account for the fact that the failure rate for new businesses has traditionally been higher in the second and third years than in the first.[7]

Entrepreneurs themselves, especially those with very small businesses, generally recommend taking the first-year figure and doubling it to arrive at start-up capital. However, some say that having too much money is potentially as dangerous as having too little. They believe that "being hungry" is a tremendous incentive to put out the extra effort that may mean the difference between success and failure.

Given the differences of opinion, and the relatively rapid changes in the economic environment of today, the safest approach to determining how much capital is needed to start a business is to get advice. Consulting one or more of those people financing entrepreneurs who are experienced in venture capitalization will probably be well worth whatever fees they charge.

Once a dollar amount has been established, the question of where to get the capital arises. There are any number of possibilities. Some people start businesses with their savings; others borrow money from a traditional lending institution. More recent alternatives include specialized venture capitalists, and financing through the Small Business Administration.

Exhibit 20.4 A Sample One-Year Estimate of Sales, Expenses, and Profit

Item	Percent of Net Sales	Total For Year	Average Month
Gross Sales	102.0%	$122,400	$10,200
Less: *Returns & Adjustments*	2.0	2,400	200
Net Sales	100.0	120,000	10,000
Less: *Cost of Goods Sold*	50.0	60,000	5,000
Margin	50.0	60,000	5,000
Less: *Controllable Expenses*			
Payroll	15.0	18,000	1,500
Advertising	2.0	2,400	200
Operating Supplies	2.0	2,400	200
Automobile & Delivery	1.0	1,200	100
Outside Labor & Professional	1.0	1,200	100
Maintenance & Repairs	0.5	600	50
Misc. Controllable Expense	1.0	1,200	100
Total Controllable Expense	22.5	27,000	2,250
Less: *Fixed Expenses*			
Rent	5.0	6,000	500
Utilities	2.5	3,000	250
Depreciation	1.3	1,560	130
Interest on Loans	1.0	1,200	100
Insurance, Licenses, etc.	0.5	600	50
Misc. Fixed Expense	0.5	600	50
Total Fixed Expense	10.8	12,960	1,080
Total Expenses	33.3	39,960	3,330
Net Profit Before Taxes	16.7%	$ 20,040	$ 1,670

Source: K. R. Van Voorhis, *Entrepreneurship and Small Business Management.* Boston: Allyn and Bacon, Inc., 1980, p. 99.

Venture Capitalists. Venture capitalists are investors, both individuals and firms, who provide funding for promising business ventures in hopes of getting a return greater than they could get in more conservative investments. Good venture capitalists not only provide capital but work with companies to help make them successful.

Finding venture capitalists has been made easier for entrepreneurs these days by the increasing popularity of venture-capital fairs. These fairs are conferences at which carefully screened entrepreneurs make presentations to groups of venture capitalists who, in turn, are given the opportunity to sign contracts with attractive prospects. The oldest such fair is sponsored by the American Electronics Association in Monterey, California, at which more than a hundred companies are given a chance to sell their ideas.

Most such fairs are very selective. For example, the 1983 high-technology fair in Atlanta admitted only seventeen out of eighty applicants. Those who are se-

Management in Action
A Business Success Story

Alan Cadan is the entrepreneurial equivalent of the one-man band. He is the owner, founder and chief executive of Alynn Neckwear Inc., as well as its head designer, bookkeeper, salesman, order-taker, typist, shipping clerk and telephone operator.

His four-year-old necktie business booked sales of $1 million last year. Mr. Cadan, 42 years old, runs the business from his house in Stamford, Conn. He is the only full-time employee.

"The only way you can run a business by yourself is to be organized," Mr. Cadan says. "You have to be on top of things." Working at home saves him commuting time, but the trade-off, he says, is that the office is always present "to remind you of all the work there is to do. You forget to take time to play."

His wife, Lynn, and their four children, ages 11 to 15, help out. Mrs. Cadan does some bookkeeping and mailing chores and tones down some of her husband's ideas for tie designs, which tend to be clever. A rodent in a jogging outfit is the figure on The Rat Race tie; a design of thumb tacks is sold as The Tacky tie.

Packing and shipping are the most time-consuming tasks. Everyone in the family packs ties, a chore that extends into the late hours during the Christmas season, when the company ships 50% of its annual volume. Mr. Cadan's 79-year-old mother drove 40 miles a day to help out last year. "It's a one-man business," Mr. Cadan's wife says, "with a lot of elves."

It's also a no-frills enterprise. The shipping department is in the basement where boxes of ties—there are 62 designs—sit on tables made of doors and sawhorses. It is equipped with an old, hand-operated tape machine and a worn bathroom scale.

Mr. Cadan's desk is a door covered with blotting paper that rests on two sawhorses. His office used to be the garage. A $10,000 computer system was acquired last year, but he prefers to use clipboards to keep track of things. The clipboards hang in neat rows on the wall behind the desk. One holds orders to be shipped; another has documents that show when fabric went from the mills to the New York tie-makers. The computer could track the inventory, but it is simpler and quicker to subtract each day's shipments from what's on hand to keep a continuous inventory count, Mr. Cadan says.

Future growth won't come from sales to retailers. Corporate ties, with logos or slogans, already account for 30% of revenue, and Mr. Cadan intends to emphasize these sales. They take as much time as a few sales to retailers but produce a lot more money. Among his corporate customers have been Ford Motor Co., RCA Corp. and American Optical Co.

Mr. Cadan doesn't want Alynn Neckwear to get too big. "I'm not," he says, "looking to grow so much I have to move out of the house."

Source: S. L. Jacobs, "By Being Organized, One Man Builds a Thriving Business," *Wall Street Journal*, February 14, 1983, p. 17.

lected, however, have good chances of being funded. The University of Michigan's Growth Capital Symposium, raising about seventy million dollars over its first four years, claims that seventy percent of its participating companies are successful.[8]

The Small Business Administration (SBA). The SBA was created in the early 1950s to provide financial, counseling, and procurement assistance to the owners of small business firms. It is the financial assistance that interests us here; its other functions will be discussed later.

In its early days, most of the financial help provided by the SBA was in the form of *direct* loans. Today, most of the assistance comes by guaranteeing up to ninety percent of a loan by a commercial bank to a prospect turned down by standard-application procedures. The borrower must fill out SBA application forms, which include all of the usual information, including **collateral** *(personal assets pledged to back up the loan) offered.* SBA loans are not free rides.

For the individual, the decision to become an entrepreneur rests on his or her own assessment of the relative rewards and costs.

Despite its purpose of helping small businesses financially, there is reason to be cautious about counting on the SBA as a last resort for financing.[9] When money gets tight, the number of guaranteed loans can drop drastically. In addition, banks are allowed to charge up to two and three-quarters percent *more* than the prime interest rate on these loans.

The Franchise Alternative. Entrepreneurs without substantial savings of their own may expect to go into debt to finance a new business enterprise; and whether they are using their own money or someone else's, they run a substantial risk of losing it. Estimates of the failure rate for new, small businesses run as high as eight out of ten.

One way to reduce the risk, if not the initial indebtedness of being an entrepreneur is to purchase an established business. Another way is to purchase a franchise, the right to do business under the trade name of an established product or service. The International Franchise Association quotes a failure rate of less than one in ten of its approximately 25,000 member outlets.[10]

Most of the more well known franchise operations are in the fast food business such as Kentucky Fried Chicken, Dunkin' Donuts, and the giant McDonald's, are in the fast food business. Chick-fil-A, small by comparison, has nonetheless experienced a yearly growth rate ranging from thirty-three percent to one hundred eighty percent a year since it began in 1968.[11]

There are franchises available to suit almost any interest—print shops, nursing homes, computer stores, automobile muffler services, car washes, hair-styling salons, exercise salons, ice-cream parlors, and preschools, to name some of the possibilities. For many, the question is not whether there is a franchise available in a business area they want, but whether they can afford the franchise fees and capital requirements.

Dwight Baumann founded the Center for Entrepreneurial Development at Carnegie-Mellon in Pittsburgh to encourage the entrepreneurial spirit.

The reduced risk of being a franchise entrepreneur stems both from the established market of a franchise, and from the training and support services provided by franchisers. Franchisers usually provide training on everything from cooking french fries to hiring and firing employees, help potential investors find financing, and may even supervise building construction. Offsetting these advantages, at least from the viewpoint of many would be entrepreneurs, are fewer profits and less autonomy.

Most franchisers collect a one-time, nonrefundable fee that ranges from a few thousand to over a hundred thousand dollars. They also collect a percentage of gross sales (royalties) and control the sale of the franchise to a third party. In addition, they can dictate every aspect of the business from wall color to products or services that can or cannot be offered. Franchisers can also terminate the agreement when the contract expires, if the investor does not conform to standards.

Owning a franchise is still owning one's own business, at least for a time, and its financial advantages can be considerable. Its greatest disadvantage, when compared with more traditional entrepreneurship, is that it does not meet the number-one personal goal of many entrepreneurs—being able to do things their own way!

Setting Up Shop

For those who decide to purchase a franchise, starting out will take work, but decision making will be minimal. Buying an established business offers more autonomy, but most decisions can be made gradually if changes are desired. The life of the entrepreneur opening a new business is considerably more complicated. Once the nature of the business and its goals have been defined, and financing obtained, he or she must confront hundreds of big and small decisions.

Many of the decisions faced by entrepreneurs in "setting up shop" are constraints on managers in other organizations, because in other organizations the decisions are made by someone else. For the entrepreneur, choices of organizational structure, organizational policy, staffing and employee compensation, and budgeting offer opportunities to do things his or her own way:

1. How many and what types of positions (work roles) are needed? (Organizing)
2. Who is going to report to whom? (Structure)
3. What kinds of employees should be hired? (Staffing)
4. What kinds of incentives will be offered and for what performance? (Directing)
5. How will business objectives be accomplished? (Planning)
6. What kind of supervision will there be for employees? (Controlling)
7. What should be emphasized—product quantity or quality or service? (Policy)

Other decisions facing the entrepreneur involve issues routinely dealt with by staff and support personnel in other organizations.

1. What day will be payday?
2. When and how often will bills be sent out and paid?
3. What arrangements will be made for office security?
4. Who is to be notified if a pipe bursts, the air conditioning fails, or there are roaches in the restrooms?
5. What if an employee becomes ill or injured?
6. What advertising media are available and which are best?
7. Where will employees and customers park?
8. Where will office supplies and other materials be bought?
9. How often will materials be delivered?

If many of the questions above seem trivial or uninteresting, remember that one of the costs of getting to make big, interesting decisions in business is having to make little, uninteresting ones, at least at first. Even if an entrepreneur has a good management team at the start or can afford the services of expert advisors, the responsibility for getting everything done remains at the top.

External Constraints and Resources

As Chapter 18 pointed out, every business must conform to federal, state, and local regulations. A significant part of setting up shop has to do with learning what must be done to conform to the external regulations that apply to the business. In this section, we will take a brief look at these regulations and at the related subject of external resources available to help entrepreneurs cope with them and with other problems facing small businesses.

Constraints. Every entrepreneur has the responsibility to determine what the new business must do to be in compliance with federal regulations regarding staffing and employee health and safety, (discussed in Chapter 18). Other recent court and government decisions relevant to running a business are shown in Exhibit 20.5.

In addition to complying with federal regulations, an entrepreneur also will have to take into account state and local regulation affecting such aspects of the operation as business license, hours of operation, employment of minors, fire safety measures, waste disposal, parking, signs, and landscaping, insurance and bonding, financial disclosure, tax assessment and payment, advertising and promotion, and pricing.

> *Entrepreneurs are managers. Like other managers, they plan, organize, direct, and control. They need to understand individual and group behavior and to exercise power, influence, and leadership in order to get things done. They rely on their skills in communicating and decision making; they use management information systems; they seek to be creative and innovative in their work. They deal with governments, unions, and ethical problems.*

On balance, while federal regulation of the various areas listed above receives more publicity, small businesses are likely to get into trouble faster by violating state or local regulations. State and local governments are often more concerned with compliance; they also have the power to withhold the license to operate as a business.

The external environment of small businesses can be a source of help and support instead of regulation and constraint. In addition to college or university courses in entrepreneurship, there are at least five major areas of assistance: pro-small-business regulation, government agencies, small business associations, publications, and suppliers.

Pro-Small-Business Regulations. Not all government laws or regulations make life harder for the entrepreneur. Some recent examples of favorable resolutions are:

1. A 1979 Federal Trade Commission regulation that protects potential franchise investors. Every company offering a franchise must provide a complete statement of franchise arrangements ten business days before contracts are signed or money changes hands. Among other items, this statement must include full documentation of any claims for the profit potential of the franchise.

2. The Equal Access to Justice Act, passed in 1980, that seeks to help small businesses fight unfair fines for rule infractions from government regulatory agencies. If the penalty is ruled unjustified, this Act provides that legal fees will be paid by the Agency involved. In the past, small businesses have paid their fines without protest, because the costs of protest were too high. This act does for small business what the Consumer Protection Act does for the individual—it provides some protection against large and more powerful organizations.

Exhibit 20.5 External Constraints on Business Owners

NEWS-LINES®

What You Can and Cannot Do If You Run a Business

as a result of recent court and government decisions

A DENTAL ASSOCIATION has been charged with violating antitrust laws by inducing its members not to cooperate with insurance companies trying to hold down the costs of dental care. The Federal Trade Commission accused the Texas Dental Association of conspiring to withhold X-rays from insurance firms using them to evaluate planned treatment that could be costly, and insisting that insurers sign "memoranda of understanding" on procedures for dealing with member dentists.

BROADCASTERS who own both a commercial television station and a cable-TV system in the same market will be forced to sell either one or the other if a rule proposed by the Federal Communications Commission is adopted. Under the proposal, the divestiture would have to be made within one year after the rule's final approval. Station owners, however, would be given an opportunity to request a waiver if they could show that the divestiture was unduly harsh and would not improve program diversity.

POLLUTERS must report oil spills to the federal government even though doing so will subject them to civil fines. That is a ruling of the Supreme Court, which overturned a lower-court decision that the penalty imposed by the Clean Water Act violates the Constitution's protection against self-incrimination. The High Court held that a breach of civil law does not trigger constitutional protections that are afforded a criminal defendant.

MANUFACTURERS face legal trouble if they impose restrictive pricing requirements in cooperative advertising programs—programs in which retailers are reimbursed for costs incurred in advertising the manufacturer's product. The FTC, in a policy statement, says that it will challenge as a per se violation of the FTC Act any cooperative ad program that inhibits advertising of discount prices. As an example, the agency said it has settled cases with two firms accused of requiring dealers to advertise at the manufacturers' suggested retail prices as a condition for reimbursement.

A RETIREE is not precluded from having a dispute over his rights arbitrated even though he is no longer an "employe" under the terms of a collective-bargaining agreement, according to a ruling of a labor arbitrator. The arbitrator said it would seem contradictory to include a provision for retirement in a collective-bargaining agreement that did not imply that a relationship existed between the retiree and the employer.

HEALTH HAZARDS associated with exposure to cadmium are coming under new government scrutiny. The Occupational Safety and Health Administration, as a result of new information on the hazards of cadmium, will inspect 50 firms involved in the manufacture and use of cadmium to see if employes are getting the protection required by current standards. Exposure can result in kidney and pulmonary disease, hypertension, liver abnormalities and possibly cancer.

EMPLOYERS who plan to buy the assets of firms adjudged bankrupt and to carry on with the same complement of employes should be wary. The National Labor Relations Board ruled that the buyer of a bankrupt firm inherited the firm's back-pay liability incurred in an NLRB unfair-labor-practice judgment eight years ago. This was so, said the board, even though the Bankruptcy Court had said that the purchase was made "free and clear of all liens." The court's order, the NLRB ruled, did not cover the unfair-labor-practice finding.

Conclusions expressed here are based on decisions of courts, government agencies and Congress. For reasons of space, these decisions cannot be set forth in detail. On written request, U.S.News & World Report will refer readers to the basic material.

Government Agencies. A number of government agencies exist specifically to help small businesses. The SBA, already discussed in another section, is the most prominent. In addition to financial assistance, the SBA offers counseling in technical areas and in the administration of a small business. It also helps small businesses to act as vendors or subcontractors for the federal government (called the procurement service).

More recently, the SBA has helped small businesses receive fair treatment relative to large corporations, and has given special assistance to women and members of minority groups who want to be entrepreneurs.[12] Other federal agencies that operate alone, or in conjunction with the SBA include:

1. The Small Business Institute (SBI). Created in 1972, this program provides small businesses with management and technical assistance from college students and provides college students with practical experience in small businesses.
2. The Service Corps of Retired Executives (SCORE) and the Active Corps of Executives (ACE). In these programs, successful retired and active business executives offer expertise and experience upon request. SCORE has been in existence for almost twenty years and is a recognized success.
3. Small Business Development Centers (SBDC). Some eighteen states now have SBDCs associated with their state university systems. These centers typically offer management services to small businesses. Most states also offer services of their own to the entrepreneur.

Formal Associations. Because entrepreneurship is synonymous with independence and attracts people who want to do things their own ways, it has been difficult to form national associations for help, protection, and pressure. Neither the nation's independent farmers nor its truckers, for example, have been highly successful in using their national associations to promote and protect their interests. Lately, however, small business seems to have overcome its reluctance. Among the national groups formed are the Council of Small Enterprise (COSE), National Small Business Association (NSBA), Coalition of Small and Independent Business Associations (COSIBA), and the National Federation of Independent Business.

The 1980 White House Conference on Small Business emphasized the impact that associations such as these can have on the environment in which small businesses operate. It set three major targets for future lobbying: tax revisions, consideration in formulating national economic policy, and action to bring minorities and women into the mainstream of American business.

Publications. There is a variety of literature specifically for the entrepreneur or small-business owner. Some is on how to get started; other publications, such as *Inc., Small Business Report, Venture Capital Journal, Successful Business, and Entrepreneur,* detail sources of assistance and current activities in the small business environment.

Suppliers. Companies that supply small businesses with materials or money have every reason to want their customers to prosper. Many progressive suppliers pro-

Exhibit 20.6 Sources of Help for Existing Small Businesses

Source	Technology of Business	
	High	Low
Small Business Administration		
Staff Counseling		X
Service Corps of Retired Executives		X
Active Corps of Executives		X
Small Business Institutes	X	X
Small Business Development Centers	X	X
Nonaccredited courses and seminars		X
Publications		X
US Department of Commerce		
Seminars and Workshops	X	X
Publications	X	X
State, county, and local governments		
Counseling		X
Seminars and workshops		X
Publications		X
Local development corporations		
Counseling		X
Seminars and workshops		X
Small-business associations		
Counseling		X
Seminars and workshops		X
Publications		X
Trade associations		
Seminars and workshops	X	X
Publications	X	X

Source: Adapted from N. C. Siropolis, *Small Business Management: A Guide to Entrepreneurship*, 2d ed. (Boston: Houghton Mifflin, 1982), p. 265.

vide their customers with advice, contacts, information, and training to help them operate more efficiently and effectively. Services run from informal tips about competition or potential new customers to formal training programs in the use of the suppliers' products or services. A summary of help for small businesses is given in Exhibit 20.6.

THE ENTREPRENEUR AS MANAGER

Entrepreneurs are managers. Like other managers, they plan, organize, direct, and control. They need to understand individual and group behavior and to exercise power, influence, and leadership in order to get things done. They rely on their skills in communicating and decision making; they use management information systems; they seek to be creative and innovative in their work. They deal with governments, unions, and ethical problems.

Entrepreneurs differ from other managers not so much in what they do, but in the ultimate responsibility that is theirs. When small businesses fail, the cause is usually poor management (See Exhibit 20.7). Entrepreneurs don't base their plans on others' plans; they initiate the whole planning process. They don't operate within a predetermined organizational structure; they create one themselves. They are not guided by long-standing policy, but develop policy themselves. They devise their own budgets and select their own staffs.

Entrepreneurship probably makes greater demands on a manager's decision-making and creative skills. We might expect stress to be greater, both because entrepreneurs usually are risking a considerable portion of their own financial assets in their venture, and because they are ultimately responsible for the short-term fates of their employees. If an entrepreneur fails, others lose money and jobs.

On the other hand, entrepreneurs don't take the plunge with the idea of failing. Success as an entrepreneur has more than financial attraction. In our society, those who start their own businesses and succeed are still regarded as heroes, as the backbone of the economy, creating jobs where none existed before. They are a part of the American dream that still lives.

The Bottom Line

Being an entrepreneur is a challenge, an opportunity, but also a risk. Being successful in a venture in which eight out of ten fail suggests the following:

1. A good, marketable idea is necessary but not sufficient for success. Most new businesses fail for financial reasons. It is better to be pessimistic in estimating financial needs, and have money left over, than to be optimistic and come up short. At the minimum, make sure you have sufficient capital to make it through the first year, then double that figure.
2. Critically evaluate your own strengths and weaknesses. Are you good at taking risks and making decisions? Can you innovate? Do you have a passion for work? Can you tolerate uncertainty and ambiguity? Are you willing to spend most, if not all, of your waking hours working or worrying about work?
3. Get help. Financial institutions, potential suppliers, government agencies, small business associations, and experienced entrepreneurs are willing and able to increase your chances for success. At the least they can help you avoid some of the mistakes that others before you have made.
4. No matter how good the idea or product, people are going to make it succeed- or fail. The people you select to staff your enterprise are crucial. Don't just hire warm bodies—they'll make your difficult job even harder. Take the time to pick good people and then make it rewarding for them to help you become a success.

SUMMARY

An alternative to a traditional management position in a company owned by others is entrepreneurship—owning and managing your own business. Such smaller companies account for a large number of jobs in the American labor force and generate almost half of the gross national product.

Exhibit 20.7   Causes of Business Failures

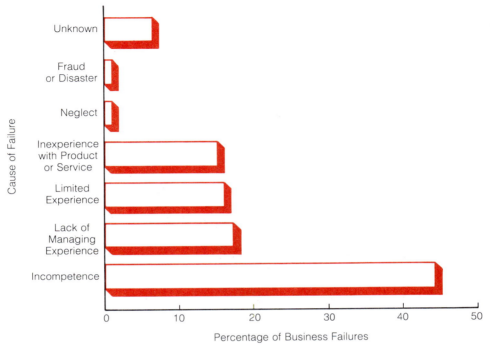

Source: Adapted from N. C. Siropolis, *Small Business Management: A Guide to Entrepreneurship*, 2d.ed (Boston: Houghton Mifflin, 1982), p. 14.

Entrepreneurship is often described as a spirit of independence, self confidence, and persistence. These and related traits may certainly make the entrepreneur's task easier. He or she must do everything the traditional manager does plus all of the things usually done by executives, staff, and support personnel in larger firms.

Being an entrepreneur requires setting personal and business goals, determining the feasibility of these goals, arranging financing, and making the hundreds of large and small decisions required to actually "set up shop." There are numerous external constraints on this process, but there are also external sources of assistance. For some, buying an established business, or purchasing a franchise, may offer an alternative to the complexities of starting a business from the beginning.

QUESTIONS FOR REVIEW AND DISCUSSION

1. Why do you think entrepreneurship is so popular despite the high risk of failure?
2. What is the difference between entrepreneurship and small business?

3. Suggest a reason, based on your understanding of behavior from Chapters 8 and 9, why many successful entrepreneurs come from families in which there is another entrepreneur.
4. Why do most entrepreneurial enterprises fail?
5. Do you think personal characteristics are more important to being a successful entrepreneur than to being a successful manager? Why or why not?
6. If you were going to be an entrepreneur, what kinds of personal goals would you have? How do you think these would fit in with your business goals?

REFERENCES AND NOTES

1. O. A. Burns, "The Hype of the Little People." *Atlanta Weekly*, April 12, 1981, 16–27, quote from page 16.
2. J. Craddock, "Why Small Business Is No Small Deal." *Florida Trend*, March 1983, pp. 55–57.
3. Quoted in A. L. Levitt, Jr., "Small Business Discovers Its Strength." *Business Week*, March 10, 1980, pp. 23–24.
4. A. L. Taylor, III., "Hard Times on Main Street." *Time*, October 26, 1981, pp. 60–61. *Business Week*, December 27, 1982, p. 16.
5. J. Komives, "Are You One of Them?" *MBA Magazine*, 1973, 7, 6, p. 5.
6. J. Merwin, "Have You Got What It Takes?" *Forbes*, August 3, 1981, pp. 60–64.
7. *The Business Failure Record.* New York: Dun and Bradstreet, 1982.
8. L. Asinoff, "Rapidly Growing Venture—Capital Fairs Evolve Into a Potent Force in the Industry," *Wall Street Journal*, April 10, 1984, p. 31.
9. S. L. Jacobs, "Lean SBA Lending." *Wall Street Journal*, October 20, 1980, p. 29.
10. S. L. Jacobs, "Operating a Franchise Often Pays, But Demands on Buyer Are Great." *Wall Street Journal*, November 3, 1980, p. 33.
11. "The Franchise Alternative." *Chicago Tribune*, January 11, 1983, Section 3, p. 7.
12. "Congress Cripples SBA Women's Program." *Wall Street Journal*, October 13, 1980.

SUGGESTED READINGS

Van Voorhis, K. R., *Entrepreneurship and Small Business Management.* (Boston: Allyn and Bacon, 1980. This book provides a good basic coverage of entrepreneurship from a practical standpoint.

Siropolis, N. C., *Small Business Management: A Guide to Entrepreneurship.* (Boston: Houghton Mifflin, 1982). The author presents a wealth of useful, well-organized information for managers of small businesses.

The Wall Street Journal and magazines such as *Forbes, Business Week,* and *MBA Magazine* frequently feature articles by and about entrepreneurs.

Inc., Entrepreneur, Venture Capital Journal, and *Small Business Report* are magazines specifically devoted to the interests and concerns of entrepreneurs and small businesses.

Report from the Field *Changing Career Goals*

Robert K. Murray runs his own company, Professional Consulting Services, Inc. which specializes in providing accounting and financial services to physicians and dentists. The company is relatively small, serving around two hundred clients. Murray keeps it small deliberately, consistent with his career goals. "Several years ago," he explains, "I sat down and worked out a set of goals for my personal and professional life, and I've tried to manage my business in a manner that is consistent with these goals.

"My goals have been to be able to see a direct correlation between my effort and the quality of my work, my own satisfaction and income; to provide consistently high-quality service for clients with whom I can develop and maintain a close professional relationship; to be my own boss; to earn enough money to maintain a comfortable standard of living for Carolyn, Rob, Mark, and myself; and to have time to enjoy my family and the outdoor activities this area provides.

"It's amazing how much these goals are different from the ones I set when I first went to work. I had all the characteristics a lot of companies were looking for at the time—a strong background in finance and accounting, my military commitment out of the way, and readiness to settle down. I finally accepted an offer from a large nationwide insurance company and went to work, ready to meet my goals.

"Fortunately, I was smart enough to figure out that it wasn't *just* the company that was the problem. It was also that my goals were not getting me what I really wanted. I had figured out that security and fringe benefits weren't really as important to me as being my own boss. I learned that retiring at 55 wasn't nearly as important as enjoying my work and my life right now. I found out that promotions and salary increases depended on too many things other than my own work and effort, and that I really wanted to see that what I did paid off. I learned that working eight to five wasn't all that great, so I revised my goals to include what I had learned about the world of business and about myself, and spent the next several months in my spare time figuring out what kind of career would suit me better.

"I finally concluded that the only company that could meet my goals was one I ran myself. Fortunately, I had worked hard and gained a great deal of experience. I had developed some relationships with professional people and realized there was a market for financial and accounting services that specialized in medical clients. So at the age of twenty-nine I took the big gamble and went into business for myself. It was a risk, but I knew if I didn't do it then, I never would, and I'd probably spend the rest of my life resigned to a career I didn't really want.

"So I left my job, started my own firm, and things have worked out fine since then. But I don't regret my earlier decisions to work for large companies, because I learned a lot from those experiences; a lot about myself as well as about business. There's no way I could have decided to work for myself without the experience of working for others.

Source: Personal Interview, January 1984.

21 / International Management

The door to his first-class compartment slid noiselessly open. The conductor, stepping halfway in, announced, "Nächste Freiburg," and was gone before Sandy Horowitz could reply.

His pulse quickened as he began gathering up his belongings in preparation for arrival. This is it, he thought, the end of a journey and the beginning of an adventure. The next stop, Freiburg, tucked into the southwest corner of Germany, was to be his home for the next eighteen months.

The job was a plum and he knew it. Getting an overseas assignment after only a year with the bank was rare. His colleagues and friends had referred to it as "just another example of the famous Horowitz luck," but Sandy knew it was more than that. It was the end result of considerable effort and planning—along with a little luck.

When he had first enrolled in German class during his sophomore year in college, his instructor had told the class, "Those of you who stay with German—or French, Russian, or Spanish for that matter—will open for yourself many opportunities you cannot yet envision." As a nineteen-year-old business major at a southwestern university, all Sandy could envision was going to Europe some summer with friends.

That trip, a six-week backpacking tour after his junior year, had whetted his appetite for living abroad. He found the countries and the people fascinating, and was both surprised and delighted with his ability to communicate in German-speaking countries. The people were warm and friendly toward Americans, especially those who could speak some German, even with a southwestern drawl.

However, it was a chance meeting at a friend's wedding back in the States that gave him the firm objective of working in international business. One of the attendants was a young woman enroute to Japan on a Rotary Club fellowship. She had finished one year of her MBA in finance at a northeastern university where she had learned Japanese as an undergraduate. The year in Japan, she explained, would develop her fluency and understanding of Japanese culture in preparation for a job in international banking. When she mentioned the salary offers she had received in anticipation of her degree, Sandy's mouth had dropped open. Of course, the demand for an American MBA with fluency in Japanese would be extraordinary, but still. . . .

Sandy had intensified his efforts in studying German language and culture as well as international business and finance. When he began job interviews during his last year of school, he concentrated on companies with overseas offices and was frank about his objective—to get assigned to a branch in a German-speaking country early in his career. He had spent his first year in Dallas at corporate headquarters, where he had distinguished himself by hard work and a persistent interest in international finance. And he had gotten the overseas assignment.

And what a place to be assigned, he thought with mounting anticipation. Freiburg was a beautiful, growing city on the edge of the famous Schwarzwald—the Black Forest, an area of mountains, woods, lakes, and picturesque villages. The food there was superb—Black-Forest bacon and peasant-style rye bread, veal Schnitzel, peppersteak, trout, sausage, onion cake, plum cake, and pastries and tortes of all kinds. And the beer—he could

already see himself sitting in the Münster-platz surrounding the thirteenth century cathedral, a liter of Dortmunder Union in his hand—beer that made Milwaukee's forgettable, to his taste. The location was ideal, only one hour by train from Switzerland to the south or France to the west, perfect for weekend or holiday trips to other parts of Europe.

His reverie was interrupted as the train began to slow for its arrival at the Freiburg Bahnhof. Could he meet the challenge of working in a foreign country? Sandy felt confident. His familiarity with the language and customs, his training and anticipation were in his favor. If he did well, he could stay. If he went back to the States, he knew the overseas assignment would be a boost to his career. All things considered, Sandy felt he was as ready as he could be.

Most American managers are to be found in their own businesses or working in a company in the United States. Like Sandy, however, increasing numbers are becoming managers in foreign firms or American firms abroad. At the beginning of this decade, it was estimated that close to a million jobs are created by American firms abroad and by foreign investment in this country. In most cases, these jobs are filled by local labor under supervision provided by managers from the company's country of origin.

The study of the special opportunities and constraints created when business crosses national boundaries encompasses the field of international business. In this chapter we will look at international business as a career opportunity and the kinds of special qualifications that are needed.

INTERNATIONAL BUSINESS: THE FIELD AND THE SYSTEM

"International business as a field of study and practice encompasses government and private business activity that affects the persons or conditions of more than one national state, territory, or colony."[1] The increasing number of firms that engage in business in several countries are called multinational corporations (MNCs) or, as a group, the multinationals. Among the more well known American members of the multinationals are Coca Cola, IBM, Standard Oil, General Electric, and McDonalds. Foreign-based MNCs with operations in the United States include Nissan (Japan), BMW (England), Seagram's (Canada), Philips (Holland), Fiat and Olivetti (Italy), Lufthansa (West Germany), and Bank Leumi (Israel).

International business covers marketing, finance, and trade as well as the particular interest here, international management. Although the famous American Graduate School of International Management, in Arizona, is now about forty years old, traditional business schools have been slow to incorporate formal courses of international business into their programs. There no longer seems any doubt, however, that they must do so if they are to prepare their students for the reality of today's business world. The American Assembly of Collegiate Schools of Business now requires its members to provide students with some exposure to international business in the curricula.

> *International business as a field of study and practice encompasses government and private business activity that affects the persons or conditions of more than one national state, territory, or colony.*

A variety of forces are pushing to create a huge interlocking, interdependent, international business system. As in smaller individual organizational systems, described in Chapter 2, events in one part of the world system have far-reaching systems effects. For example, the near-collapse of Poland's coal industry in 1980 provided enormous economic gains for Pretoria, South Africa. Pretoria was the only place that could produce the coal required to offset the reduced Polish production.[2] Grain shortages in Russia increase food prices in this country, while a trade agreement between the European Community and Hong Kong benefits textile manufacturers in Sri Lanka and the Phillipines.

All signs are that the internationalization of business will continue to increase. Most countries now actively encourage foreign firms to locate within their boundaries. Publications with a wide circulation among businesspeople frequently carry large, expensive advertisements detailing the benefits of setting up shop in a particular country (see Exhibit 21.1). German and Japan business interests continue to develop in the United States by creating and developing manufacturing plants and distributorships for their products, such as those of Nissan, Toyota, and Honda, purchasing American companies, such as Nippon Kokan's negotiations to buy Ford Motor Company's steel plant near Detroit, or through joint ventures with American companies, such as the one between Yaskawa Electric and Bendix Corporation to develop and market robots and numerical controls.[3]

In addition to seeking foreign firms to locate within their own countries, many countries are looking outside their borders for raw materials, machinery, financing, or labor, resources that have become scarce or too expensive at home. Great Britain, for example, is printing an increasing number of its books abroad, saving some twenty-five to forty percent of production costs in the process. Britain's hard-pressed publishing industry hopes that the savings will allow it to com-

Exhibit 21.1   Countries Seek Business Internationalization

pete more favorably and reverse the steady downward trend of its share of the English-language book market.[4]

Finally, the internationalization of business is being pushed forward by the direct exportation of labor, a formal government policy of sending excess labor to other countries that is similar to the more usual exporting of materials or finished goods. This policy does not include illegal aliens or voluntary individual migration to seek better employment opportunities.

One country that exports labor all over the world is China. Workers receive wages that are eight to ten times more than they could get in China; they keep seventy percent of them and the remaining thirty percent is split between the Chinese government and the sponsoring Chinese employer.[5] Other countries involved in labor export are South Korea, India, Pakistan, Taiwan, Mexico, and the Philippines.

The internationalization of business has occurred for economic and political reasons, but today it is an accepted fact of life. Businesses are facing outward almost automatically; a recent survey found that two-thirds of the 1700 high-level executives polled believed, as Sandy does, that an overseas assignment would help their careers.[6]

THE ROLE OF THE MANAGER IN INTERNATIONAL BUSINESS

There are really only two basic questions in the study of international management. The first is: What do international managers do? The second is: To what extent must they do what they do differently from the way they would do it at home? In this section, we will address the first question in a general way. In the last two parts of this chapter we will explore the issues necessary to answer the second one.

What the International Manager Does

The international manager, as the entrepreneur, does everything that his or her more typical counterparts do—plus. In addition to being a manager who plans, organizes, directs, and controls, the international manager is also a *representative* of the firm, a *representative* of the home country, a *guest* of the host country, and a *member* of a profession. Because of the multiple roles international managers must play, they are subject to the possibility of even more role conflict than their traditional counterparts. For example, carrying out the role of guest in a country where racial discrimination is still the norm can conflict directly with representing home views on the subject. In addition, representing home views can also conflict directly with personal views (intrapersonal conflict).

A manager who is not in his or her own country may do basically what would be done at home, or more. He or she is expected to see that the work gets done. However, there may also be the expectation that local personnel will be trained to take over management functions. In fact, many managers are sent to overseas operations only to bring these operations to the point of self-sufficiency. When native subordinates are capable of taking over, the manager moves on.

Given the expanded role of an international manager, there has been considerable interest in what is required to be successful. Again, there is a parallel with entrepreneurship. In both cases, the question is: what do such people need to be or to know in order to function successfully?

Personal Qualifications for the International Manager

A look at the literature on international management reveals a list of skills, knowledge, and personal resources related to success that includes all of those we have been discussing in this book—power, influence, leadership, creativity, and skills in understanding behavior, making decisions, handling information, operations, and time management. In addition, these attributes must be put to use in a different environment. In this section, we will examine three assets that experienced international managers and scholars agree are especially important.

Language.   It is possible for a manager to function in another country without knowing the local language. Many have done so, and others will do so in the future. However, those with language difficulties will experience some serious problems. Inability to speak the language of the host country can be interpreted as a belief in the superiority of the home country language or as a lack of interest in the culture and people of the host country. Such perceptions will be reinforced by the natural tendency of the manager who does not speak the host language to associate primarily with others who speak his or her own language. One of the main complaints against American managers abroad has always been their lack of visibility to subordinates and the community.

> *There are really only two basic questions in the study of international management. The first is: What do international managers do? The second is: To what extent must they do what they do differently from the way they would do it at home?*

Language is more than a means of communicating; it is a way of thinking as well. To take a simple example, the German verb *lieben*, "to love," refers only to feelings between people. While sophisticated Germans are familiar with the American peculiarity of loving everything from soap powder to soap operas, they do not think this way. As the result of such differences, even when a manager believes he or she is communicating with another satisfactorily, meaning may be lost or distorted on either side of the conversation.

Competent translators, interpreters, and English-speaking colleagues can compensate for some of the difficulties created when a manager does not speak the language of the host country. However, incredible blunders can still be made. General Motors' slogan "Body by Fisher" came out as "Corpse by Fisher" when translated for Belgians. G.M. also had a problem with the advertising of their Chevrolet Nova, because "no va" means "it doesn't go" in Spanish.[7]

The kinds of blunders mentioned above occur infrequently. Nevertheless, most successful international managers are convinced that translators and interpreters are no substitute for achieving some competence in the language of the host country. Even if the overseas tour is to be short, or a manager has a "tin ear" for languages, language training is worth both the trouble and the expense. Sandy's efforts to learn German were instrumental in getting his job assignment; his language skills will be invaluable in carrying out that assignment.

Knowledge of the Host Country.   It probably comes as no surprise to learn that an international manager will function more effectively if he or she is knowledgeable about the host country. As with language, the reasons are both practical and interpersonal. Religious beliefs and practices affect planning and organizing in many countries, for example. But learning something about such beliefs also conveys the manager's interest in local culture and new experiences.

Unfortunately, there is evidence to suggest that the average American college-educated manager is likely to be ignorant about other parts of the world. The seniors in a sample of 3500 college students on 185 campuses who recently took a general knowledge test of world affairs answered only 50 percent of the questions correctly. Even though the seniors performed better than other students, less than one in ten answered correctly two thirds of the questions.[8] Exhibit 21.2 shows one author's list of the kinds of questions managers like Sandy should be able to answer about countries to which they are sent. The author of this test points out, however, that people in other countries are curious about the manager's home country. Sandy will be expected to be familiar with the basic facts about American government, foreign policy, business systems, and living conditions.

Personal Flexibility. Most of us have heard of the "ugly Americans" who go abroad and loudly criticize everything that is not done "the way we do it back home." They want ice water, steak and baked potatoes, and a private bathroom available at all times; they continually bemoan the fact that the natives drive on the wrong side of the road, close the banks and souvenir shops at inconvenient times, and do not speak English.

The inflexible "ugly American manager" is likely to be even more unhappy than his or her tourist counterpart. He or she is not just passing through, but living and working with the natives. Both living conditions and the behavior of those at work may be quite different from those at home. Unless the manager is willing to be flexible, he or she is likely to experience disappointment, frustration, and perhaps, failure. One manager-trainee in a European firm left after five months of a scheduled one-year training program. He just could not adjust to management's policy of turning a blind eye toward drinking wine on the job.

Not all instances of culture surprise are negative. For example, the president of an American electronics firm in El Salvador noted with pride that more production was lost because of a snowstorm at its plant in the United States than was lost because of violence, sabotage, and strikes in El Salvador.[9] The workers of that country were very serious about being at work, whatever the conditions around them.

The environment of the organization in another country is different from its environment at home. Subordinates, peers, and superiors are products of that environment and bring it into constant day-to-day contact with the manager, as the story in Exhibit 21.3 illustrates.

The range of effects of cultural differences on a manager's effectiveness is wide and variable. Here we can look only at some of the special problems created by aspects of the environment on organizational functioning and the manager.

THE ENVIRONMENT OF THE INTERNATIONAL MANAGER

Remember that it is precisely because of environmental differences that many companies locate outside the borders of their own countries. Different economic policies and conditions in foreign countries often increase the availability or lower the cost of labor; government regulation or access to untapped markets often make overseas locations attractive. Even when environmental conditions are not more or

Exhibit 21.2   Questions to Test Your Knowledge of the Host Country

1. What is the form of government?
2. What role, if any, does the government play in business?
3. What taxes, if any, do expatriates pay? The people themselves?
4. How widespread is social welfare? What is covered in the welfare program?
5. What is the prevalent religion? Have you read any of the sacred writings?
6. What influence does the religion have on day-to-day life?
7. What are some of the more important social and cultural standards?
8. What are the attitudes toward divorce, remarriage, and extramarital affairs?
9. What are some words, gestures, or types of body language that are resented or considered profane?
10. What is the language?
11. What are the local attitudes toward alcohol and drugs?
12. What are some of the laws and regulations that must be obeyed or that could easily be violated through simple ignorance?
13. What are the major industries and products? The chief exports and imports?
14. What are the principal natural resources, and what importance do they play in the nation's economy?
15. What is its history?
16. Is it pro-Western, pro-Communist, or neutral?
17. What are the important holidays? How are they observed?
18. What are the favorite recreational activities of the people?
19. Who is allowed to drive? Men and women? Men only? Minors?
20. What foods are prohibited? What foods can you import for personal consumption?
21. What is the normal dress of the local men and women?
22. To what degree is makeup permitted or discouraged?
23. What is the role of women in the country? Are they allowed to work? Mingle freely with men at social affairs? Serve as hostesses at mixed gatherings in their own homes?
24. How much do housing, food, utilities, gasoline, telephone service, and automobiles cost in the country?
25. What is the local currency? What are the bills and coins? The dollar exchange rate?
26. When shopping, to what extent are you *expected* to bargain over the asking price?
27. How do people greet each other? Shake hands? Embrace? Kiss?
28. What are the local-language expressions for "Good morning," "Good night," "Hello," "How much?" "No," "Yes," "Thank you," "Please," "Yesterday," "Today," and "Tomorrow"? Will you be able to communicate with taxi drivers and waiters in restaurants?
29. What protocol is expected when you are invited to a local national's home? A gift, before or after the event? A thank-you note? Do you arrive early? Late? On time? How do you know when it is time to depart politely?

Source: Adapted from P. E. Illman, *Developing Overseas Managers—and Managers Overseas.* New York: Amacom, 1980, pp. 44–46.

less favorable, they are *different*. These differences affect the organization and can create problems different from those in the home country.

Business-Government Relations

The most striking difference between government-business relationships in the United States and other countries is probably the government ownership (nationalization) of large sectors of business commonly found in other parts of the world. The British government owns Britain's only large-scale automobile manufacturer,

BUSINESS TALKS BACK ON SOUTH AFRICA

Future electricians *learn skills at a Ford training school in South Africa.*

ACTIVISTS WHO CONDEMN American companies doing business in South Africa have dominated the debate for years—the companies have tended to speak softly if at all. Now business has begun talking back. Says William Broderick, director of international governmental affairs at Ford Motor Co.: "We're trying to show we're not the bad guys, we're the good guys."

The main institutional defender of U.S. companies with South African operations is the American Chamber of Commerce in South Africa. It represents 275 companies with a total South African investment of some $3 billion. "Our critics," says Executive Director Clark Else, "have become more vociferous, better organized, and more emotional. Our new position is to let people know exactly what we're doing here."

The first salvo is a 20-page report telling how business has improved the conditions of black workers. More than half the companies in the Chamber have signed the Sullivan code, a set of equal opportunity principles drawn up seven years ago by the Reverend Leon H. Sullivan, minister of Philadelphia's Zion Baptist Church and a director of General Motors. According to the Chamber report, U.S. companies have spent $70 million abiding by the Sullivan principles, which call for, among other things, developing training programs for blacks and improving the quality of workers' housing, schooling, and recreation. Other highlights of the report:

▶ Nearly all U.S. companies now pay whites and blacks equal wages for the same work.

▶ U.S. companies put up a large share of the funds to build a $6-million high school for 600 students in Soweto, the large black community outside Johannesburg. Some 200 companies and individuals—about half of them American—underwrite most of the $1,800 annual tuition per student.

▶ Five automobile and tire companies (Ford, GM, Volkswagen, Firestone, Goodyear) built a technical school in the southern city of Port Elizabeth for training black workers in skilled trades.

for example, and the banking industries in France and Mexico have been nationalized by their respective governments. In most countries the government owns and operates most, if not all, the airlines and railroads.

Nationalized industry can create some interesting situations for firms from other countries. For example, Occidental Petroleum Corporation found itself negotiating with the Italian government for a joint venture involving the Italian state oil company and four Kentucky coal mines.[10] When the Dutch government nationalized its oil industry in the 1970s, it made itself partners with such companies as Esso and Shell Oil. In the 1980s, the revenue-sharing arrangement between these partners became an issue in the Dutch elections. Socialists proposed to slash Esso/Shell's profit by two-thirds and put the remainder into jobs and public works, housing, and training programs.[11]

Equal Opportunity Laws

In general, equal-employment-opportunity progress in much of the world lags behind that of the United States. Discrimination on the basis of sex, race, and social standing is common in many countries, as is nepotism, giving job preference to relatives of current employees.

Even in countries with a reputation for employment equality, things are not necessarily as they seem. The U.S.S.R., for example, has long been held up as a model of sex equality in the workplace. Nevertheless, the majority of managers and decision makers in that country, even in the professions dominated by women, are men.[12]

The international manager from the United States, used to American equal-opportunity laws, may find it difficult to accept that ability to do the job is relegated to a lesser position because of other factors. The situation in multiracial societies can be especially difficult. An equal-pay-for-equal-work policy for certain races may actually be unacceptable to the forces that dominate a particular society. The moral dilemma posed by this and related situations is a corporate social-responsibility issue that has yet to be faced in any systematic way.

Unions

The formal organization of labor in any country is a process that goes through predictable stages. In the early years, there is a struggle for union recognition. Eventually, there comes acceptance of unions as management's opponent in the struggle for worker control. The outcome of this struggle may be mutual adaptation, the crushing of the unions, or a union "stranglehold" on industry.

The world today provides us with examples of all stages of union development. The workers in Africa are attempting to gain recognition for unions. Polish workers, already organized, are in a life or death struggle with the government for the survival of their union. The United States is in a relatively balanced state, while many believe union power is in the process of strangling Great Britain.

The stage of development does not tell the full story, however. Relations between unions and management can be very different even where collectivization is well established and developed. For example, the West German government asked union leaders to accept real-wage reductions for their members; Fiat won the right from union officials to lay off some fourteen percent of its work force to allow Italian companies to survive the worldwide recession.

One of the more perplexing situations that can exist occurs when a company from one country locates in a country with a different tradition. Japan, for example, encourages company loyalty and company unions. Therefore, the United Auto Workers Union has continually been frustrated in its attempts to organize Honda's American motorcycle plant in Maryland and Nissan's light truck plant in Tennessee.[13] The issue is complicated by the anger at America's replacement by Japan as the leading producer of automobiles.

Politics

In our section on the relationship of American business to its external environment, we did not discuss the role of politics. American business has and does influence political activity, but this influence is highly regulated, at least formally. From the other perspective, the influence of the American political situation on American business tends to be via current or expected policies and regulations. These political influences, while not unimportant, are nevertheless more predictable and less direct than those in many countries of the world.

In other parts of the world, direct political interference in corporate affairs is relatively common. Members of the West German government have been trying for years to bring about a merger of Germany's major aircraft companies into a national aerospace company. This pressure eventually led to a decision on the part of Connecticut's United Technologies Corporation to sell its share in one of the companies.[14]

Another aspect of the political environment in other parts of the world that is unlike our own is politically oriented terrorist activity directed against business organizations. The most publicized examples are the kidnappings of businesspeople to finance political activities. The case of William Niehous, the Owens-Illinois executive who was held hostage in Venezuela for more than three years by leftist guerrillas, is probably the most well known incident.

Over the past several years, an estimated $250 million was paid to ransom executives like Niehous, and multinational companies figure the real cost of political terrorism was at least twice that amount.[15] As a result, approximately three-quarters of the multinational firms abroad now maintain a full-time security staff, and kidnap coverage is one of the fastest growing parts of the insurance industry. Corporations, executives, and insurance underwriters are pledged to secrecy about what firms and what personnel are covered, since many feel such insurance only aggravates the problem.[16]

MANAGING IN AN INTERNATIONAL COMPANY

There are two very different situations in which international managers operate. The more common is managing in a foreign country, either for a company from one's home country, as Sandy was doing, or, more rarely, for a foreign company. The less common situation, but one that is becoming increasingly frequent, is managing for a foreign company in one's home country. Each situation imposes unique requirements for managers.

Managing in a Foreign Country

International managers find that the work situations of their foreign assignments differ from those of their home countries in three important areas: in environment and culture, in the nature of the relationship between the environment and business, and in the people. Some of the kinds of environmental differences and environment-business relationship differences that can affect organizations were discussed in the last section. People who come out of these dissimilar environments may be expected to differ with respect to religious preferences and practices, attitudes toward work, perceptions of and behavior toward authority, the relative importance given to work, and the nature of desired or expected rewards. The tangled web of relationships that can be created by the interrelationships of these three sets of variables and the possible effects on organizational or manager actions is illustrated in Exhibit 21.4.

Managing in a Foreign Company in One's Home Country

As foreign investments in this country increase, greater numbers of American managers find themselves working for foreign-owned and -operated companies in this country. While the external environment and the subordinates they manage are no different from those managers in American firms, they find themselves dealing with superiors, policies, practices, and philosophies from a different culture.

In addition to their regular functions and duties, these managers must also act as middlemen between foreign owners and American workers. They are required to implement the policies, practices, and objectives of foreign superiors in ways that are understood and accepted by their American subordinates. They must see to it that those who set objectives and policies understand the particular character of the American worker they manage.

Nissan's truck plant in Tennessee provides an example of Japanese management principles being implemented by American managers for American workers. (See the Management in Action feature for this chapter.)

How extensive are foreign holdings in this country? In 1980-81 alone, foreign companies acquired or established 2500 businesses with a million dollars or more in annual sales each, employing a total of 675,000 people. The total assets of American affiliates of foreign companies were $292 billion in 1982. These companies accounted for $412 billion in sales, and employed more than two million people. [17] Although the United States owns more affiliates in foreign countries than foreign companies own in the United States, this margin is shrinking (see Exhibit 21.5). This means that the chances that an American manager will work for a foreign company are growing.

Management in Action
Japanese Management in Tennessee

Everyone at the new Nissan light-truck plant is on a first name basis. They can't help it: it's embroidered on their uniform shirts and hats! Even company president Marvin Runyon has "Marvin" boldly scripted above the pocket on his white dress-shirts. The first name basis helps create a familial atmosphere and a level of politeness and consideration that seems out of place in the grinding ambience one expects in an assembly plant.

Nissan has sent 383 production workers and supervisors to Japan to learn teamwork and management techniques. This, management hopes, will make each feel a part of "the Nissan family." They were told to judge which techniques would work and bring back the ones they felt would work best at the Smyrna plant.

The staff decided to wear the blue Nissan uniforms, which the plant provides free (work uniforms for production workers, and blue blazer, striped Nissan tie, and gray slacks for administrative workers). They've been less enthusiastic about the optional calesthenics at 7 A.M.

In adopting the Japanese idea of minimizing the differences between executive, administrative, and production workers, the plant also adopted the idea of one cafeteria for all employees; there is no executive dining room. But Runyon and his staff decided that Japanese-style plant dormitories would not work, nor would a pay scale based on age and responsibility for aging parents and inlaws, a promotional system that requires employees to work twelve to fourteen years before being considered for a managerial job, a lump-sum retirement payment instead of a pension, or the guarantee of a lifetime job for assembly line workers.

Line workers are trained in many skills so that they—and management— have more flexibility. Runyon is convinced a multiskilled worker is happier than the specialist of Detroit.

Runyon also adopted the Japanese approach to inspection. Except for final inspections, or at one or two "quality assurance" stations between stamping, welding and paint, trim and chassis divisions, the workers who do the work are their own inspectors.

But the biggest difference between the Nissan plant and the popular recollections of oldline Detroit plants is the absence of abusive language and humiliation, the approach that would have foremen chewing out a line worker.

"I've never had a harsh word voiced to me from anyone here," said Bobby Sims, 30, who works in the production training program.

"I can ask something here and I can get an answer," said Alan Jakes, 27, a production technician, the counterpart of an assembly-line worker in a Detroit plant. "That really helps. That way you think someone really cares."

Source: R. Worthington, "Nissan's Tennessee Workers Adopt Japanese Way to a Happy Day," *Chicago Tribune*, January 9, 1983, Sec. 1, p. 10.

Exhibit 21.4 *International Environment Differences and Some Effects*

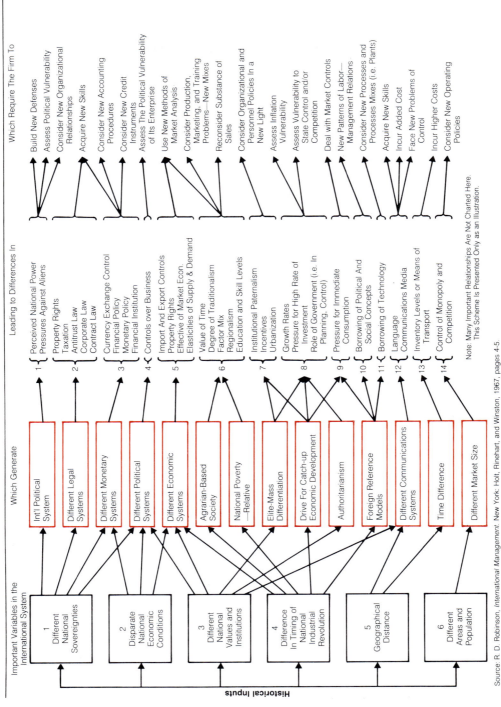

Source: R. D. Robinson, *International Management*. New York: Holt, Rinehart, and Winston, 1967, pages 4-5.

Important Variables in the International System

1 Different National Sovereignties

2 Disparate National Economic Conditions

3 Different National Values and Institutions

4 Difference In Timing of National Industrial Revolution

5 Geographical Distance

6 Different Areas and Population

Historical Inputs

Which Generate

Int'l Political System

Different Legal Systems

Different Monetary Systems

Different Political Systems

Different Economic Systems

Agrarian-Based Society

National Poverty —Relative

Elite-Mass Differentiation

Drive For Catch-up Economic Development

Authoritarianism

Foreign Reference Models

Different Communications Systems

Time Difference

Different Market Size

Leading to Differences In

1 Perceived National Power Pressures Against Aliens

Property Rights Taxation Antitrust Law Corporate Law Contract Law

2

Currency Exchange Control Financial Policy Monetary Policy Financial Institution

3

Controls over Business

4

Import And Export Controls Property Rights Effective of Market Econ. Elasticities of Supply & Demand

5

Value of Time Degree of Traditionalism Factor Mix Regionalism Education and Skill Levels

6

Institutional Paternalism Incentives Urbanization

7

Growth Rates Pressure for High Rate of Investment Role of Government (i.e. In Planning, Control)

8

Pressure for Immediate Consumption

9

Borrowing of Political And Social Concepts

10

Borrowing of Technology

11

Language Communications Media

12

Inventory Levels or Means of Transport

13

Control of Monopoly and Competition

14

Note: Many Important Relationships Are Not Charted Here. This Scheme Is Presented Only as an Illustration.

Which Require The Firm To

Build New Defenses

Assess Political Vulnerability

Consider New Organizational Relationships

Acquire New Skills

Consider New Accounting Procedures

Consider New Credit Instruments

Assess The Political Vulnerability of Its Enterprise

Use New Methods of Market Analysis

Consider Production, Marketing, and Training Problems—New Mixes

Reconsider Substance of Sales

Consider Organizational and Personnel Policies In a New Light

Assess Inflation Vulnerability

Assess Vulnerability to State Control and/or Competition

Deal with Market Controls

New Patterns of Labor—Management Relations

Consider New Processes and Processes Mixes (i.e. Plants)

Acquire New Skills

Incur Added Cost

Face New Problems of Control

Incur Higher Costs

Consider New Operating Policies

Exhibit 21.5   Direct Foreign Investment, 1970 and 1982

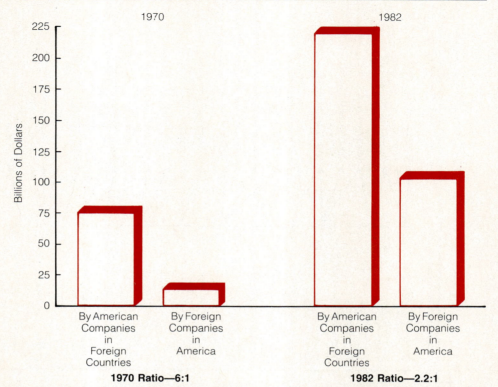

Source: Graph constructed from data taken from U.S. Bureau of the Census, *Statistical Abstract of the United States, 1984*, pp.822-824.

Comparative Management

The formal study of generalizing the theory and practice of management in one country to a different environment is called **comparative management.** Although some say flatly that American theories do not work abroad, research in this field suggests that things are not so clear cut. For example, relationships between a measure of job involvement and a variable called *locus of control,* the belief that one's life is either under self-control or is largely controlled by luck, fate, or other external forces were very similar for males in the United States, Turkey, Mexico, Yugoslavia, Thailand, and Japan, six very different countries.[18] Except for Yugoslavia, these relationships did not hold true for females. Thus, it seems that different cultures may be alike in some ways and it will have to be seen what theories can be transferred successfully from one country to another.

Measures of job satisfaction and job commitment did *not* predict turnover in a study of about eight hundred Japanese workers.[19] In this country, workers who are less satisfied with and less committed to their jobs are more likely to quit than their more committed and satisfied coworkers.

In recent years, large-scale studies across cultures have revealed patterns of differences and similarities among workers in different countries. One survey of 116,000 employees of a multinational corporation in forty countries tested employees' attitudes toward uncertainty and masculinity (See Exhibit 21.6.)[20]

The key to success in this field is flexibility. The most consistent and persistent test of this flexibility is undoubtedly the ability to cope with a different orientation toward the role of work in daily life.

The uncertainty avoidance index indicates that employees with a strong avoidance of uncertainty (high scores) welcome rules and conformity; those with a weak avoidance (low scores) can tolerate uncertainty, and have less reliance on rules and authority. The masculinity index indicates how employees feel about stereotypical "masculine" ideals (male domination, money, ambition, achievement, job performance, machismo) versus stereotypical "feminine" ideals (sexual equality, interdependence, quality of life, nurturing, service, sympathy).

The results of these two tests are summarized in Exhibit 21.6. Certain countries cluster together on these two scales (Switzerland, Germany, and Austria are all high in masculinity and about average in uncertainty avoidance). Certain countries are very different from each other (Japan is high on both scales, while Denmark and Sweden are low on both scales). The English-speaking countries are all in the same cluster, slightly below the median on uncertainty avoidance and slightly above the median on masculinity. Greece was highest on uncertainty avoidance, Singapore lowest.

Studies like this confirm that American managers overseas need to be careful in trying to apply American managerial techniques because of important differences between cultures. From Exhibit 21.6, for example, one might expect that Japanese workers would prefer more structure and authority than Swedish workers, and that Scandanavian workers would place more emphasis on quality of working-life issues than would Germanic workers.

Comparative management research points up the futility of making general statements about the similarities and differences of managing in different countries. There are cultural similarities and differences, just as there are individual similarities and differences within the same culture. If looked at as a whole, however, research and experience suggest that managers should be prepared to be flexible about the following:

1. *Relationships with subordinates.* For example, paternalism, a management practice which is generally obsolete in this country except in selected companies, is expected in other parts of the world.

2. *Recruitment and selection.* As mentioned earlier, managers may have to violate American practices in order to conform to local rules and customs. Methods may also have to be altered to adapt to different languages and different educational levels.
3. *Training.* General experience is that most workers can learn required skills if sound training principles are followed. However, they may resist doing so if the skills violate tradition. For example, workers with a strong history of hand-finished craftsmanship may balk at learning machine finishing techniques.
4. *Incentives.* A survey by an American management-consultant group illustrates the differences that may be found in rewards offered to workers. Among the fringe benefits in German companies were beauty parlor allowances, weekly flowers for women employees, and "loyalty bonuses" for long-term employees.[21]

INTERNATIONAL MANAGEMENT AS A CAREER

Most managers in other countries began their careers at home. They became international managers when the home firms sent them to a branch, subsidiary, or production facility in another country.

Occasionally Americans are hired to manage in foreign firms overseas. Generally these people are fluent in the language of the host country and have convinced their employers that their talents and training will overcome cultural difficulties. Peter Schutz, a vice-president of Cummins Engine in Indiana, was hired by a large German company to run its engine business in Cologne. After two years he had become fluent in German and was made president of Porsche, the German sports car manufacturer.[22] Like Schutz, many Americans abroad have become very successful and now see managing overseas, either for American firms or foreign firms, as a preferred career.

Although it is less common than the sequence of events already mentioned, there is an increasing tendency for some young managers to seek out international management as a first career choice. Some of these, like Sandy Horowitz, seek employment with opportunities to work abroad; a few seek employment directly with foreign firms.

Business schools are beginning to respond, both to the interests of students and to the growing internationalization of business itself. There are now several specialized international business schools as well as specialized programs in more traditional schools, such as Ohio State University, Indiana University, and the University of South Carolina. Of particular value are programs that equip managers with foreign language fluency so important to international-management success.

The manager who prepares directly for a career in international business may experience less initial culture-shock than the one who comes to it indirectly, but either way there are opportunities and challenges unavailable in other settings. Most managers who have, or had, successful careers in this field continue to stress that one key to rising to the challenges and profiting from the opportunities is flexibility. The most consistent and persistent test of this flexibility is undoubtedly the ability to cope with a different orientation toward the role of work in daily life.

Exhibit 21.6   Similarities and Differences Among Employees from Forty Countries on Uncertainty Avoidance and Masculinity

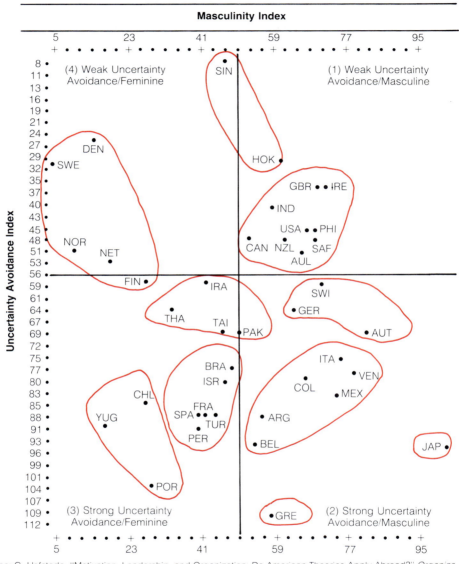

Source: G. Hofstede, "Motivation, Leadership, and Organization: Do American Theories Apply Abroad?" *Organizational Dynamics*, Summer 1980, p.54.

The effects of international competition on American industry give us ample evidence that people in the rest of the world work very hard indeed. But in no other culture does business dominate life quite to the extent that it does in the United States. A quick test of your own suitability to an international management career might be your reaction to the following:

Exhibit 21.7 New Old Mexico—Land of Opportunity?

Mexico, depending upon which international business expert is talking, is either a country ripe for direct foreign investment or one to be avoided at all costs. For years Mexico has had a reputation as a steadily developing industrial nation with good potential and a long record of political stability. Together with a large supply of labor and an increasing demand for goods and services, these factors made Mexico a quietly attractive place for other countries to acquire or build plants.

But in 1982 Mexico, hurt by the drop in oil prices, faced a possible financial collapse. Foreign investors began to withdraw capital, and President Lopez Portillo nationalized the banks. Mexico survived its crisis, in large part thanks to the conservative fiscal policies of new President Miguel de la Madrid, and foreign capital is beginning to return. American companies considering building or acquiring plants in Mexico are looking at the following factors:

Attractions	Risks
Proximity to the United States	Large federal deficits
Record of political stability	High rates of inflation
Level of industrial development	High foreign debt
Devaluation of peso	Nationalization of banks and other industries
Increasing population (More than 65% of its 75 million people are under the age of 24)	Restriction on imports
	Economy's dependence on oil
Oil resources (Mexico is the 4th largest oil producer in the world)	Unemployment

On the balance, attractions seem to outweigh risks. No major foreign companies have pulled out of Mexico, and many are continuing to increase their investments. General Electric and Scott Paper of the United States, Japan's Nissan, and Sweden's L. M. Ericsson are among those expanding their holdings in Mexico. Total American investment was $5.6 billion in 1984. To many, Mexico is a rich country, with tremendous resources, an attractive opportunity for international business.

Source: K. Labich, "The So-Far So-Good Mexican Recovery," *Fortune*, January 9, 1984, pp. 97–102.

The American manager, raised and trained on business principles and policies, should be conditioned for what he (she) will probably find abroad. In a good part of the world, he (she) won't find the same enthusiasm for productivity, achieving objectives, high performance standards, punctuality and the like that he (she) brings to the job. . . . Even Europeans fail to understand our long hours, seemingly total dedication to the job, and full briefcases. To most non-Americans, life is made up of many other pursuits of greater significance.[23]

The Bottom Line

All large businesses will eventually be involved in international trade in some form or other. Even small businesses will be affected by foreign competition and can, in turn, benefit from foreign markets, products, and ideas.

American business schools have been excruciatingly slow in responding to the increasing internationalization of business. Therefore, in order to develop an appreciation for international business:

1. Even if you have no plans to work abroad, obtain some understanding of other cultures by traveling and learning a foreign language. Even one year of a lan-

guage followed by a few weeks in a country that speaks that language will open your eyes to ideas and possibilities that those who remain ethnocentric can never imagine.

2. If you are attracted by international management, take advantage of opportunities to learn a foreign language now. Facility in another language will be one of the first things international companies look for in recruiting.

3. If you do get assigned overseas, be open and flexible. Question assumptions you make about people and operations based on your experiences in this country. Certain principles will hold true in all countries, but their interpretations will vary. For example, reinforcement of behavior is effective everywhere, but the kinds of reinforcers people respond to in one culture may differ from those people respond to in another culture.

SUMMARY

A variety of forces is pushing toward the increasing internationalization of business. Accordingly, increased opportunities will be available for pursuing a management career in a country other than the native one. The formal area of study that deals with the special challenges and opportunities of such a career is international management, one aspect of the broader field of international business, which includes international marketing, finance, competition, and trade.

Managers in international business do what managers do anywhere, but in environments that can be quite different from those to which they are accustomed. They must also fill roles as representatives of their firms and their countries, and be gracious guests of the host country. Among the special assets needed to perform these expanded duties in a different culture are knowledge of the host country's culture and language, and considerable personal flexibility.

The formal study of the similarities and differences of managing in different countries is called comparative management. Research in this area finds that cultural differences can require considerable modification of management theory and practice. At the same time, the similarities may be expected to increase as differences between countries are reduced by increasing internationalization of interests, and increased movement of people between countries.

QUESTIONS FOR REVIEW AND DISCUSSION

1. Give an example of a possible conflict between the roles of a representative of a particular company and a guest of the host country for an international manager. In your *opinion*, where does the primary responsibility lie? Briefly explain your answer.

2. What is a multinational corporation?

3. Suggest at least three practical problems not mentioned in the chapter that

could be created by the inability of an international manager to speak the language of the host country.

4. What are three ways of becoming involved in international management?
5. As a college student, you are one of a group said to have "nearly catastropic insensitivity to the rest of the world." Think about your education and experience to date and suggest some of the possible reasons for the persistent evidence that most American young people are not interested in other cultures. Can you think of any practical formal approaches to bringing about a change?
6. How extensive is direct foreign investment in the United States?
7. What do you think would be the *general* reaction in this country to fringe benefits such as flowers and beauty-parlor allowances for female employees? Explain your answer in terms of the environmental factor or factors, discussed in this chapter, that seem most relevant.

REFERENCES AND NOTES

1. R. D. Robinson, *International Management.* New York: Holt, Rinehart and Winston, 1967, p. 1.
2. D. I. Fine, "South Africa Replaces Poland as Europe's Coal Miner." *Business Week*, April 13, 1981, p. 77.
3. "International Business." *Business Week*, December 27, 1982, p. 40; "A Foreign Shopping Spree for Bendix." *Business Week*, December 15, 1982, p. 25.
4. "U. S. Publishers Invade a Troubled Book Market." *Business Week*, December 15, 1980, p. 45.
5. "Labor For Export." *Newsweek*, September 22, 1980, p. 66.
6. "Labor Letter." *Wall Street Journal*, January 8, 1980, p. 1.
7. These and other examples of corporate blunders abroad have been collected by D. Ricks, chairman of the Ohio State University international business program. *See* D. Rotbart, "To Make Mr. Rick's List, a Company Must Commit a Major Blunder Abroad." *Wall Street Journal*, January 8, 1980, p. 1.
8. "Tests Find the 'Ugly Americans' Are Now In College—in America." *The Atlanta Constitution*, April 16, 1981.
9. "El Salvador: U. S. Plants Hum Along Despite Turmoil." *Business Week*, April 13, 1981, p. 60.
10. "Italy: The Pitfalls Awaiting the Oxy-ENI Venture." *Business Week*, March 30, 1981, p. 56.
11. "The Netherlands: Multinational Profits on Gas Heat an Election." *Business Week*, March 23, 1981, p. 57.
12. "Sexual Equality More or Less." *Time*, June 23, 1980, p. 65.
13. "Honda Discord." *Time*, November 3, 1980, p. 83.
14. "West Germany: How Politics Drove Out a U.S. Plane Builder." *Business Week*, October 27, 1980, p. 73.
15. "The Fear That Haunts Corporate America." (The Figgie Report II). *Across the Board*, May 1981, pp. 47–48.

16. J. Key, "Kidnap Threat is New Headache for Business." *Chicago Tribune*, July 8, 1979, p. 4.

17. U.S. Bureau of the Census, *Statistical Abstract of the United States, 1982-83*, pp. 823–25.

18. H. J. Reitz and L. N. Jewell, "Sex, Locus of Control, and Job Involvement: A Six-Country Investigation." *Academy of Management Journal*, 1979, 22, 1, pp. 72–80.

19. R. Marsh and H. Mannari, "Organizational Commitment and Turnover: A Predictive Study." *Administrative Science Quarterly*, 1977, 22, 1, pp. 57–75.

20. G. Hofstede, "Motivation, Leadership, and Organization: Do American Theories Apply Abroad?" *Organizational Dynamics*, 1980, 9, 1, pp. 42–63.

21. A. Siegert, "German Workers Enjoy Long List of Fringe Benefits, Survey Reports." *Chicago Tribune*, 1979.

22. D. B. Tinnin, "The American at the Wheel of Porsche." *Fortune*, April 5, 1982, pp. 78–87.

23. P. E. Illman, *Developing Overseas Managers—and Managers Overseas*. New York: Amacom, 1980, 28, p. 31.

SUGGESTED READINGS

Aonuma, Y. "A Japanese Explains Japan's Business Style." *Across The Board*, February, 1981, pp. 41–50. Japan's amazing economic development in recent years has stirred up the business world to an unprecedented degree; everyone seems to be asking, "What is the secret of their success?" Aonuma's explanation is clear, balanced, and somewhat surprising.

Barrett, W. E. "Sēnor Payroll." *Southwest Review*, 1943, 29, pp. 25–29. This is a classic and entertaining reading on some unanticipated consequences of doing it "the American way" in other countries.

Kocher, E. *International Jobs (Where They Are and How To Get Them)*. Reading, Mass.: Addison Wesley, 1979. Kocher has written a book for the student who thinks he or she might be interested in a career in international management.

22 / Managing as a Career

Bill reached across the table and took his wife's hand. "Okay, now," he said, "out with it."

Pauline feigned surprise, without success. "Out with what?"

"Whatever you've been busting to tell me since I got home," he replied. "You didn't eat enough to feed a bird tonight. That means you're either sick or you've got something on your mind. You don't look sick."

"You're right—I'm not sick. I'm excited. I just wanted to wait until after dinner to talk about it," said Pauline.

"Now's the time, then," he said, easing from the table and clearing away their dessert plates. "Want some more coffee? Let's move to the other room."

"Please," she replied as she kicked off her shoes and curled up on the comfortable sofa.

Bill brought their coffee into the livingroom, turned down the stereo, and sat in the large chair nearby.

"I've got some bad news and some good news. I'll give you the bad news first—Charles Robertson is leaving the company. He's going to be the new executive vice-president at Mayport."

"No kidding. That's too bad! I really liked Charles, and I know how much you liked working for him," Bill exclaimed.

"I was really shocked when he told me." said Pauline. "He's taught me a lot, gotten me some good assignments, and backed me up when I needed it. He's always looked for ways to help other people be successful."

"Sure worked for you. You had, what, two promotions and three raises in the two years you worked for him?" asked Bill.

"That's a fact" she replied. "He's been my mentor at Dracorp, no doubt about it. My career really began to take off when I moved to his division."

"Well, he deserves to head up his own company someday. I guess he figured the odds were better somewhere else."

"That's right. That's what he told me. Of course, moving to executive VP's a step up, and so is his new salary, but it's really the shot at the top that decided it. Mayport's president is only three years from retirement. Charles figures he'll have a good chance at becoming president if he does well. At fifty-one, he'll never be named a president if he doesn't make it in the next four years, which wouldn't happen if he stayed at Dracorp."

"I know. You told me. What you haven't told me is the good news."

"The good news—at least I think it is—is that Charles wants me to go with him as part of his management team. I'd have responsibility for the whole MIS operation!"

"That's terrific, sweetheart! A big move—not to mention a big salary, no doubt." Bill sat upright, a big smile on his face. "But why do you say you think it's good news?"

"Well, for one thing, I'm not sure I want to leave Dracorp. I've done well

there, have a lot of friends, and they've treated me pretty well. If I go with Charles, that new job's gonna take a lot of time. And I'll be traveling—he told me that. I'd be gone as many as ten or twelve days a month."

"That's not too great," he agreed. "I don't know how we'd handle that. We've been lucky so far, neither one of us has had to be away from home too much, at least not since I got out of the Marines."

"I remember when we were first married. I used to hate it when they'd send you off for those two-week field exercises," she said.

"Now don't go knocking the Corps. They paid my way through college. Besides, you told me it was the uniform that attracted you anyway. You said the first time you saw me in my dress blues, you asked yourself, 'I wonder if I'll marry him?'"

"That's true, but I asked that question about every good-looking guy I saw back then. Besides, what's all this got to do with my career?"

"Nothing. Just wanted to talk about me for a while, that's all," he laughed, "and my career's pretty solid right now."

"Well, you've got to help me decide, now. We agreed that we'd make all major career decisions together, like your decision to move into project management. Charles wants a decision in two weeks."

"Does Dracorp know about all this yet?" asked Bill.

"They will tomorrow," she replied.

"Then let's wait to see what they come back with. If they think enough of you, they're gonna make you some sort of counteroffer. They can't afford to lose you all."

"I hope you're right. In a way, I guess I'd really like to stay. Charles has done a lot for me, but now I'd like a chance to make it on my own. It sure would be nice to have a sign that they wanted me. I can handle more responsibility, and Charles' leaving is going to give somebody plenty of that."

"I tell you what. Let's get out of town this weekend. We'll try to assess each situation, if you went with Charles and did all that traveling or if you stayed with Dracorp. What you would want to stay—not in money, just responsibility. That way we'll be in better shape for you to make your decision."

"That's a good idea," she said, relieved. "I know there's a lot to talk about and think about, and we'll do it better if we get away. For one thing, we won't have to cook and do dishes," she said, "and this weekend it's my turn."

The first twenty-one chapters of this book have discussed the nature of the manager's job, the wide variety of functions and activities that managers perform, some constraints with which managers must contend, and the skills and tools that managers can use to carry out their jobs. Managing, like any career, is not for everybody; too many people start out in management only to find out later that they do not like to manage or cannot manage effectively or both.

However, most of you will be interested enough to consider managing as a career because of the challenges, opportunities, or the status of managers in our society. This chapter will describe some of the patterns, compensations, and problems you may face in a managerial career.

Pauline, Charles, and Bill are three people who have embarked on management careers. Right now they are in different career stages. Pauline is trying to decide whether being a part of Charles' management team or moving into the vacuum created by his leaving will be better for her; Charles is making a calculated move for a corporate presidency, leaving the security of his old company for a corporation he thinks offers him a better chance at his goal. would Bill is in a stable period in his own career, but will have to deal with whatever changes his wife's career decision brings. However, all of them started at the same place—being recruited and selected for their first managerial job.

RECRUITMENT AND SELECTION OF MANAGERS

One advantage of management as a career is that, if you are good, employment is rarely a problem. Economic conditions sometimes leave good engineers, teachers, airline pilots, and technical staff out of work, but organizations can always use good, experienced managers. During the recession years of 1980–82, the number of managers and administrators in the United States economy actually grew by nine percent, compared to a twelve percent decline in blue-collar employment over the same period.[1] Good managers earn for their employers far more than their salaries, so they are good investments in bad economic times as well as good.

Being Recruited

Organizations recruit and select first-time managers from two sources. One source is nonmanagement personnel already working for the organization. Some organizations prefer to recruit new managers from within. Technical or specialized companies may feel that managers need to have working knowledge of the company's operations to be credible. Engineering companies typically look for engineering supervisors among their brightest young engineers. Some organizations are looking for commitment and loyalty, which they feel is best found among workers who have been with them for several years. Walt Disney Productions, for example, recruits its managers from among those young people who have already spent several years working in one of their theme parks. In addition to getting committed managers, this policy is also a sound way of rewarding workers.

The second major source of new managers is recent college graduates. A company will try to identify potential managers in several ways. First they advertise po-

The key to landing the best first job you can is to start looking early and sign up for as many interviews as you can as often as possible.

sitions through newspapers and professional publications. They also talk to individuals recommended to them by current employees or by acquaintances. Occasionally, several organizations will create recruitment centers in large cities to attract large numbers of potential employees. Finally, many companies send representatives to college campuses to recruit new managers through personal placement interviews.

From the standpoint of a prospective manager, the quickest approach is probably to contact friends, acquaintances, and relatives who may be able to bring someone they know to the attention of management recruiters. Faculty members can likewise be valuable contacts. Providing an interested professor with a job resumé and a description of your job interests may be a way to shorten the search for an initial position.

Using the college's placement service is another common method for finding that first job. The key is to start early and sign up for interviews often. Students who use the placement services at the *beginning* of their senior years are far more likely to get good jobs than those who wait until a month before graduation. Competition for good jobs is often stiff; the visibility and interviewing experience that lead to job offers go to those who make the fullest use of their campus placement centers.

Sending out unsolicited resumés to companies is a third approach, but it is also the most expensive and least productive. Remember that recruiters are managers, and managers prefer personal contact to reading written material. While a

Exhibit 22.1   A Resumé of A College Senior Seeking a Management Position

---

EMPLOYMENT OBJECTIVE
Seek an entry level position in management with a medium to large corporation leading to responsibilities in international management.

EDUCATION AND ACHIEVEMENTS
BS, Major: Business Management, Graduation: June 13, 1985.
Beta Gamma Sigma Academic Honorary.
National Golden Key Academic Honor Fraternity.
George F. Weber Scholarship Award.

ABILITIES
Leadership: Served as purchasing agent for an organization of 115.
Representative to College Scholarship Committee.
Developed new recruitment program for local service organization.

Communication: Responsible for writing and presenting weekly report concerning campus and fraternity scholarship. Organized publicity for community-charity functions. Actor in state film. Delegate to Le Congres de Francais en Floride. Four years of French study (High School). Intensive French study, Berlitz School: August 1–August 31, 1984.

Human Relations: Coordinated program bringing 60 elementary-school children in weekly contact with 50 convalescent patients. Organized social functions and transportation for a college group of 50. Responsible for aiding in comparative shopping and coordinating transportation for senior citizen group.

WORK EXPERIENCE
Eastern Federal Theatres Corporation.
Actor in Public Broadcasting Services Film, Gal Young Un, Nunez Productions.
Bartender for Professional Parties, Self-Employed.
Lawn Care and Building Maintenance for Professional Buildings.
Construction Laborer.
Adopted Grandparents Program.
Senior Citizen Action Agency.

INTERESTS
Foreign Languages, Singing, Skiing, Tennis, Theatre, Travel.

REFERENCES
List available upon request.

---

professional-looking resumé is an important part of recruitment (see Exhibits 22.1 and 22.2), by itself its chances of success are low. Students who send out as many as one hundred unsolicited resumés often receive only two or three replies from companies, if that many.

Being Selected

Organizations base their selections of new managers on five types of information: personal recommendations, academic performance, extracurricular activities, work experience, and personal interviews. The amount of weight put on any of these categories varies from company to company, and from job to job, although previous

Exhibit 22.2   Ten Common Complaints Companies Have About Resumés

1. Too long. Contains much useless information.
2. Disorganized. Information scattered, hard to follow.
3. Poorly typed and printed. Hard to read, unprofessional.
4. Not enough information. Only dates, titles, address.
5. Overwritten. Long paragraphs, saying little.
6. Not results oriented. Lists duties, not accomplishments.
7. Contains irrelevant material such as height, weight, sex.
8. Misspellings and typographical errors, poor grammar.
9. Overdone. Fancy typesetting, binders.
10. Misdirected. No reasons for candidate applying. Cover letter would help.

Source: T. Jackson, ''Writing the Targeted Resumé,'' *Business Week's Guide to Careers,* (New York: McGraw Hill, 1983), p. 26.

experience and personal recommendations usually receive a great deal of attention. Someone with a deficit in one or more areas will have to make up for that deficit by being superior in the other areas. For example, a student with no personal recommendations and no previous work experience will need an outstanding academic record, extracurricular activities, and/or an outstanding personal interview to be seriously considered for a management position.

What kinds of characteristics do recruiters look for? The first twenty-one chapters of this book provide a number of clues. Managers work hard, make decisions, analyze information, search for problems and find solutions, spend most of their time dealing with other people, and are hard-pressed for time. Recruiters are looking for evidence of characteristics that fit these requirements. Academic records describe intellectual abilities and certain kinds of technical expertise. Course loads and extracurricular activities tell something about abilities to organize time and preferences for working with people. While experience is valuable in its own right, and suggests maturity and responsibility, verbal skills and self-presentation are assessed in personal interviews. Because managing is a highly verbal, personal activity, appearance and conduct in job interviews are given a lot of weight. Showing up late, being poorly dressed, ill prepared, or inarticulate will generally eliminate a candidate from further consideration. One recruiter for a large organization revealed that she eliminated about half of her interviewees because they failed to comply with instructions regarding their interview: time, dress, and preparation.

THE FIRST JOB

Once they have been recruited and selected, most first-time managers have fairly common expectations about their jobs. Unfortunately, most of these expectations are not met. The variety in assignments is so great, even within a given company, that it is hard to describe a typical first management position. Two points can be made with some confidence, however. First, the job will differ from expectations. Second, the job will become what the new manager makes it.

Differences Between the Actual Job and Expectations

Most new managers find that their new jobs are not nearly as well-defined as they thought they would be, even in a management training position, which may be highly structured and technical, or quite ambiguous and undefined. The first job, being different from initial expectations, may be quite frustrating. A study of managerial careers describes six areas in which the new job can be particularly disappointing.[2]

Low initial challenge. Organizations often use management training programs or easy job assignments as a way of breaking in new managers. Those who are well-prepared and eager to make their mark will miss the challenge of a more demanding assignment.

Conformity. Organizations and their members will prefer custom over change. Old ways are changed with difficulty, which may frustrate those who see the old ways as outmoded or inefficient.

Lack of feedback. Students used to frequent graded assignments and exams have difficulty with the minimal performance feedback many of them encounter. Appraisals, when they do occur, may be poorly done or very infrequent.

Unrealistic expectations. Many graduates find that their expectations of power and expertise are unrealistic. At the beginning they find that they have little credibility and influence, because power and expertise must be earned *after* joining the organization, not before.

Inability to create challenge. Students used to having assignments handed out by instructors often must learn to create their own challenges. The passive roles they learned in school are not functional in a vaguely defined management position.

Defensive superiors. A new manager who reports to a new job with a good degree and a high salary may be threatening to his or her immediate superior. The superior may react by making the new manager accept a dependent and very subordinate role for an interim period.

Making the Most of the First Job

Given these problems, it is not surprising that high turnover is common among first-time managers. Over half of recent college graduates leave their first jobs within five years.[3] Their frustrations cause them to find other jobs, where they may find themselves more accepted because they now have experience. They have made a better job choice and their expectations are more realistic.

For those who stay, however, the first job is crucial; they learn that a managerial job is what they make of it. At the least, it is a learning experience. The new manager learns about the products and processes of the organization. He or she be-

comes familiar with organizational norms, communication networks, and performance standards. Identifying those who have real power and those who have little,
distinguishing those on the way up from those with no future, all are worthwhile
outcomes of the first job. The new manager who can learn what kinds of performance is valued and how he or she can contribute to the organization has not wasted
that first job assignment.

For the lucky managers who get meaningful, challenging, initial assignments,
the first year or two is no problem. Those who are not so fortunate must create
their own challenges and goals. Those who do not, who sit back and brood or sulk
about their fate, will be left behind by their more aggressive or more fortunate
peers.

MANAGEMENT APPRAISAL AND DEVELOPMENT

New managers are the executives of the future. Any competent organization strives
to identify and develop promising managerial talent to staff its future. Managerial
performance appraisal and development are major personnel functions today.

Management Appraisal

Managers are evaluated in a number of ways. One of the most difficult things for
new managers to understand is that, to a great extent, their evaluations will depend
upon the performance of their *subordinates.*

Managers get things done through people. The "things" that get done are usually done by subordinates and colleagues, rather than by the manager. We all understand that baseball managers are evaluated on their team's won-lost records. The
manager's contribution is hard to measure directly, so it is measured indirectly by
the players' performance. Just so, the performance of a manager's subordinates is
more easily observed and measured than that of the manager. Although his or her
performance may be a function of capabilities, training, tools, economics, budgets,
information, and luck, the manager is responsible for the bottom line. There are
few excuses for poor subordinate performance. Managers are expected to succeed
with what they have, and to improve upon whatever is lacking.

Managers are also evaluated upon impressions they make as reflected in their
semiannual or annual formal appraisals. An example of a management performance appraisal is provided in Exhibit 22.3. These impressions are formed by superiors' observations of the manager and his or her subordinates in action. These formal evaluations are usually carried out by the manager's immediate supervisor.
Occasionally more than one superior evaluates a manager. Peer appraisal, while
used in some professions such as medicine and law, is rare in industry.

Some organizations have developed management *assessment centers* to evaluate managerial skills and potential. An assessment center is an appraisal tool that

Exhibit 22.3   A Managerial Appraisal Form

Mark the box that most accurately describes the performance of the individual being appraised. Comment where appropriate. For items not applicable, insert "N.A." under comments.	Outstanding	High	Above Normal	Normal	Below Normal	Inadequate	**Comments**
Judgment Soundness of conclusions, decisions, and actions.	☐	☐	☐	☐	☐	☐	
Initiative Ability to take effective action without being told.	☐	☐	☐	☐	☐	☐	
Resource Utilization Ability to delineate project needs and locate, plan, and effectively use all resources available.	☐	☐	☐	☐	☐	☐	
Dependability Reliability in assuming and carrying out the commitments and obligations of the position.	☐	☐	☐	☐	☐	☐	
Analytical Ability Effectiveness in thinking through a problem, in recognizing, securing, and evaluating relevant facts, reaching sound conclusions.	☐	☐	☐	☐	☐	☐	
Communicative Ability Effectiveness in using oral and written communications and in keeping subordinates, associates, superiors, and others adequately informed.	☐	☐	☐	☐	☐	☐	
Interpersonal Skills Effectiveness in relating in an appropriate and productive manner to subordinates, associates, superiors, and others.	☐	☐	☐	☐	☐	☐	
Ability to Work Under Pressure Ability to meet tight deadlines and adapt to changes.	☐	☐	☐	☐	☐	☐	
Creativity Ability to generate worthwhile new ideas or techniques having practical applications.	☐	☐	☐	☐	☐	☐	
Security Sensitivity Ability to handle confidential information appropriately and to exercise care in safeguarding proprietary information.	☐	☐	☐	☐	☐	☐	

employs a number of methods in evaluation. It typically uses exercises, tests, simulations, games, and interviews to generate an in-depth profile of a manager's strengths, weaknesses, and potential. Assessment centers are usually run by trained staff for whom evaluation is a full-time job. Although such techniques are expensive, and typically require the manager's full time for two or more days, their popularity is increasing.[4] Among those organizations using assessment center techniques are AT&T, IBM, Sohio, and the IRS. For one thing, the validity of the center's evaluations is generally high. In addition, managers who are being evaluated and those who use the data are satisfied with the accuracy and fairness. Finally, they provide the manager with a great deal of useful feedback about his or her strengths, weaknesses, and future within that company.

Management Development

Management development programs are activities designed to provide managers with skills and knowledge useful in present and future positions. All organizations use some form of on-the-job development; most large organizations use off-the-job programs as well.

On-the-Job Development. The development of managerial talent on the job is accomplished through evaluating and counseling, transitional experience, and rotation and transfer.[5] In evaluating and counseling, a subordinate manager observes and carries out some of the superior's tasks. In this traditional method of management development, the superior is responsible for personally developing the skills and knowledge necessary for a subordinate to move into a more responsible job.

> *Two points about the first job can be made with some confidence. First, the job will differ from expectations. Second, the job will become what the manager makes it.*

Transitional experience is gained when a newly appointed manager begins to learn about his or her new job before the former manager leaves. The most striking example of transitional development occurs when the United States elects a new president. The new president and staff begin learning about their new responsibilities six to eight weeks before the new president is actually sworn in. Transitional experience is a costly process requiring that two managers, at least, are paid to do one job for the interim period. If staffs are involved, then staff costs are usually doubled.

Rotation and transfer provide the manager with a broad range of experience in the organization and an exposure to different jobs, plants, and superiors. In recent years, the high costs of moving for managers and their companies have curtailed rotation and transfer from one plant or office to another. Dual-career marriages, housing costs, inflation, and a growing emphasis on nonwork activities are causing managers to resist relocation. A research group for 750 large companies discovered that the cost of moving a homeowning employee tripled between 1975 and 1980 to an average of $30,000 per move.[6] As a result of these forces, Bell Telephone reduced its transfers by 20 percent between 1979 and 1980, and IBM reduced its transfers to 3 percent of its personnel in 1980, down from 5 percent in the mid-1970s.

Off-the-Job Development. Off-the-job development usually involves sending managers to professionally-run programs designed to provide specific skills or knowledge. These programs may be half-day seminars on new performance-appraisal techniques to complete one- or two-year MBA programs at major colleges or universities. The Armed Forces routinely send career officers to certain universities to obtain MBAs, and even Ph.Ds; suppliers of equipment and facilities run programs for customers' managers to teach them how to use their products more efficiently and effectively; government organizations often sponsor programs to acquaint managers with changes in laws and rules, particularly in the areas of taxes, investments, and overseas operations. Given the complexity and change of modern managing, you can be assured that you will not have left the classroom behind when you become a manager.

CAREERS IN MANAGEMENT

One of the more attractive features of management is that it is a profession that can be practiced in a wide variety of organizations and settings. Students seeking management careers can look for positions in any of the fifty states or can start their own businesses. Fluency in a foreign language dramatically increases their options of working overseas for an American firm, or for a foreign company overseas or here in this country.

Career Options

Although a large proportion of management positions are in business and industry, the variety of organizations makes a wide selection possible. Business and industrial groups that recruit and employ large numbers of managers each year include banking and finance, manufacturing, construction, transportation, food, and energy companies. However, the use of professionally trained and educated managers has spread beyond business and industry to:

health and hospital administration	trade and professional associations
civil service	museums and the performing arts
state, local, and federal government	the military
entertainment	law enforcement
sports	education

Management has become, and continues to be, a highly attractive field for women. In this country, the proportion of women in management and administration has increased every year during the last ten years.[7] The total number of women in managerial positions almost doubled over those ten years. By 1980, twenty-five percent of all managers and administrators were female. There is no indication that this trend will stop.

Career Planning and Development

All career planners advise prospects to set objectives as the first step in finding a job. Suggestions for objectives should include earning a specific salary by a certain age, having a specific position or title by a certain age, supervising a certain number of people by a certain age, or being an entrepreneur by a certain age.

Setting such objectives help a manager evaluate short-term career decisions and progress in light of his or her overall career objectives, just as Charles' goal of becoming a president led him to accept Mayport's offer. Goals also make it easier to tolerate short-term frustrations and disappointments which do not interfere with longer-term objectives.

These goals are not inflexible; they can be changed as the person changes. Flexibility itself can be a goal, as it was for Pauline. Flexibility may mean just gaining new experience and being able to discover and exploit opportunities that may arise. For someone who wants to remain flexible for a while, realistic short-term objectives might be performing as well as possible in every job, getting exposure by moving to a new assignment every eighteen to twenty-four months, avoiding narrowly defined jobs, and developing good relations with senior managers.

> *New managers are the executives of the future. Any competent organization strives to identify and develop promising managerial talent to staff its future.*

The goal of good relations with senior managers is useful regardless of a subordinate's other career objectives. One of the biggest advantages any beginning manager can have in his or her career is the personal support of a senior executive.

Studies of career patterns of executives reveal that a typical career evolves through several phases (see Exhibit 22.4). One of the latter stages involves assuming responsibility for others. The primary relationship which the executive seeks is that of *mentor*, the role that Charles played for Pauline in the story that opened this chapter.

A **mentor** is *an advisor, someone who fosters the career development of another manager.*[8] In this role, the mentor may act as a teacher to enhance the protégé's skills and intellectual development. The mentor guides the beginning manager through the early stages of the social and interpersonal relationships that evolve during a successful career. The mentor helps the manager develop career objectives and a plan to meet them; he or she provides counsel in times of crises or stress, and serves as a model for the less experienced manager to emulate.

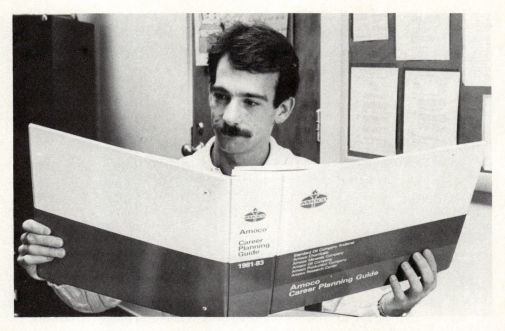

Setting objectives and doing research can help maximize the potential of a first job in terms of overall career goals.

Studies of mentors and their protegés have found that the relationship lasts from two to three years, as did Charles' and Pauline's. The mentor is usually eight to fifteen years older than the protegé. Both parties benefit from the relationship— learning, guidance, and support are obvious benefits for the protegé; the mentor obtains gratitude, an expansion of influence, and the satisfaction of helping.

One study used in depth interviews with both parties to examine fifteen mentor relationships. The study identified both same-sex and cross-sex mentor relationships. It suggested that a successful manager might have a number of such relationships during his or her career; similarly, a successful mentor might assist a number of protegés with their careers, but usually no more than one at a time.[9]

During the fourth stage of a career, the executive often exercises power in an attempt to expand and perpetuate his or her influence on the organization. An effective and common way to do this is to sponsor the career of a promising younger manager. A ***sponsor*** is *someone who nominates a promising subordinate for a key position.* The subordinate may be someone for whom the sponsor was a mentor, or perhaps someone whose performance the sponsor has followed with particular interest. Successful executives often develop management teams of subordinates whose skills complement their own, as Charles was doing with Pauline and her associates. As the executive moves up through the organizational hierarchy, or to another organization, these subordinates move as well. Becoming an important part of a successful management team is a useful step for someone with career ob-

Exhibit 22.4 Four Career Stages in Management

	Stage I	Stage II	Stage III	Stage IV
Central Activity	Helping Learning Following directions	Independent Contributor	Training Interfacing	Shaping the direction of the organization
Primary Relationship	Apprentice	Colleague	Mentor	Sponsor
Major Psychological Issues	Dependence	Independence	Assuming responsibility for others	Exercising power

Source: G. W. Dalton, P. H. Thompson, and R. L. Price, *Organizational Dynamics*, Summer 1977 © 1977 by AMACOM, a division of American Management Association, pp. 19–42. All rights reserved.

jectives of moving fast and far. If those were Pauline's objectives, she almost certainly would decide to go with Charles' management team to Mayport.

What we have described thus far has suggested that career development in many organizations is basically up to the initiative of the manager. Certainly every young manager should take as active a role as possible in his or her own career development. However, many large organizations have specific programs designed to develop the careers of their managers from their first year through retirement. Among those industries with some history of good career development are the oil industry, the airline industry, and the armed services. Exhibit 22.5 describes activities which organizations carry out as part of their career development program.

Management Compensation

Managers work long, hard hours. Among the returns for such efforts are the satisfaction of accomplishment, high status, and varied and challenging work. In addition, most managers are well paid, both in salary and in other forms of compensation.

Salary.   Starting salaries for managers vary. The field and organization that a new manager chooses, along with his or her education and experience and the geographic location of the company, will determine starting salaries. Nevertheless, surveys do provide some ideas of what salary ranges to expect. Median starting salaries for bachelor of science degrees in 1983 ranged from $17,000 to $20,000.[10] Estimated starting salaries for MBAs for 1984 were from $25,000 to $35,000 at many schools, with higher salaries for MBAs with technical backgrounds.[11]

Unless the economy collapses, one could safely predict those averages to increase by seven or eight percent each year. Most placement centers on college campuses can provide more accurate figures.

Any attempt to predict what will happen to an individual's salary after beginning a career is doomed to failure. Salary increases depend upon individual per-

Exhibit 22.5   Specific Career Activities of Organizations

Career Counseling
Career counseling during the employment interview.
Career counseling during the performance appraisal session.
Psychological assessment and career alternative planning.
Career counseling as part of the day-to-day supervisor/subordinate relationship.
Special career counseling for high-potential employees.
Counseling for downward transfers.

Career Pathing
Planned job progression for new employees.
Career pathing to help managers acquire the necessary experience for future jobs.
Committee performs an annual review of management personnel's strengths and weaknesses and
    then develops a five-year career plan for each.
Plan job moves for high-potential employees to place them in a particular target job.
Rotate first-level supervisors through various departments to prepare them for upper-management
    positions.

Human Resources
Computerized inventory of backgrounds and skills to help identify replacements.
Succession planning or replacement charts at all levels of management.

Career Information Systems
Job posting for all nonofficer positions; individual can bid to be considered.
Job posting for hourly employees and career counseling for salaried employees.

Management or Supervisory Development
Special program for those moving from hourly employment to management.
Responsibility of the department head to develop managers.
Management development committee to look after the career development of management groups.
In-house advanced management program.

Training
In-house supervisory training.
Technical skills training for lower levels.
Outside management seminars.
Formalized job rotation programs.
Intern programs.
Responsibility for manager for on-the-job training.
Tuition reimbursement program.

Special Groups
Outplacement programs.
Minority indoctrination training program.
Career management seminar for women.
Preretirement counseling.
Career counseling and job rotation for women and minorities.
Refresher courses for midcareer managers.
Presupervisory training program for women and minorities.

Source: M. A. Morgan, D. T. Hall, and A. Martin, "Career Development Strategies in Industry: Where Are We and Where Should We Be?" *Personnel*, March–April 1979, © 1979 by AMACOM, a division of American Management Associations. All rights reserved.

formance, company performance, industry performance, economic conditions, and supply and demand. All we can safely say is that managers are more likely to be overworked than underpaid. Exhibit 22.6 provides salary ranges of middle managers in selected fields in 1982.

A survey of top salaries in business will give you an idea of what is possible if you make it to the top.[12] According to the survey, Frank Rosenfelt, president of MGM was the nation's best-paid businessman, at $5.1 million. Thirty-three execu-

> *One of the more attractive features of management is that it is a profession that can be practiced in a wide variety of organizations and settings.*

tives were found who made over $1 million. Annual salaries for CEOs of larger companies typically run between $300,000 and $700,000 per year.

Lest these figures look too attractive, a small word of warning. A later survey of 824 chief executives found a large percentage of them were worried about their personal wealth despite their high salaries.[13] Inflation and high taxes still bothered most of them, who felt that their spending had to keep pace with their incomes. Few felt secure enough to stop worrying about retirement.

Other Compensation.   Executives making millions of dollars are not making it all in salary. Much of their compensation comes in other forms. *Bonuses* tied to company or division performance may range from twenty to eighty percent of an executive's salary. *Stock options*, giving an executive the right to buy common stock in the company at a specified price, act as incentives to increase company performance, so that stock prices will exceed executives' option prices. Executives can often double their salaries by exercising stock options. Other benefits include automobiles, housing, expense accounts, subsidized insurance, loans, club membership, use of company aircraft and recreational facilities, and chauffeurs. Remember, however, that a necessary prerequisite for most corporate executives is also a security staff for protection against assault or kidnapping.

CAREER ISSUES

Among the most common issues faced by managers during their careers are those of dual-career families, stress and its effects, and ethical questions.

Dual Careers[14]

Three out of every five working women are married. Economic pressures on families for two incomes, coupled with changes in values and sex discrimination laws, are increasing the ranks of dual-career families every year.

Couples who work enjoy not only the extra income but the satisfaction each gets from employment, and while the income is useful, it is often not the major reason why both people work. Young women with college degrees have experienced success, know they can compete with men, and want to put their hard-earned skills to work. Whatever the reasons, two-income families are becoming as common among white-collar workers as among blue-collar ones. When one or both

Exhibit 22.6   Salary Ranges for Selected Middle Management Positions in Medium- and Large-Sized Companies, 1982

	Range for Top Third of Managers
Technical	
*R&D executive	$60,000–79,000
*Corporate construction director	60,000–77,000
Chief industrial engineer	50,000–63,000
Finance	
*Security investments manager	50,000–76,000
*General accounting (report to controller)	45,000–68,000
*Tax compliance manager	50,000–66,000
Financial planning officer (report to controller)	50,000–62,000
Bank manager (at least $10 million deposits)	46,000–61,000
Chief internal auditor	40,000–53,000
Sales	
*National account manager	50,000–69,000
Brand manager (sales over $5 million)	30,000–63,000
International sales	45,000–59,000
Sales promotion	40,000–56,000
Personnel	
*Management training specialist/dept. head	50,000–76,000
*Personnel/human resources manager	50,000–68,000
*Labor relations executive	45,000–68,000
Employee training specialist/dept. head	35,000–47,000
Planning	
*Corporate strategic planner	50,000–70,000
Corporate economist	50,000–61,000
Manufacturing	
*Plant manager	40,000–69,000
Quality	35,000–60,000
Other	
*Management Information Systems specialist/data proc.	45,000–77,000
Federal relations executive	50,000–64,000
Corp. insurance/risk manager	45,000–63,000
Contract administrator	40,000–54,000
Purchasing manager	35,000–53,000
Media Manager	30,000–53,000

*The top dozen career slots for current middle managers of above-average abilities in medium and large-size companies.

Source: S. S. Ross, "The Twelve Top Money-Making Careers of the '80s," *Business Week's Guide to Careers* (New York: McGraw-Hill, 1983), p. 9.

spouses are managers, dual careers can present dilemmas beyond those experienced in other fields.

Some issues faced by dual-career couples in the early stages of their careers are common to all dual-career families—deciding whether or when to have children, deciding who and how to take care of meals and household chores, and finding enough time for both work and their relationship.

Another set of characteristics common to beginning professional or managerial couples leads to other problems. These characteristics include:

1. *Similar career requirements.* Both partners need to learn and develop skills and contacts. This means long hours, travel, and possibly relocation.
2. *Conflicting career-path alternatives.* One partner's best career move might mean going to another city, while the other's best alternative is to stay put.
3. *High degree of commitment to work and career.* Each may understand his or her own commitment to the job, but may not understand that the other's commitment is equally strong.
4. *Lack of preparation.* Many couples have no contingency plans to deal with job offers, children, or illness.
5. *Lack of experience in resolving conflicts.* Many young couples have never had to resolve serious conflicts in which two parties' interests conflict. They tend to view the situation as one career versus another, rather than as "our careers."
6. *Reluctance to discuss dual-career problems with their companies.* Many couples are afraid to ask for decisions or options which would alleviate dual-career problems and crises. They view corporate policy as more rigid than it may really be.
7. *Personal flexibility.* Fortunately, most young couples are willing to explore alternatives to traditional solutions. Taking turns in everything from household chores to career moves, long-distance commuting, and living apart can eventually be viewed as possible solutions to dual-career problems.

In the anecdote that introduced this chapter, Pauline and Bill are a dual-career couple who face some but not all of these problems. Although they have similar career requirements, at this time Bill's career is stable, and Pauline's potential move does not require going to another city. While both are committed to their careers, they have developed joint problem-solving skills to deal with conflicts.

What can other young couples do to survive these problems? "Survive" is the correct word, because the problems are severe enough to cause marriages to break up or careers to be ruined. Obviously, couples need to develop skills in joint problem-solving. Practice and, frequently, professional help are needed so that skills are developed *before* the first crisis, rather than during or after.

Successful dual-career couples tend to be committed to *both* careers, not one over the other. In some cases, their employers support their commitment as well. It would be a good idea to check out prospective employers' support for two-career couples.

Learning how to cope with stress and to manage time effectively are also useful skills for dual-career couples. Time demands and stress are going to be higher when both couples are involved in careers. Learning how to plan, and how to cope when plans go awry, are good survival tools.

Effects of Stress

Chapter 19 discussed the effects of stress in detail, but it is important to mention again one of the most harmful ways managers try to relieve pressure—alcohol. Because of the importance and uncertainty of their day-to-day decisions, and because management, itself, is a very social occupation, managers are particularly susceptible to alcohol abuse. More than five million workers are alcoholics, according to the National Council on Alcoholism. Alcoholism costs industry an estimated ten billion dollars annually; the average alcoholic misses twenty-two days of work per year more than the average nonalcoholic.[15]

Most alcoholics claim to be unaware that their drinking is a problem. Exhibit 22.7 provides a list of signals that drinking is no longer a pastime, but a problem.

What can be done? Rehabilitation takes two steps—recognition of the problem and professional help. Some organizations have programs for dealing with alcoholic employees; others do not, but clinics, physicians, psychiatrists, counselors, Alcoholics Anonymous, and mental health centers are available.

Ethical Dilemmas

Earlier in this chapter we described problems of beginning managers stemming from differences between their expectations for their first jobs and reality. Similarly, the early years of a career may bring about one or more ethical dilemmas for the unwary newcomer.[16]

Power vs. Rationality.   Students of management learn techniques and processes for making rational decisions. Their formal education emphasizes problem-solving, with consistent objectives of finding correct or even optimal solutions. The organizations in which these students will manage likewise stress rational decision making. The correct decision about a personnel problem may benefit one department at another's expense; the optimal decision about resource allocation may require some group to give up control over certain resources.

When problems and decisions affect individual groups and departments differently, rationality will not completely determine the final outcome. It is seldom abandoned, but individuals, groups, and departments will use their power and influence in order to protect or further their own interests. It is this struggle between rationality and power that creates problems during the early years of many careers.

Some managers reject the idea of power and influence affecting organizational decisions. They cling to the notion of objective rationality and are disillusioned when decisions that are implemented vary from their ideals. Many of them "refuse to play the power game." Others learn the system, identify powerful individuals or groups, learn to build their own power bases, and develop alliances. They learn when and for whom rationality works, and when organizational politics must be employed.

Demands for Loyalty.   First-time managers frequently learn that loyalty is a highly valued characteristic. *Loyalty* often appears as a trait used to evaluate managers in formal performance appraisals; a superior is likely to insist that his or her subordinates behave loyally.

For a new manager, dilemmas arise from trying to figure out what loyalty means. For some superiors, loyalty means obedience. What does the beginning manager do when a superior who demands such loyalty is obviously wrong? Is it loyal to obey and let the superior make an embarrassing or important error?

Exhibit 22.7   Signs of Alcoholism

Until such time that more sophisticated testing devices are developed, such as a physiological test, alcoholism can best be identified through some of the developing symptoms and behavioral expressions, such as:

Gross drinking behavior   drinking more frequently and getting intoxicated more frequently than normal drinkers

Alcoholic blackouts   suffering periods of amnesia following drinking

Loss of control   inability to stop drinking once it is begun

Marital relationships affected   family life and marital life adversely affected by drinking

Health affected   overweight, underweight, liver problems, malnutrition, or anything that has been adversely affected because of alcohol consumption

Emotional involvement   problems that arise because of excessive drinking

Financial problems   loss of income, loss of money, waste, and financial difficulties attributed to excessive intake of alcohol

Crutch drinking   drinking to solve problems, to face one's spouse, to make a sale, to meet the problems of everyday life, etc.

Alcohol-involved life   alcohol surrounding and permeating life activity, such as eating, visits of friends, participation in social activities, etc.

Loss of friends   not being invited to parties, friends avoiding you because of excessive drinking

Loss of hobbies   giving up sports, and activities, because alcohol is served at the location or because alcohol has taken over

Denial   denying the fact that the problem exists, already with an excuse for one's drinking, always finding someone else whose drinking is worse in order to rationalize one's drinking

Escape   drinking to escape surroundings, job environment, and self

Drinking when depressed   instead of seeking advice, looking for a quick and easy way out of depression and problems

Problem solving by drinking   avoiding the issue by numbing oneself instead of seeking a solution to a problem

Morning drink   to get over the hump; to clear the "cobwebs"

Withdrawal   "butterflies," hallucinating, convulsions, etc.

Employment problems   losing time from work tardiness, absenteeism, slow productivity, because of alcohol

Source: A. Brisolava, The Alcoholic Employee (New York: Human Sciences Press, 1979), pp. 47–50.

Another interpretation of a superior's demand for loyalty might be, "Protect me so that I don't look bad." This interpretation in itself conveys two possible meanings. One is to argue a superior out of a bad decision; the second meaning creates the greater problem. A superior may, in fact, expect a loyal subordinate to shift the blame and/or consequences of the superior's mistakes onto others. When a superior's demands for loyalty include covering up mistakes, the beginning manager is in a tough position. Refusal may mean loss of a job; agreement may mean feelings of guilt or worse, as we witnessed in the Watergate scandal of the Nixon administration.

Loyalty may mean simply working hard. A superior who is clearly accountable for his or her people's success will be likely to demand hard work as proof of loyalty. This is especially likely for superiors who are themselves workaholics. For managers whose sole ambition is work, such a demand is no problem, but it is a problem for those who want to get ahead yet retain or develop outside interests.

Other upwardly mobile superiors may demand loyalty in the form of success. They perceive that anything less than success reflects poorly upon them and their

Management in Action
A Career in Hotel Management

Working as a bilingual interpreter at a clinic in the Texas Medical Center (Houston), Linda Hudson felt she had little chance for advancement, and it was obvious she would never get rich. "I couldn't become a technical person and I had been there two years," she said. "I was not very happy."

One day, however, she and some of her friends were having lunch at Trader Vic's, the restaurant at the Shamrock Hilton. The bartender there was "a friend of one of my friends, and he mentioned that a lot of people who spoke Spanish stayed at the hotel, and he really thought I should apply there."

She did apply. And her career in the hotel business began.

In nine years, Hudson has gone from Houston to San Antonio to Washington, D.C. She's back in her hometown again, now as manager of the Lancaster, an old, recently reopened hotel.

Hudson's career in the hotel business began with a two-month hitch as room clerk at the Shamrock Hilton in Houston. Eventually she was transferred to the Palacio del Rio in San Antonio, where she worked for a year and a half as executive assistant manager. She then became the resident manager of the Capital Hilton (originally the Statler) in Washington, D.C., a position she held for a year and a half.

Then she heard that the Lancaster in Houston was being made into a small, luxury hotel, and that the owners were looking for a manager. "I was one of several people they interviewed, and the chemistry was right," Hudson said. "They hired me."

Investors poured millions of dollars into total renovation and remodeling. There are now eighty-five guest rooms and eight suites. Twenty four-hour room service, turndown service, and bedtime brandy are offered now, as well as an inhouse valet and limousine service.

So Hudson, 33, is the proud overseer of a small empire on the border of Texas and Louisiana. She lives in a suite near the top of the twelve-story edifice. "I live here in the hotel and I love it," she said. "You have to be close to an operation like this, and some days I have to spend eighteen hours a day here. Usually nothing major happens, but in case something does, I'm here."

Hudson says her day generally starts between eight and eight-thirty in the morning. She goes over the log left by the night manager, opens the mail, returns calls, and then starts a long series of meetings with department heads. She tries to meet some of the guests and walks the floor to see that everything is functioning smoothly. Her days may last ten hours on the average. If there are nighttime meetings or clients to entertain, it is not unusual for her to work longer hours.

Source: Tom Overton, "Faces," *The Houston Post*, March 20, 1983, p. 126.

careers, and thus suggest disloyalty on the part of the subordinate. A superior who equates loyalty with success sends his or her subordinates a message: "Succeed at all costs." When the costs of success mean unethical, immoral, or illegal behavior, the beginning manager faces a dilemma.

> *Managing is an exciting, but complex career. Any career that carries with it such powerful rewards makes demands of those who aspire to success.*

Finally, loyalty may mean telling the truth—at all times. At first blush, telling the truth would not seem to be a problem. However, at least two situations provide dilemmas for beginning managers. One is when the truth will displease a superior, as when the new manager makes a mistake, cannot meet a deadline, or disagrees. Some superiors demand the truth, yet punish those who truthfully admit to mistakes or failure. A similar problem occurs when the first-time manager is caught between demands for loyalty to a superior and to a colleague or subordinate. The superior who demands to know the source of a failure or mistake places an ethical burden on the new manager who knows that the fault lies with a colleague or subordinate.

Personal Anxiety. A third type of problem is the anxiety newer managers experience as they grow and develop in their jobs. For many, the anxiety arises from the conflict between their self-images and their behavior. For example, students of management often express values which suggest that they neither seek nor are reinforced by power or money. However, many of them discover early in their careers that, for them, money and power are reinforcing. They will behave in ways undeniably intended to increase power and wealth—such as leaving a pleasant job in comfortable surroundings for a big salary.

Beginning managers who find themselves becoming increasingly committed to their jobs or careers may likewise experience personal anxiety. As students, they saw parents or relatives whose lives were dominated by work, and they swore, "Not me!" Then they find that managing can be exciting and exhilarating. Success, praise, esteem, variety, and challenge will increase the commitment of many new managers to levels they scorned as students. Changing self-images will create personal anxiety, as the manager wonders if his or her career is becoming too important or is worth its perceived costs.

THE MANAGEMENT CHALLENGE

Managing is an exciting but complex career. It can provide powerful rewards: interesting, creative, challenging work; excitement and variety; status, power, and esteem; respect and friendship; opportunity and wealth. Any career that carries with it such powerful rewards makes demands of those who aspire to success. For most, success means, simply, hard work. Fortunately, for the majority, the work is reinforcing in itself, and thus hard work is not so costly.

Exhibit 22.8   Recent Growth Industries: Major Industries Ranked by Number of Jobs (in thousands) Created or Lost Between 1977 and 1982

Telecommunications	184.9	Appliances	(0.6)
Food, Beverage	184.5	Farm-Const Equip	(22.8)
Electronics	101.9	Containers	(44.5)
Office Equipment	88.2	Electrical	(49.5)
Chemicals	52.8	Auto—parts	(50.1)
Aerospace	36.7	Machine Tools	(67.8)
Instruments	25.7	Paper	(78.3)
Personal/Home Care	14.7	Steel	(148.8)
Fuel	14.5	Bldg Materials	(168.0)
Drugs	11.4	Auto—vehicles	(188.1)
Leisure Toys	5.6	Tire & Rubber	(199.3)
Misc. Mfg.	3.8		

Source: S. S. Ross, "Entry-Level Jobs With a Future," *Business Week's Guide to Careers*, Vol. 2, No. 1, February–March, 1984, p. 37.

For some, success means demands on time which exclude virtually everything else from their lives. While some of you may be tempted to feel sorry for those whose work is their life, don't: most of them are doing exactly what they want. Work and its outcomes are simply more reinforcing to them than anything else. They get to spend their whole lives doing what they like best, and they get paid handsomely for it.

Sadly, for some managers, as in every profession, success means abandoning ethics, morals, or principles to keep what they have or to achieve what they covet. There are proportionately no fewer of them in management than in any other profession. On the other hand, there are probably no more.

We have, from time to time, stressed the challenge of managing. Because managers get things done through people, that most complex and varied of all resources, managing will always be a challenging job. Future managers will face additional challenges. Exhibit 22.8 shows the industries where these additional jobs and challenges may come from.

The first challenge may be to understand and deal with the national and world economy. The last forty years have been years of general growth and prosperity. If, as some claim, we have entered into a new economic era of no growth, scarce and dear resources, and high or highly fluctuating interest rates, the challenge of managing will increase. Growth and abundant resources provide slack and allow for mistakes. With apologies to Isaac Asimov, a tight economy is a harsh mistress. Demands for success will be greater as the costs of failure increase.

The second challenge will be to master and exploit the ever-expanding information-systems technology. Improved information systems will help managers increase effectiveness and efficiency needed to survive in a tight economy. They will, that is, if the systems do not overwhelm the managers first. Managers who learn to cope with and master their MIS are greater bets for survival. Those who cannot cope will be dependent upon those who can.

Finally, the increasing use of robots will present a challenge of unknown proportions. There are sober, intelligent people who claim that robotics will revolutionize industry to an extent surpassing that generated by computers, and rivalled only by the revolution that spawned industry as we know it. What effects will robotics have on unions, job design, and on first-line supervisors? The challenge for managers will be to keep physical, psychological, and economic casualties of this revolution to a minimum, while using this and other new technology to get more things done efficiently and effectively.

The Bottom Line

Among the professions, managing, like practicing law, is still more of an art than a science. Despite the advent of computers, robots, and management textbooks, the bottom line is still an individual confronting an opportunity or a problem, making a decision, seeing that it's carried out, and hoping for the best.

We have talked about the more obvious allures of being a manager—the status, the money, the power. But a subtler and perhaps stronger allure for those who practice management is the element of uncertainty, the randomness of events and their outcomes. Managers try to produce order out of chaos, yet, like hunters, theirs is a controlled harvest. Chaos, in a sense, is their game, and they don't want to eliminate it, but to manage it. They claim to seek routine, but they abhor it. If they find it, they're likely to unravel it, "just to stir things up."

If the characteristics of a managerial career—uncertainty, risk, variety, as well as status, power and money—attract you, if you decide you really want to manage, and decide to start, as most do, by working for someone else:

1. Your first objective is to get a job. That means you need to find out what kind of a job you want to start out in, then write your resumé to fit that job. A good reference to use is *The Perfect Resumé* by Tom Jackson published by Doubleday & Co.
2. Prepare for interviews. Learn about the company, the industry, the problems and the opportunities. Ask questions based on your research.

SUMMARY

Getting off to a good start in a managerial career takes more than sending out resumés and waiting for job offers to come in. Having definite short-term and long-term goals, being aware of personal strengths and weaknesses, and actively seeking challenging positions through personal contacts and placement centers increases the chance of getting a good first job.

Although lack of previous experience makes it difficult for new managers to predict what a first job will be like, those who make the best of that job will gain a considerable career advantage over those who don't. Learning as much as possible about business in general, and about the industry and themselves as well, will make it easier for those who change jobs to get better ones.

One of the likely problems for new managers is the relative lack of performance feedback they receive. When they are formally evaluated, the major criteria will be the performance of their subordinates and the impressions they themselves make on superiors. Most can expect abundant opportunities to increase their expertise in management development programs throughout their careers. In larger organizations, senior managers who offer to serve as mentors and sponsors can significantly enhance the careers of younger managers.

One of the major career issues facing this generation of managers is that of dual careers. Trying to maximize two separate careers and a marriage at the same time is, to say the least, a challenging task. Fortunately, many companies are beginning to provide both flexibility and counseling to increase the chances of success.

Whether as a dual or an individual career, management is both challenging and exciting. More than most careers, it becomes what the individual makes it. Opportunities and demands will always be there for those who seek them.

Few if any managers succeed solely through their own efforts. A successful manager is one who is surrounded by successful subordinates. To a great extent, planning, organizing, directing, and controlling are all ways of creating this environment. A manager gets things done through people. Therefore, a manager's own success is a natural byproduct of the success of colleagues and subordinates.

QUESTIONS FOR REVIEW AND DISCUSSION

1. What types of information do organizations base their selection of new managers on? What does this imply for job seekers?
2. Why are new managers often frustrated in their first job? What does this imply for new recruits?
3. Why is the performance of subordinates important to managers? Can it provide a true reflection of the manager's ability?
4. Why are assessment centers gaining popularity? What are their disadvantages?
5. How do job development programs differ from assessment centers? What are ways in which the former achieve their aims?
6. What is a mentor? How are mentors helpful?
7. Besides salaries, what other forms of compensation do executives receive? How are these mutually beneficial to both executives and the organizations they work for?
8. Why do young professional couples experience problems in trying to develop a two-career marriage? How can these problems be overcome?

REFERENCES AND NOTES

1. "Management Is Still a Growth Industry," *Chicago Tribune*, May 23, 1983, Sect. 4, p. 13.
2. D. T. Hall, *Careers in Organizations* (Pacific Palisades, Calif: Goodyear Publishing Co. 1976).

3. E. H. Schein, "The First Job Dilemma," *Psychology Today*, March 1968, pp. 22–37.

4. R. B. Finkle, "Managerial Assessment Centers" in M. Dunnette, *Handbook of Industrial and Organizational Psychology* (Chicago: Rand McNally, 1976), pp. 861–888.

5. W. F. Glueck, *Management*, 2d ed. (New York: Holt, Rinehart, Winston, 1980), p. 17.

6. "America's New Immobile Society," *Business Week*, July 27, 1981, pp. 58–62.

7. The 1980 Employment and Training Report of the President (Washington: Superintendent of Documents, U.S. Government Printing Office, 1980).

8. D. J. Levinson, *The Seasons of a Man's Life* (New York: Alfred A. Knopf, 1978), pp. 97–101.

9. K. Kram, *Mentoring Processes at Work: Development of Relationships in Managerial Careers* (Unpublished Ph. D. Dissertation: Yale University, 1980).

10. S. S. Ross, "Entry Level Jobs with a Future," *Business Week's Guide to Careers*, Vol. 2, 1, February/March 1984, p. 36.

11. "Job Offers Are Chasing the New MBA's Again." *Business Week*, April 9, 1984, pp. 32–33.

12. "Top Dollar Jobs" *Time*, June 2, 1980, p. 60.

13. F. Allen, "Top Executives, Though Well-Paid, Still Worry About Wealth," *Wall Street Journal*, October 15, 1981, p. 31.

14. This section is based upon F. S. Hall and D. T. Hall, "Dual Careers—How Do Couples and Companies Cope with the Problems." *Organizational Dynamics*, Spring 1978 © 1978 AMACO, A Division of American Management Association, pp. 57–77. All rights reserved.

15. A. Brisolava, *The Alcoholic Employee* (New York: Human Sciences Press, 1979), pp. 47–50.

SUGGESTED READINGS

Hall, D. T., *Careers in Organizations* (Pacific Palisades, California: Goodyear Publishing Co., 1976). This book is a lucid summary of theory and research on a variety of careers, including management. It emphasizes the individual's role in making choices and managing his or her own career.

Belker, L. B., *The First-Time Manager* (New York: AMACOM, 1978). This practical guide for new managers describes particular personnel problems faced by first-time managers, including hiring, disciplining, and firing.

Miner, J. B., *The Challenge of Managing* (Philadelphia: W. B. Saunders Co., 1975). Designed for management development programs, this book focuses on specific problem areas faced by practicing managers. It includes a number of good cases, and a chapter in "Why Managers Fail."

Thompson, M. R., *Why Should I Hire You?* (New York: G. P. Putnam's, 1975). A practical guide to discovering what kind of job one wants and how to get it, this book covers resumé writing, interviewing techniques, and negotiation. It is an excellent reference for those seeking first time management positions.

Subject Index

Name Index

Company/Product Index

Acknowledgments

Photo Credits

Unless otherwise acknowledged, all photographs are the property of Scott, Foresman and Company.

Photos by Alan Landau for Scott, Foresman and Company: pp. 1, 3, 5, 47 (taken at Hayward Blake and Company), 182, 256, 344, 346, 508 (taken at Danilo's Restaurant, 1235 West Grand Avenue, Chicago).

p. 11	First National Bank of Chicago
p. 16	Richard Younker
p. 23	Charles Harbutt/Archive
p. 69	Courtesy of SAS Institute Inc.
p. 71	Charles Harbutt/Archive
p. 92	Courtesy of General Motors Corporation
p. 95	© Mark Weidling
p. 117	Michal Heron
p. 120	© Joel Gordon
p. 128	Courtesy of Data General Corporation
p. 152	Peter C. Poulides
p. 174	Charles Harbutt/Archive
p. 199(L)	Robert George Gaylord
p. 199(R)	Courtesy of Haworth, Inc.
p. 214(L)	Charles Harbutt/Archive
p. 214(R)	Michal Heron
p. 219	David R. Frazier
p. 237	David R. Frazier
p. 261	Courtesy of International Business Machines Corporation
p. 274	Courtesy of General Signal
p. 295(L)	Robert George Gaylord
p. 295(R)	Richard Younker
p. 308	David R. Frazier
p. 314	Henry G. Eastwood/Southern Light
p. 315	H. Armstrong Roberts
p. 320	The Toronto Star
p. 335	Mike Maple/TIME Magazine
p. 338	NASA
p. 347	Glenn N. Sanderson
p. 365	Wayne A. Bladholm

Illustration Credits

Text Credits